D1272505

THE OXFORD HANDBOOK OF

WORK AND ORGANIZATION

Nyack College Library

REF
HD
4901
·0933
2005

THE OXFORD HANDBOOK OF

WORK AND ORGANIZATION

Edited by

STEPHEN ACKROYD

ROSEMARY BATT

PAUL THOMPSON

AND

PAMELA S. TOLBERT

OXFORD

UNIVERSITY PRESS

OXFORD

UNIVERSITY PRESS

Great Clarendon Street, Oxford OX2 6DP

Oxford University Press is a department of the University of Oxford.
It furthers the University's objective of excellence in research, scholarship,
and education by publishing worldwide in

Oxford New York

Auckland Cape Town Dar es Salaam Hong Kong Karachi Kuala Lumpur
Madrid Melbourne Mexico City Nairobi New Delhi Shanghai Taipei Toronto

With offices in

Argentina Austria Brazil Chile Czech Republic France Greece
Guatemala Hungary Italy Japan Poland Portugal
Singapore South Korea Switzerland Thailand Turkey Ukraine Vietnam

Oxford is a registered trade mark of Oxford University Press
in the UK and in certain other countries

Published in the United States
by Oxford University Press Inc., New York

© Ackroyd 2005

The moral rights of the author have been asserted
Database right Oxford University Press (maker)

First published 2005

All rights reserved. No part of this publication may be reproduced,
stored in a retrieval system, or transmitted, in any form or by any means,
without the prior permission in writing of Oxford University Press,
or as expressly permitted by law, or under terms agreed with the appropriate
reprographics rights organization. Enquiries concerning reproduction
outside the scope of the above should be sent to the Rights Department,
Oxford University Press, at the address above

You must not circulate this book in any other binding or cover
and you must impose this same condition on any acquirer

British Library Cataloguing in Publication Data

Data available

Library of Congress Cataloging in Publication Data

Data available

ISBN 0–19–926 992–0

1 3 5 7 9 10 8 6 4 2

Typeset by Kolam Information Services Pvt. Ltd, Pondicherry, India
Printed in Great Britain
on acid-free paper by Biddles Ltd, King's Lynn, Norfolk

#56463480

ACKNOWLEDGEMENTS

The initial idea for this Handbook originated from David Musson, of Oxford University Press, who suggested to Paul and Stephen that they should develop a proposal. It soon became apparent, given the scope of the work, that more than the usual range of expertise would be required for the project, and so the original pair were delighted to invite Pam and Rose to join them on the editorial team. The editorial work that ensued was less onerous than might be imagined. A sequence of trans-Atlantic conference calls made the periodic editorial meetings both possible and effective, despite the distance separating the participants.

In addition, several individuals must be acknowledged for their support and help in bringing the project to a successful conclusion—especially in the later stages of the process. The contributions of Cornell staff members Judy Mead and Krista Knout to the project have been invaluable. At Oxford University Press, in addition to David Musson, we benefited regularly from the support of Matthew Derbyshire, Stuart Fowkes, Franseca Gwalchmai, and Tanya Dean. Finally, we offer thanks to our incomparable copyeditor, Lynn Deanne Childress, who, as well as being eagle-eyed and very efficient, dispensed philosophical insights and good advice all along the way.

SA, RB, PT, PT

Contents

PART I WORK, TECHNOLOGY, AND THE DIVISION OF LABOR

PART II MANAGERIAL REGIMES AND EMPLOYEE ACTIONS

LIST OF FIGURES

LIST OF TABLES

LIST OF CONTRIBUTORS

Stephen Ackroyd is Professor of Organizational Analysis in Lancaster University Management School where he is Head of the Department of Organization, Work and Technology. His current research is into contemporary organizational change and particularly the reorganization of the largest British firms retaining some manufacturing capacity. Among his recent books are *Organizational Misbehaviour* (with P. Thompson, 1999), *Realist Perspectives on Management and Organizations* (edited with Steve Fleetwood, 2000), *The Organization of Business* (2002), and *Critical Realist Applications in Organization and Management Studies* (edited with Steve Fleetwood, 2004). email: s.ackroyd@lancaster.ac.uk

Galit Ailon-Souday is a Lecturer at the Department of Sociology and Anthropology at Bar-Ilan University. Her research includes the study of organization culture and globalization and the critical analysis of managerial and organizational theory. email: ailonsg@mail.biu.ac.il

Mats Alvesson is Professor of Business Administration at Lund University, Sweden. His current research interests include knowledge-intensive firms, leadership processes, and identity construction. He has published widely in the leading academic journals in the management and organizational behavior fields. Recent books include *Reflexive Methodology* (with K. Sköldberg, 2000), *Understanding Organizational Culture* (2002), *Studying Management Critically* (edited with H. Willmott, 2003), and *Knowledge Work and Knowledge-Intensive Firms* (2004). email: Mats.Alvesson@fek.lu.se

Eileen Appelbaum is Professor of Labor and Employment Relations at Rutgers University and the Director of the Rutgers University Center for Women and Work. She was formerly the Research Director at the Economic Policy Institute. She is author of *Back to Work: Determinants of Women's Successful Reentry* (1981), *The New American Workplace: Transforming Work Systems in the United States* (with Rosemary Batt, 1994), *Manufacturing Advantage: Why High Performance Work Systems Pay Off* (with Thomas Bailey, Peter Berg, and Arne Kalleberg, 2000), and *Balancing Acts: Easing the Burdens and Improving the Options for Working Families* (2000). email: eappelba@rci.rutgers.edu

Richard J. Badham is Professor of Entrepreneurship and Technology Management at the Macquarie Graduate School of Management (Sydney, Australia) and David

Goldman Visiting Professor of Business Innovation at the University of Newcastle upon Tyne (UK). He was previously the Foundation BHP Professor of Management and Director of the Centre for Change Management at the University of Wollongong. His publications include over 100 books and articles on innovation and change, including the books *Theories of Industrial Society* (1986) and *Power, Politics and Organizational Change* (with Dave Buchanan, 1999). He is currently working on *Managing Change: A Critical Introduction* (Palgrave, Macmillan) and *Irony and Commitment in Cultural Change.* email: Richard.Badham@mgsm.edu.au

Thomas Bailey is the George and Abby O'Neill Professor of Economics and Education in the Department of International and Transcultural Studies at Teachers College, Columbia University. He is also the Director of the Institute on Education and the Economy at Teachers College. Dr Bailey holds a Ph.D. in labor economics from MIT and is an expert on the economics of education, educational policy, community colleges, and the educational and training implications of changes in the workplace. He has co-authored *Working Knowledge: Work-Based Learning and Education Reform* (with Katherine Hughes and David Moore, 2004), *Manufacturing Advantage* (with Eileen Appelbaum, Peter Berg, and Arne Kalleberg, 2000), and *The Double Helix of Education and the Economy* (with Sue Berryman, 1992). email: tb3@columbia.edu

Stephen R. Barley is the Charles M. Pigott Professor of Management Science and Engineering and the Co-Director of the Center for Work, Technology and Organization at Stanford's School of Engineering. He has written extensively on the impact of new technologies on work, the organization of technical work, and organizational culture. In collaboration with Gideon Kunda of Tel Aviv University, Barley has recently completed a book on contingent work among engineers and software developers, entitled *Gurus, Hired Guns and Warm Bodies: Itinerant Experts in the Knowledge Economy*, which will be published in July by the Princeton University Press. He is the former editor of *Administrative Science Quarterly* and current editor of the *Stanford Social Innovation Review.*

Rosemary Batt is the Alice H. Cook Professor of Women and Work at the Industrial and Labor Relations School, Cornell University. She received her Ph.D. from the Sloan School of Management, Massachusetts Institute of Technology. Her research interests include work organization and teams, service sector productivity and competitiveness, labor market restructuring, and inequality. She has published numerous book chapters and articles in such journals as *Industrial and Labor Relations Review, Academy of Management Journal, Personnel Psychology, International Journal of Human Resource Management, Industrial Relations,* and the *British Journal of Industrial Relations.* She is co-author of *The New American Workplace: Transforming Work Systems in the United States* (with Eileen Appelbaum, 1994). email: rb41@cornell.edu

Peter Berg is an associate professor at the School of Labor and Industrial Relations at Michigan State University. He received his Ph.D. in economics from the University of Notre Dame. His research interests include organizational change in the United States and Germany, high-performance work systems, work–life policies and practices in the United States and Europe, and comparative employment relations. Dr Berg is co-author of the book *Manufacturing Advantage: Why High Performance Work Systems Pay-off* (with Eileen Appelbaum, Thomas Bailey, and Arne Kalleberg, 2000) and editor of *Creating Competitive Capacity: Labor Market Institutions and Workplace Practices in Germany and the United States* (2000). email: bergp@msu.edu

M. Diane Burton is the Michael M. Koerner '49 Career Development Assistant Professor of Management at the Sloan School of Management at MIT and is affiliated with the Entrepreneurship Center and the Institute for Work and Employment Research. Her research focuses on employment relations and organizational change primarily in entrepreneurial companies. Her current major research project is a study of innovation in the cardiovascular medical device industry. She is also studying the careers of technology entrepreneurs and executives, and recently completed a large-scale study of 175 high-tech start-ups in Silicon Valley. She has published articles in a variety of academic journals including the *American Sociological Review*, the *American Journal of Sociology*, and the *Journal of Law, Economics, and Organizations*.

David L. Collinson is Foundation for Management Education (FME) Professor of Strategic Learning and Leadership at Lancaster University Management School and Head of the Department of Management Learning. His research seeks to develop a critical approach to management studies and is informed in particular by post-structuralist debates on power/subjectivity and gender/masculinity. His recent books include *Managing the Shop Floor* (2000), *Men as Managers: Managers as Men* (with Geoff Hearn, 1996), *Managing to Discriminate* (with David Knights and Margaret Collinson, 1990), and, forthcoming, *Humour and Organisations* (2005). email: d.collinson@lancaster.ac.uk

Colin Crouch is head of the Department of Social and Political Sciences and Professor of Sociology at the European University Institute, Florence. He is also the External Scientific member of the Max Planck Institute for Social Research at Cologne. He previously taught sociology at the LSE and was fellow and tutor in politics at Trinity College, Oxford, and Professor of Sociology at the University of Oxford. He is chairman, and former joint editor, of *The Political Quarterly*, and current president of the Society for the Advancement of Socio-Economics (SASE). He has published within the fields of comparative European sociology and industrial relations, on economic sociology, and on contemporary issues in British and European politics. He is currently studying processes of institutional innovation in the economy and in public policy. He is author of *Social Change in Western Europe* (1999) and *Postdemocrazia* (2003). He has co-authored recent books, including *Political Economy of Modern Capitalism: The Future of Capitalist Diversity* (with Wolfgang Streeck, 1997), *Are Skills the Answer?* (with David Finegold and Mari Sako, 1999), *Local Production Systems in Europe: Rise or Demise?* (with Patrick Le Galès, Carlo Trigilia, and Helmut Voelzkow, 2001), and *Changing Governance of Local Economies: Response of European Local Production Systems* (with Patrick Le Galès, Carlo Trigilia, and Helmut Voelzkow, 2004). email: crouch@iue.it

Virginia L. Doellgast is a Ph.D. candidate at the School for Industrial and Labor Relations at Cornell University. She is currently a visiting scholar at the Max Planck Institute for the Study of Societies in Cologne, Germany. email: vld7@cornell.edu

Stephen J. Frenkel is a Professor specializing in the sociology of work and employment relations in the Australian Graduate School of Management. Steve's research covers specific advanced societies and several developing countries in Asia. His publications include *On the Front Line: Organization of Work in the Information Economy* (1999), *Organized Labor in the Asia-Pacific* (1993), and *Industrialization and Labor Relations* (1995). His recent research focuses on service workers in Australian call centers and the management of codes of labor practice in athletic footwear supply chains, mainly in China.

Laurie Graham is currently a Visiting Associate Professor of Sociology and Women's Studies in the Department of Sociology and Anthropology at Purdue University. Her research focuses on the nature of worker resistance, emergence of gendered subcultures in work organizations, the use of temporary workers as a form of social control, and the impact of lean production systems on worker health and safety. She is the author of *On the Line at Subaru-Isuzu: The Japanese Model and the American Worker* (1995).

Robert Hebdon is an Associate Professor of Industrial Relations in the Faculty of Management at McGill University, Montreal, Canada. He started his academic career at Cornell University where he taught collective bargaining for seven years. He has also taught at the Universities of Manitoba and Toronto. His research interests include public sector labor relations and restructuring, collective bargaining, dispute resolution, and industrial conflict. He has published in a wide variety of major journals including the *American Economic Review*, the *Industrial and Labor Relations Review*, *Relations Industrielles*, the *Journal of Policy Analysis and Management*, the *Journal of Collective Negotiations in the Public Sector*, the *Labor Studies Journal*, and the *Arbitration Yearbook*. email: robert.hebdon@mcgill.ca

Bob Hinings is a Professor Emeritus and Senior Research Fellow in the Department of Strategic Management and Organization, School of Business, University of Alberta. His research interests center on strategic change in professionally based organizations such as law firms, accounting firms, consulting firms, and health care organizations. In 1999 he was the recipient of the Distinguished Scholar Award from the Organization and Management Theory Division of the U.S. Academy of Management. In 2000 he was made a Fellow of the Royal Society of Canada in the Academy of Humanities and Social Sciences and a Fellow of the U.S. Academy of Management. In 2003 he became an Honorary Member of the European Group for Organizational Studies and a JMI Scholar of the Western Academy of Management.

Arne L. Kalleberg is Kenan Distinguished Professor of Sociology at the University of North Carolina at Chapel Hill. His research focuses on topics related to the sociology of work, organizations, occupations and industries, labor markets, and social stratification. He is currently working on a book about changes in job quality and work attitudes in the United States. He is also studying changing employment relations in the United States and Norway. email: Arne_Kalleberg@unc.edu

Harry C. Katz is the Jack Sheinkman Professor of Collective Bargaining at the ILR School-Cornell University. His books include *Converging Divergences: Worldwide Changes in Employment Systems* (with Owen Darbishire, 2000), *The Transformation of American Industrial Relations* (with Thomas Kochan and Robert McKersie, 1986), *Shifting Gears: Changing Labor Relations in the U.S. Auto Industry* (1985), and *An Introduction to Collective Bargaining and Industrial Relations* (with Thomas Kochan, 2004). email: hck2@cornell.edu

John Kelly is Professor of Industrial Relations at the London School of Economics and at Birkbeck College, University of London. His recent publications include *Union Organization and Activity* (edited with Paul Willman, 2004), *Varieties of Unionism: Strategies of Union Revitalization in a Globalizing Economy* (edited with Carola Frege, 2004), *Industrial Relations: Critical Perspectives on Business and Management*, 5 vols. (editor, 2002), *Rethinking Industrial Relations: Mobilization, Collectivism and Long Waves* (1998).

Young-Mi Kim is a doctoral candidate in the Sociology Department at Cornell University. She is working in the areas of organization, stratification, inequality, and gender. Her current research interest is in exploring changes in corporate organization and their consequences in economic and social inequality. email: yk226@cornell.edu

Ian Kirkpatrick is a Senior Lecturer in Organizational Behaviour at Leeds University Business School. Ian has taught at Cardiff Business School and at Universitat Pompeu Fabra in Barcelona. He joined Leeds University Business School in 2000. Ian's research interests are in change in public services, flexible employment practices, and comparative developments in human resource management. He has published in a range of academic journals including *Public Administration, Organization, Sociological Review,* and *Work Employment and Society.* Recent work includes a co-authored volume entitled *The Management of Children's Residential Care* (with Richard Whipp and Martin Kitchener, 2004) and *The New Managerialism and Public Service Professions* (with Steve Ackroyd and Richard Walker, 2004). email: ik@lubs.leeds.ac.uk

Gideon Kunda is Associate Professor in the Department of Labor Studies at Tel Aviv University. He received his Ph.D. in Management and Organization Studies from the Sloan School of Management at MIT in 1987. Kunda's research has focused on the cultural aspects of work and organization. His book *Engineering Culture: Control and Commitment in a High-Tech Corporation* was chosen as Book of the Year by the American Sociological Association's Culture Section in 1994. His book (with Stephen Barley), *Gurus, Hired Guns and Warm Bodies: Itinerant Experts in a Knowledge Economy*, will be published in 2004 by Princeton University Press. The book examines the social organization of temporary work among engineers in Silicon Valley.

William Lazonick is an economist who specializes in the study of industrial development and international competition. He is University Professor at the University of Massachusetts, Lowell and Distinguished Research Professor at INSEAD (European Institute of Business Administration). Previously, he was Assistant and Associate Professor of Economics at Harvard University (1975–1984) and Professor of Economics at Barnard College of Columbia University (1985–1993). He has also been on the faculties of the University of Tokyo, Harvard Business School, University of Toronto, and was a visiting member of the Institute for Advanced Study in Princeton. He is the author or editor of nine books and some 80 academic articles. email: william.Lazonick@insead.edu

Karen Legge is Professor in Organizational Behaviour, Warwick Business School. Until 2003 Karen was joint editor of the *Journal of Management Studies* and has also served on numerous editorial boards including *Organization*, *Industrial Relations*, *Human Resource Management Journal*, *Gender, Work and Organization*, and the *British Journal of Industrial Relations*. Karen's research interests lie in the area of applying postmodern organization theory to HRM, change management, development of learning organizations, and organizational ethics. She has published widely in these areas, a well-known publication being *HRM: Rhetorics and Realities* (1995), a new edition of which is forthcoming in 2005.

Leslie McCall is Associate Professor of Sociology and Women's and Gender Studies at Rutgers University. Her research on wage inequality has appeared in the *American Sociological Review*, *Demography*, and *Economic Geography*, as well as in her book, *Complex Inequality: Gender, Class, and Race in the New Economy* (2001). email: lmccall@sociology.rutgers.edu

Alan McKinlay is Professor of Management at the University of St Andrews, Scotland. He has written extensively on business and labor history as well as the contemporary workplace. His books include *Strategy and the Human Resource: Ford and the Search for Competitive Advantage* (with Ken Starkey, 1992).

Glenn Morgan is Professor of Organizational Behaviour at Warwick Business School, University of Warwick. His current research interests concern comparative economic organization in Europe and East Asia, management of change, multinational firms, global financial markets, and international regulation. He is an editor of *Organization: The Critical Journal of Organization, Theory and Society.* Recent books include *The Multinational Firm* (edited with R. Whitley and P. H. Kristensen, 2001) and *Changing Capitalisms* (edited with R. Whitley and E. Moen, 2004). email: glenn.morgan@warwick.ac.uk

Paul Osterman is the Nanyang Professor of Human Resources at the MIT Sloan School of Management and the Department of Urban Planning, MIT. He is also Deputy Dean of the MIT Sloan School. His most recent book is *Gathering Power: The Future of Progressive Politics in America* (2003). In addition, he has authored a number of other books on changes in the contemporary economy and employment relations, and has written numerous academic journal articles and policy issue papers on topics such as the organization of work within firms, labor market policy, and economic development. Osterman has been a senior administrator of job training programs for the Commonwealth of Massachusetts and consulted widely to firms, government agencies, foundations, community groups, and public interest organizations.

Stephen Procter is the Alcan Professor of Management at the University of Newcastle upon Tyne Business School in the United Kingdom. He has previously taught at the Universities of Keele, Nottingham, and St Andrews. His research interests include the management of organizational restructuring and the development of team-based forms of working. He is co-organizer of the International Workshop on Teamworking and co-editor of *Teamworking* (with Frank Mueller, 2000). email: s.j.procter@ncl.ac.uk

Jill Rubery is Professor of Comparative Employment Systems at Manchester School of Management, UMIST (from October 2004 Manchester Business School University of Manchester following the merger of UMIST and the Victorian University of Manchester) and Director of the European Work and Employment Research Centre. Recent books that she has co-authored include *Fragmenting Work: Blurring Organisational Boundaries and Disordering Hierarchies* (with M. Marchington, D. Grimshaw, and H. Willmott, 2004), *The Organization of Employment: An International Perspective* (with Damian Grimshaw, 2003), *Managing Employment Change: The New Realities of Work* (with H. Beynon, D. Grimshaw, and K. Ward,

2002), and *Women's Employment in Europe: Trends and Prospects* (with Mark Smith and Colette Fagan, 1999). email: Jill.Rubery@umist.ac.uk

Chris Smith is Professor of Organizational Studies at the School of Management, Royal Holloway University of London. He was previously at the University of Aston and has held visiting positions at the Universities of Hong Kong, Sydney, Wollongong, and Griffith. His main research interests are in the sociology of professions, labour process theory, and the comparative analysis of work. His books include *Technical Workers* (1987), *Reshaping Work* (with John Child and Michael Rowlinson, 1990), *Global Japanisation?* (with Tony Elger, 1994), *Engineering Labour* (with Peter Meiksins, 1996), and *Assembling Work* (with Tony Elger, 2004).
email: chris.smith@rhul.ac.uk

David Strang is Professor of Sociology at Cornell University. His work has appeared in *Administrative Science Quarterly, American Journal of Sociology, American Sociological Review,* and *Industrial and Corporate Change.* Current projects examine the spread of TQM within a global bank, the structure of emulation on benchmarking teams, supply-side dynamics in managerial fashion, and public sector downsizing.
email: ds20@cornell.edu

Grahame F. Thompson is Professor of Political Economy at the Open University in England. His main research interests are in the political economy of the international system and the theme of globalization. In particular this concentrates upon the possible limits to globalization and on the notion of global corporate citizenship. In addition, he is working on related issues around different forms of coordination and governance. His most recent books are *Between Hierarchies and Markets: The Logic and Limits of Network Forms of Organization* (2003) and *Politics and Power in the UK* (edited with Richard Heffernan, 2004). In 2004 he will be Visiting Professorial Fellow at the University of Warwick.
email: G.F.Thompson@open.ac.uk

Paul Thompson is Professor of Organizational Analysis in the Business School at the University of Strathclyde. Among his publications are: *The Nature of Work: An Introduction to Debates on the Labour Process* (1983, 2nd edn, 1989); *Work Organizations* (3rd edn, with David McHugh, 2002), and *Organizational Misbehaviour* (with Stephen Ackroyd, 1999). He is co-organizer of the International Labour Process Conference; as well as co-editing the Palgrave Series Management, Work and Organization, and Critical Perspectives on Work and Organization.
email: p.thompson@strath.ac.uk

Pamela S. Tolbert is Professor and chair of the Department of Organizational Behavior in the School of Industrial and Labor Relations at Cornell University. Her research encompasses studies of processes of change in organizations' formal structure, the role of organizations in social stratification, and the linkages between occupations and organizations. All of these interests are reflected in her current research on the rise of non-tenure-track faculty and use of tenure systems in higher education. She is the co-author, with Richard Hall, of *Organizations: Structure, Process and Outcomes* (2004).

TEXTS AND TIMES
MAPPING THE CHANGING STUDY OF WORK AND ORGANIZATIONS

STEPHEN ACKROYD

ROSEMARY BATT

PAUL THOMPSON

PAMELA TOLBERT

In this Handbook, we bring together the work of contemporary scholars to explore the changing nature of work, employment relations, occupations, and organizations in the context of the global economy. Our purpose is to provide a map of what we know and do not know about what is happening to people at work across a wide array of settings. To this end, the map is informed by a broad range of theoretical perspectives—such as varieties of institutional theory and radical political economy as developed by European, American, Australasian, and other scholars. But the book does not claim to deliver just a map: it also claims to be a reliable map of a definite terrain. In order to deliver this, it draws on empirical research from many disciplines, including industrial and economic sociology, psychology, organization studies, industrial and labor relations, and economics.

Thus, the analyses in this book address key debates surrounding the changing nature of work and organizations from a wide range of perspectives. While the authors have their own unique analytical lenses for utilizing, appraising, and critiquing the literature on a given topic, all of the contributors use empirical research to inform their arguments and present the debates at hand. Each Handbook chapter affords readers the opportunity to learn about the current research on a given topic as well as to develop a place to stand vis-à-vis the nature of change and who has benefited or lost in the process.

This Handbook is different from others, recently published, that have a similar subject but that focus primarily on meta-theoretical literature reviews and debates over differing interpretations of organizational change. Their focus is primarily on ways of thinking about organizations, rather than on what we know about them. While useful for sorting out epistemological differences, these handbooks frequently pay short shrift to what is actually happening at work. The focus on ways of knowing has led many researchers to shift away from empirical studies to textual analyses of rhetoric. Both are needed, but in the current environment, rhetorical analysis has increasingly displaced critical-empirical investigation. Thus, in the debates over meaning we have lost sight of the reality of actual change.

In the remaining sections of the Introduction, we outline the contributions of this Handbook in greater detail. First, we provide a brief intellectual history of handbooks of work and organization studies over the last few decades. We highlight their most important analytical breakthroughs and contributions. Second, we discuss further the fundamental differences between recent handbooks on work and organization and our own. In the third section, we briefly summarize the central research questions and findings from the chapters presented here and draw out some of the key trends and patterns about work and organization in the new century.

ORIGIN OF THE PRESENT PROJECT

Not very long ago it was a fresh and compelling observation to note that each generation writes its own textbooks. If texts are products of times, they are not simply mirrors of them. For example, if the world of work and organizations is now more complex, the means of understanding it are also more fragmented as disciplines and perspectives proliferate. Nevertheless, while the history of ideas is never a simple linear acquisition of knowledge, we hope that this Handbook can take its place in a long tradition of similar writing that examines the character of work organizations and their contribution to economy and society. Several earlier handbooks with a similarly broad scope as our own are key intellectual reference points for understanding the world of work and organizations in their respective historical eras.

The first distinctive account of the new academic field of organization studies was American and identified itself as the study of organizational behavior (OB). Organizational behavior drew on an intellectual heritage with strong empirical interests and an applied focus. The title of the subject captured a useful ambiguity: it could refer to the human behavior found in organizations or the behavior of organizations themselves. The subject actually linked what people do at work with the place and role of organizations in society, designating a large territory that could be explored by research. Those who worked in this field could draw on the deep reservoirs of the American sociology of work and occupations, on the one hand, and occupational psychology, on the other. In 1962, when organizational behavior was becoming established as an academic discipline in the United States, Nosow and Form published their celebrated and very large handbook on the sociology of occupations: *Man, Work and Society.* This substantial collection contained nearly 70 articles, had over 100 authors, and comprised more than 600 pages—amounting to a surprisingly detailed account of the organization of work in North America and other parts of the developed world. It combined a wide range of historical, theoretical, and substantive work: extracts from Tilgher's *Homo Faber* (1930) and Mannheim's *Ideology and Utopia* (1936) rub shoulders with C. W. Mills on the attitudes of progressive trade union leaders and W. A. Faunce on the response of automobile workers to automation in the late 1950s. Mannheim is now unread, and Tilgher's conspectus is a historical curiosity, but the pieces by Mills and Faunce and many others continue to be a valuable record of the organization of work current at the time they were made.

The emerging field of organizational behavior successfully claimed this broad heritage, but also claimed to be more focused, empirical, and practical than other social science disciplines. The applied nature of the new field is evident in Lawrence and Seilers's text, *Organizational Behavior and Administration*, in both its title and emphasis on case examples. But the emphasis on practical relevance in the field of organizational behavior was not ubiquitous. In the same year, Rand McNally embarked on its epic handbook series, which had more than a dozen titles covering all of the social sciences. The series included James March's (1976) *Handbook of Organization,* which brought together research on the structural aspects of organizations. In part, this handbook reflected the influence of what was then the relatively new approach of contingency theory in organization studies. Work in this tradition was generally characterized by quantitative, largely ahistorical, and data-driven efforts to determine conditions under which organizations' formal structure was more likely to exhibit certain abstract properties—formalization, centralization, complexity (or differentiation), and so forth. Size and technology were primary suspects as determinants of such variations in structure, though other candidates were also occasionally examined, including organizations' relationship to their environment. The influence of contingency theory was even more prominent in Nystrom and Starbuck's (1981) *Handbook of Organizational Design*, which comprised 2 volumes, 1,000 pages, and more than 40 articles written by 70 authors. Thus, more than twenty years ago, a relatively small corner of the field of organization studies could display an impressive array of work, much of it concerned with mapping the changing shape of organizations themselves.

In the handbook that March edited, however, there was still plenty of scope for the consideration of the role of specific historical conditions and political forces in shaping organizations. The volume included consideration of the effect of social and kinship ties on organizations; the relevance of social movements to organizational processes; the connections between the judiciary, law, and organization; and the importance of intergovernmental relations.

Although the field of organizational behavior continued to record what was happening in the world of organizations, there was little questioning of the fundamental nature or value of the knowledge gained in this subject area. For many, the subject had come of age and crystallized into orthodoxy. However, it is possible to exaggerate how far organizational behavior settled into an established pattern in North America. Mundane orthodoxy, characterized by a naïve realist approach and supposedly practical subject matter, coexisted with several vibrant centers of active research and intellectual questioning.

Thus, although formalistic versions of contingency theory appeared to be fast becoming orthodoxy in organizational research in the United States by the early 1970s, there was nevertheless evidence of vibrant, alternative intellectual approaches still alive in the discipline. A key illustration of this is provided by Dubin's (1976) *Handbook of Work, Organization and Society*. Like the handbook by Nosow and Form, it is broad in scope, including case studies of particular types of work settings, accounts of different kinds of organizational forms, and comparative international analysis. The volume also included an extended comparative section on the organization of work in different economic systems (considering Japan, Poland, Israel, and Yugoslavia).

This type of comparative work, as well as the emerging field of organization studies in Europe, began to challenge widely shared assumptions about the nature of work and organization found in the North American school of organizational behavior. From its beginning, the European version of organization studies had a strong bias towards the contribution of theory and a deep concern for conceptual novelty—establishing the possibility of analytical differences arising from the adoption of different perspectives. Sometimes defined as organization theory (OT) rather than organizational behavior, such writing had strong connections to European philosophy, particularly the phenomenological and existential branches of the discipline. These have been the basis of strong anti-positivist impulses in many areas of academic endeavor. They have mounted a very serious challenge to the objectivism implicit in much thinking and research in the organizational field.

Nevertheless, some research by European scholars fit well in North American traditions of organization studies. In these instances, Europeans enriched and deepened the capacity of the field to take stock of changes in organizations and their effect on society, even when they did not redirect the field onto an entirely new path. For example, European studies rooted in the work of Marx and Weber gave rise to a more critical kind of empirical study of organizations than often produced in North America. One example is the series of influential *International Handbooks of Participation in Organizations,* first produced under the imprint of John Wiley in the early 1980s, and later for Oxford University Press (see e.g. Lammers and Széll 1989; and Wilpert and Sorge 1984). Although focusing on a number of more specialist topics in work and organization, their mapping exercises were extraordinarily wide-ranging across national and sectoral boundaries.

Other than the previously referred to volume by Dubin, work and organization handbooks have been less prominent in sociology, despite the early emergence of a micro-level 'plant sociology' tradition, whose 'special task was the study of social relations in work situations and to develop an understanding of the links between industrial systems and the wider society' (Eldridge, MacInnes, and Cressey 1991: 202). The year of publication of the Dubin volume, 1976, marked a period of change in both texts and times. Many believed that industrial sociology had begun to fragment, in part because the dominant functionalist orthodoxy was in decline and unable to explain the new trends in economic life and the world of work (Hyman 1982). The emergence of Labor Process Theory (LPT), involving a return to propositions of Marx, gave rise to new theory and research on both sides of the Atlantic. As capitalism and work were changing, Labor Process Theory offered to industrial sociology analytical and empirical tools to maintain its historic interest in the connections between the workplace and wider social system.

Researchers in the labor process tradition have published nineteen edited volumes of articles, based on the International Labor Process Conference held each year in the United Kingdom. While not published in a handbook format, these volumes have covered a remarkably wide range of topics. Nonetheless, critics of the labor process approach, with some justification, criticized its research agenda for narrowly focusing on skill, control, and work design. One reaction to a volume, *On Work,* edited by Pahl, affirmed the centrality of work relations, but sought to expand its coverage within and outside the world of employment, 'to show something of the contours of a restructured world of work' (1988: 1). In this volume of largely reprinted papers, Pahl expanded the scope of coverage by including a substantial historical and comparative dimension.

In the sheer diversity of research on different categories and levels of work and employment relations, the bigger picture can sometimes be lost in micro-level case studies or industry surveys whose causal chain ends at the factory gate. Industrial relations writers (Edwards 1992) have pushed for a broader scope of analysis, often referred to a 'political economy approach', as a signifier between workplace and national modes of labor regulation. Such a focus has been taken up in the expanding field of economic sociology. Smelser and Swedberg's handbook did an effective job of bringing together contributions that could, 'assemble, codify, systematise, and thereby advance knowledge about one of the most critical arenas in the contemporary world—economy and society' (1994: viii). Although ranging from the micro-economic to the macro-sociological, the handbook's main purpose was to carve out a legitimate intellectual territory distinct from economics, and it left areas of work and organization untouched.

Other approaches could have been used to make similar observations about locating work and organization in a broader theoretical and empirical context. One thinks, for example, of the contributions of European comparative institutional analysis or regulation theory. It is not so much that these approaches share the same basic episteme. But what all shared was a strong commitment to and concern with documenting observable, historically grounded patterns of structures and social relations that govern the workplace. This was certainly reflected in many of the classic handbooks described above.

Moving Away from Mapping Work and Organizational Change

Such attempts to grasp and describe concretely the nature of organizational reality have become much less prominent, to the point of disappearance, in some recent handbooks. The potential maps of work and organizations are just as interesting, if, arguably, also more complex. However, academics appear to be less interested in mapping exercises than in the past, or perhaps more accurately, the dominant notion of what constitutes a map has changed from description and analysis of structures and practices towards paradigmatic mapping.

Two significant influences on this trend can be identified. First, there has been a general shift in social theory away from a focus on economies and work organizations towards consumption and identity. This can be observed in the writings of leading theorists such as Beck (2000) and Gorz (1999) on the end of the 'work society', and Bauman's (1998: 24) emphasis on the move from a work ethic to the aesthetic of consumption—in which 'people are groomed and trained to meet the demands of their social identities' largely outside the realm of production. While contemporary social theorists take different positions on the extent of continuity with traditional industrial, capitalist societies, such trends are highly influenced by postmodernism, which peaked in most of the social sciences in the mid-1990s. This was manifested in what became known as the 'cultural turn'—the argument that the reproduction of everyday life and the basis of domination had shifted from the material to the symbolic (Lash and Urry 1994).

An interesting recent example is Lawrence and Philips's (2002) analysis of the growing significance of cultural industries. This sounds as if it is a promising common ground between the cultural and economic spheres, but it is not. Lawrence and Philips argue that a cultural rationality has displaced economic rationality. Cultural products are valued for their meaning not their usefulness and are consumed in an act of interpretation. Cultural industries are, in turn, defined by their mode of consumption not production. They compete in the symbolic realm. In this context, 'Managing in cultural industries is therefore not about efficiently producing a product but about creating and maintaining an organization that can produce and sell meaning' (2002: 431). The problem is that by shifting the focus from production to consumption, Lawrence and Philips are excluding employees and the employment relationship from the framework of enquiry. Such analyses are unable to answer the question—what is industrial about cultural industries? As Reed (1996) argues, such writing is typical of a new form of cultural historicism in which the source of capitalist development is no longer political economy, but the management of values and engineering of the soul.

In some countries, notably Britain, the effects of this kind of shift on the sociology of work have been dramatic and deleterious. Industrial sociology has a long and distinguished history in Britain. Yet at the beginning of a new century, the situation does not look good. Few university departments have any expertise in the area, the bookshelves are full of studies of culture and consumption rather than production and work, and the British Sociological Association has not had work and employment as a theme for its annual conference since 1984. Admittedly, many sociologists in business schools are producing relevant work in the area, but this may be a generational and institutional peculiarity.

Second, an epistemological shift has occurred, particularly among social scientists who regard their approach as being defined by its 'critical' nature. What we see is a move from ontological to epistemological skepticism. In other words, rather than challenging the maps produced by their more orthodox colleagues, critical social scientists now define themselves by an adherence to different kinds of map making. This trend draws largely on the postmodernist attitude of radical skepticism towards the idea that there is an objective reality that is to some extent knowable. From this viewpoint, as we cannot adjudicate between 'truth claims', we are left with a focus on the social construction of perspectives and how they become influential and translated for action (Czarniawska 1999). Colville,

Waterman, and Weick clearly articulate this approach: 'Theory thus works by making sense of times and situations for readers and audiences but, because this always involves rhetoric, it is a matter of words, not worlds; of maps, not territories; and of representations not realities' (1999: 130). A further example comes from the Lawrence and Philips's article discussed above. They argue that as cultural industries are embedded more in texts than physical environments, literary criticism is a better source of understanding than traditional theories of management and organization. This may be something of an extreme argument, yet it is clear that a growing number of sociologists and business and management scholars spend far more time deconstructing texts, exploring discourses, and comparing paradigms than undertaking primary research into trends in work, employment, and organization.

Both of the above shifts are strongly represented in the field of organization and management studies. Organization studies was never a unified paradigm, and despite pleas from leading theorists (Pfeffer 1993), it is never likely to become one. However, whether organizational behavior was informed by psychology or sociology, prior generations of researchers viewed organizations and organizational behavior as subjects of research whose actual character and scale of influence could be established. Now, in Europe—and to a lesser extent the United States—the conviction that real trends in organizations can or should be studied has lost authority and come under direct challenge.

What this Handbook Seeks to Do That Others Do Not

Thus, rival attempts to sum up the conspectus of contemporary organization studies, such as the *Handbook of Organization Studies* (Clegg, Hardy, and Nord 1996), have had a different sort of focus from the traditional one. That volume too begins with the intention of providing a map to help navigate around organization studies, but what kind of map and what kind of studies? It is principally about the *approaches* to organizations that are held to be important. It records and summarizes the diversity of perspectives, accurately for the most part, though not definitively, and explores the epistemological development that has occurred in this new subject. Far less emphasis is placed on substantive claims about organizations as such, the way they behave and what they are truly like, though a preference for diverse approaches does not stop the editors from endorsing in advance the idea that new forms of postmodern, networked forms of organization are in the ascendant.

A more recent *Handbook of Organization Theory* is even more explicit about focusing on 'meta-theoretical reflection on the historical development, present state, and future prospects of OT' (Tsoukas and Knudsen 2003: 1). Let us be quite clear, a desire to explore paradigmatic diversity and the status of organization theory as a social science can produce fruitful results. What we are questioning is the overall balance of interest and outcomes between meta-theoretical and paradigm debate and that of theory-led empirical research. It sometimes appears that commentators have become so paralyzed by the existence of organizational variation across time and space, and multiple rationalities, that any 'stock-taking' must of necessity embrace a sense of undecidability—concentrating on what we do not know rather than what we do. One of the problems underlying this trend is that in the paradigm wars, orthodoxy is presented not as a description of what the world looks like, but as a way of seeing. In other words, these researchers view positivism as hegemonic and as a prime problem for the development of knowledge. Even setting aside whether this is factually accurate, this tendency has created an unfortunate perception that empirical investigation into the real world necessarily entails a search for invariant laws, using particular quantitative research designs. As the editors of a recent valuable handbook in this area note, most research is conducted in the space between positivism and relativism, and is informed, explicitly or implicitly by some form of philosophical realism (Baum and Rowley 2002). That is certainly the case for most of the contributions to this volume, which leads us to what does *this* Handbook seek to do?

While recognizing that understanding work and organizations cannot be detached from the framework of assumptions that gives them meaning, we have created a handbook designed to sum up what is known of organizations across a range of key issues and areas. The methodological resources brought to the process of mapping are firmly pluralist—ranging from literature reviews and discourse analysis to primary empirical research. A similar point can be made about the theoretical resources represented in the Handbook, which include institutional, Weberian, labor process, and postmodern perspectives. All, we think, contribute to making sense of current change, however complex and multifaceted it may appear.

Taken as a whole, the contributions are also multileveled in their focus of analysis, from the micro to the macro. Chapters look across the organizational landscape and ask if it can be described and explained: from what is happening inside organizations to what is happening to occupations and on the boundaries between organizations and wider societal structures and processes. It is distinctive, not only for its comprehensive overview, but through an orientation towards factually grounded, theoretically informed accounts. Out of this diversity, we are able to highlight a series of fundamental changes that are occurring in the nature of work, employment, and organizations.

ORGANIZATIONAL RESTRUCTURING
IN THE CURRENT ERA

We take the view that work organizations, especially those that make up the developed economies, are passing through changes of significant magnitude and that compared to previous periods of decisive change, contemporary developments are less localized and more global. Of central interest in this Handbook are the interactions between social structures—such as models of capitalism—and the work, employment, and decision-making relations found in organizations. Part I begins at the workplace level; chapters focus on the changing nature of work, technology, and the division of labor. Part II puts into perspective the changes at work by analyzing alternative systems of management control and worker resistance to change. Part III considers a similar set of themes, but viewed through the lens of occupational groups—from blue-collar workers and low-wage service workers to professional and knowledge workers. Part IV places the workplace and diverse occupational groups in the context of the changing organizational and international environment. Each Part begins with an editorial introduction that outlines the distinctive contributions of the individual chapters within the context of broader intellectual debates.

So what insights and understandings into the nature of current economic and social organization does this Handbook provide? In general, the chapter authors address three issues that are fundamental to studies of work and organizations. First, what are the trends that characterize contemporary organizations and economic systems, and what are the sources of these trends? What kinds of changes are taking place in the dominant logics that govern organizations, and in the set and form of interorganizational relations? Second, how have these changes in organizations and economic systems registered in the workplace? How have they affected hierarchical relations, strategies of coordination and control, and the day-to-day experience of working? And finally, how are broad economic, organizational, and workplace trends related to changes and problems in other aspects of social life: the welfare and organization of family life, patterns of gender and racial segregation, economic inequality and social class relations, the capacity for individual and collective forms of resistance, and the evolution of institutions and government policies?

In terms of the first issue, several analyses provide testimony to the crucial changes that are taking place in what might be referred to as the demography of economic organizations (see chapters by Procter, G. Thompson, and Alvesson and P. Thompson). Increasingly, contemporary economies are characterized by giant multinationals, on one hand, and by relatively small organizations, which are often tightly networked to each other and to the multinationals, on the other. Thus, the relations between organizations that compose different strata, as well as relations within the strata, provide a critical context that must be taken into account in understanding and explaining organizational outcomes and activities.

One key focus for further exploration, in this regard, is a trend in many organizations towards the increasing use of more technologically based control strategies, as described in chapters by McKinlay, Crouch, Badham, and Alvesson and Thompson. This trend has been amplified by the pressures of global competition (see chapters by Hinings, Katz, Kunda and Ailon-Souday, and Smith) which, because of the increasing density of interorganizational networks, affect not only large multi-nationals, but many smaller, seemingly local organizations as well. Such pressures have contributed to increases in the rate of cross-national diffusion of ideas and practices across organizations (as documented in chapters by Strang and Kim, Graham, and Legge). A critical element of this diffusion is the spread of a particular organizational logic, or social action justification, often labeled as 'shareholder value'. This is described in some detail in chapters by Kunda and Ailon-Souday, and Lazonick, and its extension to the public sector in Hebdon and Kirkpatrick's chapter. However, evidence also suggests that pressures towards convergence, created by globalization, are still somewhat checked and filtered by regional and national institutions. This has resulted in the curious trend toward increasing similarity of organizational arrangements *across* countries and greater variation of arrangements *within* countries (see Katz's analysis).

Thus, the portrait of contemporary economies that emerges from these chapters is one characterized by dense organizational networks that stretch across the boundaries of nation-states and that importantly shape both public- and private-sector organizations through ideological as well as competitive processes, despite the countervailing pressures of varying local and national customs and institutions.

How have these broader transformations in economies and organizations played out on a more local level, in the workplace? We can identify crucial shifts in both work relations and employment systems. These involve the mobilization of greater discretionary effort and range of skills of workers, accompanied by a move from traditional job structures and a standard employment contract to those featuring flatter hierarchies, teamworking, and nonstandard employment contracts (see chapters by Rubery, Batt, Katz, and Osterman and Burton). At the workplace level, globalization, deregulation of product markets, and the intensification of shareholder-driven organizations have meant heightened employment and income insecurity for working people across all advanced economies.

Produced in part by the interrelated forces of global competition and international diffusion of organizational arrangements, these new work and employment relations are often marked by a sort of schizophrenia, in terms of logic and underlying values. For example, employers make use of cooperative, commitment-enhancing practices such as teams, and at the same time, take actions that loosen employer–employee ties, such as reductions in employer-provided training and increased use of outsourcing, downsizing, and contingent staffing and pay (as noted in chapters by Rubery, Crouch, Batt, Legge, Osterman and Burton, and Graham). Managers exhort workers to be more self-sufficient and ready to 'pack their own parachute', even while managerialism—strategies that exert increasing control over workers in an endless quest for higher productivity—is on the rise. Even technical and professional workers, hired to use their expertise and independent judgment, are increasingly subject to electronic monitoring, work routinization, and intense pressure to meet short-term quotas.

Researchers have observed these contradictory employment practices across the range of occupations, from traditional blue-collar workers (Graham) and low-wage service workers (Frenkel) to high-skilled technical (Barley), professional (Hinings), and knowledge workers (McKinlay). These trends have been accompanied by rising dissatisfaction among working people in most advanced economies over work intensification, longer hours, and job insecurity, as examined in the chapter by Kelly. Moreover, an unexpected outcome of shareholder-driven corporate strategies is the alienation of even operational and middle-level managers from top management—suggesting the emergence of a new class divide, as discussed by Kunda and Ailon-Souday and Lazonick.

The contradictions at work create dilemmas for individuals and the institutions and policies designed to support social and economic welfare—the third central theme addressed in this Handbook. One manifestation of these contradictions— the polarization in the demand for skill—has put enormous pressures on skill formation systems. Advanced information technologies and competitive strategies have simultaneously increased the demand for highly skilled technical and knowledge workers (Barley and McKinlay) *and* for low-skilled service work (Frenkel). But as Crouch discusses in his chapter, these forces have also created high levels of uncertainty in demand and no real understanding or ability to forecast what specific skill sets are needed. As a result of these trends, exacerbated by previously identified moves towards more fragmented employment systems, employers are unwilling to invest in skills, while public education and training systems are ill-equipped to respond to uncertainty. Thus, individuals are left to absorb the risks of investment in training that may not pay off.

The polarization in skills has also contributed to the rise in economic and social inequality. However, the new inequality is not simply the result of skill-biased technical change, as often portrayed in the economic literature. As McCall's chapter shows, organizational restructuring has intersected with gender and race discrimination to create new configurations of inequality—not only between but among social groups—among men, among women, and among ethnic and racial minorities. Similar to the example of education and training systems, our antidiscrimination policies designed to reduce inequality based on gender and race are not adequate to address these new configurations of inequality.

The demand-side changes in the economy, coupled with the supply-side changes in labor markets, have produced additional contradictions and dilemmas for working families. As employers have restructured work and reduced wage and employment security, women have entered the labor market to pursue their own careers as well as to make up for lost family income. The combined restructuring of work and household labor has led to a shift in household structures and gender relations—from a male-breadwinner/female-caregiver division of labor to a dual-earner/dual-caregiver model. Several chapters highlight the failure of social institutions to respond to these new economic challenges that working people face.

This institutional lag has left individuals on their own to craft makeshift solutions. Chapters by Rubery and Appelbaum and colleagues, for example, describe how families have absorbed the costs of corporate restructuring; and conflicts between work and family or work and personal life have become a salient pattern in the fabric of everyday life. While the structure of family institutions and social welfare systems in some countries are more supportive than in others, in all countries these institutions have lagged behind the actual changes taking place. And while some private employers have developed work/family policies, these tend to cover only a minority of workers, and typically only high-skilled technical and professional employees.

Despite this deterioration in wages, working conditions, and employment security for the majority of the working population, the potential for resistance may be limited, given the decline in union power and membership. Several chapters in this Handbook, however, point to the growth of alternative forms of resistance such as sabotage, humor, and whistleblowing (Collinson and Ackroyd); to the 'fertile grounds' for employee resistance emerging from worker cynicism towards management rhetoric and new work practices (Kelly, Graham); and to the re-emergence of tri-partite labor, management, and government dialogue that has moved beyond wages to focus on broader issues such as working time, labor flexibility, and social reforms (Katz).

The debates and unresolved dilemmas arising from organizational restructuring at the end of the twentieth century provide rich ground for future research. While they indicate how and why organizational restructuring has occurred in general, they point to large areas of social research that are undeveloped—particularly those at the boundaries of disciplines or that require interdisciplinary research to produce new knowledge and meaningful public policy solutions. Such research projects might address the intersection of work, family, and social policy; the intersection of gender, race, and class in organizational restructuring; or the feasibility of alternative political strategies for economic and social reform. Thus, our research needs to investigate a broader array of institutions that intersect with the world of work—not only labor market institutions, but gender and family institutions, immigration policies, and social welfare and security policies.

The chapters in this Handbook point to greater levels than in the past of complexity in social and political processes within and across organizational networks. They seek to develop ways of understanding connections and patterns without shoehorning trends into over-extended and frequently over-optimistic conceptions such as post-Fordism and informational society. While they offer important new insights, future research undoubtedly needs to develop more sophisticated methodologies that allow us to move beyond single units of analysis and to understand organizations at multiple levels—building theory across individuals and work groups, establishments, firms, and institutions—in order to inform public policy.

Finally, our understanding of the processes of globalization is at a very early stage. There is much need for more sophisticated cross-national research that moves beyond country-by-country comparisons and uses the same methodologies and tools to examine the same phenomenon of industrial and occupational change. Comparative international studies of work organization in service activities would be particularly valuable because the historic role of unions and other institutions that have influenced manufacturing may be lacking in many service settings. More studies examining the same multinational corporations operating in distinct national contexts would contribute much to our understanding of the relative importance of institutions and employer strategies in shaping the organization of work and related outcomes. There is also a need for more coordinated international research that compares work restructuring in advanced and industrializing economies. In sum, the chapters in this Handbook contribute to understanding what changes have occurred while also identifying the central questions that remain to be tackled.

REFERENCES

BAUM, J. A. C., and ROWLEY, T. J. (2002). 'Companion to Organizations: An Introduction', in J. Baum (ed.), *Companion to Organizations.* Oxford: Blackwell.

BAUMAN, Z. (1998). *Work, Consumerism and the New Poor.* Buckingham: Open University Press.

BECK, U. (2000). *The Brave New World of Work.* Oxford: Polity.

CLEGG, S. R., HARDY, C., and NORD, W. R. (eds.) (1996). *The Handbook of Organisation Studies.* London: Sage.

COLVILLE, I. D., WATERMAN, R. H., and WEICK, K. E. (1999). 'Organizing and the Search for Excellence: Making Sense of the Times in Theory and Practice'. *Organization,* 6/1: 129–48.

CZARNIAWSKA, B. (1999). *Writing Management: Organization Theory as a Literary Genre.* Oxford: Oxford University Press.

DUBIN, R. (ed.) (1976). *Handbook of Work, Organization and Society.* Chicago: Rand McNally.

EDWARDS, P. K. (1992). 'Industrial Conflict: Themes and Issues in Recent Research'. *British Journal of Industrial Relations*, 30: 361–404.

ELDRIDGE, J., MACINNES, J., and CRESSEY, P. (1991). *Industrial Sociology and Economic Crisis*. New York: St. Martin's Press.

GORZ, A. (1999). *Reclaiming Work: Beyond the Wage-based Society*. Cambridge: Polity Press.

HYMAN, R. (1982). 'Whatever Happened to Industrial Sociology', in D. Dunkerley and G. Salaman (eds.), *The International Yearbook of Organization Studies*. London: Routledge and Kegan Paul.

LAMMERS, C. J., and SZÉLL, G. (eds.) (1989). *The International Handbook of Participation in Organizations*, Volume I. *Organizational Democracy: Taking Stock*. Oxford: Oxford University Press.

LASH, S., and URRY, J. (1994). *Economies of Signs and Space*. London and Thousand Oaks, Calif.: Sage Publications.

LAWRENCE, P. R., and SEILER, J. A. (eds.) (1961). *Organizational Behavior and Administration*. Homewood, Ill.: Richard D. Irwin and The Dorsey Press.

LAWRENCE, T. B., and PHILIPS, N. (2002). 'Understanding Cultural Industries'. *Journal of Management Inquiry*, 11: 430–3.

MANNHEIM, K. (1936). *Ideology and Utopia*. Translated from German by Louis Wirth and Edward Shils. London: Routledge.

MARCH, J. (ed.) (1976). *Handbook of Organization*. Chicago: Rand McNally.

NOSOW, S., and FORM, W. H. (eds.) (1962). *Man, Work and Society: A Reader in the Sociology of Occupations*. New York: Basic Books.

NYSTROM, P., and STARBUCK, W. H. (eds.) (1981). *Handbook of Organizational Design*. London and New York: Oxford University Press.

PAHL, R. H. (1988). *On Work*. Oxford: Basil Blackwell.

PFEFFER, J. (1993). 'Barriers to the Advance of Organization Science: Paradigm Development as a Dependent Variable'. *Academy of Management Review*, 18: 599–620.

REED, M. (1996). 'Rediscovering Hegel: The "New Historicism" in Organization and Management Studies'. *Journal of Management Studies*, 33/2: 139–56.

SMELSER, N. J., and SWEDBERG, R. (eds.) (1994). *The Handbook of Economic Sociology*. Princeton: Princeton University Press.

TILGHER, A. (1930). *Homo Faber: Work: What it Has Meant to Men through the Ages*. Translated from the Italian by D. A. Fisher. New York: Harcourt, Brace and Co.

TSOUKAS, H., and KNUDSEN, C. (eds.) (2003). *The Oxford Handbook of Organization Theory*. London and New York: Oxford University Press.

WILPERT, B., and SORGE, A. (1984). *International Yearbook of Organizational Democracy*, Volume II. London: John Wiley.

PART I

WORK, TECHNOLOGY, AND THE DIVISION OF LABOR

Introduction

ROSEMARY BATT

How Much Has Changed?

THE changing nature of work, technology, and the division of labor in the last quarter of the twentieth century has been a central preoccupation of scholarship on organizations. Debate has centered on the extent to which a fundamental shift in employment systems has occurred—from so-called Fordist to post-Fordist models. The stylized facts portray the former as characterized by internal labor market systems in large organizations, narrow jobs in hierarchical career ladders, and long-term employment relations. The latter include decentralized organizations, flatter hierarchies, team-based forms of work organization, and shorter employment relations that reflect external market pressures.

The accumulated body of case-study and survey research over the last twenty years provides ample evidence that fundamental changes have occurred in employment systems (Appelbaum and Batt 1994). A few examples from national and cross-national surveys of work practices are instructive. First, they generally show the substantial use of 'flexible' work practices associated with post-Fordist systems, such as work teams, problem-solving groups, and total quality management. For example, the 1996 survey of Employee Direct Participation in Organizational Change (EPOC) in ten EU countries found that the overwhelming majority of workplaces had some form of direct participation scheme. A cross-national analysis comparing Europe, Japan, Canada, and the United States found that the overwhelming majority of workplaces in each region had adopted total quality management and the use of permanent problem-solving groups such as quality circles (OECD 1999).

Second, these surveys show there is wide variation in adoption of new work practices across countries, industries, and occupations. For example, in the European Union, adoption of simple forms of direct participation ranged from 61 percent of workplaces in Portugal to 90 percent in the Netherlands (OECD 1999). Across industries, 50 percent of manufacturing sites reported the use of employee involvement compared to 67 percent in banking and insurance, and 73 percent in professional services (OECD 1999). Similarly, the 1998 UK Workplace Employment Relations Survey (WERS) found that some form of team-based work system covered anywhere from 68 percent to 92 percent of non-management workers, depending on industry or occupation (Cully *et al.* 1999).

In sum, these examples suggest both an overall trend in adoption of new work practices and considerable variation in these trends across countries, industries, and occupations. Economic actors faced with the same global conditions have a range of options and responses, depending on differences in public policy, institutions, norms, and managerial choices.

Thus, something has changed, but what is it? Compared to the general participatory schemes cited above, the incidence of more radical changes in work organization—for example, the incidence of semi-autonomous or autonomous work teams—is much lower: about 40 percent of workplaces in the United States (Hunter 2000; Osterman 2000), 47 percent in Australia (Morehead *et al.* 1997), and 34 percent in the United Kingdom (Cully *et al.* 1999). Moreover, more decentralized forms of work organization are much more prevalent among higher skilled workers, such as the technical workers described by Barley in Chapter 16 or professional workers described by Hinings in Chapter 17. Non-management workers who are most in need of relief from hierarchy—the blue-collar workers captured by Graham (Chapter 14) or the frontline service workers examined by Frenkel (Chapter 15)—are the least likely to experience it. In the United Kingdom, for example, semi-autonomous or autonomous teams cover 47 percent of work-places for technical workers, but only 23 percent for craft-workers, and 18 percent for machine operators (Cully *et al.* 1999). Moreover, these estimates are for any use of these teams. The average usage rates are typically cut in half again when employers report coverage for 50 percent or more of the workers at a given site (e.g. OECD 1999).

Finally, how to assess change gets even messier when estimates from different surveys covering the same country and similar sampling frames are compared. In the United States, for example, Osterman (2000) surveyed workplaces with fifty or more workers and found that 38.5 percent used self-directed teams in 1997. Cappelli's 1997 national establishment survey covering workplaces with twenty or more workers reported an average of 18 percent using self-directed work teams (Cappelli and Neumark 2001).

These examples illustrate the complexities of interpreting the extent and nature of change in the organization of work and labor markets in the current period. Beyond a general consensus that something fundamental has occurred, estimates and interpretations diverge. The authors in this Part address these debates. They recognize that fundamental changes have taken place in the organization of work and labor markets but are critical of overly optimistic, pessimistic, or unilineal accounts of change. They have great respect for organizational and institutional context, for indeterminate and often paradoxical outcomes, and they pay close attention to empirical research on their particular topic.

In addition, the authors provide a new angle on these debates by bringing together literatures that typically are not discussed in common. The first three chapters, for example, discuss labor markets and restructuring not only as they are influenced by employer strategies but also in the context of changing families and households, social welfare institutions, and gender and race relations. They focus on labor market flexibility (Rubery), work–family conflict (Appelbaum, Bailey, Berg, and Kalleberg), and the new inequality arising from the intersection of restructuring, gender, and race (McCall). The second three chapters focus on specific aspects of restructuring of employment systems, bringing together alternative perspectives on skill formation systems (Crouch), technological change (Badham), and the organization of work (Batt and Doellgast).

Labor Market Flexibility, Work–Family Conflict, and Inequality

We begin with Jill Rubery's chapter on the rise of flexible labor markets, as it provides a broad framework for interpreting the relationship between a range of social institutions and change in employment systems. Drawing on the Supiot report (2001) on the future of employment protection in the European Union, Rubery examines four dimensions of employment systems that have fundamentally changed over the last thirty years. These are: employer organizations and the governance systems that shape product market organization and regulation; the organization of work, pay, and internal management systems; the supply of labor as influenced by family and social welfare systems; and employment regulation as shaped by labor market policy and social security systems.

She uses this framework to identify the fundamental differences between Fordist and post-Fordist employment systems. The former are characterized by bureaucracy, hierarchical job structures, a male-breadwinner/female-caregiver division of labor, and a standard employment contract. These good jobs existed primarily for male breadwinners, while women and minority workers held low-wage, dead-end jobs in secondary firms. Post-Fordist regimes, by contrast, are built on networked organizations, flatter hierarchies, teamworking and empowerment, a dual-earner/dual-caregiver model, and nonstandard employment contracts.

Having accepted the premise that a fundamental shift in employment systems has occurred, Rubery outlines a series of critiques of the literature on post-Fordism. She questions whether the model of the flexible firm (Atkinson 1984)—in which a core of loyal employees exists alongside a periphery of 'flexible' (contingent) workers—is more prescription than description of what has actually occurred. Evidence of employer adoption of this model is weak as core workers themselves have experienced greater job insecurity, downward pressure on wages, and work intensification. In addition, the model depends on the commitment of core workers to one employer when the division of labor in production chains is shifting to a multiemployer environment with more permeable boundaries. 'Peripheral' workers in supply chains often perform 'core tasks'. Moreover, the literature understates the continuing problematic nature of labor–management relations. Few studies have examined the real or potential conflicts between labor and capital or the contradictions between control and cooperation in the labor process in new organizational forms.

Rubery goes on to examine the dynamic between demand- and supply-side factors in the changing structure of labor markets for women, youth, and older workers. Women's higher labor force participation, while initially stimulated by employer demand, has subsequently become relatively autonomous as women develop their own aspirations for work and employment. While cross-national differences in the structure of family institutions and social welfare systems shape women's employment trajectories, in all countries these institutions have lagged behind the actual changes taking place in employment systems, creating heightened conflict between paid work and care work.

The implications of the intersection between labor market and household restructuring are taken up more fully in the next chapter in this part by Eileen Appelbaum, Thomas Bailey, Peter Berg, and Arne Kalleberg. They not only show how institutional mechanisms for integrating work and family life seriously lag behind actual changes; they also point to the dearth of research available to inform debates or guide firm- and public-level policies. While some countries provide better institutional support for families than others—for example, the generous paid maternity leave in most European countries compared to the ungenerous unpaid leave in the United States—all advanced economies exhibit a fundamental mismatch between the nature of institutional supports for families, on the one hand, and the changing demands at work and increased labor force participation of women, on the other. For this reason, private sector employer solutions have emerged. Appelbaum and her colleagues develop a conceptual and empirical foundation for understanding the role of employers in relation to national laws and institutions in resolving work and family conflict.

They identify two broad types of family-friendly employer policies: caregiver replacement policies, on the one hand, and those that give workers more control over their work time, on the other. The former cover child or elder care referral services, subsidized care programs, concierge services, and other services historically provided by a full-time caregiver in a traditional breadwinner/homemaker model. The latter include paid leaves, flexible work scheduling, job sharing, and other devices that allow workers to better coordinate their work and personal responsibilities. These policies provide flexibility based on workers' needs, not employers' demands. Employers are likely to adopt these policies either because they calculate that the benefits of adoption will outweigh the costs or because they respond to institutional pressures or norms to adopt them.

Few national surveys exist, however, to assess the extent of diffusion of these types of policies, despite the fact that all advanced industrial countries have moved from a full-time breadwinner model to a dual-earner/dual-caregiver model. In the United States, where several national surveys have been conducted, Appelbaum and her colleagues reached three conclusions. First, only a minority of firms offer child or elder care assistance to any of their employees. Second, while a majority of firms surveyed report that they offer some form of flexible work arrangements, the most reliable government data shows that these policies are only available to a minority of full-time employees. Third, access to firm-level policies is highly unequal across occupational groups, with professional, technical, and managerial employees most likely to have access and blue-collar workers least likely.

More generally, the authors consider international variation in public policies and cultural norms that shape firm- and individual-level behavior. Where governments provide generous parental leave policies and subsidized childcare, as in the social democratic Nordic countries, the difficulties women face in reconciling paid work and unpaid care are substantially reduced. By comparison, in liberal market-driven economies, such as the United States and United Kingdom, women and their families absorb the costs of work/family coordination; and in conservative corporatist regimes, public policy marginalizes women and encourages them to stay at home with their children.

Nonetheless, even in countries where public policy governing work–family issues is extensive and gender inequality is less, implementation of work–family policies takes place within organizations and is subject to firm-level pressures. Overall, the authors conclude that while the number of firm-level policies has grown over the last two decades in all advanced industrial economies, actual use of them is unknown, but probably low.

The process and outcomes of restructuring for workers and their families is also taken up by Leslie McCall in Chapter 3, but she focuses on our failure to understand the interaction between race, gender, and economic restructuring. The mainstream literature on race and gender in employment, like that on social welfare and work–family policy, has been divorced from the debates over organizational restructuring, employer competitive strategies, and new models of employment systems.

McCall argues that theories of discrimination—and the policy prescriptions for targeted affirmative action programs based on race or gender—are inadequate for dealing with the new inequality because they are based on the assumptions of the male breadwinner model, when employment systems were stable and internal labor markets created good jobs for white male insiders and lousy secondary jobs for women and minorities.

Over the last two decades, new configurations of inequality have emerged within as well as between social groups. For example, as (primarily white) women have sought to eradicate gender discrepancies and enter restructured professional jobs with 80-hour work weeks, they have hired immigrant women to care for their children. This intersection of work and household restructuring has created a perverse chain of global caregiving based on power and unequal relations between First and Third World women (Ehrenreich and Hochschild 2002).

The intersection of race, class, and ethnicity has produced new configurations of inequality among men as well. In the United States, for example, as manufacturing left northern cities and was replaced by service industries with a polarized demand for skills, class divisions grew, with blue-collar men—white and black alike—losing union jobs that paid middle-class wages. However, as the work of William Julius Wilson (1996) and others has shown, the interaction of race and class led to disproportionately higher inequality among black men: that is, blue-collar blacks in inner-city ghettos lost their social connections to their middle-class counterparts, and this spatial segregation diminished their access to new suburban jobs. Wilson's policy solution was not to target racial discrimination, but to suggest non-targeted policies that create good jobs in urban centers where working-class blacks and whites live, but where blacks will benefit disproportionately.

McCall, like the other authors in this Part, argues that the outcomes of restructuring are highly uncertain and context-specific. For example, there are no theoretical predictions as to how workplace restructuring or the use of new work practices such as self-directed work groups will affect existing patterns of inequality. The use of teams may increase equality by creating the same job description and pay for all members in the group; or it may result in an informal reconstruction of the division of labor, with men assuming technical jobs, and women the clerical jobs in teams. Teams may allow group members to create more egalitarian work structures and more flexible schedules to balance work and family; or the lack for formal structures may foster a 'hero' culture of long work hours and peer pressure so that people feel less able to manage family obligations or have a personal life.

Unfortunately, empirical studies of these issues are few. The only consistent finding is that groups or teams with more demographic diversity experience greater conflict and more difficulties. This is not optimistic for any theory that team-based systems are inherently more egalitarian or democratic than hierarchical structures.

McCall calls for a new generation of scholarship that examines how organizational and institutional variation, within and across nations, affects the extent and nature of inequality in our societies. This new research agenda requires a focus on a larger range of 'gender/race neutral' institutions and policies—including minimum wages, working time regulations, unions, education and training, social welfare, and tax, among others. It also requires an exploration of a wider range of outcomes, including labor force participation rates, work hours, pay, occupational segregation, job mobility, work/family integration, and work-related stress, among others.

Without a more context-rich understanding of the hidden dynamics of restructuring and inequality, policy solutions will not begin to address the problem.

Skill Formation, Technology, and Work Organization

The issues of institutional lag and indeterminate outcomes are also central themes in the chapter by Colin Crouch on how skill formation systems are adapting to industry restructuring. Crouch begins by reviewing existing systems that have supported occupational skills and economic development in advanced economies. These systems have had to overcome several dilemmas that arise from the collective goods nature of skills. While individuals need skills to work in advanced economies, training is generally too costly for them to absorb on their own. While firms benefit from a skilled workforce, they are reluctant to invest in training because they risk losing that investment to other firms that poach. The government has a general interest in educating its workforce, both to maintain social order and to build a productive workforce, but it does not want to subsidize the costs of production that would otherwise be paid for by firms.

To deal with these dilemmas, different countries have developed alternative institutional arrangements that include more or less reliance on markets, corporate hierarchies, the state, associations, and community networks. For example, the United States has relied primarily on the market and corporate hierarchies, while Germany's vocational education training (VET) system combines state support with a role for employers' associations and unions. Whatever the configuration, Crouch argues that these systems work best in a stable economy because training can be matched to employer demands for skill. The rapid change and instability brought on by new technologies and globalization at the end of the twentieth century has undermined the effectiveness of these stable systems.

This uncertainty in the demand for skills has led to several paradoxes. While there is consensus that a high-skilled workforce is necessary to compete effectively in the new economy, there is no consensus about which skills are needed. Moreover, the systems that have been viewed as very weak in their provision of stable skills, such as the United Kingdom and the United States, have adapted more successfully to current uncertainty than the more institutionalized systems, such as the German apprenticeship system.

Nonetheless, most advanced economies now face the dilemma of how to reorganize their skill formation systems in an era of high uncertainty in which innovation does not necessarily depend on codified knowledge. One response by governments and employers has been to shift the burden of training to individuals, particularly young people. However, this approach requires three conditions: a population with relatively low general education, from which entrepreneurs or risk-takers will emerge; a set of incentives to encourage people to take risks and invest in skills that have an uncertain payoff; and a large variety of jobs with relatively low skill requirements for the majority of workers who are not risk-takers. These are likely to be service jobs that must be provided in face-to-face transactions. This describes the current situation in Scandinavia, where employment in personal public services creates secure employment at relatively low wages. In the United States and other countries with income inequality, the wealthy create demand for domestic services and the commercialization of household tasks. This type of system is likely to be found where the market, in conjunction with the state, is dominant.

Crouch, however, also suggests that other scenarios are emerging. Many professions, such as law, medicine, and engineering, have been demanding more specialized skills. The uncertainty of skill demand associated with new information technologies may be related to an early stage of development, which could become more stable over time. Some VET institutions have shown the ability to adapt and reconfigure themselves into quite different models from the past. Finally, societies typically have several types of skill formation systems operating at the same time, which provide the institutional flexibility to adapt to new demands and uncertainty. In sum, where a range of system types can coexist, there are opportunities for adaptation—both in terms of the deconstruction of existing systems and the construction of new ones to codify and disseminate knowledge after innovative junctures.

The discussion of skill formation systems and their transformation makes the fundamental assumption that changes in the broader economy, and in particular new information technologies, have led to powerful changes in the demand for skills—changes that have created ambiguity and uncertainty and destabilized skill formation institutions. The subsequent chapter on technology by Richard Badham makes that assumption problematic. While recognizing that new technologies do exert external pressure on institutions, Badham seeks to create a more integrative, multidimensional approach to the concept of technological change and how it plays out at the organizational level.

He first explores what he views as traditional or one-dimensional approaches to technology as impact. While there is considerable variation among writers in this tradition of research—in terms of how technology is conceptualized and the form or degree of impact on work—they have in common an assumption that technology is a 'social fact' that shapes or constrains the nature of work and the division of labor. According to Badham, this tradition includes 'hard determinists', as exemplified by contingency theories of the impact of technology on organizational size and structure, as well as 'soft determinists' such as Shoshana Zuboff (1988), who recognizes the ways in which political and organizational factors shape the effects of technology.

Another version of the one-dimensional view, according to Badham, is research that examines how social agency shapes technology. Included here are micro-ethnographies and macro-analyses of how social, cultural, or political assumptions are embedded in the way technologies are created or implemented. This social constructionist approach predicts a range of variation in the processes and outcomes of technological change. Although different in many respects, studies of new production systems based on institutionalist, Marxist labor process, and neo-Foucauldian theories are often similar in their focus on how social and political factors shape technological outcomes.

Debate over these two perspectives in the 1980s and 1990s has led to a degree of consensus that both offer partial insights and that a more useful approach is interactionist or two-dimensional. Orlikowski's 'technology in practice' (2000) approach is exemplary: social actors implement new technologies at work, and in turn, discover new technical capabilities emerging from their decisions—a process of repeated iterations or mutual adaptations. Others want to push this approach further. Bijker (1995), for example, develops the concept of 'sociotechnical ensembles'—the idea of mutual interpenetration of the technical and social at work. Similarly, for Latour (1993), we cannot think of humans in isolation from tools, as they are so deeply embedded in our knowledge and understanding of the world. This critical examination of the literature brings Badham to three propositions: that technologies should be understood as 'sociotechnologies', or two dimensions of one phenomenon; that workplaces, similarly, should be understood as complex webs of human and nonhuman elements or social and technical configurations; and that change or innovation at work should be viewed as a process of mutual adaptation in which one sociotechnical system replaces another.

In the final chapter of Part I, Batt and Doellgast explore the ongoing debates over the reorganization of work in the last three decades. While there is growing consensus that groups have replaced individuals as the key unit of production at work, the research across disciplines does a poor job of integrating insights or developing a coherent understanding of why they are effective and what happens to workers in these systems. To foster more integration, Batt and Doellgast compare three traditions of research on teams: psychological, institutional, and critical sociological.

Micro-organizational research has concentrated on theories of why individuals in groups perform better than in isolation. One psychological explanation, building on the work of Hackman and Oldham (1980), is that team-based systems create intrinsically motivating jobs, leading to greater worker satisfaction and discretionary effort. Another explanation, at the heart of the sociotechnical systems (STS) literature, is that teams allow people to work smarter by solving problems across an entire work process. More recent versions of cognitive theory use laboratory studies to measure information processing, group cognition, and shared mental models among individuals in a group. Another recent body of literature draws on the social capital literature as it applies to organizations (Leana and Van Buren 1999). Here the argument is that team-based work systems are effective only when they build both trust among workers as well as opportunities for communication and information sharing.

While this research has helped to create a theoretical foundation for understanding groups at work, it suffers from its neglect of organizational, industrial, or institutional context. There is no serious attention to technology or the economics of production systems, which as Badham has shown, is intimately linked to how work is organized. In addition, while researchers profess to be studying performance outcomes, the focus is on a narrow set of attitudes and behaviors that may or may not be linked to operational or economic performance.

In contrast to psychological accounts, industrial relations and institutional studies of teams relate their adoption to changes in markets and technology. According to these accounts, team-based systems allow firms greater flexibility and allocative efficiency through job rotation and multitasking; they allow quicker problem-solving at the point of production by shifting operational decisions to workers; they reduce costs by eliminating indirect labor. A large body of research on high-performance work systems in many industries has demonstrated the relationship between team-based or collaborative work organization and better operational performance (e.g. Appelbaum *et al.* 2000). Workers in these environments do better where there are strong labor market institutions, such as education and training systems, unions, or works councils. These macro-organizational accounts, however, treat 'teams' as a black box so that the causal mechanisms underlying performance gains have not been clearly articulated or tested.

Critical sociologists bring to these debates a healthy skepticism about why firms have adopted team-based work systems and why they are effective. Foucauldian interpretations (Barker 1993) view teamwork as a more insidious form of control than has previously existed. Peer monitoring and control systems produce higher levels of work intensity and conformity because ties of solidarity or guilt bind workers to each other. However, these explanations are ultimately unsatisfactory because they are largely unilineal (Smith and Thompson 1999). Students of the labor process have shown that employees have a wide range of reactions to new work practices and do not necessarily buy into management rhetoric, as demonstrated in this volume by the work of Graham (Chapter 14), Collinson and Ackroyd (Chapter 13), and Kelly (Chapter 12). As of yet, however, we lack serious studies of the politics of team production—comparable to, for example, Roy's goldbricking in a machine shop (1952) or 'banana time' (1959) or Burawoy's study of the game of making out (1979), which capture the rich contradictions of formal and informal work structures, of conflict and consent at work.

In sum, while the use of team-based systems is widespread, and the research is voluminous, we have not developed a sound understanding of how and why groups work effectively in the new economy.

Future Directions

There are some topics that we did not adequately cover in this Part, such as the issue of labor mobility and migration flows across advanced and developing economies. While some have done valuable research in this area (e.g. Castles and Miller 2003; Waldinger and Lichter 2003), there is much to be done to understand how immigration flows intersect with organizational restructuring. Similarly, while some work has begun to examine the globalization of service work (e.g. Burawoy *et al.* 2000), it is so new that relatively little research has attacked this question, but it will surely become a critical topic in future research.

Together, however, the chapters in this Part point to several productive avenues for future research. First, they call for a broadening of the institutional framework for understanding change at work—one that incorporates an appreciation of workplace change in relationship to household changes, gender and family relations, and social welfare policies. Second, they suggest the need to make connections across parallel trends—as in bringing together the research on gender and race discrimination and economic restructuring. Third, they demonstrate the value of bringing together research on the same topic across disciplines—as in the research on teams at work. Fourth, they suggest the need for research at multiple levels of analysis—building theory across individuals and work groups, establishments, firms, and institutions—in order to inform public policy. Finally, they show the need for greater skepticism, more attention to the indeterminate processes of economic restructuring, and an awareness of the potential for complex and contradictory outcomes.

REFERENCES

APPELBAUM, E., and BATT, R. (1994). *The New American Workplace.* New York: ILR Press/ Cornell University Press.

—— BAILEY, T., BERG, P., and KALLEBERG, A. L. (2000). *Manufacturing Advantage: Why High Performance Work Systems Pay Off.* Ithaca, NY: Cornell University Press.

ATKINSON, J. (1984). 'Manpower Strategies for Flexible Organizations'. *Personnel Management*, 16/8: 28–31.

BARKER, J. R. (1993). 'Tightening the Iron Cage: Concertive Control in Self-Managing Teams'. *Administrative Science Quarterly*, 38: 408–37.

BIJKER, W. W. (1995). *Of Bicycles, Bakelites, and Bulbs: Toward a Theory of Sociotechnical Change.* Cambridge, Mass.: MIT Press.

BURAWOY, M. (1979). *Manufacturing Consent.* Chicago: University of Chicago Press.

—— et al. (2000). *Global Ethnography: Forces, Connections, and Imaginations in a Postmodern World.* Berkeley: University of California Press.

CAPPELLI, P., and NEUMARK, D. (2001). 'External Job Churning and Internal Job Flexibility'. NEBR working paper w8111. February. http://papers.nber.org/papers/w8111.

CASTLES, S., and MILLER, M. J. (2003). *The Age of Migration*. New York: Guilford Press.

CULLY, M., WOODLAND, S., O'REILLY, D., and DIX, G. (1999). *Britain at Work as Depicted by 1998 Workplace Employee Relations Survey*. London: Routledge.

EHRENREICH, B., and HOCHSCHILD, A. (eds.) (2002). *Global Woman: Nannies, Maids, and Sex Workers in the New Economy*. New York: Metropolitan Books.

HACKMAN, J. R., and OLDHAM, G. R. (1980). *Work Redesign*. Reading, Mass.: Addison-Wesley.

HUNTER, L. (2000). 'The Adoption of Innovative Work Practices in Service Establishments'. *International Journal of Human Resource Management*, June/11: 477–96.

LATOUR, B. (1993). *We Have Never Been Modern*. Brighton: Harvester Wheatsheaf.

LEANA, C., and VAN BUREN, H. (1999). 'Organizational Social Capital and Employment Practices'. *Academy of Management Review*, 24: 538–55.

MOREHEAD, A., Steele, M., Alexander, M., Stephen, K., and Duffin, L. (1997). 'Changes at Work: The 1995 Australian Workplace Industrial Relations Survey'. Melbourne: Addison Wesley Longman.

OECD (Organization of Economic Cooperation and Development) (1999). 'New Enterprise Work Practices and Their Labour Market Implications'. OECD Employment Outlook, Chapter 4, OECD.

ORLIKOWSKI, W. J. (2000). 'Using Technology and Constituting Structures: A Practice Lens for Studying Technology in Organisations'. *Organisation Science*, 11/4: 404–26.

OSTERMAN, P. (2000). 'Work Organization in an Era of Restructuring: Trends in Diffusion and Impacts on Employee Welfare'. *Industrial and Labor Relations Review*, 53/2: 179–96.

ROY, D. (1952). 'Quota Restriction and Gold Bricking in a Machine Shop'. *American Journal of Sociology*, 57: 427–42.

——(1959). '"Banana Time": Job Satisfaction and Informal Interaction'. *Human Organization*, 18/4: 158–68.

SMITH, C., and THOMPSON, P. (1999). 'Reevaluating the Labour Process Debate', in M. Wardell, T. Steiger, and P. Meiksins (eds.), *Rethinking the Labour Process*. Albany, NY: State University of New York Press, 205–31.

SUPIOT, A. (2001). *Beyond Employment: Changes at Work and the Future of Employment Law in Europe*. Oxford: Oxford University Press.

WALDINGER, R., and LICHTER, M. I. (2003). *How the Other Half Works: Immigration and the Social Organization of Labor*. Berkeley: University of California Press.

WILSON, W. J. (1996). *When Work Disappears*. New York: Alfred Knopf.

ZUBOFF, S. (1988). *In the Age of the Smart Machine: The Future of Work and Power*. London: Heinemann.

CHAPTER 1

LABOR MARKETS AND FLEXIBILITY

JILL RUBERY

1.1 INTRODUCTION

THE labor market has traditionally been viewed through a narrow lens, trained
directly on the market for wage labor and on the management of employment
within well-bounded organizations. This narrow lens was possible in the era of the
so-called Fordist or industrial model of employment relations. The Fordist model
focused on male workers as continuous labor market participants, employed under
standard employment contracts, and acting as subordinate labor within a single
organization. The breakdown of this model in all its different aspects has revealed
the need for a wider perspective. For example, the increasing participation of
women has called into question the exclusive focus on wage work and the standard
employment relationship. Employment contracts have become more diverse and
precarious and employment relationships more complex as employing organizations fragment and restructure. Power relations 'no longer have the clarity of a
pyramid' (Sennett 1998: 57) but operate through the decentralized systems of
performance auditing and contract specifications (Harrison 1994; Sennett 1998).
As the Supiot report on the future of employment protection in the European
Union outlined (Supiot 2001), it is necessary to move 'beyond employment', beyond
the restricted, historically contingent Fordist model, and to develop a more holistic
approach to our understanding of work, employment, and labor markets.

This broader approach also fits with the insights that have come from the expanding literature on comparative labor market systems. Differences in the organization of employment are not solely or mainly attributable to the direct institutions shaping the employment relationships, for example, the voluntary or legal systems of employment regulation. Equal or greater importance needs to be accorded to the wider societal institutions—the social welfare systems, the education and training system, the system of corporate and economic governance, the family and the form of gender relations (Crouch, Finegold, and Sako 1999; Esping-Andersen 1990; Lewis 1992; Maurice and Sorge 2000; Maurice, Sellier, and Silvestre 1986). Explaining the variety of employment systems requires an understanding of how employment fits within this broader societal system (Marsden 1986, 1999). Change in labor markets needs to be explored through a large canvas on which the interrelations between the changes in production, social

Table 1.1 From Fordist to post-Fordist employment systems

Labor market dimension	Main institutional spheres	Fordist	Post-Fordist
Employing organizations	Governance systems Product market organization and regulation	Bureaucratic organizations Dominance of manufacturing	Networked organizations Contract culture and dominance of services
Organization of work and pay	Internal management systems Training system	Taylorist and hierarchical pay and job structures Standard working hours	Flatter hierarchies Teamworking Empowerment Customer-focused Taylorism Flexible/extended working hours Performance-related pay
Supply of labor	Family Welfare system Educational system	Male breadwinner/ female carer Political objective: full employment for men	Dual-earner/dual-carer Political objective: employment opportunities for all adults
Employment regulation	Legal and voluntary regulation Social security systems Employment policy	Standard employment contract	Diversity of employment contracts

reproduction, the political and policy agenda, and the labor market can be mapped (Burchell *et al.* 2003). The current variety in employment systems provides some prima facie evidence that the path of change is historically determined. Even in a period of radical reform, that change process may be evolutionary and not susceptible to rationalist explanations such as the diffusion of best practice to meet global competition (Hall and Soskice 2001; Hollingsworth and Boyer 1997; Rubery and Grimshaw 2002; Smith and Meiksins 1995).

With these methodological issues in view, this chapter explores the nature of change in labor markets and the rise of so-called flexible labor markets. The key elements of the employment system are taken to be: (1) employing organizations and the associated pattern of work organization and pay, (2) the structure of labor supply, and (3) the form of employment relationships and contracts. Table 1.1 provides a heuristic representation of these elements in Fordist and post-Fordist employment systems, as identified in the Supiot report (2001). The empirical evidence in support of this characterization will be addressed in the sections below. The main objective is to explore the debates about how these changes are to be interpreted, particularly with respect to the now ubiquitous concept of flexibility, and to identify how change in one element is related to or reflective of changes in other dimensions.

1.2 EMPLOYING ORGANIZATIONS AND THE ORGANIZATION OF WORK

Employing organizations can be regarded as the architects of employment (Loveridge and Mok 1979), as it is within organizations that work is structured, jobs designed, labor is rewarded, and the employment relationship is forged. Surprisingly, much labor market analysis abstracts from the role of organizations and focuses on the experiences of individuals categorized by occupation, sector, human capital, or contract form without reference or knowledge of the characteristics of their employer. In the 1970s, interest began to be paid to the influence of employer policy on the shaping of skills, career structures, and payment systems through the creation of internal labor markets within large bureaucratic organizations (Doeringer and Piore 1971). Employing organizations, by determining the share of good and bad jobs in the economy and by influencing access to opportunities for skill development, were identified as contributing to the creation of labor market segments and inequalities, against the mainstream view that the labor market was a neutral reflector of social and class inequalities. According to these initial theories, access to the primary segment provided lifetime job and income security. As downsizing and flexibility spread in the 1980s and 1990s to even the most stable of employing organizations, attention refocused on the dynamics of change within employing organizations and the redrawing of boundaries between stable and unstable employment segments (Rosenberg 1989). Three strands of that debate can be identified: (1) the disintegration of internal labor markets and the development of the flexible firm, (2) the rise of new forms of production organization, and (3) the development of new human resource management styles or techniques.

1.2.1 From Bureaucratic Internal Labor Markets to the Flexible Firm?

In the segmented labor market models of the 1970s, 'modern' internal labor markets of large technologically advanced organizations coexisted alongside a residual rump of flexible secondary labor markets, employing primarily women and minorities and often based on traditional skills and modes of organization. In the 1980s flexible firm model, divisions between primary and secondary segments were redrawn to provide employers with increased flexibility of delivery and reduced risk. Employers' management dilemma is how simultaneously to harness the loyalty and skills of the workforce and yet control costs. Atkinson's (1984) flexible firm model appeared to provide organizations with a tool to achieve the best of both worlds: workers with core skills would be offered both job security and internal careers while those in the outer periphery, providing noncore or nonstrategic skills, were to be employed on a flexible basis. The periphery consisted of a ring of numerically flexible internal employees and a further layer of external peripheral workers, employed by agencies and subcontractors.

This model has been interpreted as both a prescription for how firms should manage their labor force and as a description of emerging trends. Evidence to support the latter interpretation is mixed (Heery and Salmon 2000; Pollert 1988). Extensive downsizing by large organizations and a growth of secondary-type employment indicated that a process of labor market restructuring was occurring. However, many of the flexible jobs were located in precisely those sectors that had a history of using such forms of employment (Hunter *et al.* 1993; Marginson 1989), and few firms were consciously adopting a core/periphery strategy (Hakim 1990). Moreover, despite the rising concern with job security, actual job tenure has often increased (Auer and Cazes 2001; Jacoby 1999), particularly as women have become more permanent participants in the labor market. One problem in making sense of these changes is that the stability of the employment systems in the 1960s and 1970s may have been exaggerated.

Furthermore, empirical research has cast doubt on whether a core/periphery strategy is sustainable in the long term. Subcontracting and flexible employment forms, such as temporary contracts, may deliver short-term cost savings. However, the effect may be to undermine the integrity of the production process by creating new internal divisions, for in practice peripheral workers often undertake tasks that are central to the organization's performance or brand image (Bosch, Webster, and Weibach 2000; Colling 2000; Geary 1992). Research suggests that there is no clear-cut division of tasks into core and noncore (Purcell and Purcell 1998). Decisions to subcontract or to create internal divisions may be influenced as much by issues of market power (as reflected in labor costs), as by the strategic importance of the tasks. Employers may take advantage of high levels of unemployment, weaker trade unions, and new sources of labor supply for flexible or part-time employment to offer differentiated terms and conditions of employment, either directly or through subcontracting. Labor market divisions may not necessarily be justified in part or in full by human capital differences.

International comparisons of labor markets have also called into question the ubiquity of the flexible firm approach and demonstrated that there is more than one way of responding to the new market challenges. Flexibility strategies may be categorized as positive, enabling adjustment to new challenges and opportunities created by technological and market change, or negative, aimed at cost cutting and the postponement of adjustment (Brunhes, Rojot, and Wasserman 1989). The path of labor market development depends also upon whether employing organizations are able to draw on institutional resources to pursue a 'high road' route to development. Where a society lacks such resources, employing organizations may remain locked into a low road path (Finegold and Soskice 1988; Rubery 1994).

Comparative research has highlighted the variety of ways in which labor markets are institutionalized. For example, Germany, instead of adopting the internalized labor markets of the American segmentation literature, has organized its training and employment system around occupational labor markets. Marsden (1999) has suggested a two by two categorization to describe how work and jobs are organized across societies, positing first a distinction between systems organized around a production approach and those organized around a training approach; the former seeks 'complementarities between task in the production systems' and the latter 'complementarities in worker skills' (Marsden 1999: 33). Second, he distinguishes between task-centered and function-centered rules, similar to a distinction between high and low trust systems. The production approach is argued to be dominant in the United States, France, and Japan and the training approach in the United Kingdom and Germany, while the task-centered approach is characteristic of the United States, France, and the United Kingdom and the function-centered approach of Japan and Germany (Marsden 1999: ch. 5). Changes in markets and technologies place pressure on all modes of institutionalizing and organizing employment, but the specific problems and the likely responses will vary according to the form of institutionalization. Debates over flexible labor markets have thus to consider and interact with the emerging debates on varieties of capitalism and alternative modes of post-Fordist organization (Hall and Soskice 2001).

In the 1990s, flexibility strategies appeared to be spreading to groups previously considered to be in a protected core. Cappelli, in the context of the United States, explicitly rejected the notion that the periphery acted to protect the core, stating that far from current changes being 'driven by an interest in buffering core employees... downsizing efforts increasingly strike employees who seem to be in the "core" of the workforce' (Cappelli 1995: 591). The growth of outsourcing adds instead to the competitive pressure on the remaining internalized employees to forego their previous privileges as internal protected employees. A related argument was made in the UK context where core workers were found to be continuously exposed to pressures to outsource their activities should the relative advantage between internal and external organization of the activity change (Ackroyd and Procter 1998). These arguments took the flexibility debate to a new stage where the effect was not just to redraw segment boundaries but to increase active competition between segments, a process that both spreads job insecurity and leads to work intensification (Burchell, Ladipo, and Wilkinson 2001; Green 2001).

1.2.2 New Organizational Forms and Changing Labor Markets

The flexible firm model was primarily concerned with using a more fragmented employment system to lower employment costs in situations of uncertainty. Other parallel debates took as their central concern the adaptation of production systems to meet new product market and technological conditions (Appelbaum and Batt 1994). Researchers focused on the changes required to introduce lean production (Womack, Jones, and Roos 1990), to develop market niches associated with flexible specialization (Piore and Sabel 1984), or to maximize the synergies offered by the new networked firm (Castells 1996). Employment change in this context was more a consequence of change to industrial organization than an objective sought in its own right. These changes to organizational forms involved both the internal restructuring of organizations and the development of new forms of interorganizational relations.

Lean production in practice has comparable implications for employment as the flexible firm model. It requires output to be geared more closely to consumer demand; more temporal flexibility is needed to match production to variable demands but the fragility of the system also required a loyal and committed workforce (Elger and Smith 1994), able to problem solve and unlikely to derail the system by breaking the supply chain. Thus lean production appears to require organizations to attempt to combine high commitment employment with greater flexibility and disposability for some types of staff.

The debates on flexible specialization (Brusco 1982; Piore and Sabel 1984) and the network firm (Lepak and Snell 1999; Nohria and Eccles 1992) have renewed interests in the centrality of human resources and skill to the production process. The flexible specialization thesis stresses the scope for a renaissance of craft-based systems of work organization and cooperative relations between small firms. The network firm captures the synergies that can be gained from specialization in a context of rapidly changing knowledge and new technologies that facilitate the coordination of more fragmented activities. These researchers see new systems of work organization as providing mutual gains for employers and workers by empowering workers and increasing organizational innovative capacity. However, the traditional issues of control of the workforce have tended to become invisible behind a unitarist focus on the development of productive capacity in the organization or even in the wider network. Within these new networks there is a recognized need for interorganizational relations to operate on the basis of high levels of interorganizational trust. In focusing on how to extend trust beyond the organization, the analysis glosses over the contested relations within the employment relationship and treats each organization as if all its members subscribe to a unitary purpose and pursue only mutual interests. The nurturing of trust within the internal employment relationship is thus assumed, not analyzed (Ezzamel, Willmott, and Worthington 2001; Rubery *et al.* 2002, 2003).

Organizations, according to these perspectives, have become flatter, more decentralized, and embedded in networks of interorganizational relations (Castells 1996). The consequence is that even core workers may face the prospect of unstructured careers, involving moves between multiple employers. These changes have been portrayed by some authors (Arthur and Rousseau 1996) as offering positive opportunities for individuals to manage their own careers and develop new skills. In the extreme case, the employment relationship is even reversed. Instead of managers and employees, 'everyone is a business person' (Miles and Snow 1995) and powerful employees 'hire' the organization to provide them with services (Miles and Snow 1996). Whether this analysis can be extended beyond particular knowledge-based sectors or industrial districts remains unclear. Indeed theories of flexible specialization and the network firm have been criticized for generalizing on the basis of special cases, sectors, and geographical areas (Harrison 1994), the former associated with the industrial districts of northern Italy and the latter with Silicon Valley (Saxenian 1996).

1.2.3 High Commitment Work Practices and Changing Labor Markets

Despite the extensive debate on the fragmentation of the bureaucratic firm, it is the internal management of employment that continues to dominate human resource management literature. Indeed in a more flexible market environment, employers may have even more reason to focus on ensuring that employees use their initiative in the interests of the organization. Employers do not have full knowledge of what this requires and consequently there is a perceived need to 'affect the thought processes and the decision premises of employees' (Simon 1991: 32), and to do this through the development of identity with and commitment to the organization. The importance of commitment has increased along with the delayering and decentering of the hierarchical form. Instead of compliance with organizational goals being achieved through bureaucratic rules and transparent rewards, the new flexible organization is ever more dependent upon the successful development of a strong organizational culture, underpinned by the adoption of best practice, high trust inducing human resource management techniques, and individualized reward systems and performance management (see Sisson and Storey 2000 for a review). A strong psychological contract between employer and employee should enable the employer to rely on individual employees to act in the interests of the organization even when responsibilities for behavior and action are devolved to the individual or the group (Guest 1998).

It is the changes in internal techniques and approaches to personnel management that are here driving changes in labor markets. However, the direction of change is not always clear. For example, there are continuing debates over whether organizations should decentralize human resource policy to match policy to different market conditions—the best fit approach—or retain a centralized policy to promote a strong organizational culture, thereby to underpin the psychological contract—the best practice approach (Boxall and Purcell 2002; Legge 1989; Purcell 1999). There are also obvious problems in placing increasing reliance on the notion of organizational commitment when there is increasing permeability of organizational borders (Cappelli 1995). The rise of joint ventures, alliances, subcontracting, and other arrangements are calling into question the ability of organizations to shape their own internal cultures and systems without reference to external influences. Many employees find themselves working in 'multiemployer' environments, serving the interests of clients as well as direct employers (McClean Parks, Kidder, and Gallagher 1998; Rubery et al. 2003; Scarbrough 2000). Moreover, with the downsizing of organizations and the formation of network organizations, the opportunities for single employer lifetime careers will diminish, thereby challenging the rationale for organizational commitment among employees. Indeed the level of commitment that can be expected may be at best superficial or at worst induced simply by fear. Employers may have yet to feel the impact of the demise of mutual obligations as employee performance may be kept up simply because of 'the threat of lay-off, the comparison with the jobless and the fact that most alternative employers were undergoing the same restructuring' (Cappelli *et al.* 1997: 215). Human resource management theorists are perhaps too keen to suggest that employment issues can always be resolved through the adoption of appropriate management techniques or policies (Lepak and Snell 1999; Matusik and Hill 1998). If the employment relationship is contested, any set of policies to manage employment may engender resistance and not necessarily promote commitment to the employer. Moreover, where managers of organizations find they are embedded in an environment characterized by low trust, they may not be able, even through their best efforts, to establish high trust relations with their workforce.

1.2.4 Making Sense of the Role of Organization in the Post-Fordist Labor Market

The outcomes of these rather divergent debates on the impact of changing organizations on employment can be summarized as follows. Trends towards outsourcing and fragmentation cannot be fully explained by a rational core–periphery division of activities based on their strategic importance. The advantages that internal employment offers for cooperation in and control over the labor process may be sacrificed in the search to reduce costs if outsourcing provides access to lower cost or less powerful labor. However, contracting out activities does not remove the need for such control and cooperation and may indeed complicate these requirements. That internal employment continues to offer advantages may in part explain the conflicting evidence on the extent to which organizations have embraced opportunities for fragmentation and flexibility. From very different starting points, the debates on the new organizational forms and on human resource management have both overstressed the mutuality of interests between capital and labor and the scope for management-driven initiatives to create high trust relations. The fragmentation of the bureaucratic firm has not changed the fundamental need for capital and labor to find some accommodation between their pursuit of conflicting differences and their need to cooperate in the productive process. However, new institutional systems may need to be developed and embedded in wider social structures to achieve the dual functions of protecting employee interests and promoting mutual cooperation.

1.3 LABOR SUPPLY

Changes in the structure of labor supply have been no less dramatic than the restructuring of employing organizations. There are three main forces underpinning these changes: (1) the restructuring of demand for labor, (2) changes to those social institutions that provide support mechanisms for people inside and outside the labor market, and (3) the aspirations and behavior of individuals over the lifecourse. These influences tend to be long term and not easily reversible, such that changes in demand or in institutional arrangements can set off a pattern of change that is independent of the initial stimulus. Instead, induced changes in aspirations and behavior may result in supply-side trends becoming relatively autonomous of either demand-side development or policy agendas (Humphries and Rubery 1984).

This three-pronged approach can be used to explore and explain the major changes in labor supply that are found in almost all OECD countries. These include the increasing participation of women, the declining share of young people in the labor market, and the tendency towards early retirement (Smith 2001).

The influence of demand on women's employment is clearly evident in the fact that between 1961 and 1992, 25 million out of 30 million jobs created in the European Union went to women (CEC 1994), a process of feminization of the labor force that has continued since. Women were drawn into the labor market in the phase of economic expansion in the 1960s and 1970s, but their upward employment trajectory continued through the high unemployment periods of the 1980s and 1990s. This trend towards higher female employment is to a considerable degree explained by the continuation of gender-specific demands for workers, that is, by gender difference (OECD 1994; O'Reilly and Fagan 1998; Rubery, Smith, and Fagan 1999). Gender segregation is associated both with the high demand for women in the service sector and the exposure of men to the downturn in manufacturing employment. Furthermore, the growth of flexible part-time and temporary jobs has been associated to a large extent with the employment of female labor. Thus the integration of women was to a large extent based on difference not equality. Even where women have entered previously male-dominated segments, this entry has been associated with the restructuring of the occupation and the reproduction of gender segregation, as women become concentrated in particular parts of the occupation or the whole profession moves from being male to female dominated (Crompton and Sanderson 1990; Reskin and Roos 1990). Changes in the nature of labor supply can thus be considered an integrated part of the process of employment restructuring and not a separate development (Walby 1997).

A similar dynamic between demand- and supply-side factors can explain changes in labor market participation by age. Youth entry rates to employment have declined in the face of economic restructuring that has eliminated many entry-level youth jobs and increased the demand for more educated young people—thereby postponing age of entry or leading young people to combine both education and work. The growth of a student population available for part-time or contingent work has again been an important factor in the restructuring of certain industries such as retail (Jany-Catrice and Lehndorff 2005). Similarly, the decline in older men's participation can be traced to the impact of economic restructuring and the processes of downsizing that have affected those groups deemed unsuitable for further training and redeployment (Naschold and de Vroom 1993). In countries such as the United States, this dynamic has also created a relatively autonomous supply of older workers for part-time jobs.

These general changes in demand and supply are insufficient, however, to explain the wide variations between countries in the intensity of the trends or in the levels of participation by women over the lifecycle. Here we need to understand differences between societies in social arrangements and institutions, and indeed, in policy towards labor market activity. Traditionally, economists have been primarily concerned with the decision to enter wage employment. A more interesting perspective addresses the arrangements that need to be in place to allow individuals not to have to sell their labor. The more that individuals have choices, because of a developed welfare state or family support system offering alternative means of support in sickness, old age, or times of unemployment, the less labor is treated as a commodity (Esping-Andersen 1990). While the state is a major source of support, the family is often equally important in shaping labor market participation particularly for women and young people. The family may derive part of its ability to provide support through the state—for example, through favorable tax treatment for men with dependent wives—or through education-based support for young people. It is differences in the state–family–market relations that can be used to explain many of the differences observed between advanced countries in patterns of labor supply. For example, the high participation rates of women in Scandinavian countries have been attributed to these countries' social democratic welfare states, which provided public services to support the integration of women into employment. These public services both enabled women to go out to work and generated a demand for female labor. By contrast, the continental welfare state system in, for example, Germany provided financial support to the family to support women as carers within the household but did not generate jobs or encourage participation. Differences in youth employment rates are influenced by the form of the education and training system and the associated transition from school to work (Detzel and Rubery 2002); and the pattern of early retirement reflects state policy towards the provision of benefits and pensions to those under the standard retirement age (Naschold and de Vroom 1993; Smith 2001).

However, while state policies continue to shape the pattern of labor market participation, there is also evidence that labor supply trends reflect longer-term changes in individual aspirations that are not easily controlled by changes in demand or in state policies. For example, the sustained rise in female labor market participation has been maintained by changes in the attitudes and actions of women themselves, who have become more committed, continuous participants in the labor market and who have invested heavily in education and training. This response to both state policies and demand-side opportunities has been a force pushing for more equal treatment within the labor market. Despite differences in welfare states, female employment rates have risen in all advanced countries, even in those countries with underdeveloped policies for gender equality (Mósesdóttir 2001; Rubery, Smith, and Fagan 1999). Differences between countries in the form of labor market organization—for example, the degree of wage dispersion or the share of part-time employment—will still influence whether women are able to become relatively equal breadwinners within households or whether their economic contribution to the household is still secondary to the male partner's (Rubery *et al.* 2001). The aspirations of women to be continuous participants in the labor market, therefore, now seem to be driving the process of integration. The employment rates of mothers are rising even where infrastructure support for dual-earner households in the form of publicly provided childcare is limited. Moreover, where there are problems in reconciling work and family life, it is women's fertility rate that seems to decline. Indeed 'the traditional negative correlation between female participation and fertility has now turned positive' (Esping-Andersen 2002: 65–6).

Changes in participation patterns over the lifecourse also appear to be enduring. While for young people, labor market entry initially may have been delayed in response to low demand, they now increasingly regard a period of higher education as the normal or desirable route into work. Employers accordingly have increased their entry requirements to fit the new pattern of educated labor. While longer education is generally considered a good development, there are more misgivings about the impact of early retirement on the sustainability of welfare systems. However, again there is resistance to reversals of policy as expectations of retirement before 60 have become strongly embedded in some advanced economies. Some European governments have faced major industrial unrest when attempting to reform the pension system: in France this led to the downfall of one prime minister, Alain Juppé, in the 1990s, and in 2003 a new wave of strikes was underway to protest at another government's decision to lengthen qualifying times for pensions.

If labor supply change is *relatively autonomous* of specific policy actions or demand-side patterns, there may be a lag in adjusting systems and structures to match the changed behavior of social actors. Moreover, changes to labor supply tend to be relatively long term, such that the replacement of the male-breadwinner household model by a dual-earner model is a fundamental and not easily reversible change. There are two main consequences of this development. First, it marks an end to the post-World War II Keynesian full employment consensus where male labor claimed priority in access to employment. Conflicts over the distribution of employment have become manifest in high levels of unemployment or in policies to make labor accept jobs previously considered too low paid or demeaning for unemployed male workers (Heery and Salmon 2000). Responses by some men, particularly younger members of disadvantaged groups, may be to withdraw from the labor market and engage in informal or illegal work (Freeman 1996). Similarly, among older men, there has been a retreat into, for example, reliance on long-term disability pensions (Disney 1999). The second major consequence is that there is also now no established consensus as to who should perform care work or how it is to be both funded and organized, now that the system of women providing private unpaid care has broken down. Women have begun to reject their role as primary carers, but not all societies have come up with coherent systems of replacement for female labor, leading to problems as to how care is to be provided without resulting in an absence of care or a fertility crisis (Appelbaum *et al.*, in this volume; Esping-Andersen 2002; Folbre 1994).

So far we have been discussing labor supply changes as if they are confined within a clearly defined nation state. Such an approach is becoming unsatisfactory for two reasons. First, the increasingly global production systems allow work to be more readily transferred from one nation to another. Second, migration across state borders has been growing. The development of low-paid flexible jobs has been associated with the increasing supplies of legal and illegal immigrants. Migration flows are responsive to economic push and pull factors and to rule changes on migration, but in some cases are primarily driven by political desta-bilization. The type and extent of migration takes different forms in different nation states, but it fuels labor market divisions, particularly where migrant workers are unprotected by social security, minimum wages, or by trade unions (Castles and Miller 1998).

1.4 CHANGES IN THE FORM OF THE EMPLOYMENT RELATIONSHIP

The transition to a post-Fordist employment regime has also been associated with changes in the form of the employment relationship. The characteristics of the standard or Fordist employment relationship are an open-ended commitment to relatively continuous employment (sometimes known as a permanent contract) based on full-time hours of work, with any additional hours of work subject to regulation and additional premia. Except where there are overriding reasons for continuous production processes, work was primarily scheduled for daytime hours Monday to Friday. The system provided a relatively clear division between work hours and private lives, at least for nonmanagerial workers (Supiot 2001). This standard employment relationship was established through trade union and collective organization, but backed by employment legislation and legal interpretation of the nature of the employment contract. Its influence extended beyond those organizations directly subject to collective bargaining pressure as it became established in social expectations or reinforced by legal mechanisms that extended regulation on a sectoral or labor market level (Osterman 2000).

In the post-Fordist period, there has been a seemingly relentless move towards more diverse employment relationships, based on non-permanent contracts, agency work, self-employment, short, long, and indeed variable working hours. These developments have led both to diversity of employment contracts and to changes within the standard full-time permanent contract. The OECD (1999) found a fairly widespread trend towards a reduction in employment protection during the late 1980s and 1990s. In most cases this occurred primarily through relaxation of restrictions on temporary contracts but in countries such as Spain and Portugal there were also significant reductions in protection for those on permanent contracts. Working-time arrangements have also become more flexible, blurring the clear division between work time and personal time as staff face pressure to work additional or variable hours—sometimes on an unpaid basis—and to accept responsibility for completing tasks rather than working to standard times. These tendencies, although widespread (Standing 1999), have been greater in some societies than others, depending upon the form and strength of the regulatory system (Felstead and Jewson 1999; Heery and Salmon 2000; Rubery, Smith, and Fagan 1999). Alongside and associated with the growth in nonstandard contracts, there has been a move away from a clearly bounded employment relationship between a single employer and an employee (Rubery *et al.* 2002). The growth of outsourcing, joint ventures and partnerships, agency working, and pseudo-self-employment has created ambiguities as to who the employer actually is, on the one side, and who or what an employee is, on the other.

Changes to the organization of employment, including the rise of nonstandard working, are not the outcome of abstract forces of supply and demand but instead are mediated through the specific policies and practices of organizations, the form of social and gender relations, the policies and practices of the state, and the system of labor market regulation. The importance of this social and institutional perspective is evident first of all in the differences in both the level and form of nonstandard working across advanced countries (Rubery, Smith, and Fagan 1999). Thus, while it is tempting to offer general explanations, couched, for example, in terms of globalization, the rise of the service economy, the requirements of lean production, or the increasing diversity of labor supply, the variations between countries require a more specific analysis. Such an analysis should be rooted in the following social and institutional arrangements and practices:

- the mode of integration of women into the labor market (whether into full-time or part-time work, whether on a continuous or discontinuous basis);
- the organization of service sector work (with large-scale private capital more likely to use part-time work to maximize employer flexibility than small firm, family-economy-based service sectors);
- state policies towards unemployment (for example, the degree of pressure on the unemployed to take up nonstandard work) or migration (for example, nonstandard work as informal support for excluded groups);
- the mode of organizing and funding higher education (in particular the role of part-time wage work as a supplement to state or family funding);
- the regulatory environment with respect to incentives or disincentives for outsourcing and for the use of nonstandard labor contracts;
- state and employer policies towards flexible working associated with reconciling work and personal and family commitments.

The above list represents the minimum factors that need to be taken into account to understand the differences in trends and levels of nonstandard working across advanced societies. These institutional systems, however, do not remain static over time but indeed evolve through endogenous and exogenous influences. Nonstandard employment can be considered an endogenous influence on the organization of labor markets, through the changes that it induces in social expectations with respect to standard employment. Increasingly insecurity has become associated not only with nonstandard jobs but also with standard or core jobs (Burchell, Ladipo, and Wilkinson 2001). Now core workers may be expected to build portfolio careers, to work flexibly, and to be paid according to performance rather than status within a bureaucracy.

Some states have made changes in their regulatory frameworks to adjust to, and indeed to modify in some respects, the growth of nonstandard working. For example, Spain reduced the protection offered to permanent contracts (OECD 1999) to try to reduce its very high share of temporary contracts, through reducing the disincentives to employers in creating more permanent jobs. The EU also has progressively introduced regulations to reduce the divergence in social protection offered to those on nonstandard employment contracts, including part-timers, fixed-term contract workers, temporary agency workers (legislation proposed but not yet passed), and teleworkers. These moves have been designed to avoid the development of nonstandard work as a means of evading the social costs of social protection systems (Deakin 2002).

1.5 Towards a New Model?

The disruption of the dominant Fordist model of employment has involved complex and interrelated changes in employment participation patterns, particularly by gender and age; in the structures of production and systems of work organization; and in the employment relationship. However, the changes that we observe are not necessarily moving societies towards a new logic that is either coherent or sustainable. There is no coordinated plan to move from one mode of organizing social and economic life to another. There is major scope for conflicts of interests and indeed perverse and damaging outcomes. Reliance on the automatic hand of the market may not result in either a socially acceptable or indeed efficient solution and more positive intervention may be required. The kinds of conflicts and contradictions we have in mind can be illustrated by two examples.

First, there is the conflict between wage work and care work, which is being exacerbated by both the demands for more flexible and often long working hours and by the changing patterns of household and gender relations that are reducing the specialization of women in nonmarket care work (Supiot 2001). If there are no policy initiatives to bring about a workable compromise between these conflicting pressures, the results could include more excessively stressed working parents, further reductions in the birth rate (Bettio and Villa 1998), and increased poverty among children whose parents do work full-time in the labor market (Folbre 1994).

Second, there may be increasing conflicts and contradictions between organizations' need for committed and motivated workers and the changing nature of both organizations and the employment relationship or contract. Fragmented or networked organizations are represented as lower risk organizational forms and as offering new opportunities for synergies and cross-organizational learning. However, much of the positive literature takes a very simplistic approach to the employment relationship, where organizations can overcome the contested nature of the employment relationship by adopting appropriate tools to foster organizational trust—both within the organization and vis-à-vis the other organizations in the network (Rubery *et al.* 2002, 2003). In practice it may prove more difficult than anticipated to identify core from noncore tasks and to find tools to maintain organizational loyalty in a context where employment security is decreasing. Furthermore, fragmentation may make it less likely that employers will assume responsibilities for upgrading skills, thereby leading to problems of underprovision of training unless provided through state-led initiatives.

The result of such conflicts and contradictions may be that social actors begin to think twice before pursuing some of the current policies and practices that are being promoted in the management literature, such as outsourcing. Organizations may find, for example, that subcontracting does not provide adequate quality control, or that flexible working leads to higher staff turnover, unless tailored to individual employee needs. However, reliance on 'learning by doing' to bring about a new coherent system of employment and work organization is a very risky business, particularly as individual employers may not be able to provide all the solutions to the problems themselves. For example, new ways of reconciling work and care responsibilities require new systems of infrastructure development, new ways of treating care work within systems of employment and social protection (Supiot 2001), and new rights with respect to working time arrangements, none of which are necessarily best developed and delivered at the individual employer level.

These new arrangements do therefore require a new framework for organizing employment that is not solely focused on bureaucratic, continuous careers of male workers on standard contracts. Reinstitutionalizing the labor market to meet the new needs of the post-Fordist system requires the involvement of all social actors—employers, trade unions, professional and training institutions, workers and citizens, as well as the state, at local, national, and pan-national levels. In the European Union, a process of reinstitutionalization is already underway, driven in part by the social agenda of the EU and by an increasing recognition that many of the changes that have taken place—including the integration of women and the growth of nonstandard work—are no longer marginal or peripheral developments but are central to the changing nature of economies and societies (Mückenberger 1996). However, it is not yet clear if there is sufficient momentum behind this process of reinstitutionalization to generate new forms of protection and new ways of reconciling production and social reproduction requirements. Much of the debate remains mired in the conflicts over deregulation and flexibility that began in the 1970s and 1980s and has not yet moved forward to consider what forms of regulation need to be built to provide coherent, productive, and socially acceptable labor market systems for the twenty-first century.

References

Ackroyd, S., and Procter, S. (1998). 'British Manufacturing Organization and Workplace Industrial Relations: Some Attributes of the New Flexible Firm'. *British Journal of Industrial Relations*, 36/2: 163–83.

Appelbaum, E., and Batt, R. (1994). *The New American Workplace*. New York: ILR Press/Cornell University Press.

Arthur, M., and Rousseau, D. (eds.) (1996). *The Boundaryless Career: A New Employment Principle for a New Organizational Era*. Oxford: Oxford University Press.

Atkinson, J. (1984). 'Manpower Strategies for Flexible Organizations'. *Personnel Management*, 16/8: 28–31.

Auer, P., and Cazes, S. (2001). 'Employment Stability and Flexibility in Industrialized Countries: The Resilience of the Long Duration Employment Relationship', in H. Sarfati and G. Bonoli (eds.), *Labour Market and Social Protection Reforms in International Perspective*. Aldershot: International Social Security Association and Ashgate.

BETTIO, F., and VILLA, P. (1998). 'A Mediterranean Perspective on the Breakdown of the Relationship between Participation and Fertility'. *Cambridge Journal of Economics*, 22/2: 137–71.

BOSCH, G., WEBSTER, J., and WEIBACH, H. J. (2000). 'New Organizational Forms in the Informational Society', in K. Ducatel, J. Webster, and W. Herrmann (eds.), *The Information Society in Europe: Work and Life in an Age of Globalisation*. Oxford: Rowman & Littlefield.

——and PURCELL, J. (2002). *Strategy and Human Resource Management*. Basingstoke: Palgrave.

BRUNHES, B., ROJOT, J., and WASSERMAN, W. (1989). *Labour Market Flexibility: Trends in Enterprise*. Paris: OECD.

BRUSCO, S. (1982). 'The Emilian Model: Productive Decentralization and Social Integration'. *Cambridge Journal of Economics*, 6/2: 167–84.

BURCHELL, B., LADIPO, D., and WILKINSON, F. (eds.) (2001). *Job Security and Work Intensification*. London: Routledge.

——DEAKIN, S., MICHIE, J., and RUBERY, J. (eds.) (2003). *Systems of Production: Markets, Organisations and Performance*. London: Routledge.

CAPPELLI, P. (1995). 'Rethinking Employment'. *British Journal of Industrial Relations*, 33/4: 563–602.

——BASSI, H., KATZ, D., KNOKE, P., OSTERMAN, P., and USEEM, M. (1997). *Change at Work*. New York: Oxford University Press Inc.

CASTELLS, M. (1996). *The Information Age: Economy, Society and Culture*. Volume 1. *The Rise of the Network Society*. Oxford: Blackwell.

CASTLES, S., and MILLER, M. (1998). *The Age of Migration: International Population Movements in the Modern World*. London: Macmillan Press.

CEC (Commission of the European Communities) (1994). *Employment in Europe*. Luxembourg: Office for Official Publications of the European Communities.

COLLING, T. (2000). 'Personnel Management in the Extended Organization', in K. Sisson (ed.), *Personnel Management: A Comprehensive Guide to Theory and Practice*. Oxford: Blackwell.

CROMPTON, R., and SANDERSON, K. (1990). *Gendered Jobs and Social Change*. London: Unwin.

CROUCH, C., FINEGOLD, D., and SAKO, M. (eds.) (1999). *Are Skills the Answer? The Political Economy of Skill Creation in Advanced Industrial Economies*. Oxford: Oxford University Press.

DEAKIN, S. (2002). 'The Evolution of the Employment Relationship'. ILO/French government symposium on the Future of Work, Employment, and Social Protection: The Dynamics of Change and the Protection of Workers, Lyon, January.

DETZEL, P., and RUBERY, J. (2002). 'Employment Systems and Transitional Labour Markets: A Comparison of Youth Labour Markets in Germany, France and the UK', in G. Schmid and B. Gazier (eds.), *The Dynamics of Full Employment*. Cheltenham: Edward Elgar.

DISNEY, R. (1999). 'Why Have Older Men Stopped Working?' in P. Gregg and J. Wadsworth (eds.), *The State of Working Britain*. Manchester: Manchester University Press.

DOERINGER, P. B., and PIORE, M. J. (1971). *Internal Labour Markets and Manpower Analysis*. Lexington, Mass.: Heath.

ELGER, T., and SMITH, C. (eds.) (1994). *Global Japanization?* London: Routledge.

Esping-Andersen, G. (1990). *The Three Worlds of Welfare Capitalism*. Cambridge: Polity Press.

—— (2002). *Why We Need a New Welfare State*. Oxford: Oxford University Press.

Ezzamel, M., Willmott, H., and Worthington, F. (2001). 'Power, Control and Resistance in "The Factory that Time Forgot"'. *Journal of Management Studies*, 38/8: 1053–79.

Felstead, A., and Jewson, N. (eds.) (1999). *Global Trends in Flexible Labour*. Basingstoke: Macmillan Business.

Finegold, D., and Soskice, D. (1988). 'The Failure of British Training: Analysis and Prescription'. *Oxford Review of Economic Policy*, 4/3: 21–53.

Folbre, N. (1994). *Who Pays for the Kids: Gender and the Structures of Constraint*. London: Routledge.

Freeman, R. (1996). 'Why Do So Many Young American Men Commit Crimes and What Might We Do about It?' *Journal of Economic Perspectives*, 10/1: 25–42.

Geary, J. (1992). 'Employment Flexibility and Human Resource Management'. *Work, Employment and Society*, 6/2: 251–70.

Green, F. (2001). 'It's Been a Hard Day's Night: The Concentration and Intensification of Work in Late Twentieth-Century Britain'. *British Journal of Industrial Relations*, 39/1: 53–80.

Guest, D. (1998). 'Beyond HRM: Commitment and the Contract Culture', in P. Sparrow and M. Marchington (eds.), *Human Resource Management: The New Agenda*. London: Pitman.

Hakim, C. (1990). 'Core and Periphery in Employers Workforce Strategies: Evidence from the 1987 ELUS Survey'. *Work, Employment and Society*, 4/1: 157–88.

Hall, P., and Soskice, D. (eds.) (2001). *Varieties of Capitalism: The Institutional Foundations of Comparative Advantage*. New York: Oxford University Press.

Harrison, B. (1994). *Lean and Mean: Why Large Corporations will Continue to Dominate the Global Economy*. New York: Basic Books.

Heery, E., and Salmon, J. (2000). 'The Insecurity Thesis', in E. Heery and J. Salmon (eds.), *The Insecure Workforce*. London: Routledge.

Hollingsworth, J. R., and Boyer, R. (eds.) (1997). *Contemporary Capitalism*. Cambridge: Cambridge University Press.

Humphries, J., and Rubery, J. (1984). 'The Reconstitution of the Supply Side of the Labour Market: The Relative Autonomy of Social Reproduction'. *Cambridge Journal of Economics*, 8/4: 331–46.

Hunter, L., McGregor, A., MacInnes, J., and Sproull, A. (1993). 'The Flexible Firm: Strategy and Segmentation'. *British Journal of Industrial Relations*, 31/3: 383–408.

Jacoby, S. M. (1999). 'Are Career Jobs Headed for Extinction?' *California Management Review*, 42/1: 123–45.

Jany-Catrice, F., and Lehndorff, S. (2005). 'Who Works for the Retail Trade? Working Conditions and Labour Markets in the European Retail Trade', in G. Bosch and S. Lehndorff (eds.), *Working in the Service Sector: A Tale from Different Worlds*. London: Routledge.

Legge, K. (1989). 'Human Resource Management: A Critical Analysis', in J. Storey (ed.), *New Perspectives on Human Resource Management*. London: Routledge.

Lepak, D. P., and Snell, S. A. (1999). 'The Human Resource Architecture: Towards a Theory of Human Capital Allocation and Development'. *Academy of Management Review*, 24/1: 31–48.

Lewis, J. (1992). 'Gender and the Development of Welfare Regimes'. *Journal of European Social Policy*, 2/3: 159–73.

Loveridge, R., and Mok, A. L. (1979). *Theories of Labour Market Segmentation*. The Hague: Martinus Nijhoff.

McClean Parks, J., Kidder, D., and Gallagher, D. (1998). 'Fitting Square Pegs into Round Holes: Mapping the Domain of Contingent Work Arrangements onto the Psychological Contract'. *Journal of Organizational Behaviour*, 19: 697–730.

Marginson, P. (1989). 'Employment Flexibility in Large Companies: Change and Continuity'. *Industrial Relations Journal*, 20/2: 101–9.

Marsden, D. (1986). *The End of Economic Man?* Brighton: Wheatsheaf.

——— (1999). *A Theory of Employment Systems*. Oxford: Oxford University Press.

Matusik, S. F., and Hill, C. W. L. (1998). 'The Utilization of Contingent Work, Knowledge Creation, and Competitive Advantage'. *Academy of Management Review*, 23/4: 680–98.

Maurice, M., and Sorge, A. (2000). *Embedding Organizations*. Amsterdam: John Benjamins.

—— Sellier, F., and Silvestre, J. J. (1986). *The Social Foundations of Industrial Power*. Cambridge, Mass.: MIT Press.

Miles, R. E., and Snow, C. C. (1995). 'The New Network Firm: A Spherical Structure Built on a Human Investment Philosophy'. *Organizational Dynamics*, 23/4, reprinted in R. Schuler and S. Jackson (eds.) (1999). *Strategic Human Resource Management*. Oxford: Blackwell.

——— (1996). 'Twenty-First Century Careers', in M. B. Arthur and D. M. Rousseau (eds.), *The Boundaryless Career: A New Employment Principle for a New Organizational Era*. Oxford: Oxford University Press.

Mósesdóttir, L. (2001). *The Interplay between Gender Markets and the State in Sweden, Germany and the United States*. Aldershot: Ashgate.

Mückenberger, U. (ed.) (1996). *A Manifesto for Social Europe*. Brussels: ETUI.

Naschold, F., and de Vroom, B. (eds.) (1993). *Regulating Employment and Welfare*. Berlin: De Gruyter.

Nohria, N., and Eccles, R. G. (eds.) (1992). *Networks and Organizations: Structure, Form and Action*. Boston: Harvard Business School Press.

OECD (1994). *Women and Structural Change*. Paris: OECD.

—— (1999). *Employment Outlook*. Paris: OECD.

O'Reilly, J., and Fagan, C. (1998). *Part-Time Prospects: An International Comparison of Part-Time Work in Europe, North America and the Pacific Rim*. London: Routledge.

Osterman, P. (2000). 'Work Organization in an Era of Restructuring: Trends in Diffusion and Impacts on Employee Welfare'. *Industrial and Labor Relations Review*, 53/2: 179–96.

Piore, M., and Sabel, C. (1984). *The Second Industrial Divide: Possibilities for Prosperity*. New York: Basic Books.

Pollert, A. (1988). 'The Flexible Firm: Fixation or Fact?' *Work, Employment and Society*, 2/3: 281–306.

Purcell, J. (1999). 'Best Practice and Best Fit: Chimera or Cul-de-sac?' *Human Resource Management Journal*, 9/3: 26–41.

—— and Purcell, K. (1998). 'Insourcing, Outsourcing and the Growth of Contingent Labour as Evidence of Flexible Employment Strategies (UK)'. *European Journal of Work and Organisational Psychology*, 7/1: 163–81.

RESKIN, B. F., and ROOS, P. A. (1990). *Job Queues, Gender Queues: Explaining Women's Inroads into Male Occupations.* Philadelphia: Temple University Press.

ROSENBERG, S. (1989). 'From Segmentation to Flexibility'. *Labour and Society,* 14/4: 383–409.

RUBERY, J. (1994). 'The British Production Regime: A Societal-Specific System?' *Economy and Society,* 23/3: 335–54.

—— and GRIMSHAW, D. (2002). *The Organisation of Employment: An International Perspective.* Basingstoke: Palgrave.

—— SMITH, M., and FAGAN, C. (1999). *Women's Employment in Europe: Trends and Prospects.* London: Routledge.

—— COOKE, F. L., EARNSHAW, J., and MARCHINGTON, M. (2003). 'Inter-Organizational Relationships and Employment in a Multi-Employer Environment', *British Journal of Industrial Relations,* 41/2: 265–89.

—— SMITH, M., ANXO, D., and FLOOD, L. (2001). 'The Future European Labor Supply: The Critical Role of the Family'. *Feminist Economics,* 7/3: 33–69.

—— EARNSHAW, J., MARCHINGTON, M., COOKE, F. L., and VINCENT, S. (2002). 'Changing Organizational Forms and the Employment Relationship'. *Journal of Management Studies,* 39/5: 645–72.

SAXENIAN, A. (1996). 'Beyond Boundaries: Open Labor Markets and Learning in Silicon Valley', in M. Arthur and D. Rousseau (eds.), *The Boundaryless Career.* New York: Oxford University Press Inc.

SCARBROUGH, H. (2000). 'The HR Implications of Supply Chain Relationships'. *Human Resource Management Journal,* 10/1: 5–17.

SENNETT, R. (1998). *The Corrosion of Character.* New York: W. W. Norton.

SIMON, H. (1991). 'Organisations and Markets'. *Journal of Economic Perspectives,* 5/2: 25–44.

SISSON, K., and STOREY, J. (2000). *The Realities of Human Resource Management: Managing the Employment Relationship.* Buckingham: Open University Press.

SMITH, C., and MEIKSINS, P. (1995). 'System, Societal and Dominance Effects in Cross-National Organizational Analysis'. *Work, Employment and Society,* 9/2: 241–68.

SMITH, M. (2001). 'Atypical Work and Access to Employment in the European Union'. Ph.D. thesis, Manchester School of Management. UMIST.

STANDING, G. (1999*). Global Labour Flexibility: Seeking Distributive Justice.* Basingstoke: Palgrave.

SUPIOT, A. (2001). *Beyond Employment: Changes at Work and the Future of Employment Law in Europe.* Oxford: Oxford University Press.

WALBY, S. (1997). *Gender Transformations.* London: Routledge.

WOMACK, J. P., JONES, D., and ROOS, D. (1990). *The Machine that Changed the World.* New York: Rawson Associates.

CHAPTER 2

ORGANIZATIONS AND THE INTERSECTION OF WORK AND FAMILY

A COMPARATIVE PERSPECTIVE

EILEEN APPELBAUM

THOMAS BAILEY

PETER BERG

ARNE KALLEBERG

2.1 NEW PRESSURES ON FAMILIES AND ORGANIZATIONS

DURING much of the twentieth century, industrialized economies were characterized by a rather sharp separation of the economic and social spheres and their characteristic institutions—the corporate enterprise in the economic realm and the family or household in the social realm. The socially sanctioned roles of men and women within these institutions were well defined and were assumed to be enduring. The two were linked via the male breadwinner whose income supported the family and by an employment contract that governed the relationship between work processes in large organizations and households' labor supply. In the post-World War II period, extensive trade union organization and internal labor markets provided long-term employment and career progression (rising wages and responsibility) to male workers who pursued a blue- or white-collar career in corporate enterprises. In exchange, employees and the unions that represented them agreed to be subject to the employer's instructions and to respect management's prerogatives in designing the production process (Simon 1951), although employees in some countries had a formal (e.g. Germany) or informal (e.g. Japan) consultative role in work design and corporate governance. In general, conflicts between the needs of the family and those of the enterprise were reconciled by adjustments, often negotiated by unions, to the terms and conditions of employment of the male wage earner. As industrialization proceeded, the state functioned as an implicit third party to the employment relationship by providing a system of social insurance for families, which varied across countries in its generosity, in the event that the male breadwinner was no longer available—i.e. in the event that he became unemployed, disabled, injured on the job, or died (see Piore 2002).

Economic changes in the last quarter of the twentieth century have undermined this traditional model. Women's labor force participation increased steadily over the last century as rising educational levels of women, experiences gained from wartime employment, and the growth of the service sector all encouraged women to move outside the domestic sphere. By the 1970s, a variety of developments led to the increased employment of mothers as well. In the United States, falling real wages undermined the ability of men to earn enough to support a family and pushed many homemakers into the labor market in an attempt to maintain the family's standard of living. In the Netherlands and elsewhere, prohibitions against the employment of mothers eroded as laws that allowed women to be dismissed from their jobs when they became mothers were reversed and new laws that promised women protection against discrimination in employment were enacted. In Sweden, the shift of many of the responsibilities for care of the young, the old, and the sick or infirm from the private sphere to the public sector both freed up mothers to work and created a demand for their services. There has been a dramatic increase in the employment of mothers of young children. By the end of the century, as Table 2.1 shows, about 62 percent of US mothers of children under the age of 6 were employed. The figures for other countries vary from about one-third of Japanese mothers to more than three-quarters of Swedish mothers (OECD 2001).

These labor force changes have eroded the boundaries separating the realms of the family and the workplace and pressured national governments to implement

Table 2.1 Employment rates of mothers with child(ren) aged under 6 in 1999

Country	Employment rates of mothers (in percent)	
	Mothers in couple families	All mothers with child under 6
Australia	48.0	45.0
Austria	65.7	66.5
Belgium	71.8	69.5
Canada	70.0	–
Finland	57.7	58.8
France	56.8	56.2
Germany	51.4	51.1
Greece	48.4	48.6
Ireland	45.5	44.4
Italy	44.9	45.7
Japan	33.3	–
Luxembourg	46.1	47.4
Netherlands	62.3	60.7
Norway	–	72.8
Poland	49.5	47.6
Portugal	70.2	70.6
Spain	41.5	41.8
Sweden	–	77.8
United Kingdom	61.3	55.8
United States	60.6	61.5

Source: OECD (2001: table 4.1, p. 134).

public policies that support working families. These policies include publicly subsidized childcare and/or publicly provided preschool education, paid or unpaid family or medical leave, and equal employment opportunity for men and women.

The aim of this chapter is to develop a conceptual and empirical foundation for understanding the role that employers can play in facilitating the successful resolution of the conflicting demands of employees' work and family responsibilities. Our focus is on company policies and practices and the national laws and institutions that shape them. In the next section, we examine why employers adopt various policies that support employees' efforts to integrate their work and home lives. We then summarize recent empirical studies of outcomes for firms—

improved recruitment and retention, improvements in individual employee productivity, and improvements in process efficiency—as a result of implementing these policies. The final section of the chapter examines the relationship between public policy and mothers' employment as well as the impact of public policy on employers' implementation of voluntary family-friendly policies.

2.2 EMPLOYER ADOPTION OF FAMILY-FRIENDLY POLICIES

2.2.1 Types of Family-Friendly Policies

Companies adopt two types of family-friendly policies or practices to reduce job stress and improve work–life balance for employees—(1) policies that substitute for the services of the family caregiver and (2) policies that give employees greater control over work time through paid leaves or flexibility in terms of work schedules or the location of work (den Dulk, van Doorne-Huiskes, and Schippers 2000; Glass and Estes 1997).

Caregiver replacement policies enable employees to focus on work while they are on the job by assisting with home activities, such as taking care of children or maintaining a household, that would have been carried out by a full-time caregiver in the traditional breadwinner/homemaker model. Examples include childcare referral services, on-site or subsidized childcare, after-school programs, adult day-care for elderly relatives, emergency backup care arrangements, social work services to handle housing or utility emergencies, and concierge services such as dry cleaning pick up, food shopping, or the purchase of gifts. Indeed, many of these 'life sustaining' activities are important to all employees, and company policies that assist employees in integrating these activities with the demands of their jobs may be seen as a benefit by harried workers whatever their marital or family status.

Greater flexibility in scheduling work activities helps workers better coordinate work with family care, personal, and home responsibilities. Policies that give workers some influence over the timing and duration of the workday or workweek include telecommuting, flextime, compressed work weeks, reduced work hours in the current job, self-scheduling, job sharing, paid vacations, parental leaves, and paid family and medical leaves. These policies can be useful for all employees in meeting their personal as well as their work goals. But they are likely to be especially important for employees with responsibility for the care of children or elderly family members.

2.2.2 Prevalence of Family-Friendly Policies

Evidence on the prevalence of work–life or family-friendly policies in the industrialized countries is uneven and often unreliable. Few nationally representative surveys of company policies and practices exist in any country, and there is often a problem of incompatibility of responses from employers and employees, with employers reporting higher levels of family-friendly policies. In the United States, the Families and Work Institute conducted a Business Work–Life Survey (BWLS) in 1998 of work–life policies at a representative sample of 1,057 companies and nonprofit organizations with 100 or more employees (Galinsky and Bond 1998). With respect to flexible work arrangements, they found that 68 percent of firms allow employees to periodically change starting and quitting times, 81 percent allow employees to return to work gradually after childbirth or adoption, 55 percent allow employees to work at home occasionally, and 33 percent allow them to work at home or off-site on a regular basis. In terms of child and elder care assistance, the survey found that 23 percent of companies provide elder care resource and referral services, 36 percent of companies provide childcare information and referral services, 9 percent provide childcare at or near the worksite, and 5 percent provide childcare subsidies (Galinsky and Bond 1998). However, like most surveys of employers, the BWLS survey provides information on whether a company has a particular policy in place for *any* of its employees, not whether it is available to *all or a substantial fraction* of the firm's employees. We can contrast these findings with the results of the 2001 survey of employees by the US Bureau of Labor Statistics (BLS) that examined access to flexible schedules. BLS found that only 29 percent of full-time employees reported that they are able to periodically change starting and quitting times and only 12 percent reported that they work at home on a regular basis (Appelbaum and Golden 2002).

In general, access to policies that facilitate employees' desire to combine a job with other responsibilities is unequally distributed within companies in most countries. Professional, technical, and managerial employees, and workers in healthcare and financial services industries are most likely to be covered by and have access to formal firm policies such as assistance with child or elder care, paid maternity leave, access of fathers to paid parental leave, banked hours to be used at the employee's discretion, or flexible schedules (Appelbaum and Golden 2002; Glass and Fujimoto 1995; Osterman 1995). Blue-collar workers are generally among the least likely (Appelbaum and Golden 2002; Whitehouse and Zetlin 1999). Larger organizations, including multinational firms and those with professional personnel management, are more likely to implement such policies (den Dulk 2000; Glass and Fujimoto 1995; Osterman 1995; Trifiletti 2000; Whitehouse and Zetlin 1999).

Optional work–family policies (i.e. work supports not mandated or provided by the state) are still not widely available to employees. Nevertheless, despite the weaknesses in the available data and differences in sampling frames, in respondents, and in take-up rates within firms, the evidence suggests that the number of such voluntary or optional arrangements within companies over the last two decades has increased in all of the industrialized countries. Family-friendly policies are not spread evenly among companies, and workers have unequal opportunities to use such policies. Still, employees today appear to have greater access to family-friendly policies than in the past (den Dulk 2000; Galinsky and Swanberg 2000; Lewis 2000*b*; Squirchuk and Bourke 2000).

Despite these gains, the actual use of family-friendly policies, even statutory policies, by employees may be limited because of supervisors' discretion in approving requests, negative sanctions experienced by employees who take advantage of company policies, or by a workplace culture in which expectations of workers are inconsistent with employees' family responsibilities (Bailyn, Drago, and Kochan 2001; Galinsky 1994; Lewis and Taylor 1996; Naesman 2000; Rapoport and Bailyn 1996; Williams 2000).

2.2.3 Why Companies Adopt Family-Friendly Policies

Two main theoretical perspectives inform analyses of firms' work–family practices. The rational choice perspective argues that employers will adopt family-friendly policies beyond what is legally required of them if the benefits of doing so exceed the costs. Efficiency considerations, in this view, dictate whether firms implement or reject such policies (Meyer, Mukerjee, and Sestero 2001). Efficiency arguments— making the business case—explain adoption of practices in terms of a cost-benefit calculus (Perry-Jenkins, Repetti, and Crouter 2000). Some benefits of work–family policies can be calculated in a rather straightforward manner, for example, the reduction in costs associated with absenteeism, lateness, or turnover.

Osterman (1995) argues that work–life policies—initiatives that organizations adopt to help employees manage their paid work and personal lives (Konrad and Mangel 2000; Lobel 1999)—may enable employers to more easily recruit and retain valuable employees, may reduce lateness and unplanned absences, and may encourage employees to put forth 'discretionary' effort beyond what is required in their job descriptions. In this way, work–life policies may enable firms to protect their investments in employee skills and knowledge and may yield enhanced performance for the company.

Drawing on social exchange theory, Konrad and Mangel (2000) argue that work–life initiatives can increase employee effort despite the fact that they are not tailored to individual employee contributions. Where mutual trust and commitment are present, firms that provide valuable benefits to employees as a group may obtain, in exchange, an increase in overall effort by these employees on the job as well as ideas and effort from employees that go beyond assigned responsibilities (Akerlof 1982;

Lambert 2000; Osterman 1995; Tsui *et al.* 1997). In particular, Tsui and her colleagues (1997) demonstrate empirically that, when rewards go beyond monetary compensation and include organizational concern for career advancement and the well-being of employees, performance is high on both assigned job responsibilities and overall effort beyond what is required. Konrad and Mangel's (2000) results suggest that the relationship between the provision of extensive work–life benefits and productivity may be stronger in firms that employ higher percentages of professionals and higher percentages of women.

The second theoretical perspective focuses on institutional theory and on the professionalism and values of human resource managers as explanations for firms' adoption of family-friendly policies. Institutional theory emphasizes the institutional pressures that influence organizations to respond similarly to their environments (DiMaggio and Powell 1983). These may arise as a result of social pressures or in response to professional norms (the practices HR professionals believe should be adopted). In this view, organizations adopt various innovative practices for reasons other than the need to improve economic efficiency (e.g. to enhance reputation) and may not necessarily adopt the human resource practices that make the most sense for their firm (Kossek, Dass, and DeMarr 1994; Snell 1992). There is some evidence to suggest that once certain workplace policies have become widely established in a particular organizational field, other organizations will come under institutional pressures to respond similarly (institutional isomorphism) to their environment (Glass and Estes 1997; Goodstein 1994; Kossek, Dass, and DeMarr 1994). Osterman's (1995) finding that the presence of an HR department increases the number of work–life policies and Goodstein's (1994) result that diffusion of family-friendly practices among an industry group leads other firms in that group to adopt the practice both provide support for this view.

2.3 OUTCOMES FOR EMPLOYERS

2.3.1 Differing Impacts of the Two Kinds of Family-Friendly Policies

The two broad classes of work–life policies that companies adopt to help employees manage paid work and family care responsibilities—strategies that replace the services of a caregiver and those that provide employees with greater flexibility—make very different types of demands on employers, have different implications for organizational performance, and differ in terms of the costs—organizational and financial—that they impose on companies. Short parental leaves, for example, impose relatively low financial costs on an organization, although they involve a temporary loss of human capital. Providing on-site day care, on the other hand, is extremely expensive and tends to be selective, serving only a limited number of employees (Erler 2000; Glass and Estes 1997). Flexible work schedules, which enable employees to reduce work hours or adjust their work schedules, involve few out-of-pocket costs for employers. However, they may impose different kinds of costs on the organization by requiring changes in the organization of work, increasing managers' responsibility for coordinating work, and reducing the ability of supervisors to use hours spent in the workplace to monitor work effort. These costs have usually not been carefully specified or measured in studies of the effects of work–family policies (Beinecke 1994; Brannen and Lewis 2000; Glass and Estes 1997).

Caregiver replacement policies are often part of cafeteria plans that enable employees to select from a menu of fringe benefits such as family health insurance or childcare or elder-care benefits. Caregiver replacement policies generate often-substantial administrative and financial costs. But they are like classic fringe benefits in that they do not require the company to change its work schedules, production processes, or supervisory structures. A policy such as on-site childcare, while it may be highly valued by employees and very expensive to employers, has little impact on company operations and rarely involves line managers in the planning process. Indeed, one of the goals of such caregiver replacement policies is to allow the company to maintain its traditional schedules and processes despite the changes in the demographic makeup of its workforce. Analytically, these caregiver replacement practices can be thought of as a form of compensation that, like other fringe benefits, may be highly valued by employees. Like traditional fringe benefits, however, companies can withdraw them when they come under intense economic pressure with negative consequences for morale, but little effect on organizational processes.

In contrast, flexible scheduling practices, including reduced work hours on the same or similar job with no reduction in hourly pay or benefits, usually have only modest direct costs (Hohl 1996) or may generate offsetting savings (Kim and Campagna 1981). An early review of the literature on flexible schedules found that, on balance, the benefits of flextime outweigh the costs (Golembiewski and Proehl 1978). However, these practices make extensive demands on managers' ability to coordinate production or service delivery or supervise all employees, and often require significant changes in other production and workplace practices. Line managers play a key role in implementing these practices, since they have responsibility for scheduling workers and coordinating production. Moreover, because of the wide effects on the internal operations of the firm that such practices can have, and because they may challenge company culture and a tradition of measuring employee commitment and productivity by 'face time'—long hours spent at work—flexible scheduling practices are rarely sustainable without the involvement and support of high-ranking executives.

2.3.2 Recent Empirical Studies of Employer Outcomes

Empirical analyses of the effects of work–life policies on organizational outcomes in the academic literature are mixed. Overall, this body of research is still at an early stage and cannot yet be taken as definitive. Moreover, empirical studies of the effects of family-friendly policies in Europe, Australia, and Japan are in their infancy (Erler 2000; Lewis 2000*b*; Lewis and Taylor 1996; Squirchuk and Bourke 2000). In this section, therefore, we focus on studies from the United States, where researchers have examined several key outcomes, including improved recruitment and retention, greater individual productivity and the employee attitudes and behaviors associated with higher performance, and process efficiency.

Even the US studies, however, suffer from methodological problems. For example, costs are rarely identified or measured (Beinecke 1994; Raabe 1990) and studies seldom determine whether the performance improvements are worth the program's costs to the firm (Auerbach 1990). Performance outcomes tend to be poorly specified and are often self-reported. In other cases, respondents are asked for their perceptions of outcomes (Glass and Estes 1997; Brannen and Lewis 2000). Family-friendly policies are not adequately conceptualized, intensity of employer commitment to these policies is not examined, different types of practices are not clearly distinguished, and informal practices are rarely measured (Glass and Estes 1997).

In addition, few studies focus on individual productivity and empirical studies of changes in process efficiency are especially rare. Often, studies of the effects of work–life practices on organizational outcomes rely on worker or manager perceptions, rather than on observed behavior or direct measures of organizational performance. Moreover, studies are often conducted at one workplace and are rarely longitudinal, which makes it difficult to fully assess the organizational outcomes of work–life practices.

2.3.2.1 *Recruitment and Retention*

Studies have shown that work–life policies—both those we have labeled caregiver replacement policies and those that give employees greater control over work time—have a positive influence on retention (Almer and Kaplan 2002; Aryee, Luk, and Stone 1998; Christensen and Staines 1990; Grover and Crooker 1995; Kossek and Nichol 1992), although some studies have found little evidence of this effect (Dalton and Mesch 1990). Recruitment and retention are expected to be particularly important motivations for firms to adopt such policies in occupations involving highly skilled professionals where labor markets are tight. In addition, as women account for a larger share of graduates from business, law, and other professional programs than in the past, employers may introduce such policies to avoid losing workers in whom they have made significant investments. There are, however, few empirical studies that examine the relationship between firms' investments in workers and family-friendly policies, and the evidence from such studies is mixed. One study found no effects of training costs on firms' childcare policies, although larger recruiting budgets were associated with more financial aid for workers with dependent care responsibilities (Seyler, Monroe, and Garan 1995). In another study, high commitment workplaces had significantly more work–family policies, but internal labor markets, in which companies train incumbent workers for more responsible positions, had no effect on the number of policies firms offered (Osterman 1995).

2.3.2.2 *Individual Productivity*

'Caregiver replacement' policies, such as assistance with childcare or elder-care placements or fees, may enable employees to find good quality care and to focus their attention on their jobs during working hours, thereby maximizing the amount and quality of their effort. Workers who are preoccupied with family issues or are on the phone arranging childcare or dealing with more mundane chores, such as car repair appointments, are not concentrating fully on their work. Parents may have to miss work on very short (or no) notice when their children are ill or have other types of problems, or may worry about leaving a sick child alone at home (Fernandez 1986, 1990). Policies that assist employees with childcare or that provide emergency backup care when children are sick or childcare arrangements break down are expected to increase employee productivity and reduce employee absences. In some instances, physical proximity of the childcare center to the workplace is expected to be an advantage to employees, so firms may have an incentive to provide these services directly. However, the evidence suggests that on-site childcare may not have the expected effect on absenteeism. Several studies have found no relationship between on-site childcare and employee absences (Goff, Mount, and Jamison 1990; Kossek and Nichol 1992; Youngblood and Chambers-Cook 1984), although such facilities do appear to improve recruitment and retention (Kossek and Nichol 1992; Youngblood and Chambers-Cook 1984).

Research examining the link between childcare policies and employee performance has also produced weak results at best. Kossek and Nichol (1992) found that on-site childcare is unrelated to performance. As Kossek and Nichol point out, it may be difficult to show a link between childcare and employee performance because practices such as on-site childcare are available to both high and low performers. More recently, Kossek, Noe, and Colquitt (2001) demonstrated that the relationship between childcare benefits and performance may depend on the nature and quality of the childcare arrangement and the informal culture of the organization toward work and family.

Research by Kossek and her coauthors suggests that it is difficult to justify the high cost of on-site childcare, even for highly paid professional employees at corporate headquarters, on the basis of a favorable cost-benefit analysis. The motivation for companies to offer this policy is more likely to be a result of firms modeling themselves on successful competitors (mimetic isomorphism) or firms responding to pressure from employees, union, business groups, or professional organizations (normative isomorphism).

Some employers expect a reputation for enabling workers to balance work and family life to help secure the loyalty and enthusiasm of workers, even those who do not make use of these practices. Providing work–family policies suggests that the company cares about the employees, and employers believe that these policies then induce attitudes and behaviors that affect performance, such as organizational commitment, organizational citizenship behavior, and job satisfaction. Grover and Crooker (1995), for example, found that employees who had access to family-responsive policies showed significantly lower intention to quit and greater organizational commitment. Lambert (2000) found that those who see work–life benefits as useful exhibit higher organizational citizenship behaviors when such benefits are available. In addition, Scandura and Lankau (1997) showed that women who perceive their organizations offered flexible work hours reported higher levels of organizational commitment and job satisfaction than women who did not. In any case, employees on flexible schedules are not less productive than are those on traditional schedules (Hammer and Barbera 1997; Koppelman 1986; Kossek, Barber, and Winters 1999).

Some analysts have concluded that teleworking is one type of family-friendly practice that does increase performance. Using both qualitative and quantitative analyses, Hill *et al.* (1998) showed that employees at IBM who worked remotely achieved higher productivity, flexibility, and work–life balance. However, the performance gains from telecommuting may be the result of self-selection. Those employees who know they would be more productive working remotely are able to take advantage of this option.

2.3.2.3 *Process Efficiency*

We are not aware of any quantitative studies of process efficiency. However, the case study literature suggests that organizations that adopt policies that increase employee control over work time are sometimes able to enhance process efficiency as a result (Bosch 2000; Rapoport and Bailyn 1996). The potential for such improvement results from the employer's own needs for flexibility, usually due to variations in work intensity over the course of the day or week, as employers seek to match demand for the organization's products or services to the hours that people work (Lewis 2000*a*). Companies expect this improvement in the ability to adapt labor input to demand to improve capital utilization and raise sales revenue (Golden 1996). This matching takes the form of flexible scheduling or reducing work hours for employees without reducing hourly pay or benefits.

Flexible scheduling allows variations in starting and finishing times or allows the hours of work to vary from week to week or month to month. This arrangement is expected to work best if slack times for the employer can be made to correspond to times of the day or week that are useful to employees who need to take care of personal needs (Glass and Estes 1997). In some cases, hours of work are averaged over several months (Hartz 1996; Lehndorff 2000). In Europe, where flexibility generally means greater flexibility for *employers* in scheduling work, flexible schedules usually have been accompanied by a reduction in the workweek, resulting in regularly scheduled paid time off and increased flexibility for the family (European Industrial Relations Observatory 1998).

Process efficiency can also be enhanced via greater flexibility and more options for scheduling work in organizations that have adopted just-in-time practices (Bosch 2000). The absence of inventory buffers in manufacturing and the promise of service on demand in financial, consulting, and communications services have increased the importance to firms of matching workers' schedules to variations in demand.

2.3.3 Unions Influences on Employer Work–Life Policies

Unions are credited with negotiating more generous conventional fringe benefits that are valuable to workers with family responsibilities, including in the case of the US family health benefits, paid holidays, and longer paid vacations. But the findings with respect to the effects of unions on family-friendly policies are inconsistent, with some studies finding positive effects (Galinsky 2001; Glass and Fujimoto 1995) and others finding no effects (Deitch and Huffman 2001; Osterman 1995). European unions advocated a shorter workweek in the 1980s to share work and promote job creation. But the reorganization of working time has largely increased the flexibility of employers in scheduling hours and operating on a 24/7 basis, while flexibility that provides employees with control over the duration and timing of work is less common (Mutari and Figart 2001). That is now beginning to change in Germany and elsewhere as unions negotiate limits on employers' ability to schedule work as well as new opportunities for employees to control the use of some of the time banked in working time accounts (Berg *et al.* 2003; Lehndorff 1998; Seifert 1998).

However, policies to promote individual schedule flexibility present particular challenges to unions, making it more difficult for them to monitor companies' excessive use of overtime and to limit arbitrary behavior of managers. Unions traditionally have insisted on uniform application of policies in order to guard against managerial favoritism. As the demand for greater individual control over work time has increased, however, unions have begun to rethink this approach and to focus on negotiating a transparent process open to all employees for requesting flexibility and a role for the union in monitoring the application of the process (Lehndorff 1998; Seifert 1993, 1998).

2.4 PUBLIC POLICY AND CORPORATE FAMILY-FRIENDLY POLICIES

2.4.1 Country Differences in Public Policies and Mothers' Employment

Differences between countries in the prevalence of various types of work–family arrangements rest, in part, on differences in the legal and institutional supports for working families as well as on cultural assumptions about appropriate behavior of men and women as parents and as employees (Fagnani 2002). Cross-national comparisons typically cluster countries into groups with similar characteristics, with the clustering based on national institutions. The best-known example is Esping-Andersen's (1990) three regimes of welfare capitalism—social democratic (such as the Nordic countries), conservative-corporatist (such as the continental European countries), and liberal (such as the English-speaking countries). The three regimes differ in the extent to which people possess social rights and are able to live independently of market forces. The employment of women is expected to vary across these regimes—high in the social democratic countries with its large public sector, generous parental leave policies, and extensive system of public or subsidized childcare; moderate in the market-driven liberal countries; and lower in the conservative-corporatist countries where women's work has been marginalized and public policy encourages mothers to stay home with their children.

Esping-Andersen's typology has been criticized for ignoring variations in policies and outcomes within these clusters that are especially important for women (den Dulk, van Doorne-Huiskes, and Schippers 2000; Gornick, Meyers, and Ross 1997). Among countries within each of the three regimes he identifies, the extent of government support for paid family leaves and the availability of affordable child-care is linked to the employment of mothers (Fagnani 2002; Gornick, Meyers, and

Ross 1997). Thus, the higher rate of paid employment of mothers in France than in the former West Germany is attributed to greater availability of public childcare spaces for young children in France (Fagnani 2002). Similarly, lower rates of mothers' employment in Norway than in Sweden is attributed to Norway's less generous maternity and parental leave policies.

2.4.2 Public Policies and Firms' Behavior

Public policies, most prominently childcare and parental leaves, increase the employment of mothers by reducing the difficulties women face in reconciling paid work and unpaid care responsibilities. Public policy that supports equal opportunities for women and that provides parents with extensive supports for reconciling work and family life may lead to occupational segregation. The non-profit and public administration sector is the largest employer of women in Germany, the Netherlands, Sweden, and the United Kingdom, accounting for 45–55 percent of all female employment (Gustafsson, Kenjoh, and Wetzels 2000). Thus, women may be employed mainly in the public sector, while private sector firms continue to be traditionally organized according to the male breadwinner model.

Naesman (2000) suggests that this has occurred in Sweden, where the public sector developed an extensive set of policies since the 1970s that have benefited mothers in the labor market. Generous parental leave options with a right to return to a job and public childcare and elder care make the combination of paid work and unpaid care work easier for women to manage, with the result that women's labor force participation is highest and most continuous in Sweden. Nevertheless, women are still expected to do the remaining unpaid care work at home (Siim 1991).

Within the cluster of 'liberal' English-speaking countries, government involvement in work–family arrangements is lowest in the United States and United Kingdom. Supports for working families such as publicly funded childcare are only minimally available and are targeted on the working poor (Children's Defense Fund 2002; Lewis 2000b). UK membership in the European Union has resulted in broad statutory provision of paid maternity leave, with most employed women eligible for fourteen weeks of paid leave at 90 percent of weekly pay for six weeks and a flat rate for the remainder of the leave.

For the most part, however, the development of work–family policies in the United Kingdom, as in the United States, is left largely up to individual firms, which are free to choose to implement or reject particular practices. The result is a wide divergence among firms and industries in the provision of flexible work schedules, paid leave, or subsidized childcare, and unequal access of employees to such policies (Appelbaum and Golden 2002; den Dulk, van Doorne-Huiskes, and Schippers 2000; Galinsky and Swanberg 2000; Lewis 2000*b*). Moreover, the practices that are adopted may not always coincide with the needs of employees with family responsibilities.

The lack of publicly subsidized childcare or paid family and medical leave through the social insurance system has led some employers to adopt firm policies to fill the gap, especially when they are convinced that a business case can be made for these or other family-friendly policies. However, in the absence of public policy to promote such policies, many more companies have failed to adopt practices that employees consider essential for work–family balance, especially for employees not in professional or managerial occupations (Lewis 2000*b*). In the absence of public policies that level the playing field, it is difficult for individual companies to overcome the 'collective action' problem. That is, individual firms that implement family-friendly policies may have higher costs than their competitors or may lose employees in whom they have invested to competing firms. Moreover, it is frequently very difficult for firms to put a price tag on work–family interventions or to identify their beneficiaries (Lobel and Faught 1996). The result is that practices are inconsistent (Galinsky and Swanberg 2000) and lower level employees, whose need for paid leave, subsidized day care, or flexible schedules may be greatest, often lack access to such practices (Bailyn, Drago, and Kochan 2001; Lewis 2000*b*).

Australia, like the United States and United Kingdom, exhibits a low level of government intervention in work–life arrangements within firms. Yet, it differs from the United States and United Kingdom in two important respects. First, state governments have created a mosaic of laws addressing discrimination, affirmative action, gender equity, and most recently family-friendly policies. Second, some important reforms were achieved by the centrally regulated industrial tribunals that, until recently, played a very large role in determining working conditions for the majority of employees. Important decisions include the introduction of twelve months of unpaid parental leave following the birth or adoption of a child and paid family caregiver leave to allow employees to provide short-term care for an ill family member (Squirchuk and Bourke 2000). However, the limited access to paid maternity leave by private sector employees limits the ability of mothers to take it (Earle 1999); only 14 percent of Australian companies offer paid maternity leave (Work and Family Unit 1998).

The centrally regulated system of industrial tribunals in Australia has given way, over the past decade, to a system of enterprise bargaining in which employment agreements are negotiated between workers and managers in a workplace. As in the United States and United Kingdom, this has led some companies to adopt family-friendly policies, such as paid maternity leave, flexible work hours, or subsidized childcare in order to attract and retain employees with family responsibilities (Work and Family Unit 1998). However, most organizations lag behind, and access by employees to such policies is uneven (Squirchuk and Bourke 2000; Whitehouse and Zetlin 1999).

Japan also has some limited national legislation to promote family-friendly policies in the workplace. In 1997 the Equal Employment Opportunity Law (EEOL) originally enacted in 1985 was strengthened. A legal prohibition against discrimination against women in recruitment, hiring, assignment, and promotion replaced the earlier moral duty of companies to endeavor to provide equal opportunity (Araki 1998).

Labor force participation rates of Japanese women have increased to 39.2 percent of women of working age, although it is still rare for mothers of young children to be in paid employment and women still face barriers to equality in the workplace (Araki 1998). For example, the dual-track personnel system found in most large employers provides workers with a choice among career tracks. The 'general track' involves routine jobs and employees are not required to comply with company orders to relocate. The 'career track' denotes an elite track of jobs involving discretionary decision making by employees and opportunities for training and advancement. But employees in these jobs are subject to company-wide transfers and relocation. Since women bear the responsibility for unpaid family care work, they are led to choose the general track as more compatible with their family responsibilities.

The Japanese government responded to the underrepresentation of women in career track jobs in 1991 and 1995 with laws intended to harmonize work and family life, and thus increase the employment options of women. The Child Care Leave Law of 1991 provides a worker, male or female, with the right to one year of leave following birth or adoption of a child less than 1 year old and the right to return to that job. The Employment Insurance Law pays a worker on leave 20 percent of his or her regular monthly wages as a basic allowance and an additional 5 percent if the worker returns to work at the end of the year (Araki 1998). This basic allowance was scheduled to increase to 40 percent of regular monthly wages in 2001 (private conversation at the Ministry of Labor in June 2000). The Child Care Leave Act was revised and renamed in 1995 to allow family care leave, effective as of April 1, 1999. Employees are allowed to take an unpaid leave of up to three months to care for a family member who requires care for more than two weeks (Araki 1998). It is unclear, however, how widely available such leaves are in practice.

2.5 CONCLUSION

Different national patterns of implementation of work–family policies by companies reflect in part differences in public policy and in basic cultural assumptions about gender roles and the division of tasks between women and men. Comparative research on Europe suggests that countries with more extensive statutory work–family arrangements have less gender inequality—i.e. labor force participation rates of women are higher and the gender gap in wages is smaller (den Dulk, van Doorne-Huiskes, and Schippers 1996). However, even when public policy governing work and family is extensive, the implementation of family-friendly policies takes place within organizations. Workplace climate and supervisors' attitudes continue to be a key factor in regulating employee access to formal policies. Employers still play an important role in determining whether, and how, mothers and fathers take advantage of company policies. Opportunities for career development may be more limited for those who make use of family leaves or flexible schedule policies, for example, or such employees may experience greater job insecurity. Even in highly regulated settings, the extent to which employees can make use of formal work–family practice without negative sanctions and the extent to which companies offer further options for balancing work and family above those mandated by law is a matter of employer discretion (Naesman 2000).

Limited and unequal access by workers to paid leave, childcare, and flexible schedules is a much larger problem in countries where public policy provides low levels of support for employees with family responsibilities. Unequal access to paid maternity leave or childcare is unlikely to be overcome on a voluntary basis. Intervention by national governments in the form of mandated minimum standards for family-friendly policies financed through social insurance is likely to be required to level the playing field for all employees with care giving responsibilities (Glass and Estes 1997). It is not clear that improvements in recruitment, retention, and productivity are sufficient to motivate firms to adopt work–family policies on a voluntary basis in countries like the United States, United Kingdom, Australia, and Japan. In part, this may be due to insufficient evidence to persuade employers that the benefits of such policies exceed their costs, and better research can help. More importantly, however, it may be the case that some of the policies that are most highly valued by employees are too costly for most firms to make widely available on a voluntary basis. Environmental pressures and changing societal norms may lead companies in some industries to adopt such policies despite the expense, but cost pressures are likely to limit their diffusion.

REFERENCES

AKERLOF, G. A. (1982). 'Labor Contracts as Partial Gift Exchange'. *Quarterly Journal of Economics,* 97: 543–69.

ALMER, E. D., and KAPLAN, S. (2002). 'The Effects of Flexible Work Arrangements on Stressors, Burnout, and Behavioral Job Outcomes in Public Accounting'. *Behavioral Research in Accounting,* 14: 1–16.

APPELBAUM, E., and GOLDEN, L. (2002). 'The Standard Workday or the Highway'. Washington, DC: Center for Designing Work Wisely.

ARAKI, T. (1998). 'Recent Legislative Developments in Equal Employment and Harmonization of Work and Family Life in Japan'. Tokyo: Japan Institute of Labor.

ARYEE, S., LUK, V., and STONE, R. (1998). 'Family-Responsive Variables and Retention-Relevant Outcomes among Employed Parents'. *Human Relations*, 51: 73–87.

AUERBACH, J. D. (1990). 'Employer-Supported Child Care as a Woman-Responsive Policy'. *Journal of Family Issues*, 11: 384–400.

BAILYN, L., DRAGO, R., and KOCHAN, T. A. (2001). 'Integrating Work and Family Life: A Holistic Approach'. Cambridge, Mass.: MIT Sloan School of Management.

BEINECKE, R. (1994). 'Assessing the Economic Impact of Personal Development Programs', in F. Heuberger and L. Nash (eds.), *A Fatal Embrace? Assessing Holistic Trends in Human Resources Programs*. New Brunswick, NJ: Transaction.

BERG, P., APPELBAUM, E., BAILEY, T., and KALLEBERG, A. (2003). 'Contesting Time: International Comparisons of Employee Control of Working Time'. Manuscript. Michigan State University, East Lansing, Mich.

BOSCH, G. (2000). 'Der Zusammenhang von Arbeitszeit und Qualifikation'. Gelsenkirchen: Institut für Arbeit und Technik.

BRANNEN, J., and LEWIS, S. (2000). 'Workplace Programmes and Policies in the United Kingdom', in L. Haas, P. Hwang, and R. Graeme (eds.), *Organizational Change & Gender Equity: International Perspectives on Fathers and Mothers at the Workplace*. London: Sage.

Children's Defense Fund (2002). 'Child Care Now'. Washington, DC: Children's Defense Fund.

CHRISTENSEN, K. E., and STAINES, G. L. (1990). 'Flextime: A Viable Solution to Work/Family Conflict?' *Journal of Family Issues*, 11: 455–76.

DALTON, D. R., and MESCH, D. J. (1990). 'The Impact of Flexible Scheduling on Employee Attendance and Turnover'. *Administrative Science Quarterly*, 35: 370–87.

DEITCH, C., and HUFFMAN, M. (2001). 'Family Responsive Benefits and the Two-Tiered Labor Market', in R. Hertz and N. Marshall (eds.), *Work and Family: Today's Realities and Tomorrow's Possibilities*. Berkeley: University of California Press.

deN DULK, L. (2000). 'Work–Family Arrangements in the Netherlands: The Role of Employers', in L. den Dulk, A. van Doorne-Huiskes, and J. Schippers (eds.), *Work–Family Arrangements in Europe*. Amsterdam: Thela Thesis.

——VAN DOORNE-HUISKES, A., and SCHIPPERS, J. (1996). 'Work–Family Arrangements and Gender Inequality in Europe'. *Women in Management Review*, 11: 25–35.

————(2000). 'Work–Family Arrangements in the Context of Welfare States', in L. den Dulk, A. van Doorne-Huiskes, and J. Schippers (eds.), *Work–Family Arrangements in Europe*. Amsterdam: Thela Thesis.

DiMAGGIO, P., and POWELL, W. (1983). 'The Iron Cage Revisited: Institutional Isomorphism and Collective Rationality in Organizational Fields'. *American Sociological Review*, 23: 111–36.

EARLE, J. (1999). 'The International Labour Organisation and Maternity Rights: Evaluating the Potential for Progress'. *Economic and Labor Relations Review*, 10: 203–20.

ERLER, W. (2000). 'Work–Family Reconciliation in Germany: Trends in Public and Corporate Policies', in L. den Dulk, A. van Doorne-Huiskes, and J. Schippers (eds.), *Work–Family Arrangements in Europe*. Amsterdam: Thela Thesis.

Esping-Andersen, G. (1990). *The Three Worlds of Welfare Capitalism.* Princeton, NJ: Princeton University Press.

European Industrial Relations Observatory (1998). 'Engineering Agreements Provide for Reduction in Working Time', Volume 2001.

Fagnani, J. (2002). 'Why Do French Women Have More Children Than German Women? Family Policies and Attitudes toward Child Care outside the Home'. *Community, Work & Family,* 5: 103–19.

Fernandez, J. P. (1986). *Child Care and Corporate Productivity.* Lexington, Mass.: DC Heath.

——(1990). *The Politics and Reality of Family Care in Corporate America.* Lexington, Mass.: Lexington Books.

Galinsky, E. (1994). 'Families and Work: The Importance of the Quality of the Work Environment', in S. L. Kagan and B. Weissbound (eds.), *Putting Families First.* San Francisco: Jossey-Bass.

——(2001). 'Toward a New View of Work and Family Life', in R. Hertz and N. Marshall (eds.), *Work and Family: Today's Realities and Tomorrow's Possibilities.* Berkeley: University of California Press.

——and Bond, J. T. (1998). 'The 1998 Business Work–Life Study'. New York: Families and Work Institute.

——and Swanberg, J. E. (2000). 'Employed Mothers and Fathers in the United States: Understanding How Work and Family Life Fit Together', in L. L. Haas, P. Hwang, and R. Graeme (eds.), *Organizational Change & Gender Equity: International Perspectives on Fathers and Mothers at the Workplace.* London: Sage.

Glass, J. L., and Estes, S. B. (1997). 'The Family Responsive Workplace'. *Annual Review of Sociology,* 23: 289–313.

——and Fujimoto, T. (1995). 'Employer Characteristics and the Provision of Family Responsive Policies'. *Work and Occupations,* 22: 380–411.

Goff, S. J., Mount, M. K., and Jamison, R. L. (1990). 'Employer Supported Child Care: Work/Family Conflict and Absenteeism'. *Personnel Psychology,* 43: 793–809.

Golden, L. (1996). 'The Economics of Worktime Length, Adjustment and Flexibility'. *Review of Social Economy,* 1–44.

Golembiewski, R. T., and Proehl, C. W. (1978). 'A Survey of the Empirical Literature on Flexible Work Hours: Character and Consequences of a Major Innovation'. *Academy of Management Review,* 3: 837–53.

Goodstein, J. D. (1994). 'Institutional Pressures and Strategic Responsiveness: Employer Involvement in Work–Family Issues'. *Academy of Management Journal,* 37: 350–82.

Gornick, J., Meyers, M. K., and Ross, K. E. (1997). 'Supporting the Employment of Mothers: Policy Variation across Fourteen Welfare States'. *Journal of European Social Policy,* 7: 45–70.

Grover, S. L., and Crooker, K. J. (1995). 'Who Appreciates Family-Responsive Human Resource Policies: The Impact of Family-Friendly Policies on the Organizational Attachment of Parents and Non-Parents'. *Personnel Psychology,* 48: 271–88.

Gustafsson, S., Kenjoh, E., and Wetzels, C. (2000). 'Maternity and Non-Standard Work Arrangements: Panel Study Analysis Comparing Germany, Britain, The Netherlands and Sweden', manuscript, Department of Economics, University of Amsterdam, The Netherlands.

HAMMER, L., and BARBERA, K. (1997). 'Toward an Integration of Alternative Work'. *Human Resource Planning*, 20: 28–36.

HARTZ, P. (1996). *The Company that Breathes*. Berlin: Springer.

HILL, E. J., MILLER, B. C., WEINER, S. P., and COLIHAN, J. (1998). 'Influences of the Virtual Office on Aspects of Work and Work/Life Balance'. *Personnel Psychology*, 51: 667–83.

HOHL, L. (1996). 'The Effects of Flexible Work Arrangements'. *Nonprofit Management and Leadership*, 7: 69–86.

KIM, J., and CAMPAGNA, A. (1981). 'Effects of Flexitime on Employee Attendance and Performance: A Field Experiment'. *Academy of Management Journal*, 24: 729–41.

KONRAD, A., and MANGEL, R. (2000). 'The Impact of Work–Life Programs on Firm Productivity'. *Strategic Management Journal*, 21: 1225–37.

KOPPELMAN, R. (1986). 'Alternative Work Schedules and Productivity: A Review of the Evidence'. *National Productivity Review*, 5: 150–65.

KOSSEK, E. E., and NICHOL, V. (1992). 'The Effects of On-Site Child Care on Employee Attitudes and Performance'. *Personnel Psychology*, 45: 485–509.

—— BARBER, A. E., and WINTERS, D. (1999). 'Using Flexible Schedules in the Managerial World: The Power of Peers'. *Human Resource Management*, 38: 33–46.

—— DASS, P., and DeMARR, B. (1994). 'The Dominant Logic of Employer-Sponsored Work and Family Initiatives: Human Resource Managers' Institutional Role'. *Human Relations*, 47: 1121–49.

—— NOE, R., and COLQUITT, J. (2001). 'Caregiving Decisions, Well-Being and Performance: The Effects of Place and Provider as a Function of Dependent Type and Work–Family Climates'. *Academy of Management Journal*, 44/1: 29–44.

LAMBERT, S. J. (2000). 'Added Benefits: The Link between Work–Life Benefits and Organizational Citizenship Behavior'. *Academy of Management Journal*, 43: 801–15.

LEHNDORFF, S. (1998). 'From "Collective" to "Individual" Reductions in Working Time? Trends and Experiences with Working Time in the European Union'. *Transfer: European Review of Labour and Research*, 4: 598–620.

—— (2000). 'Tertiarisation, Work Organization and Working-time Regulation', at the International Conference on the Economics and Socio-Economics of Services from International Perspectives. Brussels, Belgium.

LEWIS, S. (2000a). 'Organisational Change and Gender Equity: Case Studies from the United Kingdom', in L. L. Haas, P. Hwang, and R. Graeme (eds.), *Organizational Change & Gender Equity: International Perspectives on Fathers and Mothers at the Workplace*. London: Sage.

—— (2000b). 'Work–Family Arrangements in the UK', in L. den Dulk, A. van Doorne-Huiskes, and J. Schippers (eds.), *Work–Family Arrangements in Europe*. Amsterdam: Thela Thesis.

—— and TAYLOR, K. (1996). 'Evaluating the Impact of Family-Friendly Employment Policies: A Case Study', in S. Lewis and J. Lewis (eds.), *The Work–Family Challenge: Rethinking Employment*. London: Sage.

LOBEL, S. A. (1999). 'Impacts of Diversity and Work–Life Initiatives in Organizations', in G. N. Powell (ed.), *Handbook of Gender and Work*. Thousand Oaks, Calif.: Sage.

—— and FAUGHT, L. (1996). 'Four Methods for Proving the Value of Work/Life Interventions'. *Compensation and Benefits Review*, 1–8.

MEYER, C. S., MUKERJEE, S., and SESTERO, A. (2001). 'Work–Family Benefits: Which Ones Maximize Profits'. *Journal of Managerial Issues,* 13: 28–44.

MUTARI, E., and FIGART, D. (2001). 'Europe at a Crossroads: Harmonization, Liberalization, and the Gender of Work Time'. *Social Politics,* 8: 36–64.

NAESMAN, E. (2000). 'Sweden and the Reconciliation of Work and Family Life', in L. den Dulk, A. van Doorne-Huiskes, and J. Schippers (eds.), *Work–Family Arrangements in Europe.* Amsterdam: Thela Thesis.

OECD (2001). 'Balancing Work and Family Life: Helping Parents into Paid Employment', in *Employment Outlook.* Paris: OECD.

OSTERMAN, P. (1995). 'Work–Family Programs and the Employment Relationship'. *Administrative Science Quarterly,* 40: 681–700.

PERRY-JENKINS, M., REPETTI, R. L., and CROUTER, A. C. (2000). 'Work and Family in the 1990s'. *Journal of Marriage and the Family,* 62: 981–98.

PIORE, M. J. (2002). 'The Reconfiguration of Work and Employment Relations in the United States at the Turn of the 21st Century', in P. Auer and B. Gauzier (eds.), *The Future of Work, Employment and Social Protection.* Geneva: International Labour Organization.

RAABE, P. H. (1990). 'The Organizational Effects of Workplace Family Policies'. *Journal of Family Issues,* 11: 477–84.

RAPOPORT, R., and BAILYN, L. (1996). 'Relinking Life and Work'. New York: Ford Foundation.

SCANDURA, T. A., and LANKAU, M. J. (1997). 'Relationships of Gender, Family Responsibility and Flexible Work Hours to Organizational Commitment and Job Satisfaction'. *Journal of Organizational Behavior,* 18: 377–91.

SEIFERT, H. (1993). 'Ausmass und Effekte der Arbeitszeitverkuerzung', in P. Hampe (ed.), *Zwischenbilanz der Arbeitszeitverkuerzung.* Munich: Hase and Koehler.

——(1998). 'Working Time Policy in Germany: Searching for New Ways'. *Transfer: European Review of Labour and Research,* 4: 621–40.

SEYLER, D. L., MONROE, P. A., and GARAN, J. C. (1995). 'Balancing Work and Family: The Role of Employer-Supported Child Care Benefits'. *Journal of Family Issues,* 16: 170–93.

SIIM, B. (1991). 'Welfare State, Gender Politics and Equality Politics: Women's Citizenship in the Scandinavian Welfare States', in E. Meehan and S. Sevenhuijsen (eds.), *Equality Politics and Gender.* London: Sage.

SIMON, H. (1951). 'A Formal Theory of the Employment Relation'. *Econometrica,* 19: 293–305.

SNELL, S. A. (1992). 'Control Theory in Strategic Human Resource Management: The Mediating Effect of Administrative Information'. *Academy of Management Journal,* 35: 292–327.

SQUIRCHUK, R., and BOURKE, J. (2000). 'From Equal Employment Opportunity to Family-Friendly Policies and Beyond: Gender Equity in Australia', in L. L. Haas, P. Hwang, and R. Graeme (eds.), *Organizational Change & Gender Equity: International Perspectives on Fathers and Mothers at the Workplace.* London: Sage.

TRIFILETTI, R. (2000). 'Women's Labor Market Participation and the Reconciliation of Work and Family Life in Italy', in L. den Dulk, A. van Doorne-Huiskes, and J. Schippers (eds.), *Work–Family Arrangements in Europe.* Amsterdam: Thela Thesis.

TSUI, A. S., PEARCE, J. L., PORTER, L. W., and TRIPOLI, A. M. (1997). 'Alternative Approaches to the Employee–Organization Relationship: Does Investment in Employees Pay Off'. *Academy of Management Journal,* 40: 1089–121.

WHITEHOUSE, G., and ZETLIN, D. (1999). 'Family Friendly Policies: Distribution and Implementation in Australian Workplaces'. *Economic and Labor Relations Review,* 10: 221–39.

WILLIAMS, J. (2000). *Unbending Gender: Why Family and Work Conflict and What to Do about It.* New York: Oxford University Press.

Work and Family Unit (1998). 'Work and Family State of Play'. Canberra: Australian Department of Employment, Workplace Relations, and Small Business.

YOUNGBLOOD, S. A., and CHAMBERS-COOK, K. (1984). 'Child Care Assistance Can Improve Employee Attitudes and Behavior'. *Personnel Administrator,* 29: 49–95.

CHAPTER 3

GENDER, RACE, AND THE RESTRUCTURING OF WORK

ORGANIZATIONAL AND INSTITUTIONAL PERSPECTIVES

LESLIE MCCALL

3.1 INTRODUCTION

ECONOMIC inequality between men and women and among racial groups long pre-dates the recent period of economic restructuring. Contemporary research on gender and racial inequality developed, in fact, during the 1960s and 1970s when

I would like to thank Rosemary Batt for her helpful comments on earlier drafts of this chapter and Andrea Hood for excellent research assistance.

the underlying structure of the economy, and the advantage of men and whites within that structure, was more or less taken for granted. Much has changed since then, however. Productivity and growth rates began to decline and the earnings (in the United States) and employment (in Europe) prospects of men became more tenuous. While inequality between men and women declined nearly everywhere, inequality within groups grew in most OECD countries, and dramatically in some countries.

In this chapter, I examine these more complex dynamics using an approach that is rooted in contextual explanations of gender and racial inequality. I build on organizational and institutional approaches to inequality that highlight the substantial degree of variation in inequality across jobs, occupations, industries, firms, regions, and countries that cannot be attributed to human capital differences alone. I begin with a theoretical review of organizational and institutional theories of gender and racial inequality, follow with a brief description of the new context of economic restructuring, and then focus on the gendered and racialized aspects of economic restructuring and organization-level restructuring. I also examine the institutional differences across advanced industrial countries that have mediated the terms of women's economic incorporation during this period. While much of the existing empirical and theoretical literature I discuss draws on the United States, the approach developed here can be applied more generally. Given existing strengths and weaknesses of the literature, my primary focus is on gender, and I examine race as it intersects with gender.

3.2 ORGANIZATIONAL AND INSTITUTIONAL PERSPECTIVES

In the human capital model, an individual's economic position is determined by her productive attributes—how much education she has, how much time she spends in paid employment, and how much raw 'ability' she contributes to the production of goods and services. With the partial exception of ability, these attributes are considered the outcomes of choices and decisions made by the individual to specialize in certain kinds of activities such as unpaid labor in the home or paid labor in the market. If individuals of one group are more likely to have some attributes than others, then such individuals will have similar job and earnings profiles. Thus, women tend to have lower earnings than men in part because they have less job experience on average, owing to their absences from work for child-rearing purposes. Such earnings disparities are reinforced when employers select workers based on the perceived average characteristics of a group rather than on true individual characteristics, a form of discrimination called 'statistical' discrimination.

While no one would dispute that human capital endowments are legitimate determinants of job placement and earnings, an alternative model—or complimentary because it is concerned with the 'unexplained' component of inequality in human capital models—asks not only the prior question of why women tend to have less job experience, but why two individuals who have exactly the same observable attributes nevertheless have different earnings or 'returns' to those attributes (England 1992). For example, there are few differences in years of experience and schooling between black men and women, but yet a pay gap exists between them (England, Christopher, and Reid 1999). This is due at least in part to the segregation of black women into lower paying occupations than black men. Similarly, being married or having young children limits women's employment, but much more so for Swiss women than for American women because Switzerland has more irregular school schedules, fewer preschool and childcare provisions, and a stronger ideology of domestic motherhood (Charles *et al.* 2001: 386).

Similarly, even the same occupation can experience dramatic transformations in its sex and race typing without its human capital requirements changing. In the United States, paid domestic work was performed almost exclusively by African American women until the 1960s when the civil rights movement opened up new opportunities. But in the 1980s the occupation rebounded as a result of a greater demand by the wealthy for personal services and an increasing supply of Latina immigrants with few other options (Milkman, Reese, and Roth 1998). Under the assumption that both the supply and demand for such jobs will continue, organizers have sprung up to improve the working conditions and pay of the job (Hondagneu-Sotelo 2001). Shifts in the composition of the job, therefore, have more to do with changes or differences in its social conditions than in its human capital requirements. The entire locus of interest shifts from the attributes of individuals to the attributes of the organizations, places, and/or time periods in which they work and in which their choices are constrained. Even whether the occupation exists is an issue. Sweden, for example, has virtually no paid domestic laborers.

Although not concerned with economic restructuring per se, these examples represent an important tradition of scholarship that is a precursor to the new research on restructuring because of its emphasis on the contextual specificity of inequality. Research in this area considers everything from organizational differences across firms in the gender and racial composition of jobs in the same occupation to institutional differences across nation-states in social policies that affect the employment of women and racial minorities. The central theme is that inequality is produced within particular organizational and institutional settings and therefore tends to vary according to the particularities of those settings.

Although there is a distinct and durable 'labor queue' that ranks white men at the top and minority groups of women at the bottom, that is only part of the story (Reskin and Roos 1990).

In fact, there are several factors that are known to be important in shaping the intensity of gender and racial divisions of labor. Two such factors were already mentioned in the example of domestic work: the racial and gender composition of the local labor force and the political/cultural factors that sex-type and race-type occupations. Other factors include: (1) growth and turnover, which reduces overt competition between insiders and outsiders and pushes employers to broaden their search; (2) public oversight, which tends to be stronger in the public sector than in the private; (3) sympathetic leadership, which makes equality a priority; and (4) the younger age of a firm, since organizations tend to bear the imprint of the time of their founding and change of all kinds is more common in newer than in older, more inert and bureaucratic firms (Baron, Mittman, and Newman 1991). However, to the extent that old firms are large firms, the importance of firm size might prevail. Large firms typically have more objective hiring and promotion criteria, are more open to public scrutiny around personnel practices, consist of larger pressure groups that can press for compliance with equal employment opportunity regulations, and pay more in wages and benefits, in part because they are more likely to be unionized but also because they want to avoid unionization (Reskin and McBrier 2000; Moss and Tilly 2001).

Even among the kinds of corporations that tend to offer greater opportunities to outsiders, however, differences in context matter for how gender and racial divisions develop. Most large corporations have bureaucratic personnel systems in which both market forces and managerial discretion govern job evaluation and promotion decisions. This means that organizational history and the relative power of different social groups within a particular organization can have considerable influence over the division of labor. Local supply and demand conditions, political environment, the existence and strength of pressure groups, technological changes, and so on, also interact with such features as large firm size to produce unique outcomes. There is a rich tradition of comparative case studies of how otherwise similar jobs are filled by different racial and gender groups depending on such contextual factors (e.g. Milkman 1986). Quantitative studies also confirm that there is substantial segregation within the same occupation as a result of men, women, and racial minorities working in separate establishments (Bielby and Baron 1986).

Moreover, even the very same firm may have patterns of gender and racial inequality that differ qualitatively from one part of the firm to another. At the entry-level workers are typically hired from the external labor market, whereas at the top workers are promoted from within (i.e. via the internal labor market). Thus, an individual's firm-specific skills may be more important in determining pay at the top—where individuals are already well known—than at the bottom.

Consequently, within-job pay gaps by gender and race brought on by informal networks that favor dominant groups is more of an impediment to equality at the top than at the bottom where between-job pay gaps by gender and race brought on by separate and unequal job ladders are at issue (Bell and Nkomo 2001; Kanter 1977; Nelson and Bridges 1999).

Cross-national variation in the structure of pay systems also illustrates the importance of contextual perspectives on race and gender inequality. Wage scales for clerical and manufacturing jobs, for example, are more integrated in Germany than in England, leading to lower male/female wage differentials in Germany (Rubery 1998). Comparing Taiwan and Japan, Brinton (2001) shows that large firms in Japan have well-defined job mobility ladders for men but not for women, while small, family-owned firms in Taiwan create more opportunities for female family members to participate in the management of the firm. The connection between educational and occupational systems also shapes the process of integration. In countries such as Germany, an emphasis on early vocational specialization coupled with occupational gender typing leads to greater occupational segregation despite lower wage differentials between male and female jobs (Charles *et al.* 2001).

Finally, it is also important to consider feminist approaches that go beyond organizational and institutional approaches by arguing that all organizations are fundamentally gendered from the start. Unlike much organizational and institutional research that assumes a 'gender-neutral' and/or 'race-neutral' hierarchy of jobs, which is then overlaid with gender and racial segregation, feminist organizational theorists find that multiple systems of stratification are coevolving (Acker 1990). Other theorists have suggested that power within organizations should be understood as more diffuse and less centralized in top male-dominated positions (Martin and Collinson 1999). Gendered relationships are created in everyday interactions within organizations that have particular gender structures, and both of these—the micro relationships and the meso structures—potentially vary, along with their interaction, across organizations (see also Ridgeway 1997; Reskin 2000). In fact, the dynamics of interpersonal interaction among coworkers is of increasing interest given the growing diversity of workplaces and the perceived payoff of greater diversity in decision-making processes (Jackson and Joshi 2001).

In sum, organizational and institutional researchers of all kinds have provided us with a wide range of explanations of inequality. Identifying the precise source of inequality in turn has implications for the kinds of anti-inequality policies that are effective. On the one hand, there are well-known gender- and race-specific policies. Affirmative action policy, for one, is based on the need to move outsiders into insiders' jobs; it is a job integration strategy implemented on a person-by-person basis. Comparable worth policy, in contrast, is based on the current reality of gender and racial segregation; it is a wage integration strategy implemented on an occupation-by-occupation basis. On the other hand, this section has suggested that there are nontargeted policies that would also foster greater equality if designed in the right way, including recruitment strategies, job ladders, pay systems, workers' organizations, work/time schedules, and so on. Recent research in the United States, for example, has highlighted the importance of establishing stronger links between the bottom and top rungs of potential career ladders, especially when the rungs are organizationally separated (e.g. home health care aide and registered nurse) and credentials are needed to advance up the ladder (Fitzgerald and Carlson 2000). Equity strategies, in other words, need to be adapted to local organizational and institutional contexts.

3.3 THE NEW CONTEXT OF ECONOMIC RESTRUCTURING

While this approach to the study of gender and racial divisions of labor is helpful in emphasizing context, it developed over a period in which the full implications of economic restructuring were little known or understood. Context, I would argue, is even more important today. Here I consider how the context has changed over the past twenty to thirty years, prompting changes in the way we should think about gender and racial inequality. I first briefly outline the basic contours of economic restructuring in the remainder of this section (refer to other chapters for a fuller discussion). Next I discuss new issues in racial, class, and especially gender inequality. I then examine the gender and racial aspects of 'organizational restructuring', or how organizations (i.e. firms) have adjusted to the new context of economic restructuring.

As is well known, the world economy is still in the midst of a prolonged era of restructuring that dates from approximately the late 1960s and early 1970s. At that time, productivity growth, economic growth, and real wages began to decline and unemployment and inequality began to rise, though unevenly across and within advanced capitalist nations (Freeman 1994). Beyond these basic facts, much controversy remains over the initial and ongoing causes of this transition, and of the unexpected turnaround in the late 1990s. Most scholars agree, however, that changes in the structure of demand are central. First, in the 1960s and 1970s, an increase in international trade occurred at the same time that markets in advanced industrial countries became saturated with standardized, mass-produced goods. Second, deregulation resulted in increased domestic competition in non-trade-sensitive industries, especially in the United States, where competitors and consumers teamed up in the 1970s to break up monopolies in telecommunications and transportation. The deregulation revolution then spread to other industries, such as banking, and to other countries. Third, new information, communication, and transportation technologies were crucial in augmenting both foreign and domestic competitive advantage, by accelerating the design, improving the quality, expanding the geography, and proliferating the number of products and services. In short, intensifying competition and technological change—combined with more temporary shocks, such as inflation and increased oil prices in the 1970s—were the principal factors that precipitated and fueled the process of restructuring (Piore and Sabel 1984).

3.3.1 Gender and Race in a New Context

What are the implications of these changes for existing configurations of gender and racial inequality? As will become clear, answering this question requires a prior understanding of new forms of class and skills-based inequalities. On the one hand, increased competition and technological change have generally worked against less-skilled workers as employers seek to lower costs by automating routine tasks or outsourcing operations to lower-waged firms (e.g. temporary agencies) and/or regions around the world. This first occurred in the manufacturing sector (i.e. deindustrialization), destroying millions of high-paying jobs that required little formal education, but now increasingly occurs in the service sector as well. On the other hand, increased competition and technological change has benefited many, though by no means all, high-skilled workers by putting a premium on the kind of technical knowledge that leads to competitive innovations. On balance, skill demands have been growing over time even though technological changes have led to the deskilling and elimination of many jobs as well. The decline in demand for low-skilled workers relative to high-skilled workers is frequently considered one of the main sources of declining wages/employment at the bottom of the labor market and rising overall class inequality (Freeman 1994).

However, class inequality has not increased in all countries, and it has increased at a much faster pace in some countries, such as the United States, the United Kingdom, New Zealand, and Sweden, than in others. The causes of inequality, some argue, are therefore not so much a matter of skill-biased technological change and globalization as they are of how employers and governments have responded to these conditions. Particularly in the United States, redistributive wage-setting institutions such as unions, the minimum wage, the social wage, and internal labor markets have always been weak, but they became even weaker as power shifted decisively in favor of employers. Moreover, it is not only low-skilled workers who have been adversely affected. Work has become less stable and less secure for increasing numbers of downsized managers and high-tech workers (Cappelli 1999). While high-skilled workers may have more bargaining power with which to negotiate, they too have become more exposed to the vagaries of the market.

While flexibility is also appealing to European employers, the stronger wage-setting institutions there have insulated European workers from the falling real wages and dramatic increases in inequality typical in the United States. Instead, the cost has been unemployment and temporary employment, both of which are generally higher than in the United States. While individual nations vary in the extent to which they fall on the high-inequality/high-unemployment continuum, the trade-off between inequality and unemployment seems real enough. It is a sign of the extent to which the new competitive environment is shaped and mediated through national policies and institutions. This does not mean that full employ-ment cannot be coupled with low inequality, but it does mean that the dominant paths to flexibility have thus far followed a course of loosening either wage or employment rigidities.

Although women's economic status is also shaped in crucial ways by new and changing institutions, most researchers of women's changing economic status have emphasized institutions of a different sort—those that facilitate women's labor force attachment by relieving them of some of their family responsibilities. I discuss these important institutions in section 3.4 and consider here the changing position of women in the labor market apart from what determines the labor supply of mothers. I focus on the United States because the impact of changes in underlying economic conditions will emerge more clearly precisely because institutions, of both the wage-setting and family-care types, are so weak. I also focus on the United States because it is conceptually illuminating in its complex configuration of class, gender, and racial inequality.

While the era of restructuring is associated with rising class inequality and/or rising unemployment, gender inequality declined significantly nearly everywhere, but particularly in the United States, which moved from the bottom to the middle of the pack in its ranking on the gender wage gap (Blau and Kahn 2003). Women significantly increased their hours at work—even though their wages were not necessarily climbing, particularly at the bottom—at least in part because their paychecks were becoming increasingly central to family survival given declines in men's wages and job opportunities. In many cases, the contribution to family income by working wives and mothers prevented declines in real family income and tempered increases in overall family income inequality (Cancian and Reed 1999). As is well known, there was a substantial increase in the number of women in managerial and professional occupations as well. Their progress stemmed both from new opportunities in the service economy and more general improvements in their educational attainment and labor force attachment. This was generally the case across countries, as women were delaying marriage and childbearing, having fewer children, and returning to work sooner after childbearing (Baxter and Western 2001; Rubery, Smith, and Fagan 1999).

Although this perception of women's economic progress is generally accurate and widely held, it fails to capture the whole story of women's changing economic status—or even its most novel aspects. In particular, it differs from perceptions of economic progress by minority racial groups in the United States, who have also gained in relative terms, though more unevenly over time and less dramatically than women's progress relative to men's. In discussions of minority groups, it is common to recognize the existence of a successful middle class without assuming that the middle class status of some members represents the social status of the entire group. In other words, the black middle class and growing stratification among blacks are each well-known and well-studied phenomena, in large measure because economic restructuring provoked a rethinking of the interaction between race and inequality. I discuss this rethinking first and then turn to its implications for understanding the interaction of gender, inequality, and restructuring, including stratification among women.

In the rethinking of race and inequality, the influential work of William Julius Wilson and others in the United States were critical, highlighting the greater negative impact of deindustrialization on working-class than on middle-class blacks (especially men). The decline of manufacturing industries in northern industrial cities with large black populations and the subsequent increase in service industries with a polarized set of high-skill, high-wage and low-skill, low-wage jobs meant that working-class black men were displaced from high-wage blue-collar jobs and lacked the skills for new high-wage white-collar jobs. To Wilson, the skill and spatial mismatches brought on by deindustrialization were the proximate causes of economic hardship for working-class blacks, not racial discrimination, even though he and others have documented employer preferences for nonblacks in firms that are located in both the central city and the suburbs. Wilson therefore advocated policies that would rebuild urban economies and retrain urban workers to the benefit of white and black working-class families alike. Such policies would have broader political support than race-targeted policies but in effect would disproportionately benefit blacks (Wilson 1987, 1996).

Wilson's work also spawned research in the United States on how immigrants are affected differently than blacks by economic restructuring. Latinos never benefited from employment in high-wage manufacturing in the Midwest because they migrated to the United States during and after the period of economic restructuring (Tienda 1995). Latinos have been more likely to find precarious employment in the newly industrialized regions of the Sunbelt. These regions have their own histories of boom and bust that do not necessarily follow the chronology and character of rustbelt (de)industrialization in terms of the degree of unionization (lower), size of manufacturing plants (smaller), and technology-intensity of the production process (higher, as in electronics, and lower, as in garments and textiles)

(Moore and Pinderhughes 1993). Garment and electronics industries in particular tend to employ Asian as well as Latino immigrants in the lowest paying assembly jobs. The conditions of employment are often harsh and regulatory oversight is minimal (Lopez-Garza and Diaz 2001).

In addition, immigrant women have fueled an informal sector of sweatshops, personal services, and retail services, with sweatshops and retail establishments often owned by same-ethnic men in ethnic enclave economies. These sectors have arisen largely in response to new demands for low-wage labor by firms that are using subcontractors to cut costs. They also meet new demands by affluent individuals and dual-earner families to subcontract out a wide range of domestic work, including everything from laundry to landscaping (Sassen 1991). This is consistent with evidence that shows higher Asian/white and Latino/white wage inequality in immigrant-rich cities, even as black/white inequality is apparently unaffected by competition from immigrants, the concern most expressed by researchers in the literature on immigration and inequality (McCall 2001b). In sum, restructuring's differential impact on blacks and immigrants is clear, as is the centrality of intersections of race/ethnicity with gender and class (Browne and Misra 2003).

In contrast, women's overall economic progress has crowded out a similarly complex analysis of restructuring and growing class stratification among women (exceptions in other countries include Armstrong 1996; Larner 1996; McDowell 1991). This is surprising because, despite the overwhelming focus on men in the restructuring literature, wage inequality among men and among women is generally comparable in level and trend. Although real wages did not fall for as many women as men at the bottom, or fall as much, they too experienced declines and stagnation in wages. Meanwhile, the fastest growth in real wages came from women at the top of the education, wage, and family income distribution, far outpacing the growth of wages among men at the top (Mishel, Bernstein, and Boushey 2003).

Equally important, women are increasingly engaged in face-to-face relationships of inequality. Occupational segregation has meant that women are more likely to climb the supervisory ladder in female-dominated sectors, putting them in the position of supervising other women (Clement and Myles 1994). In addition, a whole sector of low-wage, female-dominated personal and retail service industries have developed to cater to time-crunched, high-earning women (Browne, Tigges, and Press 2001; Glenn 1999). Apart from a curiously large literature on the relationship between domestics and their employers, there is virtually nothing that explores the nature of these increasingly common relationships of inequality among women.

These trends should be of interest to all researchers of the new inequality (and not just to those interested in gender and race disparities) because women account for nearly half of the workforce. This makes inequality among women crucial for understanding overall inequality. This is especially the case if there are gender differences in the sources of inequality, which a key set of findings in the literature confirms. Consistent with the overall theme of this chapter, such research bolsters the role of institutions in explaining the rise in wage inequality in the United States. For example, the decline of the minimum wage was particularly disadvantageous to women at the bottom of the labor market who are more likely than men to work in minimum wage jobs (DiNardo, Fortin, and Lemieux 1996). There is also some evidence to suggest that in service and sales jobs, which are disproportionately filled by women, corporate restructuring strategies in the last decade have fostered greater inequality. Finally, conditions that signal more flexible and competitive labor markets—such as high levels of unemployment, temporary and part-time employment, and immigrant labor—are the most important correlates of high levels of wage dispersion among women across US labor markets (McCall 2001a). In each of these cases, where the market plays a greater role in setting wages, women on the low end appear to have been more adversely affected than women on the high end.

In sum, like researchers of the complexly evolving system of racial stratification, gender scholars have much to grapple with in exploring women's position in the new economy. Such an exploration would include a better understanding of the root causes of rising inequality among women and of the labor market policies that will foster high-wage and equitable economic growth for all groups of women as well as for low-wage earning men (Rubery, Smith, and Fagan 1999). This in turn involves a more expansive understanding of the analytical role of gender beyond its usual reference to the status of women relative to men, not least because greater female/male equality can be fostered in an environment of greater inequality among women, not to mention greater inequality among men, as has occurred over the past several decades in the United States and in other countries (e.g. Black and Strahan 2001). In short, this rethinking will involve more attention to multiple—and at times conflicting—dimensions of inequality (McCall 2001a).

3.3.2 Gender and Race in New Organizational Contexts

These large-scale changes in the nature of contemporary labor markets were carried out in no small measure by transformations in the way thousands of individual firms reorganized work. Employers have restructured their organizations in a myriad of ways: they have introduced new technology to replace some workers, upgrade the skills of other workers, and downgrade the skills of still other workers; they have changed the job structure of the firm so there are fewer job titles and broader responsibilities within each title (or, in some cases, proliferated new titles along with new products); they have moved from an individual-based to a team-based model of work; they have externalized noncore and nonspecialty functions to subcontractors, temporary workers, and part-time workers; they have introduced incentive systems based on compensation (e.g. bonuses and stock options) rather than mobility within the firm; and they have introduced other changes that at once decentralize production and services and centralize control (Rubery, Batt and Doellgast, in this volume).

At the same time that organizations have been restructuring in these ways, women have been increasing their labor force participation and antidiscrimination ideologies have become more pervasive (Cockburn 1991). The coincidence of these two dynamics—organizational change and demographic change—raises a whole set of questions that are only now beginning to be addressed in the research literature. On the one hand, change of one type can facilitate change of the other type, so that if an organization is changing its underlying structure, then it may use it as an opportunity to fully integrate equity policy into the new structure. On the other hand, change of one type can overwhelm or take precedence over change of the other type, so that equity issues become subordinated to organizational changes that are considered of greater economic necessity. Less intentional outcomes are possible as well, such as when an occupation becomes 'resegregated' as a result of restructuring—that is, its status and pay are reduced as more women and racial minorities enter it (Reskin and Roos 1990).

Preliminary research is suggestive but not conclusive on all of these questions. As one might guess, fully integrated and successful organizational and equity change is the least likely of the three outcomes. In one case, organizational scholars posed as both researchers and consultants in recommending a switch to self-managing teams in a manufacturing plant and flattened job hierarchies in a corporate headquarters. At the same time, they recommended that teams be integrated and lines of authority be broken down by gender (Meyerson and Ely 2000). In the end, the gender equity goals were sabotaged in the process of reorganization for a whole number of reasons explored by the authors as well as by Acker (2000). One intriguing reason appears to be replicated in other studies: less overtly formal authority structures foster the emergence of a 'hero' culture—working long hours, doing anything for the company, going above and beyond the call of duty, etc.—a corporate culture that is more akin to the culture of hegemonic masculinity than hegemonic femininity. In fact women who tended to engage in similar behavior were often derided as too aggressive.

Similarly, Baron *et al.* (2001) examined the connection between the propensity to hire women into core scientific and engineering positions and the organizational models of high-tech start-up firms in Silicon Valley. The model that was least likely to promote integration was termed the 'commitment' model, in which attachment to the firm is based on close relationships and cultural fit. In the banking industry in London, McDowell (1997) also found that the new emphasis on flexibility encouraged informality in the recruitment process, making one's class background and fit with the banking culture central factors in recruitment. Gender equity was never a stated coequal goal of the restructuring process, but nevertheless became an unintended casualty. Other case study researchers have come to similarly pessimistic conclusions about the equity potential of the reorganization process (see Cunningham, Lord, and Delaney 1999; Rasmussen 2001; Tienari 1999; Woodall, Edwards, and Welchman 1997).

At a more micro level, several researchers have taken a closer look at how the gender and/or racial character of the team structure itself may facilitate or impede its success. Does the sex-typing and race-typing of the jobs in the team have any impact on the success or failure of the team? Is a diverse gender or racial mix an obstacle or a benefit? When men's jobs (e.g. technician) and women's jobs (e.g. clerical) are merged into a team, a couple of studies have shown that men are more likely to resist taking on female-typed functions than women are of taking on male-typed functions, thus undermining the potential cross-functionality of the team (Kahn 1999; Ollilainen and Rothschild 2001). This is consistent with another study that found gender differences in attitudes towards the implementation of a teaming structure. Male engineers appreciated the greater degree of autonomy, while female engineers appreciated the opportunities to learn new skills and engage in more social interaction. Overall women tended to favor the team structure more than men, suggesting that teams have the potential to elevate lower-status workers when they are integrated into multi-rung teams. They may even provide a structure in which to mitigate potential gender and racial conflicts among workers as well (Daday and Burris 2002; Rasmussen 2001).

Although we have little generalizable evidence on such issues, and contextual factors appear to be important (e.g. the exact gender, racial, age, and composition of the group), on balance it appears that more evidence supports the argument that diversity creates greater conflict and turnover than not. These negative outcomes can be minimized, however, if diversity is managed from the start in a way that allows an organization to harness the productive potential that comes from having a more diverse set of talents, experiences, and information contributing to the decision-making process (Jackson and Joshi 2001).

In contrast to the origins of the teaming structure, the origins of other kinds of organizational changes have taken place as a direct result of the increasing share of women in the workplace. At the upper end of the job hierarchy, women managers and professionals have been demanding the restructuring of their professions in ways that better accommodate the care-taking responsibilities of parents. This is the 'positive' side of flexibility, in which part-time, flex-time, and telecommuting options are available to valued employees. Such accommodations may also serve as a springboard for more thorough reorganizations that increase the job satisfaction and productivity of an entire team by simultaneously loosening time constraints and tightening production schedules (Rapoport *et al.* 2002). In some organizations, however, this 'positive' side of flexibility has a downside—namely, the creation of female-dominated 'mommy' tracks in formerly male-dominated professions (Cockburn 1991; Pringle 1998). More troubling, true work schedule flexibility is less often an option for low-wage workers, who may need it the most, since they cannot afford to purchase substitute care. Moreover, the increasing employment of mothers with young children has frequently been used as a justification of less secure and less stable job arrangements, such as part-time and temporary work, when in reality these new job arrangements are introduced as cost-cutting measures. This is the 'negative' side of flexibility, which disproportionately affects female-dominated and minority-dominated jobs (Clement 2001).

3.4 GENDER AND RACE IN THE INTERNATIONAL CONTEXT

While in recent years economic and organizational restructuring have set the tone for understanding new divisions of labor, welfare state restructuring as such has not been as prominent a topic in comparative cross-national research on gender inequality (comparative research on racial inequality is rare, but see Charles 2000; Reitz 1998). Institutional changes should be a higher priority in future research—some of which is already being done on restructuring in Eastern Europe (see van der Lippe and van Dijk 2001)—but long-standing institutional differences across countries do continue to be quite stark and systematic despite extensive restructuring. In fact, variation across nations often reveals both a vivid and confounding view in the contextual nature of gender divisions of labor. This is due to two factors: (1) the large number of outcomes of interest to scholars of gender inequality, including labor force participation rates, hours at work, gender pay gaps, and occupational segregation; and (2) the large number of institutional conditions that shape such outcomes, including policies in the areas of welfare, fertility, labor supply, family leave, childcare, taxes, work time, equal employment opportunity, and occupational training (Gornick and Meyers 2003). Since I cannot do justice to these issues in so short a space, the discussion is more illustrative than exhaustive.

In terms of the complexity in outcomes, simple contrasts between countries serve to make the point. Occupational gender segregation is often thought to 'cause' gender wage inequality, but some countries facilitate gender equality in pay while reinforcing occupational segregation, such as Sweden, while other countries foster the reverse, such as East Germany and Japan. Scholars argue that differences in industrial and pay structures explain the differences in outcomes (Rosenfeld and Kalleberg 1990; Sorensen and Trappe 1995). In terms of the complexity of institutional conditions, long paid parental leave policies seem favorable but can actually reduce women's firm-based experience and increase discrimination, as the costs to hiring women are greater, thus decreasing their long-term labor market rewards (Ruhm 1998). Somewhat paradoxically, then, the one country without paid leaves, the United States, has a high level of full-time employment among women, considerable integration of women into male-dominated jobs, and rapidly rising levels of gender wage equality (though many other factors explain the US situation as well).

Multidimensionality complicates matters further. Considering interactions of class and gender, some environments are better at reducing income inequality than gender inequality (e.g. West Germany, The Netherlands, and Switzerland). Norway has a generous welfare state, which promotes post-tax household income equality, but until recently childcare was treated as a private matter contributing to high rates of part-time work among women. Even in the case of Sweden, where both gender and class inequality are low, occupational segregation is higher than in the United States, where class inequality is high. In the aggregate, however, countries with strong wage-setting institutions do tend to have both greater wage compression among men and greater wage equality between men and women (Blau and Kahn 2003), creating a virtuous effect of policies that were not principally intended to promote gender equality. To the extent that such policies are being chipped away by neoliberal restructuring, progress on gender inequality could be stalled. Indeed, this has been a concern in Sweden. But to the extent that governments acknowledge an increasing demand for women's employment and equity, progress could be accelerated as welfare states are pushed to provide more services rather than less (Orloff 2002).

To better understand cross-national variation in policies, institutions, and ideologies related to gender inequality, three types of welfare state regimes have been identified (for a recent overview, see Gornick and Meyers 2003). The first type facilitates the entrance of primary caretakers into the labor market by offering generous public services for the care of children. Such countries are referred to as 'social democratic', 'dual earner', or 'weak male breadwinner' (e.g. Sweden). The second type facilitates family formation by providing tax breaks for housewives and child credits or income grants, but lacks public childcare services. Such countries do not support the paid employment of mothers and are referred to as 'conservative', 'strong male breadwinner', and 'general family support' (e.g. Germany). Finally, the third type features few public services and limited transfers to children. Private means and markets must be relied upon to meet caretaking needs and facilitate the employment of mothers. Such countries are referred to as 'liberal' or 'market-oriented'.

In sum, not only do welfare state policies facilitate or impede the employment of mothers, they create a demand for female labor in heavily female-dominated sectors and thus shape the female labor market more generally. In the case of publicly provided services (e.g. Sweden), the work is of relatively high quality and not relegated to subordinate groups. The one drawback is that this type of system encourages occupational segregation. In the case of privately provided services (e.g. the United States), an entire sector of low-paid market care work has been filled disproportionately by racial/ethnic minorities, especially as welfare retrenchment has pushed large numbers of poor women with children into the labor market. While family formation and women's employment are promoted in the public sector model, things are much more complicated in the private sector model. Minority women's family formation is discouraged, for it is difficult to both work and raise children on little income, and women's employment is segmented along racial lines. Minority women disproportionately fill low-wage jobs in the care/household services sector while white women disproportionately pursue more financially rewarding careers (Mink 1998). In the middle between the private and public sector models of care provision are countries that facilitate family formation but not women's employment. Since women are encouraged to provide care in the home, a large and segregated female care/service sector does not exist.

3.5 CONCLUSION

Changes in the underlying economic environment have fundamentally altered the context in which to evaluate racial and especially gender inequality. When many of the underlying ideas about gender and racial discrimination were first developed, those concerned about gender and racial inequality could take a strong economy and a stable wage and employment outlook for granted, at least for white men. Overall employment and wages were growing while inequality was declining; an expanding pie could accommodate the demands for gender and racial equity.

These trends have reversed. First, economic restructuring has reduced the industrial and ideological foundation of unions, internal labor markets, and other institutions that fostered job mobility, security, and equity for insiders as well as outsiders. Second, organizational restructuring has put cost cutting and technological change ahead of equity and diversity. And, third, welfare state restructuring has scaled back the public provision of essential social services. In some cases, states have also given in to calls for restrictions on immigration to limit competition over jobs. In contrast, women have made significant progress in the labor market and in securing public support for family responsibilities. Although there is no simple and straightforward way to respond to this new environment, at a minimum gender scholars need to turn from an exclusive focus on inequality between men and women, and individual human capital explanations therein, to a broader focus on new contexts of inequality brought on by economic, organizational, and welfare state restructuring.

Such an expanded research agenda would consist of several components. First and foremost, it would seek to understand variation in women's changing economic status by education, income, household structure, race, ethnicity, and nationality. Class and skill differences in particular are becoming more salient, among both men and women. Second, it would examine the interplay of organizational restructuring and increasing racial and gender diversity in the workplace. In particular, we need to know whether the perceived urgency of organizational restructuring in the new economy has eclipsed or enhanced the prospects for gender and racial equity. Third, it would explore the potential of 'gender/race-neutral' institutions—such as the minimum wage, unions, training systems, employment agencies, work-time regulations, and non-firm-specific career ladders—for improving gender and racial equity as well as overall wage equality and job mobility. Finally, it would investigate the impact of changes in social policy regimes on relative and absolute labor market outcomes among women and racial/ethnic minorities. Such an agenda is demanding, for it requires researchers to have a foot in at least two worlds at once—the world of vast organizational and institutional change and the world of class, gender, and racial diversity. Such an agenda is necessary, however, for understanding the full range of possibilities for greater gender and racial equity in the new economic environment of the twenty-first century.

References

ACKER, J. (1990). 'Hierarchies, Jobs, Bodies: A Theory of Gendered Organizations'. *Gender and Society*, 4/2: 139–58.

—— (2000). 'Gendered Contradictions in Organizational Equity Projects'. *Organization: The Interdisciplinary Journal of Organization, Theory, and Society*, 7/4: 635–62.

ARMSTRONG, P. (1996). 'The Feminization of the Labor Force: Harmonizing Down in a Global Economy', in I. Bakker (ed.), *Rethinking Restructuring: Gender and Change in Canada*. Buffalo: University of Toronto Press.

BARON, J. N., MITTMAN, B. S., and NEWMAN, A. E. (1991). 'Targets of Opportunity: Organizational and Environmental Determinants of Gender Integration within the California Civil Service, 1979–1985'. *American Journal of Sociology*, 96/6: 1362–401.

—— HANNAN, M. T., HSU, G., and KOCAK, O. (2001). 'Gender and the Organization-Building Process in Young, High-Tech Firms', in M. F. Guillen, R. Collins, P. England, and M. Meyer (eds.), *Economic Sociology at the Millennium*. New York: Russell Sage Foundation.

BAXTER, J., and WESTERN, M. (eds.) (2001). *Reconfigurations of Class and Gender.* Stanford, Calif.: Stanford University Press.

BELL, E., and NKOMO, S. (2001). *Our Separate Ways: Black and White Women and the Struggle for Professional Identity.* Boston: Harvard Business School Press.

BIELBY, W. T., and BARON, J. A. (1986). 'Men and Women at Work: Sex Segregation and Statistical Discrimination'. *American Journal of Sociology,* 91/4: 759–99.

BLACK, S. E., and STRAHAN, P. E. (2001). 'Division of the Spoils: Rent-Sharing and Discrimination in a Regulated Industry'. *American Economic Review,* 91/4: 814–31.

BLAU, F., and KAHN, L. (2003). *At Home and Abroad.* New York: Russell Sage Foundation.

BRINTON, M. (ed.) (2001). *Women's Working Lives in East Asia.* Stanford, Calif.: Stanford University Press.

BROWNE, I., and MISRA, J. (2003). 'The Intersection of Gender and Race in the Labor Market'. *American Review of Sociology,* 29: 487–513.

——TIGGES, L., and PRESS, J. (2001). 'Inequality through Labor Markets, Firms, and Families: The Intersection of Gender and Race-Ethnicity across Three Cities', in A. O'Connor, C. Tilly, and L. Bobo (eds.), *Urban Inequality: Evidence from Four Cities.* New York: Russell Sage Foundation.

CANCIAN, M., and REED, D. (1999). 'The Impact of Wives' Earnings on Income Inequality: Issues and Estimates'. *Demography,* 36/2: 173–84.

CAPPELLI, P. (1999). *The New Deal at Work.* Boston: Harvard Business School Press.

CHARLES, M. (2000). 'Divisions of Labour: Social Groups and Occupational Allocation'. *European Sociological Review,* 16/1: 27–42.

——BUCHMANN, M., HALEBSKY, S., POWERS, J. M., and SMITH, M. (2001). 'The Context of Women's Market Careers'. *Work and Occupations,* 28/3: 371–96.

CLEMENT, W. (2001). 'Who Works: Comparing Labor Market Practices', in J. Baxter and M. Western (eds.), *Reconfigurations of Class and Gender.* Stanford, Calif.: Stanford University Press.

——and MYLES, J. (1994). *Relations of Ruling: Class and Gender in Postindustrial Societies.* Buffalo: McGill-Queens University Press.

COCKBURN, C. (1991). *In the Way of Women: Men's Resistance to Sex Equality in Organizations.* London: Macmillan.

CUNNINGHAM, R., LORD, A., and DELANEY, L. (1999). 'Next Steps for Equality?: The Impact of Organizational Change on Opportunities for Women in the Civil Service'. *Gender, Work, and Organization,* 6/2: 67–78.

DADAY, G. K., and BURRIS, B. H. (2002). 'The Effects of Teaming-Structures on Race, Ethnicity, and Gender Differences in a High-Tech Corporation: A Case Study'. Unpublished manuscript presented at the (2002) American Sociological Association meetings, Chicago.

DINARDO, J., FORTIN, N. M., and LEMIEUX, T. (1996). 'Labor Market Institutions and the Distribution of Wages, 1973–1992: A Semiparametric Approach'. *Econometrica,* 64/5: 1001–44.

ENGLAND, P. (1992). *Comparable Worth: Theories and Evidence.* New York: Aldine de Gruyter.

——CHRISTOPHER, K., and REID, L. (1999). 'Gender, Race, Ethnicity, and Wages', in I. Browne (ed.), *Latinas and African American Women at Work.* New York: Russell Sage Foundation Press.

FITZGERALD, J., and CARLSON, V. (2000). 'Ladders to a Better Life'. *American Prospect,* 11/15.

FREEMAN, R. (ed.) (1994). *Working under Different Rules.* New York: Russell Sage Foundation.

GLENN, E. N. (1999). 'The Social Construction and Institutionalization of Gender and Race: An Integrative Framework', in M. M. Ferree, J. Lorber, and B. Hess (eds.), *Revisioning Gender.* Thousand Oaks, Calif.: Sage Publications.

GORNICK, J. C., and MEYERS, M. (2003). *Work and Care: Reconciling Parenthood and Employment.* New York: Russell Sage Foundation.

HONDAGNEU-SOTELO, P. (2001). *Doméstica: Immigrant Workers Cleaning and Caring in the Shadows of Affluence.* Berkeley: University of California Press.

JACKSON, S. E., and JOSHI, A. (2001). 'Research on Domestic and International Diversity in Organizations: A Merger That Works?' in N. Anderson, D. S. Ones, H. K. Sinangil, and C. Viswesvaran (eds.), *Handbook of Work and Organizational Psychology.* Thousand Oaks, Calif.: Sage Publications.

KAHN, P. (1999). 'Gender and Employment Restructuring in British National Health Service Manual Work'. *Gender, Work, and Reorganization,* 6/4: 202–12.

KANTER, R. M. (1977). *Men and Women of the Corporation.* New York: Random House.

LARNER, W. (1996). 'The "New Boys": Restructuring in New Zealand, 1984–94'. *Social Politics,* 3/1: 32–56.

LOPEZ-GARZA, M., and DIAZ, D. R. (eds.) (2001). *Asian and Latino Immigrants in a Restructuring Economy.* Stanford, Calif.: Stanford University Press.

McCALL, L. (2001*a*). *Complex Inequality: Gender, Class, and Race in the New Economy.* New York: Routledge.

——(2001*b*). 'The Sources of Racial Wage Inequality in Metropolitan Labor Markets: Racial, Ethnic, and Gender Differences'. *American Sociological Review,* 66: 520–41.

McDOWELL, L. (1991). 'Life without Father and Ford: The New Gender Order of Post-Fordism'. *Transactions of the Institute of British Geographers,* 16: 400–19.

——(1997). *Capital Culture: Gender at Work in the City.* Malden, Mass.: Blackwell.

MARTIN, P. Y., and COLLINSON, D. L. (1999). 'Gender and Sexuality in Organizations', in M. M. Ferree, J. Lorber, and B. Hess (eds.), *Revisioning Gender.* Thousand Oaks, Calif.: Sage Publications.

MEYERSON, D., and ELY, R. (2000). 'Advancing Gender Equity in Organizations: The Challenge and Importance of Maintaining a Gender Narrative'. *Organization; the Inter-disciplinary Journal of Organization, Theory, and Society,* 7/4: 589–608.

MILKMAN, R. (1986). *Gender at Work: The Dynamics of Job Segregation by Sex during World War II.* Urbana: University of Illinois Press.

——REESE, E., and ROTH, B. (1998). 'The Macrosociology of Paid Domestic Labor'. *Work and Occupations,* 25/4: 483–510.

MINK, G. (1998). *Welfare's End.* Ithaca, NY: Cornell University Press.

MISHEL, L., BERNSTEIN, J., and BOUSHEY, H. (2003). *The State of Working America 2002/2003.* Ithaca, NY: Cornell University Press.

MOORE, J., and PINDERHUGHES, R. (eds.) (1993). *In the Barrios: Latinos and the Underclass Debate.* New York: Russell Sage Foundation.

MOSS, P., and TILLY, C. (2001). *Stories Employers Tell: Race, Skills, and Hiring in America.* New York: Russell Sage Foundation.

NELSON, R. L., and BRIDGES, W. P. (1999). *Legalizing Gender Inequality: Courts, Markets, and Unequal Pay for Women in America.* New York: Cambridge University Press.

OLLILAINEN, M., and ROTHSCHILD, J. (2001). 'Can Self-Managing Teams be Truly Cross-Functional? Gender Barriers to a "New" Division of Labor', in S. P. Vallas (ed.), *Research in the Sociology of Work*. Volume 10. *The Transformation of Work*. Amsterdam: Elsevier Science.

ORLOFF, A. S. (2002). *Women's Employment and Welfare Regimes: Globalization, Export Orientation and Social Policy in Europe and North America*. Social Policy and Development Paper No. 12. Geneva: United Nations Research Institute for Social Development.

PIORE, M., and SABEL, C. (1984). *The Second Industrial Divide: Possibilities for Prosperity*. New York: Basic Books.

PRINGLE, R. (1998). *Sex and Medicine: Gender, Power and Authority in the Medical Profession*. Cambridge: Cambridge University Press.

RAPOPORT, R., BAILYN, L., FLETCHER, J. K., and PRUITT, B. H. (2002). *Beyond Work–Family Balance: Advancing Gender Equity and Workplace Performance*. San Francisco: Jossey-Bass.

RASMUSSEN, B. (2001). 'Corporate Strategy and Gendered Professional Identities: Reorganization and the Struggle for Recognition and Positions'. *Gender, Work and Organization*, 8/3: 291–310.

REITZ, J. G. (1998). *Warmth of the Welcome: The Social Causes of Economic Success for Immigrants in Different Nations and Cities*. Boulder, Colo.: Westview Press.

RESKIN, B. F. (2000). 'Getting It Right: Sex and Race Inequality in Work Organizations'. *Annual Review of Sociology*, 26: 707–9.

—— and McBRIER, D. B. (2000). 'Why Not Ascription? Organizations' Employment of Male and Female Managers'. *American Sociological Review*, 65/April: 210–33.

—— and Roos, P. (1990). *Job Queues, Gender Queues: Explaining Women's Inroads into Male Occupations*. Philadelphia: Temple University Press.

RIDGEWAY, C. (1997). 'Interaction and Conservation of Gender Inequality: Considering Employment'. *American Sociological Review*, 62: 218–35.

ROSENFELD, R., and KALLEBERG, A. (1990). 'A Cross-National Comparison of the Gender Gap in Income'. *American Journal of Sociology*, 96: 69–106.

RUBERY, J. (1998). *Equal Pay in Europe? Closing the Gender Wage Gap*. New York: St. Martin's Press.

—— SMITH, M., and FAGAN, C. (1999). *Women's Employment in Europe: Trends and Prospects*. London: Routledge.

RUHM, C. J. (1998). 'The Economic Consequences of Parental Leave Mandates: Lessons from Europe'. *Quarterly Journal of Economics*, 113/1: 285–317.

SASSEN, S. (1991). *The Global City*. Princeton, NJ: Princeton University Press.

SORENSEN, A., and TRAPPE, H. (1995). 'The Persistence of Gender Inequality in Earnings in the German Democratic Republic'. *American Sociological Review*, 60: 398–406.

TIENARI, J. (1999). 'The First Wave Washed up on Shore: Reform, Feminization and Gender Resegregation'. *Gender, Work, and Organization*, 6/1: 1–19.

TIENDA, M. (1995). 'Latinos and the American Pie: Can Latinos Achieve Economic Parity?' *Hispanic Journal of Behavioral Sciences*, 17/4: 403–29.

VAN DER LIPPE, T., and VAN DIJK, L. (eds.) (2001). *Women's Employment in a Comparative Perspective*. New York: Aldine de Gruyter.

WILSON, W. J. (1987). *The Truly Disadvantaged*. Chicago: University of Chicago Press.

—— (1996). *When Work Disappears*. New York: Alfred Knopf.

WOODALL, J., EDWARDS, C., and WELCHMAN, R. (1997). 'Organizational Restructuring and the Achievement of an Equal Opportunity Culture'. *Gender, Work and Organization*, 4/1: 2–12.

CHAPTER 4

SKILL FORMATION SYSTEMS

COLIN CROUCH

UNTIL the mid-1990s, there was a strong consensus in both the academic and the policy literature on occupational skills around two key points. First, the creation of skills depended heavily on the existence of institutions that could overcome the tendency to free riding and poaching otherwise endemic among employers of labor in a market economy (Crouch, Finegold, and Sako 1999: ch. 1). Second, the maintenance of strong levels of good-quality employment in wealthy countries depended on high levels of skill in the workforce (Finegold and Soskice 1988; Porter 1990; Streeck 1989). From the perspective of the early years of the twenty-first century both beliefs seem less certain. Within a few years the consensus may have changed again, and it is the responsibility of academic commentators to try to look beyond the present and anticipate likely change. This will be attempted in the final part of this chapter. First, however, the two components of the earlier consensus, and their growing uncertainty, must be appraised.

4.1 SKILLS AS COLLECTIVE GOODS

Skills have to be acquired by the individuals who possess them; but their acquisition is very costly and, for the individual, there is often considerable uncertainty as to which skills will in the future bring labor-market advantages. Individuals are therefore reluctant to bear the costs of financing their own skill acquisition, unless they can see a ready connection between an affordable investment and a reliable payoff in the labor market.

For example, many young women living in large cities are willing to bear the cost of training in secretarial and other office skills because there are perceptible and durable job opportunities that make use of such skills in these locations and the cost of skill acquisition is not high. But training for the professions (e.g. medicine, the law, and engineering), even though their labor-market strength is at least as predictable as that of secretarial employment, is less often undertaken unaided by individuals. The costs are much higher. Young people already embarked on organizational careers are often willing to bear very high costs of obtaining such qualifications as an MBA because their experience has shown them that the careers of individuals who acquire these qualifications seem to progress well. Before they had started work and acquired this perception, they would probably have been reluctant to risk such investment.

Since it is employers who use skills, we might expect them always to finance their acquisition by young employees. But here simple economic analysis has long demonstrated a major problem. Assume a competitive market with many firms. Some spend money on training workers. Those who do not train have lower costs, and they can offer a proportion of what they thereby save offering slightly higher wages to recruit (or 'poach') those who have been equipped with skills by the firms who do train. Provided the wage premium needed to poach workers from these firms is less than the cost of training, the nontraining firms will be able to price their goods more cheaply than those who do train, driving the latter from the market.

The dilemma may not always be as difficult as this. Becker (1964) identified cases where skills consist of two parts: a very general level of education, such as is normally provided by national education systems, and a firm-specific component of use only to the firm concerned and therefore not easily poached. In such circumstances firms will provide training. They may in fact be expected to organize their activities so that employees' knowledge is highly specific and nontransferable. For example, they may use purpose-built machinery designed specifically for them and not widely available to competitors. However, it seems clear that this division between general and firm-specific is not universally applicable. As Margaret Stevens (1996, 1999) has shown, in many cases there are also many skills that are not provided by general education, but which are transferable from one enterprise in a sector to another. Acemoglu and Pischke (1998, 1999) have also argued that Becker ignores the imperfect competition that characterizes many labor markets, making it possible for firms to engage in training that goes beyond strictly defined firm-specific needs.

The dilemma is also softened for firms and other large organizations in oligopolistic markets or other forms of imperfect competition. For example, very large corporations with reputations for good working conditions and career prospects may find that employment with them is much preferred over working for smaller rivals. Even if these latter avoid providing training, they are unable to pay enough of a premium to attract workers away from the large corporation. This will be especially the case where the large organization dominates a regional labor market. This has often been the case with large vehicle manufacturing firms or (to take a different kind of example) public broadcasting organizations. In such cases the firm will accept the cost of training. Even if a few small firms poach some employees, these will be a small proportion of those whom the large corporation trains and easily retains (Crouch, Finegold, and Sako 1999: ch. 7).

There are also sectors where the acquisition and transmission of skill are central to the core business of the enterprise itself, and where firms who failed to train would therefore fall behind in the product market itself. This applies particularly to industries that depend heavily on a strong scientific input for their competitiveness, for example, advanced pharmaceutical firms pioneering the development of new medicines.

The problem of poaching is thus not endemic to all forms of employment. There are, however, many contexts where it is very real. In the great majority of cases where skilled labor is required by firms in competitive situations, such firms will exist only if institutions exist that assist in the resolution of the dilemma.

A different kind of problem to the classic poaching dilemma has been outlined by David Marsden (1999). Building on the social analysis of employment systems pioneered in France by Maurice, Sellier, and Silvestre (1982), he is mainly concerned with a core problem of work organization: how can workers be induced to cooperate with the requirements of management, given that management cannot exercise surveillance over employees' every move? Marsden outlines a number of different approaches that management can pursue to resolve this question. Some of these involve adapting the worker to the machinery and structures of the firm; others are built around the competences offered by the skills of the workforce. The central concern here is work organization as such rather than training, but clearly, the various alternative ways of arranging work involve different approaches to training. For Marsden particular attention focuses on interfirm structures. Given free labor markets, workers are likely to change their employers from time to time. Without detailed information about the capabilities and experience of workers, the labor market cannot function efficiently. *Pace* Becker, it is not efficient to retain everything beyond general education at a noncommunicable firm level. Again, therefore, we see a need for institutions within the training field.

Identification and analysis of these institutions has constituted the main business of the social scientific literature on skills (Backes-Gellner 1996). Authors usually treat the provision of skills as an example of the general problem of providing collective goods within a competitive market economy: that is, goods that exist outside the competitive framework, which makes the provision difficult for firms themselves. A number of such institutions have been identified in the literature (Crouch, Finegold, and Sako 1999). Not surprisingly, they can be related to the range of institutions for governance that has been developed by students of general problems of providing frameworks of order, collective goods, and other forms of regulation in market economies (Hollingsworth and Boyer 1997; Hollingsworth, Schmitter, and Streeck 1994). Briefly, the main institutions concerned are the following.

4.1.1 The State

This is the most obvious source of collective goods in modern societies. The state's activities in the production of work skills stem from two of the frequent concerns of political authorities. First is the general responsibility that all modern states assume for basic and much advanced levels of education among their populations. This responsibility stems in turn from a concern to socialize populations in the interests of social order, and a need to respond to popular striving for social advancement and mobility. Second, given that governments nearly always see their fortunes to be dependent on the strength of the national economy, and given a widespread belief that this will in turn be dependent on the quality of vocational skills in the workforce, governments are likely to take a strong interest in the provision of these skills.

'Strong interest' does not necessarily imply that the state will be a direct provider itself. It may be reluctant to bear the costs of this, and may take a view of priorities, both among different claims for its resources, and between its own spending and pressures to limit the incidence of taxation. States might well therefore under-provide training just as much as employers do. Second, there may be tension between the perspective of the state and that of employers, labor interests, and others. These may be direct political differences or differences between the priorities of state teaching institutions and those of actors in the labor market.

More mundanely, employers often complain that public institutions are slow to respond to change. For example, even though Swedish employers are very strongly represented on the committees that determine the content of vocational training courses in Sweden, individual firms began to say, during the period of rapid technological and organizational change since the 1990s, that the national vocational education and training (VET) system responds too slowly to their needs (Sweden 1992). A firm may start making rapid changes in methods of work in its response to change. However, before it could get a corresponding change in training courses it would have to lobby its own association, who would have to prioritize this question in plans being made for a revised national curriculum. These proposals would then need to be agreed with other employer associations, the unions, and government representatives. Countries with less extensive collaborative mechanisms than Sweden might not have so much delay resulting from consultation, but at the same time an individual firm in such a system might have less chance to influence the policymakers.

In some other cases the state may be confident that other institutions can carry the burden of skill provision, such that it does not need to do so itself, though even then it is likely to develop policy about how such other institutions ought to develop their role. This would be the case with the British government in the 1980s and 1990s, which believed that governments themselves should not engage in much direct provision of skills or other *desiderata* of firms' competitive strategies. It believed that the market was the best mechanism for such things. However, it remained deeply concerned about the education and skills level of the British working population, and about the ability of the existing system to equip the United Kingdom for high-skill economic activities. It resolved this tension by establishing a number of intermediary institutions that combined some government initiative with voluntary collaboration from individuals in business. Prominent examples were the Training and Enterprise Councils (TECs), eighty-one of which were established throughout England and Wales. These were public initiatives, and in fact depended heavily on highly targeted government funds for most of their activity. However, their staff did not have civil service status, they were managed by committees of local business people and had to operate commercially—indeed, one went bankrupt. Opinion is divided whether the TECs were an interesting new experiment in combined public and private governance or a timid mixture that neither asserted government policy nor gave business a chance to develop a new institution that suited its needs (Bennett and McCoshan 1993; Crouch, Finegold, and Sako 1999: 183–92; Green, with Sakamoto 2001). However, they certainly demonstrated that even governments that seek to distance themselves from economic intervention are unlikely to remain fully outside the arena of skill formation.

There are also many examples of direct state provision of VET; in some countries it constitutes the main form of such education (Crouch, Finegold, and Sako 1999: ch. 4). Sweden is one example; France and Singapore are others (for France, see Büchtemann and Verdier 1998; Rault 1994; for Singapore, see Brown, Green, and Lauder 2001). In such cases, vocational courses are provided as options within the normal public education system. Usually starting with the second stage of secondary education (post-14), young people can opt to take courses that lead them to qualify as potential practitioners of certain named occupations. In these countries and some others such provision tries to cover almost all occupations for which recognized skills are required. Elsewhere direct provision of work skills through public education exists only for specific types or levels of skill. Medicine is a particularly widespread example. No coherent theoretical account can be given of why there is direct state provision in some cases and not others. The explanation

Nyack College Library

is usually to be found far beyond the specific field of vocational education itself, in the very diverse general history of the development of different state forms. As noted above with reference to the Swedish case, there is often a problem of linking the teachers and curriculum designers of the state system to employers, the eventual users of the skills; and, as a result, a less tight link between qualifications and occupations than in apprenticeship systems of the German type (Maurice, Sellier, and Silvestre 1982).

4.1.2 The Market

Markets often figure as the source of problems of training rather than of solutions because it is market competition that produces incentives to free ride. However, we have above already encountered examples of how in certain circumstances market forces may give incentives to provide training. One group of cases would be sectors with science- or knowledge-rich products (e.g. advanced pharmaceuticals). Here, the character of the goods or services produced is such that it is not possible to succeed in the market without contributing to a learning environment. Alternatively, potential practitioners of a skill may be in situations that give them adequate incentives and knowledge to undertake the costs of their own education.

Or there are contexts like those analyzed by Becker (1964), where there is a neat division between general and firm-specific skills. For example, restaurants may be content to employ as waiters young people who come to them with the skills of numeracy, literacy, and articulacy provided by general public education. They then complement that with training in style and social presentation that they see as special to their individual enterprises. Outside these rather special cases, the market will be found operating alongside other institutions, often providing actors with the incentives to use the mechanisms provided by these others.

4.1.3 Corporate Hierarchy

Again as already noted, firms in imperfect competition will often also be direct providers of skills. These are usually large corporations able to achieve economies of scale in such provision. Where they develop long-term relations with suppliers, they may also have an incentive to ensure that these also have high skills. This model has been particularly typical of large Japanese, and to some extent Korean, corporations. These at first sight provide an almost pure example of Becker's skill division: workers are recruited from the general national education system at certain fixed points; and then the firm provides them with specific skills. However, this is made easier for these firms than it would be for those in the strongly competitive market assumed by Becker, as they have wider scope to define what is 'firm specific' (see also Acemoglu and Pischke 1998, 1999). In Japan (and in a more limited way in individual great corporations in other parts of the world) this extends to the development of specific corporate cultures, which can be 'learned' only through prolonged training and subsequent experience (Sako 1995). There is something of a 'chicken and egg' here. Firms that are able to avoid labor-market competition for skilled staff can develop cultures among such staff (who will typically remain many years with the one employer), while the development of specific cultures can be a factor limiting labor-market mobility.

The corporate hierarchy model, like the market, can exist under certain specific conditions. It is clearly of little use in sectors dominated by small and medium-sized enterprises, or even by large corporations in close labor-market competition with each other.

4.1.4 Associations

Where firms form themselves into an association and give it some authority among them, the association can perform something of the role of the state in ensuring the provision of collective goods. As organizations formed by firms themselves, associations stand a chance of avoiding the problem of remoteness that can negatively affect direct provision by the state. Associations of businesses have a number of ways of securing some kind of authority over their members (Streeck and Schmitter 1985). Unusually, but important in Austrian and German history, certain kinds of chambers of commerce and industry have been given formal state authority over their sectors (Streeck 1992). More normally, associations are purely voluntary bodies to which firms choose to adhere. For them the exercise of authority over firms is clearly more difficult than for a compulsory chamber. They are however often well equipped to make access to collective goods that they provide conditional on good behavior. This can often be used in relation to training. If firms want access to the training programs an association provides, and want to participate in shaping the programs, they have to accept rules of participation, pay their dues, etc.

Associations have provided some of the most successful forms of governance of skills provision (Crouch, Finegold, and Sako 1999: ch. 5). They are especially prominent in apprenticeship systems. Here, trainees alternate periods in a formal education institution, often a public one, with periods of serious work experience in a firm. Associations monitor the system to ensure that all firms are playing their part and taking trainees, act as intermediaries between participating firms and the public education system (including ensuring that courses are kept up to date), and frequently participate in the examination system that certifies the skills acquired. This is how the German system works (Streeck 1992). Without the associations—in this case the Kammer to which all firms are required to belong—there would be nothing to link individual participating firms and the educational institutions; firms could free ride and avoid making their contribution; the formal teaching and the work experience might become divided from each other; and firms might not trust the value of the qualifications achieved by graduates of the schemes. It is useful here to compare the fate of apprenticeship in the United Kingdom, where business associations became progressively weaker during the late twentieth century and apprenticeship almost disappeared, with that in Germany (Finegold and Soskice 1988; Thelen 2004). Such a system is also particularly useful for solving some of the tensions endemic to training: combining general with specific learning and combining the collective good characteristic of public provision with the proximity to the working world of the company level.

However, at times of rapid change in skill demands, even the skills specialists in associations can become out of touch. This is especially the case when many improvements in skill have to take place among the existing workforce rather than with new recruits. Young new entrants are usually at the point of transition from formal, usually public, education and occupational life. At that point structures that mediate between firms and the wider society—like government or associations—can most easily make their input. However, when skill upgrading is needed for existing employees, the reach of these external structures is less effective. In some cases, this means the return of the collective good dilemma, with firms, for fear of poaching, either being deterred from training their staff adequately, or distorting their growth of competences by tying training excessively to the individual firm's needs. But, when individual firms, for reasons noted above under the discussion of markets and hierarchies, do provide in-service training, a gulf may develop between this and the more collectively provided initial training, weakening the latter. There is evidence that this has been happening for some time in Germany (Backes-Gellner 1995; Sauter 1996).

4.1.5 Communities and Networks

Sociologists identify a wide range of informal social bonds outside the framework of formal associations: communities, clubs, clans, networks. Of these, communities are likely to be the most traditional and taken-for-granted; networks the most

purposive and fragile. For present purposes these distinctions are not very important. We mainly need the general idea of groups that depend for their power to
enforce collective action on informal pressures rather than the formal rules and
membership conditions of formal associations. These can sometimes be used to
ensure that individual firms do not free ride on the training activities of others.
Only rarely will such devices constitute an entire system of training. They are more
likely to be found as adjuncts to more formally constituted structures of the other
types discussed here. For example, managers of firms within a locality who otherwise engaged in arm's length market competition with each other might use the
informal pressures of local social gatherings to ostracize those who try to poach
skilled workers from those who provide training.

Communities and local networks can also be important in helping employers
and employees improve their knowledge of local labor markets and skills, particularly in regions where large numbers of small and medium-sized enterprises
cluster together (Crouch, Finegold, and Sako 1999: ch. 6; Crouch, Le Galès, Trigilia,
and Voelzkow 2001). Employers can learn of the skills of potential employees
by getting to know them through local networks. This is particularly important
in rapidly growing new sectors, such as biotechnology (Swann, Prevezer, and Stout
1998) and information technology (Saxenian 1994), where certified knowledge
is not yet widely available. This is one of the reasons why small firms in such
sectors tend to be found in geographical concentrations, as in several cases in
California. Employees are similarly able to use local networks to discover new
sources of employment and, more important for our current purposes, how skill
needs in their field are developing. This may be particularly valuable to workers
in systems where individuals are expected to ensure their own 'employability' (see
below).

The small-firm economy of central Italy is often seen as a major example of how
communities and networks may play a role in skill provision (Crouch, Finegold,
and Sako 1999: ch. 6; Regini 1995, 1996). Whether because Italians often have little
confidence in their country's formal institutions or whether because the strength of
their local communities enables them to short cut formal procedures, Italian SMEs
often prefer to rely on informal knowledge transmission and may be more likely to
base their assessments of an individual job applicant's skill on his or her local
reputation than on formal certificates.

All these informal techniques assist other systems of governance; they rarely
constitute systems themselves. Even among the industrial districts of central Italy,
where local networks are dominant, they are used to consolidate and improve on
formal state and local government provision, rather than to substitute for it (Regini
1996).

4.2 Sources of Instability and Change

Skill creation systems of all kinds operate most easily where there is stability of expectations. Where the basic pattern of economic activities and the occupations associated with them are more or less stable, it is easy for firms to communicate requirements for skills to training providers, as these change only gradually. This will be the case whether the providers are within the firm itself or external. It is also easy for the providers to respond to firms' needs and such incremental changes as they entail. It is also easy for entrants into the labor market to predict their chances of finding employment if they engage in a particular training course. Also, if skill content is stable, training can be front-loaded, in the sense that it can be imparted more or less at the start of an entrant's career. This, we have noted, is the point where vocational preparation and general education meet and therefore where collective action is most easily achieved.

On the other hand, where there is rapid change, young people are uncertain about which occupations have a viable future; employers and trainers have difficulty communicating needs; and more and more training takes the form of mid-career adjustments, away from the points where collective action of various kinds will be most effective. Where whole sectors are in decline and new ones emerging, there will even be uncertainty over what kind of preparation the new occupations need at all. Mistrust develops at all points of the skill provision system. Young people and their parents suspect governments and others of doing too little to equip them for an uncertain future; firms regard governments, schools, their own associations, possibly their own training departments, of being ignorant of their needs and slow to respond. Governments complain that business interests are not making enough of a contribution to equipping young people with skills and that young people are too reluctant to take risks.

4.2.1 High Skills and International Competitiveness

This is the situation that developed during the 1990s throughout the industrialized world. It became increasingly clear that manufacturing would become a far smaller employer of labor than for the past half century, removing a major source of apparently stable, middle-skill occupations from the perspectives of young people and education providers. The services employment that was developing in the place of manufacturing was a very diverse sector indeed, containing some activities that used the most advanced skills (such as aspects of financial and health services) with those that needed very little (such as fast-food outlets and cleaning activities)

(Crouch 1999: ch. 4). Furthermore, these changes were taking place in a context of globalization, in the sense that many manufacturing activities and some services ones could now be carried on in a far wider range of countries, with very different levels of living for labor. It seemed increasingly that workers in wealthy countries would be able to protect their wages and working conditions only if they concentrated on producing goods and services with high added value (Brown and Lauder 1996; Brown, Green, and Lauder 2001). This quality would be dependent on the existence of infrastructures that could not be rivaled by poorer countries. High levels of general and vocational education were seen to be crucial elements of such infrastructure (Streeck 1992). Economists of the endogenous growth theory school have similarly stressed the role of the improvement of the quality of human capital if countries are to retain competitiveness and increase their wealth (Romer 1990).

In a widely noted article, Finegold and Soskice (1988) distinguished between high- and low-skill equilibria, and claimed that national systems of VET would lock countries into one or the other path. Under the former, firms in countries with strong systems of VET provision were able to produce high-quality goods, which could maintain their international market share, making possible further maintenance of the skill-production system. Under the low-skill equilibrium, firms would have to compete on price alone, drawing them into a spiral of cost cutting that would prevent them (or other institutions in their countries) from investing in high levels of training. In fact, it may be doubted whether a low-skill equilibrium could be sustained as such, as increasing numbers of producers in low-cost regions of the world joined the competition.

The situation was and remains rich in paradox. On the one hand, young people, trade unions, and in some respects firms and governments have been seeking security and certainty in the acquisition of skills, while, on the other, there has been growing uncertainty over what such skills might be. All interests believed that education and training should expand; but education and training for what? At the same time, as international competition intensified, firms in many sectors sought to cut back on training to save costs; sought to escape pressure from associations to provide training; and lobbied government for lower taxation (with the implication that public services, including education, would be reduced).

We can now identify a number of perverse consequences of these paradoxes. Certainly, the low-skill equilibrium strategy of cutting back on training to save costs in order directly to fight Third World competition was doomed. Workers in Western Europe, Japan, or North America could not be pressed back to the levels of living of Indonesia or China. At the same time, the high-skill equilibrium was not only at risk if spending on training and other infrastructure was reduced, but as an employment strategy it encountered a rather predictable obstruction. Constant up-skilling of the workforce, alongside equipping it with ever-improving equipment and work organization certainly increased productivity. But that only reduced the quantity of labor needed to produce a given output. Within an industry the level of employment could be safeguarded only if improved quality increased aggregate demand for a product to compensate for the reduction in labor needed to produce a given unit of the product. This could happen only rarely.

The difficulties of such a strategy can be seen particularly clearly in the case of Germany (Green, with Sakamoto 2001; Schmidt 2002). The country possessed (and still possesses) probably the most effective training system for pursuing the high-equilibrium strategy, particularly though not solely in manufacturing. And, although by the late 1990s many German employers were seeking to free themselves of the obligations of their training system, in the sectors where Germany had important competitive advantages, it managed to sustain demand despite its goods being highly priced. But it failed completely to increase or even to sustain employment. Now, current high levels of German unemployment cannot be explained as a consequence of the country's particular skill strategy; the enormous difficulties consequent on the unification of west Germany with the former communist state of east Germany play a considerable part in the explanation. However, as we shall see further below, that strategy set alongside certain other features of the German labor market, has become less favorable for employment in that country than it was until the 1990s.

Meanwhile, policymakers increasingly focused their attention on the role of 'new' sectors of the economy in creating jobs for the future and on the importance of young people acquiring the often uncertainly defined skills that these sectors required (e.g. European Commission 1996). In these circumstances of change, governments and employers in many countries began to place responsibility for resolving the skills dilemma on to young people themselves. 'Learning how to learn' became seen as the most important skill requirement (Brown 2001: 15). Young people (and those not so young) were told that it was their responsibility to ensure their own future employability by skilling and reskilling themselves in appropriate ways. This could also imply that they should spend their own money on doing this, investing in their own future employment opportunities; or it might mean that they should take advantage of possibilities provided by government and other institutions for grants and subsidies toward the cost of education and training. These developments were linked to changes also taking place in the treatment of unemployment, all part of the overall shift from the demand-side approach to the labor market of the Keynesian period to supply-side policies. Following the growth of the US idea of 'workfare', claimants for unemployment benefit in most countries have been required to demonstrate the seriousness of their job search. This often includes demonstrating their willingness to participate in education programs. This approach has been developed particularly strongly in the United Kingdom, where the concept of unemployed has been officially replaced by that of the 'job seeker'. Only persons who have taken certain formally defined steps to acquire employment (including taking advantage of certain training opportunities) are eligible for unemployment benefit.

Young people have in effect been expected to bear the burden of risk and uncertainty concerning skills that will be needed in the future because none of the agencies normally considered to bear responsibility for this any longer understand likely patterns of skill requirements. Of course, young people are in an even worse position than governments and other formal, expert agencies to make such judgments, but they can be regarded to be entrepreneurs in a market. Provided enough of them attempt a wide range of possible alternatives, some of them will equip themselves with skills that turn out to be useful and will therefore be available for viable new forms of employment as these emerge. In taking this approach, governments and others were able to point to how skills had been developed in the information technology sector, the extraordinary growth of which during the 1990s made it appear the paradigm sector for the future economy. Since many of the skills used in it were very new, they could not be studied in pre-existing courses. Rather, individuals seemed to develop these skills teaching themselves and experimenting. Legends grew up around various extremely rich and prominent figures in the sector who had lacked formal education and had made amazing breakthroughs playing with computers in their parental homes. (Several of these accounts are brought together in Castells 2000: 38–69, a work which is overall a striking example of how academic observers become obsessed with the development of computing, the Internet, and the rest of the sector.)

This demonstrated the relative advantages of the market as a form of skills governance in a situation of high uncertainty. Given a large enough number of individuals trying to do something creative in a situation where no one knows what will bring success, statistical laws of probability alone tell us that some will chance on the new winning strategies. It can then be expected that a larger second group will quickly perceive what the early winners have started to do and will imitate them.

However, this is not a paradigm that can be generalized indefinitely. First, only a small number of sectors of the economy correspond to this model, whereby innovation owes little to existing codified knowledge. For example, another sector very important to 1990s economic success and radical product innovation, biotechnology, depended on workers with very advanced prior education in the relevant sciences, a radically different context from information technology.

Second, only a small number of attempts at innovation can and will succeed. Of the statistically available possibilities will be a large number that come to nothing. The fact that *anyone* can succeed does not mean that *everyone* can succeed. There is considerable waste. This may be unavoidable if there is true uncertainty, but the waste might induce cynicism and anger among those who take the advice to be innovative, expend their own resources, and then find that they fail.

Third, certain very specific characteristics are required of the education and training system of an economy in which increasing reliance is being placed on a combination of entrepreneurial skill among young people and statistical chance to match supply of and demand for skills:

1. There must be considerable diversity of forms of general and relatively low-level education opportunities. These are needed to provide some kind of base from which unanticipated skills might be launched. General education here is more useful than specific vocational training and skill formation, as it leaves more options open. The extension is likely to be at relatively low levels of education, partly because of the prevailing climate of declining public and private invest-ment in infrastructure, and partly because the problems of employability are concentrated at lower levels of the ability range.
2. There must be a variety of negative and positive incentives to persuade young people to take these opportunities in a situation of uncertainty where they cannot be sure which choices are likely to bring success.
3. There has to be a large variety of job opportunities, mainly in services sectors, that require low levels of skill.

This last seems inconsistent with the general thesis concerning the up-skilling of labor in the advanced economies, and therefore requires explanation (for a more detailed account, see Crouch 1998). If the main education provision is becoming general and relatively low level, and if the number of people who will therefore develop really useable skills is very low, what will become of the very large numbers who will acquire such education and not find success? It will be too late for them to acquire more strictly vocational courses, which in any case will have declined to make space for the general education opportunities. These people may be educated, but they will not be vocationally skilled. They will avoid unemployment only if there is a variety of job opportunities which make no specific skill demands. Some of these will be truly unskilled occupations; others will be those with tacit, unrecognized skills.

It is unlikely that such opportunities will be found in the production of goods and services that are internationally traded, because this runs up against the original globalization problem of competition from low-wage economies. This rules out most manufacturing and certain services—the sectors that provided stable if rather poorly paid employment for low-skilled workers in wealthy coun-tries during the pre-global period of industrialization. It leaves large areas of public service and many occupations in distribution, catering, and personal services where relatively low-wage employment can survive and even flourish in wealthy countries, without fearing being brought even lower in pay by competition with low-wage countries. This is because the services in question have to be provided close to the consumer. Competition with workers from poor countries certainly takes place in these sectors, but these appear as immigrant workers. The general difficulty of immigration, including legal restrictions on it, combined with the fact that immi-grant labor is partly subject to general conditions of labor in the country where it works, mean that this competition is not so severe as that in manufacturing, where the work can be carried out in remote sites.

Various factors affect the likelihood that a given economy will produce low-wage work of this kind. In some societies (e.g. Scandinavia) a high level of personal public services in the welfare state makes possible low-wage employment with generally stable and secure working conditions (Esping-Andersen 1999). In countries with particularly high levels of income inequality (e.g. the United Kingdom and United States), wealthy families have incomes sufficiently high and poor families have sufficiently poor income prospects that the former are able to employ the latter in a return to forms of domestic service that had flourished in most societies until the mid-twentieth century (Esping-Andersen 1999). Another model (also found in the United Kingdom and the United States) is for mothers' labor-force participation to be made possible by the commercialization of various household tasks (e.g. the rise of fast-food outlets), all of which create low-wage employment protected from international competition.

Workers in these various low-income sectors do not necessarily lack skill, but they do lack recognized skill, and their kind of employment, far from representing a contradiction of the idea of the 'knowledge' or high-skilled society, in fact make such a society possible; this is one of the major explanations of the much noted polarization of incomes in the United States and United Kingdom, the two countries that most clearly evince the model of skills (Esping-Andersen 1999; Johnson and Reed 1996; Lauder 2001). This link operates as follows: uncertainty about the skill requirements of a rapidly changing economy creates a problem for the provision of vocationally oriented skills in favor of a demand for broad, general education of a not particularly high level. This in turn provides a reservoir of useable capabilities for forms of employment that have not codified their skill needs. Compared with situations where skill needs are predictable and definable, this kind creates a large amount of 'waste' of non-specifically educated people who are not taken up by the new kinds of high-skill employment. They can be absorbed and kept from unemployment if general conditions in the economy favor the growth of one or more forms of moderately low-income employment that do not have to engage in direct competition with extremely low-wage employment in Third World countries.

This 'new' model of skill creation could in theory be provided under any kind of skill-creation regime, but in practice it is likely to be found where the market, in association with the state, is dominant. Normally a public education system is needed to produce an extensive provision of general education. It is unlikely that individuals, left to themselves or to their parents, would accept the cost of such a vaguely oriented provision. Certainly, among the advanced countries, we have no examples of countries where the state does not make such general provision. It is however the market that generates the large number of more specific, but still not precisely focused, additional courses from which young people in a system of this kind choose in order to try to anticipate some employment possibilities. Firms in such a situation of uncertainty rely on the market to provide them with suitable new recruits, as they are not certain *ex ante* what kind of employee skills they want.

The associational model of skill provision is unlikely to be involved in such a system. Where skills are evolving in rapidly growing new sectors there will often not even be associations, as the sector will not have developed the kind of identity that makes associations possible. If associations do exist, they may have relinquished the task of trying to anticipate skill needs. Similar arguments will apply to corporate hierarchy. Large firms are unlikely to develop their own training courses or those for their suppliers if the identity of skills is changing fast. They will probably prefer to discover what skills are being produced, by both demand and supply forces, in the general market. Provision by the state and other public agencies will experience severe difficulties of remoteness from rapidly changing skill needs and types. Informal community provision, always a minority mode, is however likely to survive and thrive, as it embodies the flexibility and lack of institutionalized provision required.

All this explains certain paradoxes in the development of skills provision during the 1990s. The German economy, noted for its capacity to generate the highest levels of skill for manufacturing and certain high-level services, such as banking and insurance, was for a long time unable to generate much activity in the new information-related economy. Not only is the German apprenticeship system strongly rooted in the predictable needs of established activities with clearly defined associations rather than the new and changing requirements of high-tech industries (Mason and Wagner 1998), the German economy is also particularly poorly adapted to the generation of low-skilled employment. This is partly because its system of financing social security involves employers and employees paying taxes on wages, which keep labor costs high, even for low-productivity workers. It is also partly because its welfare state concentrates on cash transfers rather than the provision of care services; and partly because German family patterns provide little demand for domestic and related services (Esping-Andersen 1999).

The French approach to education encountered fewer problems because it had engaged in a major expansion of general, state-provided education. However, expectations among young people that this would lead to the creation of high-skilled job opportunities, combined with strong welfare provision for the un-employed, made them reluctant to accept low-wage employment (Béduwé and Espinasse 1995; Verdier 1996).

It has therefore been those systems that have been seen as particularly weak in their provision of stable skills and in meeting high expectations, mainly the United Kingdom and United States, which were particularly successful in adapting to the new model. During the 1990s these economies, for the first time since the years after World War II, began to outperform many of the strong economies of continental Europe and Japan in terms of employment growth, though not in foreign trade achievements. There are, of course, other explanations of this, including the restrictions placed on demand management by those countries entering the European Economic and Monetary Union. However, developments in skill creation and labor-market policy played their part.

4.3 NEW PARADIGM OR NEW SUBSYSTEM?

During the 1990s it was common for observers to see in the rapidly growing information technology sector a paradigm for the future economy. The eventual (and in fact entirely predictable) failure of the sector to sustain its growth path, and indeed its partial collapse in the early twenty-first century, makes it possible to view the changes it introduced in a more balanced perspective.

First, the conditions that led to the demand for widespread but modest levels of general education were far from universal. It is true that, in a period of generally major and rapid technological change, many sectors experienced the radical uncertainty that led to the retreat from vocationally oriented education. But this trend could never have been strong enough to become the leading paradigm for skills. Reference has also been made to the need of the biotechnology sector for high levels of specifically trained aptitudes. Biotechnology was a highly characteristic '1990s' sector, though, like much other advanced manufacturing, it does not create large numbers of jobs. Also, professions with highly specific skill needs, such as law, medicine, or engineering, saw no tendency to dissolve these requirements. The needs of professional education were certainly changing, but they were not becoming less professional. Similar arguments apply to many occupations at the technician and skilled manual levels, though these were often declining in numbers as sources of job opportunities.

Second, many of the characteristics of the 'new' skill demands were typical of sectors undergoing the first stages of growth, when clear patterns of skill demands and specified requirements have not yet developed. In time, settled patterns emerge, and it becomes possible to codify skill and knowledge requirements and to establish training courses. The early development of the engineering industry in the eighteenth century, like that of information technology in the late twentieth century, saw relatively uneducated men experimenting in unsystematic ways. Later however their knowledge was systematized, codified, and taught. It is, of course, possible that the new industries of the 1990s will develop in permanently innovative and unpredictable ways. But it is more likely that stages of stability will be reached and they will follow the path of earlier new sectors; it becomes inefficient to keep reinventing the wheel if the techniques of wheel-making can be written down, demonstrated, and passed on.

Third, there are important examples from the past of how VET institutions that seem set heavily in their ways discover means of making slow adaptations until they produce a quite new model (Thelen 2004). There are some signs that this is happening today, suggesting that the novelty of current change has been exaggerated. For example, Baumann (2002) has shown how both German and British television and film-making companies learned during the 1990s how to adjust their approaches to training to meet both the flexible new skill demands being made of technicians and the need for new structures of governance following the decline of the role of large public broadcasters. The new structures replaced the corporate hierarchy model embodied by these broadcasters and instead developed new mixes of markets, associations, and informal networks.

Finally, and as Baumann's work reminds us, most empirical systems of skill provision incorporate examples of more than one approach to the task. The 'market' as evinced by the information technology does not constitute the American approach. The public education system plays a vast role in that society, providing not only the basic general educational level, which, as we have shown above, is an important partner of market provision; it also provides high levels of scientific and professional training. Some sectors make use of apprenticeship, though these are more likely to be provided through corporate hierarchy than through associations. What should be of interest to us is the range of system types that are able to coexist. It is this that will often determine the ability of the actors in a system to adapt and switch alongside changing requirements—whether these involve the deconstruction of an existing system to provide for newly emerging skills or measures to systematize after a period of experimentation and rapid change.

REFERENCES

ACEMOGLU, D., and PISCHKE, J. S. (1998). 'Why Do Firms Train? Theory and Evidence'. *Quarterly Journal of Economics*, 113/1: 79–119.

————(1999). 'Beyond Becker: Training in Imperfect Labour Markets'. *Economic Journal*, 109: 112–42.

BACKES-GELLNER, U. (1995). 'Duale Ausbildung und/oder betriebliche Weiterbildung? Lehren aus einem internationalen Vergleich betrieblicher Qualifizierungsstrategien'. *Berufsbildung*, 49.

——(1996). *Betriebliche Bildungs- und Wettbewerbsstrategien im deutsch-britischen Vergleich*. Munich: Rainer Ham.

BAUMANN, A. (2002). 'Informal Labour Market Governance: The Case of the British and German Media Production Industries'. *Work, Employment and Society*, 16/1: 27–46.

BECKER, G. S. (1964). *Human Capital.* Chicago: University of Chicago Press.

BÉDUWÉ, C., and ESPINASSE, J.-M. (1995). 'France: Politique éducative, amélioration des competences et absorption des diplômés par l'économie'. *Sociologie du Travail,* 37/4: 527–54.

BENNETT, R. J., and McCOSHAN, A. (1993). *Enterprise and Human Resource Development.* London: Paul Chapman.

BROWN, P. (2001). 'Skill Formation in the Twenty-First Century', in P. Brown, A. Green, and H. Lauder (eds.), *High Skills: Globalization, Competitiveness, and Skill Formation.* Oxford: Oxford University Press.

——and LAUDER, H. (1996). 'Education, Globalization, and Economic Development'. *Journal of Education Policy,* 11: 1–24.

——GREEN, A., and LAUDER, H. (2001). *High Skills: Globalization, Competitiveness, and Skill Formation.* Oxford: Oxford University Press.

BÜCHTEMANN, C. F., and VERDIER, E. (1998). 'Education and Training Regimes: Macro-Institutional Evidence'. *Revue de l'économie politique,* 198/3: 291–320.

CASTELLS, M. (2000). *The Information Age: Economy, Society and Culture.* Volume 1. *The Rise of the Network Society* (2nd edn). Oxford: Blackwell.

CROUCH, C. (1998). 'The High-Skill Society: The Latest Philosopher's Stone?' *British Journal of Industrial Relations,* 35/3: 367–84.

——(1999). *Social Change in Western Europe.* Oxford: Oxford University Press.

——FINEGOLD, D., and SAKO, M. (1999). *Are Skills the Answer: The Political Economy of Skill Creation in Advanced Industrial Countries.* Oxford: Oxford University Press.

——LE GALÈS, P., TRIGILIA, C., and VOELZKOW, H. (2001). *Local Production Systems in Europe: Rise or Demise?* Oxford: Oxford University Press.

ESPING-ANDERSEN, G. (1999). *Social Foundations of Postindustrial Economies.* Oxford: Oxford University Press.

European Commission (1996). *Living and Working in the Information Society.* Luxembourg: The Commission.

FINEGOLD, D., and SOSKICE, D. (1988). 'The Failure of Training in Britain: Analysis and Prescription'. *Oxford Review of Economic Policy,* 4/3: 21–53.

GREEN, A., with SAKAMOTO, A. (2001). 'Models of High Skills in National Competition Strategies', in P. Brown, A. Green, and H. Lauder (eds.), *High Skills: Globalization, Competitiveness, and Skill Formation.* Oxford: Oxford University Press.

HOLLINGSWORTH, J. R., and BOYER, R. (eds.) (1997). *Contemporary Capitalism: The Embeddedness of Institutions.* Cambridge: Cambridge University Press.

——SCHMITTER, P. C., and STREECK, W. (eds.) (1994). *Governing Capitalist Economies: Performance and Control of Economic Sectors.* Oxford: Oxford University Press.

JOHNSON, P., and REED, R. (1996). 'Intergenerational Mobility among the Rich and the Poor: Results from the National Child Development Survey'. *Oxford Review of Economic Policy,* 12/1: 127–42.

LAUDER, H. (2001). 'Innovation, Skill Diffusion, and Social Exclusion', in P. Brown, A. Green, and H. Lauder (eds.), *High Skills: Globalization, Competitiveness, and Skill Formation.* Oxford: Oxford University Press.

MARSDEN, D. (1999). *A Theory of Employment Systems: Micro-Foundations of Societal Diversity.* Oxford: Oxford University Press.

MASON, G., and WAGNER, K. (1998). *High Level Skills, Knowledge Transfer and Industrial Performance: Electronics in Britain and Germany.* London: NIESR.

MAURICE, M., SELLIER, F., and SILVESTRE, J.-J. (1982). *Politique d'Education et Organisation Industrielle en France et en Allemagne*. Paris: PUF.

PORTER, M. (1990). *The Competitive Advantage of Nations*. Basingstoke: Macmillan.

RAULT, C. (1994). *La Formation professionelle initiale*. Paris: La documentation française.

REGINI, M. (1995). 'Firms and Institutions: The Demand for Skills and their Social Production in Europe'. *European Journal of Industrial Relations*, 1/2: 191–202.

—— (1996). 'Le Imprese e le istituzioni: Domanda e produzione sociale di risorse umane nelle regioni europee', in M. Regini (ed.), *La Produzione sociale delle risorse humane*. Bologna: Il Mulino.

ROMER, P. M. (1990). 'Endogenous Technological Change'. *Journal of Political Economy*, 98/5: 71–102.

SAKO, M. (1995). *Skill Testing and Certification in Japan*. Washington, DC: World Bank.

SAUTER, E. (1996). 'Continuing Vocational Training in Germany', in J. Brandsma, F. Kessler, and J. Münch (eds.), *Continuing Vocational Training: Europe, Japan and the US*. Utrecht: Uitgeverij Lemma.

SAXENIAN, A. (1994). *Regional Advantage: Culture and Competition in Silicon Valley and Route 128*. Cambridge, Mass.: Harvard University Press.

SCHMIDT, V. A. (2002). *The Futures of European Capitalism*. Oxford: Oxford University Press.

STEVENS, M. (1996). 'Transferable Training and Poaching Externalities', in A. L. Booth and D. J. Snower (eds.), *Acquiring Skills*. London: CEPR.

—— (1999). 'Human Capital Theory and UK Vocational Training Policy'. *Oxford Review of Economic Policy*, 15/1: 16–32.

STREECK, W. (1989). 'Skills and the Limits of Neo-Liberalism: The Enterprise of the Future as a Place of Learning'. *Work, Employment and Society*, 3/1: 89–104.

—— (1992). *Social Institutions and Economic Performance: Studies of Industrial Relations in Advanced Capitalist Economies*. London: Sage.

—— and SCHMITTER, P. C. (1985). 'Community, Market, State—and Associations? The Prospective Contribution of Interest Governance to Social Order', in W. Streeck and P. C. Schmitter (eds.), *Private Interest Government: Beyond Market and State*. Beverly Hills, Calif. and London: Sage.

SWANN, G. M. P., PREVEZER, M., and STOUT, D. (1998). *The Dynamics of Industrial Clustering: International Comparisons in Computing and Biotechnology*. Oxford: Oxford University Press.

Sweden (1992). Arbetsmarknadsdepartementet: *Kompetensutveckling*, SOU (1992), 7. Final report of Kompetensutredningen. Stockholm: SOU.

THELEN, K. (2004). *How Institutions Evolve: The Political Economy of Skills in Germany, Britain, Japan, and the United States*. Cambridge: Cambridge University Press.

VERDIER, E. (1996). 'L'Insertion des jeunes "à la française": Vers un ajustement structurel?' *Travail et emploi*, 4: 37–54.

CHAPTER 5

TECHNOLOGY AND THE TRANSFORMATION OF WORK

RICHARD JOHN BADHAM

5.1 INTRODUCTION

OVER the last two decades, research on the social construction and dynamics of science and technology has strongly influenced investigations of technology and the transformation of work. Technology is no longer viewed simply as an exogenous influence, the impact of which can be scientifically discerned and adapted to (McLoughlin and Clark 1994; McLoughlin and Dawson 2003). Rather, scholars increasingly view technological change at work as a social process in which social agency—in the form of workplace cultures, structures, and politics—shapes how technology is designed, implemented, and used (McLoughlin 1999). Despite this recognition, speculation about the new world of work brought about by the impact of the latest batch of technologies continues to dominate popular discussion and debate. Earlier speculations about the rise of postindustrialism (Badham 1986b), post-Fordism (Badham and Mathews 1989), and the 'lights out' computer-integrated factory of the future (Badham and Schallock

1991; Valery 1987) have been reproduced in the technologically deterministic imagery of the 'virtual organization' (Preece and Laurila 2003: 12) and the 'e-economy' (Gates 2000) in a 'post-work' (Rifkin 1995) or 'post-bureaucratic' (Barley and Kunda 2001) age. In this context, how is it best for academic research to proceed?

In this chapter, I argue for the value of adopting an integrative multidimensional approach to exploring technological change at work. I argue that traditional analyses of the impact of technology, as well as more recent explorations of the role of social agency in shaping technology, are not necessarily in competition. They both address enduring and important issues in the study of technology and the transformation of work. Yet despite their value and ongoing relevance, the stronger versions of these approaches remain restricted to a one-dimensional approach to workplace transformation—investigating the effect of the 'technical' on the 'social' and vice versa. The softer versions of both approaches take up a more complex two-dimensional standpoint, recognizing the mutual influence of the technical and the social.

However, in order to further advance our understanding of technology and the transformation of work, these two-dimensional views need to be integrated with those exploring a third dimension—the emergent sphere of the 'sociotechnical', a reality sui generis with characteristics, dynamics, and effects that are not reducible to its social and technical components. This third dimension is made up of complex interwoven combinations of human and nonhuman elements, people and things. While the language used to open up this area of sociological inquiry—referring variously to 'sociotechnologies', 'sociotechnical ensembles', 'actor networks' or 'sociotechnical configurations'—sounds novel and esoteric to some (and yet not novel enough to others!), this chapter shows that the themes addressed are implicit in a number of more traditional analyses of technology and the transformation of work. The chapter concludes, however, not with an argument for the superiority of such a three-dimensional approach but, rather, the importance of integrating all three dimensions of analysis. In so doing, the dimensional perspective employed here is used to help capture the many issues involved rather than pigeonhole theorists into rigid conceptual boxes. The latter would be an exercise condemned to failure as many of the more sophisticated analysts of technology and work employ more or less frequently, and more or less self-consciously, all three approaches. As Wilbert Moore (1972: 23–4) argued more than thirty years ago, 'The question is not whether technology causes social change: it does; or whether various social changes cause technology: they do. The only interesting question is: Which changes under what circumstances?'

5.2 ONE-DIMENSIONAL VIEW (1): THE STRUCTURAL IMPACT APPROACH

Traditional and well-established impact approaches to technology focus attention on how technologies that come from 'outside' the work sphere affect the content and organization of work (Hyman and Streeck 1988). Variously described as 'technological impacts' (McLoughlin and Clark 1994; Wilkinson 1983), 'technological imperatives' (Orlikowski 1992), or 'technological determinist' (McLoughlin 1999; Preece and Laurila 2003; Thomas 1994) approaches, they differ in their view of the *nature or scope of technology*, as well as the *form and degree of impact* on work. Despite these differences, however, they all share a methodological, if not ontological, presumption that technology can usefully be examined as an 'external' 'social fact' that enables or constrains structural change and action within the world of work.

5.2.1 Nature and Scope of Technology

One of the factors bedeviling traditional structural impact approaches has been the development of precise measures of the nature of 'technology', as definitions have ranged from broad systems of production to more specific characterizations of tools, machines, and technical conditions such as degrees of complexity and uncertainty (Barley 1986). One of the most pervasive and narrower definitions of technology in the workplace has been the hardware and software of production equipment, a version of what Ogburn (1964) referred to long ago as 'material culture'. Investigations of this area have focused on such issues as: the replacement of humans using hand tools by complex machines powered by steam in the rise of the modern factory (Landes 1969; Marglin 1976); the rise of the assembly line and the creation of mass production assembly line work (Badham and Jurgens 1998; Beynon 1973; Goldthorpe *et al.* 1972; Walker and Guest 1952); and the effect of continuous process technologies in freeing up a technical workforce from being tied to particular production stations (Blauner 1964; Gallie 1978; Woodward 1958, 1965). More recently, considerable attention has been paid to the effect of information- or computer-based technologies, such as computer numerical control and computer-aided design and manufacturing, and their effect in replacing the human control of diverse complicated operations by programmed technical controls, variously interpreted as resulting in a de-skilling of traditional craft work (Cooley 1986; Shaiken 1985), the technical up-skilling of production controllers (Kern and Schumann 1984), or the creation of new professionalized forms of knowledge work (Frenkel *et al.* 1999).

Another group of scholars uses a broader definition of technology as a 'social technique'. Within this group, some characterize organizations as production systems that transform raw materials into outputs, whereby technology incorporates the wide range of tasks, techniques, tools, and knowledge involved in this process (Perrow 1970; Thompson 1967). This definition underlies contingency research focusing on the organizational impact of integrated *craft, batch, mass, and continuous process* production systems (Woodward 1958), as well as those exploring the origins and effects of more *'mechanistic'* versus more *'organic'* forms of production (Burns and Stalker 1961).

Others view technology as a form of 'knowledge', 'mindset', 'ethos', or 'spirit'— variously represented as 'mechanicism' (Mumford 1934), 'rationalization' (Weber 1974), 'instrumental rationality', or 'technique' (Winner 1977). This definition has been used to analyze the effect of mechanistic and rationalized views of the world, scientific management strategies, neo-Taylorist or post-Taylorist forms of organizational redesign, and the cultural reengineering of both manufacturing and service work (Adler and Borys 1996; Badham and Mathews 1989; Casey 1999; Hochschild 1983; Littler 1982; Mumford 1934; Ritzer 1996; Rose 1990).

5.2.2 Form and Degree of Technological Impact

5.2.2.1 *'Hard Determinism'*

Traditional 'contingency' theories of the impact of technology focused attention on the deterministic impact of production systems on organizational dimensions such as structure, size, performance, and centralization/decentralization. Woodward (1958, 1965), for example, argued that continuous process production systems reduced the tasks involved in direct human intervention in the transformation of raw materials, replacing these with new tasks requiring workers to monitor the work process; formed job content and work organization around relatively autonomous work teams; and reduced the need for personal supervision, replacing this with mechanical controls incorporated into the machinery itself. In order to achieve commercial success, Woodward argued, all organizations inevitably adopt the type of management control system most appropriate for their production system.

More recently, Donaldson (2001) has attempted to defend a sophisticated version of contingency theory as the 'structural adaptation to regain fit' (SARFIT) thesis. This approach recognizes that organizations may have a 'maladapted' structure 'out of fit' with their production system, but that the resulting failures in performance increase pressure to appropriately align the structure with the production system, leading to structural adaptation in the long run.

Donaldson (2001) builds on the classic studies by Burns and Stalker (1961), Lawrence and Lorsch (1967), Perrow (1970), Thompson (1967), and Woodward (1958, 1965) in investigating the other major theme in contingency research—the different type of organizational structure required by production systems that are more 'mechanistic' (standardized, stable, large scale, mass production, etc.) or more 'organic' (variable, changing, flexible, smaller scale, etc.). For example, Donaldson explores whether more or less 'organic' situations of degrees of task uncertainty or the factor of size are better predictors of organizational characteristics such as formalization and centralization. Donaldson concludes from a review of the evidence that at the 'micro' level of individual jobs, whatever the size of the firm, task uncertainty is accompanied by higher performance when roles are less structured (Parker and Wall 1998). However, Donaldson found that size was a greater predictor than 'technology' when it came to explaining broader more 'macro' level patterns of organizational centralization and formalization.

While Donaldson explored the impact of broader production system characteristics on jobs and organizational structures, Adler (1986) addressed the same set of issues in regard to the hardware and software of new technical systems. Adler argued that automation eliminates many routine tasks and jobs (as equipment takes over standard manual operations), increases the number of complex machine utilization tasks (as complexity and uncertainty increases due to changing products, technologies, and technical sophistication), and creates new systems development and maintenance tasks most effectively performed as close to the job as possible.

5.2.2.2 'Soft Determinism'

In contrast to such strongly deterministic arguments, however, other investigators have presented a weaker 'soft determinism' (Barley 1986: 107; Grint and Woolgar 1997: 12; Heilbroner 1972: 35). On the one hand, soft determinism modifies assumptions about the *origin* of technology—its degree of externality or autonomy (Badham 1986a). Cooley (1986) and Noble (1984), for example, seek to demonstrate the de-skilling effect of such technologies as 'numerically controlled' (NC) machine tools and 'computer-aided design' (CAD) equipment. Cooley interprets the introduction of NC and CAD equipment as removing complex work tasks from operators (such as programming decisions about machine tooling or the drafting and analysis of new designs) and creating more routine machine operation tasks (such as simple selection of pre-given programs, loading or unloading of equipment). He attributes these changes, however, to the political strategies and interests of powerful institutional actors rather than the inevitable progress of technology. On the other hand, other soft determinist approaches offer a less deterministic view of the *impact* of technology in bringing about changes in work and society. Zuboff (1988), for example, points to the dual 'automating' and 'informating' potential of information technology—involving, respectively, the substitution of technology for human labor and the generation of new and deeper levels of information about work operations. Zuboff emphasizes, however, that different organizational contexts influence the degree to which either potential is taken up and developed.

5.2.3 Beyond One-Dimensional Impact Views

Structural impact views remain one-dimensional to the degree that they focus attention solely on the impact of technology on work, with no consideration of the social factors responsible for shaping the character and dynamics of technology or mediating its effects. Such an extreme form of technological determinism is, however, quite rare. As we saw in the discussion of different definitions of technology, the portrayal of technology as a social technique or a particular mindset incorporates a range of social factors in the definition of technology itself. Similarly, in the analysis of different views of the degree of impact of technology, soft determinist views allowed some influence for social factors on either the shape or effect of technology. To the degree that such analyses allow for both the influence of technology on work and the influence of social factors inside or outside work on technology, they move towards a more two-dimensional interactive view of technology and the transformation of work. What characterizes such analyses as adherents to a broad 'impact' approach, however, is the continuing preoccupation with examining the impact of 'external' technological characteristics on the workplace.

Such broader impact views may take a number of different forms. Barley (1986), for example, adopts a sophisticated soft determinist view in seeking to retain a recognition of the materiality and determinant effects of technology, while simultaneously exploring the influence on the effect of technology of social processes in the workplace. Barley portrays technology as a 'trigger' of change, a particular type of 'exogenous shock' to a workplace social system. In the case of CT scanners, he notes how the introduction of CT scanners added a new level of technical complexity to diagnosis, with the result that the equipment operators (technicians) began exercising a greater degree of discretion in their work and relations with the medical experts (radiologists). Others are, however, more deterministic in their analysis of technological impacts—emphasizing the degree to which technologies become relatively autonomous and strongly influential in their impact despite their social origins (Heilbroner 1972; Winner 1977).

Grint and Woolgar (1997), however, criticize *all* such soft determinist approaches for assuming the existence of a socially unmediated material technology with impacts on the world of work. Arguing for a 'thoroughgoing interpretivism', they assert that all material technology is socially mediated—through the social processes involved in constructing definitions of the 'capabilities' or 'requirements' of technology, embedding individual or group interests into system designs, as well as shaping how technologies are configured, taken up, and used in the workplace. Continuing this argument, all soft determinist models ultimately assume a non-social 'technology-in-itself' and emphasize the value of understanding and adapting to the material effects of such technologies. To this degree they continue to work within a general structural impact approach—albeit in a manner that goes beyond simple one-dimensional determinism.

5.3 One-Dimensional View (2): The Social Agency Approach

In contrast to harder structural impact views of technology as developing outside the work sphere, scholars who adopt a social agency approach attempt to get inside the 'black box' of technology and reveal the social factors, both inside and outside the workplace, that shape technology and its purported 'demands' (Mackenzie and Wajcman 1999).

5.3.1 Impact of Social Agency on Technology

In recent social agency approaches, researchers have adopted a conceptualization of technology as a complex and multidimensional entity, with the effects of social agency being observed in the fundamental design of hardware and software systems, their local configuration during implementation, and their use in operation.

Investigations into the social dynamics of how workplace technologies are *designed* range from micro-ethnographies of the social dynamics of engineering design (Bucciarelli 1998; Wotherspoon 2002) to macro-sociological investigations of the institutional dynamics that allow capitalist and masculine assumptions to be embedded in the structure of workplace technologies (Cockburn 1983; Marglin 1976; Noble 1984; Shaiken 1985; Wajcman 1991). Many of the macro-analyses have addressed how assumptions about users (or desired users) are built into the hardware and software of technological systems in a manner that constrains who is able to use such systems and how they are to be used. Some of the most widely investigated examples of technology with this type of inbuilt engineering control are computer-based manufacturing systems such as NC and CAD equipment, flexible manufacturing systems (FMS), computer-aided production planning (CAPP), and computer-integrated manufacturing (CIM).

Noble (1984), for example, provided a detailed historical study of the political and institutional factors responsible for shaping such a control engineering trajectory, documenting the triumph of a de-skilling NC trajectory over an equally 'technically' and 'economically' valid (if not superior) option for the development of 'record playback' systems that retained the control and enhanced the capabilities of blue-collar machinists. Other research shows that this type of control-oriented engineering logic (Perrow 1983) continues to dominate the training of US engineers and ergonomists (Lund et al. 1993). Moreover, considerable evidence exists that the design assumptions of new hardware and software, and accompanying prescriptions for operator training and work organization, remain dominated by the engineering logic of systems developers rather than by users and their 'operational' logics (Badham 1993; Scarborough and Corbett 1992).

Whatever the assumptions built into technology designs, however, they are only effective when *implemented* in working technological systems (Badham 1993), and this always involves a degree of 'reinvention' (Rogers 1995) in the implementation context. Drawing on the social construction of science and technology, a number of analysts have emphasized the 'interpretive flexibility' of technological artifacts, and the key significance of local 'stabilization rituals' in constructing their perceived capabilities and effects (Grint and Woolgar 1997). These researchers view implemented technologies as complex multidimensional 'boundary objects', as different social worlds in the workplace frame the nature, value, and effects of these technologies in different ways (Garrety and Badham 2000). This process influences not only the interpretation but also the material substance of technologies that are reconfigured in context. Even 'harder' technologies, such as robots and computer-aided design and manufacturing (CAD/CAM) equipment, require substantial local configuration during implementation, which in turn leads to substantial variation in the content of jobs and work organization across work sites (Badham and Wilson 1993; Fleck 1999). For example, in a study of seven plants in Australia, Badham (1991) found that variation in company design and manufacturing priorities led to variation in the design and use of their CAD/CAM systems. The CAD/CAM systems differed, for example, in such dimensions as whether they were capable of complex 3D imaging or required skillful interpretation of 'wireframe' drawings, whether databases of standard designs were developed, and whether terminals were located in drafting, design engineering, or manufacturing areas. These conditions shaped whether the equipment was used by design draughtspeople, design engineers, or manufacturing engineers. In the Australian case study companies, design engineers rarely used the systems, due in part to opposition by the drafting union to engineer's use of the system and in part to the low level of in-house design capabilities. While Cooley (1986) and others predicted that the use of CAD/CAM would lead to a general de-skilling and displacement of draughtspeople due to an increased use of standardized designs and automated drafting packages, it was clear from the Australian study that the potential for CAD/CAM to have this effect was not occurring to any great extent due to alternative forms of development and use of the systems. The result of such activities is not merely the selective shaping of the technology, but also the retention or transformation of different types of skills, tasks, and forms of work organization. As detailed by Leonard-Barton (1995) in a study of thirty-four projects to develop software tools in four large US electronics companies, the outcome is a process of 'mutual adaptation' as both the technology and the work system are selectively developed and adapted to each other.

In this way, investigations of how organizational factors shape the structure of technological systems during implementation are intertwined with studies of the complex social factors that influence how technology is *used* during and after implementation. Similar technologies are often introduced into workplaces with significant differences in social and political conditions, differences that, in turn, generate ongoing variations in the outcomes and use of the technology. In *In Search of the New Working Class* (1978), for example, Gallie revealed how differences in the social context of continuous process oil refineries in France and the United Kingdom resulted in differences in class attitudes and aspirations and attitudes to employers and trade unions (the French workers being distinctly more conflictual and class conscious)—in direct contrast to the predictions of uniform increases in social integration predicted by the classical contingency analyses of Woodward and Blauner or in the neo-Marxist analyses of Mallet and Naville and colleagues (Gallie 1978: ch. 1). In his investigation of four UK Midlands manufacturing firms that introduced CNC machine tools, Wilkinson (1983) found that differences in the politics of management/worker relations led to substantial differences in work organization. In one electroplating plant, management placed the CNC controls in a locked outhouse on the other side of a brick wall from where the operators worked. In another machine tool company, the CNC machines were purchased with additional manual data input (MDI) facilities such that the skilled craftsmen operating the machines could write their own programs and enter them directly. Similarly, Sorge *et al.* (1983) found variation in the use of CNC equipment in comparable West German and UK engineering firms, with the former giving substantially greater programming responsibilities to workers than the latter. Sorge and his colleagues attributed this difference to the higher skill levels of the German workers.

5.3.2 The Nature and Scope of Social Agency

The forms of social agency that scholars privilege in such analyses reflect their prior theoretical commitments to more micro or macro, action or structure, conflict or consensus explanations in the social sciences (Knights and Murray 1994; Mackenzie and Wacjman 1999). For neo-Marxist labor process analyses, the key influencing factors are broad structural inequalities of power and control—as illustrated in the analysis by Noble (1984) above. Similarly, Cockburn and others (Cockburn 1983; Mackenzie and Wajcman 1999; Wajcman 1991) have documented how gender inequalities and patterns of domination in the development of machinery perpetuate control over jobs by skilled male workers and their unions—for example, by automating tasks that could be performed by women or children or requiring the greater developed strength or size of male workers for their operation.

This focus on structures of power and control is also found in neo-Foucauldian analyses of new production technologies as materialized 'Panopticons' for increasing surveillance and control. For example, Sewell and Wilkinson (1992) present the technologies associated with the introduction of Japanese style just-in-time systems into car plants in northern England as a form of 'electronic eye'—that monitors increasingly transparent production processes and disciplines workers' actions.

In reaction to such totalizing views of domination, neo-labor process writers have documented variable uses of technology in different product and labor market contexts (Knights, Willmott, and Collinson 1985). Power-process analyses (Thomas 1994) have shown how the 'strategic choices' of the upper level managers as well as the actions of lower level managers, workers, and engineers shape the way that technology is implemented. Theorists from both neo-Foucauldian (Knights and Murray 1994) and structuration backgrounds (Orlikowski 1992) have also developed alternative frameworks designed to better capture the fluidity of these micro/macro interactions.

Barley (1986), for example, attempts to capture this fluidity in his ethnography of the introduction of CT scanners in two US hospitals. Prior to the CT scanners' introduction, both hospitals had a similar division of labor: the radiologists with professional credentials controlled the interpretation of medical images from X-ray equipment, while radiological technologists were responsible for such tasks as running the X-ray equipment and managing patients. However, despite the same division of labor, the outcomes of introducing the same technology were different, with the first hospital shifting much more decision-making discretion from the radiologists to the technicians than the second. The differences, according to Barley, were due in part to contextual factors, in particular the fact that the first hospital made the decision to hire expert CT technicians to run the new equipment, while the second relied more on CT/technology proficient radiologists. The final outcome was, however, influenced by the micro-dynamics in each situation. When, for example, the radiologists in the second hospital attempted to hand over CT operation to the technicians, the latter lacked the competence to do the job, leading the radiologists to resume a degree of control that they had attempted to relinquish.

Barley's analysis does, however, remain restricted in its agency focus. While addressing contextual influences on the use of such scanners, he does not analyze the impact of social agency in either the design of the CT scanners or their customization and adaptation during their implementation. Were CT scanners tightly coupled systems with standardized features? Or, were there different options, and different ways of integrating them with other technologies in the radiology department? Were the overall sets of technologies, layouts, and operational procedures the same in both hospitals? Were there different perceptions of how the technology worked and how it could be used from inside and outside the radiology departments? Grint and Woolgar (1997) stress the importance of exploring such issues in examining the effect of local 'stabilization rituals' in constructing the capabilities of the technology. In her study of the different interpretations and uses of Lotus Notes software packages, Orlikowski (2000) attempts to incorporate a number of such factors.

The Lotus Notes software package was developed by a small company to provide a form of 'groupware' to support distributed electronic interaction, such as communication via electronic mail and shared discussion databases. Orlikowski found, however, that three groups used it in remarkably different ways: technologists and consultants at a large multinational consulting agency (Alpha) and IT support staff in a large software company (Zeta). These differences were shaped by the interaction between how Lotus Notes' capabilities were 'framed' (Orlikowski and Gash 1994) by each group and how the organizational context—the training, rewards, and cultural systems in each case—influenced each group. For example, Alpha's technologists viewed Lotus Notes as a radical breakthrough for cooperative learning, and thus used the system for such activities as electronic mail, knowledge sharing and collaboration, customizing templates, and adding new databases. They were highly skilled and worked in a cooperative culture. Alpha's consultants, by contrast, viewed Lotus Notes as an incremental upgrade to word processing and email. Most only used the system for email, while a minority used it to improve their individual productivity. As a group, they were technically unskilled and received very cursory training in the new system. Moreover, they were measured on billable hours, and time on Lotus Notes was not billable; and they lived in a competitive individualistic culture. Finally, the IT support staff at Zeta transformed Lotus Notes into an application that could track customer calls and document incidents, processes, and solutions. They used it to solve new problems and facilitate browsing through others' calls for ad hoc learning. This approach was consistent with the fact that they were highly technically skilled, received very useful training on the new system, and their evaluations were modified to include the effective use of the system for improved documentation and cooperative work.

5.3.3 Beyond One-Dimensional Social Agency Views

Social agency views—in a direct inverse of structural impact views—remain one-dimensional to the degree that they focus attention solely on the impact of social agency on technology, with no consideration of the role of technology in shaping the character and dynamics of social agency or mediating its effects. Again, however, such an extreme social agency approach is quite rare. What is far more common is a more two-dimensional approach, with an emphasis on the role of social agency neglected by structural impact approaches, and an attempt to combine this with a more restricted view of the influence of technology. Thus, Barley (1986: 78) emphasizes that there is substantial empirical evidence for *both* the deterministic impact of workplace technologies and for the exercise of social agency in influencing their variable consequences and uses—concluding that what is required are perspectives that encompass both sets of findings. Thomas (1994: 5) reiterates this theme in his argument for a 'power-process' perspective that presents 'a theory of how social *and* technical systems are *jointly responsible* for organization structuring and change' (emphasis added). McLoughlin and Dawson (2003) argue for a similar 'politics/process' perspective that accepts the irreducible 'materiality' of technology—urging researchers 'not to throw the technology baby out with the determinist bathwater' (Preece and Laurila 2003: 24).

Two developments have emerged from this more interactionist view. Some researchers have pushed their analyses to capture the complex processual interplay of the technical and the social during innovation and change, as in Orlikowski's (2000) investigation of 'technology-in-practice' outlined above. Such analyses can, however, be understood as remaining within the social agency perspective insofar as the *central* concern is to explore the way in which social agency shapes and uses technologies, rather than vice versa. Other researchers have engaged in more policy-oriented studies, building on the Tavistock sociotechnical tradition (van Einjatten 1993) of seeking to jointly optimize the technical and social elements of production arrangements conceptualized as sociotechnical systems. These focus on the process of mutual adaptation (Leonard-Barton 1995) of the social and the technical, undertaken in order to improve performance outcomes. They point to the economic and social costs of misalignment, the benefits of alignment, and provide recommendations for how this can be achieved (Benders, de Haan, and Bennett 1995).

5.4 THREE-DIMENSIONAL VIEW: BEYOND THE SOCIOTECHNICAL?

5.4.1 Opening Up the Conceptual Space for Going beyond a Two-Dimensional View

Underlying one-dimensional impact and agency views of technology and work are alternative deeply rooted social ontologies, methodological orientations, and value commitments (Dawe 1970). Both perspectives focus on unpeeling the onion of technology/work relations, albeit in different directions. On the one hand, impact views uncover the previously unrecognized consequences of structural technical influences on organizational life and suggest ways to adapt to the opportunities and constraints that they bring about. On the other hand, agency approaches unpack the 'objective' characteristics and 'external' demands of technology, revealing the social choices and interpretations involved in such constructions. They thereby help to inform and broaden social choice in opposition to power structures that use technicist arguments to legitimate their position of power and control. Both concerns are a priori legitimate and continue to inspire valuable research on the impact of technology on social relations at work, and the influence of social relations on the development and use of workplace technologies (Badham and Jurgens 1998).

While tensions and controversies between these two approaches dominated discussion and debate within the 1980s and 1990s, there is now a greater degree of acceptance of the partial insights provided by both perspectives. As illustrated in the work of more recent soft determinist and interactive social agency approaches, a certain degree of consensus has emerged around the value of adopting an inter-active two-dimensional approach to understanding technological change and the transformation of work. Key theoretical and empirical issues remain, of course, in regard to the form and degree of influence of technology and social relations on each other. Orlikowski (2000), for example, in arguing for a 'technology-in-practice' perspective is strongly critical of her earlier 'structuration' approach (Orlikowksi 1992). While recognizing that technologies set 'boundary conditions' on how they can be configured and used, she argues for a perspective that 'rather than starting with the technology and examining how actors appropriate its embodied structures [as assumed in her earlier structuration approach]. ... starts with human action and examines how it enacts emergent structures through recurrent interaction with the technology at hand' (Orlikowski 2000: 407). The central focus of analysis in analyzing technology use and the transformation of work, Orlikowski argues, is on recursively constituted, although frequently recurrent, work practices that condition and are conditioned by actors' interpretive schemes, technologies, and institutional structures.

Despite their sophistication and value, however, such analyses continue to operate within a two-dimensional frame, focusing investigation on the interaction between the two spheres of the 'technical' and the 'social'. This frame has been questioned by sociologists of science and technology who argue that it tends to underemphasize the mutual interpenetration of the technical and the social, and fails to pay sufficient attention to the workings of complex 'sociotechnical ensembles'. As Bijker (1995: 274) puts it, this sphere of the 'sociotechnical' 'is not to be treated merely as a combination of social and technical factors. It is sui generic. ... Society is not determined by technology, nor is technology determined by society. Both emerge as two sides of the sociotechnical coin during the construction processes of artefacts, facts, and relevant social groups.' The importance of what Law (1987) characterizes as the interdependent dynamics and simultaneous 'heterogeneous engineering' of the human and nonhuman aspects of such sociotechnical ensembles is at least implicitly recognized by prescriptive organization studies advocating the central role of line management personnel and objectives in the control of human resource management (Storey 1992), technology management (Clegg 2000), and organizational change (Schaffer and Thomson 1992).

One way of grasping the nature of such sociotechnical ensembles is to view the 'technical' and the 'social' as constituent elements which, when combined, create a sociotechnical whole that, in the words of traditional discussions of social systems, is 'greater than the sum of its parts'. This emergent entity interacts with, and defines, as well as being defined by, its social and technical components. In this sense, it is no more possible to capture the nature of emergent sociotechnical entities by simply compiling their components or investigating linear cause and effect relations between them than it is to understand the workings of a bicycle by simply listing its component parts without any comprehension of their function or role in the whole. From the perspective of this third dimension, the key issue is not, as Barley portrayed it, one of investigating the relations between CT scanners and the division of labor in radiology departments or, as Orlikowski understands it, the interaction between work practices and Lotus Notes packages but, rather, attempting to conceptualize and understand the overall nature and dynamics of embedded CT-technician-radiologist combinations or Lotus Notes-technologists/Lotus Notes-consultants/Lotus Notes-IT support staff networks.

The exact point being made here has traditionally been extremely difficult to precisely define and understand. The use of the term 'sociotechnical ensemble' by Bijker has a number of problems. It still tends to suggest that what is being discussed is an integrated assembly of independently defined social and technical elements rather than an entity that plays a significant role in defining the 'meaning' of such elements. Callon (1986) and Latour have used the term 'actor network' in order to avoid using deterministic concepts such as 'system' and 'structure', and also avoid reproducing assumptions about separate technical and social spheres that are placed in hierarchical causal relations. However, the lack of clarity in their use of both terms 'actor' and 'network' have created ongoing controversies (Crawford 1993; Latour 2002).

Another way of grasping the meaning of a third-dimensional realm of the sociotechnical is through attempts to break down modernist commonsense ideas about the existence of separate realms of the technical and the social. In *We Have Never Been Modern* (1993), Latour makes the point that modernist rhetoric of a separation between these two spheres has never been realized in practice. Despite educational systems, job classifications, and organizational functions premised on such a division, the sphere of the technical has always been thoroughly imbued with cultural symbolism, the pursuit of social interests, and individual and group passions and meaning. Similarly, the sphere of the social has always involved identities, actions, and commitments that are inextricably intertwined with the tools, knowledge, and physical environment of society's 'material culture'. For Latour, we cannot, and should not therefore, think about humans, or about nonhumans, in isolation from one another. We have, for so long, lived among and through our myriad objects that we cannot really understand who we are without taking them into account. Likewise, our tools are so deeply infused with our knowledge and intentions that they do not make much sense without us. Moreover, they do more than just reflect and embody social relations. Because we have delegated functions to them, they possess (a type of) agency (Garrety and Badham 2004). As Latour puts it, 'thanks to the hammer I become literally another man, a man who has become "other". ... This is why the theme of the tool as "extension of the organ" makes such little sense. Those who believe that tools are simple utensils have never held a hammer in their hand, have never allowed themselves to recognise the flux of possibilities that they are suddenly able to envisage' (Latour 2002: 250).

Thus, for Latour, we are all—as individuals or collectivities—'cyborgs', part-human/part-nonhuman, and the search for a historical or analytical time or space where humanity can be discerned separate from tools or technology, or where tools or technology are separate from their human creators or users, is a meaningless quest, a search inspired by a faulty 'myth of origins'. 'Nothing', states Latour (2002: 256), 'not even the human, is for itself or by itself, but always *by other things* and *for other things*.'

5.4.2 Principles Guiding Three-Dimensional Investigations of Technology and Work

Given the novelty and complexity of such a three-dimensional view, it is often difficult to understand how it would translate into an alternative form of investigation of technology and work. The following principles are, therefore, intended as a general guide to help translate these ideas into more specific guidelines for research.

5.4.2.1 *Principle 1: Technology as Sociotechnologies*

Technologies that 'enter' the world of work should be understood as 'sociotechnologies', i.e. conglomerations of techno-social techniques created and mobilized by networks or constituencies of sociotechnical agents. In his analysis of the rationalization of the world, for example, Weber (1969) made no radical distinction between 'the machine' and 'bureaucratic organization'; both were techniques involved in the building of what he saw as the 'houses of bondage' of the future. In the analysis of modern actor networks—from underground tunnel systems to regional fishing industries—Latour (1987, 1999) and others explore technological outcomes as the product of the activities of 'heterogeneous engineers' who enroll potentially wayward human and nonhuman entities as 'allies', translating their problems, interests, and investments in a manner that effectively aligns their activities with the goals of the network (Grint and Woolgar 1997; Knights and Murray 1994). Despite their differences, Weber and Latour can be seen as making a similar point: the key focus of analysis is on the development and consequences of conglomerations of techno-social 'techniques of control'.

The first principle of sociotechnical analysis, therefore, is a central focus on the nature of *sociotechnologies* introduced into the workplace. Whether these are formally characterized as 'technical' or 'organizational', they are to be understood as complex conglomerations of human and nonhuman elements, created and mobilized by human/nonhuman ('actor') networks. This involves a focus, for example, on the promotion of new sociotechnical network-based business systems rather than simply e-business, web technologies, or virtual organizations.

5.4.2.2 *Principle 2: The Workplace as a Sociotechnical Configuration*

Workplaces should be understood as sociotechnical configurations, i.e. complex webs of human and nonhuman elements that are locally configured in context in the pursuit of formal and informal, explicit and implicit purposes and goals. At a macro-level, for example, Marx attributed major significance to the dynamics between technology (forces of production) and ownership/authority relations (relations of production), yet saw both as intertwined in his overall systemic analysis of the purpose and practices of integrated sociotechnical arrangements (modes of production). For Marx, therefore, the analysis of technological change in the workplace begins with a broad focus on the goals and structures of workplace sociotechnical arrangements, a focus that is logically prior to the analysis of the dynamic and disruptive nature of new technologies, or the effect of ownership/ authority relations in developing and using such technologies as new means of control. At a more micro level, this focus is illustrated by McLoughlin, Badham, and Couchman's (2000) analysis of the introduction of cellular manufacturing (grouping different machines into product-based cells) and accompanying self-managing work teams (operating the cells as mini factories within a factory) in three Australian manufacturing firms. The varying forms of team-based cellular manufacturing that emerged were attributed to the effect of different configurations of technology, operators, and local intrapreneurs (line managers, HR personnel, engineers, and operators) involved in the pursuit of production operation and improvement.

The second principle of a sociotechnical analysis of technological change at work, therefore, is the start of analysis with a primary focus on the goals and means of workplace sociotechnical configurations—rather than beginning with the introduced technology and its interaction with social relationships in the workplace.

5.4.2.3 *Principle 3: Innovation as a Sociotechnical Practice*

The examination of technology and agency in the innovation process is not a simple matter of exploring how the social context of use influences technologies that are socially constructed in a developer context, and vice versa. The interaction is one between sociotechnologies created and mobilized by one set of sociotechnical networks and the dynamics of sociotechnical configurations present in different workplaces. It is this interactive process that is partially captured by Fleck (1999) as innofusion and Leonard-Barton (1995) as mutual adaptation. The difference for the three-dimensional view, however, is that the process of localized reinvention, or mutual shaping between the new technology and the work context, is always understood to be one of interaction between two fundamentally sociotechnical, rather than 'technical' and 'social' entities.

This approach was illustrated in a study of the introduction of 'user-centered design' methods in piloting the introduction of an intelligent manufacturing system (IMS) in an Australian steel rod mill in order to automatically control interlinked production processes (Badham, Garrety, and Kirsch 2001; Garrety and Badham 2000, 2004). This study showed how the failure of these methods to influence the architectural design of the IMS or establish a more user-centered pattern of innovation in the plant was the result of the sociotechnologies produced by the IMS project network and the sociotechnical configurations in the plant. Both the character of the user-centered design methods and practices and the plant's traditional engineering project methods and practices were locally transformed and adapted to work in context in the course of the innovation project, yet the broader contexts of both the 'external' network promoting user-centered sociotechnologies and the 'internal' sociotechnical configuration in the plant ensured that these adaptations did not stabilize in the form of a fundamental redesign of the IMS technology or a new method of involving users in technology projects in the plant.

The third principle of a sociotechnical analysis is, therefore, the examination of innovation as a complex emergent practice resulting from the interaction between two sociotechnical constellations and networks—the one responsible for the development and diffusion of sociotechnologies, the other for the operation and development of workplace sociotechnical configurations.

5.5 CONCLUSION

One-dimensional structural impact and social agency approaches, as schematically characterized in Figure 5.1 (where T stands for Technology, S for Social), offer alternative clear-cut approaches to examining the interaction between technology and the transformation of work.

Two-dimensional perspectives—as embodied in soft determinism and interactive agency views illustrated in Figure 5.2—point the way to a more comprehensive analysis, incorporating the insights of both one-dimensional views, but tend to limit analysis to the mutual interactions between the technical and the social as two independent entities.

Fig. 5.1 One-dimensional approaches

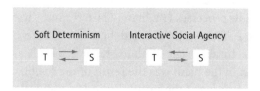

Fig. 5.2 Two-dimensional approaches

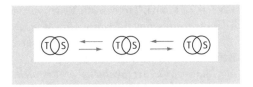

Fig. 5.3 Three-dimensional approaches

The three-dimensional sociotechnical practice perspective, as outlined in Figure 5.3, has often been presented by its proponents as an alternative view that supplants earlier approaches. Such exclusivity is, however, not warranted. While it is necessary to recognize the interwoven and emergent nature of sociotechnical combinations, explanatory issues remain surrounding the relationships of influence both within and between the various ('technical' and 'social') elements of such networks. Rather than supplanting each other these different approaches can, therefore, usefully be combined in an integrated multidimensional analysis. Consequently, the aim of this chapter has not been to outline alternative perspectives, or to simply pigeonhole particular theorists, but, rather, to open up communication between adherents of different viewpoints and contribute to the development of more comprehensive analyses of technology and the transformation of work.

REFERENCES

ADLER, P. S. (1986). 'New Technologies: New Skills'. *California Management Review*, 29/1: 9–28.

——and BORYS, B. (1996). 'Two Types of Bureaucracy: Enabling and Coercive'. *Administrative Science Quarterly*, 41: 61–89.

BADHAM, R. (1986*a*). 'Technology and Public Choice: Strategies for Technological Control and the Selection of Technologies'. *Prometheus*, 4: 288–304.

——(1986*b*). *Theories of Industrial Society*. London: Croom Helm.

——(1991). *Computer Design and Manufacturing*. Department of Industrial Relations, AGPS, Canberra.

——(ed.) (1993). 'Systems, Networks and Configurations: Inside the Implementation Process'. *International Journal of Human Factors in Manufacturing*, 3/1: 1–101.

——and JURGENS, U. (1998). 'Images of Good Work and the Politics of Teamwork'. *Economic and Industrial Democracy*, 19: 33–58.

——and MATHEWS, J. (1989). 'The New Production Systems Debate'. *Labour and Industry*, 2/2: 194–246.

——and SCHALLOCK, B. (1991). 'Human Factors in CIM Development: A Human Centred View from Europe'. *International Journal of Human Factors in Manufacturing*, 1: 121–41.

——and WILSON, S. (1993). 'Smart Sociotechnical CIM Systems: Beyond Island Solutions and Turnkey Philosophies'. *International Journal of Human Factors in Manufacturing*, 3/2: 117–33.

——GARRETY, K., and KIRSCH, C. (2001). 'Humanistic Redesign and Technological Politics in Organisations'. *Journal of Organisational Change Management*, 14/1: 50–64.

——McLOUGHLIN, I. P., and BUCHANAN, D. (1998). 'Human Resource Management and Cellular Manufacturing', in N. Suresh and J. Kay (eds.), *Group Technology and Cellular Manufacturing: State-of-the-Art Synthesis of Research and Practice*. Boston: Kluwer.

BARLEY, S. R. (1986). 'Technology as an Occasion for Structuring: Evidence from Observations of CT Scanners and the Social Order of Radiology Departments'. *Administrative Science Quarterly*, 31/1: 78–108.

——and KUNDA, G. (2001). 'Bringing Work Back In'. *Organisation Science*, 12 /1: 76–95.

BELL, D. (1976). *The Coming of Post-Industrial Society*. Harmondsworth: Penguin.

BENDERS, J., DE HAAN, J., and BENNETT, D. (eds.) (1995). *The Symbiosis of Work and Technology*. London: Taylor and Francis.

BEYNON, H. (1973). *Working for Ford*. London: Allen Lane.

BIJKER, W. W. (1995). *Of Bicycles, Bakelites, and Bulbs: Toward a Theory of Sociotechnical Change*. Cambridge, Mass.: MIT Press.

BLAUNER, R. (1964). *Alienation and Freedom*. Chicago: University of Chicago Press.

BUCCIARELLI, L. (1998). *Designing Engineers*. Cambridge, Mass.: MIT Press.

BURNS, T., and STALKER, G. M. (1961). *The Management of Innovation*. London: Tavistock.

CALLON, M. (1986). 'The Sociology of an Actor-Network: The Case of the Electric Vehicle', in M. Callon, J. Law, and A. Rip (eds.), *Mapping the Dynamics of Science and Technology: Sociology of Science in the Real World*. Basingstoke: Macmillan.

CASEY, C. (1999). 'Come, Join our Family: Discipline and Integration in Corporate Organisational Culture'. *Human Relations*, 52/2: 155–78.

CLEGG, C. (2000). 'Sociotechnical Principles for System Design'. *Applied Ergonomics*, 31: 463–77.

COCKBURN, C. (1983). *Brothers: Male Dominance and Technological Change*. London: Pluto.

COOLEY, M. (1986). *Architect or Bee*. London: Abacus.

CRAWFORD, T. H. (1993). 'An Interview with Bruno Latour'. *Configurations*, 1: 247–68.

DAWE, A. (1970). 'The Two Sociologies'. *British Journal of Sociology*, 21/2: 207–18.

DONALDSON, L. (2001). *The Contingency Theory of Organizations*. Thousand Oaks/London/Delhi: Sage.

FLECK, J. (1999). 'Learning by Trying: The Implementation of Configurational Technology', in D. Mackenzie and J. Wacjman (eds.), *The Social Shaping of Technology* (2nd edn). London: Open University Press.

FRENKEL, S., Korczynski, M., Shire, K. A., and Tam, M. (1999). *On the Frontline: Work Organisation in the Information Economy*. Ithaca, NY: Cornell University Press.

GALLIE, L. D. (1978). *In Search of the New Working Class*. Cambridge: Cambridge University Press.

GARRETY, K., and BADHAM, R. (2000). 'The Politics of Sociotechnical Intervention: An Interactionist View'. *Technology Analysis and Strategic Management*, 12/1: 103–19.

—— —— (2004). 'User-Centred Design and the Normative Politics of Technology'. *Science, Technology and Human Values*, 29/2.

GATES, B. (2000). *Business @ the Speed of Thought: Succeeding in the Digital Economy*. London: Penguin.

GOLDTHORPE, J. T., LOCKWOOD, D., BEHHOFER, F., and PLATT, J. (1972). *The Affluent Worker: Industrial Attitudes and Behaviour*. Cambridge: Cambridge University Press.

GRINT, K., and WOOLGAR, S. (1997). *The Machine at Work*. Cambridge: Polity Press.

HEILBRONER, R. (1972). 'Do Machines Make History?' in M. Kranzberg and W. H. Davenport (eds.), *Technology and Culture: An Anthology*. New York: Meridian.

HOCHSCHILD, A. R. (1983). *The Managed Heart: Commercialization of Human Feeling*. Berkeley: University of California Press.

HYMAN, R., and STREECK, W. (eds.) (1988). *New Technology and Industrial Relations*. Oxford: Basil Blackwell.

KERN, H., and SCHUMANN, M. (1984). *Das Ende der Arbeitsteilung? Rationalisierung in der Industriellen Produktion*. Munich: Beck.

KNIGHTS, D., and MURRAY, F. (1994). *Managers Divided: Organisation Politics and Information Technology Management*. Wiley: Chichester.

——WILLMOTT, H., and COLLINSON, D. (eds.) (1985). *Job Redesign*. Aldershot: Gower.

LANDES, D. (1969). *The Unbound Prometheus: Technological Change and Industrial Development in the Western World from 1750 to the Present*. Cambridge: Cambridge University Press.

LATOUR, B. (1987). *Science in Action: How to Follow Scientists and Engineers through Society*. Cambridge, Mass.: Harvard University Press.

——(1993). *We Have Never Been Modern*. Brighton: Harvester Wheatsheaf.

——(1999). *Pandora's Hope: Essays in the Reality of Science Studies*. Cambridge, Mass.: Harvard University Press.

——(2002). 'Morality and Technology: The End of the Means'. *Theory, Culture and Society*, 19: 247–60.

LAW, J. (1987). 'Technology and Heterogeneous Engineering: The Case of Portuguese Expansion', in W. Bijker, T. P. Hughes, and T. Pinch (eds.), *The Social Construction of Technological Systems*. Cambridge, Mass.: MIT Press.

LAWRENCE, P. R., and LORSCH, J. W. (1967). *Organisation and Environment: Managing Differentiation and Integration*. Boston: Harvard Business School Press.

LEONARD-BARTON, D. (1995). *Wellsprings of Knowledge: Building and Sustaining the Sources of Innovation*. Boston: Harvard Business School Press.

LITTLER, C. R. (1982). *The Development of the Labour Process in Capitalist Societies*. London: Heinemann.

LUND, R., BISHOP, A., NEWMAN, A., and SALZMAN, H. (1993). *Designed to Work: Production Systems and People*. Englewood Cliffs, NJ: Prentice Hall.

——and WAJCMAN, J. (eds.) (1999). *The Social Shaping of Technology* (2nd edn). Milton Keynes: Open University Press.

McLOUGHLIN, I. (1999). *Creative Technological Change*. Routledge: London.

——and CLARK, J. (1994). *Technological Change at Work*. Oxford: Oxford University Press.

——and DAWSON, P. (2003). 'The Mutual Shaping of Technology and Organisation: Between Cinema and a Hard Place', in D. Preece and J. Laurila (eds.), *Technological Change and Organisational Action*. London: Routledge.

——BADHAM, R., and COUCHMAN, P. (2000). 'Rethinking Politics and Process in Technological Change'. *Technology Analysis and Strategic Management*, 12/1: 17–39.

MARGLIN, S. (1976). 'What Do Bosses Do?' in A. Gorz (ed.), *Division of Labor*. London: Macmillan.

MOORE, W. E. (1972). *Technology and Social Change*. Chicago: Quadrangle.

MUMFORD, L. (1934). *Technics and Civilization*. London: Routledge.

NOBLE, D. (1984). *Forces of Production*. New York: Monthly Review Press.

OGBURN, W. (1964). 'The Culture Lag', in O. D. Duncan (ed.), *On Culture and Social Change*. Chicago: University of Chicago Press.

ORLIKOWSKI, W. J. (1992). 'The Duality of Technology: Rethinking the Concept of Technology in Organisations'. *Organisation Science*, 3/3: 398–427.

—— (2000). 'Using Technology and Constituting Structures: A Practice Lens for Studying Technology in Organisations'. *Organisation Science*, 11/4: 404–28.

—— and GASH, D. C. (1994). 'Technological Frames: Making Sense of Information Technology in Organisations'. *ACM Trans. Inform. Systems*, 2/2: 174–207.

PARKER, S., and WALL, T. (1998). *Job and Work Design: Organizing Work to Promote Well-Being and Effectiveness*. Thousand Oaks/London/New Delhi: Sage.

PERROW, C. (1970). *Organizational Analysis: A Sociological View*. Belmont, Calif.: Wadsworth.

—— (1983). 'The Organisational Context of Human Factors Engineering'. *Administrative Science Quarterly*, 28: 521–41.

PREECE, D., and LAURILA, J. (eds.) (2003). *Technological Change and Organizational Action*. London: Routledge.

RIFKIN, J. (1995). *The End of Work: The Decline of the Global Labor Force and the Dawn of the Post-Market Era*. New York: Tarcher/Putnam.

RITZER, G. (1996). *The McDonaldization of Society*. Thousand Oaks, Calif.: Pine Forge.

ROGERS, E. M. (1995). *Diffusion of Innovations* (4th edn). New York: Free Press.

ROSE, N. (1990). *Governing the Soul: The Shaping of the Private Self*. London: Routledge.

SCARBOROUGH, H., and CORBETT, J. M. (1992). *Technology and Organisation: Power, Meaning and Design*. London: Routledge.

SCHAFFER, R. H., and THOMSON, H. A. (1992). 'Successful Change Programs Begin with Results'. *Harvard Business Review*, January–February: 80–9.

SEWELL, G., and WILKINSON, B. (1992). '"Someone to Watch Over Me": Surveillance, Discipline and the Just-in-Time Labour Process'. *Sociology*, 26/2: 271–89.

SHAIKEN, H. (1985). *Work Transformed*. New York: Holt, Rinehart and Winston.

SORGE, A., HARTMAN, G., WARNER, M., and NICHOLAS, I. (1983). *Microelectronics and Manpower in Manufacturing Applications of Computer Numerical Control in Great Britain and West Germany*. Aldershot: Gower.

STOREY, J. (1992). *Developments in the Management of Human Resources*. Oxford: Blackwell.

THOMAS, R. J. (1994). *What Machines Can't Do: Politics and Technology in the Industrial Enterprise*. Berkeley and Los Angeles: University of California Press.

THOMPSON, J. D. (1967). *Organisations in Action*. New York: McGraw-Hill.

VALERY, N. (1987). 'Factory of the Future'. *The Economist*, 30(May): 6–18.

VAN EINJATTEN, F. (1993). *The Paradigm that Changed the Workplace*. Stockholm: Arbetslivcentrum.

WAJCMAN, J. (1991). *Feminism Confronts Technology*. University Park: Pennsylvania State University Press.

WALKER, C. R., and GUEST, R. H. (1952). *The Man on the Assembly Line*. Cambridge, Mass.: Harvard University Press.

WEBER, M. (1969). *The Theory of Social and Economic Organisation*. New York: Free Press.

—— (1974). *The Protestant Ethic and the Spirit of Capitalism*. London: Allen and Unwin.

WILKINSON, B. (1983). *The Shopfloor Politics of New Technology*. London: Heinemann.

WINNER, L. (1977). *Autonomous Technology: Technics Out of Control as a Theme in Social and Political Thought*. Boston: MIT Press.

WOODWARD, J. (1958). *Management and Technology*. London: HMSO.

——(1965). *Industrial Organisation*. Oxford: Oxford University Press.

WOTHERSPOON, R. (2002). *Janus: The Multiple Faces of Engineering Design*. Wollongong University.

ZUBOFF, S. (1988). *In the Age of the Smart Machine: The Future of Work and Power*. London: Heinemann.

CHAPTER 6

....

GROUPS, TEAMS, AND THE DIVISION OF LABOR

INTERDISCIPLINARY PERSPECTIVES ON THE ORGANIZATION OF WORK

....

ROSEMARY BATT

VIRGINIA DOELLGAST

6.1 INTRODUCTION

....

OVER the last fifty years, a series of debates have occurred in the workplace and in research journals over the effectiveness of teams as a strategy to organize and compensate work. Small groups and teams have been at the heart of waves of efforts to reform routinized jobs in manufacturing—from the establishment of the human relations school in the 1930s, the growth of the sociotechnical systems movement in the 1950s, and the resurgence of teams at the core of lean production in the 1980s. In contrast to engineering models that seek to maximize individual efficiency, teams have long held the promise of improving worker performance through intrinsic motivation and knowledge sharing.

It is only in the last two decades, however, that we have witnessed a widespread shift in the unit of production from the individual to the group—as firms have adopted lean production, cellular manufacturing, product development teams, and other forms of group work in order to compete more effectively. National surveys show that the prevalence of on-line teams as the unit of production, as well as off-line problem-solving groups, has increased in most advanced economies (Cully *et al.* 1999; OECD 1999; Osterman 2000). At the same time, however, more radical forms of work reorganization, such as autonomous work groups, cover only a minority of workers. In addition, new forms of Taylorized work are emerging in such service activities as retail sales, call centers, IT help desks, and other technology-mediated work.

These trends have spurred a lively and ongoing debate over whether team-based work represents the central organizing principle in 'post-bureaucratic' or 'post-Fordist' organizations. There is disagreement over the extent to which real change has occurred, the source of performance gains, and the outcomes experienced by workers. Management theorists view teams as a source of flexibility and performance gains, labor researchers as a source of liberation from Taylorism, and critics as a scheme to intensify work. Teams are often a point of contention in union–management negotiations because work reorganization fundamentally shapes the quality of jobs and working conditions of employees.

Given the enormous volume of writing on this subject, it is striking that parallel streams of research within and across disciplines have evolved with little integration of the insights from alternative traditions. At a time when firms have embraced team structures to break down bureaucratic organization, academic researchers have continued to operate in disciplinary and theoretical silos.

The purpose of this chapter is to survey and critique this varied landscape of research on groups at work, drawing out common themes and selective weaknesses with the goal of suggesting a more synthetic and informed future agenda. Our discussion is not encyclopedic, but rather focused on three quite different research traditions: those based in psychology, in industrial relations, and in critical sociology. We outline the intellectual landscape of each case and highlight areas of agreement and disagreement. We argue that this project of cross-disciplinary theory building encounters substantial challenges, but is rich in potential. These traditions differ in their theoretical assumptions, research questions and methods, and outcomes of interest. Nonetheless, we suggest that building a more multi-disciplinary research agenda is worthwhile and conclude with suggestions for further work in this direction.

6.2 Psychological Approaches
to Small Groups and Teams

Research on small groups in social psychology and organizational behavior developed some of the earliest critiques of the assumptions underlying Taylor's scientific management and helped to legitimize a shift in the unit of production from the individual to the group level. Theoretical and empirical work in these traditions analyzes the internal characteristics of groups that lead to better performance. The subject of this research is stable work groups, where members are interdependent, are perceived by others as a group, and have significant relations with other groups in a larger system (Hackman 1987).

Three traditions provide distinct theoretical explanations for why individuals perform better in groups than in isolation: sociotechnical systems (STS) theory, group effectiveness theory, and information processing theories. STS theory, originating at the Tavistock Institute in the United Kingdom in 1950 and taken up by Scandinavian researchers in the 1960s and 1970s, intersected with the primarily US-based group effectiveness theory that emerged in the 1970s and 1980s. These two traditions have involved considerable cross-fertilization (see Cordery 2003 and Tubbs 1994 for excellent reviews), but have maintained alternative causal explanations, with the former focused on group self-regulation and the latter on group motivation. Both also share a normative concern for humanizing work through team-based redesign. Information processing theory and social cognition, originating more recently, focus on performance gains from information and knowledge sharing in groups and reflect the growing interest in knowledge as a source of competitive advantage.

6.2.1 Sociotechnical Systems and Group Effectiveness Research

STS theory was an early attempt to articulate the processes that link team-based forms of work to organizational and worker outcomes (Trist and Murray 1990). It not only shifted the unit of analysis from the individual to the work group but also conceptualized workers as thinking actors rather than non-thinking extensions of dedicated machinery. Effective organizational design was conceptualized as the joint optimization of technical and social systems, thus challenging the idea that labor is a residual category in a technically engineered production system. According to STS theory, workers at the point of production jointly design work and solve problems through group self-regulation, thereby contributing to both better performance and more intrinsically satisfying work. Group learning and problem solving allow workers to work smarter—not harder or longer. STS researchers emphasized a 'systems' approach in which work groups interact with technology to ease or obstruct information flows and to foster reevaluation and redesign. These sociotechnical systems were viewed as embedded in larger organizational and institutional contexts.

The qualitative and action research methods in the STS tradition facilitated rich descriptions of actual work and organizational change processes and allowed for a comprehension of the workplace as a complex set of relationships. However, STS research has typically failed to develop testable propositions or to carefully measure constructs and outcomes. It is frequently criticized for its overzealous advocacy of work redesign as a panacea to workplace problems. In addition, while STS theory articulated the links between technology, social organization, and broader institutions, most empirical studies focused on the social organization of work—so that STS research became synonymous with self-managed teams.

While STS theory was most developed in Scandinavia (Berggren 1992), it was also influential in other parts of Europe and Australia (Badham, Couchman, and Selden 1999; Jurgens, Malsch, and Dohse 1993) and in the United States (e.g. Cohen, Ledford, and Spreitzer 1996; Kolodny and Kiggundu 1980). Most of the US literature on group effectiveness, however, drew primary inspiration from input-process-output models (e.g. McGrath 1984) and Hackman and Oldham's (1980) job characteristics model, which emphasized individual task characteristics (autonomy, variety, significance, feedback, and ability to complete a whole task) as the source of intrinsic satisfaction and motivation. Researchers empirically tested this model at the group level (Wall *et al.* 1986), and Hackman's (1987) more complex model guided many empirical studies in the 1990s (e.g. Campion, Medsker, and Higgs 1993).

The strengths and weaknesses of the US literature are in many ways a mirror image of those of the STS literature. US researchers focused heavily on measuring work group constructs (such as task design, interdependence, cohesion, and norms) and testing quantitative relationships between group characteristics and outcomes. While some scholars began to integrate organizational context into their work (e.g. Ancona and Caldwell 1992; Cohen, Ledford, and Spreitzer 1996; Sundstrom and Altman 1989), most have paid little attention to context and no attention to technology, despite exhortations by intellectual leaders to do so (e.g. Goodman 1986; Hackman 1987). While organizational behavior research has provided insights into group task design and employee behavior, it typically measures a narrow set of employee attitudes, such as satisfaction and intrinsic motivation, as outcomes. Its focus on work group characteristics has led to static models of formal structures and outcomes. While processes such as group cohesion and norms or motivation are theorized to mediate the relationship between task design and performance, these mediated models have rarely been tested.

The empirical research in both the STS and group effectiveness traditions has contributed substantially to our knowledge of how teams work and why, at least in some cases, they improve performance. It has found consistent support for the idea that workers in self-managed teams or more autonomous work groups enjoy higher levels of intrinsic satisfaction and motivation (Cohen and Bailey 1997; Cordery 2003; Guzzo and Dickson 1996; Pearce and Ravlin 1987). Researchers from both traditions also concur that these forms of teamwork are associated with better performance, especially when compared to other types of work reform—such as individual employee participation, or quality circles or other consultative groups that are parallel to the production process (Cohen and Bailey 1997).

The distinct theoretical and methodological approaches across the two traditions, however, has led to a persistent divide between European and US scholarship and has made it difficult to develop meaningful learning and integration of findings. STS theory emphasized the way that workers as a group learn from self-regulation, took a systems approach to integrating the technical and social side of work, and relied primarily on qualitative methods. The US literature, by contrast, focused on task design rather than worker agency, emphasized motivation as the key causal mechanism for improved performance, paid little attention to technology or context, and was primarily quantitative. Perhaps the most important distinction between the two is the strong orientation toward worker outcomes in the STS tradition compared to the US literature's focus on the value of teamwork for management.

6.2.2 Information Sharing and Social Cognition

In contrast to the STS and group effectiveness literature, studies of information processing and 'social cognition' are in their infancy. Research in this area is primarily concerned with the relationships between individuals' knowledge and the group's knowledge, asking what is the mental life or 'mind' of the group, and how is it similar to, or different from, the mental life of its individual members. Three main theoretical approaches have emerged: team mental models theory (Cannon-Bowers, Salas, and Converse 1993), group information sharing theory (Stasser and Titus 1985), and transactive memory (Wegner 1987).

The first approach views shared knowledge as a collective good, with each team member working from the same set of premises or 'mental model' (e.g. Cannon-Bowers, Salas, and Converse 1993). According to this theory, the shared understanding of work tasks and processes by group members should produce better coordination and efficient group functioning. To date, however, this literature lacks clear definitions and measures of cognitive structures at the group level. Furthermore, almost all of the work in this area is conceptual or based on lab studies.

The information sharing approach, by contrast, is focused on how individuals in groups deal with shared and unshared information (Stasser 1992; Stasser and Titus 1985). The assumption behind much of the literature on teams (as in STS theory, TQM, and group decision making) is that groups with diverse members should be able to pool information and thereby have access to a wider array of ideas and solutions than would otherwise be possible. Stasser and his colleagues, however, have shown that groups tend to focus on the information that is shared, to the neglect of the unshared information held uniquely by some members. This process, referred to as biased sampling, may undermine the creative problem solving assumed to be the source of performance gains from teamwork. Numerous lab studies have replicated these findings, but as field research is yet to be undertaken, we know little about why or under what conditions individuals share information or not in different team settings.

The third approach, transactive memory, refers to a collective memory system, in which individual group members know the domains of expertise of other members and are able to access and/or utilize that information for the group's benefit. The theory grows out of work by Wegner (1987), who observed that married couples develop a division of labor in which each partner knows what the other is good at and relies on the partner to carry out those tasks. At the level of work groups, members learn 'who knows what', so they are able to call on each others' area of expertise. Lab studies, for example, have shown that groups with behavioral indicators of transactive memory perform better at group tasks (Liang, Moreland, and Argote 1995). Recent research has begun to develop ways to measure this construct so that it may be used in field research (Lewis 2003). The concept is useful for understanding how groups may develop an efficient system of specialization, but it does not explain why group members are motivated to share their expertise or suggest a dynamic process of learning in groups.

These theories of groups put knowledge sharing, information exchange, expertise, and learning in the foreground of research interest, paralleling a growing focus on these more 'intangible' tools in the organizational behavior and business management literature. However, while promising, they are at a very early stage. The literature is primarily conceptual or based on lab studies, and measures of central constructs such as group mental models, knowledge or information sharing, and learning are yet to be developed. Its major contribution is to suggest both the importance and the problematic nature of knowledge sharing and learning within groups. Researchers have not yet tackled such questions as under which conditions teams do better when they have shared understandings or are able to act as interchangeable parts; or when is it important to design teams that bring together diverse areas of expertise to encourage creativity in problem solving and learning. Also yet to be addressed are more fundamental questions, such as what motivates workers to share their expertise (e.g. between experienced and novice workers) or how they learn on the job. Finally, these cognitive approaches lack the normative lens of the prior literatures and show little learning or incorporation of the findings from STS or group effectiveness research.

In sum, psychological research on teams provides a number of useful theoretical lenses on the relationship between group forms of work organization and performance. By focusing on processes and characteristics within work groups, researchers are able to carefully examine the internal variables that distinguish between successful and unsuccessful teams. Taken as a whole, however, these diverse traditions lack a coherent account of the relative importance of or interaction between different motivational and cognitive processes in groups.

More generally, an exclusive focus on social psychological processes as the explanation for work group performance fails to take seriously the economics of production systems and how these vary across industry and institutional contexts. By focusing on the work group as the unit of analysis, researchers in organizational behavior have failed to capture workers in relation to the entire division of labor. In a study of self-managed teams of technicians, for example, Batt (2001a) showed that the teams absorbed the tasks of supervisors in two-thirds less time, reducing indirect labor costs without affecting objective indicators of performance. A focus on teams as the unit of analysis alone would have failed to find these effects, and thus come to faulty conclusions about the mechanisms through which teamwork contributes to outcomes.

Finally, worker outcomes are narrowly conceptualized and tested throughout this literature. There is no attention paid to issues such as wages, work hours, overtime pay, job-related stress, employment security, or conflict at work. Scholars are overly optimistic about the potential for teams to produce mutual gains by solving production problems and simultaneously creating intrinsically interesting jobs. The tension between formal structures and informal group relations, as found in the Hawthorne studies or other early accounts of groups, is largely absent in recent theory and research. Conflicts between goals of different actors at work is thus generally viewed as an obstacle to be overcome on the road to harmonizing outcomes rather than as a constant dynamic within the workplace.

6.3 INDUSTRIAL RELATIONS AND INSTITUTIONAL PERSPECTIVES

The role of economic institutions and competing interests, lacking in the small group literature, is at the forefront of research on work organization in industrial relations. Research in this tradition integrates theories from economics and sociology to analyze how macro-level institutions shape choices in production systems at the level of the firm and establishment. Industrial relations scholars have paid close attention to the role of technology, product and labor market institutions, and public policy in driving and shaping employer decisions regarding the organization of work. They also view labor and management as social groups with different economic interests, accepting ongoing conflict and cooperation as a natural feature of employment relations. The organization of work is one arena in which labor and management contend for control, and they may or may not be able to negotiate rules for teamwork that are mutually beneficial.

Industrial relations scholars view work organization as only one element in complex production systems, such as mass production manufacturing, in contrast to the psychology-based literature's work group focus. This systems approach seeks to explain why management adopts certain combinations of employment practices within particular employment settings or historical periods. Doeringer and Piore (1971), for example, characterized mass production as including dedicated technology, Taylorized work with low skill and training requirements, seniority-based job ladders, and seniority-based pay. Osterman (1987) further elaborated this theory, identifying four interlocking dimensions of internal labor market rules: skill requirements of jobs, labor organization and deployment, compensation rules, and employment mobility and security rules. These 'rules' may be viewed as the functional equivalent of work organization and human resource practices, and different systems were expected to prevail in different kinds of workplaces, from a white-collar bureaucratic setting to a mass production factory.

This industrial relations systems approach has several methodological implications. First, the arena of research is typically a specific industry or occupation, as shaped by product and labor market institutions. This draws attention to the relationship between business strategy, technology, management practices, and labor relations. Second, industrial relations scholars view work organization or teams as part of a cluster of management practices—rather than viewing work groups as the focal point and organizational context as backdrop. Thus, the unit of analysis is typically the establishment (or entire work system), not the work group. Researchers also pay close attention to the measurement of technology and the economics of the production system—not only the social organization of work and behavioral outcomes. Finally, this focus on systems and context leads industrial relations researchers to use more context-specific measures of work practices and operational outcomes than those used by psychologists, who depend more on psychometric scales designed to be generalizable across contexts.

6.3.1 High Performance Work Systems

An influential stream of research emerging from the industrial relations tradition is found in the literature on high performance work systems (HPWS). These systems are typically defined as the opposite of the mass production model. That is, jobs require relatively high skills; work is organized to promote employee discretion and collaboration or teamwork; and employees are motivated by incentives and rewards such as investment in training, high relative pay plus some performance-based pay, and employment security (Appelbaum and Batt 1994; Appelbaum *et al.* 2000). These systems are thought to allow firms to compete more effectively on quality and customization because they allow workers to solve production problems and to use their skills more effectively. Implicit in HPWS research is the notion that these higher productivity jobs also pay off for workers, providing higher pay and more intrinsically satisfying work. Some researchers refer to these systems as 'high involvement', thereby emphasizing the involvement of workers in problem solving (Batt 2002; MacDuffie 1995), while others conceptualize them as 'high commitment', emphasizing their motivational aspects (Wood and Albanese 1995).

Research on high performance work systems in the United States relies on qualitative and quantitative studies of establishments in specific industries and addresses the empirical question of whether high performance systems (compared to mass production systems) lead to substantially better economic performance for firms. Studies set in manufacturing industries found substantial economic benefits from HPWSs in apparel (Appelbaum *et al.* 2000), auto assembly (MacDuffie 1995; Pil and MacDuffie 1996; Rubenstein 2000), medical electronics (Appelbaum *et al.* 2000), semi-conductors (Appleyard and Brown 2001; Bailey 1998), computers (Bresnahan, Brynjolfsson, and Hitt 2002), and steel (Appelbaum *et al.* 2000; Arthur 1994; Ichniowski, Shaw, and Prennushi 1997). Consistent with the systems approach, most of these studies have conceptualized bundles of practices that logically fit together, measuring these through cluster analysis or additive indices.

A second generation of research examined the same set of issues in service workplaces. They found that the systemic differences in production systems identified in manufacturing—for example, between mass and lean production—were less developed or pronounced in service settings. However, where differences in work organization were identified, these studies also found that team-based forms of work contributed to substantially better performance in airlines (Gittell 2002), hospitals (Preuss 2003), call centers (Batt 1999, 2002), and among field technicians (Batt 2001*a*).

While this research has focused on the question of organizational performance, it differs markedly from the approach found in the strategic human resource management literature (e.g. Huselid 1995; see Legge, in this volume for a discussion). The industrial relations tradition is grounded in real industries, takes technology seriously, draws on extensive qualitative field research, uses context-specific measures of work practices and performance, and often examines the role of labor–management relations.

As a body of work, HPWS research suggests two conclusions concerning the contribution of teamwork to organizational performance. First, at a general level, team-based or collaborative forms of work appear to outperform individually based Taylorized systems. However, second, there is wide variation in what teamwork or collaboration means in different work settings and the extent to which it is able to affect performance. This suggests both a universal and context-contingent interpretation of how alternative forms of work organization are associated with economic outcomes. In steel mills, for example, Appelbaum and her colleagues (2000) found that the critical performance outcome is machine uptime due to heavy investment in capital equipment. The aspect of 'teamwork' that mattered was intergroup communication and coordination across miles of rolling mills and finishing lines—so that the continuous process would not shut down. In apparel plants, by contrast, the critical performance metric involved reducing throughput time in order to respond quickly to retail demands. By shifting from the progressive bundle system to modular (self-directed) teams, whole garments could be produced by multi-skilled teams in a fraction of the time previously taken (Appelbaum *et al.* 2000). In call centers, self-directed work groups had better sales than traditionally supervised groups, not because of intergroup communication or job rotation and multi-skilling (as interdependence was low and all workers handle individual customers), but because workers in teams taught each other how to handle tough customers and how to use new software programs more rapidly (Batt 1999). In airlines, it was the use of cross-functional teams that improved on-time departures through tight coordination across departments (ticketing, baggage, mechanics, flight attendants) (Gittell 2002). In semi-conductor fabs, it is multi-occupational teams that provide better output (Bailey 1998). These findings suggest that while teamwork may be associated with better performance in a variety of settings, there are often different reasons for these performance gains due to variation in technical systems.

Despite the contributions of the US HPWS approach, there are several conceptual and methodological weaknesses. First, the 'systems' or bundle approach makes it difficult to evaluate the relative importance of different dimensions of the system—such as teams—to outcomes for firms or workers. Moreover, the focus on internal coherence among human resource practices has led researchers to pay less attention to potentially contradictory practices, such as the simultaneous use of 'commitment enhancing' teams, downsizing, and outsourcing. Critics have also argued that the US literature exaggerates the conceptual contrasts between mass production and lean production (Delbridge 1998).

The high performance literature is also theoretically undeveloped. Empirical studies have found statistical associations between management practices and performance outcomes without measuring underlying causal mechanisms. Much of the research builds on an implicit human capital model in which workers are more productive because they have higher firm-specific skills, opportunity to use those skills, and incentives to do so. This argument does not differentiate between explanations based on individual motivation (working harder), cognition (working smarter), or social behavior (e.g. working together). The HPWS literature also has failed to move beyond single organizational units, despite the fact that supply chain management has emerged as a critical organizational innovation. Finally, critics charge that the US literature has abandoned its traditional concern for worker welfare (Godard and Delaney 2000). While some studies have examined how union strategies can bring about better outcomes for workers (e.g. Frost 2000), most of the US literature is overly optimistic about the use of teams and does not seriously examine conflicts marking formal or informal labor relations in the 'new' workplace.

Like the US literature, European (British and continental) scholarship on team-work and high performance work organization is primarily based on research in manufacturing plants, especially in the auto sector. Early debates focused on the differences between STS-inspired team-based plants and Japanese-inspired lean production, with a large number of case studies showing substantially higher decision-making discretion and job satisfaction in the former cases (e.g. Berggren 1992; Buchanan and McCalman 1989). These debates are similar to those found in the US literature (Appelbaum and Batt 1994).

Beyond these similarities, however, there are substantial differences between US and European traditions. In general, the European literature on teams has been more influenced by critical perspectives, which are discussed in greater detail below. Researchers have focused primarily on outcomes for workers rather than plant performance (e.g. Procter and Mueller 2000; Whitfield and Poole 1997). More often than not, they have examined the reality of work reorganization in typical plants—rather than structured comparisons of clearly alternative approaches as in the US literature. Danford's (1998) study of seventeen Japanese electronics plants in South Wales is exemplary: he showed that most operated as classic assembly line operations; and those that adopted 'teamwork' provided workers with only minimal involvement in production-level decisions.

The qualitative case study approach used in the United Kingdom, Europe, and Australia has produced more nuanced interpretations of the benefits and trade-offs of team-based systems in different organizational and institutional contexts. While some find that the use of teams is associated with greater employee influence over work operations and greater job satisfaction (Marchington 2000), others report more mixed outcomes. In their study of self-managed teams in a continuous processing aluminum plant, for example, Wright and Edwards (1998) showed that teams experienced work intensification and inconsistent management support as well as greater autonomy, responsibility, knowledge of the production system, and satisfaction. Analyses of the British Workplace Employment Relations Survey

(WERS) data also provide mixed accounts, showing that benefits from teams and HPWSs, such as greater influence, discretion, satisfaction, commitment, and job security, are accompanied by higher job strain (Ramsay, Scholarios, and Harley 2000). Delbridge and Whitfield's (2001) analysis showed that workers in establishments with greater use of quality circles and work teams reported having more influence at work than those in more traditional workplaces; however, those with representative (union) participation had greater influence. The central message in this literature is that work restructuring is a complex and contradictory process. The central problem is that concepts are not clearly defined or consistently applied, making comparisons across studies difficult (Marchington 2000). In addition, case studies often attribute outcomes to 'teamwork' when in fact the organization of work is only one element of organizational restructuring.

6.4 CRITICAL SOCIOLOGY

Beyond simply adding complexity to the story of organizational restructuring and performance, critical scholars in sociology provided a healthy antidote to the generally optimistic assessment of teams and teamwork found in the psychological and HPWS literatures. Focused on outcomes for workers and skeptical of the extent to which real change has occurred, they have drawn attention to 'the "dark side" of new production systems' (Smith and Thompson 1999: 210). In this section, we compare current research on teamwork from two influential critical traditions—labor process theory and postmodern approaches. While there are significant areas of disagreement between the two, they share a common concern with dynamics of conflict, coercion, and consent within the workplace. Both typically use intensive field-based studies to explore their theoretical assumptions and approach teamwork as part of management's strategies to control worker effort and output, rather than as potentially emancipatory forms of work organization.

6.4.1 Labor Process Theory

Labor process scholars are centrally concerned with explaining how management effectively controls worker effort and appropriates the surplus value of labor (Braverman 1974; Burawoy 1979; Thompson 1983). An important debate in this tradition is whether new forms of work organization represent continuity or discontinuity from past management practices, and, further, whether they represent any meaningful change for workers—both fundamentally different questions than those posed in the HPWS literature. In Braverman's (1974) classic portrayal of the deskilling of clerical work under Taylorism, management controls the labor process through the 'separation of conception from execution'. The reintegration of tasks and devolution of management functions to workers associated with post-Fordist, team-based production systems represents a challenge to this deskilling thesis. A variety of new interpretations of teamwork have followed, seeking to place it within the context of evolving management strategies to extend control over worker effort and output.

One interpretation holds that new management practices should be understood as a particular moment in a progression of stages or cycles in which distinct strategies of control dominate during different historical eras. In Edwards's influential theory of historical stages of management control (1979), corporations moved from simple or coercive control in the late nineteenth century to technological control in the Fordist assembly line, and then to bureaucratic control in the hierarchical organization of the mid-twentieth century. At each stage, the mechanism of appropriation changed. Under Fordism, management control over the labor process occurred through the separation of conception from execution and the detailed division of labor. In post-Fordist regimes, the use of teams to reintegrate conception and execution of tasks represents an alternative mechanism of control.

Labor process researchers have stressed the continuity of new forms of work with Taylorism, defining new production systems not as 'post-Fordist' but 'neo-Fordist'. They have relied heavily on evidence from lean production team settings, arguing that the use of off-line 'quality circles', multi-skilling, and just-in-time production techniques typically involve little substantive redistribution of responsibility to workers. Instead, the central mechanism of performance improvement is work intensification combined with strategies to mine workers' tacit knowledge in pursuit of continuous improvement. The result is the reproduction of hierarchical control coupled with more effective mechanisms to secure worker consent. Adler's (1995) study of the GM-Toyota NUMMI plant, for example, depicts lean production as 'democratic Taylorism'. Parker and Slaughter (1988) provide a similar, if more negative, analysis of the NUMMI system, describing it as 'a kind of super-Taylorism' where teamwork is little more than 'management by stress'. Moreover, the union's role in defending worker interests is undermined when it cooperates in implementing the system and accepts restrictions on its grievance-processing role. Garrahan and Stewart (1992) critique lean production as constraining union power and bolstering management's control over labor, while Delbridge (1998: 204) argues that Japanese lean production techniques are little more than 'an extension of the principles of Taylor through the systematic standardization and proceduralization of tasks within a context of heightened managerial dominance and control'. Other studies in this vein include Rinehart, Huxley, and Robertson's (1997) study of the

CAMI auto plant in Canada, and Babson's (1995) compilation of critical studies of lean production in autos.

These accounts of lean production in the auto industry suggest that its effectiveness as a strategy of work organization stems from its success at securing workers' commitment while intensifying their exploitation. This echoes the themes found in Burawoy's (1979) politics of production in which workers consent to their own exploitation, but adds a focus on production efficiency and conflicts over controlling worker knowledge essential to improving that efficiency. Accounts vary in the extent to which they give space to conflict on the shop floor. Unions are often viewed either as potential collaborators in the exploitation of employees or as marginalized actors in more encompassing systems of control. This helps to explain limited union success in certain Japanese transplants, but does not engage with examples from the institutional literature of union involvement in democratizing teamwork and improving employee outcomes.

Labor process scholars' recognition of workplace conflict and attention to the historical and economic context of shifting management strategies shares much conceptual ground with industrial relations and institutional traditions. However, their use of tools of analysis provided by critical theory combined with in-depth ethnographies of workplaces allows them to explore the interaction between formal and informal shop-floor dynamics often missing from institutional accounts. Perhaps most importantly, by analyzing resistance as a response to relationships of control extending beyond the firm, these theorists challenge scholars to be wary of emancipatory rhetoric accompanying teamwork and flexible production. Instead, they suggest, the disciplines of capital markets and increased global competition have created often contradictory pressures for rationalization and enhanced employee discretionary effort.

6.4.2 Postmodern and Foucauldian Interpretations

In contrast to the focus on lean production in the labor process literature, postmodern theorists have used self-managed teams as a setting for theory building (e.g. Barker 1993; Ezzamel and Willmott 1998; Sewell 1998). In doing so, they have emphasized more discontinuity than continuity with the past. Barker's ethnography of self-managed teams in an electronics plant, for example, begins with Tompkins and Cheney's (1985) theory that new forms of work organization represent a fourth stage of 'concertative' control, building on Edward's schema of progressive changes in management strategy. In place of hierarchical rules imposed by an impersonal bureaucracy, self-managed teams shift the locus of control to workers. These workers then develop a consensus around core values and norms, formalize them as rules of proper behavior designed to maximize quality and productivity, and enforce these rules through peer group pressure and monitoring. They work harder, longer, and are under more stress than before, but paradoxically reject a return to prior forms because they enjoy and take pride in their work. Sewell (1998) shares Barker's concern with the insidious effects of new, normative forms of control in self-managing teams, but argues that teams are often complementary to hierarchical forms of control. He, too, identifies a 'new disciplinary mode' in his ethnography of an electronics firm, which he terms 'chimerical control'. Teams set their own sanctions and rewards (horizontal control), while management information systems identified quality errors, flagging good and bad performers with 'traffic lights' (vertical control).

These two accounts interpret teamwork as a more insidious form of management control than that found under Fordism. Management traps the worker within an 'iron cage' or a web of control limited only by the reach and scope of the surveillance system. In later work (1993), Barker links his theory more fully to postmodern rhetorical theory and Foucault's vision of society as a panopticon, or a prison in which inmates are under constant surveillance from both the guards and one another. These authors share the small group literature's emphasis on employee motivation as the source of performance gains from teams, but they argue that the source of this motivation is coercion rather than the more neutral idea of employee attitudes and goal alignment. Indeed, this focus on the dynamics of worker motivation seems to turn on its head the STS and small group literature's preoccupation with employee satisfaction and organizational commitment.

A notable drawback of these studies is that despite their qualitative methods, they often neglect important aspects of organizational and institutional context. Barker's theory, for example, relies on identity formation in teams, without considering other sources of identity formation such as race, gender, community, religion, or political affiliation. The focus of Foucauldian accounts on encompassing or totalizing control has also drawn criticism from scholars who object to the lack of worker agency or to the neglect of the economic or institutional structures in which workplaces are embedded. One version of this critique holds to a postmodern interpretation of the mechanisms of control in modern teamwork, but argues that worker resistance may be an unintended consequence of power when it conflicts with other forms of worker identity (Knights and McCabe 1998). Ezzamel and Willmott's (1998) case study of work reorganization in an apparel factory traces the shift from a piece-rate system to a team-based pay system, finding that workers refused to assume new self-managing responsibilities due to conflicts with their identities as mates and collaborators. Thus, employees may react differently to the demands of teams as their practical concerns—described here as self-identity or subjectivity—mediate between structure and outcome.

Other critical scholars object to these attempts to bring postmodern traditions to bear on analysis of the labor process, arguing that the distinctive dynamics of control and resistance in capitalism are obscured by a preoccupation with expressions of worker identity and their subjugation to normalizing disciplines (Smith and Thompson 1999). Heated debates have ensued between labor process and Foucauldian theorists. Several case studies have shown that workers do not easily buy into management rhetoric. In their study of several Volvo truck plants, for example, Thompson and Wallace (1996) found little evidence that management used teams as a means of normative regulation. A study of the Scottish Spirits industry showed that workers were positive about the principles of teamwork and relations with coworkers; but they remained critical of management, saw normative training as 'brainwashing', and their attitudes about teamwork were juxtaposed against their overall concerns about job insecurity and instability (Findlay *et al.* 2000). Similarly, in their study of a Scottish electronics plant, McKinlay and Taylor (1996) showed that workforce resistance combined with competitive pressure led to the unraveling of a comprehensive peer review system. Students of the labor process have also paid somewhat more attention to the implications of work reorganization for unions (Ackers, Smith, and Smith 1996; Bacon and Storey 1995; Garrahan and Stewart 1992).

In summary, the labor process and postmodern traditions contribute important insights into debates over the relationship between modern forms of teamwork and Taylorist production strategies, and present work intensification as a more plausible mechanism through which teams influence performance. Research from both traditions draws attention to continuities in dynamics of power, control, and resistance in teams, casting doubt on optimistic visions of a flexible and empowered post-bureaucratic workplace. Similar to the psychological literature, however, neither tradition has given the kind of attention to the economics of production systems and mechanisms of performance gains that are the hallmark of the HPWS literature.

6.5 CONCLUSIONS: COMPLEMENTARITIES ACROSS TRADITIONS

Our review of alternative approaches to team-based work highlights important differences in the kinds of research questions raised, the methods used, and the outcomes of interest across several research traditions. Some of these differences are fundamental—such as theoretical assumptions regarding the level of conflict between labor and management at work. These assumptions also shape alternative research methodologies. The epistemological models underlying each tradition stem from radically different assumptions about the linearity of relationships among phenomena, the role of the researcher, and the validity and generalizability of qualitative versus quantitative methodologies.

Some differences, however, are probably less fundamental. Here, we believe that incremental steps can be made to increase learning across disciplines and theoretical traditions. For example, students of organizational behavior have long argued that their research on groups at work must incorporate a richer understanding of organizational context, but few have done so in a convincing manner. They could learn much from industrial relations scholarship, particularly regarding the relationship between work organization and technology and the importance of understanding the economics of production. This would allow them to articulate a broader array of relevant outcomes and to move away from 'context as backdrop' in order to develop richer insights into how organizational conditions shape implementation. Researchers in organizational behavior would also benefit from the skepticism found in the critical literature on teams. While some have studied interpersonal versus substantive conflict within groups (e.g. Jehn 1995), they have not paid attention to issues such as peer group pressure or conflicts between work teams and management or other occupational groups at work.

Similarly, students of industrial relations, who are strong on context but weak on theory, would benefit from examining alternative theories of information processing and social cognition to better understand how individuals in groups solve problems, share knowledge, and learn from each other in ways that affect their performance. While studies of high performance systems provided explanations of how and why team-based work is associated with better performance, they have not developed careful measures of processes at work nor have they tested mediating mechanisms. Some recently developed measures of knowledge sharing in the organizational behavior literature (e.g. Lewis 2003) could provide a point of integration.

Another arena for complementary work is across US and European traditions. The US research in high performance work organization has focused primarily on performance outcomes, using large-scale quantitative data across establishments to generate results. European studies have focused more on implications for workers, often relying on qualitative case studies. These differences, however, are beginning to change. Examples include the large-scale study of performance among auto suppliers by Delbridge and colleagues and analyses of the British WERS that test the links between management practices and performance (Ramsay, Scholarios, and Harley 2000). Similarly, recent studies in the United States have focused on the relationship between HPWS and workers' outcomes, including wages, satisfaction, and stress (Appelbaum *et al.* 2000); wage inequality (Batt 2001*b*); and wages and layoffs (Osterman 2000). A 2004 special issue of *Industrial Relations* on outcomes for workers concluded that many programs have no effect on worker pay, but that on average, workers realize a small increase in wages after the introduction of new work systems with higher employee involvement (Handel and Levine 2004).

One area where debate and dialogue have occurred is among critical scholars in the labor process and Foucauldian traditions. As our review indicates, while team-based work may involve greater peer group pressure and surveillance in some instances, a large number of case studies have shown that this is probably not a dominant pattern. Rather there is a wide range of variation in outcomes, which depend importantly on such factors as history, institutional context, and the strategies of employers and unions. This research would benefit, however, from input from psychologists trained in defining and measuring certain of their concepts more precisely—such as the meaning of peer group monitoring, group cohesion, normative control, and surveillance.

Beyond these incremental steps, there are several areas where common ground appears to be growing. First, there is greater recognition of the need to define and measure different dimensions of team-based work more carefully. While this is a long-standing concern of organizational behavior researchers, those in industrial relations and critical studies also have recognized that using different definitions prevents meaningful comparisons across studies. Marchington (2000) provides a useful framework, which captures the degree, scope, level, and form of teamwork. Alternatively, Thompson and Wallace (1996) distinguish between the technical, governance, and normative dimensions of teams.

Second, there is growing awareness of the need to examine a broader array of outcomes from team-based work organization. For workers, these include not only conventional measures of job satisfaction, commitment, and the like, but job security, pay, workloads, job-related stress, and work–family conflict. Similarly, organizational performance measures need to capture not only specific operational measures of quality and efficiency, but labor inputs such as hours of work and labor costs. As research on service activities grows, there is also a need to understand the relationship between management practices, worker experiences, and consumer outcomes.

A third area of growing consensus is the desirability of multi-method studies that focus on particular industries and occupations. Multiple methods include careful field research and observation, interviews at various levels of the organization, surveys to quantify what is observed in fieldwork, and matching of perceptual and archival datasets. One-off case studies of convenience make meaningful comparisons difficult and often yield little beyond descriptive stories.

Fourth, many see the need to move beyond a single unit (the work group, the organization) and examine work organization at multiple levels of analysis. This goes beyond the idea of placing teams in organizational or institutional context. Rather, it is about studying the relations within and across work groups and organizational units. This approach may be particularly useful for studies of supply chain management. New statistical packages such as hierarchical linear modeling also facilitate this type of analysis. More importantly, many have seen the theoretical limits of studying fixed structures and are beginning to conceptualize groups at work in terms of ongoing relationships and processes. This has led scholars to explore the concept of organizational social capital—the relations of trust and knowledge sharing among employees—as a mechanism for performance gains (Leana and Pil 2002). It has also led to experiments with social network analysis, as in Rubenstein's study of the role of the union at the Saturn auto plant (2000).

Fifth, the awareness of globalization has highlighted the need for more sophisticated cross-national research. Other than the rich literature on the international auto sector and the role of national institutions in shaping alternative management practices, few international comparisons of work organization in other industries have occurred. Comparative international studies of work organization in services would be particularly valuable because the historic role of unions and other institutions that have influenced manufacturing may be lacking in many service settings. Studies examining the same corporations operating in distinct national contexts would contribute much to our understanding of the relative importance of institutions and employer strategies in shaping the organization of work and related outcomes.

These directions point to the need for large-scale research projects that bring together psychologists, sociologists, and industrial relations scholars with complementary strengths and expertise. There is also a need for more coordinated international research that compares work restructuring in advanced and industrializing economies. These types of endeavors require major commitments in terms of time and resources, and academics often have limited incentives to undertake such projects. Academic disciplines and journals continue to discourage interdisciplinary work. New systems of management in academia have also pushed scholars to publish large quantities of articles, often recycling their data sets and arguments. It is time, however, to move beyond separate silos and narrow research agendas in order to develop a more theoretically rich and integrated understanding of the organization of work in the next century.

REFERENCES

ACKERS, P., SMITH, C., and SMITH, P. (eds.) (1996). *The New Workplace and Trade Unionism.* London: Routledge.

ADLER, P. (1995). '"Democratic Taylorism": The Toyota Production System at NUMMI', in S. Babson (ed.), *Lean Work: Empowerment and Exploitation in the Global Auto Industry.* Detroit: Wayne State University Press.

ANCONA, D. G., and CALDWELL, D. F. (1992). 'Demography and Design—Predictors of New Product Team Performance'. *Organization Science,* 3/3: 321–41.

APPELBAUM, E., and BATT, R. (1994). *The New American Workplace.* Ithaca, NY: Cornell University ILR Press.

—— BAILEY, T., BERG, P., and KALLEBERG, A. L. (2000). *Manufacturing Advantage: Why High Performance Work Systems Pay Off*. Ithaca, NY: Cornell University Press.

APPLEYARD, M. M., and BROWN, C. (2001). 'Employment Practices and Semiconductor Manufacturing Performance'. *Industrial Relations*, 40/3: 436–74.

ARTHUR, J. B. (1994). 'Effects of Human Resource Systems on Manufacturing Performance and Turnover'. *Academy of Management Journal*, 37/3: 670–87.

BABSON, S. (ed.) (1995). *Lean Work: Empowerment and Exploitation in the Global Auto Industry*. Detroit: Wayne State University Press.

BACON, N., and STOREY, J. (1995). 'Individualism and Collectivism and the Changing Role of Trade Unionism', in P. Ackers, C. Smith, and P. Smith (eds.), *The New Workplace and Trade Unionism*. London: Routledge.

BADHAM, R., COUCHMAN, P., and SELDEN, D. (1999). 'Alternative Socio-technical Systems in the Asia–Pacific Region: An International Survey of Team-based Cellular Manufacturing', in S. Clegg, E. Ibarro, and L. Bueno (eds.), *Global Management: Universal Theories and Local Realities*. London and Thousand Oaks, Calif.: Sage Publications.

BAILEY, D. E. (1998). 'Comparison of Manufacturing Performance of Three Team Structures in Semiconductor Plants'. *IEEE Transactions on Engineering Management*, 45/1: 1–13.

BARKER, J. R. (1993). 'Tightening the Iron Cage: Concertive Control in Self-Managing Teams'. *Administrative Science Quarterly*, 38: 408–37.

BATT, R. (1999). 'Work Organization, Technology, and Performance in Customer Service and Sales'. *Industrial and Labor Relations Review*, 52/4: 539–64.

—— (2001a). 'The Economics of Teams among Technicians'. *British Journal of Industrial Relations*, 39/1: 1–24.

—— (2001b). 'Explaining Wage Inequality in Telecommunications Services: Customer Segmentation, Human Resource Practices, and Union Decline'. *Industrial and Labor Relations Review*, 54/2A: 425–49.

—— (2002). 'Managing Customer Services: Human Resource Practices, Quit Rates, and Sales Growth'. *Academy of Management Journal*, 45/3: 587–97.

BERGGREN, C. (1992). *Alternatives to Lean Production*. Ithaca, NY: Cornell University ILR Press.

BRAVERMAN, H. (1974). *Labor and Monopoly Capital: The Degradation of Work in the Twentieth Century*. New York: Monthly Review Press.

BRESNAHAN, T. F., BRYNJOLFSSON, E., and HITT, L. M. (2002). 'Information Technology, Workplace Organization, and the Demand for Skilled Labor: Firm-level Evidence'. *Quarterly Journal of Economics*, 117: 339–76.

BUCHANAN, D., and McCALMAN, J. (1989). *High Performance Work Design: The Digital Experience*. London: Routledge.

BURAWOY, M. (1979). *Manufacturing Consent: Changes in the Labor Process under Monopoly Capitalism*. Chicago: University of Chicago Press.

CAMPION, M. A., MEDSKER, G. J., and HIGGS, A. C. (1993). 'Relations between Work Group Characteristics and Effectiveness—Implications for Designing Effective Work Groups'. *Personnel Psychology*, 46/4: 823–50.

CANNON-BOWERS, J. A., SALAS, E., and CONVERSE, S. A. (1993). 'Shared Mental Models in Expert Team Decision Making', in N. J. Castellan, Jr. (ed.), *Individual and Group Decision Making: Current Issues*. Hillsdale, NJ: LEA.

COHEN, S., and BAILEY, D. (1997). 'What Makes Teams Work: Group Effectiveness Research from the Shop Floor to the Executive Suite'. *Journal of Management*, 23/3: 229–90.

COHEN, S. G., LEDFORD, G. E., and SPREITZER, G. M. (1996). 'A Predictive Model of Self-Managing Work Team Effectiveness'. *Human Relations*, 49/5: 643–76.

CORDERY, J. (2003). 'Team Work', in D. Holman, T. Wall, C. Clegg, P. Sparrow, and A. Howard (eds.), *The New Workplace: A Guide to the Human Impact of Modern Working Practices*. Chichester, NY: Wiley & Sons.

CULLY, M., O'REILLY, A., MILLWARD, N., FORTH, J., WOODLAND, S., DIX, G., and BRYSON, A. (1999). *Britain at Work: As Depicted by 1998 Workplace Employee Relations Survey*. New York: Routledge.

DANFORD, A. (1998). 'Work Organisation inside Japanese Firms in South Wales: A Break from Taylorism?' in P. Thompson and C. Warhurst (eds.), *Workplaces of the Future*. London: Macmillan.

DELBRIDGE, R. (1998). *Life on the Line in Contemporary Manufacturing*. Oxford: Oxford University Press.

—— and WHITFIELD, K. (2001). 'Employee Perceptions of Job Influence and Organizational Participation'. *Industrial Relations*, 40/3: 472–89.

DOERINGER, P. B., and PIORE, M. J. (1971). *Internal Labor Markets and Manpower Analysis*. Lexington, Mass.: Heath Lexington.

EDWARDS, R. (1979). *Contested Terrain: The Transformation of the Workplace in the Twentieth Century*. New York: Basic Books.

EZZAMEL, M., and WILLMOTT, H. (1998). 'Accounting for Teamwork: A Critical Study of Group Based Systems of Organizational Control'. *Administrative Science Quarterly*, 43: 358–96.

FINDLAY, P., MCKINLAY, A., MARKS, A., and THOMPSON, P. (2000). 'In Search of Perfect People: Teamwork and Team Players in the Scottish Spirits Industry'. *Human Relations*, 43/12: 1549–74.

FROST, A. (2000). 'Explaining Variation in Workplace Restructuring: The Role of Local Union Capabilities'. *Industrial and Labor Relations Review*, 53/4: 559–78.

GARRAHAN, P., and STEWART, C. (1992). *The Nissan Enigma: Flexibility at Work in a Local Economy*. London: Cassell.

GITTELL, J. H. (2002). 'Supervisory Span, Relational Coordination and Fight Departure Performance: A Reassessment of Post-bureaucracy Theory'. *Organization Science*, 12/4: 367–82.

GODARD, J., and DELANEY, J. (2000). 'Reflections on the "High Performance" Paradigm's Implications for Industrial Relations as a Field'. *Industrial and Labor Relations Review*, 53/3: 482–502.

GOODMAN, P. S. (1986). 'Impact of Task and Technology on Group Performance', in P. S. Goodman and Associates (eds.), *Designing Effective Work Groups*. San Francisco: Jossey-Bass.

GUZZO, R. A., and DICKSON, M. W. (1996). 'Teams in Organizations: Recent Research on Performance and Effectiveness'. *Annual Review of Psychology*, 47: 307–38.

HACKMAN, J. R. (1987). 'The Design of Work Teams', in J. Lorsch, *Handbook of Organizational Behavior*. New York: Prentice Hall.

—— and OLDHAM, G. R. (1980). *Work Redesign*. Reading, Mass.: Addison-Wesley.

HANDEL, M., and LEVINE, D. (2004). 'Introduction' to Special Issue: 'The Effects of New Work Practices on Workers'. *Industrial Relations*, 43/1: 1–43.

HUSELID, M. (1995). 'The Impact of Human Resources Management Practices on Turnover, Productivity, and Corporate Financial Performance'. *Academy of Management Journal*, 38: 635–72.

ICHNIOWSKI, C., SHAW, K., and PRENNUSHI, G. (1997). 'The Effects of Human Resource Management Practices on Productivity: A Study of Steel Finishing Lines'. *American Economic Review*, 87/3 (June): 291–313.

JEHN, K. A. (1995). 'A Multimethod Examination of the Benefits and Detriments of Intragroup Conflict'. *Administrative Science Quarterly*, 40: 256–82.

JURGENS, U., MALSCH, T., and DOHSE, K. (1993). *Breaking from Taylorism: Changing Forms of Work in the Automobile Industry*. Cambridge: Cambridge University Press.

KNIGHTS, D., and McCABE, D. (1998). 'Dreams and Designs on Strategy: A Critical Analysis of TQM and Management Control'. *Work, Employment and Society*, 12/3: 433–48.

KOLODNY, H., and KIGGUNDU, M. (1980). 'Towards the Development of a Systems Model in Woodlands Mechanical Harvesting'. *Human Relations*, 33: 623–45.

LEANA, C. R., and PIL, F. K. (2002). *Social Capital in Public Schools*. University of Pittsburgh. Working Paper.

LEWIS, K. (2003). 'Measuring Transactive Memory Systems in the Field: Scale Development and Validation'. *Journal of Applied Psychology*, 88/4: 587–605.

LIANG, D. W., MORELAND, R., and ARGOTE, L. (1995). 'Group versus Individual Training and Group-Performance—the Mediating Role of Transactive Memory'. *Personality and Social Psychology Bulletin*, 21/4: 384–93.

MACDUFFIE, J. P. (1995). 'Human Resource Bundles and Manufacturing Performance: Organizational Logic and Flexible Production Systems in the World Auto Industry'. *Industrial and Labor Relations Review*, 48: 197–221.

McGRATH, J. E. (1984). *Groups: Interaction and Performance*. Englewood Cliffs, NJ: Prentice Hall.

McKINLAY, A., and TAYLOR, P. (1996). 'Power, Surveillance and Resistance: Inside the Factory of the Future', in P. Ackers, C. Smith and P. Smith (eds.), *The New Workplace and Trade Unionism*. London: Routledge.

MARCHINGTON, M. (2000). 'Teamworking and Employee Involvement, Terminology, Evaluation, and Context', in S. Proctor and F. Mueller (eds.), *Teamworking*. London: Macmillan.

OECD (Organization of Economic Cooperation and Development) (1999). 'Employment Outlook: The EPOC Survey'. OECD.

OSTERMAN, P. (1987). 'Choice of Employment Systems in Internal Labor Markets'. *Industrial Relations*, 26/1: 46–67.

—— (2000). 'Work Reorganization in an Era of Restructuring: Trends in the Diffusion and Effects on Employee Welfare'. *Industrial and Labor Relations Review*, 53/2: 179–96.

PARKER, M., and SLAUGHTER, J. (1988). *Choosing Sides: Unions and the Team Concept*. Boston: South End Press.

PEARCE, J. L., and RAVLIN, E. (1987). 'The Design and Activation of Self-Regulating Work Groups'. *Human Relations*, 40: 751–82.

PIL, F. K., and MACDUFFIE, J. P. (1996). 'The Adoption of High-Involvement Work Practices'. *Industrial Relations*, 35/3 (July): 423–55.

PREUSS, G. (2003). 'High Performance Work Systems and Organizational Outcomes: The Mediating Role of Information Quality'. *Industrial and Labor Relations Review*, 56/4: 590–605.

PROCTER, S., and MUELLER, F. (2000). 'Teamworking: Strategy, Structure, Systems and Culture', in S. Proctor and F. Mueller (eds.), *Teamworking*. London: Macmillan.

RAMSAY, H., SCHOLARIOS, D., and HARLEY, B. (2000). 'Employees and High-Performance Work Systems: Testing inside the Black Box'. *British Journal of Industrial Relations*, 38/4: 501–31.

RINEHART, J., HUXLEY, C., and ROBERTSON, D. (1997). *Just Another Car Factory?* Ithaca, NY: ILR Press.

RUBENSTEIN, S. (2000). 'The Impact of Co-management on Quality Performance: The Case of the Saturn Corporation'. *Industrial and Labor Relations Review*, 53/2: 197–220.

SEWELL, G. (1998). 'The Discipline of Teams: The Control of Team-Based Industrial Work through Electronic and Peer Surveillance'. *Administrative Science Quarterly*, 43/2: 397–416.

SMITH, C., and THOMPSON, P. (1999). 'Reevaluating the Labour Process Debate', in M. Wardell, T. Steiger, and P. Meiksins (eds.), *Rethinking the Labour Process*. Albany, NY: State University of New York Press.

STASSER, G. (1992). 'Information Salience and the Discovery of Hidden Profiles by Decision-making Groups: A "Thought Experiment"'. *Organizational Behavior and Human Decision Processes*, 52/1: 156–81.

—— and TITUS, W. (1985). 'Effects of Information Load and Percentage of Shared Information on the Dissemination of Unshared Information during Group Discussion'. *Journal of Personality and Social Psychology*, 53: 81–93.

SUNDSTROM, E., and ALTMAN, I. (1989). 'Physical Environments and Work Group Effectiveness', in L. L. Cummings and B. Staw (eds.), *Research in Organizational Behavior*, Vol. 11. Greenwich, Conn.: JAI Press.

THOMPSON, P. (1983). *The Nature of Work: An Introduction to Debates on the Labour Process*. London: Macmillan.

—— and WALLACE, T. (1996). 'Redesigning Production through Teamworking'. Special Issue on Lean Production and Work Organization, *International Journal of Operations and Production Management*, 16/2: 103–18.

TOMPKINS, P. K., and CHENEY, G. (1985). 'Communication and Unobtrusive Control in Contemporary Organizations', in R. D. McPhee and P. K. Thompkins (eds.), *Organizational Communication: Traditional Themes and New Directions*. Beverly Hills, Calif.: Sane Publications.

TRIST, E., and MURRAY, H. (eds.) (1990). *The Social Engagement of Social Science: A Tavistock Anthology*. Philadelphia: University of Pennsylvania Press.

TUBBS, S. (1994). 'The Historical Roots of Self-Managing Work Teams in the 20th Century', in M. Beyerlein and D. Johnson (eds.), *Advances in Interdisciplinary Studies of Work Teams*. Greenwich, Conn.: JAI Press.

WALL, T. D., KEMP, N. J., JACKSON, P. R., and CLEGG, C. W. (1986). 'Outcomes of Autonomous Workgroups: A Long-Term Field Experiment'. *Academy of Management Journal*, 29/2: 280–304.

WEGNER, D. M. (1987). 'Transactive Memory: A Contemporary Analysis of the Group Mind', in B. Mullen and G. R. Goethals (eds.), *Theories of Group Behavior*. New York: Springer-Verlag.

WHITFIELD, K., and POOLE, M. (1997). 'Organizing Employment for High Performance: Theories, Evidence, and Policy'. Special Issue on High Performance Work Organization, *Organization Studies*, 18/5: 745–65.

WOOD, S., and ALBANESE, M. (1995). 'Can We Speak of High Commitment Management on the Shopfloor?' *Journal of Management Studies*, 32: 215–47.

WRIGHT, M., and EDWARDS, P. (1998). 'Does Teamworking Work, and If so, Why? A Case Study in the Aluminium Industry,' *Economic and Industrial Democracy*, 19: 59–90.

PART II

MANAGERIAL REGIMES AND EMPLOYEE ACTIONS

INTRODUCTION
UNMANAGEABLE CAPITALISM?

PAUL THOMPSON

WHEN considering how to conceptualize the practice of management, we can identify countervailing tendencies. On the one hand, there is the legacy of classical writings in which management is treated as a single, unproblematic category and generalizable knowledge and practice. While this view is, perhaps, no longer widely accepted, it is, as Armstrong (2002) observes, sustained intellectually by popular business writings and institutionally by consultants and senior executives who benefit from a view of management as decontextualized and transferable expertise. One might add that it is also sustained by the diminished ranks of functionalist-positivist theorists, who argue for a professionalized management drawing on a rational science and agreed body of knowledge (Donaldson 1995). Ironically, such writers see popular business literatures, with their emphasis on fads and fixes, as the enemy, rather than fellow soldiers in the search for a positive science (Hilmer and Donaldson 1996 and see Morgan and Hampson 1998 for a critical commentary).

In contrast to the above, as Hales (1999) notes, most research has given up searching for commonalities in managerial work. We are much more likely to find descriptive, idiographic accounts that see management primarily in terms of micro-level actors concerned with personal survival and 'keeping the show on the road'; or research charting the social construction of management in inherently varied historical and contemporary settings. For example, Grint (1995: 46, 62) argues that managerial work is defined by the context not the content of the activity and that we can only assess what they do by reconstructing and interpreting their motives from their own and other's accounts.

While there is obvious value in such approaches, they are an overreaction to classical views with the attendant danger that what managers do is seen as 'a catalogue of disconnected actions, events and encounters' (Hales 1999: 336). Contrary to social constructionists, management consists of real sets of actors and practices. The concept of managerial regime is useful in this respect as it can refer to practices at a number of levels. There is a generic character to managerial practices—the control of complex organizations or aspects of them—derived from the agency role on behalf of employers. At a more macro level, that is expressed in formulations such as managerial capitalism in which hierarchy performs the primary coordinative role within modern corporations (Chandler 1977). More specifically, a managerial regime might refer to a particular group of functional practices, such as high trust, high skill arrangements for the management of knowledge workers. This level will be our main concern in Part II of the Handbook. Yet, if management is an agency, it has to be achieved and is therefore always contested and context-specific. With this in mind, it is also necessary to analyze management in terms of competing rhetorics and interests.

Management: A Contested Terrain

An important source of such analysis is Armstrong's (1984, 1989) accounts of interprofessional competition and competing managerial agencies. Combining a Weberian emphasis on expert bodies of knowledge as a means of collective power and mobility, with a labor process analysis of alternative managerial control strategies, he explores the varying fortunes of engineers, accountants, and personnel groupings. Within this framework, management is conceived less as a set of tasks and techniques and more as an agency relationship with capital in which occupational groups attempt to convince employers and senior managers to transfer trust to them as the most credible way of resolving control and coordination problems.

'To give a much over-simplified illustration: it may be cheaper for senior managers to trust a management accountant to monitor the activities of operational managers than to pay the premium involved in creating a trust relationship with the operational managers themselves' (Armstrong 1989: 316).

Real life outcomes will be dependent on a variety of factors including the predilections of senior managers and the power resources (including serviceable rhetoric) of rival groups in particular historical, economic, and institutional contexts. Nevertheless, while knowledge and practices may be constructed in specific locations, they seldom remain there. As Strang and Kim show in this Part, there have long been international flows between nations. Using the cases of the diffusion of scientific management from the United States to Japan and quality practices in the other direction, they highlight the significance of distinctive *diffusion infrastructures* in shaping the capacity and type of learning. Stimulated by perceived performance gaps, diffused practices are always promoted by but mediated and translated for a domestic context by *communities of experts*. The authors compare the steadier and more stable evolution of managerial innovation in Japan, where agencies such as the Japanese Union of Scientists and Engineers have close state and corporate links, with the US situation of decentralized competition among consultants that produces 'faddish trajectories'.

The latter observation highlights that one of the problems with identifying the production of rhetoric is to assess the extent to which it corresponds to the realities of organizational life. This is not easy and not simply because of the difficulties of establishing clear cause and effect relationships. As part of the internationalization process, management 'theory' itself has become a global commodity. Its role is as much to legitimate as to describe or guide action and those forms of legitimation may not correspond closely or indeed at all with actual practices. For example, a rhetoric of changing and turbulent times—of which the idea of the post-bureaucratic organization is a prominent theme—has been a permanent fixture of managerial discourse, at least from the 1950s, irrespective of whether and in what ways the economy and organizations have really changed (Eccles and Nohria 1992; Thompson and O'Connell Davidson 1994). Theory and rhetoric act as a resource through which managers seek to persuade not only employees but also themselves and rival managerial groups.

One of the most influential accounts of the historical ebb and flow of rhetoric and practice was provided by Barley and Kunda in their 1992 article. The framework utilized is one in which culture sets the terms and boundaries within which managerial discourses develop, but material, economic forces determine when new surges of theorizing occur and such surges tend to be championed by a specific managerial subgroup (1992: 392–3). Kunda and Ailon-Souday revisit that argument in this Part. They find the previously dominant normative rhetoric—expressed through emphases on organizational culture and quality—to be declining and displaced by one of market rationalism. This rhetoric envisages organizations as 'lean, managerially diluted and dispersed networks of members', and managers as mobile, self-regulating, and instrumental. To evaluate the nature and impact of competing rhetorics, it is not enough to count publications and chart the rise and fall of fashions (see e.g. Kieser 1997). As Kunda and Ailon-Souday observe, organizational reality is much more complex than depicted in managerial rhetoric. Yet, by drawing on a wide range of secondary evidence they argue that there is a broad approximation between the rhetoric of market rationalism and the realities of downsizing, restructuring, and outsourcing. There seems little doubt that such descriptions of organizational change are accurate as Chapter 24 in Part IV by Lazonick demonstrates. What about agency under market rationalism? It certainly is not traditional middle management, who as Kunda and Ailon-Souday assert, have become 'the primary victims of organizational restructuring'. A new group, focused on project managers, has to an extent filled the coordination gap, but while they have employable, 'portfolio' skills, as a group they lack substantial power resources. Senior or corporate management are the beneficiaries of the new market conditions, protected from the negative effects and receiving much of the benefits of restructuring. Where does that leave other key managerial agencies such as human resource and knowledge managers?

The End of Managerial Capitalism?

Market rationalism apparently does not have time for culture and is more inter-ested in reducing then transforming the workforce. This does not appear to be good news for human resource management (HRM), which has been at the center of business and public policy rhetoric for at least the last twenty-five years. Pfeffer's (1998) *The Human Equation: Building Profits by Putting People First* sums up the central tenet of competitive advantage expressed through a variety of forms, from human capital theory, resourced-based views of strategy, HRM/High-Performance Work Systems (HPWS), through to the latest manifestation in theories of the knowledge economy.

Legge provides a comprehensive overview of the relevant literatures in this Part. As she notes, one of the anomalies is that the bulk of evidence is skeptical on the extent and depth of implementation of HPWS, which is puzzling if there is or should be such a demonstrable link to organizational performance. There is obviously a range of potential explanations for this shortfall. Legge's discussion rests partly on the distinction between hard and soft models of HRM. The former primarily seeks a fit between human resource policies and broader business strat-egy, with employees considered as a flexible headcount resource. Drawing on a developmental humanist tradition, the emphasis of the latter is employees as a valued asset through their commitment and skills, and therefore on a more internal 'fit' between clusters of mutually supportive work and employment practices. The possibilities for integration are always highly contingent on organizational or societal context.

The degree of emphasis on 'hard' and 'soft' options, Legge argues, may also be contingent. For example, the strategic choice can depend on the type of market in which the organization is competing. In a high-volume, low-cost sector treating employees as a valued asset may be a luxury. Market differentiation is undoubtedly important as a factor that influences strategic choices, but this kind of distinction between 'hard' and 'soft' HRM practices is not always easy to sustain. For example, most call centers are oriented towards the economies of scale that derive from centralized, high-volume customer management and the need to extract value from labor where such costs are frequently 60 percent of the total (Callaghan and Thompson 2002). Yet their managerial regime is typically a hybrid where low-discretion, routinized work is combined with a high-commitment model drawing on a variety of intensive human resource practices (notably in recruitment and training) and normative control measures (Houlihan 2002).

Another way of interpreting the shortfall is that 'soft HRM' provides the legit-imating rhetoric for the management of change, while 'hard HRM' predominates in the real world of bottom-line judgments. The rhetoric–reality gap is a consistent and necessary staple of radical critique of management practices, but it is unneces-sary to deny a potentially positive link between soft HRM and enhanced performance. The key problem in such literatures is not the desirability of such practices, but how to explain their low take-up and fragility. An additional layer of explanation shifts the focus from product and labor to capital markets. Within the former, HPWS envisages a 'bargain' in which employees deliver greater discretionary effort in the work process in return for employer investment in human capital through measures such as enhanced training, job stability, and career structures (Appelbaum *et al.* 2000; Huselid 1995).

However that bargain has proved to be hugely unstable. First, there is a fundamental tension between collectivization of effort in the labor process and decollectivization of risk in the employment relationship (Burchell *et al.* 1999). Discretionary effort from employees is coinciding with declining investment in training and skill development, while many employers are unable to deliver on any degree of job security (Beynon *et al.* 2002; Cappelli 1999). The primary causal mechanism undermining HPWS is the increasing influence of capital markets on firm behavior. The pursuit of shareholder value and the increased dominance of institutional investors in deregulated and globalizing markets has led to pressures for increased rates of return as markers of financial performance (Froud, Johal, and Williams 2002). Among the consequences are the kinds of downsizing, acquisition and divestment, and perpetual restructuring described by Lazonick in Chapter 24. Of crucial importance, work by researchers such as Konzelmann and Forrant (2003) shows that tensions between what they call 'creative work systems' and 'destructive markets' affects even those firms that have achieved gains in productivity and market share through the appropriate HRM measures. Although expressed in different language, this explanation is consistent with Legge's argument that a search for external fit between human resource policy and broader business strategy may be inconsistent with the objective of internal fit among work and employment measures.

These trends raise the issue of agency and levers—what is driving organizational change and who are the beneficiaries? Kunda and Ailon-Souday argue that the modern division is between 'top executives and everyone else'. While this perhaps underestimates the complexity of managerial layers and interests, there is a strong degree of truth in the observation. The push for shareholder value in the 1980s arose in part from attempts to find ways of disciplining managerial behavior and to realign their interests with those of owners. In this they have clearly been successful, enriching a layer (admittedly small) of senior managers along the way and encouraging the kind of speculative and sometimes corrupt behavior of which Enron was an extreme case.

At a more analytical level, it can be argued that this is a form of capitalism, at least of the Anglo-American kind, in which there is a double disconnection: between policies pursued in the work and employment spheres, and between management of the workplace and corporate governance (Thompson 2003). Human resource managers may want to pursue higher performance and high commitment policies, at least in some sectors, but the levers they are pulling are often outweighed or countermanded by corporate decision makers in thrall to financial markets. Indeed, one could extend that argument to plant or unit level managers more generally. In contrast to popular business writings that claim a more decentralized pattern of decision making, it may be that we have to reconsider the whole idea of managerial capitalism in an era of increasingly financialized economies.

Where does this leave the other currently most feted regime, that of knowledge management? The idea of a knowledge economy has become the driving force of intellectual debate and public policy. Like HRM the high policy rhetoric has soft, human capital assumptions, such as that knowledge is the inherent property of the producer, 'it remains with the employee and in no real sense is it ever of the firm ... it is impossible to separate knowledge from the knower' (Despres and Hiltrop 1995: 11). As a consequence, self-management through teams and 'communities of practice' is more appropriate than controls and rules. The characteristics of knowledge management as an alternative general regime are outlined by Adler (2001). He argues that the growing dominance of knowledge as a force of production requires a focus on the management of innovation, new products and processes. In turn, this necessitates a shift from market and hierarchy as mechanisms of coordination to community and trust.

However, the status of knowledge management as universal argument or even as primary tendency is highly questionable. Job growth is highest in low-skill, personal service sectors where the conditions of access to and use of specialized knowledge is limited (Thompson, Warhurst, and Callaghan 2001). In addition, as our previous discussion about firms under financialized capitalism indicates, broader dynamics in the economy are unfavorable to knowledge management regimes. This is a territory largely ignored in the mainstream literature, but it has been recently explored by Littler and Innes (2003). Using longitudinal firm-level data on organizational restructuring, they show that the dominant pattern is downsizing and that this is associated with a 'de-knowledging of the firm'; in other words a loss of key skills and knowledge as occupational recomposition takes place. There are a minority of 'knowledge-intensive growers', and as Barley's contribution to Part III demonstrates, technical and scientific occupations are taking an increasing share of total employment. But even by grouping all categories of occupations together, the total reaches 5 percent. Given this kind of evidence, it is clear that idea of knowledge management itself needs to be downsized.

While there are some revealing micro-level accounts of the social relations of expert labor, the same cannot be said of its management. Like much contemporary business literature, the knowledge management thesis is strong on optimism and normative prescription, while weak on power and agency. In other words, who is being managed, how and why? As McKinlay demonstrates in this Part, there have been significant new competitive pressures on product development or 'molecule to market' conditions, that, in turn, produce new and contradictory pressures on the management of labor. Knowledge management is not often a universal and distinctive regime in its own right, but rather a partial and uneven set of practices, with a specific focus on identifying, converting, codifying, and disseminating the tacit knowledge of expert labor, most often within a project management framework. McKinlay argues that the idea of communities of practice has been appropriated for managerialist purposes. Firms are being encouraged to engage more inventively with such informal organization in an effort to direct the flows of knowledge. As his own and wider evidence illustrates, this is easier said than done. There are inherent tensions in the balance between control and autonomy, knowledge as private and public good, career paths, and organizationally specific requirements.

Despite the high concept rhetoric attached to knowledge management and the attempts to make a distinction between information and knowledge, the evidence from surveys and case studies is that though an increasing number of companies claim to be undertaking knowledge management initiatives, they are largely focused on technology-driven instruments such as intranets, data warehousing, decision-support tools, and groupware (Scarbrough 2003). Furthermore, they are led by Information System's professionals, already empowered by growing organizational reliance on IT infrastructure, and by consultants with a vested interest in commodifying the tools and metrics of managing knowledge. McKinlay argues, however, that these efforts have not been effective in terms of innovative process and product. As it stands, knowledge management is largely top-down and underpinned by a utopian unitarism that assumes that all employees will gladly participate as donors and recipients. This brings us to the role of labor.

Labor is Still a Significant Actor

The end of a particular type of managerial capitalism does not lead to the conclusion that the employment relationship is irrelevant, merely that its management is different from what we might expect from the dominant rhetorics. One further aspect of such orthodoxies is a view that economic, cultural, and political changes diminish the prospects for union organization and work resistance. All the final three chapters in Part II reject this doom and gloom scenario and in their own way demonstrate that managerial regimes continue to shape and be shaped by the actions and interests of labor.

It is true that globalization and deregulation give additional opportunities and power resources to industrial relations managers and pose considerable problems for unions. Yet the picture is not straightforward. As Katz shows in this Part,

'A special dilemma for industrial relations managers in the multinational corporation arises from the fact that culture, laws, and institutions retain much of their institutional diversity at the same time that globalization has increased the premium on coordination and central control.' Pattern analysis shows a number of distinctive employment systems across countries, within a common trend towards pushing the location of management of the employment relation downwards. This, in turn, is partly driven by the kind of decentralization of corporate structures discussed earlier. Elsewhere, the author (Katz and Darbishire 2000) describes this trend as a process of converging divergences. The tension between these processes is fundamental to a number of contributions to the Handbook. Whereas Strang and Kim emphasize the relative stability of diffusion mechanisms and national differences, Smith identifies the complex interactions between systemic and contingent influences on work and employment relations. Both analyses are important in finding a middle ground between the universalizing assumptions about managerial regimes present in mainstream business literatures and the overemphasis on national diversity in traditional social science. In other words, diversity in employment systems continues within a changing and more constrained context. As Katz shows, some countries choose to continue or even develop tripartite coordination of industrial relations, though such coordination is not inconsistent with decentralization of industrial relations. This reinforces the continued significance of the state as an actor and the persistence of varieties of capitalism, albeit within tightened conditions of competition (Elger and Burnham 2001; Hall and Soskice 2001).

In such discussions, labor as an agency can be obscured, or subsumed within forms of collective organization and representation. The chapters by Kelly, and Collinson and Ackroyd, offset this tendency. Labor and unions are frequently treated as helpless victims of globalization and postindustrial changes: the assumption being an inevitable decline in the power resources and mobilizing capacity of labor. In the history of social science, this is not the first time we have been down this route. Yet, as Kelly argues, 'There is no simple causal chain running from global competition, production, and investment to labor decline.' To move away from such assumptions, it is necessary to expand our understanding of labor organization beyond particular and conventional forms of collective representation and action. There is considerable evidence that new management practices and organizational restructuring provide fertile grounds for injustice and the formation of employee grievances.

Kelly believes that mobilization theory offers a more innovative framework for linking micro and macro developments. In practice, whether such grievances can be mobilized in coherent and collective forms remains an open question, but they are present in a variety of forms. This view is taken further in the final chapter by Collinson and Ackroyd. They illustrate how much of the most innovative research and writing on employee resistance and misbehavior is taking place across and beyond disciplinary boundaries, through diverse sources such as labor process theory, post-structuralism, and feminism (though there are also continuities to older traditions such as industrial anthropology). There is often a different emphasis on the micro, informal dimension and on practices such as sabotage, workplace humor, and time wasting. The ability of workplace research to move away from a purely management-centered approach depends in part on ethnographic and other qualitative modes of enquiry (Hodson 2001).

An obvious objection is that compared to traditional literatures on collective organization and action, such practices are trivial. However, the characteristics of employee action shift as the objects of managerial regimes change. In the past twenty years we have seen increased attempts by organizations to mobilize the identities and emotions of employees through initiatives such as corporate culture and customer service programs. Employee cynicism towards and dissent from such initiatives, as well as action to maintain dignity and positive identity at work, are in this context as much a form of resistance in its broadest sense as traditional effort bargain struggles. The importance of new ways of thinking about employee action lies in their capacity to do for labor what innovative research has done for management: to open it up as a category, to grasp its diversity, and to explore the complex interplays between interests and identities.

Conclusion

The idea of a universal body of management theory and practice that develops in evolutionary and enlightened manner is well past its sell-by date. There is, however, a reverse problem, that awash with competing fashions and discourses, and aware of multiple contingencies, we simply drown in diversity. Concepts such as managerial regime signal an intent to identify dominant patterns and their causes, while recognizing that any idea of regime needs to be multileveled and multifaceted in order to deal with the different sets of pressures and practices that shape organizations.

While the search for universality does not stretch very far beyond the territory of popular business books, social scientists are still powerfully attracted to the idea of holistic, integrated regimes. This is understandable, after all research tells us, for example in the case of HPWS, that such approaches can have positive payoffs for a variety of stakeholders. Unfortunately, the same research also indicates that such coherent regimes are few and far between. Most organizations, whether in the private or public sector, are hybrids of managerial practices and control structures. This point is picked up on by Adler (2001) in his previously referred- to article on changing forms of coordination. Although he claims a shift away from hierarchy and market towards trust mechanisms, it is noted that there are complex three-way tensions and that the three modes can be mutually supportive if designed and implemented appropriately.

Unfortunately, as discussed earlier, this may be overestimating the design capacity of managerial agents in a context where it is harder to pursue stable, long-term, and coherent strategies under financialized capitalism. This is not to deny that some routes are more effective and more capable of generating consent and mutual gains among stakeholders than others. But if 'there is no "one best way" of managing these contradictions, only different routes to partial failure' (Hyman 1987: 30), even this kind of success may be getting more difficult to generate and to sustain. The world, or at least the workplace, is, for the time being, becoming less manageable.

REFERENCES

ADLER, P. S. (2001). 'Markets, Hierarchy and Trust: The Knowledge Economy and the Future of Capitalism'. *Organization Science*, 21 (March–April): 4–34.

APPELBAUM, E., BAILEY, T., BERG, P., and KALLEBERG, A. L. (2000). *Manufacturing Advantage: Why High Performance Work Systems Pay Off*. Ithaca, NY: ILR Press.

ARMSTRONG, P. (1984). 'Competition between the Organizational Professions and the Evolution of Management Control Strategies', in K. Thompson (ed.), *Work, Employment and Unemployment*. Milton Keynes: Open University Press.

—— (1989). 'Management, Labour Process and Agency'. *Work, Employment and Society*, 3/3: 307–22.

—— (2002). 'The Politics of Management Science'. *International Journal of Management and Decision-Making*, 31/2: 2–18.

BARLEY, S. R., and KUNDA, G. (1992). 'Design and Devotion: Surges of Rational and Normative Ideologies of Control in Managerial Discourse'. *Administrative Science Quarterly*, 37: 363–99.

BEYNON, H., GRIMSHAW, D., RUBERY, J., and WARD, K. (2002). *Managing Employment Change*. Oxford: Oxford University Press.

BURCHELL, B. J., DAY, D., HUDSON, M., LADIPO, D., MANKELOW, R., NOLAN, J. P., REED, H., WICHERT, I. C., and WILKINSON, F. (1999). *Job Insecurity and Work Intensification*. London: Joseph Rowntree Foundation.

CALLAGHAN, G., and THOMPSON, P. (2002). '"We Recruit Attitude": The Selection and Shaping of Call Centre Labour'. *Journal of Management Studies*, 39/2: 233–54.

CAPPELLI, P. (1999). *The New Deal at Work*. Boston: Harvard Business School Press.

CHANDLER, A. (1977). *The Visible Hand*. Cambridge, Mass.: Harvard University Press.

DESPRES, C., and HILTROP, J. M. (1995). 'Human Resource Management in the Knowledge Age: Current Practice and Perspectives on the Future'. *Employee Relations*, 17/1: 9–23.

DONALDSON, L. (1995). *For Positivist Organization Theory*. London: Sage.

ECCLES, R. G., and NOHRIA, N. (1992). *Beyond the Hype: Rediscovering the Essence of Management*. Boston: Harvard Business School Press.

ELGER, T., and BURNHAM, P. (2001). 'Labour, Globalization and the "Competition State"'. *Competition and Change*, 5/2: 1–23.

FROUD, J., JOHAL, S., and WILLIAMS, K. (2002). 'Financialisation and the Coupon Pool'. *Capital and Class*, 78: 119–51.

GRINT, K. (1995). *Management: A Sociological Introduction.* Cambridge: Polity Press.

HALES, C. (1999). 'Why Do Managers Do What They Do? Reconciling Evidence and Theory in Accounts of Managerial Work'. *British Journal of Management*, 10: 335–50.

HALL, P. A., and SOSKICE, D. (eds.) (2001). *Varieties of Capitalism: The Institutional Foundations of Comparative Advantage.* Oxford: Oxford University Press.

HILMER, F. G., and DONALDSON, L. (1996). *Management Redeemed: Debunking the Fads that Undermine Corporate Performance.* Sydney: Free Press.

HODSON, R. (2001). *Dignity at Work.* Cambridge: Cambridge University Press.

HOULIHAN, M. (2002). 'Tensions and Variations in Call Centre Management Strategies'. *Human Resource Management Journal*, 12/4: 67–85.

HUSELID, M. (1995). 'The Impact of Human Resource Management Practices on Turnover, Production and Corporate Financial Performance'. *Academy of Management Journal*, 38: 635–72.

HYMAN, R. (1987). 'Strategy or Structure? Capital, Labour and Control'. *Work, Employment and Society*, 1/1: 25–55.

KATZ, H., and DARBISHIRE, O. (2000). *Converging Divergences: Worldwide Changes in Employment Systems.* Ithaca, NY: ILR/Cornell University Press.

KIESER, A. (1997). 'Rhetoric and Myth in Management Fashion'. *Organization*, 4/1: 49–74.

KONZELMANN, S. J., and FORRANT, R. (2003). 'Creative Work in Destructive Markets', in B. Burchell, S. Deakin, J. Michie, and J. Rubery (eds.), *Systems of Production: Markets, Organization and Performance.* London: Routledge.

LITTLER, C. R., and INNES, P. (2003). 'Downsizing and Deknowledging the Firm'. *Work, Employment and Society*, 17/1: 73–100.

MORGAN, D., and HAMPSON, I. (1998). 'The Management of Organizational Structure and Strategy: The New Professionalism and Management Redemption'. *Asia Pacific Journal of Human Resources*, 36/1: 1–24.

PFEFFER, J. (1998). *The Human Equation: Building Profits by Putting People First.* Boston: Harvard Business School Press.

SCARBROUGH, H. (2003). 'The Role of Intermediary Groups in Shaping Management Fashion: The Case of Knowledge Management'. *International Studies of Management and Organization*, 32/4: 87–103.

THOMPSON, P. (2003). 'Disconnected Capitalism: Or Why Employees Can't Keep Their Side of the Bargain'. *Work, Employment and Society*, 17/2: 359–78.

THOMPSON, P. and O'CONNELL DAVIDSON, J. (1994). 'The Continuity of Discontinuity: Managerial Rhetoric in Turbulent Times'. *Personnel Review*, 24/4: 17–33.

——WARHURST, C., and CALLAGHAN, G. (2001). 'Ignorant Theory and Knowledgeable Workers: Interrogating the Connections between Knowledge, Skills and Services'. *Journal of Management Studies*, 38/7: 923–42.

CHAPTER 7

THE DIFFUSION AND DOMESTICATION OF MANAGERIAL INNOVATIONS

THE SPREAD OF SCIENTIFIC MANAGEMENT, QUALITY CIRCLES, AND TQM BETWEEN THE UNITED STATES AND JAPAN

DAVID STRANG
YOUNG-MI KIM

7.1 INTRODUCTION

COMPARATIVE organizational research provides an opportunity to build socially grounded theories of organization. While the business literature often adopts a narrow efficiency logic, examination of the way organizations vary across countries suggests the importance of cognitive models, national historical trajectories, the relationship between firms and the state, and variation in legal, labor markets, and employment regimes.

Much comparative work lies within the rubric of a convergence/divergence debate. A 'logic of industrialism' (Kerr *et al.* 1960) contends that organizations become more similar over time as the requirements of industrial society eliminate primordial social and cultural differences. Many Marxist accounts also anticipate convergence, arguing that market flexibility, decentralization, and deregulation lead to more homogeneous national economies after the collapse of Fordism (Hyman and Streeck 1988).[1] Meyer *et al.* (1997) contend that models of bureaucratic structure and employment relations are increasingly global in scale.

'Divergence' theories counter that national differences are large and persistent over time. Maurice, Sorge, and Warner (1980) document substantial cross-national differences in organizational structure linked to variation in schooling systems and labor markets. Hofstede (1980) and Triandis (1995) locate nationally-specific cultural orientations towards fundamental issues like inequality, individualism versus collectivism, and competition versus cooperation. Dobbin (1994) and Hamilton and Biggart (1988) argue that cross-national variation reflects the state's organization and bases of legitimacy, while Gooderham, Nordhaug, and Ringdal (1999) point to the effect of legal institutions on human resource practices. Guillen (2001) argues that path dependency in economic development leads to the widening of organizational differentials over time.

Perhaps the most common comparison is between Japan and the West. Early organizational research anticipated convergence on the Western model, with Harbison confidently concluding that otherwise 'Japan is destined to fall behind in the ranks of modern industrialized nations' (1959: 254). But Japan's remarkable success in the postwar period made the opposite conclusion credible. Most notably, Dore (1973) and Lincoln and Kalleberg (1992) argue that the combination of lifetime employment, seniority-based wages, and company unions provides a powerful recipe for effective cooperation within the firm. Dore contends that Japan's twentieth-century industrialization allowed it to avoid the class conflict that marked the British workplace.

The success of Japan and other 'late developers', in company with an expanding knowledge base in comparative organizational studies, has led to a variety of ideas about how to transcend or enrich the convergence/divergence debate. In this volume, for example, Harry Katz argues that a pattern of 'converging divergence' is emerging where national business communities show standardized forms of

---

[1] Other recent Marxist work emphasizes how organizational constraints and the regulatory role of the state create diversity across varieties of capitalism (see e.g. Coates 2000).

diversity, while Chris Smith's model of system, societal, and dominance effects describes forces promoting both convergence and divergence.

Whether viewed in simple or complex ways, the convergence/divergence debate tends to focus on cross-sectional variation rather than on the movement of organizational practices from one place to another. But arguments like the 'advantages of backwardness' imply an important role for contact and communication across national boundaries—it is knowledge of the problems others faced and how they sought to resolve them that distinguishes early and late developers. We think it is useful to start from an assumption that international linkages are pervasive.

Multinationals embody the most explicit sort of organizational tie, where business units in different countries are managed under a single authority and ownership structure. Kostova and Roth (2002) examine how management practices are transferred from headquarters to national subsidiaries, with varying reception depending on their fit to national institutional environments. Influence may also flow in the opposite direction; for example, Cole (1999) found that Hewlett-Packard's quality program was based on the experience of its Japanese subsidiary. Other forms of direct organizational contacts include partnerships, strategic alliances, and joint ventures like New United Motor Manufacturing Inc. (NUMMI) (Adler 1993).

Firms are also linked by transnational communities of experts. The papers collected in Alvarez (1998), for example, provide a rich account of the burgeoning management knowledge industry. Industry boards and associations, professional associations, business journals, consultants, and schools of management are all growing apace, and show much homogeneity across national borders. These experts act as key carriers of management ideas by advocating, explaining, and often implementing organizational innovations.

Given this thick web of interconnections, it seems more useful to think of organizational practices and structures as diffusing from one place to another than as being independently constructed in each location. This perspective suggests new questions. 'What linkages facilitate the movement of a practice across national borders?' 'What sorts of practices are quick to move, and which are not?' 'What determines the direction of diffusion?' 'How are practices translated as they diffuse?'

Rather than try to comprehend a 'global diffusion system', we limit our attention to the flow of management practices between two countries—the United States and Japan. Much research has sought to explicitly link or implicitly contrast these two organizational communities, for a number of good reasons: the size of each national economy and critical role of both American and Japanese corporations in global markets, the cultural and institutional distance between the two, and the degree to which the two countries have provided each other with organizational models. The relationship between the United States and Japan should not be assumed typical, but it is certainly important.

We examine three 'moments' in the diffusion of managerial ideas between the United States and Japan. These are the flow of scientific management (from the United States to Japan), quality control circles (from Japan to the United States), and company-wide quality control (from Japan to the United States).

7.2 FROM AMERICAN SCIENTIFIC MANAGEMENT TO JAPANESE PERSONNEL MANAGEMENT

'Scientific management' is perhaps the most distinctive American contribution to the theory and practice of the corporate organization (treatments from different perspectives include Braverman 1974; Jacoby 1979; Litterer 1961; Shenhav 1999). The approach is most strongly associated with the work of Frederick W. Taylor. But Taylor's proposed science was just part of a broad family of efforts to apply the new professional disciplines of industrial engineering, mechanical engineering, and cost accounting to managerial work.

As a concrete technology, Taylorism emphasizes systematic analysis of product-ive tasks with an eye to locating 'the one best way', testing employees to optimally match them to work roles, and the use of piece rates to motivate workers to maximize production. Proponents of scientific management like Taylor and the Gilbreths developed time study and motion study to achieve these aims, while engineers like Henry Gantt formalized production charts.

Scientific management embodies a social mobility project for industrial engineers (Stark 1980). By separating planning and execution, scientific management enlarged the role of professionals (and possibly managers, though see Shenhav 1999) and diminished that of foremen and workers. In case anyone missed the implications, Taylor made them explicit:

This work is so crude and elementary in its nature that the writer firmly believes that it would be possible to train an intelligent gorilla so as to become a more efficient pig-iron handler than any man can be. Yet it will be shown that the science of handling pig iron is so great and amounts to so much that it is impossible for the man who is best suited to this type of work to understand the principles of the science, or even to work in accordance with these principles without the aid of a man better educated than he is. (Taylor 1967 [1911]: 40–1).

But scientific management was not presented as a system for deskilling workers and improving the bargaining position of owners. Taylor posed his approach as a response to increasing levels of labor–management conflict in American business, and in fact attention to scientific management rose and fell with the strike rate in the decades following the turn of the century (Shenhav 1995). Outflanking earlier appeals to a preindustrial commonality of interests and to employer benevolence, Taylor argued that opposition between workers and employers would diminish as the size of the pie grew.

Data on the spread of organizational practices associated with scientific management in the United States is scanty. One percent of American firms had adopted Taylorist methods in 1909 (Kogut and Parkinson 1993: 182). By the mid-1930s, between a quarter and a third of companies surveyed by the National Industrial Conference Board utilized time study with increased implementation over the decade (Guillen 1994). Piecework was more common, with about half of all firms making use of the practice. Manufacturers and large firms were the most prominent users of scientific management.

As a managerial ideology, scientific management experienced a checkered career in the United States. In part, this reflected competition among the many versions of the approach. Taylor, Frank and Lillian Gilbreth, Harrington Emerson, Henry Gantt, and Charles Bedaux all touted the distinctiveness of their methodologies. And as scientific management became fashionable, a horde of 'upstart' efficiency experts appeared on the scene. Frederick Colvin, editor of the *American Machinist*, complained:

Science was in a fair way to becoming another religion or cult, if one could judge by the columns and columns of space in the increasing number of Sunday supplements. ... [This trend] brought in its train a fair number of charlatans or thimbleriggers who figuratively set up their medicine shows in the public square and sold flummery and hocus-pocus in the name of science (Colvin 1947: 154)

Scientific management was also opposed by organized labor, which rejected piece-rate compensation and the rule of the time study man. Taylor's most publicized 'intervention', the implementation of scientific management at the Watertown Arsenal, led to a strike and federal investigation. Workers saw Taylorism as infringing on traditional methods and usurping control over their own labor (Braverman 1974; Jacoby 1979). Even managers resented the overweening claims of the industrial engineers (Shenhav 1999).

While Taylor's dream of industrial peace was scarcely credible, scientific management became emblematic of a distinctively modern approach to the organization of work. From an operational point of view, it offered a new set of concrete technologies (such as time study) around which Fordist mass production could build. From a cultural perspective, scientific management promoted a rationalist vision of the organization that identified managers and engineers as the key actors and control over work processes as a fundamental goal.

As the United States overtook Great Britain as the world's leading industrial and technological power, scientific management came to represent 'the' American organizational model to the rest of the world. Enthusiasts included French organizational experts and the Communist Party of the Soviet Union, which saw Taylorism as a model for technological rationalization and growth. In countries like Great Britain, by contrast, scientific management made little headway because of resistance from organized labor (Kogut and Parkinson 1993) and the lack of a strong and independent engineering profession (Guillen 1994).

Late nineteenth-century Japan is often depicted as a 'rational shopper' (and possibly a compulsive one as well). After the Meiji Restoration in 1868, Japanese governmental and industrial elites vigorously searched the West for new organizational models. As Westney (1987) details, Japan selected purposively among the institutional designs offered by different countries, modeling its new navy after Britain, its army after Prussia, and its judicial and police system after France. In the field of industrial management, Japanese attention focused on the American system of mass production and rationalized management (Greenwood and Ross 1982).

Scientific management was rapidly disseminated in Japan (Littler 1982; Warner 1994). Frederick Taylor's *The Principles of Scientific Management* was translated into Japanese in 1912, just a year after it was published in the United States, and sold more than a million copies in a version revised for workers. Enthusiastic exponents of Taylor's approach included Yoichi Ueno and Araki Toichiro (Gordon 1989; Greenwood and Ross 1982). In 1921, the Industrial Efficiency Research Institute (Sangyo noritsu kenkyujo) was formed under Ueno's leadership to promote the methodology of scientific management.

Scientific management moved to Japan as a set of concrete practices as well. Some Japanese corporations adopted motion-saving techniques as early as 1913 (Cole 1989). Firms like Mitsubishi Electric and Nippon Electric took the lead, as did manufacturers like Kannebo and Toyobo in textiles.

These developments took place in the industrial context far removed from the openly conflictual American industrial scene of the first decades of the twentieth century. In Japan, business associations like Ryumonsha and Kogyo Kyokai pictured the factory as a moral community where employer benevolence and employee loyalty replicated the feudal patron–client bond (Kinzley 1991). Japanese policy makers and elites sought to prevent the emergence of American-style class conflict by appealing to traditional communal values. In key debates over Factory Law legislation in the late nineteenth century, both proponents and opponents conceived of workplace relationships within a framework of natural friendship and intimacy (Kinzley 1991: 17).

Within this context, Japanese interpretations of scientific management were linked to ideas about personnel management in Japan that directly opposed the core meanings of Taylorism in its birthplace (Gordon 1989; Hazama 1977). In the United States, scientific management stood for sweeping away 'industrial betterment' schemes that posed a false moral community in favor of clarifying the functional interdependence of manager and employee, and for replacing the traditional authority of the foreman and craftsman with the science wielded by the engineer and manager. In Japan, scientific management was seen as building rather than simplifying employee skills, and strengthening rather than deflating preindustrial understandings of community. The notion of systematically improving production techniques was accepted, while individualizing incentives like piece rates were rejected.

Japan's Industrial Efficiency Research Institute noted above was thus established within Kyochokai, the 'Harmony and Cooperation Society'. Formed in 1919 by the state and leading corporations, Kyochokai conducted education and research aimed at the alleviation of labor conflict. The Industrial Efficiency Research Institute's emphasis was on increasing worker commitment and improving industrial training rather than on radical deskilling. Its first director, Yoichi Ueno, was a psychologist whose disciplinary background was in sharp contrast to the engineering and technical experience of American proponents of scientific management (Kinzley 1991; Shenhav 1999).

The assimilation of Taylorism into what would be seen in the United States as an alternative 'human relations' frame appears in industry experience as well. For example, the Japanese National Railway was an early formal adopter of scientific management principles in the mid-1920s. But it delayed implementation of motion study until 1929 in favor of group discussion and problem-solving teams (Levine and Kawada 1980: 201). Japan's version of scientific management led toward a personnel management system that combines rationalized production with participatory activities and themes of industrial harmony, a combination that reappeared after World War II in the Japanese quality movement.

7.3 FROM JAPANESE QUALITY CONTROL CIRCLES TO AMERICAN QUALITY CIRCLES

Quality control circles developed in Japan to involve foremen and workers in quality control. They consist of a small group drawn from a workshop or unit that studies and applies quality control methods, particularly careful observation and statistical analysis, to production problems. They are *jishusei*, a term often translated as voluntary, but closer in meaning to autonomous. Japanese managers might set up quality control circles throughout the firm, but would not direct them or make them responsible for carrying out official duties.

Quality control circles stemmed not from a single author or network of competing consultants (as Taylorism had), but from a collective one: the Japanese Union of Scientists and Engineers (JUSE). Established in 1946 during the period of American occupation, JUSE began by promoting American statistical quality control techniques like Shewhart's control chart and sampling inspection methods. In 1950 JUSE invited W. Edwards Deming, a student of Shewhart and director of SQC (statistical quality control) training in the US War Production Board, to give eight days of workshops. When Deming declined the honorarium for the talks, JUSE used the funds to establish the Deming Prize for Quality Control.

In spite of Deming's personal popularity and JUSE's efforts, statistical quality control methods per se were little followed in Japan, perhaps because they failed to meet the needs of Japan's war-ravaged firms. For Tsutsui, these sophisticated statistical techniques were no less than 'fitting jet engines on wooden biplanes' (1996: 315). Japanese quality control moved towards broader organizational strategies for improving product quality, methods which drew on the tradition of forming problem-solving groups in the workplace (Ishikawa 1984).

As the poster child of a major professional association, quality control circles can be quite precisely dated. The idea was promulgated in 1962, when the Japanese Union of Scientists and Engineers first published *Genba-to-QC* (Quality Control for the Foreman) and launched a drive to encourage the formation of quality control circles in Japanese industry. The first QCC was registered in May 1962 (the Matsuyama Carrier Equipment Circle of Japan Telephone and Telegraph).

QC circles spread widely and rapidly throughout Japanese industry. By 1970, 30,000 circles were registered with JUSE, and a decade later the count had risen to more than 100,000 (Lillrank and Kano 1989). While never the 'management secret' they were touted to be in the American business press, quality control circles played a substantial and well institutionalized role as the participatory wing of Japanese quality control.

Information about quality circles was disseminated from Japan to the United States and around the world in several ways. Quality control experts like Joseph Juran returned from trips to Japan with news of how shop-floor workers were solving manufacturing problems (Juran 1951).[2] Japanese quality circles toured

---

[2] The American literature often credited Juran and fellow quality expert W. Edwards Deming with introducing the quality control circle to Japan. This view exaggerates a grain of truth. Deming and Juran's lectures on quality control had been greeted with enthusiasm in Japan, and their ideas (about statistical quality control and company-wide quality efforts) are compatible with the QC circle. But neither man envisaged or promoted the concrete organizational practice of the QC circle.

American and European businesses describing their approach, and delegations from abroad made the return trip.

The first major quality circle program within the United States was started in 1974 at Lockheed's Aeronautics division in Santa Clara, California. Lockheed's circle program was stimulated by the visit of a touring quality circle party from Japan, followed by a return visit by American managers to Japan in 1973. They enjoyed considerable success, reporting a cost savings of $3 million, tenfold reduction in defects, a 600 percent return on investment, and improved morale. Lockheed manufacturing manager Wayne Rieker, QC coordinator Donald Dewar, and QC training manager Jeff Beardsley advertised their success widely, preparing presentations at the American Society for Quality Control. All three ultimately left Lockheed to become business consultants setting up circles elsewhere.

The idea of QC circles generated little initial interest within American industry. In the mid-1970s, QC programs were located mainly in the aerospace and electronics industries and propagated mainly via interorganizational networks. For example, Lockheed managers suggested that their colleagues at Honeywell might find quality circles useful, and in turn Honeywell passed the idea on to Westinghouse.

As circles gained currency in the United States, they were renamed 'quality circles' (the term 'quality control circle' had some initial currency, but was gradually dropped from American discourse). The American quality circle model builds on its Japanese parent, but it also differed from it in crucial respects. First, while Japanese circles focused on quality control, American quality circles were understood as potentially addressing almost any workplace problem or issue. Second, while Japanese QC circles formulated and carried out workplace improvements, American quality circles centered on making recommendations to management.

These differences were not random copying errors, but instead modifications produced by the concerns, interpretive framework, and structural conditions of American business. Problematic issues included the undesirable connotations of 'control' for a participatory managerial practice, a desire to limit the role of the QC Department, the small role of foremen and cohesive work groups within American industry relative to Japan, and the oppositional character of management–labor relations. All of these conditions led quality circles to play a more passive role (see Cole 1989 for an extensive and insightful analysis).

Paul Lillrank (1995; Lillrank and Kano 1989) argues that American efforts at quality circles were further hampered because they wrenched the practice out of its organizational context. American managers were drawn to circles as a stand-alone technology whose success would flow naturally once the neglected resource of worker knowledge and cooperation was tapped. This view minimized the social and technical infrastructure needed to make circles self-sustaining over time. Lillrank (1995) provides a glimpse of the managerial infrastructure behind QC circles in Japan:

to keep the circles active and working on relevant problems, strict management guidance was necessary. For this, a parallel support structure was constructed, made up of steering committees at various levels. Top management strategies were broken down into objectives for each level. While most of the circles could still choose the topics to work with, management suggestions, annual policy proclamations, slogans and campaigns provided the circles with indirect guidance on what types of issues to focus on.

Quality circles took off within American organizations in the late 1970s and early 1980s, a time when Japanese dominance of core American markets had brought the search for 'Japanese management secrets' to a fever pitch. A national association (the inaccurately named 'International Association of Quality Circles') was established in 1978 and experienced exponential growth, doubling in membership until 1983 (Cole 1989: 183). As Figure 7.1 shows, journal articles on quality circles peaked in the United States in 1981 (Abrahamson and Fairchild 1999), as did business consultants listing quality circle services (Strang and Macy 2001: 150–1). Organizational surveys found quality circles in more than 40 percent of large manufacturers (Freund and Epstein 1984).

But the quality circle movement was short-lived within the United States, in sharp contrast to its longevity in Japan. In 1985 Lawler and Mohrman (1985) published a widely cited critique of quality circles in the *Harvard Business Review*, arguing not only that circles were relatively unprogressive but also that

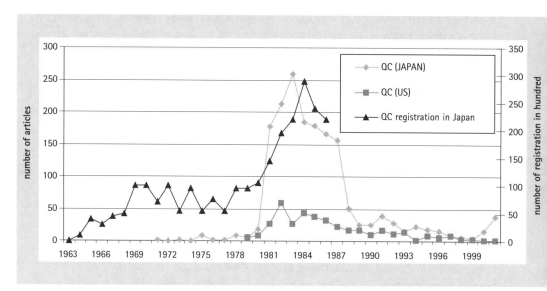

Fig. 7.1 QCC: Trends in Japan and the United States

Note: The original source for the number of QC registration is *Continuous Improvement* (Lillrank and Kano 1989: 231). The numbers of registrations are presented in hundreds in the right axis.

'as everyone knows, it's a fad'. Attention in the business press and among consult-ants dwindled, and close inspection of quality circle programs showed them to be short-lived (Drago and Turnbull 1988). By the late 1980s, quality circles were coded in American business discourse as an example of irrational exuberance gone bad.

American interest in quality circles did last long enough, however, to provoke a remarkable 'boomerang' in Japan. As Figure 7.1 shows, by the 1970s QC circles had become institutionalized in Japanese industry. High and consistent levels of activity are indicated by the fact that some 5,000 to 10,000 QC circles are registered each year. But very few articles on QC circles appeared in the Japanese academic or business press, suggesting that the approach had become taken-for-granted.

American attention to quality circles around 1980 led to a huge increase in Japanese QC circle discourse and activity. Apparently, Japanese managers and quality experts concluded that there must be something more to their ideas if the United States and the rest of the world took them so seriously! The number of QC circles in Japan increased about threefold, with some 300,000 circles registered with JUSE by 1984. And managerial discourse rose even more rapidly, reaching as many as 350 articles per year in 1983 before declining to 1970s levels at the end of the decade.

7.4 FROM JAPANESE COMPANY-WIDE QUALITY CONTROL TO AMERICAN TQM

Japanese quality control circles were only one wing of a vigorous national quality control movement. While quality control circles mobilized foremen and front-line employees to measure and solve workplace problems, complementary strategies were promoted at other organizational levels as well. Senior managers established quality plans and emphasized the strategic opportunity to out-compete rivals on both quality and cost. Middle managers conducted quality audits that helped align these plans with production targets. Engineers sought to simplify work processes to simultaneously improve product quality and reduce cycle times. Marketing and design personnel sought to measure customer satisfaction and integrate consumer concerns into the design process.

Three main organizations promoted the development and spread of these quality control activities. As with quality control circles, the Japanese Union of

Scientists and Engineers played a core role. In addition, the Japanese Standards Association (JSA) and the Japan Productivity Center (JPC) organized workshops and published standardized QC texts, providing a common language and strengthening communication networks across Japanese firms. All three organizations were strongly linked to the Japanese state: most of the directors of the JSA and JUSE were former officials within MITI, and the JPC was sponsored by MITI.

Japan's new quality model marked a clear departure from traditional inspection and statistically based notions of quality control (see Cole 1999 and Hackman and Wageman 1995 for more detailed discussion). Features of the new approach included:

- *customer focus*: a proactive emphasis on introducing customer concerns and reactions into the definition of quality goals and integrating quality and design issues
- *process focus*: the notion that all aspects of what an organization does can be understood in terms of work processes that cross functional specializations
- *measurement focus*: an emphasis on 'management by fact' based on quantitative summaries and analysis
- *employee involvement and participation*: all employees should be directly and meaningfully involved in improving quality, in their own individual work, as members of production teams, and as contributors to various work processes
- *kaizen or continuous improvement*: a strategy of continually streamlining work processes and reducing production errors.

This complex of ideas and supporting practices became widespread in the 1960s, a period when trade liberalization reinforced the importance of product quality for Japanese firms (Nonaka 1995). In 1968 the term 'Company Wide Quality Control' (CWQC) was proposed to describe the evolving quality model.[3] Kaoru Ishikawa, the 'father' of Japanese quality control, defines CWQC as 'all-department participation', 'all-employee participation', and 'integrated process control' (1984).

American interest in Japan's company-wide quality methods was again delayed by about two decades. It is difficult to date this rise in the way that quality circles can be temporally located because both the new model and its reception in the United States were more complex. In fact, Cole (1999: 18–21) represents the growth of the new quality movement as a sequence of mini fads. For example, the quality circles boom was followed by attention to quality function deployment and Taguchi methods in the early 1980s, customer focus and continuous improvement in the mid-1980s, and annual objectives and ISO 9000 in the late 1980s.

---

[3] The Japanese approach had previously been described under the rubric of Feigenbaum's notion of Total Quality Control. TQC (*sogoteki hinshitsukanri*) and CWQC (*zenshatecki hinshitsukanri*) are almost indistinguishable in Japanese. Hence Western interpreters often use Japanese quality control or Japanese TQC to refer to CWQC.

Overall, American efforts to learn from Japan's quality model came of age in the late 1980s. In 1987 the establishment of the Malcolm Baldrige National Quality Award signaled that the total quality movement had gained national prominence as well as the support of leading corporations. And in the late 1980s, the term 'total quality management' (TQM) gained currency as a way of integrating the complex of quality methods that American companies were learning from Japan.

As with quality circles, America's renewed attention to Japan stemmed in large part from Japan's competitive success. The US economy grew at a significantly slower pace than Japan's throughout the 1980s, with a severe dip at the end of the decade—just the time when American quality efforts coalesced around the Baldrige. Key industries like automobiles, electronics, and computer hardware continued to lose market share to Japanese firms both globally and domestically. And consumers continued to view the quality of Japanese products as significantly higher than those of American companies.

American TQM also grew out of lessons learned from earlier, more partial innovation attempts. While quality circles had failed in most firms, they laid the groundwork for more aggressive efforts by introducing the notion of quality as a 'strategic issue' and by sponsoring the growth of a consulting community with expertise in quality techniques. Philip Crosby's 'Zero Defects' program played a similar role in introducing many American companies to a homegrown version of quality management that combined traditional elements with newer ones (Cole 1999; Easton and Jarrell 1998). Quality 'gurus' such as Deming, Juran, and Feigenbaum became prominent during the quality circle fad, and these experts all argued that deeper managerial commitment was needed.

The quality journey was not a smooth one, however. Robert Cole (1999) details the difficulty that managers at Hewlett-Packard had in comprehending and following the Japanese quality model. Early on, HP managers faced strong psychological as well as cognitive barriers: they felt they had little to learn from the Japanese, and regarded the assumptions of the new quality model (particularly the lack of conflict between quality and other organizational goals) as implausible. During the 1980s, top manager communication of quality successes at HP-Yokohama stimulated interest in and acceptance of major elements of TQM in the manufacturer's American divisions. Nevertheless, Cole portrays even a quality exemplar like Hewlett-Packard as having learned to 'surf quality fads' rather than having established a coherent, well-institutionalized program.

Organizational surveys show widespread development of TQM in American industry by the late 1980s. Easton and Jarrell (1998) examine forty-four companies with 'advanced' TQM programs: of these, about half had begun implementation after 1985. Lawler, Mohrman, and Ledford's (1992, 1995) surveys of the Fortune 1000 indicated that about three-quarters had TQM programs in the early 1990s, with modest increases in usage and program coverage by 1995.

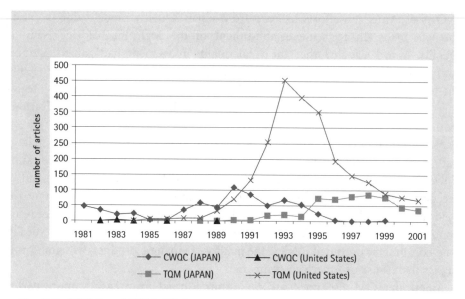

Fig. 7.2 CWQC and TQM: Bibliometric trends in Japan and the United States

Source: Database for Japan: Nichigai, http://www.nichigai.co.jp. Database for United States: ABI/Inform Global.

Figure 7.2 gives bibliometric trends in American and Japanese management discourse around new quality approaches for the last two decades.[4] It underlines the late but rapid rise of interest within the American business community. The boom in TQM discourse occurred in the late 1980s and early 1990s, with a peak in 1993. This peak was followed by a rapid falloff in interest, as the hype surrounding TQM lost credibility. This falloff can also be seen in the number of business consultants offering TQM services (David and Strang 2003), though the maximum number of TQM consultants occurred later and was followed by the stabilization of TQM services rather than a decline towards zero.

The Japanese bibliographic pattern shows a different pattern. Discussion of CWQC/TQM is stable over time, unlike the characteristically American 'boom and bust' cycle in business discourse. If we sum the two Japanese curves, there is little temporal variation between 1980 and 2000. What does change, however, is the label, with Japanese usage once again remarkably responsive to American managerial discourse. By 1994 the American term 'TQM' had become widespread in Japan, with the references to CWQC slipping into the background.

Figure 7.2 also reminds us that the overall level of Japanese management discourse is much smaller than that of American discourse. In 1993 we count some 453 articles focusing on TQM in American journals. By contrast, the largest number of

---

[4] American TQM articles included are those where 'TQM' or 'total quality management' appears in the title. (A keyword search on TQM retrieves a larger number of articles, but the trend over time is little changed.) Japanese CWQC articles are those indexed by the keywords 'CWQC' or '*zenshatecki hinshitsukanri*'. Japanese TQM articles are those indexed by the keyword 'TQM'.

TQM or CWQC articles published in Japan in any given year was 108. Over the twenty-year period, American references substantially outweigh Japanese references (6,872 to 2,863 articles).

While relative market size surely explains some of this differential, we think it is more importantly a product of the different ways that managerial innovation is organized in the two countries. In the United States, management practices are discussed in public forums, and academics, consultants, and journalists compete with each other to promote different ideas and techniques. In Japan, academia is less tightly connected to the business world and key organizations (like JUSE and JPC) promote management practices through direct contact with companies rather than within a public marketplace of innovation advocacy and debate.

At the level of concrete practices, American TQM is not readily distinguished from its Japanese parent. For example, an American-headquartered bank we observed implemented a total quality initiative between 1997 and 2000. This initiative involved training of all employees in a statistical language and methodology for analyzing error rates (Motorola's Six Sigma™ system), formation of more than a thousand cross-functional process improvement teams to reduce organizational errors and speed up work processes, measurement of organizational units on the basis of 'quality metrics' targeting customer interactions, and efforts to share information with suppliers. All of these practices are widespread in both Japanese CWQC and American TQM.

While many of the techniques involved in Japanese CWQC were followed in the United States, they were often implemented in a way that reversed core meanings. For example, Osterman (2000) found a positive correlation between TQM programs in the United States and employee layoffs, and a negative relationship between TQM and gain-sharing programs. The 'employee unfriendly' context of much American TQM contrasts with Japan, where at least until recently, quality efforts are supported by lifetime employment and cooperative labor–management relations (Nakamura and Nitta 1995).[5] Scholarly debate over TQM in the West has largely centered on whether it empowers workers or intensifies managerial control (see e.g. Adler 1993; Parker and Slaughter 1998; Wilkinson 1997).

Management–labor conflict is one reason quality programs are more fragile in the United States than in Japan. In studying the American-based multinational described above, for example, we were struck by how strongly program efforts and success varied across national settings. In the United States, the bank's quality initiative faced skepticism from managers and low rates of quality team formation

---

[5] Japanese firms avoided mass layoffs during the first oil shock in 1973 and the second in 1978. Although there were significant reductions in force during economic downswings in the 1980s, Japanese conglomerates sought to minimize their impact by transferring employees to subsidiaries or other affiliated firms. By the 1990s this strategy was no longer viable, and observers suggest that pillars of the postwar firm such as lifetime employment and seniority-based wages are no more (Numura 1998; Takeuchi 1998).

(Sine and Strang 2001; Strang 2003; Strang and Jung 2004). Many questioned whether the quality program would lead to downsizing. Tensions over the empirical meaning of 'empowerment' also ran high; for example, one team studied by the first author experienced much conflict over whether its high-ranking sponsor would control the team's communications.

By contrast, the bank's quality program was implemented extensively outside the United States. The largest volume of quality activity emerged in Southeast and East Asian operations, with teams from Japan and the Pacific Rim far exceeding American efforts despite the much greater scale of US-based operations. And most remarkably, Asian divisions within the bank continued to pursue quality team efforts despite the eventual loss of headquarters support for the program, while American activities tailed off rapidly once the program lost senior management support.

7.5 REGULARITIES IN DIFFUSION AND DOMESTICATION

The cases of scientific management, quality (control) circles, and CWQC/TQM provide both a historical record of connections between Japanese and American management and a set of examples of the diffusion of organizational practices. We comment on several apparent regularities.

First, the flow of practices from one country to another seems driven by performance gaps, where firms and entire business communities seek to learn from success (for discussions of performance gaps in American industrial history, see Abrahamson 1997; Barley and Kunda 1992 also see Strang and Macy 2001 for a formal model of emulating success). Japan pursued scientific management to learn from American industrial success in the 1910s and 1920s. American firms returned the favor in the 1980s and 1990s, when Japanese quality control circles and company-wide quality control were the focus of efforts in the United States to 'catch up with the Japanese'.

Japan and the United States cannot be described as equally susceptible to each other's practices, however. The Japanese business community was very quick in attending to and incorporating American management models, while the United States was reluctant to learn from Japan. Scientific management was rapidly disseminated in Japan, with Taylor's key treatise translated within a year and early development of an organizational infrastructure within Japan. By contrast,

Japanese quality practices were introduced in the United States long after their development in Japan. Quality circles became popular in the United States more than fifteen years after their dramatic launching in Japanese industry, and it took more than twenty years for Japanese company-wide quality control to be recognized within the American business community.

Asymmetry is also evident when we consider 'boomerang' effects: how the exporter of management practices is affected by the diffusion of its ideas abroad. As far as we know, proponents of scientific management in the United States were uninfluenced by the interest their ideas generated in Japan. By contrast, Japanese business was keenly aware of American interest in quality circles and TQM. Japanese quality circle registrations skyrocketed after the American quality circle fad was launched, and the label of 'company-wide quality control' was discarded in Japanese management discourse in favor of the American label 'TQM'.

In an insightful discussion of the sources of American sluggishness, Cole (1998) emphasizes the emotional as well as cognitive difficulty that American managers had in acknowledging that they had something to learn from Japan. More structurally, America's early technological lead and often hegemonic position within the global economy and polity promoted an internal focus. Japan's late industrialism and politically subordinate position after World War II led to an emphasis on learning from abroad (for a more general argument about the impact of national position within the global economy, see Arias and Guillen 1998).

Asymmetries in diffusion appear on a broader scale as well. One can argue that the American business community is relatively unsusceptible to external influence but at the same time highly infectious. This is particularly evident if we consider the dominant position of the United States in international consultancy, business education, professional associations, and organizational research. For example, Engwall (1998) details trends towards homogenization of management models within Europe and the leading role of American management journals and texts.

These differentials in responsiveness notwithstanding, organizational practices moved from Japan to the United States as well as from the United States to Japan. In both cases, we are struck by the fact that practices were not imported wholesale. Instead, foreign management practices were domesticated in transit.

A good example of domestication is the way Americans reinterpreted Japan's autonomous quality control activities based on small groups within the workplace as voluntary groups that made recommendations to management. 'Sponsored but autonomous' QC circles made little sense in American firms lacking a strong foreman role and experiencing sharp labor–management conflict. Similarly, Japanese business was enthusiastic about scientific management techniques like time and motion study, but not about its emphasis on piece-rate incentives.

Firms and innovation experts in each country thus selected from those compnents of foreign management, the ideas that appeared most compatible with domestic concerns and agendas. In Japan, scientific management was assimilated into efforts to maintain a preindustrial sense of community, while in the United States Taylorism was presented as an alternative to hoary notions of industrial betterment (Barley and Kunda 1992). American firms combined TQM with downsizing, making its implementation an occasion for intensified rather than reduced workplace conflict.

The domestication of diffusing practices provides an opportunity to see 'institutions' in action. As Guillen (1994) argues, institutions are both cognitive models for behavior and structures of power. For example, American managers and consultants developed a simplified, context-independent notion of the quality circle that fit American notions of 'participatory management'. And the oppositional structure of American labor relations and the hegemonic position of top management led American TQM to be combined with downsizing rather than revive the notion that employment represents an implicit social contract.

Finally, the United States and Japan possess qualitatively different 'diffusion infrastructures': patterned ways of learning about and disseminating new practices (see Cole 1989 for insightful discussion along these lines for the case of small group activities). In the United States, all three practices described here spread via a decentralized market for organizational innovation. Frederick Taylor, the Gilbreths, and a horde of 'efficiency experts' touted their own versions of scientific management after the turn of the century. A flurry of independent consultants from Lockheed and elsewhere promoted quality circles, and TQM's early spread involved competition between gurus like Feigenbaum, Juran, and Deming. This competition occurred in a very public way through the business press as well as less visibly through managerial networks.

In Japan, by contrast, corporate innovation was promoted in centralized fashion by publicly supported organizations. The Industrial Research Institute, the Japanese Union of Scientists and Engineers, and the Japanese Standards Association all enjoyed a combination of government and corporate sponsorship that no American consultant could lay claim to (and that rivals would have sharply attacked as 'un-American' if it had). These associations directly promulgated best practices through ties to top managers and leading corporations rather than through a media free-for-all.

These different modes of innovation diffusion are obviously related to the contrast between the 'boom and bust' cycle characteristic of American managerial innovation versus the Japanese pattern of relative stability and internal evolution. In the United States, consultants tend to converge on popular innovations, increasing the volume of unsustainable claims as competing advocates seek to distinguish their approach and undercut their rivals. Since an innovation's popularity raises managerial expectations while diminishing average levels of consultant experience and expertise, a proclivity towards faddish cycles is reinforced (David and Strang 2003). In Japan, by contrast, direct ties between peak associations of experts and major firms generate better prospects for 'continuous improvement' (though perhaps fewer new ideas).

7.6 CONCLUSIONS

This chapter has examined the spread of managerial practices between Japan and the United States, possibly contributing to overmuch attention to this particular dyad. After all, cross-national diffusion is marked by multiple centers of innovation and varied relationships between exporters and importers of practices. The ISO 9000 movement, for example, is strongest in the United Kingdom, Europe, and the British Commonwealth (Mendel 2002), with the number of countries issuing certificates rising from 48 to 129 between 1993 and 1997 (Guler, Guillen, and Macpherson 2002).

We have also focused on a specific set of organizational practices. Scientific management, quality circles, and TQM are all 'named' innovations that received extraordinary levels of attention, and their patterns of spread may differ from those of practices perceived to be simply 'business as usual'. And the story could be continued: in particular, analysis of the Japanese reception of the practices described by Kunda and Ailon-Souday (in this volume) as 'market rationalism'—reengineering, downsizing, and outsourcing—would extend and test the argument developed here.

Of the lessons suggested by the three instances of diffusion examined here, we put particular stress on two. The first is the stability of diffusion mechanisms over time. It is often argued that the world has entered a new and qualitatively different phase of globalization, that in the words of one wag 'the whole world is going global'. While the growth of a global community of management experts deserves close attention, we would emphasize continuities over the twentieth century. The spread of managerial practices across countries is not a new phenomenon. In fact, the diffusion of scientific management from the United States to Japan was in many ways more rapid and extensive than the reverse flow of quality methods more than a half century later.

Second, the process of diffusion provides a site for studying the sources of national difference as well as the sources of convergence and homogenization. Firms and organizational communities do not blindly imitate the managerial practices of other countries. Instead, they interpret them in light of their own theories of effective action and implement them in ways that reflect power relations within the firm. The history of connections between American and Japanese managerial practices can thus be read as an account of the reproduction of characteristic modes of work within each country.

REFERENCES

ABRAHAMSON, E. (1997). 'The Emergence and Prevalence of Employee Management Rhetorics: The Effects of Long Waves, Labor Unions, and Turnover, 1875 to 1992'. *Academy of Management,* 40: 491–533.

——and FAIRCHILD, G. (1999). 'Management Fashion: Lifecycles, Triggers, and Collective Learning Processes'. *Administrative Science Quarterly,* 44: 708–40.

ADLER, P. S. (1993). 'The Learning Bureaucracy: New United Motors Manufacturing Incorporated', in B. M. Staw and L. L. Cummings (eds.), *Research in Organizational Behavior* 15. Greenwich, Conn.: JAI Press.

ALVAREZ, JOSE, L. (ed.) (1998). *The Diffusion and Consumption of Business Knowledge.* New York: Macmillan.

ARIAS, M. E., and GUILLEN, M. (1998). 'The Transfer of Organizational Techniques across Borders: Combining Neo-Institutional and Comparative Perspectives', in J. L. Alvarez (ed.), *The Diffusion and Consumption of Business Knowledge.* New York: Macmillan.

BARLEY, S. R., and KUNDA, G. (1992). 'Design and Devotion: Surges of Rational and Normative Ideologies of Control in Managerial Discourse'. *Administrative Science Quarterly,* 37: 363–99.

BRAVERMAN, H. (1974). *Labor and Monopoly Capital: The Degradation of Work in the Twentieth Century.* New York: Monthly Review Press.

COATES, D. (2000). *Models of Capitalism.* Oxford: Oxford University Press.

COLE, R. E. (1989). *Strategies for Learning: Small-Group Activities in American, Japanese, and Swedish Industry.* Berkeley: University of California Press.

——(1998). 'Learning from the Quality Movement: What Did and Didn't Happen and Why?' *California Management Review,* 41: 43–72.

——(1999). *Surfing Quality Fads: How American Business Learned to Play the Quality Game.* Oxford: Oxford University Press.

COLVIN, F. H. (1947). *60 Years with Men and Machines.* New York: McGraw-Hill.

DAVID, R., and STRANG, D. (2003). 'In and Out of Fashion: Management Consulting Firms and Total Quality Management'. *Annual Meetings of the Academy of Management.*

DOBBIN, F. (1994). *Forging Industrial Policy: The United States, Britain and France in the Railway Age.* Oxford: Oxford University Press.

DORE, R. (1973). *British Factory, Japanese Factory: The Origins of National Diversity in Industrial Relations.* Berkeley: University of California Press.

DRAGO, R., and TURNBULL, G. K. (1988). 'Individual vs. Group Piece Rates under Team Technologies'. *Journal of the Japanese and International Economies,* 2: 1–10.

EASTON, G., and JARRELL, S. (1998). 'Patterns in the Deployment of Total Quality Management', in R. E. Cole and W. R. Scott (eds.), *The Quality Movement and Organization Theory.* Thousand Oaks: Sage.

ENGWALL, L. (1998). 'Mercury and Minerva: A Modern Multinational Academic Business Studies on a Global Scale', in J. L. Alvarez (ed.), *Diffusion and Consumption of Business Knowledge.* New York: Macmillan.

FREUND, W. C., and EPSTEIN, E. (1984). *People and Productivity: New York Stock Exchange Guide to Financial Incentives and the Quality of Work Life*. Homewood, Ill.: Dow-Jones-Irwin Professional Publication.

GOODERHAM, P. N., NORDHAUG, O., and RINGDAL, K. (1999). 'Institutional and Rational Determinants of Organizational Practices: Human Resource Management in European Firms'. *Administrative Science Quarterly*, 44: 507–31.

GORDON, A. (1989). 'Araki Toichiro and the Shaping of Labor Management', in T. and K. N. Yui (eds.), *Japanese Management in Historical Perspective*. Tokyo: University of Tokyo Press.

GREENWOOD, R., and ROSS, R. H. (1982). 'Early American Influence on Japanese Management Philosophy: The Scientific Management Movement in Japan', in S. Lee and G. S. Lee (eds.), *Management by Japanese Systems*. New York: Praeger.

GUILLEN, M. F. (1994). *Models of Management: Work, Authority, and Organization in a Comparative Perspective*. Chicago: University of Chicago Press.

—— (2001). *The Limits of Convergence: Globalization and Organizational Change in Argentina, South Korea, and Spain*. Princeton: Princeton University Press.

GULER, I., GUILLEN, M. F., and MACPHERSON, J. M. (2002). 'Global Competition, Institutions, and the Diffusion of Organizational Practices: The International Spread of ISO 9000 Quality Certificates'. *Administrative Science Quarterly*, 47/2: 207.

HACKMAN, J. R., and WAGEMAN, R. (1995). 'Total Quality Management: Empirical, Conceptual, and Practical Issues'. *Administrative Science Quarterly*, 40: 309–42.

HAMILTON, G. G., and BIGGART, N. W. (1988). 'Market, Culture, and Authority: A Comparative Analysis of Management and Organization in the Far East'. *American Journal of Sociology*, 94: S52–S94.

HARBISON, F. (1959). 'Management in Japan', in F. Harbison and C. A. Myers (eds.), *Management in the Industrial World: An International Analysis*. New York: McGraw-Hill.

HAZAMA, H. (1977). 'Formation of the Management System in Meiji Japan: Personal Management in Large Corporations'. *The Developing Economy*, 15/4: 402–19.

HOFSTEDE, G. (1980). *Cultures and Organizations*. London: McGraw-Hill.

HYMAN, R., and STREECK, W. (eds.) (1988). *New Technology and Industrial Relations*. Oxford and New York: Blackwell.

ISHIKAWA, K. (1984). *Quality Control Circles at Work*. Tokyo: Asian Productivity Organization.

JACOBY, S. (1979). 'The Origins of Internal Labor Markets in Japan'. *Industrial Relations*, 18: 184–96.

JURAN, J. M. (ed.) (1951). *Quality Control Handbook*. New York: McGraw-Hill.

KERR, C., DUNLOP, J. T., HARBISON, F., and MEYERS, C. (1960). *Industrialism and Industrial Man*. Cambridge, Mass.: Harvard University Press.

KINZLEY, W. D. (1991). *Industrial Harmony in Modern Japan: The Invention of a Tradition*. London and New York: Routledge.

KOGUT, B., and PARKINSON, D. (1993). 'The Diffusion of American Organizing Principles to Europe', in B. Kogut (ed.), *Country Competitiveness: Technology and the Organizing of Work*. Oxford: Oxford University Press.

KOSTOVA, T., and ROTH, K. (2002). 'Adoption of an Organizational Practice by Subsidiaries of Multinational Corporations: Institutional and Relational Effects'. *Academy of Management Journal*, 45/1: 215–33.

LAWLER, E. E., and MOHRMAN, S. A. (1985). 'Quality Circles after the Fad'. *Harvard Business Review*, 63/1: 64–71.

——— and LEDFORD, JR., G. E. (1992). 'The Fortune 1000 and Total Quality'. *Journal for Quality and Participation*, 15/5: 6–10.

——————— (1995). *Creating High Performance Organizations: Practices and Results of Employee Involvement and Total Quality Management in Fortune 1000 Companies*. San Francisco: Jossey-Bass Publishers.

LEVINE, S. B., and KAWADA, H. (1980). *Human Resources in Japanese Industrial Development*. Princeton: Princeton University Press.

LILLRANK, P. (1995). 'The Transfer of Management Innovations from Japan'. *Organization Studies*, 16: 971–90.

—— and KANO, N. (1989). *Continuous Improvement: Quality Control Circles in Japanese Industry*. Ann Arbor: Center for Japanese Studies.

LINCOLN, J. R., and KALLEBERG, A. L. (1992). *Culture, Control and Commitment: A Study of Work Organization and Work Attitudes in the United States and Japan*. New York: Cambridge University Press.

LITTERER, J. A. (1961). 'Systematic Management: The Search for Order and Integration'. *Business History Review*, 35: 461–76.

LITTLER, C. R. (1982). *The Development of the Labor Process in Capitalist Societies: A Comparative Analysis of Work Organisation in Britain, the USA and Japan*. London: Heinemann.

MAURICE, M., SORGE, A., and WARNER, M. (1980). 'Societal Differences in Organizing Manufacturing Units: A Comparison of France, West Germany, and Great Britain'. *Organizational Studies*, 1: 59–86.

MENDEL, P. (2002). 'The Global Diffusion of International Management Standards: A Trans-National Analysis of ISO 9000 Certificates', paper presented at the Academy of Management Annual Meeting, Denver, Colorado.

MEYER, J. W., BOLI, J., THOMAS, G. M., and RAMIREZ, F. O. (1997). 'World Society and the Nation-State'. *American Journal of Sociology*, 103: 144–81.

NAKAMURA, K., and NITTA, M. (1995). 'Developments in Industrial Relations and Human Resource Practices in Japan', in R. Locke and T. Kochan (eds.), *Employment Relations in a Changed World Economy*. Boston: MIT Press.

NONAKA, I. (1995). 'The Recent History of Managing for Quality in Japan', in J. M. Juran (ed.), *A History of Managing for Quality*. Milwaukee: ASQC Quality Press, 517–52.

NUMURA, M. (1998). 'Japan's "Total Employment" and Its Decline'. *Japanese Economy*, 26/1: 55–101.

OSTERMAN, P. (2000). 'Work Reorganization in an Era of Restructuring: Trends in Diffusion and Effects on Employee Welfare'. *Industrial & Labor Relations Review*, 53: 179–97.

PARKER, M., and SLAUGHTER, J. (1998). 'Should the Labor Movement Buy TQM?' *Journal of Organisational Change Management*, 6: 43–57.

SHENHAV, Y. (1995). 'From Chaos to Systems: The Engineering Foundations of Organization Theory'. *Administrative Science Quarterly*, 40: 557–85.

—— (1999). *Manufacturing Rationality: The Engineering Foundations of the Managerial Revolution*. Oxford: Oxford University Press.

SINE, W. D., and STRANG, D. (2001). 'On the Road Again: Quality Teams and National Culture in a Global Bank'. *American Sociological Association*, Anaheim, Calif.

STARK, D. (1980). 'Class Struggle and the Transformation of the Labor Process'. *Theory and Society*, 9: 89–130.

STRANG, D. (2003). 'The Diffusion of TQM in a Global Bank', in J. A. C. Baum and O. Sorenson (eds.), *Geography and Strategy: Advances in Strategic Management* 20. Amsterdam and London: Elsevier/JAI.

—— and JUNG, D. (2004). 'Organizational Change as an Orchestrated Social Movement: Determinants and Implications of Recruitment to a Quality Initiative', in G. Davis, D. McAdam, W. R. Scott, and M. Zald (eds.), *Social Movements and Organizational Theory*. Cambridge: Cambridge University Press.

—— and MACY, M. W. (2001). 'In Search of Excellence: Fads, Success Stories, and Adaptive Emulation'. *American Journal of Sociology*, 107: 147–82.

TAKEUCHI, Y. (1998). 'The End of Company-ism'. *Japanese Economy*, 26/1: 33–54.

TAYLOR, F. W. (1967[1911]). *Principles of Scientific Management*. New York: Harper.

TRIANDIS, H. (1995). *Individualism and Collectivism*. Boulder, Colo.: Westview.

TSUTSUI, W. M. (1996). 'W. Edwards Deming and the Origins of Quality Control in Japan'. *Journal of Japanese Studies*, 22/2: 295–325.

WARNER, M. (1994). 'Japanese Culture, Western Management: Taylorism and Human Resources in Japan'. *Organization Studies*, 15: 509–34.

WESTNEY, E. (1987). *Imitation and Innovation: The Transfer of Western Organizational Patterns to Meiji Japan*. Cambridge, Mass.: Harvard University Press.

WILKINSON, A. (1997). 'Bouquets, Brickbats, and Blinkers: Total Quality Management and Employee Involvement in Practice'. *Organization Studies*, 18: 799–819.

CHAPTER 8

....

MANAGERS, MARKETS, AND IDEOLOGIES

DESIGN AND DEVOTION REVISITED

....

GIDEON KUNDA

GALIT AILON-SOUDAY

8.1 INTRODUCTION

....

In a paper titled 'Design and Devotion' published in 1992 in *Administrative Science Quarterly*, Barley and Kunda examined the historical evolution of managerial ideology in the United States between the late nineteenth and late twentieth century. Managerial ideology, in their view, is 'a stream of discourse that promulgates, however unwittingly, a set of assumptions about the nature of ... corporations, employees, managers, and the means by which the latter can direct the other two'.[1] Based on bibliometric analysis and content analysis of a wide range of managerial texts, they argued that managerial rhetoric developed in periodical surges of theorizing that alternated between two distinct types of ideology:

---

[1] Barley and Kunda's study drew inspiration from Bendix's classical study of managerial ideology and joined a small but steady stream of scholars who attempted to account for the substance of managerial rhetoric in both its academic and practitioner-oriented form. These include Abrahamson (1997) and Czarniawska-Joerges (1988).

normative and rational. Normative ideologies see the organization as a locus of shared values and moral involvement in which control rests on shaping workers' identities, emotions, attitudes, and beliefs. Rational ideologies, on the other hand, view the organization as a machine consisting of calculative actors in which control rests on managerial ability to manipulate systems. The specific periodized surges they identify lasted approximately two decades each. They are: the normative rhetoric of Industrial Betterment (1870–1900), the rational rhetoric of Scientific Management (1900–1923), the normative rhetoric of Human Relations (1925–1955), the rational rhetoric of Systems Rationalism (1955–1980), and, finally, the normative rhetoric of Organizational Culture and Quality (1980–1992).[2]

Following the logic of Barley and Kunda's model one might have predicted that the rhetoric of culture and quality with its associated notions of corporate communities, guiding values, and committed, loyal employees would continue its surge well into the last decade of the twentieth century and perhaps beyond. However, the twists and turns of history are never as neat and predictable as the models designed to capture them would suggest. In fact, as Barley and Kunda were researching and writing their paper, a new rhetorical surge—consisting of terms such as 'reengineering', 'downsizing', 'outsourcing', 'distributed work', to name a few—was gathering momentum and ultimately came to dominate American managerial discourse in the 1990s. This new paradigm, which we call 'market rationalism', uses the root image of the market and of the patterned relationships between rational market actors to capture, understand, and describe corporate realities and to guide managerial practice.

In this chapter we use Barley and Kunda's framework to illustrate and interpret the main themes of market rationalism in the American context.[3] Then, based on a review of the research literature, we discuss some of the actual transformations in the organization of work that appear to be related to the managerial rhetoric of the period. We conclude by offering some speculative thoughts on the nature of managerial ideology and on its future directions.

---

[2] Barley and Kunda (1992) explored various material explanations for this pattern of alternating surges. They found little or no connection between this pattern and the quality of labor relations, but did find evidence linking particular surges to changes in the long-term business cycle.

[3] To accomplish this, we studied managerial texts published in the United States between 1988 and 2002. We were not able, within the confines of this study, to create a broad and representative database of texts, nor did we employ the bibliometric techniques that Barley and Kunda used to support their claims. Instead, we read and interpreted a selection of the most widely distributed and broadly recognized texts culled from the managerial best-seller lists and the most popular managerial publications, and attempted to identify the underlying ideological orientations characteristic of them. It is not always easy to distinguish rhetoric from research. The distinction we make is between texts aimed at the academic community that use data and evidence of a scientific nature and those that are driven by a commercial interest.

8.2 MARKET RATIONALISM: PREINDUSTRIAL MARKETS IN POSTINDUSTRIAL TIMES

Market rationalism's starting point is the claim that the environment of business has dramatically changed. As proponents of this view argue, falling trade barriers and rapid technological advances create new rules of competition. In order to survive in global markets, companies have to adjust themselves to the soaring and changing demand of customers who are no longer satisfied with mass produced, standardized products. Rather, today's customers expect instantaneous, cheap, and customized gratification and can look anywhere in the world to find it (Davidow and Malone 1992; Hammer and Champy 1993; Peters 1992). Thus, market rationalism depicts a worldwide expansion of markets characterized by heightened, ever-changing, and constantly accelerating competition that collapses space and time boundaries and makes customers unprecedentedly powerful.

These new realities, it is claimed, present the American corporate world, and by extension America itself, with a serious challenge. Proponents of this view repeatedly warn readers of America's eroding status as an economic empire, especially in relation to the Far East on one hand, and a resurgent European bloc, on the other. Apprehensions such as, 'by the year 2015 the United States will either be a leader ... or it will be a postindustrial version of a developing country' (Davidow and Malone 1992: 2) seem designed to evoke a sense of urgency. In this limitless, placeless, timeless market, many competitors are positioning themselves to take America's place. Business leaders and managers are thus exhorted not only in the name of their corporate responsibility but also as a patriotic duty to do what it takes to prevail once again.

The good news, Market Rationalists maintain, is that the battle is not lost. 'Yes, We're Down', claims the title of a *Business Week* special report, but 'No, We're Not Out' (Pennar 1990: 34). There are measures that can be taken and these are framed as fundamental: tough measures for tough times. For example, speaking of 'a crisis that will not go away', Michael Hammer and James Champy, authors of the bestselling *Reengineering the Corporation* (1993: 7) argue that 'American corporations must undertake nothing less than radical reinvention of how they do their work'. Similarly, Thomas H. Davenport, author of *Process Innovation* (1993: 1), claims that 'today's firms must seek not fractional, but multiplicative levels of improvement ... radical levels of change'.

Ironically, however, the 'new business revolution' draws on imagery that is older than organizations themselves. What seems to underpin most of the prescribed solutions is the idea that organizations should so thoroughly internalize the new dictates of the market, so completely tune into its demands, so smoothly flow along its currents, that they should literally assume its form. In other words, they should be undergoing 'marketization' by *blasting the violent winds of the marketplace into every nook and cranny in the firm*' (Peters 1992: 14, original emphasis). Put in theoretical terms made popular by Williamson (1975), these prescriptions call on managers to metamorphose hierarchies, the fundamental form of organization and the backbone of bureaucracy, back into the markets from which they originally sprung during the industrial era. By doing so, they argue, managers will inject into the corporations they manage some of the characteristics that made America great in the first place—individualism, self-reliance, and an entrepreneurial willingness to take risks.

What are managers to actually do in order to effectively adopt Market Rationalist principles in their firms? While there are a plethora of proposed schemes ranging, as is always the case with managerial rhetoric, from the academic to the eccentric, it is possible to divide the prescribed actions into two major groups, both of which appear in one form or another in most managerial writings. First, all the internal bureaucratic and administrative arrangements that stand in the way of firms' efficient behavior should be eliminated.[4] Unlike the proponents of strong cultures who called for a reform of bureaucracy by infusing its denizens with values, norms, belief systems, and emotions that would change their behaviors to the firm's advantage, Market Rationalists seem to have little patience for culture, no matter how strong. Instead, they call for a radical restructuring that generally involves reducing rather than transforming the workforce, eliminating hierarchical layers and functional departments, and 'outsourcing'—subcontracting away most anything apart from what came to be called 'core competencies' (e.g. Prahalad and Hamel 1990; Quinn and Hilmer 1994).

Thus, these prescriptions challenge past assumptions that 'bigger means better' (Cameron, Freeman, and Mishra 1991: 71) and that strength lies in diversification of activities coupled with unification of values. Instead, they turn to what is perhaps the most powerful aesthetic ideal of our times by equating organizational thinness, or leanness, with flexibility, speed, and health. All that interferes with the efforts of organizations to get as close and become as adaptive as possible to the market has to be 'dieted' away. From the ruins of bloated, stumbling bureaucracy, with its large, loyal staffs, its wordy mission statements and hierarchical reporting relationships, functional departments, economies of scale, and so forth, new organizational creatures are waiting to be born.

---

[4] Efforts to accomplish moderate or radical reform of bureaucratic organizations have accompanied the rise of the large corporation throughout the twentieth century (Barley and Kunda 1992). In recent years both their academic and managerial versions focused on promoting, studying, or debunking the 'post-bureaucratic' organization. From our point of view, it is worth noting that 'post-bureaucratic' imagery accompanies not only the recent rise of a new market-oriented rational rhetoric, but was also part of earlier normative rhetorics. See e.g. Kunda (1992) on the post-bureaucratic rhetoric of the 'strong corporate culture' fad.

The second group of prescribed actions consists of a variety of ideas about how these new creatures should be structured. Like proponents of rational ideologies of the past, when called upon to translate the principles of their ideology into prescriptions for organizational design, Market Rationalists turned to the most prevalent technological imagery of the time. Just as Scientific Management appropriated the image of automation and Systems Rationalists used computer metaphors (Barley and Kunda 1992), Market Rationalists conceptualize the organization in terms of the cutting-edge technology of the day: the computer network. More specifically, they envision the organization as consisting of flexible collections of small, self-contained yet interrelated units, free-standing 'businesses', or horizontal, multifunctional, at times even interorganizational teams. Organized around key processes or shifting projects, these self-contained units, 'businesses', and teams should, in this view, strongly rely upon IT systems that enable flexible interconnectedness according to market demands, customers' whims, and competitors' maneuvers. Work life in these organizations may consequently become freeflowing, dynamic, nonhierarchical, and boundaryless, resembling a carnival (Peters 1992: 15) or a jam session (Bohl *et al.* 1996: 13; Kao 1997), but, like them, nevertheless based on an underlying order.

The orderly operation of the potentially chaotic organizational network is governed by the logic of the market. The people who work in such organizations, they claim, are only those who 'add actual value'. Companies wishing to adapt themselves to new realities are called upon to subject their entire workforce to critical evaluation. Indeed, so strong is this dictum, that even CEOs have periodically been subjected to it. Several *Business Week* cover stories and special reports, for example, declare compensation at the top 'out of control' (Byrne, Foust, and Therrien 1992: 38), and accuse CEOs of becoming unjustifiably 'pampered, protected, and perked' (Byrne, Symounds and Siler 1991: 38). But, paradoxically, the greatest attack launched by Market Rationalists was aimed at the prime consumers of their writings: middle managers (see Jackson 1996: 577). In what seems to cast some doubt upon attempts to link between managerial ideologies and managerial interests (e.g. Shenhav 1999), the latest wave of rhetoric primarily challenges the power and status of managers themselves. Tom Peters, in *Liberation Management* (1992: 758), observes: 'Am I a middle-management basher? Yes. Are most of the people who attend my seminars middle managers? Yes. Why do they come? Beats me.'

Peters was not alone. Managerial writers of the period seem united in their efforts to turn middle-management positions into a 'Death Zone' (Hammer and Stanton 1995: 35) of restructuring efforts. In the name of the same ideals that were once middle managers' main source of legitimacy—profitability, competitiveness, cost reduction—these texts declare most of them redundant, and many of their functions replaceable by sophisticated information systems. Consequently, they remain little more than an unnecessary and costly 'glue' (Hammer and Champy 1993: 30). Divorced from the market, the logic goes, they contribute to nothing but their own power and status. In fact, managers' reported resistance to restructuring was often provided as proof of their tendency to be primarily concerned with protecting their own turf. Middle managers, in short, are depicted as relics of a bureaucratic past that will, to a great extent, vanish, and their resistance as little more than proof of this assertion.

This should not, however, be taken to imply that Market Rationalists sought to eliminate management altogether. Managerial layers, they claimed, should indeed vanish, but management should not. It should transform itself. Thus, employees themselves should be 'empowered'. In this view customers are the ultimate source of authority, and organizational leaders should delegate responsibility for many of the traditional managerial tasks to those who are closest to the market—the employees doing the actual work. Workers, in other words, are, to a greater extent than previously imagined, to manage themselves. When necessary, they are to be organized in autonomous, geographically dispersed, mixed-and-matched teams or projects that coalesce around a particular task and then break up in order to form a new configuration (Davidow and Malone 1992). Here too, however, they are expected to manage themselves, having the right and duty to oversee entire processes rather than merely execute specific tasks within the division of labor. Their jobs thus 'enriched', they are urged to act as their own bosses, while their 'real' bosses—senior executives and remaining managers—are urged to learn to trust them (e.g. Webber 1993). As Champy (1995: 205), one of the reengineering gurus maintained, 'We are in the grip of the second managerial revolution, one that's very different from the first. The first was about the transfer of *power*. This one is about an access of *freedom*. ... Free markets need free men and women to invent the future' (original emphases).

8.2.1 From Management to Workers

In this imagery of empowered workers embedded in networks and governed by market forces, senior managements' role largely fades into the shadows. Since they are the farthest away from the daily realities of the ever-changing market, they are no longer portrayed as experts, decision makers, or strategists in the traditional sense. And since market-based organizations are devoid of communal concerns, there is also no need to highlight their social and symbolic leadership functions. Thus, the rhetoric of market rationalism downplays both the technical and the normative prescriptions for senior managers' behavior typical of earlier managerial rhetorics. Instead, it portrays them as facilitators or enablers who provide inspiration and encouragement, offer guidance, and design the work environment according to market principles (e.g. Halal 1994). In this scheme, however, they themselves are, to a great extent, insulated from potential negative effects of market dynamics. Apart from periodic concerns with excessive compensation, discussions concerning their own added value seem to be the last remaining 'fuzzy' rhetorical element, exempt from the tyranny of the 'bottom line'. Apparently, then, a rhetoric set on dismantling and decentralizing management in the name of 'marketization' allowed senior management to elude the strictures of rhetorical scrutiny.

In the gap between senior managers and empowered workers left by their rhetorical deconstruction of the traditional middle manager, Market Rationalists highlight the emergence a new type of middle manager: the project manager. A 'market-driven antitype of a sinecurist hierarch' (Stewart 1995: 122), this new management type is charged with ensuring the smooth flow of organizational processes.[5] Project managers are the epitome of middle management in a market environment: they are expected to take initiative, to assume responsibility without authority, to live with uncertainty. Taken to the extreme, this view also renders it plausible to put 'zanies' (Peters 1992: 14) or 'mavericks' (Fierman 1995) in managerial positions, because—it is suggested—those whose vision is different from everyone else's could help attain a competitive edge in ways that others cannot conceive of. Managers too, then, are to be empowered: just as subordinates are to think as managers, managers are to broaden their mental horizons beyond the solid boundaries of traditional bureaucratic rationality that once defined and delimited their jobs.

Between the lines of proclamations of empowerment, however, lurks an image of control that puts clear constraints on organizational members' new found 'freedom'. Members are perhaps not subjected to the bureaucratic controls of their work behavior typical of earlier rational ideologies, nor to attempts to shape their beliefs and feelings characteristic of normative rhetorics (Kunda 1992), yet they are still to be subjected to a well thought out scheme of control. The scheme consists of an old stick and a new carrot. The old stick is the constant threat of discharge. Forging a new employment contract that fosters no expectations for job security (and often glorifies its opposite), market rationalism implies or openly suggests that employers should offer employees their trust, but not their commitment. Employees are to be treated as entrepreneurs, as a 'business' within a business, each of them responsible to develop a 'portfolio of skills they can sell' (Nussbaum 1991: 42–3) and to sustain a market for themselves within the organization. Competing with anyone else who can do their job, they have to realize that in contemporary organizations there are no long-term promises, no strings attached. It is up to them to rise above the competition, up to them to survive, up to them to

---

[5] Project Management is increasingly recognized in managerial circles as a managerial specialty with its own unique expertise that is generalizable across situations and organizational contexts. The professionalization of 'project management' is marked, for example, by the establishment of the 'Project Management Institute' in Pennsylvania and the publication of the 'Project Management Body of Knowledge' by its 'Standards Committee' in 1996.

sustain their own career. Thus, for example, Andrew S. Grove, CEO of Intel Corp., summarized this view in an article published in *Fortune*:

As a general rule, you have to accept that no matter where you work, you are not an employee; you are in a business with one employee—yourself. You are in competition with millions of similar businesses, millions of others all over the world, picking up the pace, capable of doing the same work that you can do and perhaps more eager. The point is, the clichés of globalization and the information revolution have real meaning—potentially deadly meaning—for your career. The sad news is, nobody owes you a career. You own it as a sole proprietor. (Grove 1995: 141)

According to market rationalism, then, employees' motivation is accomplished by causing them to act toward the business at hand as if they had an ownership stake in it. The focus, in other words, is on causing workers to behave like an organization rather than inspire them to feel for the organization, as the normative logic of past ideological surges dictated. Workers are to be treated as the 'sole proprietors' of their professional destinies, liable to be discharged as quickly and easily—and, it is implied, with as much justification—as any failing business in an unregulated market.

Along with the old stick built into market relations with employees, there is also a new carrot. This is the promise of the future economic potential created by current employment, a promise of potential that came to be known in Human Resource Management circles as 'employability' (Bridges 1994). Further building on the theme that employees need to take charge of their own careers, 'employability' suggested that through hard work in one firm, employees learn skills and gain experience useful to other firms. Thus, the main benefit of employment—the new carrot intended to motivate and shape employees' investment of their best efforts in the firms' interest—is an attractive résumé and the advantages it brings in external job markets.

What does all this add up to? The organization as envisioned by the late twentieth-century Market Rationalists is a lean, managerially diluted, and dispersed network of members. Its employees are depicted as 'central processing units' embedded in larger networks that possess all of the necessary capabilities to perform complex functions from beginning to end. They are controlled by being empowered, and their relationship with the organization is purely instrumental: members have to continually guard from competition, face the constant threat of discharge, and expect to get nothing from the organization but financial rewards and a marketable line on their résumé. The underlying logic of market rationalism thus marks a return to the utilitarian notions of employee control that undergirded earlier surges of rational rhetoric. Yet, as far as workers are concerned, there is also a sign of progress, at least in a metaphorical sense. Once conceptualized by proponents of Scientific Management as mere cogs in a machine and by Systems Rationalists as components of a computer (Barley and Kunda 1992), workers have advanced up the technical evolutionary scale to the metaphorical level of an entire computer embedded in a communication network. This metaphor conveys two distinct meanings. On the one hand, workers are self-sufficient machines worthy of empowerment and trust within an organizational network. On the other hand, like all machines, no matter how intelligent, they lack both the desire and the need for community. The technical imagery of market rationalism, in short, constructed the perfect market actor for 'marketized' organizations.

Market rationalism is a managerial rhetoric. We turn now to an examination of how and to what extent its images play themselves out in the practices of contemporary American organizations.

8.3 LIFE IN THE SHADOW OF THE MARKET

The surge of the rhetoric of market rationalism was accompanied by many practical changes in the world of work. These changes bear evidence of a strong connection between managerial ideology and managerial practice.[6] In *The New Deal at Work*, for example, Cappelli (1999) offers evidence for the increasing prevalence of a new market-based employment relationship that essentially brings market logic into firms. Concomitantly, many writers document widespread trends of downsizing and restructuring (see e.g. Belous 1989; Cappelli 1999; Cappelli *et al.* 1997; Freeman and Cameron 1993). Their evidence shows that many firms shed layers of 'fat' through layoffs, while, at the same time, reconfiguring internal structures by compressing job categories and creating autonomous, dispersed, multilevel work teams. Finally, if evidence is needed, there are reports of increased investment in and use of information technology in organizations (see e.g. Brynjolfsson *et al.* 1994).[7]

These transformations, Useem and Cappelli (1997) argue, are likely to gain further momentum. Along with other factors associated with changes in the

---

[6] Whether managerial ideology precedes and leads to managerial action or merely follows and legitimizes it, and whether there are direct causal links between them or the two are only loosely coupled, if at all, are long-standing and oft debated questions that lie well beyond the scope of our discussion. See in this regard Barley and Kunda (1992). While proponents of different views may find support for their positions in our claims, we prefer not to take a position. Instead, our interest is in establishing the close correspondence between formulations of market rationality and practices that promote market-based organizational arrangements.

[7] This should not be taken to imply sweeping changes in the world of organizational practices. As Barley and Kunda (1992) claim, practical organizational arrangements do not change as dramatically as the rhetorics purporting to describe them (see Alvesson and Thompson, in this volume).

economy and the labor force, they pose mounting challenges to many industrial institutions that once seemed solid and unshakable, blurring many taken-for-granted, work-related categories and distinctions and replacing them with new ones. In what follows, we offer a three-section summary of research findings concerning the changes that accompanied the surge of market rationalism and a discussion of their implications.

8.3.1 Peripheries Invade the Center

Contemporary researchers concur that in many organizations work conditions that were once typical of peripheral employees are now shared by core employees. As the logic of market rationalism takes hold along with its central practice of downsizing and outsourcing, the traditional implicit bargain struck with the salaried employees of companies' middle and upper ranks no longer holds (Kunda and Van Maanen 1999). Principles of secure, long-term employment, internal career development, and stable pay, are, in Cappelli's (1999: 35) words, 'largely dead'. Instead, as Christensen (1991: 140) suggests, 'Many companies now think of their personnel in the same manner as they do of their inventories, striving for a just-in-time staffing strategy to parallel their just-in-time inventory systems.'

The implications of these changes are far-reaching. As Kunda and Van Maanen (1999: 66) claim, they imply that 'surviving residents of the core of the business firm are beginning to experience conditions once reserved—indeed thought natural—for their distant neighbor, the hourly workforce of blue, pink, or no collar'. More specifically, core employees under such corporate regimes face reductions in employment security, declining investment in internal human resource development, increases in risks, and, with the collapse of stable internal wage structures, rising uncertainty concerning pay, if not actual stagnation of wages and benefits (Cappelli 1997b; 1999; Osterman 1997; Rifkin 1995). Moreover, with the declining (often downsized) number of employees who share the load, the work of organizational members has become increasingly long and stressful (Rifkin 1995; Cappelli 1997b; Schor 1992). Witnessing the organization do away with many of their fellow workers, and, along with them, many of its family-inspired values (Hochschild 1997), they are also often inflicted with a 'layoff survivor sickness' (Noer 1993), suffering anger, diminished morale, and even guilt (Cappelli 1997b). While some claim that restructurings have also made work more challenging, creative, and engaging (Osterman 1997; Useem and Cappelli 1997),[8] the bottom line seems

---

[8] This is stated with regard to restructuring rather than downsizing. As Useem and Cappelli (1997: 59) claim, however, the two are generally inseparable: 'Companies that had taken downsizing steps, thereby increasing employee insecurity and stress, were also found to have introduced the work redesign measures, which increased employee attachment and productivity.'

to be that 'more is expected of employees while less is offered to them' (Cappelli 1997a: 10).

Nevertheless, those holding on to their jobs still seem better off than the growing number of those who are laid off and displaced. With regard to this latter group, it is reported, for example, that job displacement shifts many to the lower end of the income distribution (Cappelli 1997b) and that it tends to involve extended post-displacement joblessness (Ruhm 1991). The luckier victims of downsizing often begin a 'boundaryless career' (Arthur and Rousseau 1996) of inter-organizational job-hopping. In their employment experience, 'The imagery of love and marriage fades into obscurity, replaced by short-term affairs or one-night stands' (Kunda and Van Maanen 1999: 73). While this is not necessarily bad for some, particularly high end temporary workers (Barley and Kunda 2004) during periods of tight labor markets, when there is a downturn in the economy it implies heightened uncertainty and anxiety.

With so many organizations undergoing similar processes, the invasion of the periphery asserts itself on higher levels of analysis as well. At the industry level, for example, conditions thought 'natural' for the manufacturing sector and for blue-collar work have been diffusing into virtually every sector and collar color scheme. Most evidently, reports suggest that dislocation is distributed throughout the economy, and white-collar unemployment, relative to overall unemployment rates, has risen steadily since the 1980s (Cappelli 1999).

Furthermore, there is evidence for an invasion of the periphery at an even higher level of analysis: a global periphery. With the emergence of a single, global marketplace, American workers are forced to compete with an international labor pool. Contemporary technological developments heighten the labor competition (see e.g. Aronowitz and DiFazio 1994; Aronowitz *et al.* 1998; Brynjolfsson *et al.* 1994; Rifkin 1995), in part by affording employers the flexibility to locate work anywhere in the world. Thus, at least some of the changes we discussed could be interpreted as a sign of the diffusion of some of the conditions that are characteristic of industrializing countries into the postindustrial center of the world.

8.3.2 The Transformation of Management

Middle managers, researchers argue, took the greatest blow during the 1990s because for them the changes during this period marked the sharpest departure from the past. Often the target of downsizing, managers went from one of the most secure organizational occupations to one of the least (Cappelli 1992, 1999). Furthermore, since their work is largely governed by internal standards and their skills often organizationally-specific, displacement often had a devastating effect upon their careers. Many have had little chance of finding an equivalent job with comparable benefits (Rifkin 1995). Often suffering periods of unemployment, some have had to leave the managerial field altogether and others have gotten used to more horizontal career paths and interorganizational mobility (Useem 1991). In many cases managers themselves bore the cost of adjusting to the model of the market by paying outside management coaches and mentors for skill development and career advice (Cappelli 1999). Facing 'broken ladders' (Osterman 1996), a 'new deal' that is poorly suited for their occupation (Cappelli 1999), and, consequently, sharp drops in morale (Cappelli 1997b), their situation marked a steep decline from past glories.

In a sense, during the 1990s, middle managers faced a worse situation than that of blue-collar workers, for they had none of the protections of the 'traditional' proletariat. More specifically, they had neither the protection of unions nor of labor laws (Cappelli 1999), which, though sometimes inefficient and even counterproductive (Rifkin 1995), still seem to bestow some power and offer safety nets for the laboring class. Ironically, all this occured at a time in which managers themselves embraced the entrepreneurial rhetoric. As their situation worsened, they tended to conform to the ideological fashion by donning the mask of the independent, self-regulating, and active agent, albeit while realizing that they had actually become much less powerful (Kunda and Van Maanen 1999).

But if this, indeed, is the trend, who is left to play elite? Some managers, it is no surprise, are spared. Top executives have not only been out of the woods but even seemed to have flourished during the past decades. As Cappelli (1997a, 1999) shows, senior executives' contracts typically offer them special protection from restructuring not enjoyed by other employees and extraordinary compensation packages, ensuring that much of the productivity gains and increased profit margins of the past decades flow to them (Rifkin 1995). Thus, it appears that the traditional hierarchical division within most workplaces between supervisors and supervisees, managers and workers, while still clearly in place, has been overshadowed, or at least complemented, by a new division between the small number of top executives who are protected from market forces and everyone else. Perhaps it is not going too far to speculate that senior executives' privileged place in the division of managerial labor, coupled with adherence to the principles of market rationalism—a managerial ideology stripped of normative prescriptions and moral concerns—contributed to the prevalence of the self-serving and even illegal managerial behaviors that have recently become a matter of public concern with the exposure of executive misbehavior at Enron and subsequent reports of managerial excess.

8.3.3 The Rise of Contingent Work

While estimates of the extent of contingent work in the United States vary, largely because of disagreements as to how it should be defined, there seems to be agreement that it is substantially growing.[9] More and more companies increasingly institute a two-tier system composed of a shrinking, salaried core that is augmented by an expanding pool of contingent workers who have weak ties to the company, are generally hired for finite periods, and typically receive no benefits (Christensen 1991). These contingent workers bolster the temporary employment industry which, in turn, is becoming much more sophisticated and diversified (Peck and Theodore 1998). No longer confined to clerical workers, it incorporates workers in every position, industry, and sector and of virtually any profession (see e.g. Aronowitz and DiFazio 1994; Barker and Christensen 1998; Barley and Kunda 2004; Rifkin 1995).

Despite increased diversification, it is still customary to divide the contingent labor force into two major groups: the low-skilled and the high-skilled. For low-skilled workers, research shows that contingent work involves many disadvantages. Specifically, contingent workers are often paid less than permanent employees, receive fewer if any benefits, must bear greater risk and insecurity, and have a limited ability to develop or change careers (Barker and Christensen 1998; Belous 1989; Cappelli 1999). Moreover, they often face de-skilling, devaluing, and alienation (Rogers 1995, 2000); stigmatization and eroded self-esteem (Henson 1996); and vulnerability to exploitation (McAllister 1998). Indeed, these workers are also less protected than 'regular' employees: outsourcing allows companies to bypass unions (Belous 1989; Rifkin 1995), US Labor Law is inadequate to protect contingent workers (duRivage, Carré, and Tilly 1998), and nonstandard jobs limit their capacity for collective action (Smith 1998). Thus, contingent workers face many problems and hardships due to their employment conditions, but have little means to change or affect them.

As far as high-skilled, professional contingent workers are concerned, the contingency trend alters a century-long historical process in which the once 'free professions', bound only by the norms developed by their professional community, were subjected to bureaucratic constraints and supervision. While this historical subjection often involved conflicts between professional and bureaucratic models

---

[9] Broadly the estimates vary between Belous's (1989) figure of 25 to 30 percent of the workforce to the much lower estimates published by the BLS, the least conservative of which is 4.9 percent. See Cohany *et al.* (1998) for further estimates by the BLS. It should also be mentioned in this regard that Diebold, Newmark, and Polsky's (1997) paper offers data that is inconsistent with the claim concerning the growth of contingent work. Specifically, the paper reveals that there has been little to no change in workers' overall job tenure. According to Barker and Christensen (1998), however, the definition of tenure in that study is problematic as far as co-employment relationship of agency temporaries is concerned (see pp. 5–6). See Barley and Kunda (2004) for a review.

of authority, professionals had generally been treated well in bureaucratic settings. Like managers, they had often come to expect continuous salary growth, regular career promotions, and life long company employment (Useem 1991). Now it seems that many of them lose or leave their permanent jobs only to return as 'contractors' who sell their expertise on a part-time or contingent basis (Barley and Kunda 2004).

Research on contingent professionals is somewhat inconclusive in terms of how advantageous or disadvantageous contingency is for these workers. For example, in Barker's (1998) study of adjunct instructors—the temporary professional workers of higher education—she claims that for them, like for low-skilled temporary workers, contingency involves exclusion, stigmatization, devaluation, and long-term difficulties such as the accumulation of career deficits that hamper future prospects. In a study of highly-skilled technical contractors, however, Barley and Kunda (2004) reveal a different picture. They report that while many contractors did indeed experience a sense of estrangement, uncertainty, and insecurity, most of them found contracting to be more lucrative than permanent employment, consciously preferred it, and accepted its risks. Furthermore, many of them found contracting professionally advantageous, feeling that it offered autonomy and enabled them to develop and exercise expertise. In order to shield themselves from some of the disadvantages of being lone individuals in the market, they developed professional networks and communities to satisfy needs such as training and job seeking (see also Kunda, Barley, and Evans 2002). Thus, for them the 'marketization' of the organization actually seemed to have inspired the creation of a socially meaningful alternative that was in some ways more consistent with their professional identity. To a large extent, they adapted to the new situation and learned to make the most of it.[10]

This ability of contingent workers to adapt will perhaps someday be seen as the origin of the challenges that are beginning to be voiced against market rationalism. Organizations, it seems, are learning that while offering flexibility and cutting costs, contingency also involves disadvantages. Most critically, organizational disloyalty apparently fuels employee self-loyalty. It drives employees to think more like members of traditional occupations and professions whose ultimate allegiance is to their skills and careers and who have little reason to identify with their current, but probably temporary, employer (Cappelli 1999). Indeed, popular writers such as Bridges (1994) encourage labor to stop thinking like employees and develop a self-serving and independent mindset toward their work. While many elements in the present-day economic and legal environments erode workers' ability to do so (Barker and Christensen 1998), by the mid-1990s enough commitment had been withdrawn from organizations to turn a book like *The Loyalty Effect* (Reichheld

---

[10] Barley and Kunda (2004) coin the term 'itinerant professional' to capture the unique attributes of this type of technical professional worker and to set if off from the traditional typology of 'free professionals', employees of professional firms and corporate professionals.

1996) into a best-seller. Chances are that as labor markets tighten, the legal environment changes, and employment policies are altered, the situation will change even more dramatically (Barley and Kunda 2004; Cappelli 1999; duRivage, Carré, and Tilly 1998; Kunda and Van Maanen 1999). When that time comes, change might be both institutionalized and far-reaching. Employers who have been busy cultivating an efficient market-based ideology for organizing workers in the 'New Economy' may then discover that these workers have already set their hearts and minds elsewhere.

8.4 Conclusion

In this chapter we have discussed the attributes, associated practices, and some social consequences of the American version of a managerial ideology that we termed market rationalism. This, we argue, surged during the decade of the 1990s following the heyday of 'Corporate Culture and Quality'. It promulgated an image of an unrelenting, ever-changing global market, and used it both as a justification and as a model for organizational change. To survive in this market, its proponents claimed, organizations should internalize its logic. Broadly speaking, this means posing customers as the ultimate source of authority, orienting work processes to the projects of gratifying the customers' transient, fluid, and increasingly fussy needs, dissolving traditional hierarchies and replacing them with networks governed by market principles, empowering those who 'add value', and 'dieting away' those who do not.

Put in historical perspective, 'market rationalism' marks an interesting twist in the evolution of managerial thought. While seeming to conform to the elegant pattern of alternating surges of normative and rational rhetoric that Barley and Kunda revealed in 1992, it exposes new continuities and discontinuities. The most evident continuity concerns technological metaphors. Constituting the third instance of a rational rhetoric (after Scientific Management and Systems Rationalism), it suggests that there is a tight-coupling of utilitarian logic and technologically inspired images of order. In the case of market rationalism the image is that of the network: a fluid, mix-and-match sort of interconnectedness that draws on the most prominent technological development of our time. Very much like the way that automated machines captured the imagination of proponents of Scientific Management and computer systems inspired Systems Rationalists, the network was now promulgated by writers as a model for conceptualizing and structuring organizational processes.

Market rationalism also marked two historical discontinuities. First, it broke away from the century-long process of institutionalization of the managerial profession. In contrast to previous managerial ideologists who were characterized by an underlying commitment to enhancing the legitimacy and status of the managerial role (albeit in different ways), Market Rationalists threatened to undermine it. Reexamining prior taken-for-granted convictions concerning the managerial profession, they questioned its 'added value' and turned managers into one of the primary targets of organizational restructuring. Second, market rationalism undermined hard-earned achievements of workers. While 'empowering' and conceptualizing them in terms that seemed to give them more credit and respect than ever before, it also seriously contested beliefs concerning the social conditions and protections that they had achieved over the course of the twentieth century. Most evident in this regard is the decline, if not the disappearance, of the notion of employment as membership in a community of work and concomitant notions of job security. Thus, stripped of its high-tech imagery and popular catch phrases, the new 'post-bureaucratic' market rationalism bears a striking, almost eery, resemblance to its 'pre-bureaucratic' ancestors: late nineteenth-century proponents of laissez-faire economics and advocates of the doctrine of Social Darwinism and 'the survival of the fittest' that justified and legitimized it.

Our review of the empirical research literature suggests that many of market rationalism's principles and prescriptions have clear correlates in the world of practice. While there is considerable debate as to the extent of such phemonena (see Alvesson and Thompson, in this volume), and, as always, a shortage of data, there can be little doubt that over the last decade and perhaps for longer, many organizations—and workers—are indeed undergoing processes of 'marketization' and that this has affected organizational and work life in ways both dramatic and mundane. We have, in this brief review, touched, of course, only the tip of the iceberg: the question and challenge of contingent labor, the tensions between core and periphery, and the changing nature of management. Much remains to be revealed.

A review of the historical development of managerial ideology does, however, suggest one more concluding thought about the future of managerial ideology, speculative as it may be. Like other managerial rhetorics, the implementation of market rationalism in the organizational world has also produced additional, perhaps unintended consequences. Most crucially, psychological and sociocultural dimensions of work that the Human Relations and Organizational Culture and Quality perspectives addressed head-on and incorporated into their rhetoric did not disappear once Market Rationalists downplayed or ignored them. They currently seem to be resurfacing in the form of discussions of 'problems' such as employee 'disloyalty', turnover, difficulties in preserving intellectual capital, and unconstrained, and at times unethical, executive actions (Kunda and Van Maanen 1999). Organizational reality, we learn again, is much more complex than the way managerial rhetoric depicts it. While adopting the notion that this is an 'Age of

Unreason' (Handy 1990), Market Rationalists used prevalent images of order—the market, the network—to produce 'reason' that was perhaps fashionably elegant but, like many fashionable notions, was quickly revealed as somewhat superficial. As practitioners and observers of management now grapple with the problems that have been produced or magnified by market-based restructuring, a new ideological surge might be waiting in the wings, soon to be thrust onto the stage of managerial thought as *the* solution to management's ever-present problem of control.

REFERENCES

ABRAHAMSON, E. (1997). 'The Emergence and Prevalence of Employee Management Rhetorics: The Effects of Long Waves, Labor Unions, and Turnover, 1875 to 1992'. *Academy of Management Journal*, 40/3: 491–533.

ARONOWITZ, S., and DiFAZIO, W. (1994). *The Jobless Future: Sci-tech and the Dogma of Work*. Minneapolis: University of Minnesota Press.

——ESPOSITY, D., DiFAZIO, W., and YARD, M. (1998). 'The Post-Work Manifesto', in S. Aronowitz and J. Cutler (eds.), *Post Work: The Wages Cybernation*. New York: Routledge, 31–80.

ARTHUR, M. B., and ROUSSEAU, D. M. (eds.) (1996). *The Boundaryless Career: A New Employment Principle for a New Organizational Era*. New York: Oxford University Press.

BARKER, K. (1998). 'Toiling for Piece-Rates and Accumulating Deficits: Contingent Work in Higher Education', in K. Barker and K. Christensen (eds.), *Contingent Work: American Employment Relations in Transition*. Ithaca, NY: ILR and Cornell University Press, 195–220.

——and CHRISTENSEN, K. (1998). 'Controversy and Challenges Raised by Contingent Work Arrangements', in K. Barker and K. Christensen (eds.), *Contingent Work: American Employment Relations in Transition*. Ithaca, NY: ILR and Cornell University Press, 1–20.

BARLEY, S. R., and KUNDA, G. (1992). 'Design and Devotion: Surges of Rational and Normative Ideologies of Control in Managerial Discourse'. *Administrative Science Quarterly*, 47: 363–99.

————(2004). *Gurus, Hired Guns and Warm Bodies: Itinerant Experts in a Knowledge Economy*. Princeton: Princeton University Press.

BELOUS, R. S. (1989). *The Contingent Economy: The Growth of the Temporary, Part-Time and Subcontracted Workforce*. Washington: National Planning Association, Report No. 239.

BOHL, D. L., SLOCUM, J. W., LUTHANS, F., and HODGETTS, R. H. (1996). 'Ideas That Will Shape the Future of Management Practice'. *Organizational Dynamics*, Summer: 7–13.

BRIDGES, W. (1994). *Job Shift: How to Prosper in a Workplace Without Jobs*. Reading, Mass.: Addison-Wesley.

BRYNJOLFSSON, E., MALONE, T. W., GURBAXANI, V., and KAMBIL, A. (1994). 'Does Information Technology Lead to Smaller Firms?' *Management Science*, 40/12: 1628–44.

BYRNE, J. A., FOUST, D., and THERRIEN, L. (1992). 'Executive Pay'. *Business Week*, March 30: 38–44.

——SYMOUNDS, W. C., and SILER, J. F. (1991). 'CEO Disease'. *Business Week*, April 1: 38–44.

CAMERON, K., FREEMAN, S. J., and MISHRA, A. K. (1991). 'Best Practices in White-Collar Downsizing: Managing Contradictions'. *Academy of Management Executive*, 5/3: 57–73.

CAPPELLI, P. (1992). 'Examining Managerial Displacement'. *Academy of Management Journal*, 35/1: 203–317.

—— (1997a). 'Introduction', in P. Cappelli, L. Bassi, H. Katz, D. Knoke, P. Osterman and M. Useem (eds.), *Change at Work*. London: Oxford University Press, 3–14.

—— (1997b). 'The Effects of Restructuring on Employees', in P. Cappelli, L. Bassi, H. Katz, D. Knoke, P. Osterman and M. Useem (eds.), *Change at Work*. New York: Oxford University Press, 173–207.

—— (1999). *The New Deal at Work: Managing the Market-Driven Workforce*. Boston: Harvard Business School Press.

P. CAPPELLI, L. BASSI, H. KATZ, D. KNOKE, P. OSTERMAN and M. USEEM (eds.) (1997). *Change at Work*. New York: Oxford University Press.

CHAMPY, J. (1995). *Reengineering Management: The Mandate for New Leadership*. New York: HarperBusiness.

CHRISTENSEN, K. (1991). 'The Two-Tiered Workforce in U.S. Corporations', in P. Doeringer et al. (eds.), *Turbulence in the American Workplace*. New York: Oxford University Press, 140–55.

COHANY, S. R., HIPPLE, S. B., NARDONE, T. J., POLIVKA, A. E., and STEWARD, J. C. (1998). 'Counting the Workers: Results of a First Survey', in K. Barker and K. Christensen (eds.), *Contingent Work: American Employment Relations in Transition*. Ithaca, NY: ILR and Cornell University Press, 41–68.

CZARNIAWSKA-JOERGES, B. (1988). *Ideological Control in Nonideological Organizations*. New York: Praeger.

DAVENPORT, T. H. (1993). *Process Innovation: Reengineering Work through Information Technology*. Boston: Harvard Business School Press.

DAVIDOW, W. H., and MALONE, M. S. (1992). *The Virtual Corporation: Structuring and Revitalizing the Corporation for the 21st Century*. New York: HarperBusiness.

DIEBOLD, F. X., NEWMARK, D., and POLSKY, D. (1997). 'Job Stability in the United States'. *Journal of Labor Economics*, 15/2: 206–33.

duRIVAGE, V. L., CARRÉ, F. J., and TILLY, C. (1998). 'Making Labor Law Work for Part-Time and Contingent Workers', in K. Barker and K. Christensen (eds.), *Contingent Work: American Employment Relations in Transition*. Ithaca, NY: ILR and Cornell University Press, 263–80.

FIERMAN, J. (1995). 'Winning Ideas from Maverick Managers'. *Fortune*, February 6: 40–6.

FREEMAN, S. J., and CAMERON, K. S. (1993). 'Organizational Downsizing: A Convergence and Reorientation Framework'. *Organization Science*, 4/1: 10–29.

GROVE, A. S. (1995). 'A High-Tech CEO Updates His Views on Managing and Careers'. *Fortune*, September 18: 141–2.

HALAL, W. E. (1994). 'From Hierarchy to Enterprise: Internal Markets are the New Foundation of Management'. *Academy of Management Executive*, 8/4: 69–83.

HAMMER, M., and CHAMPY, J. (1993). *Reengineering the Corporation: A Manifesto for Business Revolution*. New York: HarperCollins.

—— and STANTON, S. A. (1995). *The Reengineering Revolution: A Handbook*. New York: HarperBusiness.

HANDY, C. (1990). *The Age of Unreason*. Boston: Harvard Business School Press.

HENSON, K. D. (1996). *Just a Temp*. Philadelphia: Temple University Press.

HOCHSCHILD, A. R. (1997). *The Time Bind*. New York: Metropolitan Books.

JACKSON, B. G. (1996). 'Re-Engineering the Sense of Self: The Manager and the Management Guru'. *Journal of Management Studies*, 33/5: 571–90.

KAO, J. (1997). *Jamming: The Art and Discipline of Business Creativity*. New York: Harper-Business.

KUNDA, G. (1992). *Engineering Culture: Control and Commitment in a High-Tech Corporation*. Philadelphia: Temple University Press.

—— and VAN MAANEN, J. (1999). 'Changing Scripts at Work: Managers and Professionals'. *Annals, AAPSS*, 561: 64–80.

—— BARLEY, S. R., and EVANS, J. (2002). 'Why Do Contractors Contract? The Experience of Highly Skilled Technical Professionals in a Contingent Labor Market'. *Industrial & Labor Relations Review*, 55: 234–61.

MCALLISTER, J. (1998). 'Sisyphus at Work in the Warehouse: Temporary Employment in Greenville, South Carolina', in K. Barker and K. Christensen (eds.), *Contingent Work: American Employment Relations in Transition*. Ithaca, NY: ILR and Cornell University Press, 221–42.

NOER, D. M. (1993). *Healing the Wounds: Overcoming the Trauma of Layoffs and Revitalizing Downsized Organizations*. San Francisco: Jossey-Bass.

NUSSBAUM, B. (1991). 'I'm Worried about My Job!' *Business Week*, October 7: 42–6.

OSTERMAN, P. (ed.) (1996). *Broken Ladders: Managerial Careers in the New Economy*. New York: Oxford University Press.

—— (1997). 'Work Organization', in P. Cappelli, L. Bassi, H. Katz, D. Knoke, P. Osterman and M. Useem (eds.), *Change at Work*. New York: Oxford University Press, 89–121.

PECK, J., and THEODORE, N. (1998). 'The Business of Contingent Work: Growth and Restructuring in Chicago's Temporary Employment Industry'. *Work, Employment & Society*, 12/4: 655–74.

PENNAR, K. (1990). 'Yes, We're Down. No, We're Not Out'. *Business Week*, December 17: 34–5.

PETERS, T. (1992). *Liberation Management: Necessary Disorganization for the Nanosecond Nineties*. New York: Fawcett Columbine.

PRAHALAD, C. K., and HAMEL, G. (1990). 'The Core Competence of the Corporation'. *Harvard Business Review*, May–June: 79–91.

Project Management Institute (1996). Project Management Body of Knowledge. PMI Communications.

QUINN, J. B., and HILMER, F. G. (1994). 'Strategic Outsourcing'. *Sloan Management Review*, Summer: 43–55.

REICHHELD, F. F. (1996). *The Loyalty Effect: The Hidden Force behind Growth, Profits, and Lasting Value*. Boston: Harvard Business School Press.

RIFKIN, J. (1995). *The End of Work: The Decline of the Global Labor Force and the Dawn of the Post-Market Era*. New York: G. P. Putnam's Sons.

ROGERS, J. K. (1995). 'Just a Temp: Experience and Structure of Alienation in Temporary Clerical Employment'. *Work & Occupations*, 22/2: 137–66.

—— (2000). *Temps: The Many Faces of the Changing Workplace*. Ithaca, NY: ILR and Cornell University Press.

RUHM, C. J. (1991). 'Labor Displacement in the United States', in P. Doeringer *et al.* (eds.), *Turbulence in the American Workplace*. New York: Oxford University Press, 46–63.

SCHOR, J. (1992). *The Overworked American: The Unexpected Decline of Leisure*. New York: Basic Books.

SHENHAV, Y. (1999). *Manufacturing Rationality: The Engineering Foundations of the Managerial Revolution.* Oxford: Oxford University Press.

SMITH, V. (1998). 'The Fractured World of the Temporary Worker: Power, Participation, and Fragmentation in the Contemporary Workplace'. *Social Problems,* 45/4: 411–30.

STEWART, T. A. (1995). 'The Corporate Jungle Spawns a New Species: The Project Manager'. *Fortune,* July 10: 121–2.

USEEM, M. (1991). 'Restructuring Managerial and Professional Work in Large Corporations', in P. Doeringer *et al.* (eds.), *Turbulence in the American Workplace.* New York: Oxford University Press, 156–78.

—— and CAPPELLI, P. (1997). 'The Pressures to Restructure Employment', in P. Cappelli, L. Bassi, H. Katz, D. Knoke, P. Osterman and M. Useem (eds.), *Change at Work.* New York: Oxford University Press, 15–65.

WEBBER, A. M. (1993). 'What's So New about the New Economy?' *Harvard Business Review,* January–February: 24–42.

WILLIAMSON, O. E. (1975). *Markets and Hierarchies.* New York: Free Press.

CHAPTER 9

....

HUMAN RESOURCE MANAGEMENT

....

KAREN LEGGE

9.1 INTRODUCTION

....

THE concept of human resource management (HRM) has always proved conten-
tious, though the grounds of contention have changed. An early concern of UK
writing was to try to identify the differences between HRM and personnel management (Legge 1989, 1995; Storey 1989, 1992). The implicit assumption was that HRM
was something new or an improved version of personnel management. Hence the
accompanying debate about why HRM 'emerged' in the United Kingdom in the
late 1980s. At one level we might say that HRM is still the same activity as personnel
management. It is about the management of the employment relationship and of
the indeterminacies in the employment contract. In any case, this focus was short-
lived. It became displaced partly due to US dominance in setting research agendas.
There is little point in discussing the niceties of the differences between personnel
management and HRM when, in the United States, HRM is just another term for
personnel management and because of the quickly established consensus on the
issues involved.

With hindsight it can be seen that this was something of an artificial
debate. Whether HRM was considered to be different from personnel management
largely depended on the point of comparison: sharp distinctions and contrasts
emerged if the normative aspirations of HRM were compared with the descriptive

practices of personnel management, but otherwise faded into several different emphases, all of which, though, pointed to HRM, in theory at least, being, in essence, a more central and strategic task than personnel management (Boxall 1992). Nor is there any interest in continuing to discuss reasons for the rise in HRM, when there is a consensus about the influence of globalization and the 'Japanese Janus', deregulation, sectoral changes, electronic technologies, enterprise cultures, decline in trade union power, and the changing nature of the workforce, in awakening senior managers to the importance of human resources to competitive advantage. So research moved on to focus on more substantive issues: the impact of HRM on organizational performance and employees' experience of work.

This chapter will focus on two streams of theory-driven empirical research on HRM. The first is the 'mainstream', predominantly survey-based research on the nature of 'strategic' high-commitment/high-performance human resource management (HRM) and its relationship to organizational performance. This work derives from a positivist and often unitarist position and is well represented by North American researchers, with its UK adherents representing a more pluralistic approach. Given its dominance in present HRM research agenda-setting in the most prestigious North American journals, I will devote most space to discussing this stream of research. The second stream is the work that derives from critical, often case-study-based, research, informed by a labor process tradition that has been reinvigorated by Foucauldian and discourse analysis perspectives.[1] This research has focused on employees' experience of HRM in the context of lean production, teamworking, and new work sites, whether Japanese manufacturing implants or call centers. It has also been concerned with issues of employee subjectivity, identity, and resistance. Prominent researchers in this stream are typically, but not exclusively, European.

The first stream of work to consider is that which focuses on the relationship between strategic HRM and organizational performance, within the general framework of resource-based value theory (RBV).

---

[1] Due to constraints of space and the editorial brief to focus on empirical studies of HRM, I have largely omitted discussion of some influential Foucauldian inspired analysis (Townley 1993, 1994) and of some of its initiatives, such as cultural change programs (see e.g. Willmott 1993). There is also no discussion of HRM from a discourse or social constructionist perspective that emphasizes the role that language and imagery has played in the development of HRM (Grint 1994; Guest 1990; Keenoy 1999; Keenoy and Anthony 1992: 238–9; Legge 1995). Finally, there has been no attempt to assess the role played by management consultants and gurus in packaging HRM-related ideas, about the search for excellence and competitive advantage, for the easy consumption of practitioners (Clark and Fincham 2002; Fincham 1999).

9.2 STRATEGIC HRM AND ORGANIZATIONAL PERFORMANCE

9.2.1 What is Strategy?

Strategy may be defined as a set of fundamental choices about the ends and means of an organization (Child 1972). More recently, it might be defined as policies and procedures that are aimed at securing, first, viability and, second, if this is achieved, sustained competitive advantage (Boxall and Purcell 2002). That said, there are several different approaches in exploring the question 'what is strategy?' Some focus on the *content* of strategy and its positioning in relation to factors internal or external to the organization that might be salient to securing viability/sustained competitive advantage. An example of the internal, firm-focused approach would be the RBV view of the strategy of the firm (Barney 1991; Wernerfelt 1984). This perspective defines firms as bundles of resources and suggests that the route to developing sustained competitive advantage is to develop resources internally that meet the criteria of value, rarity, inimitability, nonsubstitutability, and appropriability (capable of providing a superior return to the firm's shareholders). Examples of the latter, market-focused approach might be Porter's (1980) generic strategies (low cost, differentiation, segment, or niche) in relation to his 'five forces' model or Miles and Snow's (1978) categorization of firms as prospectors, analyzers, defenders, and reactors, both models emphasizing market-oriented choices. Theories that bring together internal and external perspectives are life cycle theories of the firm or product (e.g. the Boston Consultancy Group's portfolio planning growth share matrix and SWOT analysis). Of course, this distinction between internal and external factors is somewhat artificial. As Porter (1991: 108) argues in relation to RBV theory, 'resources are not valuable in and of themselves, but because they allow firms to perform activities that create advantages in particular markets'.

A second approach, which can subsume the content approaches, focuses on the *processes* of strategy making. A famous distinction is that between 'planned' and 'emergent' strategy (Mintzberg 1978; Mintzberg and Walters 1985). Building on this is Whittington's (1993) useful typology based on two axes relating to continua of outcomes (profit-maximizing/pluralistic) and processes (deliberate and emergent). Four perspectives on strategy are identified: the 'classical' (profit maximizing/deliberate, Ansoff 1965), 'evolutionary' (profit maximizing/emergent, Hannan and Freeman 1988), 'processual' (pluralistic/emergent, Mintzberg and Walters 1985), and 'systemic' (pluralistic/deliberate, Granovetter 1985). The processes of strategy making that are 'deliberate' are comprised of rational, planned, top-down decision making ('classical') and decision making shaped by the social systems in which organizations are embedded ('systemic'). 'Emergent' processes are those that reflect the very bounded, incremental, and political nature of decision making (processual) or, in contrast, the population ecology view of the competitive processes of natural selection, where the market picks the winners and where managers' attempts at strategic decision making are illusory (evolutionary). Presently, the 'fashionable' approaches to strategizing are the processual and the systemic. The orthodoxy is that classical approaches are too inflexible in a world of globalized competition[2] and that the 'evolutionary view' denies any significant role to managerial agency, but is useful in conjunction with institutional theory in explaining organizational similarities and in analyzing the fall from grace of erstwhile highly successful companies, such as Marks and Spencer, that no longer 'fit' their niche.

9.2.2 What is Strategic HRM?

Two quotations point us in a popular direction. A manager in Grant and Oswick's (1998: 187) research study on practitioners' views of HRM was reported as saying that 'my own view is that HRM joins the management of people and the business strategy together'. A decade earlier, a prominent figure in the UK Institute of Personnel and Development commented that the real difference between HRM and personnel management was 'not what it is but who is saying it. In a nutshell HRM represents the discovery of personnel management by chief executives' (Fowler 1987: 3). In other words, strategic HRM is about how the employment relationships for all employees can be managed in such a way as to contribute optimally to the organization's goal achievement. Boxall and Purcell (2002), having identified first, viability and, second, sustained competitive advantage as the central, 'first order', strategic goals for all organizations, suggest that HRM's contribution to such goal achievement is through meeting three 'second order' goals, namely desired types and levels of labor productivity, organizational flexibility and social legitimacy. How is this to be done?

Different commentators espouse different models and approaches. An early distinction was between the 'hard' model of the Michigan school (Fombrun, Tichy, and Devanna 1984), reflecting what has been termed a *utilitarian instrumentalism* and the 'soft' mutuality model of the Harvard school (Beer and Spector 1985; Walton 1985), more reminiscent of *developmental humanism* (Hendry and Pettigrew 1986). The hard model stresses HRM's focus on the crucial importance of the close integration of human resources policies, systems, and activities with business strategy, requiring that they are not only logically consistent with and supportive of business objectives, but achieve this effect by their own coherence. From this perspective, employees are regarded as a headcount resource to be

---

[2] See Boxall and Purcell (2002: 228–30) for a critique of this view.

managed in exactly the same rational, impersonal way as any other resource, i.e. to be exploited for maximal economic return. Thus, its focus is on human *resource management* and the implied perspective on strategy seems to have much in common with Whittington's 'classical', profit-maximizing, deliberate model of strategy.

In contrast the soft, developmental humanism model, while still emphasizing the importance of integrating HR policies with business objectives, sees this as involving the treatment of employees as valued assets, a source of competitive advantage through their commitment and adaptability of skills and performance. Employees are proactive and resourceful rather than passive inputs into the productive process. Rather than exploitation and cost minimization, the watchwords in this model are investment and value-added, of *human resource* management. In Whittington's terms, the strategic perspective here is pluralistic and rooted in a resource-based view of strategy.

This latter model, throughout the 1990s and well into this century, in both the United Kingdom and United States, has come to be seen as the exemplar of what HRM, as a distinct normative philosophy of managing the employment relationship, is all about (see Pfeffer 1994, 1998). In the United Kingdom this tends to be termed the 'high-commitment' model (HCM), emphasizing the importance of employee motivation and commitment (Wood 1996). But increasingly, in both the United Kingdom and United States, the preferred term is 'high-performance work systems' (HPWS), emphasizing the importance of employee 'empowerment' and increased involvement in operational decision making (Appelbaum and Batt 1994; Appelbaum *et al.* 2000; Lowe, Delbridge, and Oliver 1997). Either way, at operational level, this model of HRM comprises such policies as:

- Careful recruitment and selection with emphasis on traits and competencies
- Extensive use of systems of communication
- Teamworking with flexible job design
- Emphasis on training, learning, and knowledge management
- Involvement in decision making with responsibility ('empowerment')
- Performance appraisal linked to contingent reward systems

However, it would be a mistake to see these two contrasting models of HRM as necessarily incompatible. If the stress is on integrating HRM policies with business strategy, in certain situations choosing HCM/HPWS policies may be appropriate to driving the business strategy. They appear to be the logical choice where employee knowledge, skills, and discretion are crucial to the delivery of added value and reciprocal high-trust relations are essential to organizational performance. Such a situation is often equated with organizations pursuing a strategy of producing high value-added goods and services, in a knowledge-based industry, where it adopts a policy of organic growth rather than asset management. But if the organization's chosen business strategy is to compete in a labor-intensive, high-volume, low-cost industry, generating profits through increasing market share by cost leadership, such a policy of treating employees as assets may be deemed an expensive luxury. For such an organization the HR policies that may be most appropriate to driving strategic objectives are likely to involve treating employees as a variable input and cost to be minimized. Further, echoing Boxall and Purcell's (2002) comments about viability and sustained competitive advantage, *human resource* management, in line with the 'soft' HCM model, is only viable if the organization is economically successful or 'hard', if it achieves effective human *resource management*.

At the heart of the distinction between hard and soft models of HRM lies the fundamental and age-old contradiction that personnel management/HRM—whatever the nomenclature—is called upon to mediate: the need to achieve both the control and consent of employees that are '*both* dependable *and* disposable' (Hyman 1987: 43). Integration with business strategy may require the design and interpretation of an employment contract that veers towards control (with assumptions of labor as a commodity, embedded structural conflict, low trust, and transactional contracts) for some groups of employees, but consent (with assumptions about the employee as a valued asset, a unitary frame of reference, high-trust, and relational contracts) for others. Moreover, both approaches may exist within the same organization, as evidenced by the very idea of core/periphery workforces deemed crucial in the achievement of the so-called flexible firm.

9.2.3 Resource-Based View of the Firm

The popularity of the HCM/HPWS models of HRM reflects the present fashion for the RBV perspective on business strategy (Hamel and Prahalad 1993, 1994; Leonard 1998). As already touched upon, resources are considered to be any feature of the firm that is value creating and preferably rare, inimitable, non-substitutable, and appropriable (Barney 1991). This includes the talents and interactions of employees, even if, unlike proprietary technologies and systems, the firm does not own them. While resources are not immune to 'Schumpeterian shocks', or radical innovations that redefine technologies and the nature of businesses, barriers to imitation have been identified. These include such factors as unique timing and learning (first mover advantage, path dependency), social complexity (complex patterns of teamwork and coordination inside and outside the firm, strong clusters of 'human and social capital') (Lovas and Ghoshal 2000: 883, cited in Boxall and Purcell 2002: 77), and causal ambiguity (about the cause/effect relations that explain a firm's performance).[3]

---

[3] The latter characteristic is somewhat controversial and debated. See Boxall and Purcell 2002; McWilliams and Smart 1995; Priem and Butler 2001.

The RBV perspective argues that a firm's ability to achieve success in the long run rests on its ability to understand its core competencies or those that it needs to develop for future viability as well as competitive advantage. Hamel and Prahalad (cited in Boxall and Purcell 2002: 79) identify a 'core competency' as:

- A bundle of skills and technologies that enables a company to provide particular benefits to customers
- Not product-specific
- Represents ... the sum of learning across individual skill sets and individual organizational units
- Must ... be competitively unique
- Is not an 'asset' in the accounting sense of the word
- Represents a 'broad opportunity arena' or 'gateway to the future'

Leonard's (1998) approach is similar, presenting what she terms 'core capabilities' as 'knowledge sets' composed of four dimensions: 'content' dimensions (which include relevant employee skills, knowledge, and technical systems) and the process dimensions (which include managerial systems, values, and norms). Because these dimensions are interlocking and systemic, they can become 'core rigidities' over time, unless firms can renew themselves by 'double-loop' organizational learning (Argyris and Schon 1978). Capabilities are dynamic: over time one firm's core capability (such as outstanding quality or customer service) is likely to be copied by competitors and firms that seek sustained competitive advantage must discover new ways in which to differentiate themselves. What starts as a firm's distinctive capability within a particular business sector, over the years, tends to become a 'table stake' or 'ticket to play', the norm within that sector (Hamel and Prahalad 1994: 226). An example would be quality and reliability in cars, once the distinctive capability of Japanese manufacturers and now the global norm. The crucial factor then in the RBV approach to organizational analysis is the recognition that 'it is the firm's ability to learn faster than its rivals, and adapt its behaviour more productively, that gives it competitive advantage' (Boxall and Purcell 2002: 83; see also Kamoche and Mueller 1998). From this perspective firms should place a high priority on becoming 'learning organizations' and developing 'organizational agility' (Brown and Duguid 1991).

It is hardly surprising then that the RBV view of organizations, by treating employees and HR systems as potentially a source of sustained competitive advantage, is popular with reflective HR practitioners and academics alike and, even among the less reflective, may become the next consultant/practitioner fad. Fitting HR policy to business strategy always leaves HR policy and practice as reactive, if no longer as powerless as traditional personnel management. The RBV perspective accords a more proactive role to HRM as it can be valued not just for reinforcing predetermined business strategies, but for developing strategic capability, improving the long-term resilience of the firm.

9.2.4 Universalistic 'Best Practice' or Contingent 'Best Fit'?

If strategic HRM centrally involves the integration of HRM with business strategy, we need to reflect on just what is meant by 'integration'. Where there is the belief that HRM 'best practice' will *always* deliver enhanced performance, irrespective of business context and strategy, it can just mean senior management committing themselves to best practice HRM policies and practices and implementing them consistently. More technically, following Baird and Meshoulam (1988), integration appears to have two meanings: integration or 'fit' of HR policy and practice with the organization's stage of development and business strategy (external fit) and the integration or complementarity and consistency of HCM/HPWS employment policies aimed at generating employee commitment, flexibility, and quality (internal fit). Well-known models of external fit are those of Kochan and Barocci (1985) (match between critical HRM activities and organizational life cycle); Schuler and Jackson (1987) (match between Porterian business strategies, required employee role behaviors and supportive HR practices); and Miles and Snow (1984) (match between strategic behavior and HRM systems). Desirable internal fit has been categorized by Baron and Kreps (1999) as involving three types of fit: 'single employee consistency' or mutually consistent and supportive policies in relation to employees—this should involve no 'deadly combinations' to use Delery's (1998) colorful phrase; 'among employee consistency' or consistency of employment conditions for employees doing similar work; and 'temporal consistency' or consistency in how employees are treated over a reasonable period of time.

Unfortunately, these forms of integration and their interrelationships are problematic at a conceptual, empirical, and prescriptive level (Boxall and Purcell 2002; Legge 1995). At a conceptual level the external matching process assumes the classical rationalistic approach to strategy making and ignores the other three approaches. This allows the presentation of clear, simplistic models that assume a top-down, unitaristic planning process and that business strategy formulation will inevitably and logically precede the development of HR strategy. It ignores the systemic approach that allows strategy formation to be embedded in organizational and societal cultures and institutions, shaped by numerous stakeholders and the processual approach that recognizes it to be a multilevel, multistage, iterative, incremental, 'messy', and political process. It downplays the necessary match or psychological contract between the organization and the employee and the issues involved if the pursuit of a particular business strategy disrupts this contract. It fails to recognize the limitations of life cycle (issues of organizational renewal) and Porterian models (dubious assumption of the necessary discreteness of the different strategies). It takes little account of the sheer diversity of business strategies pursued by diversified companies. It underestimates the historical, cultural, institutional, and often financial constraints on managers' freedom of choice in pursuing a preferred business strategy.

It is not surprising then that there is only *limited* empirical support for any widespread and close matching of business strategy and HR policy and practice (see Legge 1995, for a discussion of the evidence pre-1995 and Boxall and Purcell 2002, post-1995). Furthermore, from a prescriptive position, there is an argument that this is not necessarily desirable as it may inhibit the flexibility required to cope with new opportunities and market changes (Boxall 1992; Wright and Snell 1998). Similarly, it has been suggested that advocacy of close internal integration 'over-simplifies the paradoxical elements involved in managing people' (Boxall and Purcell 2002: 57). For example, an organization may require a highly committed, 'empowered' workforce, while at the same time pursuing a strategy of downsizing, as is the case for companies in the airline and car manufacturing industries (Pil and MacDuffie 1996, cited in Boxall and Purcell 2002: 57). External fit may undermine the possibility of achieving internal fit.

A further problem is that while external fit with business strategy would argue a *contingent* design of HRM policy, internal fit or consistency—at least with the 'soft' human resource values associated with HCM/HPWS—would argue a *universalistic* approach to employment policy. Can this contradiction be reconciled without stretching to the limit the meaning of HRM as a distinct approach to managing people at work? Indeed, should we focus on HRM as a special variant of personnel management, reflecting a particular ideology about how employees should be treated? Or should we regard it as potentially a variety of very different policies and practices designed to achieve the desired employee contribution, judged solely 'against criteria of coherence and appropriateness (a less rigid term than "fit")'? (Hendry and Pettigrew 1986: 8–9).

This distinction is critical as the contingent and universalistic approaches rest on very different and contradictory theoretical perspectives about organizational competitiveness. The universalistic approach is consistent with institutional theory and arguments about institutional isomorphism (DiMaggio and Powell 1983). In other words, the assumption here is that organizations that survive and prosper do so because they identify and implement the most effective, 'best' policies and practices. As a result successful organizations get to look more and more like each other through practices such as benchmarking. Here we have echoes of Whittington's 'evolutionary' perspective on strategy. In HR terms this equates with the belief that treating employees as assets via the HCM/HPWS model will always pay off, irrespective of circumstance and that the effects are additive (the greater the number of 'best' HR practices implemented, the greater the positive effect on performance) (see e.g. Pfeffer 1994).

Further, in what is sometimes described as a configurational approach, it is also claimed that an integrated 'bundle' of HCM/HPWS practices will have positive, nonlinear, synergistic effects on performance (MacDuffie 1995).

Contingency approaches, on the other hand, are consistent with the RBV theories, referred to earlier, that argue that sustained competitive advantage rests not on imitating so-called best practice, but on developing unique, non-imitable competencies (Barney 1991). This approach rests on the recognition of the importance of *idiosyncratic* contingencies that result from path dependency, social complexity, and causal ambiguity (Collis and Montgomery 1995). From this perspective organizational performance is not enhanced by merely following 'best' HR practice (the HCM/HPWS model) but from knowledge about how to combine, implement, and refine the whole potential range of HR policies and practices to suit the organization's idiosyncratic contingencies (Boxall 1996).

There has been some attempt to reconcile these two approaches. For example, Boxall and Purcell (2002: 69) suggest that it is helpful to distinguish between the 'surface level' of HR policy and practices in an organization and an 'underpinning level' of processes and principles. They write:

We are most unlikely to find that any theorist's selection of best practices (the surface layer) will have universal relevance because context always matters, as descriptive research demonstrates. It is, however, possible to argue that there are some more effective ways of carrying out the generic HR processes (such as selection) which all firms would be wise to follow. More powerfully, it is possible to argue that there are certain *desirable* principles which, if applied, will bring about the more effective management of people. (authors' emphasis)

Further, building on the work of Wright and Snell (1998), Guest (2001: 1093) proposes what he terms a 'contingent strategic contingency model'. In other words, it might be argued that, in capital-intensive manufacturing, a HPWS model may always be preferable as labor costs are a small proportion of total costs and high quality, committed labor can facilitate the optimum exploitation of high-cost plant and materials. In the service sector, however, there is a choice, depending on business strategy, between the 'high road' of HPWS and the 'low road' of a low-waged, Tayloristic, highly controlled employment strategy. Empirical research has yet to provide clear support for this proposition.

This brings us to what has become the key research question about strategic HRM, in both the United States and United Kingdom: what is its relationship to organizational performance?

9.2.5 Strategic HRM and Performance

Is strategic HRM linked to organizational performance on a universalistic (additive), configurational (patterned), or contingency (idiosyncratic) basis (Delery and Doty 1996)? The greatest support appears to be for the universalistic model: that the greater the extent to which the characteristics of the HCM/HPWS model are adopted, the better the organizational performance (see e.g. empirical studies in both the United Kingdom and United States by Delery and Doty 1996; Guest 1997,

1999; Huselid 1995; MacDuffie 1995; Patterson *et al.* 1997). For support of the contingency position, see Arthur (1992, 1994) and Sanz-Valle, Sabater-Sanchez, and Aragon-Sanchez (1999). However, on examination, the empirical evidence for such universalism is more equivocal than it might appear at first sight.

The problems stem from methodological concerns with research design (see Becker and Gerhart 1996; Edwards and Wright 2001; Guest 2001; Legge 2001; Wright and Gardner 2002) and from empirical observation (see Cully *et al.* 1999; Gittleman, Horrigan, and Joyce 1998; Osterman 1994). Methodologically speaking there are problems associated with the specification and measurement of 'best' HR practices and of performance variables. There are also problems associated with the nature of the cross-sectional, survey-based research that give rise to issues concerning the inference of causality, which are further exacerbated by the artifact of what has been termed 'implicit performance theories' (Gardner, Wright, and Gerhart 1999) and by potential Hawthorne effects. Then there are problems with inappropriate and mismatched levels of analysis. Finally, little has been done to unlock the 'black box' of the processes that link HRM with organizational performance and the attempts that have been made have produced highly equivocal results (see e.g. Ramsay, Scholarios, and Harley 2000).

Turning to empirical observation, we are confronted by puzzling findings. If we are to accept at face value the research studies that suggest there is a universalistic relationship between HCM/HPWS and organizational performance, why do we find such relatively little implementation of this model of HRM? In the United Kingdom, for example, the 1998 Workplace Employee Relations Survey (Cully *et al.* 1999) found that only 14 percent of the responding workplaces have 'soft' HRM fully in place (defined as eight plus out of fifteen 'high-commitment' management practices) as opposed to 29 percent which had three or less, 22 percent of which, with three or less HCM practices and no unions, may be defined in Guest's (1995: 125) memorable phrase as constituting a 'black hole'. Similarly, in the United States, Gittleman, Horrigan, and Joyce's (1998) comprehensive survey found that of six work organization practices (teamwork, TQM, quality circles, peer review of employees' performance, worker involvement in purchase decisions, and job rotation) 58 percent of firms had none of these practices. Putting the findings of the empirical studies together (including those of Osterman 1994), there seems to be a consensus that HPWS are more prevalent in sectors competing on quality, whether in products or services, exposed to international competition and employing more advanced technology. As far as workplaces are concerned, HPWS are more likely to be found on the greenfield sites of large (and in the United Kingdom) foreign-owned and unionized organizations. But all this would point to the logic of the contingency, 'best fit' approach rather than that of 'best practice'.

Indeed, as several commentators have observed, the implementation of any management 'best practice' is likely to fall foul of vested interests, politicking, organizational history and culture (Pfeffer 1998). What is defined as 'best practice' is going to be influenced by national culture and institutions, as is clear from the differing HR implications of the 'patient capital', social democratic institutions of the coordinated market economy of Germany as compared to the short-termism of market-driven Anglo-American liberal market models (Hall and Soskice 2001). These are the factors that undermine the exercise of the classical model of strategizing, but which are central to the systemic and processual models. Indeed, it has been suggested that in the Anglo-American world, in the last fifteen years or so, the dominant emphasis in practice has been on short-term survival rather than the development of long-term resource-based advantage, with the widespread, ad hoc adoption of 'hard' policies of delayering, downsizing, and increasingly contingent forms of employment, even if, simultaneously, senior management aspire to a committed, involved workforce (Boxall 1996; Pil and MacDuffie 1996).

9.3 CRITICAL PERSPECTIVES ON HRM PRACTICES

In contrast to the strategic HRM and performance research stream, the 'critical perspectives' stream of research, at a more micro level, focuses on the experience of work under 'new' HPWS regimes. These constitute a useful external check on what have been primarily debates internal to the framework. Given space restrictions, I will concentrate on some representative research on employees' experience of lean production systems and of teamworking and its impact on identity.

   The success of the Japanese economy in the 1980s and particularly the degree of its export penetration and FDI gave rise to much research and managerial commentary on Japanese production methods, both in Japan and in its overseas implants (Kenney and Florida 1993; Oliver and Wilkinson 1992; Wickens 1987; Womack, Jones, and Roos 1990). From an HRM point of view, consistent with a focus on the relationship between strategic HRM and organizational performance, there was an interest in the symbiotic relationship between JIT/TQM production techniques and commitment-inducing HRM systems in order to generate a high-performance work system of reliable and flexible employees to combat the inherent fragility of lean production. MacDuffie's (1995) work, cited earlier, is an example of this interest. But more descriptive research from the International Motor Vehicle program (Womack, Jones, and Roos 1990) and eulogistic accounts from managerial authors (Wickens 1987) made more sweeping claims than MacDuffie as to the universal applicability and success of HPWS. Womack, Jones, and Roos (1990: 225) stated unequivocally that 'lean production is a superior way for humans to make things. ... It follows that the whole world should adopt lean production, and as quickly as possible.' Wickens, writing as Personnel Director at Nissan Sunderland, spoke of lean production, involving mutually supportive teamworking, flexibility, and TQM, as constituting a 'tripod of success'.

There followed a series of case-study-based research studies designed to explore these claims, often by researchers from a pluralistic or labor-process perspective, predisposed to step outside a purely managerial agenda and examine the impact of HPWS on the workers and from their perspective (Delbridge 1998; Delbridge and Turnbull 1992; Garrahan and Stewart 1992; Oliver and Wilkinson 1992; Parker and Slaughter 1988). Their early results suggested an alternative interpretation of working in a lean production system: that such systems exerted high levels of management control and resulted in high stress levels and labor intensification. Indeed, on the basis of their reappraisal of lean production at Nissan Sunderland, Garrahan and Stewart (1992) redefined Wickens' 'tripod of success', as a 'tripod of subjugation': flexibility equating with labor intensification and management-by-stress; quality with control and management-through-blame; teamworking with peer surveillance and management-through-compliance.

Proponents of lean production would argue, however, that in contrast to the high-control, low-trust regimes of Fordism, lean production values the cognitive inputs of shop-floor employees and reverses the Tayloristic separation of conception and execution, so that workers 'work smarter, not harder', with increased autonomy and empowerment (Adler 1993; MacDuffie and Pil 1997; Wickens 1995). Such empowerment is often seen as embodied in kaizen activities in the context of teamworking. Against this background, it is interesting to juxtapose three critical studies of teamworking.

Rinehart, Huxley, and Robertson (1997) report a longitudinal study of the CAMI Automotive car assembly plant, a joint venture between General Motors and Suzuki, organized on lean production principles, in Ontario, Canada. The research was jointly conducted by academics and the Canadian Auto Workers' trade union and involved employee surveys, interviews, and observations conducted by the research team between early 1990 and mid-1996. When the plant opened, workers were promised a different working environment from traditional car assembly plants, one that would be characterized by team-based empowerment and high-trust, cooperative labor relations. The study then documents the extent to which the plant lived up to the aspirations of empowerment, *kaizen*, open communications, and team spirit. According to Rinehart, Huxley, and Robertson (1997), the initial enthusiasm felt by workers during their recruitment and induction was steadily eroded, as was their willingness to be involved in discretionary, participative activities. As far as teamworking was concerned, workers questioned the degree of experienced autonomy, reported the significance and divisiveness of peer pressure, and recognized that management's desire to operate without waste and with maximum efficiency resulted in labor intensification and high levels of stress. Almost 90 percent of respondents considered that CAMI was no different from other car plants. Although one might question whether the union involvement in the research might have biased the findings, they are consistent with other studies, referenced above and below.

Barker, Sewell, and Wilkinson shed a critical light on the reality of autonomy and empowerment in teams. From a labor process 'frontiers of control' and Foucauldian 'disciplinary practices' perspectives and on the basis of case-study research in two consumer electronic plants, they argue that, through teamworking, management exercises even tighter control over the labor process than was the case under Fordist bureaucratic regimes, thus tightening the 'iron cage' (Barker 1993; Sewell 1998; Sewell and Wilkinson 1992). This is through the exercise of what Barker (1993) termed 'concertive' control, that is when workers reach a consensus on how to shape their behavior according to a set of core values aimed at increasing rationalization of production, using peer pressure within the team to induce conformity to these self-imposed norms. Control is via peer scrutiny, whereby self-disciplining workers normalize their productive efforts around the activities of the best performers. Sewell (1998: 422) argues that this control becomes even more effective, from a managerialist point of view, when combined with panoptic surveillance to create a form of 'chimerical' control, where 'the constant and supportive interaction of electronic surveillance and the peer group scrutiny allows organizations to cede a degree of discretion to teams while increasing the probability that it is exercised in line with the organization's goals and objectives'.

Finally, drawing on formal and informal interview data from the 'bewitched, bothered and bewildered' employees of an automobile company, analyzed from a Foucauldian perspective to explore issues of subjectivity, identity, and resistance, Knights and McCabe reveal subtle nuances in employee experience of teamworking (Knights and McCabe 2000; McCabe 2000). First (by far the minority of those interviewed) there are those who seem to have been 'bewitched' by the discourse of teamworking and who, in a wholehearted manner, have internalized its norms and values. Second, there are those who are 'bothered' by teamworking in the sense that they are disturbed by what they perceive to be its incessant intrusion into their lives. They are concerned that some of their colleagues seem to be enthralled by the team discourse and alarmed at what they see as psychological warfare waged by management through an ideology of teamworking. Third, there are employees who are 'bewildered' by teamworking less because of its ideological overtones than because of its attack on established working practices and trade demarcations that reflect and reinforce their own sense of identity. The bewildered are ambivalent or confused because, while approving of the quality standards promoted by teamworking, they feel no necessity to change their practices to achieve them. Rather, such changes threaten their pride (and hence their identity) in having always worked to high standards.

Such research embodies both the weaknesses and strengths of case-study research: the inability to test causal relationships and to generalize, but the opportunity to explore, through 'thick description' (Geertz 1973), people's *situated* sense-making through processes of human action and interaction (Weick 1995). Indeed, the importance of context and the contingent nature of HRM systems and implementation emerges clearly from case-study research on HRM. For example, as mentioned earlier, depending on business strategy, either a 'high road' and 'low road' approach to designing and implementing work systems may be adopted, whether in manufacturing industry, call centers, or teleworking (Ackroyd and Procter 1998; Bacon and Blyton 2000; Holman 2003; Travic 1998). Yet even here there is no completely consistent pattern. For example, some mass service call centers adopt high-commitment work practices (Batt 2000) and some high-commitment services call centers adopt mass service work practices (Kinnie, Purcell, and Hutchinson 2000). Contingencies other than business strategy, such as local labor market conditions, may intervene.

9.4 FUTURE DIRECTIONS OF RESEARCH ON STRATEGIC HRM

Earlier, some of the problems associated with mainstream research on the nature of strategic, high-commitment/high-performance HRM and its relationship to organizational performance were discussed. In spite or perhaps because of these difficulties, whether from a practitioner or academic viewpoint, interest in the HRM/performance relationship seems here to stay. Most commentators already cited have made suggestions for the improvement of research designs. For example, more within-industry, business, and plant level designs; more consistent and valid measures of HR practices; more longitudinal studies; a 'balanced scorecard' approach to organizational outcomes; opening up the 'black box'. Guest (1997) and Purcell (1999) present two contrasting ways forward, one from a universalistic and one from a contingent perspective.

Guest (1997, 1999) suggests that expectancy theory might provide a theory of process to link HRM practices and performance, as it links motivation and performance. Specifically, expectancy theory proposes that, at the individual level, high performance depends on high motivation, coupled with the necessary skills and abilities and appropriate role design and perception. This equates skills and abilities with quality, motivation with commitment and role structure, and perception with flexibility. HR practices designed to foster these HR outcomes—selection and training for skills and abilities/quality; contingent pay and internal promotion for motivation/commitment and teamworking design for appropriate role design and perception/flexibility—should facilitate high individual performance, which in turn should contribute to high-performance outcomes such as high productivity, low absenteeism, and labor turnover, giving rise (other things being equal) to desired financial outcomes. In an empirical study of employees' reactions to HCM/HPWS policies (Guest 1999; Guest and Conway 1997), Guest suggests that the psychological contract may be a key intervening variable in explaining the link between such HR practices and employee outcomes such as job satisfaction, perceived job security, and motivation. Furthermore, although Guest's research is cross-sectional and, hence, raises the usual caveats about causality, the inferred direction of his empirical findings is supported by a similar longitudinal study (Patterson *et al.* 1997).

Nevertheless, Guest acknowledges the limitations of these models in terms of explaining organizational outcomes. While we may be able to measure the impact of HR practices on *HRM* outcomes (quality, commitment, and flexibility), the measurable impact on *organizational* and *financial* outcomes is likely to become progressively weaker because of the range of potentially intervening variables. Guest also suggests that we need a theory about the circumstances when human resources matter more and a theory about how much of the variance between HR practices and performance can be explained by the human as opposed to other factors.

Purcell (1999: 36–8), building on the resource-based view of strategy, has some interesting observations here. He recognizes that, on the one hand, claims that bundles of 'best practice' HCM/HPWS are universally applicable leads into 'a utopian cul-de-sac', ignoring dual labor markets, contingent workers, and business strategies that do not require such expensive practices to achieve financial success. On the other hand, the search for a contingency model of HRM is a 'chimera', 'limited by the impossibility of modeling all the contingent variables, the difficulty of showing their interconnection, and the way in which changes in one variable have impact on others, let alone the need to model idiosyncratic and path dependent contingencies'. The way forward, Purcell argues, is the analysis of how and when HR factors come into play in the management of strategic change. Purcell suggests that we should explore how organizations develop successful transition management, build unique sets of competencies and distinctive organizational routines and, in situations of 'leanness', with greater dependency on all core workers, develop inclusivity and trust. The focus of research on strategic HRM (indeed, the focus of strategic HRM itself) should be on 'appropriate HR architecture and the processes that contribute to organizational performance in the short and medium term, and which positively contribute to the achievement of organizational flexibility and longevity'.

Whether the future research on strategic HRM focuses on the psychological contract or the processes of transition management, it can only benefit from the insights derived from qualitative, critical case studies. In particular, such studies, by their ability to explore in depth contextual contingencies and employee sense-making, can contribute to opening the 'black box' of the processes that link HRM to organizational performance.

REFERENCES

ACKROYD, S., and PROCTER, S. (1998). 'British Manufacturing Organization and Workplace Relations: Some Attributes of the New Flexible Firm'. *British Journal of Industrial Relations*, 36/2: 163–83.

ADLER, P. (1993). 'The "Learning Bureaucracy": New United Motor Manufacturing, Inc.'. *Research in Organizational Behavior*, 15: 111–94.

ANSOFF, H. (1965). *Corporate Strategy*. Harmondsworth: Penguin.

APPELBAUM, E., and BATT, R. (1994). *The New American Workplace*. Ithaca, NY: ILR Press.

—— BAILEY, T., BERG, P., and KALLEBERG, A. (2000). *Manufacturing Advantage: Why High-Performance Systems Pay Off*. Ithaca, NY: ILR Imprint, Cornell University Press.

ARGYRIS, C., and SCHON, D. (1978). *Organizational Learning*. Reading, Mass.: Addison-Wesley.

ARTHUR, J. B. (1992). 'The Link between Business Strategy and Industrial Relations Systems in American Steel Minimills'. *Industrial and Labor Relations Review*, 45: 488–506.

—— (1994). 'Effects of Human Resource Systems on Manufacturing Performance and Turnover'. *Academy of Management Journal*, 37: 670–87.

BACON, N., and BLYTON, P. (2000). 'High Road and Low Road Teamworking: Perceptions of Management Rationales and Organizational and Human Resource Outcomes'. *Human Relations*, 53/11: 1425–58.

BAIRD, L., and MESHOULAM, I. (1988). 'Managing the Two Fits of Strategic Human Resource Management'. *Academy of Management Review*, 13/1: 116–28.

BARKER, J. R. (1993). 'Tightening the Iron Cage: Concertive Control in Self-Managed Teams'. *Administrative Science Quarterly*, 38: 408–37.

BARNEY, J. (1991). 'Firm Resources and Sustained Competitive Advantage'. *Journal of Management*, 17/1: 99–120.

BARON, J., and KREPS, D. (1999). 'Consistent Human Resource Practices'. *California Management Review*, 41/3: 29–53.

BATT, R. (2000). 'Strategic Segmentation in Front Line Services: Matching Customers, Employees and Human Resource Systems'. *International Journal of Human Resource Management*, 11: 540–61.

BECKER, B., and GERHART, B. (1996). 'The Impact of Human Resource Management on Organizational Performance: Progress and Practice'. *Academy of Management Journal*, 39/4: 779–801.

BEER, M., and SPECTOR, B. (1985). 'Corporate Wide Transformations in Human Resource Management', in R. E. Walton and P. R. Lawrence (eds.), *Human Resource Management, Trends and Challenges*. Boston: Harvard Business School Press, 219–53.

Boxall, P. (1992). 'Strategic Human Resource Management: Beginnings of a New Theoretical Sophistication.' *Human Resource Management Journal*, 2/3: 60–79.

—— (1996). 'The Strategic HRM Debate and the Resource-Based View of the Firm'. *Human Resource Management Journal*, 6/3: 59–75.

—— and Purcell, J. (2002). *Strategy and Human Resource Management*. Basingstoke: Palgrave.

Brown, J., and Duguid, P. (1991). 'Organizational Learning and Communities of Practice'. *Organizational Science*, 2: 40–57.

Child, J. (1972). 'Organizational Structure, Environment and Performance: The Role of Strategic Choice'. *Sociology*, 6: 1–22.

Clark, T., and Fincham, R. (eds.) (2002). *Management Consulting*. Oxford: Blackwell.

Collis, D. J., and Montgomery, C. A. (1995). 'Competing on Resources: Strategy for the 1990s'. *Harvard Business Review*, July/August: 118–28.

Cully, M., Woodland, S., O'Reilly, A., and Dix, G. (1999). *Britain at Work*. London: Routledge.

Delbridge, R. (1998). *Life on the Line in Contemporary Manufacturing*. Oxford: Oxford University Press.

—— and Turnbull, P. (1992). 'Human Resource Maximisation: The Management of Labour under a JIT System', in P. Blyton and P. Turnbull (eds.), *Reassessing Human Resource Management*. London: Sage, 56–73.

Delery, J. (1998). 'Issues of Fit in Strategic Human Resource Management: Implications for Research'. *Human Resource Management Review*, 8/3: 289–309.

—— and Doty, D. (1996). 'Modes of Theorizing in Strategic Human Resource Management: Tests of Universalistic, Contingency, and Configurational Performance Predictions'. *Academy of Management Journal*, 39/4: 802–35.

DiMaggio, P., and Powell, W. (1983). 'The Iron Cage Revisited: Institutional Isomorphism and Collective Rationality in Organizational Fields'. *American Sociological Review*, 48/2: 147–60.

Edwards, P. K., and Wright, M. (2001). 'High Involvement Work Systems and Performance Outcomes: The Strength of Variable, Contingent and Context-Bound Relationships'. *International Journal of Human Resource Management*, 12/4: 568–85.

Fincham, R. (1999). 'Rhetorical Narratives and the Consultancy Process'. Paper presented at the BAM Conference, Manchester, September 1–3.

Fombrun, C., Tichy, N. M., and Devanna, M. A. (eds.) (1984). *Strategic Human Resource Management*. New York: Wiley.

Fowler, A. (1987). 'When Chief Executives Discover HRM'. *Personnel Management*, 19/1: 3.

Gardner, T. M., Wright, P. M., and Gerhart, B. (1999). 'The HR-Firm Performance Relationship: Can It be in the Mind of the Beholder?' Working Paper, Center for Advanced Human Resources Studies, Cornell University, Ithaca, NY.

Garrahan, P., and Stewart, P. (1992). *The Nissan Enigma: Flexibility at Work in a Local Labour Economy*. London: Mansell.

Geertz, C. (1973). *The Interpretation of Cultures*. New York: Basic Books.

Gittleman, M., Horrigan, M., and Joyce, M. (1998). '"Flexible" Workplace Practices: Evidence from a Nationally Representative Survey'. *Industrial and Labor Relations Review*, 52/1: 99–115.

Granovetter, M. (1985). 'Economic Action and Social Structures: The Problem of Embeddedness'. *American Journal of Sociology*, 91/3: 481–510.

GRANT, D., and OSWICK, C. (1998). 'Of Believers, Atheists and Agnostics: Practitioner Views on HRM'. *Industrial Relations Journal*, 28/3: 178–93.

GRINT, K. (1994). 'Reeengineering History: Social Resonances and Business Process Reengineering'. *Organization*, 1/1: 179–201.

GUEST, D. E. (1990). 'Human Resource Management and the American Dream'. *Journal of Management Studies*, 27/4: 378–97.

—— (1995). 'Human Resource Management, Trade Unions and Industrial Relations', in J. Storey, (ed.), *Human Resource Management, A Critical Text*. London: Routledge, 110–41.

—— (1997). 'Human Resource Management and Performance: A Review and Research Agenda'. *International Journal of Human Resource Management*, 8/3: 263–76.

—— (1999). 'Human Resource Management—The Workers' Verdict'. *Human Resource Management Journal*, 9/3: 5–25.

—— (2001). 'Human Resource Management: When Research Confronts Theory'. *International Journal of Human Resource Management*, 12/7: 1092–106.

—— and CONWAY, N. (1997). *Employee Motivation and the Psychological Contract*. London: IPD.

HAMEL, G., and PRAHALAD, C. (1993). 'Strategy as Stretch and Leverage'. *Harvard Business Review*, 71/2: 75–84.

—— —— (1994). *Competing for the Future*. Boston: Harvard Business School Press.

HANNAN, M. T., and FREEMAN, J. (1988). *Organizational Ecology*. Cambridge, Mass.: Harvard University Press.

HENDRY, C., and PETTIGREW, A. (1986). 'The Practice of Strategic Human Resource Management'. *Personnel Review*, 15/5: 3–8.

HOLMAN, D. (2003). 'Call Centres', in D. Holman, T. D. Wall, C. W. Clegg, P. Sparrow, and A. Howard (eds.), *The New Workplace, A Guide to the Human Impact of Modern Working Practices*. Chichester: Wiley, 115–34.

HUSELID, M. (1995). 'The Impact of Human Resource Management Practices on Turnover, Productivity, and Corporate Financial Performance'. *Academy of Management Journal*, 38: 635–72.

HYMAN, R. (1987). 'Strategy or Structure? Capital, Labour and Control'. *Work, Employment and Society*, 1/1: 25–55.

KAMOCHE, K., and MUELLER, F. (1998). 'Human Resource Management and the Appropriation-Learning Perspective'. *Human Relations*, 51/8: 1033–60.

KEENOY, T. (1999). 'HRM as a Hologram'. *Journal of Management Studies*, 36/1: 1–23.

—— and ANTHONY, P. (1992). 'HRM: Metaphor, Meaning and Morality', in P. Blyton and P. Turnbull (eds.), *Reassessing Human Resource Management*. London: Sage, 233–55.

KENNEY, M., and FLORIDA, R. (1993). *Beyond Mass Production: The Japanese System and its Transfer to the United States*. Oxford: Oxford University Press.

KINNIE, N., PURCELL, J., and HUTCHINSON, S. (2000). 'Managing the Employment Relationship in Call Centres', in K. Purcell (ed.), *Changing Boundaries in Employment*. Bristol: Bristol Academic Press, 163–94.

KNIGHTS, D., and McCABE, D. (2000). 'Bewitched, Bothered and Bewildered: The Meaning and Experience of Teamworking for Employees in an Automobile Company'. *Human Relations*, 53/11: 1481–517.

KOCHAN, T., and BAROCCI, T. (1985). *Human Resource Management, Text, Readings and Cases*. Boston: Little, Brown.

LEGGE, K. (1989). 'Human Resource Management—A Critical Analysis', in J. Storey (ed.), *New Perspectives on Human Resource Management*. London: Routledge, 19–40.

——(1995). *Human Resource Management, Rhetorics and Realities*. Basingstoke: Macmillan (now Palgrave).

——(2001). 'Silver Bullet or Spent Round? Assessing the Meaning of the "High Commitment Management"/Performance Relationship', in J. Storey (ed.), *Human Resource Management: A Critical Text* (2nd edn). London: Thomson Learning, 21–36.

LEONARD, D. (1998). *Wellsprings of Knowledge: Building and Sustaining Competitive Advantage*. Boston: Harvard Business School Press.

LOVAS, B., and GHOSHAL, S. (2000). 'Strategy as Guided Evolution'. *Strategic Management Journal*, 21: 875–96.

LOWE, J., DELBRIDGE, R., and OLIVER, N. (1997). 'High-Performance Manufacturing: Evidence from the Automotive Components Industry'. *Organization Studies*, 18/5: 783–98.

McCABE, D. (2000). 'The Team Dream: The Meaning and Experience of Teamworking for Employees in an Automobile Manufacturing Company', in S. Proctor and F. Mueller (eds.), Basingstoke: Macmillan, 203–21.

MacDUFFIE, J. P. (1995). 'Human Resource Bundles and Manufacturing Performance: Organizational Logic and Flexible Production Systems in the World Auto Industry'. *Industrial and Labor Relations Review*, 48/2: 197–221.

——— and PIL, F. (1997). 'Changes in Auto Industry Employment Practices: An International Overview', in T. Kochan, R. Lansbury, and J. P. MacDuffie (eds.), *After Lean Production: Evolving Employment Practice in the World Auto Industry*. Ithaca, NY: ILR Press, 9–42.

McWILLIAMS, A., and SMART, D. (1995). 'The Resource-Based View of the Firm: Does It Go Far Enough in Shedding the Assumptions of the S-C-P Paradigm?' *Journal of Management Inquiry*, 4/4: 309–16.

MILES, R. E., and SNOW, C. C. (1978). *Organizational Strategy, Structure and Process*. New York: McGraw-Hill.

——— (1984). 'Designing Strategic Human Resources Systems'. *Organizational Dynamics*, Summer: 36–52.

MINTZBERG, H. (1978). 'Patterns in Strategy Formation'. *Management Science*, 24/9: 934–48.

——— and WALTERS, J. A. (1985). 'Of Strategies, Deliberate and Emergent'. *Strategic Management Journal*, 6: 257–72.

OLIVER, N., and WILKINSON, B. (1992). *The Japanization of British Industry: New Developments in the 1990s*. Oxford: Blackwell.

OSTERMAN, P. (1994). 'How Common is Workplace Transformation and Who Adopts It?' *Industrial and Labor Relations Review*, 47/2: 173–88.

PARKER, M., and SLAUGHTER, J. (1988). *Choosing Sides: Unions and the Team Concept*. Boston: Labor Notes.

PATTERSON, M., WEST, M., LAWTHOM, R., and NICKELL, S. (1997). 'Impact of People Management Practices on Business Performance'. *Issues in People Management No. 22*. London: Institute of Personnel and Development.

PFEFFER, J. (1994). *Competitive Advantage through People*. Boston: Harvard Business School Press.

——(1998). *The Human Equation: Building Profits by Putting People First*. Boston: Harvard Business School Press.

PIL, F. K., and MacDUFFIE, J. P. (1996). 'The Adoption of High Involvement Work Practices'. *Industrial Relations*, 35/3: 423–55.

PORTER, M. (1980). *Competitive Strategy*. New York: Free Press.

——(1991). 'Towards a Dynamic Theory of Strategy'. *Strategic Management Journal*, 12/S: 95–117.

PRIEM, R., and BUTLER, J. (2001). 'Is the Resource-Based "View" a Useful Perspective for Strategic Management Research?' *Academy of Management Review*, 26/1: 22–40.

PURCELL, J. (1999). 'Best Practice and Best Fit: Chimera or Cul-de-Sac?' *Human Resource Management Journal*, 9/3: 26–41.

RAMSEY, H., SCHOLARIS, D., and HARLEY, B. (2000). 'Employees in High-Performance Work Systems: Testing Inside the Black Box'. *British Journal of Industrial Relations*, 38/4: 501–31.

RINEHART, J., HUXLEY, C., and ROBERTSON, D. (1997). *Just Another Car Factory? Lean Production and its Discontents*. Ithaca, NY: ILR Press.

SANZ-VALLE, R., SABATER-SANCHEZ, R., and ARAGON-SANCHEZ, A. (1999). 'Human Resource Management and Business Strategy Links: An Empirical Study'. *International Journal of Human Resource Management*, 10/4: 655–71.

SCHULER, R. S., and JACKSON, S. E. (1987). 'Linking Competitive Strategies with Human Resource Management Practices'. *Academy of Management Executive*, 1/3: 209–13.

SEWELL, G. (1998). 'The Discipline of Teams: The Control of Team-Based Industrial Work through Electronic and Peer Surveillance'. *Administrative Science Quarterly*, 43: 397–428.

——and WILKINSON, B. (1992). ' "Someone to Watch Over Me": Surveillance, Discipline and the Just-in-Time Labour Process'. *Sociology*, 26/2: 271–91.

STOREY, J. (ed.) (1989). *New Perspectives in Human Resource Management*. London: Routledge.

——(1992). *Developments in the Management of Human Resources*. Oxford: Blackwell.

TOWNLEY, B. (1993). 'Foucault, Power/Knowledge, and its Relevance to Human Resource Management'. *Academy of Management Review*, 18/3: 518–45.

——(1994). *Reframing Human Resource Management: Power, Ethics and the Subject at Work*. London: Sage.

TRAVIC, B. (1998). 'Information Aspects of New Organizational Designs: Exploring the Non-Traditional Organization'. *Journal of the American Society for Information Science*, 49: 1224–44.

WALTON, R. E. (1985). 'Toward a Strategy of Eliciting Employee Commitment Based on Policies of Mutuality', in R. E. Walton and P. R. Lawrence (eds.), *Human Resource Management: Trends and Challenges*. Boston: Harvard Business School Press.

WEICK, K. (1995). *Sensemaking in Organizations*. Thousand Oaks, Calif.: Sage.

WERNERFELT, B. (1984). 'A Resource-Based View of the Firm'. *Strategic Management Journal*, 5/2: 171–80.

WHITTINGTON, R. (1993). *What is Strategy and Does It Matter?* London: Routledge.

WICKENS, P. (1987). *The Road to Nissan*. Basingstoke: Macmillan.

——(1995). *The Ascendent Organization*. Basingstoke: Macmillan.

WILLMOTT, H. (1993). ' "Strength is Ignorance, Slavery is Freedom": Managing Culture in Modern Organizations'. *Journal of Management Studies*, 30/4: 515–52.

WOMACK, J. P., JONES, D., and ROOS, D. (1990). *The Machine that Changed the World*. New York: Rawson Macmillan.

WOOD, S. (1996). 'High-Commitment Management and Payment Systems'. *Journal of Management Studies*, 33/1: 53–77.

WRIGHT, P., and GARDNER, T. M. (2002). 'Theoretical and Empirical Challenges in Studying the HR Practice–Firm Performance Relationship', in D. Holman, T. D. Wall, C. W. Clegg, P. Sparrow, and A. Howard (eds.), *The New Workplace: People, Technology and Organisation*. London: Wiley.

—— and SNELL, S. (1998). 'Towards a Unifying Framework for Exploring Fit and Flexibility in Strategic Human Resource Management'. *Academy of Management Review*, 23/4: 756–72.

CHAPTER 10

KNOWLEDGE MANAGEMENT

ALAN MCKINLAY

FEW would dispute the increased centrality of knowledge as a force of production and as a critical factor in a firm's competitiveness (Teece 1998). The rise of knowledge management as an arena of theory and practice reflects management's efforts to cope with this shift in the nature of competition. The central argument of this chapter is that knowledge management is an attempt by corporations to come to terms with new competitive pressures within capitalism for perpetual innovation in products, services, and organization by leveraging the tacit knowledge of their employees (Boisot 1998; Kenney 1997: 88). Understanding, codifying, and mobilizing employees' social competencies has emerged as a key driver of corporate human resource policies. Here lies one of the paradoxes of knowledge management. On the one hand, knowledge-intensive firms confront powerful competitive pressures to accelerate every phase of the product development process. Time constraints on innovation, on the other hand, also place enormous pressure on the creative space ceded to expert labor to experiment. None of these tensions—between creativity and cost; autonomy and management control—are new. What is novel, however, is the intensity of management focus upon the nexus between knowledge, innovation, and competitiveness coupled with the awareness that Taylorist technologies of control necessarily compromise creativity.

Knowledge management is much more than a purely theoretical project. Yet a trawl through the overlapping literatures on the management of knowledge is far from illuminating. They are dominated by prescriptive, implicitly managerialist perspectives. Ironically, despite the declaratory, business-like tone of this discourse one would search in vain for practical guidance about what systems to install, any rough guide to the scale of investment necessary, the timescales for measurable results or, indeed, how one would conduct an impact assessment. Equally unclear would be on what parts of the organization management would be well advised to focus its initial efforts: for instance, occupational groups that may be the most receptive—or hostile—to knowledge management.

Given these limitations, it is wiser to take a step back and begin with the antecedents of the management problem—workplace knowledge itself. This is particularly appropriate as the debates on the nature of knowledge *work* and knowledge *management* have proceeded largely independently.

10.1 WORKPLACE KNOWLEDGE: CHANGING CONDITIONS AND CHARACTERISTICS

The key distinction running through debates has been that between 'tacit' and 'codified' knowledge. Codified knowledge is generic and not bound to a particular time, place, or workgroup. Rules, regulations, and manuals of standard operating procedures are examples of codified knowledge. Tacit knowledge, by contrast, is dynamic, is developed and transferred orally, and is necessarily embedded in the collective experience of a particular work group or occupation. With this distinction in mind, the problem of managing knowledge is not new: all work is and always has been, in an important sense, 'knowledge work' and its management has always been contested. For example, the labor process perspective has long looked to enclaves of skilled workers encircled by management projects that seek to encroach, if not dislodge, skills and knowledge that provide workers with some alternative moral authority and practical power base.

Admittedly, knowledge work is most clearly associated with professional or expert labor who have access to formal bodies of abstract knowledge. Yet, even the most highly choreographed, intensely supervised labor processes require that individuals and groups develop capabilities to comprehend and cope with contingencies in the technical and social divisions of labor. All work requires the mobilization of 'tacit' and embodied knowledge to be viable and to open up unmanaged social spaces. Tacit knowledge exists not just at the margins of routine procedures but is the necessary precondition of the functioning of formal systems. Nevertheless, for management, tacit knowledge is often covert, occasionally capricious, and sometimes oppositional. This is because the nature, trajectory, and value of tacit knowledge is necessarily difficult for management to monitor, far less control (Swan and Scarbrough 2001). For Taylorism, tacit knowledge was little more than the daily ruses of the 'cunning workman' to thwart effective management. Scientific management was the antidote: the method of prising tacit knowledge away from obdurate workers. Knowledge management shares this objective to a large degree.

10.1.1 Boundaries of Knowledge Work

It is important to recognize that not all knowledge work requires the individual or group to draw upon abstract, codified expertise in the form of either organizational or professional knowledge. Nor does all knowledge work require *constant* improvisation and innovation. The emphasis upon innovation downplays or ignores the repertoires of routine practices defined as tacit knowledge, not because of any intrinsic features but because the organization has carefully ignored their existence or discounted their importance. Even the most intensely routinized service work can involve the development of tacit knowledge by employees. In exceptional cases, even call center operators, that most routinized of contemporary occupations, do not simply articulate scripts but deploy individual diagnostic skills to clarify the nature of the consumer's enquiry and to move efficiently to *specific* system-programmed responses. Diagnostic skills and informal, personalized finding aids are extracted and developed by the individual call center operator from the mass of official procedures. For the operator, the dialogue was not simply the articulation of scripted prompts and responses but inevitably involved judgment.

Thus, it would be more apt to regard the existence of tacit knowledge in call centers as testimony to the *inevitability* of knowledgeability at work in even the most 'codified' of environments. In the rationalized environment of most call centers, mobilizing tacit knowledge is clearly not the main driver of management strategy. Indeed, for management, the elimination of the need for operators to develop and deploy any tacit knowledge is critical to increased efficiency. The existence of tacit knowledge alone, then, cannot be used either as the sole criteria in defining 'knowledge work' or as a sufficient condition for the emergence of formal knowledge management regimes.

If so, what else should we be looking for? The influential view of Robert Reich (1993: 178) is that the defining feature of knowledge work is that the value-adding activity is *symbolic* rather than material:

Symbolic analysts solve, identify, and broker problems by manipulating symbols. They simplify reality into abstract images that can be rearranged, juggled, experimented with, communicated to other specialists, and then, eventually, communicated back into reality. The tools may be mathematical algorithms, legal agreements, financial gimmicks, scientific principles, psychological insights about how to persuade or to amuse, systems of induction or deduction, or any other set of techniques for doing conceptual puzzles.

We might quibble with the ethereal tone of this definition or remain uneasy about the manner in which 'work' and 'play' are elided, but Reich undoubtedly captures something of the range of tasks and occupations that fall into the category of 'knowledge work'.

In addition, knowledge work requires the capacity to broker information by mobilizing work and social networks. The relational and fluid nature of organizing knowledge work is at least as important as any technical expertise. In software development, for example, 'the possession of technical competencies—familiarity with a particular software language, the ability to think analytically about a software problem, and being able to construct and debug a piece of code—was seen as a necessary, but not sufficient condition for successfully working within the labour process' (Marschall 2002; Woodfield 2000: 74). For the new hybrid professional of contemporary software development, no less important were the interpersonal skills necessary to evaluate and regulate relationships with clients and colleagues. This is true even in software development houses that have experienced significant use of project management techniques to increase temporal predictability and to tighten control over the work process:

on a day-to-day basis ... work routinely involves substantial technological use, often related to technological production, across international boundaries. These workers merge technical skills, largely centred around communication and information technologies, and knowledge of their social environment to solve managerial and technical problems, create new markets, and find alternative partners in their global enterprises. They work in a web of shifting interdependencies in which building trust among strangers becomes an important set of skills (English-Lueck 2002: 91).

The primary means of managerial control of knowledge work is the regulation of employees' *self* rather than work flows or task. The socialization of novice consultants is as much about assimilating and embodying the cultural norms of a firm as mastering techniques (Grey 1994). Normative controls involve the demonstration of commitment through long hours or a readiness to understand—or at least represent—work as play (Gabriel 1995; Grugulis, Dundon, and Wilkinson 2000). 'Soft control' can, however, be compromised and constrained by a variety of factors, such as shifts in management strategy or of organizational structure, particularly by the trading of expertise between different divisions that results in the marketization of social relationships (Robertson and Swan 1998).

A word of caution is required here. We share Warhurst and Thompson's (1998, forthcoming) unease that the descriptive and analytical value of the term 'knowledge worker' is threatened by imprecision and overgeneralization, and are sympathetic to the distinction they make between the increased significance of *knowledgeability* at work and a more restricted category of knowledge workers.

Yet for all that, 'knowledge work' does capture important aspects of contemporary work experience. Undoubtedly, much of today's 'knowledge work' is little more than yesterday's expert or professional labor with the addition of those in professional services (such as consultancy) or the creative industries (advertising executives, graphic designers, and new media producers). But knowledge or knowledgeable work also signifies an increasing amount of mainstream administrative and clerical activities in manufacturing, services, and the professions. The job-stretch of white-collar work echoes the degree of empowerment and up-skilling 'enjoyed' by blue-collar manufacturing workers for almost two decades. As organizations become more complex and fluid amalgams of hierarchy, market, and network modes, so the 'knowledge work' that binds these restless structures together will increase in importance.

10.1.2 Managing Knowledge

The management problem, however, is that knowledgeable work is difficult to observe, and, even for knowledge workers, awkward to verbalize, far less to codify and measure (Davenport, Jarvenpaa, and Beers 1996: 54–5). The value of knowledge products and services is no less difficult for peers and clients to evaluate (Alvesson 2001). The social nature of knowledge work means that it exists as isolated tasks in a sea of social exchanges. Tasks may be technical in nature but also incredibly compressed in terms of time and distributed between parallel project teams, perhaps even operating in different continents. The duration and complexity of any technical task has no necessary relationship to its value. In surveys of high-end knowledge workers in the pharmaceutical industry, an awareness of informal organizational processes was rated much more highly than abstract or technical knowledge (McKinlay 2003). Knowledge work requires the ability to juggle formal requirements for information flows and data management, for project management and budgetary control. However thorough, formal procedures cannot be comprehensive and were little guide to the practical management of workflows that are increasingly concurrent rather than linear. The ambiguous nature of knowledge work makes it an awkward subject for conventional and critical analysis alike.

Nevertheless, the rise of knowledge management (KM) speaks of a growing managerial self-confidence that no longer regards workers' practical expertise as something to be nullified. Rather, KM begins from the premise that tacit knowledge is no longer necessarily hidden and oppositional but to be treated as a public good. The myriad expertise that was laid under siege by Taylorism is now to be freed as a common resource to be shared by all, not monopolized by management. Taylor's grinding world of unlimited ignorance is to be replaced by one of continual personal and collective learning. This is the paradox at the core of KM. On the one hand, it is legitimized as a managerialist project by speaking of the imperatives of competitiveness. On the other hand, KM is underpinned by a utopianism that assumes that all employees will gladly participate, both as donors and as recipients, in this collective project if only appropriate capture/conversion mechanisms can be embedded in everyday routines. From this unitarist starting-point, the *only* obstacle that KM has to overcome is technical.

10.2 KNOWLEDGE MANAGEMENT: HARD SYSTEMS AND THEIR LIMITS

As we indicated earlier, the rise of KM can be understood as, in part, a response to a series of competitive and organizational tensions. On the one hand, there are the pressures, derived from the perpetual innovation demanded of products and services, the compression of product life cycles, and, as a result, the need to extract and mobilize more knowledge from expert labor, ever more rapidly. Yet this need must be met in the context of the instability of contemporary work organizations and daily routines, allied to corporate downsizing and restructuring. KM is therefore tied to a growing hybridity of organizational structures, as can be seen in the chapter by Alvesson and Thompson.

The stark polarization of market and hierarchy is giving way to a range of intermediate or hybrid forms that regulate internal and external processes by combining hierarchy, market, and community mechanisms. The associated modes of coordination and incentives are, in turn, authority, price, and trust (Adler 2001). Adler goes on to argue that organizations are turning to forms of soft control that prioritize trust as the key mechanism to elicit the active consent of knowledge workers.

Yet we cannot understand KM solely in terms of broad structural drivers. New managerial regimes also require particular mechanisms and agents. A useful place to start is the global consulting firms that have been the most important source and key disseminators of the new practices. Consultancies are 'knowledge-intensive firms' both in terms of the strategic priority of knowledge over other resources and the dominance of well-qualified, often relatively scarce employees (Starbuck 1992). Consultancies differ from professional service firms, such as law and accountancy practices, in their greater reliance upon embodied or encultured knowledge contained in organizational routines and in individuals (Blackler 1995). The global consultancy firms have invested heavily in KM systems inside their own organizations, partly as a marketing tool for this new product. McKinsey estimates that it allocates around 10 percent of revenue on knowledge management (Davenport and Prusak 1998). Such systems rely upon portfolios of databases categorized by, for instance, client, sector, engagement information, business process, and an internal expert directory.

From broad statements of intent in the early 1990s, the global consultancy firms' internal KM systems have grown rapidly. Within just a few years, the major consultancies typically have developed several thousand distinct databases, each with tens of thousands of records. The scale of data warehousing has, in turn, stimulated the development of increasingly sophisticated navigational tools (Dunford 2000). The sheer scale of on-line information constantly threatens to outpace the capability of navigational tools and overwhelm the individual consultant's ability to interrogate, synthesize, and utilize information, particularly when there is quasi-market competition between databases for consultants' attention (Hansen and Haas 2001). Issues of scale and navigability are compounded by the immense technical and organizational difficulties of minimizing information redundancy and maximizing relevance and timeliness. A failure to address these issues results in extremely limited use of the system's technical capability or the creation of expensive 'information junkyards' (McDermott 1999; McKinlay 2000).

Consulting firms have, of course, also been prominent in attempting to use IT systems to diffuse KM more widely. Service delivery by knowledge-intensive firms requires close interaction with clients, a process that almost inevitably results in the two-way transfer of tacit knowledge (Sivula, van den Bosch, and Elfring 2001). Similarly, leading consultancies have attempted to institutionalize KM through co-development processes with major clients (Abell and Oxbrow 2001: 195; McKinlay 2000). However, as Scarbrough (2003: 95) observes, 'the protean nature of knowledge in organizations ... the indeterminacy of the available means of exploiting it' made it intensely difficult for the global consultancy firms to commodify 'the high-concept rhetoric' of KM.

Nevertheless, such developments help to explain why IT specialists and Information Systems departments have been by far the leading organizational function in introducing and developing KM, with human resources playing a minor role in what tends to be defined initially as an exclusively technical process (KPMG 2000; Scarbrough 2003). KM projects have largely been driven by the development of extensive intranet repositories coupled with sophisticated navigational tools and some interactive capacity. Ruggle's (1998) survey of over 400 US and European organizations showed that creating intranets and knowledge repositories, plus implementing decision tools and groupware were the four most common KM practices. The main objective is to capture and transfer incremental innovations from the local level throughout the organization. Filtering and categorizing information inevitably involves selection and the emergence of organizational intermediaries between producer and user in KM systems. Intermediation, especially when identified with a specific functional group, both compromises the immediacy favored by KM systems and reduces their claim to neutrality in terms of organizational politics.

More recently, there has been an abrupt shift away from 'hard' technological definitions of knowledge management towards conceptions that stress the social construction of knowledge at work. This does not represent the complete failure of 'knowledge' technologies such as groupware, intranets, and shared databases, but the inevitability that success is, at most, partial and fragile. Rather, sustained innovation and the relative effectiveness of information technology tools have highlighted the importance of management, organizational structures and processes, and the informal, social dimension of work organization (Carberra and Carberra 2002: 704). Despite substantial and sustained investment, even inside the major consultancies, employee participation in KM systems has proved uneven, with significant differences in use between enthusiastic junior staff and reluctant senior partners; consultants measured by billable hours rather than their contribution to a 'public good' system; and a general unease about surrendering personal expertise to an organizational repository (Weiss 1999; similarly Coombs and Hull 1998). The extent to which a knowledge codification wins the support of professional staff may be determined by their perception of its appropriation of *surface information* and its irrelevance to the *deep knowledge* demanded by their practice (Morris 2001). A generic difficulty of KM highlighted by the experience of the consultancy industry is that, at best, technological systems have had a modest impact on organizational performance. No consultancy has established robust metrics to measure the local impacts of KM, far less upon patterns of innovation, employee learning, or comparative advantage at the organizational level.

The construction of large-scale data repositories is of little value without the transfer of knowledge (Huysman and de Wit 2003: 52–3; Kluge, Stein, and Licht 2001: 108). A Swedish cross-sectoral study of twenty-five organizations demonstrated the extraordinary difficulty of diffusing learning from a project-specific setting to the organization as a whole, despite the support of senior management and practitioners (Ekstedt *et al.* 1999: 202). The context-dependent and experiential nature of tacit knowledge gained in various projects rendered it impossible to encapsulate the knowledge in a database in any meaningful form.

European and North American studies of 'best practice' have reached two broad conclusions. The first is that highly codified KM systems are most effective where they capture outward-facing, largely client-based information, including some assessment of sales and delivery methods. Examples include consultancies' databases holding 'soft' information on key contacts in client firms or coded messages between physicians concerning patients. Such standardized systems have been used successfully by multinational consulting firms (Mertins, Heisig, and Vorbeck 2000). Unfortunately, the few studies that have sought to identify the impact of these systems have focused exclusively upon the *organization* as the unit of analysis.

Given the highly contextualized nature of knowledge work, an organizational approach is unlikely to allow an assessment of the development of individual or collective knowledge and its impact upon specific labor processes. Moreover, there have been no cross-sectional, longitudinal studies of knowledge management using a common methodology and performance measures. There have been no quantitative impact assessments of knowledge management techniques upon specific occupations or work organizations. There is nothing approaching panel data on the impact of different forms of KM projects on, for instance, client satisfaction, or the productivity or diagnostic capability of employees.

The second conclusion is that in the few instances where knowledge management systems have been judged relatively successful this has been in 'high-end professions', with a well-established external knowledge base, and low levels of ambiguity in terms of alternative methods of task performance (Davenport and Glaser 2002). Thus, knowledge management systems are more successful when deployed *with* the grain of professional development in occupations with secure status anchored in deep expertise. This widely shared understanding has shifted the focus of interest to theories and practices that emphasize the *social* rather than physical technologies.

10.3 COMMUNITIES OF PRACTICE?

One of the most important theoretical developments concerning the nature of tacit, collective knowledge in the contemporary workplace has been the deployment of the anthropological concept of 'communities of practice'. This research has revealed or, more accurately, rediscovered the importance of the collective, hidden knowledge of workers in even the most routinized work. In an important sense this is a rediscovery of the existence of the subterranean world of skills and knowledge that parallels formal, managed work processes (see, *inter alia*, Ackroyd and Thompson 1999; Gouldner 1954).

Access to the liminal spaces at the edge of formal procedures and the ill-defined intersections of organizational structures is critically important for several reasons (Brown and Duguid 1991; Lave and Wenger 1991). First, it permits communication beyond the formal. That is, a community of practice is defined, in part, by reflexive participation in formal organizational domains, a reflexivity that finds a voice and authority precisely through the participant's mastery and ability to synthesize, adapt, or critique formal procedures or the shared body of knowledge of a profession or occupation.

Second, participation in a community of practice requires both novices and masters to develop their practical expertise in situ, not just to disseminate and refine an established repertoire of techniques. A community of practice is centered upon a dynamic of knowledge and practice that is, at most, only partly visible to management. In contemporary organizations that experience almost constant structural upheaval, a vital form of 'knowledge' is that which allows individuals and work groups to cope with procedural ambiguities by sidestepping formal communication channels. It is such tacit knowledge of the gaps in organizational processes that *enables* formal structures and processes to function effectively.

Third, liminality implies both a certain open-endedness and boundedness. The community of practice is necessarily bound to a technology, a set of techniques or an organization—that is to a common referent from which all participants evaluate the authority or skill of their peers and the organization. Just as it is impossible to identify the origins of a community of practice, so its development turns upon the interactions of its members with each other and with the formal routines and structures of the organization.

Fourth, communities of practice exercise varying degrees of self-regulation but all develop sets of values, skills, and reciprocal expectations that are independent of the formal organization. In some cases, gaining full membership of a community is marked by a rite of passage. Individuals validate themselves not through formal status but through their peers' recognition of their expertise.

Finally, participation in a community of practice allows individuals not just to improve their ability to cope with the demands of the organization but also to develop a deeper understanding of the limits of official systems. The necessary symbiosis between learning and practice establishes the basis for grassroots innovation. The explicit purpose of the 'communities of practice' research is to alert managers to the necessary existence and social organization of tacit knowledge in the workplace. The central management objective becomes not the perfection of planning and formal procedures but accepting and shaping the communities of practice that inevitably emerge in liminal organizational spaces. Effective management turns upon the sensitivity of managers to the dynamics of communities of practice, the ability to intervene while going with the grain of the informal organization.

Just as Taylorism aspired to be a science of work organization that separated knowledge from the worker as a knowing subject, so the 'communities of practice' approach aims at a similar appropriation of workforce knowledge. Unlike Taylorism, however, management is conceived of as an art or a craft, rather than a science; the ideal manager is no longer the rational economic planner but the instinctive, knowing anthropologist. The key management skills are not those of the rational technocrat but the ability to become dispassionately immersed in a community of practice in order to translate and diffuse knowledge but without deep emotional attachment (Seely Brown and Duguid 1998). The growing body of research into 'communities of practice' is not, then, neutral social science but a thoroughly managerialist project. Competing interests, power, and conflict are entirely absent from this unitarist literature; individual and collective learning is divorced from all managerial or market pressures (Easterby-Smith 1997: 1095).

Ironically, the growing research into communities of practice does not consider 'knowledge work' in the sense proposed by Reich. Rather, the key texts in this literature examine skilled forms of work with tangible tasks, technologies, and material products: photocopier technicians, midwives, butchers, and army quar-termasters (Orr 1996; Wenger 1998). But such groups are linked together by technology, task, and technique that are relatively durable over time and space. These workers occupy stable organizational environments, have enduring skills that are easily comprehensible to their peers, *not* the ephemeral tasks, transient technical and symbolic skills, and project-based environments of knowledge work. In many respects, these groups bear some of the hallmarks of craft work. In craft work, apprentices were assigned to an experienced worker who determined the manner of the novice's learning. At the very least, the allocation of work always involved negotiation between management and craft groups. For the craft group, work was allocated according to notions of equity that did not necessarily coincide with efficiency. Older craft-workers, for example, would be allocated less physically demanding work by their junior peers, who were secure in the knowledge that they would receive similar treatment in later years. To belong to a craft was to accept a moral code that stretched across generations and was not limited to a particular organization. While the apprentice absorbed basic techniques, they were also socialized into the occupational culture of the craft: autonomy, uniqueness, and a shared responsibility to protect the boundaries of the craft from incursion or erosion by management or other occupations. Management had very little control over this dual learning process. Highly developed manual and conceptual skills rested upon a claim for monopoly control over specific tools, tasks, and materials. The informal rules of the craft community were jealously guarded and involved the individual in a complex web of obligations that included strangers, not just their immediate workmates. Moreover, these obligations remained binding on the individual for their entire working life. To be a craft-worker *necessarily* entailed resistance to managerialism.

The contemporary 'community of practice' is but a pale shadow of the rich cultural milieu and the robust autonomy of the craft tradition. Full participation in Wenger's community of practice is not predicated upon the lengthy novitiate or the absorption and ritual celebration of the skill and autonomy protected by the craft tradition. The technical skills of the community of practice are derived from managerially codified procedures. To achieve the status of a master inside a community of practice is also to develop a range of coping mechanisms that allows the individual to exercise judgment about which managerial rule to follow and which to ignore, to prioritize tasks according to their own circumstances, and, most important of all, to invest this learning process with meaning (Wenger 1998: 40–1). Membership of a community of practice has none of the lifetime obligations of craft or professional work and is tied to a specific time, task, and organization. Communities of practice are highly localized phenomena and membership is neither transferable nor necessarily recognized even by cognate communities. If the craft tradition was based upon autonomy, equity, and independence, then the ethic of the contemporary community of practice is bound by individual and collective pragmatism. The craft union—or professional association—plays a role not just in the workplace but also in the labor market: regulating entry, negotiating national standards in training and competence, and representing their members. Conversely, knowledge work has no 'natural' representational voice, no body that seeks to play a similar role to that of a trade union or professional association. Undoubtedly, the concept of community of practice captures something of the indeterminancy and transience of 'skill' and 'knowledge' in the contemporary rationalized workplace. However, the term sheds little light upon the dynamics of different social and digital milieu: there is no attempt to develop metrics that would allow some comparison of populations, roles, and interactions. In any case, while such metrics would increase our understanding of the nature of communities of practice, this would be both retrospective and offer little opportunity for real-time managerial interventions.

10.4 KNOWLEDGE MANAGEMENT IN PRACTICE: TENSIONS AND REFLECTIONS

The previous section highlighted the need to be cautious about overstating the scope and depth of collaboration in KM 'communities'. One of the problems is that we have few in-depth studies of corporate attempts to realize KM in practice. This section considers some of them, beginning with those carried out by the author (McKinlay 2000, 2002). In partnership with Ernst and Young, 'WorldDrug' launched a major KM project. The basis for KM was the on-line archiving of the 'Lessons Learned' reports through established debriefing processes at the end of phases of projects. The formal 'Lessons' process had largely degenerated into a practical irrelevance, with no overarching corporate system. The objective of 'Warehouse' was to capture *process* knowledge. Essentially, for all the ambition of its rhetoric, 'Warehouse' simply integrated all 'Lessons' in a hypertext-linked intranet. Navigational aids were designed to search only for solutions to queries rather than by generic themes, far less to enable dialogue between individuals or groups. The highly instrumental purpose underlying 'Warehouse's' design left little space for innovation. Measured by volume and usage, 'Warehouse' was a major success. But the system's architects were careful to avoid any assessment of its impact upon productivity or innovative capability.

At the edge of the formal KM program, there was a significant attempt to develop an alternative vision of knowledge management as a conversation between experts. Modeled upon the ideal of a dispersed 'community of practice', 'Café' was based upon interviews with key players in development projects. Using rich navigational aids, conversations were interrogated as much for the contrasting perceptions they revealed as for the best practice they articulated. 'Café's' aim was to enable participants to experience—and reflect upon—something of the rich linguistic texture of working in project teams. 'Café' was predicated upon an infinitely looser, less hierarchical discursive structure than 'Warehouse'. 'Café' was linked to the shared web repositories used by development teams, but this provided only the most tenuous and fragile bond to administrative routines. Ironically, the very marginality that allowed the emergence of 'Café' was also its undoing. Without the executive support and sheer scale of 'Warehouse' as protection, 'Café' was defined as abstract and impractical and starved of funding necessary for expansion and for the development of metrics that allowed analysis of conversations inside 'Café'. Just as the controlled rollout of 'Warehouse' engulfed 'Lessons', so 'Café' was squeezed out as the budgets and labor processes that supported 'Warehouse' became subject to greater management scrutiny and control. Far from stimulating radical innovation in work organization and a deeper managerial appreciation of the dynamics of tacit knowledge, 'WorldDrug's' KM project proved intolerant of experimentation and executive support extended no further than the centrally controlled and increasingly rationalized 'Warehouse' system.

Other companies, such as Siemens, consider their development of on-line international networks of peers as a significant success in terms of durability and participation (Franz *et al.* 2002). An average Siemens 'KEC Community' survives to just over 3 years old and comprises between 10 and 35 'active' and over 100 'passive' members. 'Active' denotes an ongoing contribution to the network, whereas 'passivity' refers to colleagues who only receive information. Clearly, 'passive' encompasses several categories: from those who have temporarily withdrawn from active engagement; those whose membership was determined by their formal job title rather than any real commitment to the community; or others for whom 'community' information is just so much organizational spam. There has been no attempt to allow 'active' or 'passive' members to evaluate the value of their membership to themselves or to specific projects. Perhaps this is because such an evaluation could show that there is no necessary link between 'passivity' or lapsed membership and the value derived by the individual from a short engagement with an expert community. Or it might reveal that 'active' membership does not signify any deep attachment to a community but simply a longer-run instrumental calculation of the relative gain in exchanges of technical and organizational expertise.

In France Telecom, for instance, three-quarters of 'general' intranet sites registered zero or minimal traffic but remained extant. More focused 'expert' sites proved more likely to experience sustained interactions with intense spikes of activity, but their character was also significantly altered by the visibility of their 'success'. Specifically, comparatively high levels of traffic drew sites to management's attention, which then intervened to shift discussion from purely technical issues to include those of project management and productivity (Beaudoin, Cardon, and Mallard 2001). In turn, this resulted in a sharp drop in site activity and user engagement. In other words, the majority of site users simply stopped being 'active', a shift that registered passive resistance against managerialism. The tension generated by attempts to *manage* expert sites and chat rooms is even greater where informal, electronically-mediated communities already existed prior to the adoption of an overarching knowledge management strategy.

Software developers in 'CoreTech' were accustomed to participating in informal, real-time expert newsgroups (Callaghan 2002). 'CoreTech's' adoption of a knowledge management strategy centered upon the construction of a centrally regulated intranet system that set the protocols for all web documents and links to electronic newsgroups. Centralized managerial control conflicted with the workforce's expectation of high degrees of personal and collective autonomy. For management, the problem was both the impossibility of measuring the value in heterogeneous forms of information exchange and blurring of the boundary between work and non-work. Software developers would flit in and out of newsgroups, alternately tracking and contributing to the exchange while waiting on their machine to complete a parallel task. Inevitably, the closure of the informal newsgroups was extensively discussed in the new, more controlled environment, as a violation of the professionals' right to exchange information and opinion informally and autonomously.

Thus, the introduction of a knowledge management system can disrupt rather than extend existing grassroots networks of experts and reduce the likely success of the formal system. Failure to pursue a strategy that treats KM as an organizational as well as technical project and that is sensitive to the balance between central coordination and local involvement dooms any initiative to almost certain failure. This was the experience of a multinational bank that developed an intranet to integrate client and process knowledge. The rapid proliferation of local development of intranet sites resulted in a poorly coordinated system that reinforced pre-existing organizational boundaries rather than eroding or displacing them (Newell 1999). Subsequent attempts to improve coordination by centralizing control over system development resulted in a sharp drop-off in employee participation in all related KM projects. Ironically, then, the limited longitudinal evidence suggests that knowledge management techniques may have the least purchase upon highly ambiguous and improvisational knowledge labor processes.

While we can piece together some of the dynamics of discrete digital KM regimes, however hesitantly, we must be even more tentative about the interaction of different types of KM initiatives. Accounts of KM in practice focus upon digital or group-based projects as if these were mutually exclusive categories. In practice, in industries such as software, the formation of robust, organic networks of experts—special interest groups—has been well established for several decades. The novelty of KM lies in the attempts by management to initiate such networks and spread them beyond self-selecting groups of technical experts, to monitor their behavior, and to assess their value. Equally, attempts to capture the 'lessons learned' from projects are not new and are part of the fabric of team-based organizations.

For all the above difficulties, in industries such as pharmaceuticals, the combination of increasingly globalized corporations and the drive to compress the developmental or 'molecule to market' process drives the determination to identify and diffuse incremental innovations in working practices from the work group throughout the organization. Furthermore, technical innovation in clinical trials and the introduction of simultaneous data testing delivered major gains in process efficiency (Chiezza and Manzini 1997; McKinlay 2002; Pisano 1998).

10.4.1 Implications for Employees

If the impact of KM has been mixed for corporate management, the same can be said for the knowledge *workers* involved in such processes. While, WorldDrug's KM system failed to deliver on its ambitious promises, it did have a significant impact upon work organization and the experience of expert labor. Web repositories compressed, internationalized, standardized, and subtly altered the work process in WorldDrug. Formerly, the application of statistical tests and their interpretation was a distinct phase of a sequential and highly compartmentalized labor process that had little direct contact with the field teams or the contract firms that generated raw clinical data. Parallel teams of biometricians worked on national or regional data sets with little management oversight or coordination. Over time, point solutions to specific difficulties had eroded similarities in the tools and techniques used by American and European biometric teams. Significant concentrations of customized software, in particular, constituted a major barrier to work standardization and to the integration of data sets.

Virtual working on web-shared data repositories triggered a sharp shift towards international teams using common tools and techniques, reducing processing time by more than one-third. Web technology erased the boundaries between previously distinct projects and teams, an erasure that was predicated upon the standardization of statistical interrogation and interpretation. Virtual and international collaboration reshaped the nature of work for the individual biometrician. Where the statistician was previously a commentator or impartial 'judge' of the integrity of the data produced by clinical trials, the massive compression of processing schedules has pushed them towards greater involvement in the data collection phase. Commenting upon his change of role, one biometrician, educated to doctoral level—who defined himself as a knowledge worker—implicitly lamented his feeling of loss of expertise and status:

I used to be a statistician pure and simple. My job started when the data was clean, locked-down. *Then* I interpreted it and pointed out weaknesses. We always worked to tough deadlines but now they are impossible. *Now* I've got to work with 'early' clinical data and have a much closer relationship with regulatory affairs and the development teams. I suppose now I'm a 'customer relationship manager'.

The standardization of technical work and the compression of timescales resulted in a rapid and significant increase in the range and depth of coordinative work. The clean, distinct role of the biometrician was blurred by technical and organizational change as it lost its singular place in the division of labor as it became enmeshed in a much more complex web of social relationships (Star 1995). Expertise was no longer sanctioned and sheltered by educational or professional qualifications. Inside knowledge-intensive organizations, personal authority can no longer be guaranteed by an individual's expert or professional status. It may be an exaggeration to state that all claims to individual knowledge are ephemeral, but managerial and expert authority is now more perilous, more regularly and more formally evaluated by colleagues than in the past. The KM project is suffused by a rhetoric of radical democratization that claims *all* knowledge is, in principle, accessible to everyone. Ironically, this organizational denial of the value, perhaps even the existence, of *deep* expertise cuts across the possibility of individuals building a career based upon the gradual accretion of professional competence and organizational experience. While this process was not initiated by the knowledge management project, it does represent a significant shift in the nature of authority relations inside the firm. In short, to define oneself as a knowledge worker does not necessarily mean a gain in self-esteem or labor market opportunity but can be experienced as a loss of professional autonomy and reduction in personal authority. In organizations in which career paths remain dependent upon the individual's ability to demonstrate their distinctive expertise there is a clear tension with KM's drive to make *all* knowledge available to everyone (Hull 2000: 156).

10.5 CONCLUSION

Academics, consultancies, and corporations are all stumbling towards some under-standing of the dynamics of knowledge creation and transfer at work. Debates in this area have, on the whole, generated more heat than light. Analytically, there is a danger that 'knowledge', much as 'skill' before it, has become a careless portman-teau term that embraces everything and reveals little or nothing. Ironically, such a thoroughly managerialist literature has only the most limited practical value for management practice. One will search in vain for any guidance in terms of how management should deal with any resistance to a KM project, the threshold levels at which real value is added, or even the value to be derived by the individual.

How can the overall trends be summed up? The evidence from newer know-ledge-intensive industries is that organizations are experimenting with a repertoire of control practices within emergent knowledge management regimes. Studies of the mobilization of creative and knowledge labor in industries such as advertising and new media suggest that rival, if not competitive, organizational logics coalesce in individual firms, regional clusters, or projects. The product development process for new media products, for example, is typically both ephemeral and defined through the complex interactions of several stakeholders. In such cases, product negotiations are sifted through relationships that are complex amalgams of market, hierarchy, project, and network (see Grabher 2001, 2002; Pratt 2002; Wittel, Lury, and Lash 2002). The precise balance of these elements is not wholly defined in advance of the product development process. Rather, the organizational form emerges in parallel with the evolution of the product development and product market process. The exact organizational configuration is dependent upon the nature of the product and the interaction of firms and individuals. While there is evidence that organizational structures familiar to 'old economy' patterns re-emerges as product markets mature (Pries and Abel 2004), participation in such complex social processes requires individual firms to continue to be highly adaptive and reflexive in order to understand, mobilize, and anticipate the different organ-izational logics in play.

What KM does signify is the increased pace of product and organizational innovation, compounded by the new possibilities of collaborative, on-line work organization. If KM theory veers uncertainly between metaphysics and a gauche managerialism, then the few longitudinal studies of the impact of KM in practice reveal its contradictory dynamics. The defining paradox of the knowledge manage-ment project represents the attempt by corporate management to render the hidden, social dimension of working knowledge a more public and private good simultaneously. That is, to expand the creation and consumption of working knowledge as a shared resource while also appropriating this knowledge as a private, corporate good. Ironically, KM initiatives are more likely to be sustainable if they begin from the premise that all forms of knowledge are not the sole prerogative of management. Equally, more durable KM projects will accept the inevitability of its limits: that important working knowledge will remain tacit, partly due to its highly contextual and ephemeral nature but also because workers can draw upon this resource to regulate their working lives; to sustain practices that are geared toward equity rather than efficiency; and to erect barriers against managerial incursions into professional, occupational, or individual ethics. KM projects based upon solving widely recognized, practical problems tend to enlist greater workforce support than top-down initiatives triggered by possibilities offered by information and communication technologies. Inevitably, however, this creates tensions between short-term success and long-term viability. Equally, to achieve their promise, KM projects are necessarily pitched beyond specific operational difficulties and aspire to encompass the entire organization, and beyond. This necessarily increases the scale of the project, and, when focused on information and communication technologies, creates a definition of knowledge as a 'stock' rather than a 'flow'. KM remains vulnerable to inherent problems of measurement of process, effectiveness, and value of outputs. The elusive nature of 'knowledge' labor processes goes a long way to explaining the lack of robust longitudinal evaluative studies of the impact of knowledge management projects. Undoubtedly, the next phase of knowledge management research and practice will be the search for convincing measures of the impact of different knowledge management regimes. Knowledge management awaits the arrival of its F. W. Taylor.

REFERENCES

ABELL, A., and OXBROW, M. (2001). *Competing with Knowledge: The Information Professional in the Knowledge Management Age*. London: Library Association.

ACKROYD, S., and THOMPSON, P. (1999). *Organization Misbehaviour*. London: Sage.

ADLER, P. (2001). 'Market, Hierarchy, and Trust: The Knowledge Economy and the Future of Capitalism'. *Organization Science*, 12/2: 215–34.

ALVESSON, M. (2001). 'Knowledge Work: Ambiguity, Image and Identity'. *Human Relations*, 54/7: 863–86.

BEAUDOIN, V., CARDON, D., and MALLARD, A. (2001). 'De clic en clic: Créativité et rationalisation dans le usages des intranets d'enterprise'. *Sociologie du Travail*, 43: 309–26.

BLACKLER, F. (1995). 'Knowledge, Knowledge Work and Organizations: An Overview and Interpretation'. *Organization Studies*, 16/6: 1021–46.

BOISOT, M. (1998). *Knowledge Assets*. Oxford: Oxford University Press.

BROWN, J. S., and DUGUID, S. (1991). 'Organizational Learning and Communities of Practice: Towards a Unified View of Working, Learning and Innovation'. *Organization Science*, 2/1: 40–57.

CALLAGHAN, J. (2002), *Inside Intranets and Extranets: Knowledge Management and the Struggle for Power*. London: Palgrave.

CARBERRA, A., and CARBERRA, E. (2002). 'Knowledge-Sharing Dilemmas'. *Organization Studies*, 23/5: 687–710.

CHIEZZA, V., and MANZINI, R. (1997). 'Managing Virtual RandD Organizations: Lessons from the Pharmaceutical Industry'. *International Journal of Technology Management*, 13/5: 471–85.

COOMBS, R., and HULL, R. (1998), ' "Knowledge Management Practices" and Path Dependency in Innovation'. *Research Policy*, 27/3: 239–55.

DAVENPORT, T., and GLASER, J. (2002). 'Just-in-Time Delivery Comes to Knowledge Management'. *Harvard Business Review*, 107–11.

——and PRUSAK, L. P. (1998). *Working Knowledge: How Organizations Manage What They Know*. Boston: Harvard Business School Press.

——JARVENPAA, S., and BEERS, M. (1996). 'Improving Knowledge Work Processes'. *Sloan Management Review*, Summer: 53–65.

DUNFORD, R. (2000). 'Key Challenges in the Search for the Effective Management of Knowledge in Management Consulting Firms'. *Journal of Knowledge Management*, 4/4: 295–302.

EASTERBY-SMITH, M. (1997). 'Disciplines of Organizational Learning: Contributions and Critiques'. *Human Relations*, 50/9: 1085–113.

EKSTEDT, E., LUNDIN, R., SODERHOLM, A., and WINDENIES, H. (1999). *Neo-Industrial Organising: Renewal by Action and Knowledge Formation in a Project-Intensive Economy*. London: Routledge.

ENGLISH-LUECK, J. A. (2002). *Cultures@siliconvalley*. Stanford, Calif.: Stanford University Press.

FRANZ, M., SCHMIDT, R., SCHOEN, S., and SENFERT, S. (2002). 'KEC Networking—Knowledge Management at Infinean Technologies AB', in T. H. Davenport and G. Probst (eds.), *Knowledge Management Case Book: Siemens Best Practices*. Berlin: John Wiley.

GABRIEL, Y. (1995). 'The Unmanaged Organization: Stories, Fantasies and Subjectivity'. *Organization Studies*, 16/3: 477–501.

GOULDNER, A. (1954). *Patterns of Industrial Bureaucracy*. New York: Free Press.

GRABHER, G. (2001). 'Ecologies of Creativity: The Village, the Group, and the Heterarchic Organisation of the British Advertising Industry'. *Environment and Planning A*, 33: 351–74.

——(2002). 'Cool Projects, Boring Institutions: Temporary Collaboration in Social Context'. *Regional Studies*, 36/3: 205–14.

GREY, C. (1994). 'Career as a Project of the Self and Labour Process Discipline'. *Sociology*, 28: 479–97.

GRUGULIS, I., DUNDON, T., and WILKINSON, A. (2000). 'Cultural Control and the "Culture Manager": Employment Practices in a Consultancy'. *Work, Employment and Society*, 14/1: 97–116.

HANSEN, M., and HAAS, M. (2001). 'Competing for Attention in Knowledge Markets: Electric Document Dissemination in a Management Consulting Company'. *Administrative Science Quarterly*, 46: 1–28.

HULL, R. (2000). 'Knowledge Management Practices and Innovation', in B. Andersen, J. Howells, R. Hull, I. Miles, and J. Roberts (eds.), *Knowledge and Innovation in the New Service Economy*. Cheltenham: Edward Elgar.

HUYSMAN, M., and DE WIT, D. (2003). 'A Critical Evaluation of Knowledge Management Practices', in M. S. Ackerman, V. Pipek, and V. Wulf (eds.), *Sharing Expertise: Beyond Knowledge Management*. Cambridge, Mass.: MIT Press.

KENNEY, M. (1997). 'Value Creation in the Late Twentieth Century: The Rise of the Knowledge Worker', in J. Davis, T. A. Hirschl, and M. Stack (eds.), *Cutting Edge: Technology, Information Capitalism and Social Revolution*. London: Verso.

KLUGE, J., STEIN, W., and LICHT, T. (2001). *Knowledge Unplugged: The McKinsey and Company Global Survey on Knowledge Management*. Basingstoke: Palgrave.

KPMG (2000). *Knowledge Management Research Report*. London: KPMG Consulting Reports.

LAVE, J., and WENGER, E. (1991). *Situated Learning: Legitimate Peripheral Participation*. Cambridge: Cambridge University Press.

McDERMOTT, R. (1999). 'Why Information Technology Inspired but Cannot Deliver Knowledge Management'. *California Management Review*, 41/4: 103–17.

McKINLAY, A. (2000). 'The Bearable Lightness of Control: Organisational Reflexivity and the Politics of Knowledge Management', in C. Pritchard, R. Hull, M. Chumer, and H. Willmott (eds.), *Managing Knowledge: Critical Investigations of Work and Learning*. New York: St. Martin's Press.

—— (2002). 'The Limits of Knowledge Management'. *New Technology, Work and Employment*. 17/2: 19–31.

—— (2003). 'Smart Workers, Dumb Organizations', in K. Starkey, A. McKinlay, and S. Tempest (eds.), *How Organizations Learn*. London: Thomson Press.

MARSCHALL, D. (2002). 'Internet Technologists as an Occupational Community: Ethnographic Evidence'. *Information, Communication and Society*, 5/1: 51–69.

MERTINS, K., HEISIG, P., and VORBECK, J. (eds.) (2000). *Knowledge Management: Best Practices in Europe:* Berlin: Springer.

MORRIS, T. (2001). 'Asserting Property Rights: Knowledge Codification in the Professional Service Firm'. *Human Relations*, 54/7: 819–38.

NEWELL, S. (1999). 'EBank: A Failed Knowledge Management Initiative', in H. Scarbrough and J. Swan (eds.), *Case Studies in Knowledge Management*. London: Institute of Personnel Development.

ORR, J. E. (1996). *Talking about Machines: An Ethnography of a Modern Job*. Ithaca, NY: ILR Press.

PISANO, G. (1998). *The Development Factory*. Cambridge, Mass.: Harvard Business School Press.

PRATT, A. (2002). 'Hot Jobs in Cool Places. The Material Cultures of New Media Product Spaces: The Case of South of the Market, San Francisco'. *Information, Communication and Society*, 5/1: 27–50.

PRIES, L., and ABEL, J. (2004). 'Shifting Patterns of Labour Regulation: Highly Qualified Knowledge Workers in German New Economy Companies'. Paper prepared for International Workshop on Studying New Forms of Work in Cultural Industries and Beyond. Berlin, March.

REICH, R. (1993). *Work of Nations*. New York: Random House.

ROBERTSON, M., and SWAN, J. (1998). 'Modes of Organizing in an Expert Consultancy: A Case of Knowledge, Power and Egos'. *Organization*, 5/4: 543–64.

RUGGLES, R. (1998). 'The State of the Notion: Knowledge Management in Practice'. *California Management Review*, 40/3: 80–99.

Scarbrough, H. (2003). 'The Role of Intermediary Groups in Shaping Management Fashion: The Case of Knowledge Management'. *International Studies of Management and Organization*, 32/4: Winter 2002–3: 87–103.

Seely Brown, J., and Duguid, P. (1998). 'Organizing Knowledge'. *California Management Review*, 40/3: 90–111.

Sivula, P., van den Bosch, F., and Elfring, T. (2001). 'Competence-Based Competition: Gaining Knowledge from Client Relationships', in R. Sanchez (ed.), *Knowledge Management and Organizational Competence*. Oxford: Oxford University Press.

Star, S. L. (1995). 'The Politics of Formal Representations: Wizards, Gurus, and Organizational Complexity', in S. L. Star (ed.), *Ecologies of Knowledge: Work and Politics in Science and Technology*. New York: SUNY Press.

Starbuck, W. (1992). 'Learning by Knowledge-Intensive Firms'. *Journal of Management Studies*, 29/6: 713–40.

Swan, J., and Scarbrough, H. (2001). 'Knowledge Management: Concepts and Controversies'. *Journal of Management Studies*, 38/7: 913–21.

Teece, D. (1998). 'Capturing Value from Knowledge Assets: The New Economy, Markets for Know-How, and Intangible Assets'. *California Management Review*, 40/3: 55–79.

Warhurst, P., and Thompson, P. (1998). 'Hands, Hearts and Minds: Changing Work and Workers at the End of the Century', in P. Thompson and C. Warhurst (eds.), *Workplace of the Future*. London: Macmillan.

—— —— (forthcoming). 'Measurement by Proxy: Problems in Mapping Knowledge in the Economy and Workplace'. *Work, Employment and Society*. December 2004.

Weiss, L. (1999). 'Collection and Connection: The Anatomy of Knowledge Sharing in Professional Service Firms'. *Organization Development Journal*, 17/4: 61–78.

Wenger, E. (1998). *Communities of Practice: Learning, Meaning and Identity*. Cambridge: Cambridge University Press.

Wittel, A., Lury, C., and Lash, S. (2002). 'Real and Virtual Connectivity: New Media in London', in S. Woolgar (ed.), *Virtual Society? Technology, Cyberbole, Reality*. Oxford: Oxford University Press.

Woodfield, R. (2000). *Women, Work and Computing*. Cambridge: Cambridge University Press.

CHAPTER 11

....

INDUSTRIAL RELATIONS AND WORK

....

HARRY KATZ

11.1 INTRODUCTION

....

THIS chapter focuses on the changing nature of labor, management, and government interactions in advanced industrialized countries with particular emphasis on how modifications in industrial relations intersect with the organization of work. The evidence shows increased variation in industrial relations patterns within countries as a result of the growth of nonunion alternatives to previously dominant union systems; the rise of human resource employment patterns as alternatives to traditional collective bargaining; and the polarization of collective bargaining into participatory and adversarial alternatives. Variation across countries is declining due to similarities in the *process* of industrial relations. Although these process changes are particularly evident in workplaces that make use of high-performance work processes, they are common elsewhere. There are also similarities in industrial relations *outcomes* across countries involving commonalities in employment patterns and work practices.

The other key development examined in this chapter is the increasing role of a level of industrial relations activity above traditional collective bargaining. In some countries (e.g. Italy, Ireland, The Netherlands, and Germany) tripartite dialogue and agreements surprisingly reemerged to play a significant role in the 1990s. In addition, multinational corporations adjusted to increasingly important regional trade pacts and the consolidation of production through the creation of a regional level of industrial relations and human resource management (HRM) activity (and a stronger role for corporate headquarters). It is telling that neither tripartite activity nor regional corporate industrial relations activity is proving to be inconsistent with the decentralization occurring in the structure of industrial relations.

This higher level of industrial relations activity has a number of implications for work practices and work organization. Tripartite activities, for example, often include the promotion of workplace participation and high-performance practices. Notably, this distinguishes recent tripartite dialogue from earlier corporatism. Corporate regionalization, in turn, is often used to promote work restructuring and participatory patterns of industrial relations and work organization.

11.2 GROWING VARIATION IN EMPLOYMENT SYSTEMS

One important aspect of the change that has appeared in employment systems in industrialized countries in recent years has been the decline of union strength and membership. This has led to increased variation in the employment conditions employees experience through the lower wages paid in the nonunion sector as compared to the union sector, and the differences that appear in union versus nonunion work practices, including differences in how employee complaints are resolved.

Yet, within both the union and nonunion sectors the extent of variation in wages, work practices, and other employment conditions has also increased. This variation is particularly pronounced in workplaces that are adopting contingent compensation (such as profit sharing) or individualized pay procedures. Variation also is growing in work organization and related work practices in part as a result of the fact that certain plants use team concepts of work organization while others do not.

An important factor contributing to variation in employment practices within the union sector is the expansion of work and union participation processes at some unionized work sites while conflict-laden labor–management relations prevail at other unionized sites. In the process, the middle ground of traditional labor–management relations that had included a bounded amount of conflict is becoming less common. While increased variation in employment relations is more obvious in the union sector, variation has also been spreading in nonunion firms with some investing heavily in an HRM approach that emphasizes extensive individualized communication and pay practices while other nonunion firms use low wage and informal work practices. Meanwhile, in many countries the spread of Japanese investments or efforts to imitate Japanese employment practices in domestically owned firms has led to the spread of a distinctive set of work practices and thereby added another source of variation in employment conditions. Although developments in the United States represent an extreme case of employment system variation, with that country experiencing heavy doses of both concessionary and participatory collective bargaining and rapid growth in nonunion and Japanese employment systems, similar types of variation in employment relations have appeared in other countries.

11.3 PREVIOUS DEBATES AND EVIDENCE

The causes and consequences of increased variation in employment systems have been the source of much debate. Economists have drawn attention to a widening in the distribution of income that has been occurring within nearly all industrialized countries in recent years (Levy and Murname 1992). Yet, there has been more limited attention paid to the role that increased variation in firm-level employment relations has played as a source of that income variation. Furthermore, the focus by economists on income distribution has largely ignored the extensive variation appearing in other employment outcomes.

Declines in union membership and bargaining concessions have led many observers to see this era as involving a fundamental decline in union strength and an increase in the discretion and authority of management and market forces. Union membership and bargaining power have declined sizably since the early 1980s in most countries. While there is no simple measure of union bargaining power, a variety of indicators suggest that union power also has been declining even in countries such as Germany where union membership has not sizably declined. Although these declines do not explain the breadth of the variation appearing in employment systems within and across countries, these declines clearly have played an important role in promoting increased variation.

The most obvious sign of union bargaining power decline appears in the concessions that unions have accepted in collective bargaining in recent years. Concession bargaining first appeared in the early 1980s in a number of industries and countries and typically included either pay cuts or pay increases that were below historical standards. Concession bargaining also has been manifest in changes made to work organization (i.e. fewer job classifications or the weakening of seniority rights) that reverse gains unions had achieved in previous bargaining. Although the form and depth of concessions has varied substantially within and across countries, union membership declines, actual or threatened declines in employment, plant closings, and other factors reduced union power, evident in the limited gains achieved by unions in strike actions, even in countries where union membership has to date held up.

A more extreme claim is made by Leo Troy (1990) who views union decline as a permanent and an inevitable result of increased international competition and globalization. Unable to maintain strong multinational organizations, unions have not been able to (and according to Troy, will never be able to) expand their jurisdiction commensurate with the widening jurisdiction of the marketplace and thus the decline in union power is said to be irreversible. John Purcell (1995) also makes a gloomy forecast for the labor movement, although he sees the central challenge arising from managerial strategies that replace, or at least deflect, demand for unionism, through the elaboration of communication strategies and the individualization of personnel practices.

A less gloomy vision of the future is provided in the argument that employment relations are converging toward Japanese-style practices. The claim here is that Japanese employment relations practices are linked to Japanese manufacturing (and organizational) practices that together produce superior economic performance through their heightened attention to quality and flexibility, and relatively low cost. Favorable performance outcomes are said to derive from continuous improvement efforts, low inventories, and other features of the Japanese production system that are facilitated by Japanese employment practices (MacDuffie 1996; Womack, Jones, and Roos 1990). The net effect of this shift to Japanese-style employment relations is alleged to be a movement toward more enterprise-oriented employment relations including very decentralized bargaining structures, team-oriented work practices, and lifetime employment (at least for a core of the workforce). Interestingly, among those who offer strong evidence of this shift there are some analysts, such as Dore (1992), who are attracted to the increased organizational orientation in Japanese practices and others, such as Babson (1995) and Parker and Slaughter (1988), who claim these practices increase employee stress and union subservience.

Given the strong employment growth experienced in the United States in the 1990s, especially when compared to the high unemployment rates that have characterized the labor markets in most European countries since the late 1980s, other observers have claimed that a new international convergence to US-style flexible labor markets (and deregulated product markets) is now underway (Krugman 1996). A related claim in this line of argumentation is that a key competitive advantage has emerged in the United States through the early and heavy reengineering of managerial practices, which helped promote an American model of lean management (Hammer and Champy 1993). While put in very different terms, it is interesting to note the common claim of American superiority found in this new school of thought and the earlier convergence notions of Kerr *et al.* (1964).

Kerr *et al.* claimed that industrialization would lead to a common 'structuring' of the workforce across and within countries, a structuring process that appeared to have a relatively strong role for unions. Although it is not obvious exactly what these analysts expected industrial relations systems to converge toward, Kerr *et al.* appear to have expected that unionism would grow to much higher levels of representation and influence (unions represented one-third of the workforce in the early 1950s in the United States when they were conducting their research). They also expected industrialization to proceed relatively smoothly across the globe and in the process transform industrial relations systems around the world, so they would become similar to the collective bargaining system that appeared to be maturing in a number of core American industries in the mid-1950s.

A number of influential comparative social scientists earlier had rebutted the Kerr *et al.* convergence thesis by developing sophisticated analyses of the particularities of the industrial relations systems of various countries. The thrust of scholars such as Cole (1971), Dore (1973), and Streeck (1984) (and much of the comparative industrial relations literature that followed in the footsteps of these researchers) is that there is wide and persistent variation in industrial relations across countries in part due to the influence of nationally specific institutional factors (i.e. laws, customs, history). With persistent national differences in employment relations as the backdrop, much comparative research examines the extent to which there was commonality in the adjustment strategies being pursued in particular industries across countries (as in the auto industry, see Streeck and Katz 1984).

A major extension of comparative industrial relations analysis comes in the work of Richard Locke (1992) who, drawing on research examining the changes occurring in employment relations in Italy in the 1980s, notes the wide variation appearing within employment relations in Italy. In the face of this variation, and the forecast that this variation would increase in the future, Locke sees no evidence of cross-country convergence to any common pattern. He also questions the relevance of notions of distinct national systems of employment relations in the face of the widening variation in employment relations occurring within countries.

11.4 FOUR KEY GROWING PATTERNS OF WORK PRACTICES

Research closely related to the work of Locke suggests that a similarity in employment system changes in part derives from the fact that four common patterns of work practices are spreading (Katz and Darbishire 2000). The core elements of the four patterns of work practices that are growing are outlined in Table 11.1. This analysis utilizes the notion that employment practices cluster within firms that creates discreet patterns of employment practices across firms, a clustering arising from the fact that various employment practices reinforce one another and are linked to one another. Pattern analysis uses concepts developed in Arthur (1992), Katz and Kochan (2000), Kochan, Katz, and McKersie (1994) and Purcell and Ahlstrand (1994). A related, but somewhat distinct, way to interpret these changes is to see them in terms of a contrast between coordinated and uncoordinated decentralization (Traxler 1996).

Column 2 of Table 11.1 describes a low-wage employment pattern characterized by work practices that afford management substantial discretion and power. Work

Table 11.1 Growing Patterns of Workplace Practices

Type	Low wage	HRM	Japanese-oriented	Joint team-based
Work practices	Managerial discretion with informal procedures	Corporate culture and extensive communication	Standardized procedures	Joint decision making
	Hierarchical work relations	Directed teams	Problem-solving teams	Semi-autonomous work groups
	Low wages with piece rates	Above average wages with contingent pay	High pay linked to seniority and performance appraisals	High pay with pay-for knowledge
	High turnover	Individualized career development	Employment stabilization	Career development
	Strong anti-union animus	Union substitution	Enterprise unionism	Union and employee involvement

practices in this pattern are informally applied and this pattern typically operates on a nonunion basis. The HRM employment pattern (Column 3 in Table 11.1) focuses on individualized rewards and career development. The HRM approach, for example, includes teams that are more centrally directed by management when compared to the large role supervisors play in team-related and other work practices found in the Japanese-oriented pattern. However, like the Japanese-oriented system, the HRM approach attempts to sustain a strong managerially driven corporate culture through extensive corporate communication, although the communication channels differ from the supervisory-based channels found in the Japanese-oriented workplaces.

In the United States, the HRM pattern developed primarily in nonunion firms and is closely linked to efforts by those firms to stay nonunion. Interestingly, while this HRM pattern is now spreading in other countries (as in Italy), there it is often being adopted as a complement, and not an alternative to, collective bargaining procedures (Ferner and Hyman 1992).

Column 4 of Table 11.1 describes a Japanese-oriented workplace pattern. This pattern is distinguished from a more joint team-based approach (Column 5 of Table 11.1) in part based on the extent to which workers are granted autonomy to decide how and when they carry out their job tasks. In the Japanese-oriented employment pattern, jobs are highly standardized, and although workers may have input into this standardization process, once job tasks are standardized, there is little, if any, room for worker or team discretion, as found in the joint team-based pattern. Furthermore, in the Japanese-oriented workplace, supervisors have very strong roles whereas in the joint team-based system workers themselves take on many of the responsibilities previously carried out by supervisors and the number of supervisors is relatively low.

There is much variation regarding how each of these workplace patterns is actually implemented in each country in addition to the cross-country differences noted above. Important factors are the roles workers are asked to play and the roles any unions choose to play. In some joint team-based systems, for example, unions and workers participate extensively in business decisions. An extreme example of this pattern is the GM Saturn Corporation where UAW representatives serve as co-managers and are engaged in numerous managerial decisions including the selection of parts suppliers and the development of corporate business plans (Rubenstein and Kochan 2001). Less extreme illustrations of the joint team-based approach are more widespread in the auto, telecommunications, and other industries where unionists influence managerial decisions through their involvement in plant-level business committees or through worker representation on corporate boards.

There is variation in the practices followed by Japanese-owned firms that is similar to other forms of the variation found in employment systems. All the firms that are owned by a Japanese parent company have not adopted a Japanese-oriented workplace pattern. A number of Japanese-owned plants in the United

States, for example, follow a low-wage pattern of employment relations including informal personnel policies, high job turnover, low wages, and similar examples can be found in the United Kingdom and Australia (Milkman 1991). Evidence of significant variation in the practices in Japanese-owned firms operating in Europe is provided in Elger and Smith (1998).

At the same time, there is a growing influence of Japanese practices through either direct Japanese investments or the imitation of Japanese practices in domestically owned firms (MacDuffie 1996). This influence of Japanese-style practices has contributed to the richness of the variation that is appearing, however, there is little indication that employment relations are converging towards a Japanese-style pattern.

11.5 THE INFLUENCE OF NATIONAL INSTITUTIONS

While there are many commonalities in the work practices that make up the key employment patterns that are spreading across countries, the relative proportion of the different workplace patterns, and the extent to which these patterns operate on a nonunion basis, vary much across countries. In the United States and the United Kingdom, for example, and to a lesser degree in a number of the other countries, the low-wage, human resource management, and Japanese-oriented workplace practice patterns operate on a nonunion basis. In this way growing employment system variation is linked to declines in the fraction of the workforce that is represented by unions.

Country-specific institutions also influence the mix of workplace practice patterns and the degree of unionization. For example, German regulations that can extend the terms of negotiated framework collective bargaining agreements to firms that are not members of the relevant employers' association have helped produce limited growth in low-wage and nonunion employment patterns. Furthermore, the legal rights of German works councils have contributed to the relatively high degree of standardization in complaint resolution procedures and the structure of employee representation. As a result, for example, the sort of variation found across US auto transplants in grievance procedures, or the different bargaining roles played by 'company councils' at Nissan and Toyota in the United Kingdom, for example, are not issues in Germany. Likewise, in Germany the rights of works councils lead to less variation in the information employee representatives receive at either the plant or company level. In Australia, the political strength of the labor movement and the continuing importance of a national wage tribunal system similarly have served to limit the growth of low-wage employment.

Although it is not always obvious how labor market or regulatory institutions exert their influence, the outcomes are rather striking (Smith and Elger 1997). For example, in the United States nonunion Japanese transplants have made substantial inroads into the auto assembly sector, while in Australia all auto assembly transplants remain unionized. In Italy and Sweden, even though the work practices that fit the human resource management pattern are spreading, as a result of existing institutions and the continuing strength of the labor movement, these practices are complementing collective procedures and are not associated with the spread of nonunion employment relationships. While it remains to be seen if institutions continue to constrain to such a high degree the spread of nonunion employment relationships in countries such as Italy, Sweden, and Germany, to date institutions have clearly strengthened unions in these countries especially when developments are contrasted with events in the United States and the United Kingdom (Katz and Darbishire 2000).

The patterns of workplace practices outlined in Table 11.1 typically complement pay, work organization, bargaining structure, and many other employment policies and practices that affect employment relations and labor market outcomes in each country. This is one of the ways existing country-specific labor market structures and institutions critically affect employment systems. For example, the joint team-based pattern of work practices operates very differently and has very different consequences for labor and management in German versus other countries because of the important role exerted by the German dual system of employee representation.

The effects of and outcomes produced by the various employment patterns depend on the basic employment relations institutions in each country and also upon the extent and nature of the representation afforded to workers and unions in each country. For example, the extent to which semi-autonomous work groups lead to enhanced worker involvement in decision making differs in the United States and Germany because the latter already includes an extensive amount of worker involvement mandated through national codetermination laws.

Institutions also influence the extent to which variation in employment systems appears within a given country. Thus, it is just as important to understand, for example, why Germany and Japan have experienced less extreme variation in employment systems in comparison with the variation found in the United States and the United Kingdom, as it is to note the similarities that appear across countries.

The influence of national institutions suggests that to fully account for the nature and consequences of employment system variation it is necessary to understand the variation that prevailed in employment systems within each country as each entered the critical 1980s. In the United States, for example, a wide diversity of employment systems had developed over the post-World War II period within and between the union and nonunion sectors. Union and nonunion firms differed substantially in the wages provided to workers (with unionized firms paying wages that were on average 10–20 percent higher) and in work rules (with work practices in the union sector regulated by negotiated seniority rules). In the nonunion sector in the United States, research has documented the existence of a rule-bound 'bureaucratic' pattern that lacked the flexibility and individualized nature of the work practices that now appear in the HRM approach (Katz and Kochan 2000). A low-wage pattern of employment relations also has long prevailed in many 'secondary' labor market sectors in the United States.

In Germany, in contrast, there has long been much less extreme variation in employment relations given the presence of national codetermination laws and procedures that extend the terms of regional negotiated collective bargaining agreements to firms whether or not they are unionized. In Australia, to take another example, the wage tribunal system has helped assure employment system standardization. While the traditional employment patterns differ much across countries, and serve as a template upon which the four patterns have diffused, the spread of the employment patterns described in Table 11.1 has led to declines in the role played by the traditional employment patterns in each country.

11.6 VARIATIONS IN WORK ORGANIZATION WITHIN COUNTRIES

A key source of work organization variation within each country is the differences appearing in the detailed policies that implement particular work practice patterns. For example, analysis of the evolution of auto employment relations reveals wide variation in the nature of team systems that are being adopted as part of the joint team-based pattern (Katz and Darbishire 2000). Among other things, differences appear across plants and even within plants in the methods used to select team leaders and in the roles and responsibilities of team leaders and team members. The roles of team leaders, for example, vary much across auto plants in the United States, Germany, and Italy. Another instance of within-pattern work practice variation is the differences in the particular policies being adopted to promote individualized career development as part of the HRM pattern.

Variation within countries also is growing due to the fact that work practices increasingly vary across individuals and pay outcome variation is also being spurred by the spread of contingent pay procedures. There is much interaction across these various practices illustrated in the way that greater individualized rewards are often linked to the expansion of contingent compensation payment methods. In the British and Australian telecommunications industries, for example, individualization of employment relations has been promoted in the ranks of senior managers through individual contracts that replace traditional collectively negotiated contracts. This is expanding to include all managers, and even some sections of the non-managerial workforce, as the use of contingent pay grows.

Contingent compensation is spreading in a number of countries, although there is wide variation in the form and extent of the use of contingent pay. Contingent pay is particularly evident in the auto industry as the share of worker compensation that is set through annual bonuses, pay-for-knowledge, or payments linked to individual assessments has been rising in recent years. In Japan, for example, the variation in the annual bonuses received by autoworkers at the primary auto assemblers has increased sizably in recent years (Katz and Darbishire 2000). In the United States, across the Big Three auto assemblers, where hourly pay had long been standardized, from the mid-1980s on annual pay has varied substantially as a result of variation in company profit-sharing payouts, and also varied within companies due to variation in the use and form of pay-for-knowledge plans. In Sweden, where autoworker unions had long resisted perform-ance-based compensation schemes, there is a recent expansion in the use of contingent (and more individualized) pay procedures, as in Italy. Likewise, a similar trend is occurring in Germany, where there are, in particular, emerging differences in pay between companies as a result of concession bargaining as firms' performance levels vary, and as works councils negotiate company-level employ-ment security clauses.

Substantial diversity also appears even within firms (or plants) that are following a particular pattern of work practices. This diversity in part arises from the fact that the decentralization that has occurred within managerial and corporate struc-tures has shifted decision-making authority regarding employment relations to the shop floor. Thus, for example, where team systems of work are utilized, there is much variation in the specific job duties assigned to the team leader or to team members. As team members directly take on more problem-solving tasks, they often develop particular solutions to workplace problems that further spur variety in work practices. This variety is one of the reasons why team systems are attractive as a mechanism to lower costs and improve quality and productivity.

The growth in variation in employment conditions within firms is often linked to a decentralization occurring within businesses, a decentralization that is frequently associated with the rise in the importance of business units or profit centers within organizations. In the telecommunications industry, for example, there is a tendency for firms to oscillate between centralized and decentralized organizational forms as these firms search for a structure that fits well with the more deregulated and uncertain economic environments.

Another common process change is decentralization in the structure of collective bargaining. In the United Kingdom, United States, and Sweden, for example, decentralization has entailed a decline in the proportion of collective bargaining occurring at the multiemployer level and an increase in company- and plant-level bargaining. Even where formal structures of bargaining have not changed in these countries, the strength of pattern bargaining has weakened as company- and increasingly plant-level variation emerges in pay and working conditions.

In Germany and Japan, in contrast, the formal structure of bargaining has not been decentralized, as these countries already had relatively decentralized structures for workplace change, while adjustments within existing structures are allowing increased variation in pay and other labor market outcomes. Yet, even in Germany there has been massive decentralization *inside* existing institutional structures, as works councils have played an increasingly important role in determining basic employment conditions. In Japan, the enterprise unions, particularly in the auto industry, have increasingly taken on a mediating role between workers on the shop floor and corporate management in the process of facilitating workplace adjustments.

Meanwhile in Italy, earlier formal decentralization of collective bargaining structures has been partially reversed in recent years (Regalia and Regini 2004). Nevertheless, in all countries a downward shift in the locus of employment relations is being driven by decentralization in corporate structures, work reorganizations, and increases in the direct participation of employees in production and business decision-making. Another important change in the structure and processes of employment relations that is spreading across and within countries is an increase in direct communication between employees and management. More direct employer–employee communication has been associated with the more decentralized production methods that are being adopted at many work sites.

In addition, management at many plants has utilized more direct communication with employees as part of the more informal and more continuous negotiation that is being adopted as an alternative to traditional arm's length forms of labor–management relations. Enhanced direct communication is also linked to the work restructuring that is occurring including the use of team systems of work organization and other techniques used to settle production problems and disputes more quickly on the shop floor. In the process of communicating its case more directly with employees, management has been either circumventing existing union-related negotiation structures or creating alternatives to union representation, such as individual contracts. The latter is particularly evident in work sites using human resource management work practices.

11.7 FACTORS CONTRIBUTING TO WITHIN-COUNTRY VARIATION IN EMPLOYMENT SYSTEMS

In part, the growing variation in employment systems that appears within countries has resulted from a shift in bargaining power in management's favor at the same time there is pressure to reorganize work practices. A combination of these factors has led management to push for changes in the process of labor–management relations, and workplace restructuring. The shift in relative power is also illustrated in that a number of the key patterns of workplace practices outlined in Table 11.1 frequently operate on a nonunion basis, and the continuing growth in nonunion work sites is clearly associated with a decline in union power.

Within the unionized sector, one of the key ways bargaining power has been affecting the variation in employment systems is through management-led whip-sawing of plants and local unions. Management bargaining leverage is greater where there are alternative production sites and the production process allows a separation of the various aspects of production. For example, management has gained concessions from autoworkers where it can outsource the production of a part or operation, particularly where a low-wage nonunion supplier is available. This sort of outsourcing has proven to be more difficult, although increasingly available, in the telecommunications services sector, where management-led whip-sawing is constrained by the need to coordinate service provision along the basic telephone network, and in other industries. Where management is gaining whipsaw leverage a wide variety of concessions are emerging, and the ensuing variation in work practices is often linked to work restructuring proceeding at the plant level.

Although unions and workers are often disadvantaged by concessionary whip-sawing, work restructuring is providing advantages to the workforce in the form of enhanced shop-floor involvement or through changes in work organization, such as teamworking, that at least some of the workforce prefer to traditional work methods. Work restructuring may well have intensified even if management power had not increased. Yet, in point of fact, since increases in managerial power are so closely interconnected with the spread of work restructuring, it may be futile to try to distinguish the independent influence of each as a cause of the growing variation in employment practices.

11.8 THE REEMERGENCE OF TRIPARTITE DIALOGUE IN SOME COUNTRIES

Another key change occurring in industrial relations that has critical implications for work organization is the reemergence of tripartite labor, management, and government dialogue concerning labor policy in various countries from the early 1990s on. In Ireland, The Netherlands, Germany, and Italy, for example, social dialogue and partnership and other national-level interactions between representatives of labor, management, and the government (i.e. tripartism) have played a positive role addressing critical economic and social problems (Bosch 2004; Regalia and Regini 2004; Slomp 2004; Teague and Donaghey 2004).

Recent tripartism differs much from previous corporatism. In a number of social democratic countries in the 1960s and 1970s, corporatism involving dialogue between representatives of labor, management, and government focused on efforts to control inflation (incomes policy) and often involved political exchanges whereby tax and other government policies were traded for wage (and price) moderation. In recent years, however, tripartism has come to focus more on working time flexibility and the promotion of part-time work than on previous concerns about inflation. Tripartite dialogue also has expanded beyond traditional corporatist partners to include women's groups, representatives of senior citizens, and other representatives of 'civic society'.

With the limited success that incomes policies had in restraining inflation in a number of countries in the 1960s and 1970s, one might have expected that tripartism had lost its appeal. In this light, in the 1990s the negotiation of prominent tripartite accords in Ireland, Italy, and The Netherlands, and the national employment pact in Germany is quite surprising.

While recent tripartite pacts have much in common with previous incomes policies given the central importance of wage moderation, the specific pressure for such moderation such as the need for monetary discipline in order to conform to European Union and related monetary union pressures, has added a new twist to the exercise. In addition, recent pacts seem to be broader in scope as compared to earlier corporatism with an emphasis on workplace and employment flexibility, promotion of participatory processes, and inclusion of social security reforms.

There was much theorizing in previous research about the factors that influenced the success of neocorporatism including the degree of encompassing interest representation, union democracy, and social democratic political strength (Baccaro 2000; Crouch 1985; Regini 1997, 2000; Schmitter 1981; Streeck 1982). While Schmitter (1979) argues that mechanisms that shielded union leaders from popular pressures assisted corporatism in the 1970s and 1980s, Baccaro (2002) claims that it was the spread of internal democracy in unions that was a key to the success of tripartism in Italy in the 1990s.

The structure of labor, management, and government interactions are changing in critical ways beyond the replacement of corporatism with more varied forms of tripartite dialogue and policymaking in countries where the latter flourishes. Analysis of recent developments in Japan, Korea, Australia, and the United States, for example, finds that, although tripartism has not been central to economic policymaking in recent years in those countries, as in countries where tripartism flourishes, a variety of other 'coordinating' mechanisms provide interactions that help shape employment conditions and labor policy (Katz, Lee, and Lee 2004). The fact that there has been so much vibrancy in these coordinating mechanisms goes against the notion, popular in some quarters, that there is an overpowering unilateral decentralizing shift underway in labor–management interactions. These coordinating functions are increasing as a result of pressures promoting greater flexibility in work organization and working time.

11.9 THE ROLE OF GLOBALIZATION AND REGIONALIZATION

The expansion of global trade, regional trade pacts (such as the European Union and the North American Free Trade Agreement), and the growth of multinational corporations have spurred globalization and regionalization, and these are among the key factors promoting shifts in the structure of labor–management interactions. For example, in Europe, a new cross-national tier of labor–management interaction has been spurred by the European Union's requirement, as of 1996, that multinational corporations operating in more than one country facilitate the formation of European-wide works councils.

Regionalization also appears in the restructuring of internal industrial relations and human resource staff functions within multinational corporations. The pressures for decentralization have led many corporations to shift area management or business unit structures to gain flexibility in industrial relations administration and in some cases, bargaining power advantages. Yet, globalization pressures are leading to potentially cross-cutting shifts in the internal operations of multinational corporations. A special dilemma for industrial relations managers in the multinational corporation arises from the fact that culture, law, and institutions retain much of their international diversity at the same time that globalization has increased the premium on coordination and central control.

Cross-national differences in culture, law, and institutions have long created control and coordination problems for multinational firms. Traditionally, multinational firms responded to this problem by maintaining a high degree of local control (decentralization) in the internal direction of industrial relations (Kujawa 1980). Previous analysis of multinational firms generally showed that the administration of industrial relations was more decentralized than other management functions such as finance or marketing. Multinationals found that there were substantial benefits to be gained from the decentralization of industrial relations. These benefits include the ability to respond flexibly to various kinds of diversity. By allowing local managers in each country to fashion industrial relations policies, these managers could create policies and procedures that fit with local conditions and events. Yet, there is accumulating evidence that shifts are underway in multinational corporate strategy and structure due to the pressures of globalization.

Although corporations might still prefer to keep the everyday conduct of collective bargaining localized, in order to better respond to local differences and avoid potentially uplifting employment condition comparisons, more extensive coordination of labor policies and work practices is emerging within multinational corporations. For example, so-called centers of excellence give multinational corporations the capability to take greater advantage of scale economies and more continuous operation of advanced process technologies. In this environment, labor disputes that in the past would have effects in only one country now potentially affect a multinational corporations regional or global 'supply chain'. This in turn is stimulating greater corporate concern for labor relations and human resource practices in regional production centers and is creating a push for a regionalization in corporate labor relations and human resource activities.

Further pressure for greater corporate involvement in labor relations comes from the fact that multinational corporations see advantage in the coordination of work reorganizations occurring around their global operations in order to take advantage of successful and innovative cases. The similarities in work restructuring concerning teams and participatory work systems and contingent pay practice or continuous operations stimulate the need for mechanisms through which multinational corporations can transfer information and learning across operating sites and national boundaries. These factors are leading to the formation of a new regional level of human resource management and greater corporate coordination of labor relations policies and practices in multinational corporations (Katz 2004).

The increasing cross-national coordination of corporate and union industrial relations strategies are aspects of the increased coordination apparent both in countries, such as the United States, that lack national-level tripartite activities and in those countries that have tripartite activities. The widespread increased coordination of labor and management interactions, which in some cases includes government, provides a commonality across countries that contrasts with the extremely varied use of tripartite dialogue and policymaking.

11.10 RESEARCH AGENDAS

The growing variation in employment systems within countries suggests that a key task for future research is documenting the distribution of various employment patterns within countries. With more refined knowledge of the distribution of work practices it might then become feasible to analyze what, if any, relationship exists between work practice patterns and economic performance. This would allow for informed extension of the 'varieties of capitalism' debate and clarification as to whether there is one best way or multiple paths to economic advantage.

Further research also is needed to identify the implications of the spread of decentralized collective bargaining and coordinating mechanisms that span different bargaining levels. For example, while current evidence suggests that decentralization and tripartism are not inconsistent, this may not prove to be true in the long run. Nor is it yet clear whether the trend toward more regional corporate industrial relations and cross-national unionism will continue and if so, lead to substantive changes in collective bargaining outcomes and work practices. With the spread of more decentralized and informal labor–management interactions, the vocabulary of industrial relations, developed to understand the traditional formal institutions of labor relations, should correspondingly change. There is a clear need for new theory to analyze the implications of the shifts underway in the process of labor–management interaction.

It is already apparent that simple predictions of cross-national convergence or uncontrolled decentralization in collective bargaining need to be replaced by more sophisticated analyses of the changes underway in work and industrial relations. And perhaps even more importantly, even with the decline of unionism, there remain many developments in the field of industrial relations and in the world of work worthy of further analysis.

REFERENCES

ARTHUR, J. B. (1992). 'The Link between Business Strategy and Industrial Relations Systems in American Steel Mini-Mills'. *Industrial and Labor Relations Review*, 45/April: 488–506.

BABSON, S. (1995). 'Whose Team? Lean Production at Mazda U.S.A.', in S. Babson (ed.), *Lean Work: Empowerment and Exploitation in the Global Auto Industry*. Detroit: Wayne State University Press.

BACCARO, L. (2000). 'Centralized Collective Bargaining and the Problem of "Compliance": Lessons from the Italian Experience'. *Industrial and Labor Relations Review*, 53/July: 579–601.

—— (2002). 'Negotiating the Italian Pension Reform with the Unions: Lessons for Corporatist Theory'. *Industrial and Labor Relations Review*, 55/April: 413–31.

BOSCH, G. (2004). 'The Changing Nature of Collective Bargaining in Germany: Coordinated Decentralization', in H. Katz, W. Lee, and J. Lee (eds.), *The New Structure of Labor Relations: Tripartism and Decentralization*. Ithaca, NY: Cornell University Press.

COLE, R. E. (1971). *Japanese Blue Collar*. Berkeley: University of California Press.

CROUCH, C. (1985). 'Conditions for Trade Union Wage Restraint,' in L. Lindberg and C. Maier (eds.), *The Politics of Inflation and Economic Stagnation*. Washington, D.C.: Brookings Institution.

DORE, R. (1973). *British Factory—Japanese Factory: The Origins of National Diversity in Industrial Relations*. Berkeley: University of California Press.

—— (1992). 'Japan's Version of Managerial Capitalism', in T. Kochan and M. Useem (eds.), *Transforming Organizations*. New York: Oxford University Press.

ELGER, T., and SMITH, C. (1998). 'Exit, Voice, and "Mandate"—Labour Strategies and Management Practices of Japanese Firms in Britain'. *British Journal of Industrial Relations*, 36/June: 185–207.

FERNER, A., and HYMAN, R. (1992). 'Italy: Between Political Exchange and Micro-Corporatism', in A. Ferner and R. Hyman (eds.), *Industrial Relations in the New Europe*. Cambridge, Mass. and Oxford: Basil Blackwell.

HAMMER, M., and CHAMPY, J. (1993). *Re-engineering the Corporation: A Manifesto for Business Revolution*. New York: HarperBusiness.

—— (2004). 'United States: The Spread of Coordination and Decentralization without National-level Tripartism', in H. Katz, W. Lee, and J. Lee (eds.), *The New Structure of Labor Relations: Tripartism and Decentralization*. Ithaca, NY: Cornell University Press.

—— and DARBISHIRE, O. (2000). *Converging Divergences: Worldwide Changes in Employment Systems*. Ithaca, NY: ILR and Cornell University Press.

—— and KOCHAN, T. A. (2000). *An Introduction to Collective Bargaining and Industrial Relations* (2nd edn). New York: Irwin-McGraw Hill Inc.

—— LEE, W., and LEE, J. (eds.) (2004). *The New Structure of Labor Relations: Tripartism and Decentralization*. Ithaca, NY: Cornell University Press.

KERR, C., DUNLOP, J. T., HARBISON, F., and MYERS, C. (1964). *Industrialism and Industrial Man*. New York: Oxford University Press.

KOCHAN, T., KATZ, H. C., and McKERSIE, R. (1994). *The Transformation of American Industrial Relations* (2nd edn). Ithaca, NY: ILR and Cornell University Press.

KRUGMAN, P. (1996). *Pop Internationalism*. Cambridge, Mass.: MIT Press.

KUJAWA, D. (1980). 'Labor Relations of U.S. Multinational Abroad', in B. Martin and E. Kassalow (eds.), *Labor Relations in Advanced Industrial Societies*. New York: Carnegie Endowment for Peace.

LEVY, F., and MURNAME, R. J. (1992). 'U.S. Earnings Levels and Earnings Inequality: A Review of Recent Trends and Proposed Explanations'. *Journal of Economic Literature*, 30/September: 1333–81.

LOCKE, R. M. (1992). 'The Decline of the National Union in Italy: Lessons for Comparative Industrial Relations Theory'. *Industrial and Labor Relations Review*, 45/January: 229–49.

MacDUFFIE, J. P. (1996). 'International Trends in Work Organization in the International Auto Industry: National-Level vs. Company-Level Perspectives', in K. Wever and L. Turner (eds.), *The Comparative Political Economy of Industrial Relations*. Madison, Wis.: IRRA.

MILKMAN, R. (1991). *Japan's California Factories: Labor Relations and Economic Globalization*. Los Angeles: UCLA Institute of Industrial Relations.

PARKER, M., and SLAUGHTER, J. (1988). *Choosing Sides: Unions and the Team Concept*. Boston: South End Press.

PURCELL, J. (1995). 'Ideology and the End of Institutional Industrial Relations: Evidence from the UK', in C. Crouch and F. Traxler (eds.), *Organized Industrial Relations in Europe: What Future?* Hants: Avebury.

——and AHLSTRAND, B. (1994). *Human Resource Management in the Multi-Divisional Company*. Oxford: Oxford University Press.

REGALIA, I., and REGINI, M. (2004). 'Collective Bargaining and Social Pacts in Italy', in H. Katz, W. Lee, and J. Lee (eds.), *The New Structure of Labor Relations: Tripartism and Decentralization*. Ithaca, NY: Cornell University Press.

REGINI, M. (1997). 'Still Engaging in Corporatism? Recent Italian Experience in Comparative Perspective'. *European Journal of Industrial Relations*, 3/November: 259–78.

——(2000). 'Between Deregulation and Social Pacts: The Responses of European Economies to Globalization'. *Politics and Society*, 28/March: 5–33.

RUBENSTEIN, S. A., and KOCHAN, T. A. (2001). *Learning from Saturn*. Ithaca, NY: Cornell University Press.

SCHMITTER, P. (1979). 'Still the Century of Corporatism?' in P. Schmitter and G. Lehmbruch (eds.), *Trends toward Corporatist Intermediation*. London: Sage.

——(1981). 'Interest Intermediation and Regime Governability in Contemporary Western Europe and North America', in S. Berger (ed.), *Organizing Interests in Western Europe*. New York: Cambridge University Press.

SLOMP, H. (2004). 'The Netherlands: Resilience in Structure, Revolution in Substance', in H. Katz, W. Lee, and J. Lee (eds.), *The New Structure of Labor Relations: Tripartism and Decentralization*. Ithaca, NY: Cornell University Press.

SMITH, C., and ELGER, T. (1997). 'International Competition, Inward Investment and the Restructuring of European Work and Industrial Relations'. *European Journal of Industrial Relations*, 3/November: 279–304.

STREECK, W. (1982). 'Organizational Consequences of Corporatist Cooperation in West German Labor Unions', in G. Lehmbruch and P. Schmitter (eds.), *Patterns of Corporatist Policy-Making*. Beverly Hills, Calif.: Sage.

—— (1984). *Industrial Relations in West Germany: A Case Study of the Car Industry*. London: Heinemann.

—— and KATZ, H. C. (1984). 'Labor Relations and Employment Adjustments', in A. Altshuler *et al.* (eds.), *The Future of the Automobile*. Cambridge, Mass.: MIT Press.

TEAGUE, P., and DONAGHEY, J. (2004). 'The Irish Experiment in Social Partnership', in H. Katz, W. Lee, and J. Lee (eds.), *The New Structure of Labor Relations: Tripartism and Decentralization*. Ithaca, NY: Cornell University.

TRAXLER, F. (1996). 'Collective Bargaining and Industrial Change: A Case of Disorganization? A Comparative Analysis of Eighteen OECD Countries'. *European Sociological Review*, 12: 271–87.

TROY, L. (1990). 'Is the U.S. Unique in the Decline of Private Sector Unionism?' *Journal of Labor Research*, 11/Spring: 111–43.

WOMACK, J. P., JONES, D. T., and ROOS, D. (1990). *The Machine That Changed the World*. New York: Rawson Associates.

CHAPTER 12

....

LABOR
MOVEMENTS AND
MOBILIZATION

JOHN KELLY

12.1 INTRODUCTION

....

ONE increasingly influential account of contemporary employment relations runs as follows. Union membership rose significantly in many countries through the late 1960s and into the 1970s, as a growing range of workers protested against reductions in pay and increases in the intensity of labor. Unions deployed labor market power, through the strike weapon, as well as political power, through corporatist relations with governments, in order to protect and improve the interests of their members. But in the global recession that gathered pace from the late 1970s, many of the foundations of union membership, power, and activity were swept away and with them went union influence.

Across the advanced capitalist world they have lost members on an unprecedented scale, and it is now rare for them to organize more than a minority of the labor force. Their influence within the workplace has declined as employers have moved away from joint regulation of terms and conditions of employment towards unilateral control over the labor process. The percentage of workers whose pay is fixed by union–management negotiation—the coverage of collective bargaining—

has fallen significantly in line with union membership. In Britain, bargaining coverage fell from 83 percent in 1980 to 41 percent in 1998 and similar trends occurred in the United States and Japan (Cully *et al.* 1999: 242; Golden, Wallerstein, and Lange 1999: 203). As union power has diminished, its most dramatic manifestation, the strike, has become a rare event. Inside companies, new types of payment system and sophisticated forms of 'human resource management' have increasingly aligned the objectives and interests of workers and employers, rendering unions increasingly unnecessary and irrelevant, as employment relations have become less adversarial and more cooperative. Unions have also been weakened by global product market competition and the threat of capital relocation into the union-free 'export processing zones' of Third World countries (Jessop and Gordon 2000). They have also had to contend with the recomposition of the economy and the labor force. Union heartlands in large manufacturing plants and publicly owned corporations have shrunk while employment growth has been concentrated in weakly unionized private services. The workforce is no longer dominated by the archetypal union member—a full-time, male manual worker with a strong sense of collectivism—but has become more diverse through employment growth among women, part-timers, and white-collar workers who are thought to have far more individualistic orientations to employment. Finally, the state has played a significant role in many countries as an agent of increased market regulation and has often served to weaken trade unionism still further.

Tables 12.1 and 12.2 show union density and strike rates for the major advanced capitalist countries since 1960 and the evidence is largely consistent with the story of union decline. Some commentators have argued that these trends in the structure of the economy and the workforce require corresponding adjustments in the policies and modes of action of trade unions. From the proposition that there

Table 12.1 Trade union density, six countries, 1960–1997 (% of workers in unions)

	1960	1970	1980	1985	1990	1997
France	24.1	19.5	22.2	18.5	13.9	9.9
Germany	34.7	32.0	34.9	34.3	32.1	27.1
Italy	24.7	37.0	49.6	42.3	39.1	36.8
Japan	31.3	34.5	30.3	27.8	25.4	24.0
United Kingdom	44.9	49.8	56.3	50.4	42.8	34.4
United States	29.4	25.9	20.2	17.2	14.8	14.2

Sources: France, Germany, Italy, and the United Kingdom: Ebbinghaus and Visser (2000: table WE.13/14a); Japan and the United States: Golden, Wallerstein, and Lange (1999: table 7.1).

Table 12.2 Working days lost through strikes per 1,000 workers, six countries, 1960–1999 (annual averages)

	1960–4	1971–5	1980–4	1990–5	1995–9
France	352	232	90	36	98
Germany	34	57	50	17	1
Italy	1,220	1,367	950	148	33
Japan	302	188	10	3	2
United Kingdom	242	1,186	480	29	23
United States	722	484	160	33	13

Sources: 1990–9: Davies (2001*a*: table 3); 1980–4: Bird (1991: table 1); 1971–5: *Employment Gazette*, 90/2: 69, 1981; 1960–4: *Department of Employment Gazette*, 79/2: 164, 1971.

has been a decline in the incidence of collectivist values, some writers have deduced that unions must develop more individualistic modes of representation. Unions could act as a servicing agent, advising workers on employment contracts, job opportunities, and training requirements or as an advocate, representing workers' claims for individual legal rights. Other writers have interpreted the decline in collective action as the harbinger of a new era of more cooperative industrial relations and urged unions to embrace a role of partnership with the employer in the promotion of competitive success, a policy that might also prove more acceptable to organizationally committed white-collar workers (Heckscher 1996; Kochan and Osterman 1994). Each of these modes of action is complex; partnership for instance can take different forms, depending on the balance of power between the parties and on the degree to which union and worker rights are legally protected (Kelly 2004). Nor are they exclusive, and indeed they might even be combined with other, more traditional forms of action such as political lobbying.

This account of contemporary developments is both plausible and coherent and appears consistent with the kind of evidence shown in Tables 12.1 and 12.2. But a deeper examination of organizational life and of current employment relations suggests that it is actually superficial and misleading.

12.2 TRADE UNIONS AND WORKPLACE DISCONTENT

In analyzing the future of trade unions we need to understand how and why employees join them and under what conditions employers and states will recognize them as legitimate and powerful bodies with whom they must enter some form of enduring relationship. These two themes are interconnected: unions that cannot establish and maintain bargaining relations with employers or engage in political exchange with states will find it extremely difficult to sustain their membership. The reason is that most workers join unions for instrumental reasons, in other words, they expect that the union will be able to provide them with benefits they have been unable to secure through their own action as individuals. In the absence of such benefits, and assuming they have freedom of choice, workers are unlikely to maintain their membership (Clark 2000: 32–9).

The processes through which workers join unions turn out to be similar to those involved in the formation and growth of other social movements. According to mobilization theory, it is not simply dissatisfaction at work which triggers unionization, but a sense of injustice, a breach of legal or collective agreement rights, or of widely shared social values (Kelly 1998). Such rights could be either procedural (the right to a fair hearing on a disciplinary charge) or substantive (the right to overtime pay for example). In a workplace where there is no union presence, such grievances must be felt by substantial numbers of workers in order to generate a shared sense of group identity. Workers who identify with one another in this way are more likely to form a cohesive group that can withstand managerial pressure against the formation of a union. Before getting to that stage however workers must either attribute blame for their problems to the employer or must feel the employer can remedy them. Attributions for injustice that focus on impersonal forces such as 'the market' or 'global competition' are disabling (regardless of their validity) because they fail to provide a target for collective action (Javeline 2003). Finally people must have a sense of agency (or efficacy), i.e. the belief that collective organization and action can make a difference.

These sets of beliefs, known as 'collective action frames' (Klandermans 1997: 17), are necessary but not sufficient for workers to join and act through unions. There must also be a collective organization that can provide the resources necessary for such action; a leadership willing and able to mobilize members for action; a balance of power favorable to such action; channels through which demands can be placed, such as bargaining structures; and minimal costs, e.g. state or employer repression, associated with collective organization and activity (Kelly 1998; Tilly 1978). One immediate implication of this framework is that the absence of collective action, such as strike activity, tells us very little about injustice at the workplace; it could just as easily signify a deficiency in union leadership, for example, or an unfavorable balance of power.

The logic of social movement theory is that the fortunes of labor movements therefore depend, *inter alia*, on the scale of injustice at the workplace, the attitudes of employees towards management, and the effectiveness of union organization and action. People's beliefs about these issues will in turn depend on the actions and rhetoric of union leaders and their opponents and on the structural conditions that shape union power, in particular the state of labor and product markets (unemployment and competition, respectively) and the forms of legal regulation of union activity.

We first examine evidence about contemporary work and workers and then move on to examine worker attitudes and responses towards management and trade unions. Evidence will be drawn from as wide a range of countries as possible, but survey data on worker attitudes tends to come from the United Kingdom and the United States. In the light of this material we can then reexamine the initial arguments about the decline of unions and collective action.

12.3 WORKERS AND WORKPLACES

Other chapters in this Handbook have documented the many types of 'new' managerial practices that have spread throughout workplaces in the advanced capitalist world and developments in the experiences of work for many employees. Nevertheless it is worth summarizing some key points here about improvements in terms and conditions of employment in recent years. Between 1979 and 1998 real pay increased significantly for the overwhelming majority of workers in the OECD countries. For full-time men (excluding the United States) average weekly earnings rose 22.6 percent, while for women the increase was even higher at 31.6 percent. In the weakly unionized United States, men's earnings actually fell over the past two decades, by 5.5 percent while women's earnings did rise, but by 15.3 percent, about half the OECD figure as a whole (Blau and Kahn 2002: 50). A growing percentage of British employees has experienced a rise in levels of skill and job responsibility. In 1986, 52 percent reported skill increases over the previous five years but in 1992 that figure had risen to 63 percent. For responsibility, the corresponding figures were 60 and 65 percent, respectively (Gallie *et al.* 1998: 34, 37). Finally, although unemployment in the advanced capitalist world rose steeply throughout the 1980s, and in 2003 was still well above the levels of the 1970s, it has fallen significantly in recent years (Blau and Kahn 2002: 21). Yet despite the evidence of increases in pay and skill levels, there is a growing body of evidence on the dark side of 'the new workplace'.

Between the early 1980s and the late 1990s, there was a dramatic increase in the number of complaints about employment lodged at the drop-in offices of the free British legal advice service, the Citizen's Advice Bureaux, from around 450,000 per year to about 650,000 (see Table 12.3). Here are just two typical examples:

A single mother-to-be working in a shop ... had been dismissed with one month's notice after informing her employer of her condition, on the grounds that a 'pregnant woman is not an attractive sight to customers'. (NACAB 2001: 26)

A CAB in Avon reports a 19-year-old client who was employed at a gardening centre. He worked from 8 am to 5 pm six days a week, at an hourly rate of £2.00. He had no written contract. His hours were gradually increased to 70 per week, with no overtime pay. When he protested, he was sacked. (NACAB 1993: 11)

And similar stories have been reported in the United States:

Anne is ... a casting operator for a company that makes rubber belts ... she began to notice some unusual physical reactions, ... including a burning sensation inside her nose and mouth. ... Anne told her boss that she wanted to learn more about the chemicals in use and their exact nature. ... Her supervisor told her that was a good idea. The next day she was fired. (Rothschild and Miethe 1994: 261–2)

There has also been a rising trend in the number of applications to British Employment Tribunals (ETs) for redress against violations of legal rights.[1] The

Table 12.3 Worker complaints to the Citizens' Advice Bureaux (CABs) and applications to Employment Tribunals (ETs) in Britain, 1982–2001

	Employment complaints to CABs	Number of registered ET applications
1982–3	469,000	43,660
1986–7	625,735	38,385
1989–90	709,570	34,697
1992–3	882,257	71,821
1996–7	610,000	88,910
1997–8	584,000	80,435
1998–9	616,000	91,913
1999–2000	686,841	103,935
2000–2001	631,768	130,408
2001–2002	601,227	112,227

Sources: Kelly (1998: 45); www.citizensadvice.org.uk; Hawes (2000: 19); www.ets.gov.uk

[1] The CAB numbers need to be interpreted with some caution because of changes in the method of recording introduced in 1994. However, as these changes postdate the major rise in complaints between the mid-1980s and 1993, they do not invalidate the inference that more employees are complaining to the CAB today than twenty years ago (Abbott 1998: 259). In the case of applications to Employment Tribunals, the number of legal rights covered by British tribunals increased throughout the period in question, so we might have expected some increase in applications. But at the same

majority of CAB and ET complainants have come from nonunion firms in the service sector, a fact that has two important implications. First, it supports the theoretical proposition that the absence of collective organization and action does not necessarily indicate the absence of perceived injustice (Abbott 1998: 259). And second, it shows that the rise in employee complaints is not being driven by restructuring in the declining sectors of the industrial economy but by employment relations in the expanding service sector.

Other evidence suggests that the past twenty years has witnessed a significant intensification of work as employers have successfully sought to squeeze more effort out of employees. This has occurred both within the working day, leading to complaints of being pressured and overworked, and through extending the working day itself. In a 1992 survey of almost 3,500 British employees, 62 percent reported they had to expend more effort in their jobs than five years previously and 53 percent said that stress levels had increased. Another British survey, carried out in 1998 but using management respondents, found as many as 39 percent stating that employee effort levels had risen during the previous five years, discounting the idea that reports of intensification reflect employee biases (Green 2001: 66, 68). Comparative data from twelve European countries shows a similar trend. In 1991, 24 percent of employees in these countries said they had to work at 'very high speed' but by 1996 the figure had risen to 31 percent (Green and McIntosh 2000: table 1). Again, interview quotes from qualitative research convey the flavor of the phenomenon:

Jobs built up that I had no control over completing and I wasn't being able to—as hard as I worked, and I worked all the hours under the sun—but every day things would be added to my list that would never get done. So I ended up, well, I got stressed . . . (Utilities manager quoted in Wichert 2002: 101)

The big thing is going home at night time and not being able to relax because you've got work spinning round in your head and you're thinking 'God, I'll never get it all ready.' (College lecturer quoted in Nolan 2002: 121)

The strongest predictor of the international rise in effort levels is change in trade union density, a crude measure of union power (Green and McIntosh 2000: table 6). Countries with the steepest declines in union density—Britain and Ireland, for example, compared to say Spain and Denmark—have recorded the sharpest increases in effort levels, an association that suggests it is the changing balance of power at the workplace that has permitted employers to drive up effort levels.

The average working week has altered very little in Britain in recent years but this stability conceals a significant process of polarization. On the one hand, there has

---

time successive governments also placed more obstacles in the path of potential applicants in order to discourage them. On balance it seems reasonable to assume these two sets of factors may cancel each other out so that the rise in numbers probably does reflect a real increase in the level of applications (Dickens 2002: 71–2).

been an increase in part-time workers; on the other hand, there has been a rise in the proportion of employees working very long hours. For example, in 1983, 25 percent of British men worked at least 48 hours per week but by 1998 the figure was 30 percent (and that despite a reduction of almost one-third in the numbers working in manufacturing, a traditional site of long hours) (Green 2001: 60). Similar trends have been reported in other countries particularly Australia, Canada, Denmark, Ireland, and the United States (OECD 1998: 158). It is clear from British data that the extension of working hours does not simply reflect employee choice, a new trade-off between work and leisure. While 51 percent of British women were satisfied with their working hours in 1992, the figure had fallen dramatically to just 29 percent in 2000 (the figures for men were 35 and 20 percent, respectively) (Taylor 2002: 10).

Evidence on job insecurity is mixed and not easy to interpret. Comparative data exploring the perceived probability and costs of job loss suggests there was a significant increase in employees' feelings of insecurity between 1992 and 1996 in many countries, including France, Germany, Italy, Japan, the United Kingdom, and the United States, though not in Ireland, Finland, The Netherlands, and Norway (OECD 1997: 135).[2] Taking a longer-term view, it appears that while levels of employee concern about job security rise and fall with the prevailing level of unemployment, they are also higher now than twenty years ago (Bryson and McKay 1997: 28). One reason, as with labor intensity, is the balance of power between workers and employers, as reflected in trade union membership and influence: the greater the fall in trade union density and bargaining coverage, the sharper the rise in employees' feelings of job insecurity between the mid-1980s and the mid-1990s (OECD 1997: 150).

The decline of trade unionism has yielded one further consequence for employees and that shows up in figures on pay distribution, where there has been a substantial rise in inequality between those at the top and bottom of the earnings distribution. This trend has been especially pronounced in the liberal market economies of the United States, the United Kingdom, Ireland, and New Zealand (by contrast with the Nordic countries). In other words, where union membership and influence fell steeply, pay levels stagnated or even fell at the bottom of the distribution and rose very quickly at the top end (Machin 1999: 189–91; OECD 1996: chart 3). Throughout this period a growing percentage of employees in Britain came to believe that the gap between 'high and low incomes' at their own workplace was too large. In the mid-1980s a little under 40 percent of employees held this view but by the late 1990s the figure had climbed to almost 50 percent (Jowell *et al.* 1998–2001; Kelly 1998: 46).

---

[2] Changes in question wording over time may account for some of the apparent rise in felt insecurity in the OECD data, but it is clear from other datasets that insecurity is higher in the mid-1990s than it was in the mid-1980s (at least in Britain) (Bryson and McKay 1997: 28; Burchell 2002: 64–5).

So to sum up, it appears from both survey and case-study evidence in a number of countries, that despite real increases in earnings and skills and falling unemployment, and despite the rhetoric of 'human resource management', a growing proportion of employees has become dissatisfied with their working lives. This trend is reflected in a growth of complaints about employment to external agencies and in rising discontent about effort levels and working hours, about pay inequalities, and job insecurity. In order to understand the roots of collective organization and action we must explore how far employees blame management for these workplace issues.

12.3.1 Attitudes towards Management and Unions

Before doing so, it is worth reminding ourselves of the far-reaching changes that have been carried through by British and American employers over the past twenty years. As worker representation through trade unionism has declined, British employers have moved towards direct systems of employee communications (see Table 12.4). Likewise, in both union and nonunion workplaces, employers have tried to link workers' rewards to those of the enterprise via profit-sharing or share ownership schemes. US surveys have focused more on the labor process, documenting the sharp rise in 'High-Performance Work Practices' since the early 1980s. For example, in 1992 it was found that 27 percent of US workplaces used problem-solving groups that covered at least half their core workforce; by 1997 the figure had risen to 57 percent (Osterman 1999: 99). Similar trends were found for job rotation, total quality management, and profit-sharing schemes through the 1980s and 1990s (Appelbaum and Batt 1994: 60–8).

Table 12.4 British management practices, 1980–1998 (% of all workplaces)

	1980	1984	1990	1998
Regular meetings between workers and management	N/A	34	41	48
Briefing groups	N/A	36	48	65
Profit sharing	N/A	19	44	46
Employee share ownership	13	22	30	24

Source: Millward, Bryson, and Forth (2000: 118, 214).

Table 12.5 British worker attitudes to management, 1983–2000

	1983	1987	1990	1993	1996	2000
Management–worker relations at own workplace:						
Very/quite good	84	82	82	78	79	78
Not very good/not at all good	15	18	17	20	20	21
Own workplace was:						
Very/quite well managed	80	80	81	78	78	77
Not well managed	20	20	19	21	22	22

Sources: Kelly (1998: 47); Jowell et al. (1997, 2001).

Despite these sea-changes in the management of employment relations the most remarkable feature of British worker attitudes to management is their stability (see Table 12.5).

Since the early 1980s, an unvarying 80 percent of employees has reported their workplace was 'well managed' compared to an equally stable 20 percent who thought it 'not well managed'. The proportion describing relations as not very good (or worse) rose significantly from around 15 percent to 20 percent through the 1980s and has remained pretty stable ever since (Bryson and McKay 1997: 29). In view of the resources devoted by managements to changing employment relations in British workplaces over the past twenty years, this would have to go down as a disappointing set of results. Equally striking is the proportion of employees who remain dissatisfied with the amount of say they have over workplace decisions, despite managerial attempts to convince them their views are taken seriously. Thirty-seven percent of employees were dissatisfied with their say in decisions affecting their work back in 1985. After the rise of briefing groups and direct communications in the ensuing years (but following the decline in union representation) that figure actually rose to 54 percent in 1989 and has hardly changed since (Kelly 1998: 46; Jowell et al. 1997, 2001). Curiously a US employee survey carried out in 1994 arrived at much the same estimate of what the authors described as 'the representation gap', the difference between the amount of influence employees said they wanted and the amount they actually exercised. According to Freeman and Rogers (1999: 48–9), 53 percent of US employees had less involvement in workplace decisions than they would have liked. We should not make too much of the similarity in numbers because of differences in question wording and in levels of union influence between Britain and the United States. Nevertheless it is interesting that a small majority of both British and US employees appears dissatisfied with management's organization of decision making and involvement.

On the face of it, these findings seem inconsistent with evidence that HRM or 'High-Performance Work Practices' have enhanced employee commitment and satisfaction. A study of the US clothing, steel, and electronics industries found a range of such work practices enhanced employee participation in decision-making autonomy which in turn increased organizational commitment and job satisfaction (Appelbaum *et al.* 2000: 184–94; Freeman and Rogers 1999: 109–11). British data has reported the same links between work practices and employee commitment (Gallie, Felstead, and Green 2001). In fact however many employers have simultaneously adopted other practices that have impacted negatively on employees such as curbing on-the-job discretion or laying off workers (Gallie, Felstead, and Green 2001; Osterman 2000). It may be that these two sets of practices have often cancelled out each others' effects so the overall impact on employees has been more or less neutral.

This evidence is suggestive of employee discontent with management, but how far will this translate into collective organization and activity? Recent survey data from nonunion employees in both Britain and the United States suggests that a substantial minority would join a union if one were available at their workplace. In 1998, for instance, 41 percent of a sample of 653 British nonunion employees said they would be 'very or fairly likely' to join a union if it were available at their workplace and similar figures were reported in a 2001 survey (Charlwood 2002). A US study in 1994 found that 32 percent of nonunion employees would vote for a union if an election were held at their workplace (Freeman and Rogers 1999: 69). These surveys have all reported evidence on general attitudes so it does not necessarily follow that they would be closely linked to particular behaviors: there could be perceived opposition on the part of management, for example, or other perceived costs involved in voting for or joining a union. We therefore need to look more closely at union organizing efforts in recent years in order to see how far unions have been able to translate employee discontent into collective organization and activity.

12.4 Union Organizing and Collective Action

In 1997 the British Trades Union Congress (TUC) followed the example of its US counterpart, the AFL–CIO and created an educational institution, the Organizing Academy, to train union activists in the skills of organizing. After almost two decades of membership decline, the new leadership at the head of the TUC had come to realize that membership recovery would only happen with a substantial diversion of resources away from servicing existing members into the recruitment and organization of new members and workplaces. Labour's election victory in 1997 had signaled a change in the political environment with the promise of a National Minimum Wage and a union recognition law, eventually embodied in the Employment Relations Act (1999). Under the Act employers would be obliged to negotiate with a union where it had demonstrated majority employee support. Throughout the 1990s more and more unions had created specialist organizing departments and appointed organizing officers (Heery, Kelly, and Waddington 2003). The result of all these changes was that the decline in British trade union membership, which began in 1979, came to a halt in 1997–8. In 1998 total union membership rose by 50,589 and in the next year it rose again, by 45,615. In the following two years however (2000, 2001) membership gains through recruitment were more than cancelled out by membership losses from manufacturing closures and redundancies (Certification Officer). During these years some famous nonunion companies have been forced to recognize unions, including car manufacturer Honda and transport company Eurotunnel. US unions have also scored some notable organizing victories, including the telecommunications company Verizon and overall membership rose slightly, by 165,000, between 1997 and 2001 (www.bls.gov). Why have employees joined unions in the course of these campaigns? Case-study evidence is largely consistent with the propositions of mobilization theory and suggests that perceived injustice at the workplace is the factor that commonly triggers unionization. Attributing workplace problems to management is critical and so too is a belief that unions can make a difference (Taylor and Bain 2003). US case studies of recent organizing drives among immigrant workers in California suggest a similar story and also underline the importance of activists in conveying a coherent 'collective action frame' that targets management (Milkman and Wong 2000; Zabin 2000).

A small proportion, less than 20 percent, of new union agreements in Britain have involved some formal commitment to labor–management cooperation or 'partnership' (Gall 2003: 14). However the total number of thoroughgoing partnership agreements is very small, both in Britain and the United States. Many of the longer-standing and well-known cases are employer-dominant agreements signed by unions in weak bargaining positions. The available evidence suggests they have done little to protect jobs, improve wages and conditions, raise union membership, or increase employee influence at work (Guest and Peccei 2001; Kelly 2004).

If we turn to union activity in the rest of Europe, it is important to bear in mind that union density figures grossly underestimate union influence because of the key role of extension clauses. Collective agreements on pay and conditions negotiated by unions are typically extended to cover most employees throughout the economy. For example, union density in France is 9 percent but bargaining coverage is around 90 percent; union density in Germany is 30 percent, bargaining coverage 80 percent (the figure for EU bargaining coverage as a whole) (European Commission 2000: 11).

Before we turn to collective action, it is worth recalling a point made elsewhere in the Handbook, that employee resistance to managerial control can take a wide range of both individual and collective forms, including absenteeism, theft, petty sabotage, work restriction, and whistleblowing (Ackroyd and Thompson 1999; Hodson 1995). It would therefore be quite inappropriate to infer high levels of employee consent and cooperative employment relations from low levels of strike activity. Although the current rate of strike action is at historically low levels throughout the advanced capitalist world (Table 12.2), social movement theory suggests this could be for a variety of reasons, of which better industrial relations is only one. Part of the explanation lies in lower levels of union membership and organization because generally speaking strikes are organized by unions and participated in by union members. Another part of the story is structural: traditionally strikes were heavily concentrated in manufacturing industry so the decline in size of the industrial workforce in conjunction with high unemployment and intense product market competition has weakened industrial unions. Where these conditions do not exist to the same degree, i.e. where labor demand is stable, competition less intense, and unions more powerful, we would expect strikes to persist and that is indeed what we find across Europe, where most recent strikes have been in the 'public or protected sectors' (European Commission 2000: 44). In Britain, for example, almost half the working days lost during 2000 were accounted for by strikes in health, education, and government (Davies 2001b: 304).

There is another reason for doubting the idea of a generalized decline in worker willingness to strike and that comes from evidence of support for union-initiated general strikes or protests against state policy. In June 2002 Spanish unions mobilized several million workers in a one-day strike around pension reforms; in April 2002 Italian unions claimed 13 million workers stayed at home and 3 million joined demonstrations against a relaxation of dismissal laws; early in 2002 the German metalworkers' union IG Metall mobilized approximately half a million workers in pay strikes. Going back a little further we find evidence of well-supported general strikes and demonstrations in a range of countries over different issues: Austria 2001 over social insurance reforms, Belgium 1998 over social security reforms and in 1996 over pay, Denmark 1998 over pay, and France 1995 over pensions and public spending cuts, to name just a few examples (www.eurofound.ie). Workers in these countries now strike very rarely, but it is significant that when their unions have recently attempted to mobilize large numbers of workers on one-day strike actions, they have enjoyed widespread support. Both the mobilizing capacity of unions and the willingness of workers to strike therefore appear far higher than the strike statistics would suggest.

Another reason for the low level of strike activity is that union movements across Europe have sought to deploy political power as a way of overcoming labor market weakness. In recent years they have negotiated and reached agreements with governments on a wide range of labor market issues, including traditional items such as wages and working time in addition to welfare topics, principally pensions, social security, and employment protection. Social pacts, as they are now known, have appeared in Belgium (from 1998), Finland 1995, Ireland 1987, Italy 1995, The Netherlands 1993, and Spain 1996 (European Commission 2000: 80–5). The significance of these agreements however, should not be overstated, despite their apparent similarity with corporatist agreements of the 1970s. The latter involved powerful, militant, and growing union movements negotiating with governments in a context of relatively full employment. The modern social pacts have emerged at a period of much higher (though falling) unemployment and low levels of militancy. Nevertheless these pacts do reflect a degree of state dependency on labor movements for the purpose of carrying through the economic and social restructuring entailed by European integration and monetary union (Pochet and Fajertag 2000). That process of restructuring has borne down heavily on well-organized public sector workers because the convergence criteria for monetary union laid down a strict limit (3 percent) on public sector debt as a proportion of Gross Domestic Product. The consequent reforms of public sector employment relations throughout Europe have allowed unions to position themselves as the key representatives of the workforce and, from time to time, to mobilize workers in opposition to particular reforms.

Union political action has taken other forms in the liberal market economies of the United States and the United Kingdom. In the absence of social pacts, union movements have concentrated on electoral activity, trying to maximize voter turnout among pro-Democrat and pro-Labor union members. Evidence suggests that despite the US Republican victory in 2000, union campaigning made a significant difference. Voter turnout from union households was significantly higher than the national average and helped ensure Democrat victories in several key states (Hurd, Milkman, and Turner 2003). In Britain too, union personnel and finance raised voter turnouts for Labour in 2001 (Ludlam 2002).

Finally, we come to international union action. Often disregarded in the industrial relations literature or dismissed as being relatively inconsequential because of the power and mobility of multinational corporations (MNCs), this type of action has now become far more significant in part because of the increased globalization of capitalist production (Dicken 2003; Sklair 2000). Three main forms can be identified: solidarity action with groups of striking workers, in industries such as port transport; mobilizations in conjunction with other social movements targeted on the Third World plants of particular companies; and mobilizations focused around international agencies such as the World Trade Organization (WTO). Solidarity action, especially in industries such as port transport, is a long-standing and familiar feature of labor internationalism, although in recent years it has been facilitated by global communications technology. Not only do most unions now have their own websites, but there are several sites mainly devoted to disseminating information about disputes around the world, e.g. www.labourstart.org and www.labornet.org. Actions have also been targeted at particular companies such as Shell, Nike, shirtmaker Philips-Van Heusen, and the holding company Peabody and Hanson (Anner 2000; Klein 2000; Zinn 2000). Unions organized in the US branches of these companies have sometimes used strike action, but more often have sought to mobilize power resources through alliances with other groups, such as shareholders, religious organizations, unions in Third World countries, and students. National and international media have also been used to generate negative publicity and damage the reputation of companies whose marketing is based on positive consumer images of the brand name (Nike is an example). Labor practices of MNCs in Third World countries have featured prominently in such campaigns and have included issues such as the use of child labor, payment of poverty wages, and health and safety violations (Klein 2000: ch. 9). Research suggests that such campaigns are more likely to succeed where there is vibrant local union organization, a condition found in many parts of Central and Latin America, notably Mexico and also in parts of South East Asia, such as South Korea and Indonesia (though less so in China and Singapore) (Anner 2000).

A number of corporate campaigns, such as those involving Nike, have intersected with the growing volume of protest about the consequences of global capitalism. Sometimes misleadingly called antiglobalization protests, the largest demonstrations in recent years have involved trade unions and a variety of other social movements at meetings of bodies such as the WTO or the G8 nations. An estimated 70,000 protestors took part in the WTO demonstrations in Seattle in December 1999 while approximately 300,000 participated in protests at the G8 summit in Genoa in July 2001 (Bircham and Charlton 2001: 340–1). To date there have been few concrete outcomes from these mobilizations, but they have succeeded in placing onto the political agenda a set of issues around labor rights, fair trade, and ethical investment that might otherwise have been marginalized (cf. for instance the edited collection by Gunnell and Timms *After Seattle* (2000) and Amnesty International's 2000 booklet on global trade and labor rights).

12.5 THE CONTRADICTIONS OF GLOBAL CAPITALISM

Evidence about an apparent revival of international labor activity does however raise an important theoretical question, touched on at the beginning of this chapter. If the globalization of capitalist production, trade, and investment is part of the reason for the decline of labor movements, then how can we account for what may be a revival of union organization and activity? The answer to this question is complex but essentially falls under two headings: the limitations of 'globalization' in explaining the fate of labor movements around the world and the contradictions of globalization itself.

First, the globalization of production and services has hardly affected some of the most well-organized workers employed in public sector services such as education, health, social security, and transport, at least not directly. This degree of shelter from the competitive forces that affect manufacturing industry is one reason for the persistence of high levels of union organization and militancy among public sector workers throughout the world (see above). It is true there is an indirect effect of globalization on the public sector, mediated through the stringent fiscal requirements for European Monetary Union, but to date this has facilitated rather than inhibited collective action, as noted earlier. In addition, many private sector establishments such as retail stores, restaurants, hotels, leisure centers, garages, and residential homes for the elderly, supply goods and services to local consumers in local markets and are largely unaffected by the cost and quality of service provision in other parts of the world.

A second limitation of the 'globalization leads to labor decline thesis' is that 'institutions and politics matter'. There is no simple causal chain running from global competition, production, and investment to labor decline. National states still enjoy some discretion in how to regulate domestic labor markets, a fact that is clear from the enormous differences in labor rights and protections between the liberal market economies of the United Kingdom and the United States, on the one hand, and the coordinated market economies of say Germany and Sweden, on the other (Hall and Soskice 2001). Not only are there differences in labor (and other) institutions between countries but there are also differences in policies between Left and Right governments that make a difference to workers' rights and conditions even in the face of a globalizing capitalism. Wage inequality, minimum wages, and the level and composition of unemployment, for instance, are all affected by governmental action and differ significantly under governments of the Left and Right (Boix 1998; Garrett 1998).

The globalization of production however is a process replete with its own contradictions. At a general level, the expansion of capitalist production into hitherto less developed areas of the world has also expanded the working classes of those countries. A combination of repressive state and employer policies, super-exploitation of labor, and the growth of international activity by First World trade union movements have all facilitated the rise of organized labor in countries such as Indonesia, South Korea, and Taiwan (Kuruvilla *et al.* 2002). Second, where the production chain is integrated across countries, as in parts of the electronics industry, for example, then the production process as a whole becomes that much more vulnerable to disruption. Third, while it is true that MNCs can to some degree play off one host country government against another as each seeks inward investment, it is also true that some MNCs compete among themselves for investment locations, thus providing governments with a degree of leverage (Dicken 2003: chs. 7 and 8). Finally the uncritical and Panglossian rhetoric of some proponents of global capitalism has invited critics to take such rhetoric at face value and judge capitalism in its own terms. Claims about who gains from foreign direct investment, for example, have been judged against the evidence of working conditions in Third World factories, figures on profits remitted from Third to First World countries, or the salaries of corporate chief executives in First World countries. The gap between 'rhetoric and reality' has provided abundant fuel for a wide range of global anticapitalist protests (Bircham and Charlton 2001; Klein 2000).

12.6 CONCLUSIONS

Capitalist economies are recovering from the recession of the 1980s, with higher growth rates and sharp falls in unemployment. Real wages and skill levels have been increasing and many firms have tried to raise employee commitment through a range of organizational practices, such as briefing groups and increased information flows. Some commentators have linked these trends to the simultaneous decline of the trade union movement in many countries, reflected in its loss of membership and influence and the fall in strike rates.

However a closer examination of trends and developments around work and labor movements suggests a different and more complex picture. The decline of trade unionism has been strongly associated with a sharp increase in pay inequalities, in job insecurity, and in the intensity of labor. So even though many employees are earning more than they did ten years ago, they are also having to expend more effort and to work longer hours in jobs that are often less secure. Nor have these developments gone hand in hand with increased employee voice at the workplace, since workers have become more critical of their lack of influence at work. All of these trends have expressed themselves in a rising volume of complaints about employment, at least in Britain, as aggrieved employees have sought redress for the injustices experienced at work. One further result has been a remarkably high level of support for trade unionism among nonunion employees. When unions have tried to organize such workers, in Britain and to a lesser degree in the United States, they have often succeeded in building up membership and securing bargaining rights from the employer.

Yet even these two union movements, with a heavy commitment to organizing nonunion workplaces—in the United Kingdom and the United States—have done little more than stabilize their membership in recent years; there is no sign yet of an imminent surge in membership on the scale of the 1970s. Why this should be the case is an interesting question for further research. Employer opposition may be part of the story, especially in the United States, since that raises the costs to workers of union membership and activity. But other factors also need to be looked at. To what extent are employees convinced unions are powerful enough to make a difference at the workplace? Do they perhaps see the pursuit of individual legal rights as an alternative means of redress to unionism? Does the low level of strike activity in these countries suggest to many workers that unions are weak? If so, perhaps union organizing needs to be accompanied by a greater willingness on the part of unions to take industrial action if workers are to be convinced they can make a difference. But higher levels of strike activity could in turn jeopardize union promotion of partnership with employers, leaving them with an interesting strategic dilemma.

It is clear from the high levels of worker support for political and general strikes throughout Europe in recent years that the mobilizing capacity of unions remains high. Moreover the influence of these unions remains extensive, because of high rates of bargaining coverage and because of the 'social pacts' with governments that have emerged over the past few years. But again questions can be asked about both these sources of union power. If union density continues to fall, will not some employers start to question the value of their bargaining relations with unions, as is happening already in Germany and The Netherlands? By the same logic, will governments start to question their own involvement in social pacts with unions, as the German government did in spring 2003?

Finally, the globalization of production, trade, and investment has had contradictory effects on trade unionism. On the one hand, the mobility of capital has been used to undermine trade union organization in industries such as clothing, textiles, and vehicle production. On the other hand, it has also given birth to new forms of labor internationalism involving alliances between unions and a variety of social movements concerned about the impact of capitalist production on workers' wages and conditions. Many questions still remain unanswered about these recent alliances: how can they withstand employer repression in Third World countries?

While international pressure can be effective in influencing events in small Third World countries, what about the large and more powerful economies of China or Indonesia?

To conclude, many of the points in this chapter reflect an observation made long ago by two of the most acute observers of the capitalist mode of production: 'In proportion as the bourgeoisie, i.e. capital, is developed, in the same proportion is the proletariat, the modern working class, developed' (Marx and Engels 1848: 114).

REFERENCES

ABBOTT, B. (1998). 'The Emergence of a New Industrial Relations Actor—the Role of the Citizens' Advice Bureaux?' *Industrial Relations Journal,* 29/4: 257–69.

ACKROYD, S., and THOMPSON, P. (1999). *Organizational Misbehaviour.* London: Sage.

Amnesty International (2000). *Global Trade, Labour and Human Rights.* London: Amnesty International.

ANNER, M. (2000). 'Local and Transnational Campaigns to End Sweatshop Practices', in M. E. Gordon and L. Turner (eds.), *Transnational Cooperation among Labor Unions.* Ithaca, NY: ILR Press.

APPELBAUM, E., and BATT, R. (1994). *The New American Workplace: Transforming Work Systems in the United States.* Ithaca, NY: ILR Press.

—— BAILEY, T., BERG, P., and KALLEBERG, A. (2000). *Manufacturing Advantage: Why High-Performance Systems Pay Off.* Ithaca, NY: ILR Press.

BIRCHAM, E., and CHARLTON, J. (2001). *Anti-Capitalism: A Guide to the Movement.* London: Bookmarks.

BIRD, D. (1991). 'International Comparisons of Industrial Disputes in 1989 and 1990'. *Employment Gazette,* 99/12: 653–8.

BLAU, F. D., and KAHN, L. M. (2002). *At Home and Abroad: U.S. Labor Market Performance in International Perspective.* New York: Russell Sage Foundation.

BOIX, C. (1998). *Political Parties, Growth and Equality: Conservative and Social Democratic Economic Strategies in the World Economy.* New York: Cambridge University Press.

BRYSON, A., and MCKAY, S. (1997). 'What about the Workers?', in R. Jowell *et al.* (eds.), *British Social Attitudes: The 14th Report.* Aldershot: Ashgate.

BURCHELL, B. (2002). 'The Prevalence and Redistribution of Job Insecurity and Work Intensification', in B. Burchell, D. Ladipo, and F. Wilkinson (eds.), *Job Security and Work Intensification.* London: Routledge.

Certification Officer (various years). *Annual Report.* London: Certification Office for Trade Unions and Employers' Associations.

CHARLWOOD, A. (2002). 'Why Do Non-Union Employees Want to Unionize?' *British Journal of Industrial Relations,* 40/3: 463–91.

CLARK, P. F. (2000). *Building More Effective Unions.* Ithaca, NY: ILR Press.

CULLY, M., WOODLAND, S., O'REILLY, A., and DIX, G. (1999). *Britain at Work as Depicted by the 1998 Workplace Employee Relations Survey.* London: Routledge.

DAVIES, J. (2001a). 'International Comparisons of Labour Disputes in 1999'. *Labour Market Trends*, 109/4: 195–201.

—— (2001b). 'Labour Disputes in 2000'. *Labour Market Trends*, 109/6: 301–14.

DICKEN, P. (2003). *Global Shift: Reshaping the Global Economic Map in the 21st Century* (4th edn). London: Sage.

DICKENS, L. (2002). 'Doing More with Less: ACAS and Individual Conciliation', in B. Towers and W. Brown (eds.), *Employment Relations in Britain: 25 Years of the Advisory, Conciliation and Arbitration Service*. Oxford: Blackwell.

EBBINGHAUS, B., and VISSER, J. (2000). 'A Comparative Profile', in B. Ebbinghaus and J. Visser (eds.), *Trade Unions in Western Europe since 1945*. London: Macmillan Reference.

European Commission (2000). *Industrial Relations in Europe 2000*. Luxembourg: Office for Official Publications of the European Communities.

FREEMAN, R. B., and ROGERS, J. (1999). *What Workers Want*. Ithaca, NY: ILR and Cornell University Press.

GALL, G. (2003). 'Introduction', in G. Gall (ed.), *Union Organizing: Campaigning for Trade Union Recognition*. London: Routledge.

GALLIE, D., FELSTEAD, A., and GREEN, F. (2001). 'Employer Policies and Organizational Commitment in Britain 1992–1997'. *Journal of Management Studies*, 38/8: 1081–101.

—— WHITE, M., CHENG, Y., and TOMLINSON, M. (1998). *Restructuring the Employment Relationship*. Oxford: Clarendon Press.

GARRETT, G. (1998). *Partisan Politics in the Global Economy*. New York: Cambridge University Press.

GOLDEN, M., WALLERSTEIN, M., and LANGE, P. (1999). 'Postwar Trade Union Organization and Industrial Relations in Twelve Countries', in H. Kitschelt, P. Lange, G. Marks, and John D. Stephens (eds.), *Continuity and Change in Contemporary Capitalism*. New York: Cambridge University Press.

GREEN, F. (2001). 'It's Been a Hard Day's Night: The Concentration and Intensification of Work in Late Twentieth Century Britain'. *British Journal of Industrial Relations*, 39/1: 53–80.

—— and McINTOSH, S. (2000). 'Working on the Chain Gang? An Examination of Rising Effort Levels in Europe in the 1990s'. University of Kent: Unpublished MS.

GUEST, D., and PECCEI, R. (2001). 'Partnership at Work: Mutuality and the Balance of Advantage'. *British Journal of Industrial Relations*, 39/2: 207–36.

GUNNELL, B., and TIMMS, D. (eds.) (2000). *After Seattle: Globalisation and Its Discontents*. London: Catalyst.

HALL, P. A., and SOSKICE, D. (2001). 'An Introduction to Varieties of Capitalism', in P. A. Hall and D. Soskice (eds.), *Varieties of Capitalism: The Institutional Foundations of Comparative Advantage*. New York: Oxford University Press.

HAWES, W. R. (2000). 'Setting the Pace or Running Alongside? ACAS and the Changing Employment Relationship', in B. Towers and W. Brown (eds.), *Employment Relations in Britain: 25 Years of the Advisory, Conciliation and Arbitration Service*. Oxford: Blackwell.

HECKSCHER, C. (1996). *The New Unionism: Employee Involvement in the Changing Corporarion*. Ithaca, NY: ILR Press.

HEERY, E., KELLY, J., and WADDINGTON, J. (2003). 'Union Revitalization in Britain'. *European Journal of Industrial Relations*, 9/1: 79–97.

HODSON, R. (1995). 'Worker Resistance: An Underdeveloped Concept in the Sociology of Work'. *Economic and Industrial Democracy*, 16/1: 79–110.

HURD, R., MILKMAN, R., and TURNER, L. (2003). 'Reviving the American Labor Movement: Institutions and Mobilization'. *European Journal of Industrial Relations*, 9/1: 99–117.

JAVELINE, D. (2003). 'The Role of Blame in Collective Action: Evidence from Russia'. *American Political Science Review*, 97/1: 107–21.

JESSOP, D., and GORDON, M. (2000). 'Organizing in Export Processing Zones', in M. Gordon and Lowell Turner (eds.), *Transnational Cooperation among Unions*. Ithaca, NY: ILR and Cornell University Press.

JOWELL, R., *et al.* (eds.) (various years). *British Social Attitudes*. Aldershot: Ashgate.

KELLY, J. (1998). *Rethinking Industrial Relations: Mobilization, Collectivism, and Long Waves*. London: Routledge.

—— (2004). 'Social Partnership Agreements in Britain: Labor Cooperation and Compliance'. *Industrial Relations*, 43/1: 267–92.

KLANDERMANS, B. (1997). *The Social Psychology of Protest*. Oxford: Blackwell.

KLEIN, N. (2000). *No Logo*. London: Flamingo.

KOCHAN, T. A., and OSTERMAN, P. (1994). *The Mutual Gains Enterprise: Forging a Winning Partnership between Labor, Management, and Government*. Boston: Harvard Business School Press.

KURUVILLA, S., DAS, S., KWON, H., and KWON, S. (2002). 'Trade Union Growth and Decline in Asia'. *British Journal of Industrial Relations*, 40/3: 431–61.

LUDLAM, S. (2002). 'Unions Give Party More Than Cash'. *Labour Research*, 91/5: 10–12.

MACHIN, S. (1999). 'Wage Inequality in the 1970s, 1980s and 1990s', in P. Gregg and J. Wadsworth (eds.), *The State of Working Britain*. Manchester: Manchester University Press.

MARX, K., and ENGELS, F. (1848). 'Manifesto of the Communist Party', in K. Marx and F. Engels (eds.), *Selected Works* (Volume 1). Moscow: Progress Publishers, 1969.

MILKMAN, R., and WONG, K. (2000). 'Organizing the Wicked City: The 1992 Southern California Drywall Strike', in R. Milkman (ed.), *Organizing Immigrants: The Challenge for Unions in Contemporary California*. Ithaca, NY: ILR and Cornell University Press.

MILLWARD, N., BRYSON, A., and FORTH, J. (2000). *All Change at Work? British Employment Relations 1980–1998, as Portrayed by the Workplace Industrial Relations Survey Series*. London: Routledge.

NACAB (National Association of Citizens Advice Bureaux) (various years). *Annual Reports*. London: National Association of Citizens Advice Bureaux.

—— (1993). *Job Insecurity*. London: National Association of Citizens Advice Bureaux.

—— (2001). *Birth Rights: A CAB Evidence Report on Maternity and Paternity Rights at Work*. London: National Association of Citizens Advice Bureaux.

NOLAN, J. (2002). 'The Intensification of Everyday Life', in B. Burchell, D. Ladipo, and F. Wilkinson (eds.), *Job Insecurity and Work Intensification*. London: Routledge.

OECD (Organization of Economic Cooperation and Development) (1996). 'Earnings Inequality, Low-Paid Employment and Earnings Mobility'. *OECD Employment Outlook*, 59–108.

—— (1997). 'Is Job Insecurity on the Increase in OECD Countries?' *OECD Employment Outlook*, 129–60.

—— (1998). 'Working Hours: Latest Trends and Policy Initiatives'. *OECD Employment Outlook*, 153–88.

OSTERMAN, P. (1999). *Securing Prosperity: The American Labor Market: How It Has Changed and What to Do about It*. Princeton, N.J.: Princeton University Press.

——(2000). 'Work Reorganization in an Era of Restructuring: Trends in Diffusion and Effects on Employee Welfare'. *Industrial and Labor Relations Review*, 53/2: 179–96.

POCHET, P., and FAJERTAG, G. (2000). 'A New Era for Social Pacts in Europe', in G. Fajertag and P. Pochet (eds.), *Social Pacts in Europe: New Dynamics* (2nd edn). Brussels: European Trade Union Institute.

ROTHSCHILD, J., and MIETHE, T. D. (1994). 'Whistleblowing as Resistance in Modern Organizations: The Politics of Revealing Organizational Deception and Abuse', in J. M. Jermier, D. Knights, and W. R. Nord (eds.), *Resistance and Power in Organizations*. London: Routledge.

SKLAIR, L. (2000). *The Transnational Capitalist Class*. Oxford: Blackwell.

TAYLOR, P., and BAIN, P. (2003). 'Call Center Organising in Adversity: From Excell to Vertex', in G. Gall (ed.), *Union Organizing: Campaigning for Trade Union Recognition*. London: Routledge.

TAYLOR, R. (2002). *Britain's World of Work—Myths and Realities*. London: Economic and Social Research Council.

TILLY, C. (1978). *From Mobilization to Revolution*. New York: McGraw-Hill.

WICHERT, I. (2002). 'Stress Intervention: What Can Managers Do? in B. Burchell, D. Ladipo, and F. Wilkinson (eds.), *Job Insecurity and Work Intensification*. London: Routledge.

ZABIN, C. (2000). 'Organizing Latino Workers in the Los Angeles Manufacturing Sector: The Case of American Racing Equipment', in R. Milkman (ed.), *Organizing Immigrants: The Challenge for Unions in Contemporary California*. Ithaca, NY: ILR and Cornell University Press.

ZINN, K. (2000). 'Solidarity across Borders: The UMWA's Corporate Campaign against Peabody and Hanson PLC', in M. E. Gordon and L. Turner (eds.), *Transnational Cooperation among Labor Unions*. Ithaca, NY: ILR Press.

CHAPTER 13

RESISTANCE, MISBEHAVIOR, AND DISSENT

DAVID COLLINSON

STEPHEN ACKROYD

13.1 INTRODUCTION

IT was not until the second half of the twentieth century that academics developed a significant understanding of organizations as sites of dissenting behavior and of resistance to authority. True, the early business consultants Taylor, Gantt, and Bedaux (Littler 1982; Taylor 1911) and consultancy orientated social scientists (Mayo 1934; Roethlisberger and Dickson 1939) noticed that not all work behavior was compliant and dutiful, and sought to counter these tendencies. However, it was not until later in the century that systematic study began. Knowledge was initially developed from the standpoint of a number of disciplines, each having its own perspective and understanding. The field is still not unified, despite recent attempts to bring findings together and to formulate a systematized area of knowledge. Today, commentators use a number of terms to refer to employee practices that have an oppositional or subversive intent or effect. These include resistance (Jermier, Knights, and Nord 1994), dissent (Tilly, Tilly, and Tilly 1975), secondary adjustments (Goffman 1968), antisocial behavior (Giacalone and Greenberg 1997), and misbehavior (Ackroyd and Thompson 1999).

The title of this chapter implies a continuum of oppositional workplace practices ranging from resistance (with connotations of behavior that is overt, principled, and perhaps formally organized), through misbehavior (defined as self-conscious rule-breaking), to dissent (which foregrounds linguistic or normative disagreement). These may be seen as a subset of protesting behavior: from rebellions, insurrections, and riots, shading through strikes and other types of formally organized resistance in workplaces through sabotage, theft to destructiveness, work limitation, absenteeism, and time-wasting, to the cynical debunking of management pretensions and the satirical mockery of managers and authority figures. It can be objected that some of the above are rejections of or reactions to the state and civil society, and so not a fit subject for inclusion in a book about work and organization. Prasad and Prasad's typology (1998) envisages a continuum from open confrontation in work, through subtle subversions to ambiguous accommodation and disengagement. Clearly, however, misbehavior at work has been closely connected with disturbances beyond the workplace at many points in history, and may be so again.

The fact is that approaches to this particular subject area are typically limited in their range. Given the complexity of the subject matter and the fact that it is partly defined by normative criteria, somewhat arbitrary limitations are endemic. This is a field in which there are a large number of arbitrary exclusions from the definition of the subject area: researchers often examine informal group organization, but seldom look at bullying (Ishmael 1999); they sometimes study pilferage (Mars 1982), but seldom venture far into the field of socially organized crime and the grey or black economies (Henry 1987). Much of the available literature tends to be Anglo-American (e.g. Ditton 1972; Jermier, Knights, and Nord 1994; Mars 1982), concentrating on the most visible and collective oppositional practices such as strikes (Hyman 1972), output restriction/work to rule (Roy 1952), and sabotage (Brown 1977; Jermier 1988; Taylor and Walton 1971). These studies also tend to focus primarily upon male, manual workers in the traditional, unionized manufacturing sectors. Yet, there are many other oppositional practices that are more covert and less collective and/or organized. These include absenteeism and turnover (Edwards and Scullion 1982), theft/pilfering/doing foreigners (Mars 1982), indifference/foot dragging (Scott 1985), and even irony and satire (Rodrigues and Collinson 1995). Resistance practices that are more covert and subterranean (Gabriel 1999; Knights and McCabe 2000) are inevitably more difficult to identify and research.

Finally, until recently, few researchers have concerned themselves with managerial misbehavior. Employee absenteeism, pilferage, and work limitation have been studied in detail; yet there is little difference in principle between managerial and employee misbehavior except that managers decide what is misbehavior and what is not. It is probably impossible to avoid limitations of this kind entirely. The best one can hope for is that, as far as possible, researchers are self-conscious about the limitations of the perspectives that inform their thinking. Clearly, there is a danger of excessive focus on the minutiae of employee behavior and, possibly at the same time, of adopting a managerialist frame of reference. But what managers and employers do often includes comparable conduct, not to mention the possibility of such practices as stock dumping, insider trading, and company fraud, which are opportunities for misbehavior not usually available to ordinary employees. Recently, there have been welcome signs that managerial misbehavior is being taken seriously by some authors (Geis, Meier, and Salinger 1995; Holcomb and Sethi 1992; Punch 1996).

This chapter is organized into three sections. First, there is a review of the disciplines that initially revealed this subject area. Not including the early consultancy studies, it is within the last fifty years that this subject area was even noticed, and it was well after this that it began to be seen as a field of study. There is no claim here that resistance, misbehavior, and dissent had entirely escaped attention before 1950, but, rather, there was little recognition of the range of related behavior that might be studied. In this section, then, we ask what were the steps in which some perception of this field was first constructed. Second, there is a review of the main perspectives on this field of study today. Arguing that the field is still deeply divided, we distinguish four distinct perspectives: managerialist organizational behavior, labor process, post-structuralism, and feminism. These approaches do have connections, overlaps, and similarities but are far from constituting a unified field of study. Third, we look at resistance and misbehavior in different kinds of contemporary organizations.

13.2 INITIAL PERSPECTIVES: UNCOVERING THE SUBJECT

13.2.1 Consultancy and Other Early Studies

In the early twentieth century, management consultants such as Taylor (1911) noted some effective worker resistance to management control. Taylor acknowledged that there was a natural tendency to effort limitation (natural soldiering), and this objective could be systematically pursued by workers (systematic soldiering). Taylor's efforts to control work performance, exposed some of the ways that workers utilized their specialized knowledge of production to control shop-floor output and thus protect jobs. Taylor's assumption was that managers could and should become much more systematic in their approach. By separating the conception of work tasks from their execution, and by reorganizing and measuring shop-floor work (in the process de-skilling it), the purpose of scientific management was to obtain greater output from employees. The extent to which employees might effectively prevent this was the limit of Taylor's interest in resistance. He, and the many other management consultants who followed him such as Gantt, the Gilbreths, and Bedaux, all naively assumed that there was an underlying similarity in the interests between managers and workers, and the benefit of all would be served if the profits from redesigned work could result in the marginally increased wages. Their understanding of the origin and nature of resistance was extremely limited.

The work of the human relations writers, who argued that employee behavior was more complicated than assumed by management consultants, developed in the 1920s. Mayo and other human relations writers differed in the way they understood work behavior. While Mayo argued that worker behavior was subject to social motivations that were progressive in a historical context (1934), others, following the ideas of the Italian economist Pareto, argued that worker behavior was, for the most part, straightforwardly irrational (Ackroyd 1976). However, this group of writers, like the management consultants, thought worker resistance was something that might be relatively easily overcome by intelligent managerial action. This did not prove to be the case and the practice of systematic soldiering has been found to be deeply rooted. Indeed, it later became a central focus of industrial sociologists who addressed it from a rather different perspective.

13.2.2 Social History

As was remarked by the radical historian and political commentator G. D. H. Cole in 1938, for a long period the only social and economic history written was a history of the powerful. It was concerned with the activities of royal families and/or key members of the ruling elite. Social historians discovered ordinary people as significant historical actors at a remarkably late stage. The work of the Hammonds (1919) on town workers, and Cole and Postgate's more general history of working people a generation later (1938), were important pioneering studies, but, at the time of their publication, they received little notice. After World War II, however, a series of works by Marxist historians made more impact (Hobsbawm 1959; Rude 1964; Thompson 1963, 1978) and brought to a wider readership the historical study of the activities of peasants and workers in history.

There were several things about this new literature making it relevant to this discussion. The impact of industrialism on the behavior of working people was a matter of special importance to these historians. They also asked how and to what extent organized activities in response to industrialism—such as the formation of trade unions and the development of strike action—was linked to general insurrectionary movements. As this line of research continued, it remained broad in its frame of reference but became, if anything, more theoretically informed (Moore 1967; Tilly, Tilly, and Tilly 1975). The subject area soon came to be concerned with the social bases of obedience and revolt, and to consider the question of the extent to which modern history could or could not be considered a path towards greater and more effective regulation of behavior. Some of this was compelling intellectual work, but although it contributed to the creation of new fields of historical research, it seldom connected with other areas of research into social and economic conflict.

13.2.3 Industrial Relations

Industrial relations as a field of study emerged in many Western countries in the first half of the twentieth century, becoming firmly established in Britain (Webb and Webb 1911), France, and the United States (Commons 1917) by the interwar period. Academics with interests in industrial relations were sometimes politically influential, being able to shape economic and industrial policy. For example, American scholars had some influence on the forms in which collective bargaining was institutionalized in the United States in the 1930s. Academics from the victorious powers influenced the institutional framework imposed on Germany after both World Wars. The dominant perspectives of these scholars were functionalism and pluralism, implying that institutions such as trade unions allowed the channeling of industrial conflict in ways that allowed effective representation and conflict resolution. Industrial conflict in the form of strikes and other mass confrontations of capital and labor were perceived as the failure of effective conflict resolution.

Clegg (1970), the doyen of British industrial relations specialists, argued that collective bargaining was misnamed and was more appropriately thought of as joint regulation. This was clearly not simply a minor readjustment of the terms used to describe the central concern of this field of study. By his redefinition Clegg implied that the collectivity referred to comprised capital and labor jointly (rather than merely the totality of labor), and the matter at issue was not bargaining over the distribution of surplus product from industry, but nothing less than the regulation of the industrial system. In this way, it is argued that the extensive institutionalization of industrial bargaining machinery is functional for the society of which it is part. This definition of the subject of industrial conflict clearly was in sympathy with (and gave additional impetus towards) tripartite and corporatist political regimes, in which industrial policy was supposedly formed by the cooperative efforts of industry, government, and organized labor.

For many years, understanding of dissent and resistance was dominated by the study of formal industrial relations, in which attention was focused on the institutions that channeled, expressed, and represented collective worker discontents. Writers in this tradition concentrated on strike patterns and had much less to say about more informal but clearly related behavior such as overtime bans, working to rule, and going-slows (Edwards and Scullion 1982; Flanders 1970; Hyman 1972, 1987). Whatever the merits of this approach in other ways, it is clear that it drew attention away from the informal aspects of industrial behavior.

13.2.4 Industrial Anthropology and Industrial Sociology

Another direction of study was the application of anthropological techniques to the study of industrial behavior. In the United States, this was shaped by symbolic interactionist sociology, an approach to social life first applied to occupations by scholars at Chicago and elsewhere. In the early 1950s, studies were undertaken in industrial settings (Dalton 1948; Roy 1952, 1953, 1954). In Britain the development of this perspective took longer (Cunnison 1964; Lupton 1963; Sykes 1966). Both the Americans and the British discovered, through close observation of work groups, the extent of the adaptation of operatives to management practices. These studies focused on the social factors underpinning production norms. Their key finding concerned the economic rationality of workers in response to industrial regimes, and the way that practical behavior at work aimed at adjusting wage–effort exchanges in their favor. Industrial misbehavior was found to be concerned with the practical readjustment of the wage–effort exchange.

Industrial anthropologists give a new slant to misbehavior in that, by and large, the misbehaving responses of workers are in employee interests, implying that management has inadequately gauged the extent of economic rationality and the effectiveness of informal organization in supporting this. By being collectively in agreement about the level at which timings allow gravy (Roy 1952) to be earned, a degree of control is achieved by operatives who generally follow customary output norms. The work of the American authors identifies the politics of informal relations that grow up surrounding the administration of piecework payments systems (Collins, Dalton, and Roy 1946). This finding could be and was generalized in different ways. In a penetrating series of case studies, researchers at Columbia University showed how interconnected activities in organizations are. In perhaps the most insightful of these, Gouldner (1954) showed that disturbance of the customary patterns of exchange of work for rewards could cause industrial action as well as more conventional forms of work limitation. In his seminal work on mental hospital patients, Goffman (1961: 172) highlighted patients' tendency to engage in oppositional practices. Goffman referred to these as secondary adjustments, by which he meant, 'any habitual arrangement by which a member of an organization employs unauthorized means, or obtains unauthorized ends, or both, thus getting around the organization's assumptions as to what he [*sic*] should do and get and hence what he should be'.

By the 1960s a general theory of the basis of exchanges of work for wages in the industrial setting was worked out by Baldamus (1961) and Behrend (1957). These researchers proposed that a contract of employment does not specify the amount of work that any worker is obliged to do. For this reason usually (a) social norms fix the general level of effort typically put forth and (b) practical negotiation about the amount of effort to be expended in particular work is ubiquitous. Through meticulous studies of absenteeism and turnover in particular, these writers came to the conclusion that what they called the effort bargain regulated the amount of work done in work settings. By the 1970s, there was emerging agreement that bargaining over rewards was a key insight. It was applied in various areas of research. A second generation of industrial anthropologists revealed just how extensive the development of economically motivated workplace organization can be (Ditton 1977*a*; Mars 1973, 1982). A study by Ditton suggested that the same kinds of work limitation practices that were prevalent under piecework systems were also present with day work (1977*b*) and absenteeism could be connected with time-wasting (1972, 1978). Ditton's studies also made clear that, like output restriction, fiddling cash was a particular form of making out in the effort bargain (1977*a*, 1977*b*). Industrial relations analysts, interested in the formal organization of the workplace, also tended to use this perspective.

Not long after, landmark research by Edwards considered a range of dissenting behavior (Edwards 1986; Edwards and Scullion 1982). Thus, the idea of the effort bargain was taken up by industrial relations specialists and industrial sociologists. In this tradition of thought there is the broadest consensus yet to emerge concerning misbehavior.

13.2.5 Applied Psychology

Psychologists have usually assumed that poor work performance and misbehavior are aberrations that can be avoided. Study began by attempting to find out the actual pattern of work performance with the examination of the output achieved by workers in munitions factories in World War I. This showed that fatigue reduced performance in typical ways. It also revealed that managers had little appreciation of the effects involved, pointing to the need for more research. The assumptions here were more sophisticated than those involved with scientific management and came along with the realization that attempts to maximize the amount of work from employees could well be counterproductive. Nevertheless, the conclusion of the early psychologists was similar to that of the early consultants, the effects of fatigue and worker stress could be minimized and job performance maximized by effective job design.

The emerging field of work psychology was enormously enriched by the contribution of German researchers, many of whom, like Lewin and Adorno, were émigrés from Nazi Germany who went to America in the 1930s. Because of their origins, they had the problem of authoritarian control in organizations high on their list of concerns. A consequence of this tradition of thought was that many researchers were preoccupied with the extent of conformity in organizations and how to render people and organizations responsive to democratic rather than autocratic control. The research question here had considerable vitality, and concern with the extent of authoritarian control and the degree to which punitive supervisory behavior could be induced in research subjects continued until long after World War II (Asch 1951; Milgram 1974).

Whether focused on conformity or deviation, psychologists have tended to see misbehavior and dissent as primarily individual acts. In consequence, they have often regarded the oppositional practices of subordinates as the irrational behavior of poorly motivated individuals. Such explanations tend to limit perceptions of resistance to an individualistic account of pathology. In particular, this approach explicitly rejects the proposition that conflict is embedded in the social organization of production by employees and that this is supported by social norms.

13.3 CONTEMPORARY PERSPECTIVES

We now distinguish four contemporary perspectives on organizational misbehavior. Although there are significant areas of overlap, they are more conspicuous for their differences, and their exponents would certainly think of them as being necessarily different from other positions.

13.3.1 Managerialist Organizational Behavior: Obedience and Compliance

The interest of many American scholars in organizational misbehavior began less than ten years ago, occurring within the discipline of organizational behavior (OB) (Fox and Spector 1999; Giacalone and Greenberg 1997; Vardi and Weiner 1996). For many years OB, particularly as it was practiced in the United States, tended to assume that the majority of behavior at work was responsible. In obvious ways many OB researchers shared the values of managers themselves: both groups tended to think that if employees were treated reasonably, then responsible behavior would ensue. The differences between OB specialists and liberal managers turned simply on how deeply one had to think about employee expectations to ensure good conduct.

In recent years these assumptions came under increased questioning in response to a number of incidents of workplace aggression and violence. As a result the understanding of misbehavior held by some OB writers is shaped by a perception that behavior is often unprincipled and even dangerous. Giacalone and Greenberg explicitly call their subject matter the dark side of organizational behavior. This approach is motivated by the desire to find solutions to what they conceive of as a new organizational problem. The concepts used to characterize the subject matter include workplace deviance (Robinson and Bennett 1995, 1997), organizational misbehavior (Vardi and Weitz 2003), antisocial behavior (Giacalone and Greenberg 1997), dysfunctional behavior (Griffin, O'Leary-Kelly, and Collins 1998), aggression (Neuman and Baron 1998), counterproductive behavior (Fox and Spector 1999), retaliation (Skarlicki and Folger 1997), and revenge (Bies, Tripp, and Kramer 1997).

Exponents of this perspective typically view organizational misbehavior as a negative phenomenon because of the harmful consequences it may bring to organizations. Robinson and Bennett (1995, 1997) argue that all three elements of intentionality, violation of some norm or standards, and harmful effects need to be present before managers can legitimately decide whether an event constitutes serious workplace misbehavior (or to use their term, workplace deviance). Despite the authors' circumspection, there is no disguising the fact that they are aiming to facilitate management decision making concerning how to identify unacceptable behavior and whether or not to impose sanctions. Defining their subject normatively as they do, writers have little difficulty in identifying with organizations and their problems. Robinson and Bennett (1995) have argued for instance that dumping toxic waste into rivers or lakes is not a form of misbehavior if the organization's norm strongly encourages such practices as a cost-saving device. It seems clear that one objective of much of this writing is to help in the construction of the obedient and compliant employee (Ackroyd and Thompson 1999; Hollway 1991).

13.3.2 Labor Process Theory and Recent Industrial Sociology: Conflict and Contradiction

In sharp contrast with organizational behavior assumptions, labor process (LP) theory and some recent industrial sociology share a different orientation. A central tenet of LP literature is that there is incipient, structured antagonism between management and labor within capitalist organizations (Burawoy 1979; P. K. Edwards 1986; R. Edwards 1979; Thompson 1989). Employee resistance is a consequence of the control imperative established by the agency relationship of managers to employers and the competitive pressures that require capital to continually transform the conditions of work and extract greater value from labor (Braverman 1974).

However, LP writers argue that no matter how asymmetrical power relations are, managerial control is never complete and employees invariably find ways of resisting (Beynon 1980). Many LP writers highlight the contradictory nature of capitalist employment relations in that they are built upon both divergent interests and interdependence between management and labor (Cressey and MacInnes 1980). Accordingly, they demonstrate how managerial control is inherently contradictory in its attempts to treat employees as both disposable and dependable labor (Hyman 1987). Typically, managers seek to harness employee commitment and creativity while limiting this very same worker's discretion because that might be applied in ways deemed unacceptable. These contradictory managerial practices seek to manufacture consent while also exercising coercion (Burawoy 1979). Thus, they often result in a shifting emphasis: for example, insisting first upon direct control and then, subsequently, shifting to reliance on employees to exercise responsibility when controls are relaxed (Friedman 1977). Employee resistance may well be instrumental in exposing the failure of managerial techniques and policies to secure long-term employee commitment.

Sociologists can take the view that resistance is not intrinsic to capitalist employment relations so much as reactive to particular management behavior. Thus, Hodson (1995: 80) defines employee opposition as 'any individual or small group act intended to mitigate claims by management on workers or to advance workers' claims against management'. Hodson (1995) contends that the logic of diverse managerial control systems provides openings for different types of worker resistance. He argues that where the direct control of supervisors is abusive, workers may resist by venting frustration through sabotage, theft, and pilferage and through widespread collective support and solidarity. Where technical control predominates, resistance is likely to focus more upon the intensity and duration of work (playing dumb, output/effort restriction, tardiness, work avoidance, absenteeism, and quitting). These arguments reaffirm the point that to understand resistance we need to examine such practices in relation to workplace discipline and managerial control. Having said that, asymmetrical power relations are unlikely to produce employee resistance in any simple or predetermined way. The outcomes of the complex interrelations between capital and labor can produce consent and accommodation, as well as control and resistance.

Recently writers from the LP perspective have begun to use the term 'organizational misbehavior' to denote informal practices of subordinates. In their approach the definition of misbehavior is held to be within managerial prerogative. While management both identifies misbehavior and imposes sanctions on employees who have misbehaved, its decision to do so is not automatic. Rather, whether misbehavior is punished or otherwise depends on management decision (Ackroyd and Thompson 1999). Managers do not always consider misbehavior illegitimate and act against it; sometimes they accommodate to it, and even encourage it under certain circumstances, especially when this is related to business expediency (Webb and Palmer 1998). In this view workplace misbehavior is differentiated from resistance. Ackroyd and Thompson (1999: 163) argued that the term 'misbehavior' is not intended to replace resistance but to recognize that 'there is another realm of workplace behaviour that should not be understood merely as a form or step towards what has become identified with the term resistance' (165). Although the authors maintain that misbehavior and resistance are two distinct concepts, many studies tend to equate misbehavior with resistance because these practices appear to share similar behavioral domains.

13.3.3 Post-Structuralism: Surveillance and Subjectivity

Drawing particularly on Foucault's (1977) ideas on discipline, post-structuralist writers seek to show how contemporary managerial control is often exercised through new forms of workplace surveillance (computers, CCTV, appraisal, performance targets) and how these disciplinary processes significantly impact on employees' selves. Some post-structuralists are concerned to demonstrate the disciplinary effectiveness of surveillance regimes (Casey 1995; Sewell and Wilkinson 1992; Willmott 1993;). Others argue that the emergence of resistance itself can reinforce power and discipline. It can have the unintended effect of reinforcing managerial control because opposition is then rendered more visible and known. For example, Burrell (1988) argues that the effects of resistance frequently strengthen control: 'discipline can grow stronger knowing where its next efforts must be directed' (1988: 228).

While increased disciplinarity is certainly one possible outcome, other post-structuralists have countered that this is by no means inevitable and that not all forms of resistance end in defeat for subordinates. They suggest that these arguments are overly deterministic and are inconsistent with Foucault's (1977) own assertion that power invariably produces resistance, especially in the form of local acts of defiance. In certain cases managerial attempts to render misbehavior the target of further discipline may actually reinvigorate worker resistance. Ezzamel (1994) found that subordinates used their technical knowledge of budgeting successfully to challenge a redundancy program in a UK university. Highlighting different strategies of resistance, Collinson (2000) argued that persistence was a more effective (but less common) strategy than distancing. Shop-floor workers distanced themselves from management and the organization, but paradoxically their counterculture had the effect of reinforcing managerial prerogative and power. By contrast, employees who sought to render those in power more visible and accountable, through the persistent demand for more information and the questioning of decisions, were relatively more effective in achieving change. These strategies of resistance tended to reflect and reinforce quite distinct employee subjectivities, both of which contained important paradoxes, ambiguities, and ironies.

For many post-structuralists, resistance is not only a primary means by which employees express discontent, but is also a way for subordinates to construct alternative, more positive identities to those provided, prescribed, or circumscribed by the organization. Challenging conventional notions of identity as a fixed and objective essence, post-structuralists contend that oppositional selves are open, negotiable, shifting, ambiguous, and potentially contradictory (Collinson 2003). They tend to view actors as decentered selves whose multiple identities are frequently characterized by insecurities, contradictions, and creative tensions (Kondo 1990). Questioning assumptions about subjectivity, post-structuralists argue that social scientists need to rethink the ways they typically conceptualize particular practices as resistance (Jermier, Knights, and Nord 1994). While earlier radical writers might be inclined to emphasize and even celebrate (all) forms of workplace resistance, post-structuralist approaches also caution against this tendency automatically to impute a revolutionary motive, subversive impetus, or transformative effect to resistance. Given these subjective complexities, post-structuralists suggest that any examination of resistance needs to explore its interrelated conditions (that give rise to misbehavior), processes (meanings, motives, and diverse practices), and consequences (impact on selves and organizations).

13.3.4 Feminist Studies: Gender and Sexuality

Feminist studies reveal the gendered nature of workplace power relations, of employees' oppositional practices, and of the various identities that are constructed in organizations. Writers illustrate how managerial control is often sustained through gendered job segregation (Collinson, Knights, and Collinson 1990) and through the desexualization of the workplace (Burrell 1992). They show how gender and sexuality frequently shape employee resistance and misbehavior. For example, various studies describe how male-dominated shop-floor countercultures are typically characterized by masculine breadwinner identities, aggressive and highly sexualized forms of humor, and the elevation of 'practical' manual work/engineering skills as a confirmation of working-class manhood, independence, and opposition to management (Cockburn 1983; Collinson 1992).

Research on female-dominated workplaces suggests that women also often engage in aggressive, joking, and sexualized countercultures that resist managerial control strategies (Pollert 1981; Pringle 1988; Westwood 1984). While these studies point to similarities between male- and female-dominated workplace countercultures, they also reveal differences between the masculine and feminine character of specific workplace cultures. Burrell (1992) demonstrates that heterosexual and homosexual men and women find ways of resisting management's concern to desexualize the workplace. Feminist studies also reveal some of the contradictions of subordinate resistance. They show, for example, how a shared sense of masculinity between male workers may not only facilitate, but also constrain worker opposition. Walby (1986) illustrates how male-dominated oppositional workplace forms can reproduce gender divisions and women's subordination. Hence, male worker resistance against the employer (over the breadwinner wage) can simultaneously constitute a form of gendered control (through the exclusion/segregation of female labor). Similarly, Willis (1977) describes how working-class 'lads' creatively construct a counterculture that celebrates masculinity and the so-called freedom and independence of manual work. Yet, despite its apparent oppositional nature, the counterculture also facilitated the lads' smooth transition into precisely the kind of shop-floor work that then subordinated them, possibly for the rest of their working lives.

In her study of gender relations in a Japanese factory, Kondo (1990) highlights the contradictory outcomes of oppositional processes. She describes how the countercultures of Japanese shop-floor workers that frequently expose managerial inconsistencies can themselves be caught up in contradictions, simultaneously legitimizing as they challenge dominant organizational and gendered discourses. While Japanese workers criticized management and questioned the dominant notion of the company as family, they simultaneously took pride in belonging to the organization. Kondo outlines how women part-time shop-floor workers were highly effective in asserting their gendered identities (often as surrogate mothers to the younger male artisans) that creatively challenged the masculine celebration of prowess on the job. Yet simultaneously these identities relied on conventional discourses about women, having the effect of reinforcing their marginality as workers, excluded from the central masculine discourses of artisan work. By casting themselves as mothers, women claimed power over the younger men but simultaneously reproduced their own exclusion. Paradoxically, they asserted and marginalized themselves simultaneously.

Hence, feminist studies of workplace resistance focus on that which is frequently taken for granted in much of the earlier literature on resistance, misbehavior, and dissent. They highlight the importance of taking gender and sexuality into account when examining workplace processes of power, resistance, and misbehavior.

13.4 CONTEMPORARY RESISTANCE

Many contemporary studies continue to find examples of employee resistance and misbehavior. Hodson (2001) recently analyzed more than eighty book-length studies of different kinds of work groups, which reveal far more behavioral similarities than differences, including tendencies to misbehave in response to management neglect and abuse. Although, much of this research was not written in the recent past, contemporary research, as we shall see, suggests that its insights continue to be of relevance. Similar resistance, misbehavior, and dissent have not gone away with the decline of trade unions or organized industrial action, or the introduction of new technologies and new working practices. Unlike strikes, which were concentrated in particular industries and geographical locations, misbehavior continues to be ubiquitous and, in many circumstances, is more difficult to control.

An important feature of current employee resistance appears to be a highly cynical employee orientation to management and work. In one sense this is not new—there have always been such reactions to the gap between management words and deeds. However, this gap has, arguably, been widening and changing its character. For example, Deal and Kennedy (2000) argue that managerial innovations over the past twenty years (from soft practices such as corporate culture initiatives and quality circles, to the harder edged BPR, JIT, outsourcing, and downsizing) have intensified employee job insecurity and distrust of management, and produced a culture of cynicism. Wright and Smye (1998) contend that the current adoption of lean production and the widespread use of performance measurement reinforce intimidatory managerial styles that often involve corporate abuse, scapegoating, and cultures of blame.

The use of sophisticated and powerful management information systems has allowed many businesses to operate with a minimum of staff. The few remaining staff are required to be highly responsible in their attitude to corporate assets and interests. In these circumstances some managers adopt quite contradictory attitudes: on the one hand, they tend to regard labor as a considerable cost, as potentially disposable, and as a subject of discipline. On the other hand, they recognize how highly vulnerable undermanned systems are to sabotage and to a lack of continued responsibility and diligence. This leads to managerial attempts to specify the details of work behavior in ways that patronize employees and reinforce their cynicism.

Several studies have shown that employees' cynicism is often fuelled by their awareness of significant discrepancies between official managerial policies and actual practices. Graham (1995) examined teamworking in the new US Subaru Isuzu plant and found that disaffection was widespread. Workers detected inconsistencies between the teamworking ideal (with its emphasis on cleanliness, *kaizen*, and quality) and the speedup of the production process. Employee cynicism was expressed by refusal to participate in corporate rituals (such as morning exercises and the daily collection of information on defects) and by their sending highly critical anonymous letters to the company. Others used humor to make light of the company's teamworking and continuous improvement philosophies. Graham also found a range of more demonstrative activities that signify actual misbehavior and not simply ideological dissent.

Similar patterns concerning employee cynicism have been documented in different work settings. Fleming (2002) examined employee cynicism in an Australian call center. He argues that in the face of an all-pervasive corporate culture that treats workers like children, cynicism enabled employees to refuse to become a 'Sunray (the company) self' and to construct a new, different, and opposing identity. Through humorous cynicism workers made fun of the organization, paradoxically, in order to be taken seriously, and to construct an identity as a dignified adult. Fleming contends that employee cynicism does not necessarily signify capitulation as is often assumed (Casey 1995; Kunda 1992; Willmott 1993), but may constitute an effective form of resistance. So, rather than treat employee cynicism as a form of psychological distancing, Fleming argues that it is better understood as an attempt to create a new and alternative identity to that offered by the organization. Work by Taylor and Bain, also in call centers, suggests that responses to this kind of work can vary a good deal, but where the work is highly routinized, resisting behavior may well be reminiscent of responses to industrial work (Taylor and Bain 1999).

Recent studies in retailing and the leisure industries reveal that subordinate cynicism may also be expressed towards customers. For example, Van Maanen (1991) found that despite close surveillance at Disneyland, employees still found ways of resisting difficult or abusive guests. He argues that workers were motivated by the need to restore self-respect, particularly when customers stepped beyond definitions of acceptable behavior. Similarly, Leidner (1993) argues that routinized, interactive service work can increase workers' control over work processes, not least over difficult customers. Under pressure to work faster, employees were particularly hostile to customers who slowed them down (through indecision, changing their minds, or simply striking up a conversation when the store was busy).

In many cases employee cynicism would seem to be justified in a broader sense. The pressures for profit and success can lead to managers cutting corners to reach corporate goals. Indeed, following an in-depth study of numerous corporate scandals, Punch (1996) has argued plausibly that corporate business is crimogenic. By this he means that business executives have to lie and cheat to maintain their positions and to advance the interests of their businesses. Recent corporate scandals, such as those at Enron and Worldcom, suggest that corporate misbehavior may well not only be extensive in some companies, but systemic in the contemporary political economy. Instances of executive illegality can set up huge tensions for employees who see the rule breaking and who cannot readily overlook community and other interest. Not surprisingly, these tensions have resulted in some employees feeling compelled to translate their cynicism into action, typically to disclose information outside their own organization. This is the practice of whistle-blowing (Miceli and Near 2002).

Initially, often loyal and conscientious rather than oppositional workers, as the process develops they become increasingly frustrated and cynical with those in senior positions (Rothschild and Miethe 1994). The case of whistle-blowing suggests that workplace resistance can be a relatively individualized oppositional practice and one that also involves more senior-level employees (La-Nuez and Jermier 1994). Nonetheless, for whistle-blowers the costs of their actions through corporate reprisals are potentially extensive (Collinson 2000). Accordingly, for many employees a detached cynicism remains a central and preferred response to the contradictory managerial controls they often experience.

13.5 CONCLUSION

This chapter has reviewed some of the key analytical developments in the study of employee misbehavior. We have suggested that the scope of resistance has always been wider than often acknowledged and has become wider still as management has made greater demands on employee effort and identity. Such broadened scope of employee resistance and misbehavior can complement the more conventional forms of collective action documented elsewhere in this section of the Handbook by Kelly and Katz. However, we have also suggested that despite its interest and importance, the field of employee resistance remains far from coherent. The fact that we have discussed the topic using the labels resistance, misbehavior, and dissent itself suggests that there are differences of view about the relevant terminology and how the field should be defined. There also remain important theoretical differences and disagreements between the various frameworks used to interpret employee practices. Writers draw on a diversity of paradigms and perspectives from anthropology, sociology, psychology, industrial relations, organizational behavior, labor process theory, and neo-Marxism, to feminism and post-structuralism. These approaches reflect and reinforce the plurality of theoretical perspectives, backed by supporting ontologies and epistemologies that characterize organization studies more broadly.

While the terms 'resistance', 'misbehavior', and/or 'dissent' have informed our discussion, we also acknowledge their inadequacy as descriptors of employee practices. Some take it as axiomatic that the implications of these terms have become significantly limited. As Kondo (1990) observes, there is no such thing as a 'true resister' or an entirely 'authentic' or 'pristine space of resistance'. Notions of 'resistance' may thus appear inadequate because oppositional practices are frequently characterized by ironies, contradictions, and unintended outcomes, while employees often 'consent, cope, and resist at different levels of consciousness at a single point in time' (Kondo 1990: 224). Hence, while it is certain that there is a need to develop new theories and concepts that can more adequately reflect the complexity of employee practices, that this should necessarily limit their potential political significance is more doubtful. That resistance has somehow been contained because it is compromised and incomplete, is still open to debate.

Our discussion also suggests that the empirical coverage of resistance and misbehavior is seriously incomplete, and there are new terrains in which conflict can be expressed. For example, the increasingly global reach of organizations, and associated tendency to escape from their national framework of regulation, raises important questions regarding opposition and dissent. While trade unions are seeking to cooperate across national boundaries, some of the most effective forms of opposition have emerged through the protests of citizens outside traditional organizations (e.g. NGOs like Friends of the Earth and Greenpeace and even investigative journalists). Klein (2000) has examined these new forms of resistance, exploring global campaigns and protests against the World Bank, the IMF, and the World Trade Organization as well as more specific, but highly coordinated and international campaigns against companies like Nike, Reebok, McDonald's, Pepsi, and Shell. Highlighting how this resistance is no longer confined to specific countries, Klein points to the importance of the Internet as the tool of choice for spreading information about multinationals around the world. A classic example is that of the campaign that flowed from the writs issued by McDonald's in 1990 against two Greenpeace activists over the contents of a leaflet highly critical of the company's practices. This led to a trial lasting 313 days, the longest civil case in English history. During the case all of McDonald's practices were scrutinized and the McSpotlight web site was created. It offers a debating room where McDonald's workers can exchange horror stories about working for the company. This site became one of the most popular on the web, being accessed over 65 million times (Klein 2000: 394).

In obvious ways, the accounts of resistance and misbehavior discussed in this chapter are mainly Western in origin and/or inspiration. More often than not, they are adaptations of Anglo-American perspectives. There are few studies of organizational misbehavior originating in other places, particularly from developing societies. Partly this is due to straightforward political oppression, the governments of developing societies have little sympathy with scholars wishing to draw attention to dissent and resistance. But even where social science has been allowed to flourish, studies of dissent and misbehavior such as there are mostly involve the transplantation of Western assumptions and perspectives. To take one example, Malaysia has been the context for some celebrated studies of dissent and resistance. From this one country we have the radical anthropology of Scott (1985) and insightful industrial study by Ong (1987), which concern the responses of Malaysian factory workers to the disciplines of Western industrialism.

Finally, despite the suggestion by some that resistance and misbehavior may have no future (because, among other things, managers and authorities have acquired effective techniques of behavioral control), it seems that studies of these phenomena continue to be undertaken. In what appear to be increasingly disciplinary, insecure, and highly stressful workplace conditions, it is indeed notable that employees continue to find ways to enact discontent and express dissatisfaction. The 'post 9/11 era' is likely to be characterized by intensified surveillance and the further corrosion of trust relations in civil society (Lyon 2003). Insofar as these developments will be mirrored by ever more extensive forms of technological and behavioral monitoring within organizations, employees may well need to find new coping strategies and new ways of 'misbehaving' and resisting these disciplinary regimes. Although employee misbehavior may not always lead to significant change, it is likely to remain a crucially important feature of workplace life, one that will continue to require detailed examination by critical scholars of work and organizations.

References

ACKROYD, S. (1976). 'Sociological Theory and the Human Relations School'. *Sociology of Work and Occupations*, 3: 379–410.

—— and THOMPSON, P. (1999). *Organisational Misbehaviour*. London: Sage.

ASCH, S. (1951). 'Effects of Group Pressure on the Modification and Distortion of Judgements', in H. Guetzkow (ed.), *Groups, Leadership and Men*. New York: Carnegie Press.

BALDAMUS, W. (1961). *Efficiency and Effort*. London: Tavistock.

BEHREND, H. (1957). 'The Effort Bargain'. *Industrial and Labour Relations Review*, 10: 503–15.

BEYNON, H. (1980). *Working for Ford*. Harmondsworth: Penguin.

BIES, R. J., TRIPP, T. M., and KRAMER, R. M. (1997). 'At the Breaking Point: Cognitive and Social Dynamics of Revenge in Organisations', in R. A. Giacalone and J. Greenberg (eds.), *Antisocial Behaviour in Organisations*. Thousand Oaks, Calif.: Sage.

BRAVERMAN, H. (1974). *Labor and Monopoly Capital*. New York: Monthly Review Press.

BROWN, G. (1977). *Sabotage: A Study in Industrial Conflict*. Nottingham: Spokesman Books.

BURAWOY, M. (1979). *Manufacturing Consent: Changes in the Labor Process under Monopoly Capitalism*. Chicago: Chicago University Press.

BURRELL, G. (1988). 'Modernism, Postmodernism and Organisational Analysis: The Contribution of Michael Foucault'. *Organisation Studies*, 9: 221–35.

—— (1992). 'Sex and Organizational Analysis', in A. J. Mills and P. Tancred (eds.), *Gendering Organizational Analysis*. London: Sage.

CASEY, C. (1995). *Work, Self and Society: After Industrialism*. London: Routledge.

CLEGG, H. (1970). *The System of Industrial Relations in Great Britain*. Oxford: Blackwell.

COCKBURN, C. (1983). *Brothers: Male Dominance and Technological Change*. London: Pluto.

COLE, G. D. H., and POSTGATE, R. (1938). *The Common People*. London: Methuen.

COLLINS, O., DALTON, M., and ROY, D. (1946). 'Restriction of Output and Social Cleavage in Industry'. *Applied Anthropology*, 5: 1–14.

COLLINSON, D. L. (1992). *Managing the Shopfloor: Subjectivity, Masculinity and Workplace Culture*. Berlin: William de Gruyter.

—— (2000). 'Strategies of Resistance: Power, Knowledge and Subjectivity', in K. Grint (ed.), *Work and Society: A Reader*. Cambridge: Polity Press.

—— (2003). 'Identities and Insecurities: Selves at Work'. *Organization*, 10: 527–47.

—— KNIGHTS, D., and COLLINSON, M. (1990). *Managing to Discriminate*. London: Routledge.

COMMONS, J. (1917). *Labor and Administration*. New York. Macmillan.

CRESSEY, P., and MacINNES, J. (1980). 'Voting for Ford: Industrial Democracy and the Control of Labour'. *Capital and Class*, 11: 5–33.

CUNNISON, S. (1964). *Wages and Work Allocation*. London: Tavistock.

DALTON, H. (1948). 'The Industrial Rate Buster'. *Applied Anthropology*, 7: 5–18.

DEAL, T. E., and KENNEDY, A. A. (2000). *The New Corporate Cultures*. London: Texere.

DITTON, J. (1972). 'Absent at Work: How to Manage Monotony'. *New Society*, 21/533: 679–81.

—— (1977a). *Part-time Crime: An Ethnography of Fiddling and Pilferage*. London: Macmillan.

—— (1977b). 'Perks, Pilferage and the Fiddle: The Historical Structure of Invisible Wages'. *Theory and Society*, 4: 39–71.

—— (1978). 'Baking Time'. *Sociological Review* 27: 157–67.

EDWARDS, P. K. (1986). *Conflict at Work*. Oxford: Blackwell.

—— and SCULLION, H. (1982). *The Social Organization of Industrial Conflict*. Oxford: Blackwell.

EDWARDS, R. (1979). *Contested Terrain: The Transformation of the Workplace in the Twentieth Century*. London; Heinemann.

EZZAMEL, M. (1994). 'Organizational Change and Accounting: Understanding the Budgetary System in its Organizational Context'. *Organization Studies*, 15: 213–40.

FLANDERS, A. (1970). *Management and Unions: The Theory and Reform of Industrial Relations*. London: Faber and Faber.

FLEMING, P. (2002). 'Diogenes Goes to Work: Culture, Cynicism and Resistance in the Contemporary Workplace'. Doctoral Thesis. Department of Management, University of Melbourne, Australia.

FOUCAULT, M. (1977). *Discipline and Punish*. London: Allen and Unwin.

FOX, S., and SPECTOR, P. E. (1999). 'A Model of Work Frustration-Aggression'. *Journal of Organisational Behaviour*, 20: 915–31.

FRIEDMAN, A. (1977). *Industry and Labour: Class Struggle at Work and Monopoly Capitalism*. London: Macmillan.

GABRIEL, Y. (1999). 'Beyond Happy Families: A Critical Re-evaluation of the Control-Resistance-Identity Triangle'. *Human Relations*, 52: 179–203.

GEIS, G., MEIER, R. F., and SALINGER, L. M. (eds.) (1995). *White Collar Crime: Classic and Contemporary Views* (3rd edn). New York: Free Press.

GIACALONE, R. A., and GREENBERG, J. (1997). *Antisocial Behaviour in Organisations*. Thousand Oaks, Calif.: Sage.

GOFFMAN, E. (1961). *Encounters*. Harmondsworth: Penguin.

——(1968). *Asylums*. Harmondsworth: Penguin.

GOULDNER, A. W. (1954). *Patterns of Industrial Bureaucracy*. New York: Free Press.

GRAHAM, L. (1995). *On the Line at Subaru-Isuzu*. Ithaca, NY: ILR Press.

GRIFFIN, R. W., O'LEARY-KELLY, A., and COLLINS, J. (1998). 'Dysfunctional Work Behaviours in Organisations', in C. L. Cooper and D. M. Rousseau (eds.), *Trends in Organisational Behaviour*. Chichester: John Wiley.

HAMMOND, J. L., and HAMMOND, B. (1919). *The Town Labourer 1760–1832*. London: Longmans.

HENRY, S. (1987). *The Hidden Economy: The Context and Control of Borderline Crime*. Oxford: Martin Robertson.

HOBSBAWM, E. (1959). *Primitive Rebels*. Manchester: Manchester University Press.

HODSON, R. (1995). 'Worker Resistance: An Underdeveloped Concept in the Sociology of Work'. *Economic and Industrial Democracy*, 16: 79–110.

——(2001). *Dignity at Work*. London: Cambridge University Press.

HOLCOMB, J. M., and SETHI, S. P. (1992). 'Corporate and Executive Criminal Liability: Appropriate Standards, Remedies and Managerial Responses'. *Business and the Contemporary World*, 41 (Summer): 81–105.

HOLLWAY, W. (1991). *Work Psychology and Organizational Behaviour*. London: Sage.

HYMAN, R. (1972). *Strikes*. London: Fontana Collins.

——(1987). 'Strategy or Structure? Capital, Labour and Control'. *Work, Employment and Society*, 1: 25–55.

ISHMAEL, A. (1999). *Harassment, Bullying and Violence at Work*. London: Industrial Society.

JERMIER, J. (1988). 'Sabotage at Work: The Rational View'. *Sociology of Organisations*, 6: 101–34.

——KNIGHTS, D., and NORD, W. R. (1994). *Resistance and Power in Organisations*. London: Routledge.

KLEIN, N. (2000). *No Logo*. London: Flamingo.

KNIGHTS, D., and McCABE, D. (2000). 'Ain't Misbehaving? Opportunities for Resistance under New Forms of "Quality" Management'. *Sociology*, 34: 421–36.

KONDO, D. K. (1990). *Crafting Selves: Power, Gender and Discourses of Identity in a Japanese Workplace*. Chicago: University of Chicago Press.

KUNDA, G. (1992). *Engineeering Culture: Control and Commitment in a High-Tech Corporation*. Philadelphia: Temple University Press.

LA-NUEZ, D., and JERMIER, J. M. (1994). 'Sabotage by Managers and Technocrats: Neglected Patterns of Resistance at Work', in J. M. Jermier, D. Knights, and W. R. Nord (eds.), *Resistance and Power in Organisations*. London: Routledge.

LEIDNER, R. (1993). *Fast Food, Fast Talk: Service Work and the Routinisation of Everyday Life*. Berkeley: University of California Press.

LITTLER, C. (1982). *The Development of the Labour Process in Capitalist Societies*. London: Heinemann.

LUPTON, T. (1963). *On the Shopfloor*. Oxford: Pergamon.

LYON, D. (2003). *Surveillance after September 11*. Cambridge: Polity Press.

MARS, G. (1973). 'Chance, Punters and the Fiddle: Institutionalised Pilferage in a Hotel Dining Room', in M. Warner (ed.), *The Sociology of the Workplace*. London: Allen and Unwin.

——(1982). *Cheats at Work*. London: Counterpoint.

MAYO, E. (1934). *The Human Problems of an Industrial Civilisation*. New York: Macmillan.

MICELI, M. P., and NEAR, J. P. (2002). 'What Makes Whistle-Blowers Effective? Three Field Studies'. *Human Relations*, 55: 155–67.

MILGRAM, S. (1974). *Obedience and Authority*. London: Tavistock.

MOORE, W. B. (1967). *Social Origins of Democracy and Dictatorship*. Harmondsworth: Allan Lane.

NEUMAN, J. H., and BARON, R. A. (1998). 'Workplace Violence and Workplace Aggression: Evidence Concerning Specific Norms, Potential Causes, and Preferred Targets'. *Journal of Management*, 24: 391–419.

ONG, O. (1987). *Spirits of Resistance and Capitalist Discipline: Factory Women in Malaysia*. New York: SUNY Press.

POLLERT, A. (1981). *Girls, Wives and Factory Lives*. London: Macmillan.

PRASAD, A., and PRASAD, P. (1998). 'Everyday Struggles at the Workplace: The Nature and Implications of Routine Resistance in Contemporary Organisations', in P. A. Bamberger and V. J. Sonnenstuhl (eds.), *Research in the Sociology of Organisations*. Greenwich, Conn.: JAI Press.

PRINGLE, R. (1988). *Secretaries' Talk: Sexuality, Power and Work*. London: Verso.

PUNCH, M. (1996). *Dirty Business*. London: Sage.

ROBINSON, S. L., and BENNETT, R. J. (1995). 'A Typology of Deviant Workplace Behaviours: A Multidimensional Scaling Study'. *Academy of Management Journal*, 38: 555–72.

————(1997). 'Workplace Deviance: Its Definition, Its Manifestations, and Its Causes', in R. J. Lewicki, R. J. Bies, and B. H. Sheppard (eds.), *Research on Negotiation in Organisations*. Greenwich, Conn.: JAI Press.

RODRIGUES, S. B., and COLLINSON, D. L. (1995). '"Having Fun": Humour as Resistance in Brazil'. *Organisation Studies*, 16: 739–68.

ROETHLISBERGER, F., and DICKSON, W. (1939). *Management and the Worker*. Cambridge, Mass.: Harvard University Press.

ROTHSCHILD, J., and MIETHE, T. D. (1994). 'Whistleblowing as Resistance in Modern Work Organizations', in J. Jermier, D. Knights, and W. R. Nord (eds.), *Resistance and Power in Organisations*. London: Routledge.

ROY, D. (1952). 'Quota Restriction and Goldbricking in a Machine Shop'. *American Journal of Sociology*, 57: 427–42.

——(1953). 'Work Satisfaction and Social Reward in Quota Achievement: An Analysis of Piecework Incentives'. *American Sociological Review*, 18: 507–14.

——(1954). 'Efficiency and the "Fix": Informal Inter-Group Relations in a Piecework Machine Shop'. *American Journal of Sociology*, 60: 427–42.

RUDE, G. (1964). *The Crowd in History*. New York: John Wiley.

SCOTT, J. C. (1985). *Weapons of the Weak: Everyday Forms of Peasant Resistance*. New Haven, Conn.: Yale University Press.

SEWELL, G., and WILKINSON, B. (1992). '"Someone to Watch over Me": Surveillance, Discipline and the Just-in-time Labour Process'. *Sociology*, 26: 271–90.

SKARLICKI, D. P., and FOLGER, R. (1997). 'Retaliation in the Workplace: The Rules of Distributive, Procedural, and Interactional Justice'. *Journal of Applied Psychology*, 82: 416–25.

SYKES, A. J. (1966). 'Joking Relationships in an Industrial Setting'. *American Anthropologist*, 68: 188–93.

TAYLOR, F. W. (1911). *The Principles of Scientific Management*. New York: Harper.

TAYLOR, L., and WALTON, P. (1971). 'Industrial Sabotage: Motives and Meanings', in S. Cohen (ed.), *Images of Deviance*. Harmondsworth: Penguin.

TAYLOR, P., and BAIN, P. (1999). 'An Assembly Line in the Head: Work and Employee Relations in the Call Centre'. *Industrial Relations Journal*, 30: 101–17.

THOMPSON, E. P. (1963). *The Making of the English Working Class*. London: Gollancz.

—— (1978). 'Eighteenth Century English Society: Class Struggle without Classes?' *Social History*, 3: 133–65.

THOMPSON, P. (1989). *The Nature of Work*. London: Macmillan.

TILLY, C., TILLY, L., and TILLY, R. (1975). *Rebellious Century*. Cambridge, Mass.: Harvard University Press.

VAN MAANEN, J. (1991). 'The Smile Factory', in P. Frost *et al.* (eds.), *Reframing Organizational Culture*. Newbury Park, Calif.: Sage.

VARDI, Y., and WEINER, Y. (1996). 'Misbehaviour in Organisations: A Motivational Framework'. *Organisation Science*, 7: 151–65.

—— and WEITZ, E. (2003). *Misbehavior in Organizations*. Mahwah, NJ: Lawrence Erlbaum.

WALBY, S. (1986). *Patriarchy at Work*. Cambridge: Polity Press.

WEBB, M., and PALMER, G. (1998). 'Evading Surveillance and Making Time: An Ethnographic View of the Japanese Factory Floor in Britain'. *British Journal of Industrial Relations*, 36: 611–27.

WEBB, S., and WEBB, B. (1911). *The History of Trade Unionism*. London: Longmans Green.

WESTWOOD, S. (1984). *All Day, Every Day: Factory, Family, Women's Lives*. London: Pluto.

WILLIS, P. (1977). *Learning to Labour*. Aldershot: Saxon House.

WILLMOTT, H. (1993). 'Strength is Ignorance, Slavery is Freedom: Managing Culture in Modern Organisations'. *Journal of Management Studies*, 30/4: 515–52.

WRIGHT, L., and SMYE, M. (1998). *Corporate Abuse*. New York: Simon and Schuster.

PART III

OCCUPATIONS AND ORGANIZATIONS

Introduction

PAMELA S. TOLBERT

The chapters in this Part examine contemporary economic and organizational changes that are analyzed in other Parts of this book, but from a somewhat different vantage point—that of occupations. Shared occupational identities provide a foundation for the recognition of common economic interests (Weber 1968; Weeden 2002). Consequently, occupational membership can serve as an important basis for collective action that is aimed at defining both material and social relationships within organizations (Berlant 1975; Larson 1977; Weber 1968).

Such action may be directly focused on employing organizations, targeted at enhancing occupational members' control of work and setting terms of exchange. This typically takes the form of unionism, although it can also involve less formal arrangements, such as the formation of committees within organizations that are intended to address specific organizational issues raised by occupational members. Alternatively, collective action may focus on the broader political economy, seeking to secure the interests of occupational members by persuading the public that members have unique, specialized knowledge that is needed to carry out certain tasks. Such recognition provides the basis for the creation of licensing and other market closure arrangements that may affect the supply of individuals available to carry out certain kinds of work, and thus broadly affect the economic situation of an occupational group (Abbott 1988; Berlant 1975; Larson 1977; Leicht and Fennell 2001; Weeden 2002).

The latter form of collective action also may shape occupational members' social relations and work arrangements within organizations by providing the underpinning for what Freidson (1994) refers to as the 'occupational principle', a logic that may govern relations within organizations, and which he contrasts with the 'administrative principle'. Although both logics are consistent with rational legal authority (Ritzer 1973; Satow 1975), they are not completely compatible with each other (Gouldner 1973; Scott *et al.* 2000); the dominance of one or the other principle in work organizations is significantly related to how much power and authority individuals have in their daily relationships based on their occupational membership. As a way of setting the chapters of this Part in context, it is useful to consider these two principles in more detail.

Occupational vs. Administrative Principles of Organization

Following the administrative principle, decisions about the organization of work and execution of work tasks are vested in organizational agents based on their hierarchical position. This principle is, of course, a core element in Weber's (1968) depiction of the modern form of organization, the ideal type of bureaucracy. In this context, authority rests on the implicit assumption that the attainment of higher level positions is correlated with knowledge of organizational requirements, resources, and constraints. Thus, individuals at higher hierarchical levels presumably have greater knowledge of organizational needs and capabilities and this knowledge allows them to make efficient and effective (and ergo, legitimate) organizational decisions.

In contrast, according to the occupational principle, decisions about the appropriate bases and form of the division of labor, how to carry out work tasks, and how to evaluate work outcomes are left primarily, if not entirely, in the hands of members of a designated occupational group. Authority, in this context, is based on social and legal recognition of members' unique, specialized knowledge in some substantive area of application, knowledge that is deemed necessary for the effective execution of certain types of tasks (Abbott 1988). Thus, authority rests on the assumptions that only individuals with detailed knowledge of the means and ends relations involved in particular work processes are able to respond to situational requirements of work appropriately, and that such knowledge generally requires membership in a particular occupational group. By token of the latter, organizational agents who are not occupational members are assumed not to possess requisite knowledge needed to make all organizational decisions. Consequently, following this principle entails organizational administrators' concession of relatively greater control to employees, not only over their own work, but over the work of their colleagues, i.e. of supervisory responsibility (Freidson 1986: 134 *et passim*).

The Occupational Principle and Contemporary Organizations

We usually identify such authority with those occupations that have been assigned the honorific title of 'professions', but it is also often invoked in other occupations whose professional status is more questionable—e.g. those that are characterized as creative (musicians, artists, actors, etc.), as well as those that are regarded as highly technical (computer programmers and analysts, data managers, various types of technicians, etc.). Indeed, prior to the advent of scientific management techniques, the occupational principle was also operative in many traditional blue-collar occupations (Braverman 1998). Even today, more recent managerial efforts to collect and codify tacit knowledge held by blue-collar workers, through 'quality circles', 'continuous improvement programs', and similar arrangements, attest to the lurking presence of this principle in these occupations (Graham 1995). Thus, the occupational principle has historically been an important force in shaping work relations within organizations, though to varying degrees and in varying forms across occupational groups. So how does this principle fare in various occupations today?

Other chapters in this Handbook analyze core changes that have taken place in many national economies and organizations over the last quarter century or so. These include broad economic changes, particularly the increases in international competition among business firms that are associated with rapid globalization— i.e. the spread and relocation of production centers across the world and the accompanying creation of worldwide labor markets for many organizations and occupations (see Smith's chapter in Part IV). Changes in work technologies have occurred in tandem with such economic changes: advances in computer-based production technologies have resulted in progressive declines in labor intensity in many organizations, along with increased speed and quality in production; and advances in communication technologies have enabled the coordination of geographically far-flung work sites (see Rubery's chapter in Part I). Concomitantly, common organizational changes have often resulted from pressures for greater efficiency and the diffusion of employment arrangements that are assumed to enhance efficiency and quality (see Strang and Kim's chapter in Part II). These changes have affected different occupations somewhat differently and through different mechanisms.

Overview of Chapters

We begin by considering the impact of these forces on traditional blue-collar occupations. This category spans a wide range of workers, from skilled mechanics and craftsmen to relatively low-skilled mining and construction laborers; but at least since the turn of the century, machine operators and assemblers in factories have served as the prototype of this group. By the mid-twentieth century, a third to nearly a half of all employees in most industrialized economies fell into this occupational category (International Labour Office 1990), but partly as a consequence of technological changes, the relative size of the occupational group has declined steadily throughout the second half of the century. With the notable exception of Japan, in most of the countries where this occupational group once dominated, today less than a quarter of workers fall within this category (International Labour Office 2002).

As Laurie Graham notes in her chapter on production-level, manufacturing employees, the occupational principle, based on workers' tacit knowledge of manufacturing work processes, was severely undercut in the first part of the twentieth century through the application of scientific management techniques. In the wake of its decline, industrial unions emerged, driven by the economic downturns of the 1930s and increasing labor unrest, to protect workers from complete hierarchical domination. Such protection entailed, in part, matching the codification of worker knowledge with the codification of work rules that bounded management's exercise of discretion.

Graham's analysis documents the way in which recent changes that have taken place in many organizations, partly as a consequence of globalization and technological forces, have undercut unions' ability to moderate administrative control. These changes, which Graham refers to as Japanese Manufacturing System Management (because they reflect many Western countries' efforts to emulate Japan's economic success in the 1970s and 1980s by adopting common organizational arrangements), have led to a sharp decline in the implementation of structures that traditionally provided the basis for unions' control over work: delimited and well-defined job classifications, use of seniority as a criterion for career advancement, and contractually specified rules concerning the posting of job openings, overtime arrangements, and use of grievances procedures to handle worker/management disputes. Thus, in this case, although the impact of the decline of the occupational principle on workers' control of work was temporarily stayed by the emergence of unions in the mid-twentieth century, the weakening of unions' power at the end of this century has allowed the logic of the administrative principle to fully dominate. In theory, the contraction in the ranks of lower-level managerial and supervisory employees produced by restructuring and re-engineering activities (see Kunda and Ailon-Souday's chapter in Part II) and the rise of team-based designs in many organizations in the last two decades might be expected to provide a basis for more effective collective action by members of these occupations (see Batt and Doellgast's chapter in Part I). One could imagine how these changes might permit workers to accumulate new, non-managerially controlled knowledge of production processes, and thus serve as a source of occupationally grounded power. However, Graham notes that, although workers have resisted the diminution of the power associated with JSMS both individually and collectively, such efforts have so far been limited and not systematic, and for now, the prospects for workers' ability to resist further dimunition appear dim.

In the next chapter, we turn to an occupational group that has sometimes been referred to as the 'new blue collar', service workers. Stephen Frenkel argues that as a group, they are distinguished from the traditional blue-collar occupations that Graham analyzes by virtue of their production output: namely, services involving assistance, advising, and/or care to individuals or representatives of organizations. On the other hand, he also differentiates them from what are sometimes referred to as 'knowledge workers'—the technical workers discussed in the chapter by Barley and professional workers as analyzed in Hinings's chapter—by the relatively limited range of knowledge and skills required for production. Again, however, this category encompasses a rather broad range of occupational subcategories that vary considerably in required skills and in their potential for the application of the occupational principle.

This is reflected in the variations in management strategies used with these workers. Frenkel describes two key forms, which he refers to as the mass services model, characterized by highly routinized work, low wages, and unstable work arrangements, and the mass customized model, characterized by relatively broadly defined jobs, higher wages, and greater work stability. McDonald's and other fast-food restaurants offer a prototype of the former strategy, while call centers often are taken as typifying the latter. The mass customized model, which involves a greater delegation of decision-making responsibilities to individual workers, is more compatible with the occupational principle. However, there is limited evidence of the development of occupational identities and/or collective organization and action among service workers, even those in jobs characterized by mass customization, as yet.

Frenkel's analysis suggests a complex of factors involved in this, ranging from worker demographics (high proportions of younger workers and/or immigrants) to employer demographics (high proportions of small and marginal businesses) to the nature of the work itself (the ability to attribute work dissatisfaction to customers/clients rather than the employment situation). In this context, it is notable that a large proportion of service workers are female. Various studies have provided evidence that female-dominated jobs are less likely to receive societal recognition of the skills and knowledge that are required of workers, compared to similar, male-dominated jobs (Steinberg 1990). This may undercut the development of occupational identities even among service workers whose jobs are relatively more skilled. In addition, traditional wisdom also suggests that women are more difficult for unions to organize, although whether this is in fact a reflection of unions' investments in organizing female workers or women's own resistance to unionization is subject to debate. Teaching and nursing, however, as two prominent, female-dominated occupations that have become progressively unionized over time may contribute to a shift in older gender distinctions in unionization, and this may, in the long run, have implications for occupationally based efforts to assert greater workplace control by service workers. As with the traditional manufacturing line-workers described by Graham, though, at present the administrative principle appears to be firmly in place as the dominant logic governing the organization of work for this occupational group.

The following chapter by Stephen Barley considers a category of workers in which we might expect the occupational principle to predominate, those occupations whose members are now sometimes fashionably referred to as 'knowledge workers': engineers, scientists, and affiliated technicians. Unfortunately, as his analysis suggests, the various theoretical lenses worn by those who have studied such occupations have made it difficult to assess the empirical validity of this expectation. He begins by chronicling a number of views of technical occupations that have been offered by different theorists over time: oppressed workers desiring the sort of autonomy associated with the occupational principle, but suffering the shackles of the administrative principle in their work; victims of inexorable, cross-occupational pressures by capitalists to reduce labor costs and limit workers' power through 'de-skilling'; beneficiaries and willing accomplices of capital in the devel-opment of de-skilling processes for other workers; and so on. Along the way, he documents how various empirical studies failed to validate the theoretical imagery holding sway at a particular point in time, and thus led to the rise of alternative theoretical images, which in turn were called into question by still other evidence from studies of technical workers. Despite the evolution of theories and evidence, he argues that, overall, we in fact have relatively little knowledge of whether and to what extent technical workers seek and are able to exercise occupationally based control over their work. Just as Frenkel's work emphasizes the high degree of differentiation among service workers, the contemporary comparative studies that Barley describes suggest that the importance of the occupational principle as a governing logic depends on a variety of factors, including the level of develop-ment of an industry, specific occupational segments or areas of specialization, the culture of employing organizations, as well as national definitions of the status of technical work.

In the following chapter, Bob Hinings considers the work organizations of yet another occupational group, those referred to as 'professions'. The effort to clearly define the boundaries between professions and other occupational groups has largely been abandoned (despite hard pursuit in much work in the latter half of the twentieth century). Instead, contemporary research typically reflects the rather broad definition offered by Abbott (1988: 9), who defines professions as 'exclusive occupational groups applying somewhat abstract knowledge to particular cases'. Following this definition, the classification of an occupation as a profession depends on the degree to which members are able to exercise control over how to conduct particular tasks and the evaluation of their outcomes; this is based on social acceptance of the relevance of their specialized and esoteric knowledge—i.e. on the application of the occupational principle in their work organizations. Hinings's analysis of the prototypical form of professionals' work organization, what he refers to as the P^2 (professional partnership) form, suggests that the logic of this principle has indeed traditionally predominated in many occupations we think of as professions—law, accounting, medicine, etc.

However, his analysis also identifies a competing form that has gained promin-ence in many professions over the last thirty years or so, one that has been labeled the managed professional business (MPB). In this form, the logic of the adminis-trative principle plays a more dominant role: decisions about which jobs should be undertaken, what procedures are most appropriate, and what criteria are to be used in evaluating work outcomes are increasingly vested in a subset of organizational members on the basis of their organizational, hierarchically determined expertise, rather than on occupationally based criteria.

Hinings identifies a variety of factors that have contributed to the development of the MPB form, including: the growth in the business services market, which has led to increased interprofessional competition for this market; developments in technology which have contributed to both the routinization of some professional tasks; the ability of clients to access information once confined to members of a particular occupation; and globalization, which has led client organizations to demand a simultaneous increase in the breadth and speed of delivery of professional services. In short, this analysis suggests that even in the work organizations that we might expect to be a bastion of the occupational principle, the administrative principle is gaining ground. However, like the authors of other chapters, Hinings also underscores the importance of considering intra-occupational differences, by occupational segment and by organization, in understanding the logics that govern work organizations. This is an avenue for future research that merits considerably more attention, and the sort of close, detailed analyses of social relations in practice that Barley advocates in his chapter.

In the final chapter, Paul Osterman and Diane Burton focus attention on recent shifts in within-organization career patterns, changes that shed additional light on the blue-collar occupations analyzed by Graham, as well as on an occupational group not yet considered, managers and administrators. Although 'blue collar' and 'white collar' have often been treated as occupational antonyms, these two groups traditionally have shared at least one key occupational feature, careers built around internal labor markets, or a common pattern of structured, upward job moves within an employing organization. While the operation of internal labor markets is typically more explicit and formalized in blue-collar occupations (due to unions' influence, as Graham's chapter suggests), research suggests that their operation is— or was—equally important to the careers of many managerial employees.

In this context, Osterman and Burton's chapter examines evidence of the alleged demise of internal labor markets and the implications of such for understanding contemporary careers. Their careful analysis of different pieces of evidence provides some support for the contention that internal labor markets have declined overall in the last three decades, though perhaps less dramatically than some analysts have suggested; it also suggests that the impact of this decline has fallen largely on one demographic group of workers, middle-aged men. However, the increased use of outsourcing arrangements and temporary workers, which can be viewed as a related aspect of declines in internal labor markets, affects a much broader segment of workers. Likewise, changes in compensation patterns—greater use of pay-for-performance arrangements and a higher proportion of variable pay in total compensation—that are also consistent with the declining influence of internal labor markets have wide-ranging impacts. Taken altogether, the evidence that Osterman and Burton present suggests a gradual, but significant shift in standard employment structures, and in particular, a decline in arrangements that promoted long-term employer–employee relationships.

Conclusion

As a set, the chapters in Part III illuminate some of the impacts of changes in organizations and labor markets suggested by chapters in other Parts of the book, and some of the contradictions in contemporary changes in the workplace. They suggest, on one hand, the increasing prominence and prevalence of the administrative principle as a governing logic—the trumping of occupational, worker-based control of work by hierarchical control—even in occupations that have traditionally been dominated by the occupational principle.

On the other, they also suggest a weakening of the incentives organizations have traditionally used to induce compliance with the administrative principle: fewer, less assured opportunities for continuing employment and upward mobility within a given employer. Declining internal labor markets and greater reliance on short-term employment relations might seem likely to lead to stronger occupational identities, as occupational networks become more important determinants of career patterns (Tolbert 1996). In the current environment of global competition, this would seem to require the formation of much stronger, cross-national occupational groups, and it is not clear whether there is any movement in that direction. But insofar as occupations do represent an important potential source of resistance to increasing administrative domination, understanding the nature of occupations could well become important for understanding how changes in global markets, work and communication technologies, and gender and family roles play out in the evolution of employment arrangements and organizational designs.

References

ABBOTT, A. (1988). *System of Professions*. Chicago: University of Chicago Press.
BERLANT, J. (1975). *Profession and Monopoly*. Berkeley: University of California Press.
BRAVERMAN, H. (1998). *Labor and Monopoly Capitalism: The Degradation of Work in the Twentieth Century*. New York: Monthly Review Press.
FREIDSON, E. (1986). *Professional Powers: A Study of the Institutionalization of Formal Knowledge*. Chicago: University of Chicago Press.

—— (1994). *Professionalism Reborn: Theory, Prophecy and Policy.* Chicago: University of Chicago Press.

GOULDNER, A. (1973). 'Bureaucratic vs. Craft Forms of Organization', in W. V. Heydebrand (ed.), *Comparative Organizations: The Results of Empirical Research.* Englewood Cliffs, NJ: Prentice Hall.

GRAHAM, L. (1995). *On the Line at Subaru-Isuzu: The Japanese Model and the American Worker.* Ithaca, NY: Cornell University Press.

International Labour Office (1990). *Yearbook of Labour Statistics: Retrospective Edition on Population Censuses, 1945–1989.* Geneva: International Labour Office.

—— (2002). *Yearbook of Labour Statistics.* Geneva: International Labour Office.

LARSON, M. S. (1977). *The Rise of Professionalism.* Berkeley: University of California Press.

LEICHT, K. T., and FENNELL, M. L. (2001). *Professional Work: A Sociological Perspective.* Malden, Mass.: Blackwell Publishers.

RITZER, G. (1973). 'Professionalism and the Individual', in E. Freidson (ed.), *The Professions and their Prospects.* Beverly Hills, Calif.: Sage.

SATOW, R. L. (1975). 'Value Rational Authority and Professional Organizations: Weber's Missing Type'. *Administrative Science Quarterly*, 20: 526–31.

SCOTT, W. R., RUEF, M., MENDEL, P., and CARONNA, C. A. (2000). *Institutional Change and Healthcare Organizations: From Professional Dominance to Managed Care.* Chicago: University of Chicago Press.

STEINBERG, R. (1990). 'Social Construction of Skill'. *Work and Occupations*, 17: 449–82.

TOLBERT, P. S. (1996). 'Occupations, Organizations and Boundaryless Careers', in M. B. Arthur and D. M. Rousseau (eds.), *The Boundaryless Career.* New York: Oxford University Press.

WEBER, M. (1968). *Economy and Society: An Outline of Interpretive Sociology,* ed. G. Roth and C. Wittich. New York: Bedminister Press.

WEEDEN, K. A. (2002). 'Why Do Some Occupations Pay More Than Others? Social Closure and Earnings Inequality in the United States.' *American Journal of Sociology*, 108: 55–101.

CHAPTER 14

··

MANUAL WORKERS
CONFLICT AND CONTROL

··

LAURIE GRAHAM

In 1950 production workers in manufacturing constituted about 40 percent of the
total workforce. By 1970 this had dropped to 35 percent; 1990 saw a drop of another
9 percent and by the 2000 census, manufacturing workers made up only 25 percent
of the total US workforce.[1] Although this is a drastic decline, production workers
continue to be an important, relatively highly paid segment of the workforce, with
unionized workers averaging $16.81 to $21.03 per hour and nonunion workers
averaging $15.36 to $17.84.[2] Similarly, job loss within this portion of the workforce
is of concern to other Western industrialized nations partly because of pay levels:
the average European production worker in manufacturing made $18.47 an hour in
2000 (Sparks, Bikoi, and Moglia 2002), and in 2001, manufacturing production
workers in Germany alone averaged $22.86. Comparable workers in the United
Kingdom earned $16.14, and US counterparts averaged $20.32 per hour (http://
www.dol.gov/ilab/media/reports/oiea/chartbook/chart12.htm).

---

[1] Figures based on data from Series D 182-232 in *Historical Statistics of the United States: Colonial
Times to 1970* (U.S. Bureau of Census) and from table 10 in http://www.bls.gov/opub/rtaw/stattab2.
htm. Workers that fall within this occupational category include precision production, craft, and
repair workers, operators, fabricators, and laborers.

[2] From http://www.laborresearch.org website for Labor Research Association, 'Union v. Non-
Union: Average Hourly Earnings in 2001'. Source: *Union Membership and Earnings Data Book* (Bureau
of National Affairs, 2002); data from the Current Population (U.S. Census Bureau).

This chapter examines the nature of recent changes that have taken place in organizational structures in unionized manufacturing settings, changes that contribute to this downward trend. When applied in their most effective manner, the changes limit the ability of this occupational group to exercise its historically strong influence on the shop floor. Workers are finding it difficult to maintain the status quo as job controls that they fought for and enjoyed for decades are under attack and rapidly disappearing.

A new transfer of power is taking place, a transfer from worker to company. Those experiencing the greatest effect are workers with high levels of seniority (length of service with the company) as their ability to transfer to much preferred and less physically demanding jobs is diminished. The historical shop-floor division between newly hired workers and more senior employees is intensified as new workers benefit from the loss of control of more senior workers. This transfer of power and increased divisiveness has occurred because so many companies have adopted a new set of organizational practices, referred to here as Japanese-Style Management System (JSMS), without strong union intervention.

The introduction of JSMS systems has resulted in a wide body of research including studies that question the negative effects of this management system. For example, when Smith (1996) studied the introduction of JSMS into a nonunion white-collar service work setting, she found it had a positive effect for workers as opportunities were created to learn new skills and to provide meaningful input. However, when researchers have focused on unionized, manufacturing settings, especially those in decline, many have found that the negative effects of JSMS on the worker far outweigh the positive (Babson 1995; Fantasia, Clawson, and Graham 1988; Hodson 1995; Rinehart, Huxley, and Robertson 1997). The difference between the two work settings is probably the main reason for the conflicting results. Many unionized workers in declining areas of manufacturing have established long-standing formal and informal shop-floor controls backed up by union strength. Therefore, they seemingly have more to lose than their nonunion counterparts in the expanding, white-collar service industry.

The chapter is divided into six sections. It begins with an introduction to labor process theory and a brief history of shop-floor control. This is followed by a general description of JSMS and its impact on organizational change. How JSMS works to undermine worker control is addressed in the next two sections. These sections examine first, formal controls that union workers established through negotiated contract language and second, informal controls such as solidarity arrangements that workers created to benefit each other. The last two sections include examples of worker resistance and concluding remarks.

14.1 LABOR PROCESS THEORY AND THE HISTORY OF SHOP-FLOOR CONFLICT

To better understand the nature of these changes and the impact that they have on the individual worker, it is useful to frame the discussion in the context of shop-floor control and Labor Process Theory (Braverman 1974; Burawoy 1979; Edwards 1973; Thompson 1983). In a capitalist system, it is necessary for companies to continually find ways to maximize profits. This forces companies to increase productivity by devising methods to capture their workers' 'extra effort'. In such a system, the principle role of a supervisor is, simply put, to get as much work out of each individual as possible; everyone must work as fast as they can every second of every minute. A company's goal is to increase the pace and productivity of each worker, while a worker seeks to exercise some autonomy and control over his or her work, in part to ensure that the pace leaves some time and energy at the end of the day to participate in the lives of family and friends. As this struggle ensues between management and labor, one can see the conflict that emerges on the shop floor between profit maximization and a worker's desire to control how his or her time is spent.

14.1.1 Historical Background

Methods for capturing a worker's 'extra effort' have changed historically with the nature of the production process (Thompson 1983). For example, when the dominant form of production was based on skilled craftwork, craft-workers used their exclusive unions and training hierarchy to maintain control over the speed of work. They used a variety of formal and informal mechanisms. Formal controls were maintained through their unions by deciding on the rate of production. Union members also decided who was allowed to join, learn the craft, and also when a worker was ready to advance. On the shop floor, workers controlled production informally through 'soldiering' (Montgomery 1979). Production workers have not enjoyed this level of control since the advent of Taylorism and mass production.

Production methods changed drastically with Frederick Taylor's system of de-skilling work. His goal was 'to separate the worker's head from his hands', and in this way capture control of the knowledge base of the craft (Taylor 1911). Once that was accomplished, control over hiring and training began to shift from craft-workers and their unions to companies. Henry Ford added to Taylor's methods with the refinement of the assembly line giving employers mechanical control over the pace of work. When workers protested through quitting and sabotage, Ford increased wages and created a system of control based on ever-increasing technology and high wages (Ford 1924; Milkman 1991) known today as Fordism.

As the struggle for control continued, production workers responded to mass production by organizing into industrial unions and forcing companies to recognize them through the union contract. Industrial unions differed from craft unions because they welcomed unskilled as well as skilled workers; therefore the industrial unions' focus shifted from protecting the integrity of the craft to controlling the arbitrary actions of management. The first contracts were fought to gain union recognition and wage increases. Subsequent contracts included seniority clauses, work rules, job classifications, and grievance machinery. These negotiated contract provisions gradually shifted certain aspects of control over production from the company to the workers through union protection. For example, seniority, work rules, and job classifications combined to create a system of 'job ownership'. As a person's seniority increased, he or she was able to bid on a more desirable job. In turn, work rules protected individuals from working outside of their job classification or from someone else performing their job. Such measures interfered with management's flexibility in directing the workforce and bolstered union workers' job security.

Historically, other forms of worker control emerged informally outside the contract. Workers formed 'solidarity arrangements' with coworkers and, sometimes, even supervisors. For example, workers figured out ways of 'doubling up' where one would work doubly fast and take over the job of another for a brief period of time, allowing the other person to rest (Hamper 1986). Another informal method, 'making out' was to work ahead and make quota to create spare time (Burawoy 1985). These systems relied on the tacit approval of supervisors. It was a mutually beneficial system to both workers and supervisors as quotas were met and conflict was kept to a minimum. In order for workers to gain these informal means of control over their time, it was necessary for them to discover faster, more efficient ways of doing their jobs. If they were to use this knowledge to keep control over their spare time, they had to maintain secrecy over their discoveries.

With the advent of JSMS, both the formal union negotiated controls and the informal worker solidarity arrangements are under attack. JSMS is successfully shifting the traditional balance of control that emerged during mass production and Fordism away from the individual worker back to the company.

14.2 The Japanese-Style Management System

JSMS practices are based on the Toyota Production System and have been referred to as Lean Production (Womack, Jones, and Roos 1990), the Japanese Management Model (Graham 1995), Total Quality Management and Continuous Improvement (Deming 1986), and the Japanese Management System (Liker, Fruin, and Adler 1999). They all have several components in common, but only one component seems to occur in each system, the team concept.

Although JSMS is known for its team concept and organizing work around a team, several other features are also important in this system of control. Such features include: (1) a suggestion program used for continuous improvement; (2) highly standardized and recorded work processes with each work station electronically connected to a mainframe computer for purposes of surveillance and monitoring; (3) just-in-time production that eliminates buffers of inventory stock; (4) a corporate culture of 'cooperation' intent on mobilizing workers to identify their interests with company goals rather than identifying with their coworkers; and finally (5) a rigorous system of pre-employment screening with ongoing training in quality control and work standardization.

Another adaptation of the Japanese management system has led to the use of atypical (or 'nonstandard') employees who are hired at lower wages and without benefits enjoyed by core manufacturing workers (Gottfried 2000). In the United States this is reflected in the increasing use of temporary and contract workers in unionized as well as nonunion plants (Graham 1997). Temporary workers under JSMS potentially undermine many of the traditional rights of a union worker and are an effective method for increasing discipline over the workforce.

The application of JSMS varies in terms of which components are used and how the various components are packaged. As stated above, the consequences of JSMS on work life depends on one's position on the seniority list. Under this new management system, the longer you have worked for a company, the more control you have to lose, especially in terms of securing better jobs based on seniority rights.

The use of language plays an important role in instilling JSMS corporate culture and control. Language is used to engage the worker in the company's competitive struggle (Barker 1999; Delbridge 1998; Garrahan and Stewart 1992; Oakes, Townley, and Cooper 1998). For example, company rhetoric extols the virtues of the team player as workers are called upon to join with the company in its battle against the competition (Delbridge 1998; Graham 1995; Rinehart, Huxley, and Robertson 1997). Concurrently, the language of the global marketplace disciplines the workforce as it threatens to eliminate jobs by moving them to lower wage countries.

Workers are told that increasing the intensity of their work will increase profits and thus lead to greater job security. In reality, however, workers experience the implementation of JSMS quite differently as the overriding goal is to continually find ways to decrease the number of workers.

Workers experience job loss under JSMS in two ways. First, the goal and philosophy of JSMS is continuous improvement, manifested in a system that constantly uncovers methods for cutting jobs from the workforce (Graham 1995).[3] This forces the remaining workers to speed up their pace and work even more efficiently. Workers find that under the new work system they are often 'working' themselves right out of a job. Second, working at the fast, repetitive pace required under JSMS can lead to permanent repetitive stress injuries and job loss due to the inability to do the work (Babson 1995; Besser 1996; Graham 1998). In a recent discussion the author had with a group of union autoworkers, they described their reaction to continuous improvement and company pressures to increase their output:

If you work to full capacity, they only push for more.

I'd be working myself out of a job.

I want to be able to do things with my kids after work. At this pace I won't have anything left.

These comments reflect the daily conflict between workers and management as companies search for new ways to capture a worker's extra effort.

Threats to relocate production in lower wage nations are often used to force workers to accept JSMS. Outside pressures are also used to force both company managers and workers to adhere to JSMS practices. For example, in order to fully participate in today's global marketplace, US manufacturers are increasingly forced to comply with global auditing systems such as International Organization for Standardization commonly referred to as ISO.

To gain and retain ISO certification, company managers and workers are required to comply with many JSMS practices. ISO constantly monitors industry 'best practices' to develop benchmarks for all companies within the same industry. In order for ISO to make meaningful comparisons, companies have instituted work standardization and record-keeping processes found in JSMS. Under ISO guidelines, each employee is required to record the exact details of his or her job on standardized work sheets. Through mandatory ISO compliance, a worker's knowledge of a particular job process can be transferred not only from worker to company, but also from company to industry. Theoretically, the most efficient work practices across an entire industry are standardized, recorded, and implemented. At the same time, this external pressure, which pushes companies to tighten up and enforce the most efficient work practices, greatly enhances a company's ability to move work overseas as each job has been recorded in the

---

[3] This is referred to as the philosophy of *kaizen* in Japanese transplants.

most intricate detail. Consequently, both JSMS and ISO compliance produce disciplining effect on the workforce. Workers find themselves forced to accommodate outside forces that may ultimately lead to the extinction of their jobs. Such global competitive pressures create a compelling reason for companies to force changes in the traditional union contract and to attack long-standing shop-floor solidarity arrangements.

14.3 FORMAL CONTROLS: THE UNION CONTRACT

Workers located in US manufacturing plants that were unionized during the heyday of mass production are experiencing the greatest challenges. This is particularly true in highly automated, unionized sectors such as auto, steel, rubber, and meatpacking. All of these industries have undergone extensive restructuring and plant closings due to global economic competition. Because of these larger economic forces and the low level of unionization in the United States, workers have had to accept major changes in their union contracts—changes that weaken their ability to defend their traditional means of control over work. This represents a shift from collective to individual forms of regulation and bargaining.

With JSMS, industrial relations are no longer guided by the sanctity of the union contract. The traditional contract is replaced by a 'living document' and industrial relations are subsumed under a company philosophy of cooperation. This philosophy rests on the notions that workers should be flexible and decisions ought to be made by 'consensus' in accordance with company goals. Some of the more radical changes in the contract include reducing the number of job classifications, changing long-standing work rules, shifting the application of seniority, and undermining the strength of the grievance procedure.

14.3.1 Job Classifications and Seniority

Prior to JSMS, in traditional union manufacturing settings, contractually defined job classifications often evolved into highly specialized systems of worker control. Key to control was a worker's position on the company's seniority list. For example, unions traditionally negotiate a clause in their contracts that makes seniority one of the most important factors in deciding job transfers and promotions. In this way, the more seniority a worker accumulates, the greater his or her choice of jobs. Also, in cases of layoff and recall, the person with higher seniority is the last to leave and the first to be called back to work. This has meant that, as workers aged and accrued more seniority, they were able to bid on less demanding jobs and continue working at the company until retirement. Many workers refer to this use of seniority as 'buying a job'. In this way, one can see the economic as well as the cultural significance of the principle of seniority. To many it has been as important in the unionized workplace as wages—a form of 'job ownership'. Seniority has led to greater job security, higher wages, and greater individual control as workers are able to bid on more appealing jobs during their tenure at a plant.

In a JSMS plant, one of the first features to disappear in the union contract is the system of multiple job classifications. Under the most extreme form of JSMS, all production workers generally fall under a single classification, thus eliminating an individual's 'right' to bid on a better job. With JSMS, workers are attached to a team rather than a specific job and are required to perform multiple tasks within the team. The goal is for every member of a team to become proficient in all jobs within that team's domain, enabling workers to rotate among those jobs or similar jobs. If someone is missing from the team, the other team members are required to 'pick up that work'. Additionally, because there is only one job classification, unless specifically prevented through contract language, the company is able to move workers to other jobs and teams as it sees fit. This constant threat of change is often disruptive and can be very stressful. Under traditional rules, this could not occur as a worker would not be forced to work outside of his or her specific job classification. This is but one aspect of the type of flexibility companies have attained through the team and JSMS.

One can see from the above example why workers with more seniority tend to resent JSMS and the team concept, while workers with very little seniority often prefer it. In the short run, they gain some power from JSMS at the expense of more senior workers. On the other hand, as these new workers gain more seniority and become aware that they have less and less control over the increasing pace of work, this may change.

14.3.2 Work Rules

In traditional unionized manufacturing plants, work rules are clearly spelled out in the contract and obeyed by all parties. If a supervisor ignores one of the rules, a worker can file a grievance against the company for violating the contract. Many work rules have evolved to address favoritism and prevent arbitrary actions by management. A few examples of such work rules include how job openings are filled, how much notice workers must be given in order to work overtime, when and how long breaks will occur, and what work is performed within a particular job classification.

Under JSMS, many work rules, such as those noted above, have disappeared. Nebulous statements about behaving according to company philosophy and mission have taken their place. These are often followed by a list of team member responsibilities focusing on individuals' behavior and attitudes. For example, the following is one of the 'absolutes' for team members under a typical JSMS contract. (Although the contract language contained in this chapter is hypothetical, the examples are based on examination of real life contracts.)

Team members must accept responsibility for personal behavior, support and abide by reasonable standards of conduct and work within Company guidelines and philosophies.

Although this appears to be a perfectly reasonable rule, none of these guidelines are spelled out in the contract, and specific work rules—especially those related to the job classification system have disappeared. In the absence of clearly defined rules, workers are once again vulnerable to arbitrary actions by management. In this context, the significance of seniority and its protection against such things as favoritism is substantially eroded.

14.3.3 Grievance Procedures

Contract language involving grievance procedures has also changed. First, the definition of what constitutes a grievance is often very narrow under JSMS. Second, workers are encouraged to represent their own case to management instead of having union representation at the first step in the grievance process. Finally, many potential grievance issues have been eliminated from outside, binding arbitration.

The following examples of grievance procedures are from a single manufacturing plant that switched from a traditional contract to a JSMS contract after it was spun off from a large corporation. First is an example of the initial step of the traditional grievance procedure, when a worker first believes that he or she has a legitimate grievance against the company. This step defines what constitutes a grievance according to the contract and where the worker should turn for help to resolve the situation.

Traditional Language: Step One
Any employee having a grievance, or one designated member of a group having a grievance, should first take the grievance up with the foreman who will attempt to adjust it. *Any employee may request the foreman to call the union steward to handle a specified grievance with the foreman. The foreman will send for the steward without undue delay and without further discussion of the grievance.* (All emphases in contract language are the author's.)

If the grievance is not adjusted by the foreman, it shall be reduced to writing and signed by the employee involved and a copy given to the foreman. The steward shall then take the grievance up with higher supervision.

The first sentence provides a broad definition of a grievance by not limiting it to any specifically defined items. It also gives a worker the right to file a 'group' grievance as well as a grievance involving an individual problem. The highlighted sentence is important because it gives the grievant the right to union representation at the very beginning stage before the company has an opportunity to interrogate the worker.

What follows is typical grievance language found in a team concept plant using JSMS principles.

JSMS Language: Step One

Team members who have issues or disputes concerning the meaning, interpretation or application of the Agreement (including whether discipline or discharge was for just cause) must bring such issues or disputes to the attention of the Area Leader for their Work Team within 3 working days of the occurrence giving rise to the dispute. The Area Leader will then have 24 hours to initiate steps to resolve it (union stewards may participate as required/ requested).

Team Members who have issues concerning other day-to-day matters not involving the interpretation of this Agreement may bring those issues to the attention of their Area Leader, who will then attempt to facilitate resolution of the issue within the Work Team using the conflict resolution principles: (see 'Consensus Process' below).

Several items are important in this grievance procedure. First, the definition of the grievance is limited to the language contained in the contract itself. If a worker has any problem that is not covered by contract language, he or she is required to take it through the company's Consensus Process. The dispute does not constitute an official grievance and the union is never involved. When one considers that this contract is a total of 25 pages (compared to the 510 pages contained in the former local contract before the plant was sold and JSMS was instituted), the definition of what constitutes a grievance is indeed very narrow. The second item of importance is that the company is not required to include the worker's union steward at this step.[4] Additionally, according to this language, if the worker has a problem that is not related to discipline or discharge, such as a problem with workload, unequal treatment, or even harassment, it is not clear that the company will consent to involve the union at this point. There is nothing to stop the company from considering it a 'day-to-day problem' and requiring the worker to attempt to solve it through the company's Consensus Process.

---

[4] Under federal labor law, if discipline or discharge is a possibility then, if the worker specifically requests union representation, the company is required to summon union representation before any further discussion can take place. (Note that it is the responsibility of the worker to know that this legal right exists. If he or she does not make the request, the company can legally proceed without the worker gaining union protection.)

Some sort of consensus process is usually found in a JSMS negotiated contract. The following Consensus Process section illustrates typical language found in many JSMS contracts.

14.4 CONSENSUS PROCESS

The parties recognize that adversarial relationships between Team Members and management or between fellow Team Members are not compatible with the Work Team Concept and can only interfere with the achievement of the company's ultimate mission and vision. Accordingly, the parties agree that the consensus process, as outlined below, should be the primary method for making decisions and resolving disagreements.

1. Resolution is achieved through the joint efforts of the parties in discovering creative solutions to the day-to-day issues within the company.
2. The joint solutions must provide a high level of acceptance for all parties and support the overall business needs and objectives.
3. Once an agreement is reached, the parties must be totally committed to the solution and its implementation.
4. Different viewpoints are encouraged; however, the parties have an obligation to work through concerns and reach a consensus on the issue.
5. The joint effort is aimed at discovering the best decision/resolution within the context of the company's philosophy and mission.

Several features of the above JSMS language in this example are noteworthy. First, although the process is referred to as consensus, decisions must support 'overall business needs and objectives' and must fall within the company's 'philosophy and mission'. This has the effect of unfairly shaping the outcome, giving the company's interest undue weight over individual concerns. Second, whenever a union is not involved in representing an employee, an unequal power relation exists, putting the worker in a vulnerable position. Finally, when an individual tries to negotiate with an organization that has control over his or her work life, the idea that a consensus can be reached that is truly equitable is ludicrous. Operating by consensus reinforces discipline and control within a workforce. This is especially true when backed up by the indirect controls that emerge from coworker peer pressure and team conformity in a team concept plant (Barker 1999; Delbridge 1998; Garrahan and Stewart 1992; Graham 1995).

In a traditional contract the second step of the grievance procedure occurs after the union steward has made a verbal argument with the immediate supervisor but is unable to reach a settlement. The grievance is then formalized by putting it in writing and it progresses to a higher level within the company and the union. At each step, the union and company meet as adversaries on equal footing—the union presenting its grievance and the company presenting its side of the issue. In this format the worker's grievance is argued from a position of power. The following is an example of step two:

Traditional Contract: Step Two

If the case is not adjusted at Step One, it may be referred to the Union Grievance Committee. The committee will further investigate the grievance and the grievance will be taken up with Local Management within 15 working days. Written answers will be given by the Management to all written grievances presented by the Grievance Committee.

In the above traditional contract language, the grievance has become the property of the union: it is no longer the individual worker's complaint. The union as an organization is fighting for the issue and will support its progress toward a possible resolution.

The following is step two of the JSMS contract:

JSMS Contract: Step Two

Issues not resolved at Step One may be appealed to the Plant Review Board. The party seeking appeal (or his/her designated representative) must make a written request for appeal within 24 hours of the Step One decision in order to have the matter reviewed by the *Plant Review Board*. The Board will then have 48 hours to attempt to resolve the matter.

The Board will consist of the Team members' Union Steward, the company Personnel Representative, Area Leader, and Plant Manager or his designee.

With respect to day-to-day issues not concerning the interpretation of this Agreement, the Plant Review Board has the right to return to the Team issues that should have been resolved at the Team level for further application of conflict resolution principles.

In the above JSMS contract language, the grievance is submitted to an in-house committee or 'board' at Step Two. Note that representation on the Board is unequal, with three company representatives and only one union representative, the worker's steward. Also, if the worker has not involved the union in the previous step, then this will be the first time that the problem will have come to the union's attention. In the meantime, the company has had ample opportunity to investigate and prepare its case. The fact that the company has already been actively involved and has interviewed the worker without union representation potentially contaminates the process and shifts the outcome in the company's direction. Finally, when the union becomes a member of the company's appeals board, it can easily undermine its role as adversary. Instead of defending the rights of the worker up front, the union finds itself strapped by the language of the company's Consensus Process. Delbridge found a similar result with the 'company advisory board' (or CAB) in his study of a fictionally named British plant under Japanese ownership (Delbridge 1998: 166–74).

The third step in a traditional contract is usually the point at which the union decides if the grievance merits arbitration by a neutral outside party chosen by both the company and the union. The arbitrator's decision will be final and binding to both parities:

Traditional Contract: Step Three
If the grievance is not adjusted at Step Two the union Grievance Committee will further discuss and investigate the grievance. If it believes it has grounds to appeal the Plant Management decision ... the Committee will prepare the grievance to be submitted to an outside neutral third party agreeable to both Management and Union for final and binding arbitration.

The third step in a JSMS plant differs drastically as illustrated by the following example:

JSMS Contract: Step Three
Issues that are not resolved at Step Two by the Plant Review Board may be appealed to the Policy Review Committee for its review within 24 hours of the Board's decision. The Policy Review Committee will consist of the Personnel Representative, a representative from Human Resources, and the designated representatives from the Shop Committee.

Decisions of the Policy Review Committee regarding issues that do not involve the meaning, interpretation or application of this Agreement shall be final and shall not be appealable to arbitration.

Disputes concerning the meaning, interpretation, or application of this Agreement (including whether discipline or discharge was for cause), which are not resolved by the preceding steps, may be taken to arbitration.

During the third step in the JSMS contract, the grievance progresses to a second in-house committee that reviews the decision made by the first in-house committee. This is where the fact that the definition of what constitutes a grievance, and the fact that it has been narrowly defined, really come into play. If the Committee determines that the problem is not a dispute over contract language, a disciplinary action, or actual discharge, then the Committee's decision is final. There is no chance for the issue to go before an outside, independent arbitrator.

14.5 INFORMAL CONTROLS: SOLIDARITY ARRANGEMENTS

Under mass production, workers have developed many informal controls outside of the formally, negotiated union contract. These informal controls are particularly the targets of attack under JSMS. Informal mechanisms referred to above, such as 'doubling up' and 'making out', are methods that workers have used to maintain control over how their own 'extra effort' is spent. JSMS has a philosophy of continuous improvement that is aimed at appropriating the tricks and secrets that a worker has devised to save and control a portion of his or her time.

Virtually all continuous improvement programs begin with some mechanism for soliciting worker suggestions. Workers are sometimes encouraged to participate with rewards, but more often they are expected to participate simply because continuous improvement is the company's mission and philosophy and they are contractually bound to do so. Basically, the program works by soliciting suggestions from workers on how to make their own workstations more efficient. Suggestions are reviewed by management on a regular basis and changes are implemented that save time and money. On the surface, this seems very appealing and is often referred to in JSMS literature as 'worker empowerment', since workers contribute their ideas to the company and their suggestions are given serious consideration. In reality, however, the goal of continuous improvement is to get rid of jobs, not to empower the workforce. This is another example of the importance that language and company rhetoric play in JSMS.

Continuous improvement aims to capture the 'secrets' that a worker has learned from doing his or her job to make it more efficient. These tricks enable an individual to work ahead and gain a few seconds of time. By incorporating continuous improvement as a company mission and then contractually binding workers to comply with that mission, JSMS moves a step beyond Taylorism in its attempt to gain control over a worker's creative knowledge. In mass production plants before JSMS, a worker's knowledge about ways of saving time was safely guarded and used to the benefit of that individual worker. Continuous improvement not only captures those secrets for gaining spare time, once management appropriates that knowledge, it controls when and where those ideas are implemented (Graham 1995).

In addition to the suggestion program, workers are forced to make their workstations more efficient through the use of sophisticated technology that closely monitors each worker's and team's progress. One example of such technology is found in assembly lines that use the Andon system. With this system each workstation is connected to a mainframe computer by means of a yellow warning device. When a worker runs into trouble on the line she pulls on the yellow cord located at her station. Once pulled, several things happen in rapid succession. First, the team leader is alerted to the problem. Second, a switch is triggered in the computer system recording which team and station pulled the cord. Third, the team leader runs over to the station, takes it over and pulls the same yellow cord to prevent the line from stopping.

The following example illuminates how management uses this information to eliminate jobs and increase the pace of work. As part of continuous improvement, supervisors and/or engineers meet on a regular basis to review the suggestions turned in by workers. Their goal is to figure out how to combine those suggestions and ultimately eliminate a job. In this way, they are continuously improving productivity and gradually downsizing the workforce. Company managers ascertain which teams are best able to handle the loss of a team member through the record keeping provided by the Andon system. The team that seldom pulls a yellow cord is targeted. A worker is transferred off that team and the rest of the team members are forced to juggle their own processes so that they can incorporate the extra load. The team will undoubtedly pull the yellow cord numerous times as it figures out the best way to absorb the extra work. Finally, however, it will meet with success and stop pulling the cord. Ironically, the team's success in incorporating the extra work makes it more vulnerable to future adjustments and speedup. In this way, continuous improvement leads to speedup and is directly forced upon workers under JSMS.

Andon and its computer system create a kind of 'workstation bookkeeping', a ledger of each individual's failings and capabilities. In turn, that information is used to control the output of the team. One might compare this type of record keeping with Foucault's concept of internal accounting as a mechanism of control and close surveillance (McKinlay and Starkey 1998: 6).

14.6 WORKER RESISTANCE/RESPONSE

As part of the ongoing struggle for control, workers have discovered informal solidarity arrangements to combat speedup caused by JSMS. For example, teammates will cooperate with each other to make certain that the yellow warning devise is triggered on a regular basis to discourage the company from increasing their workload. In other cases, workers with high seniority within a team have simply not cooperated with rules of rotation by choosing one workstation and refusing to rotate to other jobs. Workers also have been found to manipulate a company piece-rate system to resist speedup (Delbridge 1998). Such arrangements disrupt company efforts to increase flexibility over assigning work and undermine continuous improvement speedups.

On a more formal level, some union contracts have begun to address both the role and the process for choosing the team leader in an effort to shape the nature of the team—to change it from a company-centered team to a more worker-centered team (Babson 1995). Other locals have gone out on strike to force the company to hire additional workers to address injuries from overwork and inability to take time off (Graham 1998).

These formal and informal responses are encouraging signs and will surely continue as part of the ongoing struggle on the shop floor. However, these do not represent a unified, coherent union movement response. The author argues that most unions have no idea of the potential havoc that this system can wreck on the shop floor both in terms of divisiveness and loss of individual control. One case in point is the AFL–CIO's support of the 'High Performance' workplace (Baugh 1994). The AFL–CIO lists five principles for a model work organization:

1. Reject the traditional dichotomy between thinking and doing. Workers are in the best position to decide how their work can most efficiently and effectively be accomplished.
2. Redesign jobs to include a greater variety of skills and tasks and, more importantly, greater responsibility for the ultimate output of the organization.
3. Substitute a flatter management structure for the traditional multilayered hierarchy of work organization.
4. Ensure workers, through their unions, a decision-making role at all levels of the enterprise, not just the workplace level.
5. Distribute the rewards realized from transforming the work organization of equitable terms agreed upon through negotiations between labor and management (Baugh 1994: 16).

None of the above principles prevent changes in contract language and the use of continuous improvement tactics that weaken the worker's position. They do not address how JSMS undermines solidarity through peer pressure and generational divisions, or how it cuts jobs through information collection and close surveillance. Finally, the 'high-performance' workplace does not address the negative effects on the union's role in the grievance procedure. Delbridge (1998: 174–7) found the same lack of organized, adversarial response to be true of the union movement in Great Britain.

14.7 Conclusions

Economic pressures from global competition, combined with pressures for companies to implement industrial benchmarking and work standards, has led to a historical shift in the ongoing struggle for shop-floor control for production workers in manufacturing. One can see that without direct union intervention members of this occupational group will continue to lose controls that they have enjoyed for decades in unionized settings. However, with the low level of unionization in the United States and weak and unenforceable labor laws, it is difficult to anticipate what the union response will be.

The formal changes that JSMS brings to the union contract truly affect the quality of life of the individual worker. The narrow definition of a grievance limits what workplace issues can be resolved potentially in favor of workers' interests. The consensus process undermines the adversarial role of the union on the workers' behalf. Workers are no longer able to use their seniority to ensure their continued ability to stay with a company. Finally, close surveillance and worker 'involvement' through continuous improvement undermines traditional solidarity arrangements that protect workers from speedup and overwork. Without aggressive union intervention, the transformation in worker control will continue as each individual workplace transforms itself into a 'model of cooperation and empowerment' under the Japanese-Style Management System.

REFERENCES

BABSON, S. (1995). 'Whose Team? Lean Production at Mazda U.S.A.', in S. Babson (ed.), *Lean Work and Exploitation in the Global Auto Industry*. Detroit: Wayne State University Press.

BARKER, J. (1999). *The Discipline of Teamwork: Participation and Concertive Control*. Thousand Oaks, Calif.: Sage Publications.

BAUGH, R. (1994). *Changing Work: A Union Guide to Workplace Change*. Washington, DC: AFL-CIO Human Resources Development Institute.

BESSER, T. (1996). *Team Toyota: Transplanting the Toyota Culture to the Camry Plant in Kentucky*. Albany: State University of New York Press.

BRAVERMAN, H. (1974). *Labor and Monopoly Capital*. New York: Monthly Review Press.

BURAWOY, M. (1979). *Manufacturing Consent: Changes in the Labor Process under Monopoly Capitalism*. Chicago: University of Chicago Press.

——(1985). *The Politics of Production*. New York: Verso.

DELBRIDGE, R. (1998). *Life on the Line in Contemporary Manufacturing: The Workplace Experience of Lean Production and the 'Japanese' Model*. Oxford: Oxford University Press.

DEMING, W. E. (1986). *Out of the Crisis: Quality, Productivity, and Competitive Position*. Cambridge: Cambridge University Press.

EDWARDS, R. (1973). *Contested Terrain*. New York: Basic Books.

FANTASIA, R., CLAWSON, D., and GRAHAM, G. (1988). 'A Critical View of Worker Participation in American Industry'. *Work and Occupations*, 15: 468–88.

FORD, H. (1924). *My Life and Work*. London: Heinemann.

GARRAHAN, P., and STEWART, P. (1992). *The Nissan Enigma: Flexibility at Work in a Local Economy*. London: Mansell Publishing Limited.

GOTTFRIED, H. (2000). *The Weakness of a Strong Breadwinner Model: Part-time Work and Female Labour Force Participation in Germany and Japan*. Detroit: College of Urban, Labor and Metropolitan Affairs, Wayne State University.

GRAHAM, L. (1995). *On the Line at Subaru-Isuzu: The Japanese Model and the American Worker.* Ithaca, NY: ILR/Cornell University Press.

—— (1997). 'Permanently Temporary: The Japanese Model and the Reproduction of Social Control', in R. Hodson (ed.), *Research in the Sociology of Work: The Globalization of Work,* 6. Greenwich, Conn.: JAI Press.

—— (1998). 'Worker Health in Two Auto Assembly Plants: A Comparison of Policy in Union vs. Nonunion Environments', in S. Babson and H. Juarez Nunez (eds.), *Confronting Change: Auto Labor and Lean Production in North America.* Benimerita Universidad Autonoma de Puebla and Detroit: Wayne State University Press.

HAMPER, B. (1986). *Rivethead: Tales from the Assembly Line.* New York: Time Warner.

HODSON, R. (1995). 'Worker Resistance: An Underdeveloped Concept in the Sociology of Work'. *Economic and Industrial Democracy,* 16: 79–110.

LIKER, J., FRUIN, W. M., and ADLER, P. (1999). *Remade in America: Transplanting and Transforming Japanese Management Systems.* New York: Oxford University Press.

McKINLAY, A., and STARKEY, K. (eds.) (1998). *Foucault, Management and Organization Theory: From Panopticon to Technologies of Self.* London: Sage Publications.

MILKMAN, R. (1991). 'Labor and Management in Uncertain Times: Renegotiating the Social Contract', in A. Wolfe (ed.), *America at Century's End.* Berkeley: University of California Press.

MONTGOMERY, D. (1979). *Worker's Control in America: Studies in the History of Work, Technology, and Labor Struggles.* Cambridge: Cambridge University Press.

OAKES, L., TOWNLEY, B., and COOPER, D. (1998). 'Business Planning as Pedagogy: Language and Control in a Changing Institutional Field'. *Administrative Science Quarterly,* 43/2: 257–92.

RINEHART, J., HUXLEY, C., and ROBERTSON, D. (1997). *Just Another Car Factory? Lean Production and Its Discontents.* Ithaca, NY: Cornell University Press.

SMITH, V. (1996). 'Employee Involvement, Involved Employees: Participative Work Arrangements in a White-Collar Service Occupation'. *Social Problems,* 43: 166–79.

SPARKS, C., BIKOI, T., and MOGLIA, L. (2002). 'A Perspective on U.S. and Foreign Compensation Costs in Manufacturing'. *Monthly Labor Review,* 125/6: 36–50.

TAYLOR, F. (1911). *The Principles of Scientific Management.* New York: Harper.

THOMPSON, P. (1983). *The Nature of Work: An Introduction to Debates on the Labour Process* (2nd edn). Atlantic Highlands, NJ: Humanities Press International.

WOMACK, J. P., JONES, D., and ROOS, D. (1990). *The Machine that Changed the World.* New York: Rawson Associates.

CHAPTER 15

SERVICE WORKERS IN SEARCH OF DECENT WORK

STEPHEN J. FRENKEL

This paper is dedicated to the memory of Susan Eaton,
service-work scholar and friend for too short a time.

15.1 INTRODUCTION

SERVICE workers represent a large and growing proportion of the workforce. They come a close second (17.9 percent) in size to professionals and related (paraprofessional and technical) workers (18.4 percent) (Hecker 2001: 60). Moreover, this is an underestimate because some administrative and clerical workers and many routine sales workers are in fact service workers. In addition, service workers have grown faster than the total workforce. In the decade to 1998, service workers grew by 21.5 percent, posting the fourth largest growth after professionals (31.7 percent), technical workers (27.6 percent), and marketing and sales personnel (23.8 percent). Future growth is likely to be even stronger. Service workers are projected to grow

Thanks to Rose Batt and Randy Hodson for pointing me to some valuable ethnographic materials and to Pam Tolbert and Markus Groth for useful comments on a previous draft.

the second fastest, after professionals. Taking into account the relative size of the employment pool, labor turnover, and growth, service work is likely to be the largest source of employment generation through 2010 (Hecker 2001: 64).

Job growth is one element of decent work; the other element is job quality, i.e. extrinsically and intrinsically rewarding work (ILO 2001). From this perspective, the future is less promising. In general, service work is comparatively low paid and less secure than most other kinds of work. US official data show that service workers earn the least, on average, of all occupational groups (US DOL 2001a: 1–9). And service workers typically receive lower fringe benefits than workers in other major occupational categories (see Pierce 2001: 1509). Indeed, persons engaged in service work comprise the largest single occupational category of those earning below the official poverty level (US DOL 2002a: 1–2).

Survey evidence spanning four recent years (1996, 1998, 2000, and 2002) shows that the average median tenure for service workers is more than one-third less than that for workers in all occupations (US DOL 2002b: table 6). This is related to a relatively high proportion of service workers who are employed as contingency workers (i.e. temporary or casual workers). Part-time work is also common: 45.4 percent of women service workers are part-timers compared to 28.7 percent men (US DOL 2001b: table 4). In some service industries, for example, hospitality and retail, standard full-time work is the exception rather than the rule (Walsh 1990). In short, much service work is not well rewarded and is emotionally exacting (Ehrenreich 2001); service workers are one of the major risk bearers of a more fragmented, less egalitarian society (Beck 2000: 80–91).

Before continuing, let me clarify what I mean by service work. I use three main criteria. First, service work is interactive; it is a front-line activity, involving workers serving, assisting, advising, or caring for individuals or representatives of organizations. Although not always appropriate (e.g. in custodial or professional settings), I will refer to these persons as customers. Second, service work is not especially complex; it is located at the lower range of the skills, creativity, and knowledge continuum (Frenkel *et al.* 1999: 66). Third, service work contributes to the informal or formal economy: it is paid work.

Service work varies in content and technology, extent of worker discretion, and context in which it is undertaken. Some service work is highly dependent on technology (e.g. call centers and airline ticketing), but this is less true for most personal services such as waiting, fitness training, and nursing assistant work. Within the same technological environment, workers may work from variable locations including home and customer sites. This depends on job design, which also influences the amount of discretion that service workers are expected to exercise (Batt 2000). The type of controlling organization is a relevant institutional factor—whether a privately or publicly owned company, a not-for-profit, or a state-owned institution—that shapes management's values and goals and hence influences work organization and service workers' responses (Eaton 2000).

Four main implications follow from this analysis. First, the customer is a central figure in relations between management and employees (Frenkel *et al.* 1999; Leidner 1993). Although much service work is structured to standardize and coordinate the interests of the three parties, where service workers enjoy more discretion, they can exercise some power over management through their ability to satisfy customers. Second, variations in reliance on the use of workers' discretion to satisfy customers results in differences in the nature of management control over service workers. Routine service workers are controlled by a combination of technological and supervisory control, while service workers engaged in more complex work are subject to socionormative control (culture and peer norms) characteristic of knowledge work settings (Frenkel *et al.* 1999: 148–54). Third, customer involvement broadens management expectations of employees. Tensions may arise over the way workers present themselves physically (aesthetic labor) and how emotion is used to further the organization's goals (emotional labor). Fourth, since it is impossible to stockpile service labor to meet swings in customer demand, service workers are expected to be flexible. This takes several forms: shift working, working in a temporary capacity, altering work hours to match demand, and intensifying work effort (Oliva 2002).

As we shall see, management has pursued a variety of strategies to organize service work. The most salient differences are associated with cost-reducing and value-adding approaches. The former is embodied in what I refer to as the mass services model. Standardization and tight control over narrowly prescribed work are emphasized (Frenkel *et al.* 1999: 13–14; Ritzer and Stillman 2001). Work associated with this model is relatively low paid and unfulfilling; in short, it is indecent work (ILO 2001).

In contrast, when firms adopt a value-adding approach by providing customized, quality service, they rely on the discretion of front-line service workers. This mass customized form of work organization, which is associated with more complex work (within limits), is less hierarchical than the mass service organizational form. Control is based on prevailing norms and is more self-regulated. Workers employed in this kind of organization are more assertive and are better off than their mass service counterparts. Nevertheless, their pay and employment conditions remain well below those of knowledge workers. Much of this work too is indecent. Consequently, I shall argue that service workers in the information-based, service society are analogous to the proletariat of industrial capitalism, demonstrating a similar heterogeneity in the detail of their work but often lacking a collective occupational identity.

The chapter is organized in three sections. The first section focuses on the way management organizes service work, including a brief overview of management strategies and tactics, and their implications for service workers. The second section examines workers' experience of work, including strategies used to defend and promote workers' interests. The concluding section points to feasible strategies aimed at promoting the growth of decent service work, thereby contributing to a more humane and egalitarian society.

Before proceeding, a caveat is worth entering. I have relied mainly on US data because the United States is the largest and most technologically advanced country and is also the largest source of relevant information. Even so, there is no comprehensive set of American service worker studies. I therefore draw heavily on research focusing on fast-food workers to highlight mass service work and call center employees to illustrate mass customized work. Any generalizations that I make are therefore provisional and should be regarded as working hypotheses.

15.2 THE WORK OF MANAGEMENT: RATIONALIZING AND CUSTOMIZING

Standardized practices limit costs and provide service consistency. These attributes help to differentiate high-volume, low-price service providers from their competitors targeting different segments of the same market; examples include organizations in the fast foods, supermarket, large-scale entertainment, and three-star hotel sectors. In these settings, service workers are expected to demonstrate the right attitude toward customers—being friendly and attentive—but their jobs are relatively simple, based on scripts and procedures devised by management. These workers must also be flexible: being available for work virtually on demand, and hence prepared to vary their work schedules in accordance with changes in market demand.

In this *mass service model*, jobs are therefore often narrow in task range and nonstandard (part-time and/or on short-term contract). Wages tend to be low and there is minimal training (Buchanan 2002; Stack 2002). Many of these jobs—for example, cleaning, food serving, and security guard work—have very limited promotion opportunities.[1] However, such work does transmit useful skills to young employees, including timekeeping, multitasking, teamworking, managing interpersonal relations, and planning (Buchanan 2002: 60; Stack 2002: 33). Nevertheless, these mass service employment conditions, especially when coupled with a predominantly young workforce, lead to high levels of labor turnover (see later). Although some firms have attempted to remedy this by offering limited benefits,

---

[1] Large brand fast-food outlets are an exception. Workers can be promoted to 'crew trainer', and then to 'crew chief' and to 'swing manager'. Leidner (2002: 19) notes that most fast-food workers do not wish to remain in the industry and are therefore not interested in promotion.

such as service bonuses, medical insurance, and promotion opportunities, these additional elements are often unattractive to employees mainly interested in higher pay and better working conditions (Leidner 2002: 25).[2]

The mass service form of work organization is not typical of all service work. Customer centrality means that anticipating and satisfying customer needs can be a competitive advantage. Adding value through service quality is a strategy often favored by specialized, smaller service providers—e.g. boutique stores, fine dining restaurants, nightclubs, and fitness training firms. Some larger service organizations such as five-star hotels, casinos, and nursing homes also favor this approach. Front-line work in this *mass customized model* that is not strongly shaped by technology is appropriately described by Herzenberg, Alic, and Wial (1998) as 'unrationalized labor intensive'. Alternatively, IT can be used to automate routine work and facilitate work restructuring to create more complex, better paid jobs (Herzenberg, Alic, and Wial 1998: 64). IT-enabled mass customization is most evident in financial services, communication (telephone and TV), health, and the educational service sector. In recent years these services have been offered through telephone call centers that now include email communication.

Managers in mass customized settings generally acknowledge that service workers contribute to organizational effectiveness by satisfying customers. They are therefore generally rewarded more highly than their mass service counterparts (Herzenberg, Alic, and Wial 1998: 46–51),[3] although some customized service work involves unacknowledged skills (associated with sexism and a weak labor market), and thus remains low paid. Nurses' aides employed in public hospitals are an example.

Regardless of strategic intent, there exists a tension between standardizing and customizing practices and structures (Frenkel *et al.* 1999; Shamir 1978). Because relentless competition in saturated markets encourages management to pursue short-term profit by constantly seeking to reduce costs, this contradiction is especially evident in organizations pursuing a value-adding strategy (Appelbaum *et al.* 2003; Bernhardt, Dresser, and Hatton 2003; Korczynski 2002: 97–8;). Here there is a temptation to prioritize both value adding and cost reduction. Managing

---

[2] Some hospitals have reorganized the work of food service workers and nurses aides, making these more challenging and fostering worker flexibility and higher service quality. The results have not been as positive as anticipated, in part because these changes were not accompanied by sufficient additional training. Employees did seem to value the higher pay (see Appelbaum *et al.* 2003).

[3] Frenkel *et al.* (1999: 103–4) found that training accounted for around 5 percent of revenue in six call centers. Almost all of this was initial rather than ongoing training, although informal learning from supervisors and peers was a continuing feature that contributed to worker performance. In regard to promotion opportunities, management sought to retain effective employees and workers expected training and promotion opportunities to be provided. Consequently informal, truncated career ladders were common. These mainly took the form of opportunities to learn and advance to team leader and supervisor roles, and occasionally to transfer to other parts of the company (Frenkel *et al.* 1999: 104–6; Batt, Hunter, and Wilk 2003).

the employee relations aspects of this dilemma can be seen by reference to recent call center research where mass customized bureaucratic settings predominate (Frenkel *et al.* 1998). Customer service representatives (CSRs) working in these organizations are typically expected to answer customer queries covering a large range of products and offer suggestions tailored to customer needs. Each day they face the twin demands of achieving high productivity (low average time per customer) and high service standards (tailoring service to customer needs, usually implying longer time per customer). Call center managers have addressed this problem by adopting one of four human resource strategies. These are referred to below as sacrificial, high commitment, oscillation, and empowerment strategies.

First, and most commonly, management have prioritized productivity subject to meeting a minimum quality service standard. One way to achieve this objective is to pursue what Wallace, Eagleson, and Waldersee (2000) label a 'sacrificial human resource strategy'. In effect, workers are selected on the basis of a high customer service orientation and are employed in low discretion work roles under close management control. This leads to emotional exhaustion and employee with-drawal, which are influenced by negative customer interactions, scripted rules, management's productivity focus, a high workload, work routinization, lack of promotional opportunities, limited call length, control over call completion time, insufficient team leader support, and two personal variables: low positive affectivity and inferior physical health (Deery, Iverson, and Walsh 2002: 486–7). Management accepts an average worker tenure of around eighteen months after which burnt-out workers are replaced by new employees. In short, in lieu of developing human resource policies that limit worker dissatisfaction, workers are sacrificed in order to satisfy cost-reduction and profitability objectives (Wallace, Eagleson, and Waldersee 2000: 178).

The second strategy seeks to engender high worker commitment. It is designed to alleviate the stress and dissatisfaction arising from a high productivity, low-cost business strategy. In three of the four call centers studied by Houlihan (2002), management developed policies to counteract a regime of repetitive, unfulfilling front-line work. Common features included relatively flat reporting structures, teams, self-management, ongoing training, communication mechanisms, and pay related to performance. Two of the three call centers went further: in one case by providing superior physical working conditions and in the other case by offering additional skill development and career opportunities. This high commitment approach appears to be relatively common (Batt, Hunter, and Wilk 2003; Frenkel *et al.* 1999).

Oscillation is a third type of approach. Management oscillates between the goals of productivity and service quality. According to Holtgrewe and Kerst (2002), and Taylor and Bain (1999: 116), call center managers switch priorities when the costs of following one route begin to outweigh the benefits. For example, productivity targets may be reduced in response to rising worker turnover and service quality standards may subsequently be relaxed when lengthening queues, in part, arising from longer, higher quality service calls, begin to threaten short-term revenue targets.

The fourth strategy is designed to empower employees and is more commonly associated with knowledge workers employed on help-desks (the higher level counterpart of call centers). Quality service takes priority over productivity in what resembles the empowered organization model (Frenkel *et al.* 1999: 14). Houlihan's (2002) fourth call center featured more complex work associated with educational counseling and career guidance. A short career path enabled workers to progress from the position of information provider to learning adviser. Batt, Hunter, and Wilk (2003) refer to four call centers specializing in human resource benefits administration, controlled by a single professional services firm. In this case, CSRs handled more complex issues with relatively few customers each day. Although initial training was relatively short (six weeks), half the CSRs were college graduates. Teamwork was integral to the job and there were career opportunities within the call center (promotion to specialized and supervisory positions) and in the organization more generally. Pay, however, was moderate, varying between $28,000 and $33,000 a year (in 2001).

Call centers that combine wider, more interesting service work roles organized in teams, with high commitment human resource practices—comprising recruitment of tertiary educated workers, ongoing training, relative employment security and high pay, availability of promotion opportunities, and a low level of electronic performance monitoring—have been shown to perform better and experience lower labor turnover than their counterparts serving the same customer segment. Moreover, the more complex the work associated with employees serving different customer segments, the higher the call center performance (Batt and Moynihan 2002). Although this argument has yet to be demonstrated using financial data, it suggests that business strategies that prioritize service quality over productivity, supported by appropriate bundles of human resource practices, may be more profitable than alternative models.

This finding chimes with research that underpins the influential service profit-chain model. This claims that service workers with higher levels of satisfaction and organizational understanding interact more positively with customers generating higher customer satisfaction, which in turn, leads to superior performance, including higher profitability (Heskett, Sasser, and Schlesinger 1997; Rucci, Kirn, and Quinn 1998).[4] Service worker satisfaction is said to depend on job design, effective

---

[4] It is puzzling why so few firms appear to have adopted this model. One reason may be lack of knowledge about best practice organization; another reason may be that leading firms are reticent to publicize, what is, in effect, their competitive advantage. A third reason may be that management is skeptical about the cost-effectiveness of this high-value strategy, and fourth, management may be discouraged by implementation difficulties including cost constraints and middle management opposition to a reduction in their power.

technology, and congenial physical employment conditions. Other factors include management that inspires, communicates, and encourages customer focus and teamwork, especially between interdependent parts of the organization (Gittell 2002).

Apart from these general human resource strategies, managers often use tactics that may either reinforce or undermine worker commitment. Much depends on the prevailing culture whose alignment to the human resource strategy is sometimes problematic. By requiring workers to conform to certain aesthetic and emotional display rules, managers attempt to control workers' self-identities and they foster particular feelings of optimism, fun, energy, good health, beauty, etc. (Sturdy and Fineman 2001: 139–40). Managers (and customers) also use informal tactics such as joking and flirting to 'butter up' (flatter), 'soften up' (intimidate), or 'put down' (punish) workers. Members of minorities (based on ethnic, religious, or sex-preference lines), and women, who tend to be concentrated in subordinate work roles, may be discriminated against in these ways and are particularly sensitive to such tactics. In addition, since social skills and aesthetic criteria feature in the recruitment process, male managers tend to favor hiring younger women to subordinate positions. Designating these as gender attributes means that women's social and organizational skills may go unacknowledged and unrewarded (LaPointe 1992: 386–7). In addition, rules governing aesthetic and emotional labor reflect male-dominated preferences. As noted below, some women have challenged these practices.

15.3 SEEKING MEANING AND SATISFACTION: SERVICE WORKERS' STRATEGIES

I begin this section by focusing on responses that distinguish service workers from other, more skilled workers, and then compare mass service workers' strategies to the way mass customized workers respond to what is often a more complex environment characterized by the competing logics of standardization and customization.

15.3.1 Avoiding Conflict with Management and Covert Responses

The relatively weak labor market position and lack of strategic power in the labor process means that service workers are unlikely to overtly challenge management authority. Where management acts unfairly, service workers will withdraw cooperation or covertly undermine company policies. Where they exercise more power, or are mobilized by forces outside the organization, they will occasionally take collective action. However, in general, they are more likely to seek ways to control their work, squeezing satisfaction out of the most routine of tasks, often in association with coworkers or customers.

Customer interaction varies between mass service and mass customized workers. In the former case, it usually takes the form of encounters—short, nonrepeatable interactions that provide little positive feedback to employees (Gutek 1995). In the latter case, workers may have longer and occasionally repeatable interactions with specific customers. These more meaningful interactions have been termed quasi-relationships (Frenkel *et al.* 1999: 211–14). Where workers are required to represent the organization to customers in ways that are inconsistent with their own experience, we have what Gutek (1995) refers to as pseudo-relationships. All of these relationships entail emotional labor—the expenditure of emotional effort in accordance with management's expectations. Where workers have minimal discretion, do not personally identify with the work role, and feel overworked, emotional labor leads to dissatisfaction, exhaustion, and alienation (Hochschild 1983; Troyer, Mueller, and Osinsky 2000: 9; Wharton 1993). These conditions are more likely to be found in mass service work settings including fast-food outlets, retail outlets, and ticketing agencies. Alternatively, in mass customized settings such as tourist agencies and call centers, workers are able to exercise a little more control over their interaction with customers. Part-time work gives some emotional relief from long periods of customer contact, although where workers lack the power to control their work schedules, employees may be disoriented by alterations in working hours that interrupt their sleep patterns.[5]

Given their limited market and workplace power, one might expect service workers to further their interests by participating in trade unions. Institutional barriers, however, limit free choice in this regard. In 2001, 9.1 percent of service workers (excluding more heavily unionized protective services employees) were members of a union or an employee association, not much different from the 9.0 percent for US private sector wage and salary earners (US DOL 2002c: table 42: 218). Collective bargaining coverage is similarly low (Herzenberg, Alic, and Wial 1998: table A-3: 177). Where service workers have the least power—in routinized jobs with a high proportion of contingent and/or part-time workers—union density appears to be lowest (4.5 percent; in retail trade and 0 percent in fast food) (Leidner 2002: 15; US DOL 2002c: table 42: 218).

---

[5] Young workers, who often depend on stretches of long working hours, may be unable to manage the 'time crunch' and undertake the further study required to escape from 'dead end' jobs (Newman 1999: 130; Stack 2002: 43). However, Newman (1999: 106–16) observes that young workers in deprived areas who attempt to combine work and school begin to socialize with friends at work, creating a community that offers some protection against youth ensnared in drug and crime cultures.

In addition to the nature of employment, there are six further reasons why service workers remain largely unorganized. First, at least in the United States, labor law confers few rights on workers and inhibits union organizing (Bronfenbrenner 2000; Leidner 2002: 13–15). A second institutional reason concerns employer characteristics. These include the elusiveness and small scale of many employers (especially contractors), and the antiunion ideologies espoused by most managers, reflected in selective hiring based on workers demonstrating 'the right attitude' toward working with customers (Callaghan and Thompson 2002; Ehrenreich 2001: 13–14, 58–59). A third reason relates to worker demographics, particularly the dominance of vulnerable groups such as the young and inexperienced, recent immigrants, ethnic minorities, and women. Fourth, the triangular nature of service work relations means that customers rather than management are often seen as the problem (Leidner 1993: 145). Fifth, service workers' high rates of labor turnover militate against unions developing a stable core of organized workers to promote unionization (Korczynski 2002: 176). Sixth, and finally, the advantages of unionism—higher wages, greater employment security, fairer allocation of work assignments, and assistance in skill upgrading—may not be widely communicated by unions to service employees.

Lacking power and an institutional means of collectively expressing their dissatisfaction, service workers rely more on emotional withdrawal and covert opposition. This is sometimes manifested in high rates of labor turnover and absenteeism; although such behaviors may not be entirely work-related, most are. In 2001, after 'administrative support, including clerical', service workers recorded the second highest absence rate among six major occupational categories (US DOL 2002d: table 47: 223). Regarding labor turnover, in the absence of occupational data, industry data shows that for services, the average monthly quit rate over five recent survey periods (December 2000 to April 2001) was 1.8, higher than for manufacturing (1.3) over the same survey periods (US DOL 2002e: table 7). In addition, recall that service workers' employment tenure was more than one-third lower than for workers in general. This suggests a high turnover rate, though some of this could be involuntary.

15.3.2 Service Workers' Responses in Mass Service Work Settings

Despite the high rates of turnover and absenteeism, a few comments on routinized work should alert us to overestimating dissatisfaction among mass service workers. Some workers like routine work. They value role clarity and being virtually free from the arbitrary demands of managers and customers. Routinization instills a sense of time awareness and discipline, while permitting psychological disengagement and protection from critical managers and abusive customers (Leidner 1996: 44). Disneyland ride operators, for example, 'go robot' or put themselves on 'automatic pilot' to avoid distressing encounters with customers (Van Maanen 1991: 75). Other reasons for preferring routinized work have to do with workers going beyond their expected role. Thus, Leidner (1993: 134–8) refers to fast-food workers finding satisfaction in adding a personal touch in order to please customers. Risking management detection, they sometimes avoided or minimized those parts of the job that caused the most dissatisfaction. An example is suggestive selling, which sometimes invited hostility from customers. Finally, avoiding dissatisfaction is also achieved by emphasizing particular goals (e.g. speed of delivery) at the expense of others that workers found demeaning (e.g. the emotional labor of appearing to be friendly and courteous).

In a more positive vein, satisfaction can be derived from a greater sense of self-control, outside and inside the workplace. Earnings from work contribute to a sense of self-respect, for there is less dependence on family or the state (Newman 1999: 136). At work, some control can be achieved vis-à-vis customers. For example, Soares (2001: 116) shows how supermarket cashiers hide checkout errors by persuading customers to purchase an additional item to balance sales with cash register records. In another context—that of experienced waitresses—Paules (1991) observes:

Like all social actors the waitress monitors her projected personality and manipulates her feelings in the course of social interaction, but she does so knowingly and in her own interests. ... With experience, her ability to separate front and backstage expressions of subservience and conviviality increases and she may silently applaud her powers of deception even as she stands before her audience of customers. (p. 162)

There are also factors that compensate for the routine nature of work. These include efforts by some management to assist young workers by minimizing conflicts between work and school schedules (Newman 1999: 104) and by injecting a sense of fun and respect into the workplace (Leidner 1993: 136–7). More important is coworker camaraderie and helpfulness that comprise the work culture, although as Hodson's (2001: 229–30) research indicates, there is both greater solidarity and more infighting among service workers in highly interdependent work settings like restaurants and the media. Workers do assist one another in learning work tasks, including machine repair (see Newman 1999: 139), and the socialization process helps workers to develop and improve their social skills. Workers are encouraged to listen to and communicate with customers, to interpret customer and coworker needs, to regulate their relations with customer and managers, and to more successfully manage their self-perceptions (Smith 2001: 42–9). Marginal groups like young workers and immigrants are able to gain a sense of self-worth and achieve some measure of social integration in a work culture (Newman 1999: 106; Stack 2002: 33). Colleagues support each other by building a 'rebuttal culture' (Newman 1999: 104) that challenges customers' discriminatory behavior and defends workers' dignity (Guerrier and Adib 2000: 699–700; Soares 2001: 118).

Occasionally a service worker will risk a confrontation with a customer or manager. These conflicts usually occur when a worker's self-identity is disparaged, when for example, servility rather than civility is demanded, or when discrimination on gender or ethnic grounds is openly expressed (Paules 1991: 153–8). Workers learn from coworkers how to inflict damage on customers without being detected. Disneyland ride operators, for example, create 'accidents' by exercising control over mechanical equipment (Van Maanen 1991: 71–2), while waiters may 'get the jump on' abusive customers by slowing down service or by serving very hot food (Mars and Nicod 1984: 83–8). Directly confronting customers is risky for it is likely to escalate out of control and can lead to dismissal, especially if a manager is directly involved. Moreover, it has social significance: a loss of the small amount of control that is vested in the mass service workers' work role.

In sum, mass service workers typically lack the resources and the will to influence management either directly or through their influence on customers. So, they accommodate and challenge in less direct ways. This said, there are exceptions, including two recent inspirational union campaigns waged by, and on behalf of, Los Angeles building cleaners—the so-called Justice for Janitors Campaign (Erickson *et al.* 2002)—and the Service Employees' International Union drive to organize home care workers (Osterman *et al.* 2001: 114–16). We return to these developments in the concluding section.

15.3.3 Service Workers' Responses in Mass Customized Service Work Settings

Compared to knowledge workers, mass customized service workers are less trusted by management and have less of a stake in the success of the enterprise. Consequently, they are more equivocal about the corporate culture. However, compared to their mass service counterparts, they appear to be relatively satisfied with work and accordingly have less reason to resist management. Frenkel *et al.* (1999: 243) found that the job satisfaction of workers employed in call centers (primarily) depended on the intrinsic nature of their work (interesting and challenging tasks, and influence over work-related decisions), promotion prospects, and the effectiveness of the technology with which they worked.[6] Although they reported being less intrinsically satisfied than both knowledge workers and sales workers, these

---

[6] In descending order of importance, these workers valued pay, promotion prospects, job security, the intrinsic nature of work, and relations between coworkers as the five most important attributes of work (Frenkel *et al.* 1999: 85).

service workers reported being less stressed, and being as satisfied with work overall, compared with these other two kinds of workers (Frenkel *et al.* 1999: 89–90; 286–7, appendix 5). Holman (2001) compared job satisfaction, anxiety, and depression in call center workers, clerical workers, and blue-collar, manufacturing employees. He found that the call center workers were neither more dissatisfied nor more anxious or depressed than clerical and shop-floor workers.[7]

Workers in mass customized settings enjoy more autonomy but often expend more emotional labor than their mass service counterparts. Under appropriate conditions, assisting customers is one of the most satisfying aspects of customized service work (Frenkel *et al.* 1999: 207–43; Holman 2001). However, where jobs are inappropriately designed and receive little management support, particularly in dealing with emotional labor, employees risk being burnt out (Deery, Iverson, and Walsh 2002). Burnout is especially common in caregiving contexts—working with the infirm, the elderly, the handicapped, and with children. In these labor-intensive, customized settings, workers often subscribe to a strong helping ethic but resources are thin and additional costs may be imposed by organizations having to abide by state regulations. Because action taken to defend their interests almost invariably discomfits care receivers, workers can more easily be exploited (see Foner 1994: 132). They have however developed strategies to protect themselves. These include avoidance of rate-busting, turning a blind eye to coworkers' rule infringements, not venturing across job territory lines, and supporting the union if workers are union members (Foner 1994: 132–7).

Experienced customized service workers develop strategies to manage emotional overload and conflict with customers, managers, and colleagues. Although some of these have been touched on in our discussion of mass service workers' strategies, six frequently used strategies are worth noting.

1. *Emotional distancing.* This avoids personalizing and is often accompanied by an emphasis on problem solving.
2. *Seeking informal assistance.* For example, workers may get help from managers or colleagues to resolve a problem and obtain emotional support.
3. *Redefining the worker–customer relationship.* For example, workers may take control, in order to limit conflict or simply to relieve tension.[8]
4. *Acting unilaterally against management in a covert manner.* For example, hotel desk clerks may go on a 'smile strike' (Fuller and Smith 1991) or be unavailable for overtime.

---

[7] Only at the call center where work was highly routinized did workers report lower intrinsic and extrinsic work satisfaction than clerical workers. Depression scores were also higher. Compared with shop-floor workers, intrinsic satisfaction at this same call center was significantly lower, however extrinsic satisfaction was higher and anxiety lower. There was no difference in regard to depression.

[8] Callaghan and Thompson (2002: 13) quote a UK call center worker as saying: 'They [customers] can't see us so we can actually take the mickey out of them while they're trying to speak to us' (CSR1).

5. *Negotiating with management (or a customer) in order to reach agreement.* For example, workers may appeal to management values—e.g. quality service, communication, teamworking, etc.—at team meetings to attain their objectives. Threatening to quit at times of a labor shortage can also be effective (Taylor and Bain 1999: 112).

6. *Pursuing a formal request or challenging a rule infraction by management through an institutionalized procedure* (Sturdy and Fineman 2001: 144–9). Rules regulating electronic monitoring of call center workers are spreading in several countries and are likely to be closely monitored (see Holtgrewe, and Kerst 2000; Frenkel *et al.* 1999: 158; Taylor and Bain 1999: 114; Arzbächer).

15.4 CONCLUSION

In this chapter I have argued that service work comprises regular customer contact and the use of limited skills, knowledge, and creativity. Its importance was indicated by its role in delivering valued services, its size relative to other broad occupational categories, and its contribution to future employment. Nevertheless, I suggested that most service work is indecent in the sense that it is often poorly rewarded and provides little intrinsic satisfaction. However, I cautioned against accepting such a categorical and bleak assessment. We noted differences between mass service and mass customized work, and showed that the latter includes opportunities for workers to exercise autonomy and influence customers and managers. This has the potential to bring both more pleasure and more pain, the extent of each depending on management strategy and its execution, particularly in attempting to reconcile the opposing logics of standardization and customization. In regard to mass service work, we noted that management occasionally provides conditions that improve employee satisfaction, but most often it is the workers themselves who create the conditions for making work more tolerable. In discussing service workers' strategies, I argued that pragmatic acceptance of management authority and covert tactics, sometimes directed at customers, were more common than either enthusiastic endorsement of corporate culture or overt collective opposition to management. Nevertheless, more powerful mass customized workers did sometimes seek to influence management directly and there have been instances of union participation. Indeed, there is evidence that institutional barriers, rather than worker disaffection with unions, stand in the way of service workers pursuing more assertive, collectivist strategies to further their interests.

Despite efforts by workers to make work more satisfying, and management recognition that customer satisfaction, especially in mass customized settings, depends on worker satisfaction and commitment, we noted the predominant logic of cost reduction. This encourages work standardization accompanied by low pay and jobs with limited employee discretion and few opportunities for development—in short, indecent work. What can be done to stop this trend? The short answer is to find ways to accelerate the expansion of higher quality service jobs. The longer answer suggests different strategies depending on the type of service work being addressed.

Regarding mass services and other labor-intensive work driven by a cost-reducing management strategy, the primary aim should be to improve job quality, complemented by efforts to encourage job growth where possible, predicated on higher quality work. In the case of both high-volume (mass) and low-volume (labor-intensive) customized work, there should be equal emphasis on job expansion and on improving the quality of these jobs. Some recently introduced programs suggest ways to proceed. There is also the potential for workers to use their voice through unions and workplace structures.

The extent to which mass service work can be improved is limited by high-volume, low-cost business strategies that lead management to emphasize standardized processes and high productivity. Job rotation and job enrichment may provide some additional intrinsic satisfaction and lower labor turnover (Bernhardt, Dresser, and Hatton 2003). But more improvement is likely to be made by increasing pay and benefits, and offering promotion opportunities. The latter may be less costly for employers and more easily justified by higher worker morale that translates into higher productivity and reduced labor turnover. By providing more support for education and training aimed at achieving an accredited industry or occupational qualification, organizations would enhance workers' chances of internal or external progression. This could be facilitated by a government grant scheme. A variation on this theme is provided by the Cape Cod Hospital 'Career Ladders' program and by a Burger King franchise owner who, according to Herzenberg, Alic, and Wial (1998: 126), arranges career opportunities for outstanding employees, not in his own firm, but with local manufacturers. This scheme is designed to attract higher quality workers and to reduce labor turnover. Less common are employer consortia that fund and manage training and accreditation schemes that promote upward worker mobility within a specific industry or regional labor market. Examples include the San Francisco Hotels Partnership Project and the Wisconsin Regional Training Partnership (Finegold, Wagner, and Mason 2000: 510; Herzenberg, Alic, and Wial 1998: 127–8, 134–7). In addition, as Newman (1999: 286–9) has argued in relation to deprived areas, local government development agencies should coordinate and support links between business owners in these areas and more prosperous firms in adjacent locations. This would help competent employees from the deprived areas find better jobs elsewhere.

Although unions are key participants in most of the initiatives cited above, two recent union campaigns—Justice for Janitors and the Service Employees' International Union drive to organize home-care aides—show that service workers can achieve their goals through more assertive activity. Both campaigns resulted in a more organized workforce and improvements in pay and working conditions. The key to their success, and to other living wage campaigns conducted in around fifty US cities since 1994 (Neumark 2002: 720–2; Osterman *et al.* 2001: 135–8), seems to lie in community-based organizing that includes alliances with ethnic, religious, and consumer groups, and substantial efforts to influence the media and local politics. In this regard, mass service workers are able to appeal to three important American values: equality of opportunity (by escaping from poverty through training and career progression); individual independence (by avoiding dependence on state welfare benefits through work that is often highly visible); and dignity through work (by raising the status of service work currently stigmatized as 'dead end'). These values appear to strike a chord with a wide section of public opinion.

Since customized service work typically offers more extrinsic and intrinsic satisfaction than mass service work, it is important to create more of this type of work while also seeking to improve the quality of these jobs. Worker participation in job-related decisions is the key to creating decent work. Through workplace forums such as team meetings, service quality workshops, off-line project teams, and union meetings, customized service workers can support management efforts to pursue high value, customizing strategies that bring satisfaction to both workers and customers. Cost-reducing, standardizing strategies that limit customer contact to encounters or pseudo-relationships should be automated. This is important because as we noted, many managers have adopted a hybrid or compromise model with a tendency toward cost-reducing strategies that have adverse effects on job quality and worker satisfaction. Employee groups and unions should actively encourage and disseminate the findings of studies that demonstrate the benefits of work customization and high commitment human resource strategies. These could be used as a basis for action research projects and experimentation designed to strengthen the customizing tendency and help realize the joint goals of management and employees. Baldridge or similar prize applications could also be supported as a way of emphasizing workers' commitment to models of service that contribute to both profitability and decent work.

Developing stronger learning and career building opportunities are especially critical for maintaining ongoing worker commitment. In particular, efforts should be made to foster relations among employers, high schools, and colleges to keep education curricula relevant and to place more promising students in jobs. Furthermore, nationally recognized occupational qualifications should be created that articulate with paraprofessional competencies. Examples include a possible nurses aide→licensed practical nurse→registered nurse stream, a childcare worker→ teacher stream (Herzenberg, Alic, and Wial 1998: 128–9), and CSR→call center supervisor→human resource manager or customer relationship manager stream. Service workers could then plan a career targeting a related set of service occupations without being dependent on any single employer.

To conclude: as I have argued, even within the present conservative political context, much can be done to transform service work into decent work. But the larger picture of a polarized society, with constraints on political reform should be kept in mind. For there are some changes—e.g. greater opportunities for union organizing, improved rights for part-time and contingent workers—that require broader coalitions of service workers and other groups who share a vision of a more egalitarian and free society. These political changes are essential complements to the occupational reforms required to ensure that decent work is not a privilege of the few but ultimately a right of all workers.

REFERENCES

APPELBAUM, E., BERG, P., FROST, A., and PREUSS, G. (2003). 'The Effects of Work Restructuring on Low-Wage, Low-Skill Workers in U.S. Hospitals', in E. Appelbaum, A. Bernhardt, and R. Murnane (eds.), *Low Wage America*. New York: Russell Sage Foundation.

ARZBÄCHER, S., HOLTGREWE, U., and KERST, C. (2000). 'Call Centers: Constructing Flexibility', in U. Holtgrewe, C. Kerst, and K. Shire (eds.), *Re-Organising Service Work*. Ashforth: Ashgate Publishing.

BATT, R. (2000). 'Strategic Segmentation in Front-Line Services: Matching Customers, Employees and Human Resource Systems'. *International Journal of Human Resource Management*, 11/3: 540–61.

—— and MOYNIHAN, L. (2002). 'The Viability of Alternative Call Center Production Models'. *Human Resource Management Journal*, 22/4: 14–34.

—— HUNTER, L., and WILK, S. (2003). 'How and When Does Management Matter? Job Quality and Career Opportunities for Call Center Workers', in E. Appelbaum, A. Bernhardt, and R. Murnane (eds.), *Low Wage America*. New York: Russell Sage Foundation.

BECK, U. (2000). *The Brave New World of Work*. London: Polity Press.

BERNHARDT, A., DRESSER, L., and HATTON, E. (2003). 'The Coffee Pot Wars: Unions and Firm Restructuring in the Hotel Industry', in E. Appelbaum, A. Bernhardt, and R. Murnane (eds.), *Low Wage America*. New York: Russell Sage Foundation.

BRONFENBRENNER, K. (2000). 'The American Labour Movement and the Resurgency in Union Organising', in P. Fairbrother and C. Yates (eds.), *Trade Union Renewal and Organising*. London: Mansell.

BUCHANAN, R. (2002). 'Lives on the Line: Low-Wage Work in the Teleservice Economy', in F. Munger (ed.), *Laboring below the Line*. New York: Russell Sage Foundation.

CALLAGHAN, G., and THOMPSON, P. (2002). 'We Recruit Attitude: The Selection and Shaping of Routine Call Centre Labor'. *Journal of Management Studies*, 39/2: 233–54.

DEERY, S., IVERSON, R., and WALSH, J. (2002). 'Work Relationships in Telephone Call Centres: Understanding Emotional Exhaustion and Employee Withdrawal'. *Journal of Management Studies*, 39/4: 472–96.

EATON, S. (2000). 'Beyond "Unloving Care": Linking Human Resource Management and Patient Care Quality in Nursing Homes'. *International Journal of Human Resource Management*, 11/3: 591–616.

EHRENREICH, B. (2001). *Nickel and Dimed: On (not) Getting by in America*. New York: Metropolitan Books.

ERICKSON, C. L., FISK, C. L., MILKMAN, R., MITCHELL, D. J. B., and WONG, K. (2002). 'Justice for Janitors in Los Angeles: Lessons from Three Rounds of Negotiations'. *British Journal of Industrial Relations*, 40/3: 543–68.

FINEGOLD, D., WAGNER, K., and MASON, G. (2000). 'National Skill-Creation Systems and Career Paths for Service Workers: Hotels in the United States, Germany and the United Kingdom'. *International Journal of Human Resource Management*, 11/3: 497–516.

FONER, N. (1994). *The Care Giving Dilemma: Work in an American Nursing Home*. Berkeley: University of California Press.

FRENKEL, S., KORCZYNSKI, M., SHIRE, K., and TAM, M. (1998). 'Beyond Bureaucracy? Work Organisation in Call Centres'. *International Journal of Human Resource Management*, 9/6: 957–79.

————————(1999). *On the Front Line: Work Organization in the Service Economy*. Ithaca, NY: ILR/Cornell University Press.

FULLER, L., and SMITH, V. (1991). 'Consumers' Reports: Management by Customers in a Changing Economy'. *Work, Employment and Society*, 5/1: 1–16.

GITTELL, J. H. (2002). 'Relationships between Service Providers and Their Impact on Customers'. *Journal of Service Research*, 4/4: 299–311.

GUERRIER, Y., and ADIB, A. S. (2000). 'No, We Don't Provide That Service: The Harassment of Hotel Employees by Customers'. *Work, Employment & Society*, 14/4: 689–705.

GUTEK, B. (1995). *The Dynamics of Service*. San Francisco: Jossey-Bass.

HECKER, D. (2001). 'Occupational Employment Projections to 2010'. *Monthly Labor Review*, 124/11: 57–84.

HERZENBERG, S., ALIC, J., and WIAL, H. (1998). *New Rules for a New Economy: Employment and Opportunity in Postindustrial America*. Ithaca, NY: Cornell University Press.

HESKETT, J. L., SASSER, Jr., W. E., and SCHLESINGER, L. A. (1997). *The Service Profit Chain: How Leading Companies Link Profit and Growth to Loyalty, Satisfaction, and Value*. New York: Free Press.

HOCHSCHILD, A. (1983). *The Managed Heart*. Berkeley: University of California Press.

HODSON, R. (2001). *Dignity at Work*. New York: Cambridge University Press.

HOLMAN, D. (2001). 'Employee Well Being in Call Centres'. *Human Resource Management Journal*, 12/4: 34–49.

HOLTGREWE, U., and KERST, C. (2002). 'Researching Call Centres: Gathering Results and Theories'. Paper presented to the 20th Annual International Labour Process Conference, Glasgow, University of Strathclyde, April 2002.

HOULIHAN, M. (2002). 'Tensions and Variations in Call Centre Management Strategies'. *Human Resource Management Journal*, 12/4: 67–85.

International Labour Office, Geneva (2001). Report 1(A) Report of the Director-General: Reducing the Decent Work Deficit—A Global Challenge.

KORCZYNSKI, M. (2002). *Human Resource Management in Service Work*. London: Palgrave.

LaPointe, E. (1992). 'Relationships with Waitresses: Gendered Social Distance in Restaurant Hierarchies'. *Qualitative Sociology*, 13/4: 377–93.

Leidner, R. (1993). *Fast Food, Fast Talk*. Berkeley: University of California Press.

——(1996). 'Rethinking Questions of Control: Lessons from McDonald's', in C. MacDonald and C. Sirianni (eds.), *Working in the Service Society*. Philadelphia: Temple University Press.

——(2002). 'Fast-Food Work in the United States', in T. Royle and B. Towers (eds.), *Labour Relations in the Global Fast-Food Industry*. London, New York: Routledge.

Mars, G., and Nicod, M. (1984). *The World of Waiters*. London: G. Allen & Unwin.

Neumark, D. (2002). 'Drawing the Lines', Comment on P. Osterman et al., *Working in America*. *Industrial & Labor Relations Review*, 55/4: 716–23.

Newman, K. S. (1999). *No Shame in My Game: The Working Poor in the Inner City*. New York: Knopf and Russell Sage Foundation.

Oliva, R. (2002). 'Tradeoffs in Responses to Work Pressure in the Service Industry'. *California Management Review*, 43/4: 26–43.

Osterman, P., Kochan, T., Locke R., and Piore, M. (2001). *Working in America*. Cambridge, Mass.: MIT Press.

Paules, G. F. (1991). *Dishing It Out*. Philadelphia: Temple University Press.

Pierce, B. (2001). 'Compensation Inequality'. *Quarterly Journal of Economics*, 116/4: 1493–1525.

Ritzer, G., and Stillman, T. (2001). 'From Person to System-Oriented Service', in A. Sturdy, I. Grugulis, and H. Willmott (eds.), *Customer Service*. Basingstoke: Macmillan/Palgrave.

Rucci, A. J., Kirn, S. P., and Quinn, R. T. (1998). 'The Employee–Customer Profit Chain at Sears'. *Harvard Business Review*, 76/1: 82–97.

Shamir, B. (1978). 'Between Bureaucracy and Hospitality—Some Organisational Characteristics of Hotels'. *Journal of Management Studies*, 15/3: 285–307.

Smith, V. (2001). *Crossing the Great Divide: Worker Risk and Opportunity in the New Economy*. Ithaca, NY: ILR/Cornell University Press.

Soares, A. (2001). 'Silent Rebellions in the Capitalist Paradise: A Brazil–Quebec Comparison', in R. Baldoz, C. Koeber, and P. Kraft (eds.), *The Critical Study of Work, Labor, Technology and Global Production*. Philadelphia: Temple University Press.

Stack, C. (2002). 'In Exile on Main Street', in F. Munger (ed.), *Laboring below the Line*. New York: Russell Sage Foundation.

Sturdy, A., and Fineman, S. (2001). 'Struggles for the Control of Affect—Resistance as Politics *and* Emotion', in A. Sturdy, I. Grugulis, and H. Willmott (eds.), *Customer Service: Empowerment and Entrapment*. Basingstoke: Palgrave.

Taylor, P., and Bain, P. (1999). 'An Assembly Line in the Head: Work and Employee Relations in the Call Centre'. *Industrial Relations Journal*, 30/2: 101–17.

Troyer, L., Mueller, C. W., and Osinsky, P. I. (2000). 'Who's the Boss?' *Work and Occupations*, 27/3: 406–27.

US Department of Labor (US DOL). (2001a). *National Compensation Survey, 2000, NCS: Occupational Wages in the United States*, Supplementary Tables. www.bls.gov/ocs/sp/ncb10402.pdf

——(2001b). *Table 4. Employed Contingent and Noncontingent Workers by Occupation and Industry*, February 2001. www.bls.gov/news.release/conemp.to4.htm

—— (2002*a*). Bureau of Labor Statistics, March. 'A Profile of the Working Poor, 2000'. Report 957.

—— (2002*b*). Table 6: Median years of tenure with current employer for employed wage and salary workers by occupation, selected years, 1983–2002. www.bls.gov/news.release/tenure.to6.htm

—— (2002*c*). Household Data, Annual Averages. Table 42: Union affiliation of employed wage and salary workers by occupation and industry.

—— (2002*d*). Household Data, Annual Averages. Table 47: Absences from work of employed full-time wage and salary workers by occupation and industry.

—— (2002*e*). *Job Openings and Labor Turnover Survey*. Table 7: Quits rates by industry and census region, JOLTS Historical Data: December 2000–April 2001, www.bls.gov/jlt/jlt_hto7.htm

VAN MAANEN, J. (1991). 'The Smile Factory: Work at Disneyland', in P. Frost, L. Moore, M. Louis, C. Lundberg, and L. Martin (eds.), *Reframing Organisational Culture*. Newbury Park, Calif.: Sage.

WALLACE, C. M., EAGLESON, G., and WALDERSEE, R. (2000). 'The Sacrificial HR Strategy in Call Centres'. *International Journal of Service Industry Management*, 11/2: 174–84.

WALSH, T. (1990). 'Flexible Labour Utilisation in the Private Service Sector'. *Work, Employment and Society*, 4/4: 517–30.

Website (not referred to above): ACSI 2002 http://asci.asq.org

WHARTON, A. S. (1993). 'The Affective Consequences of Service Work'. *Work and Occupations*, 20/2: 205–32.

CHAPTER 16

··

WHAT WE KNOW (AND MOSTLY DON'T KNOW) ABOUT TECHNICAL WORK

··

STEPHEN R. BARLEY

16.1 INTRODUCTION

··

EVERY economic era has archetypical occupations; lines of work that become prominent during the era and that are iconic of the era's primary mode of production. The farmer and the merchant were the archetypical occupations of the preindustrial era, when economic activity revolved around agriculture and mercantile capitalism. As we move deeper into what some have called a postindustrial or knowledge economy, we cannot know for sure which occupations historians will eventually consider archetypical. But as Daniel Bell (1973) noted three decades ago, the candidates will most surely include engineers, scientists, programmers, computer scientists, and technicians; lines of work colloquially known as 'technical occupations'.[1]

Since World War II, technical occupations have consistently ranked among the fastest growing occupations in the United States. Whereas total employment between 1900 and 1950 grew by a little over 100 percent, the number of engineers increased 1,300 percent! Because the US Census did not count scientists and technicians as distinct occupational categories in 1900, it is not possible to determine growth rates for these occupations for the first half of the twentieth century. However, in the second half of the century, employment of scientists grew by almost 700 percent and employment of technicians grew by over 900 percent, while total employment increased by only 162 percent.

Moreover, these figures do not include computer scientists, engineering managers, sales engineers, information technology managers, computer operators, computer repairers, and computer control programmers. If one counts these occupations as well, then technical occupations now represent 5 percent of the total workforce. Technical occupations hold a similar place in the economies of other Western nations (Barley 1996a), but the importance of technical occupations goes beyond sheer numbers: software developers, engineers, and technicians are responsible for designing almost every technology that we use, as well as most of the production processes by which those technologies are made.

Yet, sociologists of work and occupations have paid scant attention to technical work relative to other occupational groups. Research on computer occupations and on technicians remains nearly an empty set. Studies of engineers are more numerous, but because most have been motivated by theoretical issues of concern to sociologists, rather than by an attempt to understand what engineers do, these studies tell us surprisingly little about the actual work of engineers. Studies of scientific practice are more common, thanks to sociologists of science and knowledge who championed laboratory ethnographies in the 1980s (e.g. Knorr-Cetina and Mulkay 1983; Latour and Woolgar 1979; Lynch 1985). But because contemporary sociologists of science have been interested primarily in epistemological issues, even our understanding of scientific work, especially in industrial contexts, is limited. This situation has led a number of observers to acknowledge that despite their importance and prevalence, technical workers remain an 'invisible' workforce (Downey, Donovan, and Elliott 1989; Fleischer and Liker 1992; Shapin 1989). The goal of this chapter is to prompt sociologists to rectify this situation.

I begin by briefly reviewing two major clusters of research on technical work, both developed after World War II when the employment of scientists and

---

[1] There is no accepted definition of a technical occupation. For the purposes of this chapter we shall confine its use to scientific, engineering, and computer-related occupations and to technicians, which roughly approximates the term's use in everyday speech. A broader definition of technical work would certainly include many health care occupations and a significant proportion of the craft and repair occupations.

engineers began to attract attention. The first cluster, which I shall call the Weberian literature, emerged in the 1950s when industrial sociologists were actively exploring the implications and limitations of Weber's (1968/1922) theory of bureaucracy.[2] The second cluster ascended during the 1970s, drew its inspiration primarily from Marx and later Braverman (1973), and focused on questions about the place of technical occupations in the class structure. My objective in this review is to show how sociology's tendency to place theory before description has left us with anemic images of technical work.

The second part of the chapter lays out a research agenda for developing our substantive knowledge of technical work and its social organization, drawing eclectically on more recent studies that have taken steps toward a more comparative, grounded, situated and emic understanding of what technical work entails. Because the perspectives that I discuss cut across research on different technical occupations, I shall weave together studies of engineers, programmers, technicians, and, where relevant, scientists. By necessity, however, the discussion is weighted toward engineers because studies of engineers comprise the bulk of the literature on technical workers.

16.2 THE WEBERIAN LITERATURE

16.2.1 Professionals in Bureaucracies

Research on scientists and engineers emerged in the late 1950s under the influence of Parson's (1939, 1951), Hughes's (1958), and Merton's (1942, 1957) writings on bureaucracy, professions, and science. All three argued, albeit from somewhat different perspectives, that bureaucratic and professional forms of organizing rested on conflicting principles. In contrast to the bureaucratic principle, which invests social control and authority in the hierarchical structure of organizations, professionalism invests control in the occupational group and the voluntary associations that represent professional practitioners (Blau and Scott 1962).

---

[2] Others have referred to this as the literature on 'engineers as professionals' and have emphasized its ties to functionalism (Downey and Lucena 1995; Downey, Donovan, and Elliott 1989; Meiksins and Smith 1996; Watson and Meiksins 1991; Whalley 1986b; Zussman 1985). As noted in the text, the Weberian cluster did focus on questions of professionalism and it was also structural-functionalist in orientation. But I prefer the label 'Weberian' because it emphasizes how the literature's roots in the study of the limits of bureaucracy shaped the questions that researchers asked.

Given this general premise, students of organizations and occupations anticipated that the influx of engineers, and especially scientists, into industrial labs that
occurred at the end of World War II would result in significant personal tension and
strain for these employees because of inherent conflicts between bureaucratic
and professional forms of organizing. Between 1960 and the early 1970s, industrial sociologists conducted a number of studies in government and large
industrial laboratories, especially in the aerospace industry (Abrahamson 1964;
French 1967; Glaser 1963, 1964; Goldner and Ritti 1967; Hinrichs 1964; Kornhauser
1962; LaPorte 1965; Lee 1971; McKelvey 1969; Marcson 1960; Miller 1967; Pelz and
Andrews 1966; Ritti 1968, 1971; Sheldon 1971; Souder 1974). Except for Marcson
(1960) and Ritti (1971), all relied exclusively on surveys that explored the attitudes
and opinions of technical personnel, the career aspirations of scientists and engineers, the formal organization of R&D labs, and the ways in which firms attempted
to motivate technical employees in light of their professional allegiances and
identities.

This literature evolved through two periods as accumulating data repeatedly
failed to conform to the Weberians' expectations. Initially, research focused entirely
on scientists or treated scientists and engineers as if they were alike. These early
studies repeatedly found that technical professionals seemed more satisfied, more
oriented to their firms, and less oriented to their disciplines than sociological
theory expected. To be sure, some scientists and engineers resembled 'cosmopol-
itans' and others resembled 'locals' (Merton 1957), but a significant number seemed
to hold both orientations simultaneously: they identified with their profession as
well as their employer.

The early studies also pointed to consistent differences in the attitudes and
aspirations of 'applied researchers', who were usually engineers, and 'basic researchers', who were usually scientists. In general, applied researchers were less interested
in publishing, less concerned with contributing to knowledge, less devoted to
developing a reputation in their field, more interested in contributing to the success
of their firm, and more interested in having a managerial career.

Finally, researchers found that firms employed an array of techniques for 'motivating' technical professionals that were consistent with popular and theoretical
images of what scientists valued. These included encouraging technical professionals to publish, patent, and participate in professional associations as well as
allowing them to work on 'bootleg' projects of personal interest. Large firms had
also instituted 'dual ladders' that enabled firms to 'promote' technical professionals
without moving them into managerial careers.[3] However, the evidence suggested
that technical professionals did not view these motivational techniques as

---

[3] In a dual ladder system, a technical hierarchy is created to parallel the managerial hierarchy. As
engineers and scientists ascend the technical ladder they are given greater control over the substance of
their work and larger salaries, but they typically do not supervise the work of others or have greater say
over the direction of the firm.

particularly effective (see Allen and Katz 1986; Epstein 1986; Goldner and Ritti 1967; Kornhauser 1962; Pelz and Andrews 1966; Shepard 1958).

In light of these findings, Weberian researchers turned, in the late 1960s, to explicating the differences between scientists' more 'professional' and engineers' more 'bureaucratic' orientations to work (Bailyn 1980; Goldner and Ritti 1967; Miller 1967; Miller and Wager 1971; Perrucci and Gerstl 1969; Ritti 1968). The consensus of the second period of research was that engineers were not professionals, at least as sociologists then understood the term.

16.2.2 Engineering as a Profession

This consensus meshed well with the image of engineering emerging from a second stream of research that sought to explain why some occupations could be considered professions while others could not. At the time, a paradigm shift was occurring among students of the professions. While earlier work had focused on identifying a distinctive constellation of characteristics that distinguished professions from other, run-of-the-mill occupations (Carr-Sanders and Wilson 1933; Goode 1957; Greenwood 1957), by the early 1970s, the emphasis on classification had given way to an emphasis on process, exploring professionalization as an ongoing effort by occupational groups to secure autonomy, status, power, and, ultimately, monopolistic control over the rendering of particular services (Bucher and Strauss 1961; Friedson 1970, 1973; Larson 1977; Wilensky 1964). Both approaches called the professional status of engineering into question.

Most who examined engineering in light of specific criteria concluded that it lacked the attributes and power of a strong profession (e.g. Perrucci and Gerstl 1969; Rothstein 1969; Wilensky 1964). Although university-trained engineers certainly possessed technical knowledge, a significant proportion of the engineers' acumen was practical and contextual. Furthermore, having a specialized degree was not necessary for entering the occupation. Employers had thwarted attempts by engineers to build strong professional societies, efforts to establish accreditation standards had had limited success, and engineers remained, by and large, subordinate to the direction of their clients (their employers) who controlled the economic demand for their services (Calhoun 1960; Larson 1977; Layton 1971; Meiksins 1988; Whalley 1986b; Zussman 1985). Engineering appeared to be a heterogeneous collection of practitioners who lacked a common identity or the sense of community characteristic of strong professions (Perrucci and Gerstl 1969).

In the end, Weberian sociologists drew conflicting interpretations from the research on technical occupations. The most common conclusion was that engineering represented a 'new' kind of profession, one born within the confines of bureaucracy and, hence, potentially paradigmatic of the future (e.g. Hall 1968;

Wilensky 1964). Wilensky wrote: 'The occupational group of the future will combine elements from both the professional and bureaucratic models. … Mixed forms of control … are the likely outcomes' (p. 157). Perrucci (1971) took a less sympathetic stance. He concluded that engineering's lack of professionalism made engineers the handmaidens of management and 'servants of power'. Consistent with the spirit of social criticism of the day, he chastised engineering for failing to live up to its obligations as a profession.

Having reached the conclusion that engineering was, at best, a weak profession and that engineers accommodated easily to the demands of bureaucracy, Weberian studies of technical occupations largely ceased. What remained of the tradition were occasional studies of the careers of scientists and engineers that focused on the transition into management (Bailyn 1980; Bailyn and Lynch 1983; Biddle and Roberts 1994; Roberts and Biddle 1994; Rynes, Tolbert, and Strausser 1988). As the Weberians left the field, studies of technical work took a more critical turn.

16.3 THE MARXIST LITERATURE

Whereas the Weberians approached technical work as a critical case for studying the limits of bureaucracy, Marxists used engineering to explore how capitalism and class relations had evolved over the twentieth century. Because of their macrosocial perspective, most Marxists eschewed workplace studies and focused, instead, on the social history of engineering and other technical occupations. Marxist scholarship on technical work fell roughly into three clusters: a literature that portrayed engineers as agents of de-skilling, a literature that argued that technical work was itself being de-skilled, and a body of work on how technical occupations fit into the class structure.

16.3.1 Agents of De-skilling

In *Labor and Monopoly Capitalism*, Harry Braverman (1973) argued that the essence of twentieth-century capitalism was the separation of cognition from execution, accomplished by devising ways to separate the mental from manual aspects of jobs. By various techniques, capitalists succeeded in 'de-skilling' craftsmen and clerical workers, thus robbing them of their expertise and, hence, their shop-floor power.

Braverman traced the ideology of de-skilling to Frederick Taylor and the scientific management movement, whose advocates were primarily mechanical and industrial engineers who practiced in the last decades of the nineteenth and the first decades of the twentieth centuries (see Nelson 1975; Shenhav 1999). Like Perrucci (1971), Braverman saw engineers as servants of power. In fact, Braverman intimated that management could not control labor were it not for engineers, because engineers design the machines and work processes that allow de-skilling.[4]

The publication of *Labor and Monopoly Capitalism* triggered a flurry of research on de-skilling in a variety of occupations (see Crompton and Reid 1982; Wood 1982; Zimbalist 1979) and gave rise to what we now call 'labor process studies'. In *America by Design*, Noble (1977), a historian, depicted the integral role engineers played in the emergence of corporate capitalism in late nineteenth and early twentieth centuries. Noble's analysis depicted engineers as actively involved in yoking science and university education to industrial goals and in persuading the federal government to champion and fund applied R&D. He also documented the historical links between engineering education and management education, the latter of which can properly be said to have evolved from the former, regardless of how separate they may be today. Noble emphasized that engineers were prominent among the early capitalists who designed modern corporations.

Several years later, Noble (1979, 1984) turned his attention to the problem of explaining why numerical control had preempted record-playback (or tracer) technology, which would have automated machining while granting machinists greater centrality in developing programs. Although Noble left no doubt that some managers and engineers saw numerical control as a way to de-skill machinists, his story was more complex than a simple tale of de-skilling. Noble showed that numerical control had emerged from a confluence of agendas including the scientific aspirations of mathematicians at MIT's Servo-Mechanism Lab, the Air Force's need for finely machined parts for jet aircraft, as well as the Air Force's willingness to subsidize contractors that purchased numerically controlled tools. Moreover, Noble's examination of numerical control at GE indicated that corporate management's de-skilling agenda was hampered by the machinists'

---

[4] Braverman was a former machinist. At the time he wrote, machine tools that used punched paper tapes were the state of the art in numerical control. Consequently, his observations on the separation of programming from the running of machine tools were partially tied to the constraints and affordances of tape technology. He failed to anticipate the development of machine tools controlled by microcomputers that would alter the division of labor in the machinists' favor (see Kelley 1986, 1989; Shaiken 1984). Braverman was a determinist, but his determinism was rooted in idealism not materialism.

union as well as by GE engineers at the level of the plant who opposed using numerical control to de-skill.

More recently, Steven Vallas (Vallas 1998, 2001; Vallas and Beck 1996) published a series of ethnographic papers examining the role that production engineers play in de-skilling operators in highly automated paper mills. In contrast to Braverman and Noble, who depicted engineers as the capitalists' henchmen, Vallas drew on Abbott (1988, 1991) to argue that production engineers were motivated to maintain and strengthen the boundary between mental and manual work because they sought to protect their occupational jurisdiction. Although jurisdictional concerns often shaped engineers' choices, Vallas noted that some engineers saw things differently and were willing to recognize the 'legitimacy of craft knowledge' (Vallas and Beck 1996: 351). Zuboff (1989) found much the same thing in her studies of automated pulp paper mills. Similarly, Thomas's (1994) case studies of the introduction of automated technologies in a number of firms and industries indicated that contests over de-skilling were typically fought between different groups of engineers with competing occupational and organizational agendas, and that engineers used the rhetoric of labor costs largely to convince top management to authorize technologies that the engineers wished to purchase or develop for reasons that had little to do with labor relations.

These studies point to cracks in the Marxists' monolithic image of engineers as agents of de-skilling, suggesting that such images are, at best, underspecified or, at worst, wrong on several grounds. First, Braverman and his theoretical descendants failed to appreciate engineering's heterogeneity. Thomas's (1994), Vallas's (1998, 2001), and Zuboff's (1989) research shows that even among industrial and production engineers, there is variation in engineers' objectives and philosophies. More importantly, most contemporary engineers (e.g. electrical engineers, software engineers, structural engineers) work in contexts where issues of de-skilling are irrelevant. Thus, de-skilling theory is, at best, useful for describing the rhetoric and, in some cases the ethos, of engineering in production environments. Second, although technological change has, without doubt, de-skilled and even eliminated some occupations (printing, for instance), Braverman's global predictions have failed to materialize. The consensus that has emerged over the last twenty years is that technological and organizational changes have brought about either no net change or a slight rise in skill requirements throughout the economy (Adler 1992; Attewell 1987, 1992; Gallie 1994; Salzman 1992; Wright and Martin 1987). Finally, Braverman, Noble, and others failed to recognize that engineers are themselves employees who are subject to managerial control. This realization motivated a second group of Marxist scholars, who argued that technical workers were themselves being de-skilled.

16.3.2 De-professionalization

While Braverman and others were writing about the de-skilling of the blue-collar and clerical labor, other sociologists began to argue that the power of the professions was similarly eroding through the process of de-professionalization (Antley and Antley 1973; Derber 1982a, b; Haug 1975, 1977; McKinlay 1982; Toren 1975). Four developments presumably drove this change: automation (especially expert systems), an increasingly well-educated workforce for whom the professional's knowledge was less of a mystery, the bureaucratization of professional practice, and attempts by corporations to limit the discretion of the professionals they employed. Although the fate of medicine garnered most of the attention (for reasons that are now obvious in a world of HMOs and managed care), a handful of scholars sought to show that de-skilling was also occurring among technical workers.

Drafting and computer programming were taken as prominent examples. Cooley (1980) and Shaiken (1984) both claimed that computer aided design (CAD) systems, often touted by marketers as a means of reducing labor costs by simplifying work, would de-skill drafters and designers, whose drawing skills had long been crucial to engineering and architecture. Similarly, Kraft (1979a, b) and Greenbaum (1979) warned that computer programmers were being de-skilled by a push for greater efficiency and predictability in software development. Ensmenger's historical studies of the perennial 'software crisis' (Ensmenger 2001, 2002; Ensmenger and Aspray 2001) provided evidence for Kraft's and Greenbaum's claims that corporate management's agenda was to control the IT labor force. But between conception and execution, once again, fell a shadow.

Contrary to de-skilling theory's expectations, Salzman (1989) found that aerospace and automobile firms dramatically increased their employment of drafters and designers in the 1980s while simultaneously investing heavily in CAD systems. His studies of designers of printed circuit board indicated why: CAD systems demanded skilled designers because the software was buggy and constantly changing, because automated routing and placing functions produced inferior products, and because even the most advanced software was unable to automate the more complex, analytic aspects of chip design. In fact, designers argued that CAD made their work more challenging! Henderson (1998) also observed that CAD had done little to eliminate hand drawing and sketching, and that designers used CAD most often to store and create documents for use by customers. Furthermore, empirical evidence indicates that there is little reason to believe that either structured programming or a more elaborate division of labor have de-skilled programmers (Kuhn 1989). Rather, as Orlikowski (1988) pointed out, as firms became increasingly dependent on an IT infrastructure, programmers and other IT occupations actually gained power in organizations. In addition, continual labor shortages and the ease of switching employers have granted programmers considerable market power. It appears that de-skilling theorists mistook specialization for the fragmentation of work. Unlike fragmentation, specialization brings control over narrower but also more esoteric knowledge, which usually enhances autonomy and control. Specialization does, however, engender jurisdictional battles (Abbott 1988, 1991), and Ensmenger (2001) has suggested that we interpret firms' ongoing but largely ineffective attempts to tighten the leash on computer work as just such a battle.

16.3.3 New Class Theories

A third body of Marxist scholarship focused on the problem that technical occupations posed for class analysis. Traditional Marxism divided society into three classes: capitalists, workers, and the petty bourgeoisie. Technical workers did not easily fit this framework. Although they were employees, they had considerably more status than most other workers and, more important, they controlled crucial scientific and technical knowledge that firms required. Moreover, even if technical workers did capital's bidding, most were not themselves managers. To circumvent the theoretical dilemmas posed by these occupations, most class theorists simply elected to force engineers to one side of the class divide or the other.

Observing that French technicians had played central roles in a number of strikes and protests in the late 1960s, Gorz (1967) and Mallet (1975) proclaimed that technical workers represented a 'new working class'. Like Veblen (1965/1921) many years before, new working-class theorists argued that engineers and technical workers resented the fact that they had little say over corporate goals and that in time they would (and should) join with other workers, leveraging their control over the technical means of production to take command away from managers and capitalists.

Carchedi (1977) agreed that technical workers were employees, but unlike Gorz and Mallet, he emphasized that engineers had also historically held supervisory positions. As such, Carchedi argued that technical workers were situated between capitalists and workers. Carchedi (1977) and Wright (1976) asserted that firms were gradually routinizing the work of engineers and technicians who were, therefore, better viewed as new 'new proletarians' that lacked any clear identity with the working class. Wright later changed his mind, when his own analysis of US occupational data indicated a decline rather than an increase in proletarianization among American workers during the 1970s (Wright and Martin 1987).

Poulantzas (1978) and eventually Gorz (1976) adopted yet another view. Engineers and technical workers were not only staunchly middle class, they were allied with capital for several reasons: they often held managerial positions; their work was primarily mental; and most important, they employed their knowledge to assist capitalists in controlling labor.

New class theories did not lend themselves easily to empirical investigation and the few researchers who put them to the test quickly found them to be insufficiently nuanced. For instance, Roberts *et al.* (1972) and Smith (1987) conducted field studies of technicians in industry, drawing on new class theory, only to discover that the daily realities of technical work were far more complex than class theorists anticipated. In particular, the attributes of technical work seemed to vary considerably across occupation, task, and organization.

By the late 1980s all three clusters of Marxist scholarship on technical work had dissipated. Each had been driven by a theoretical agenda whose interpretations were unable to withstand empirical scrutiny. Part of the problem lay in the fact that Marxists almost never examined what engineers did; they simply presumed they knew. Like the Weberians, the Marxists also failed to recognize that engineering had become a collection of occupations whose members did radically different work in radically different contexts. Even worse, new class theorists lumped engineers together with technicians and with operatives in automated production plants to create a murky conceptual and empirical morass. The end result was that whatever else they may have achieved, Marxists scholars told us even less about the realities of technical work than the Weberians who preceded them.

16.4 TOWARD GROUNDED STUDIES OF TECHNICAL WORK

16.4.1 The Columbia Studies

In the early 1980s under the guidance of Alan Silver, three doctoral students at Columbia University—Peter Whalley, Robert Zussman, and Stephen Crawford—began dissertations that would break received theory's stranglehold on sociological studies of engineering, paving the way for more grounded, ethnographic research on technical occupations. Guided by the recognition that the Weberian and Marxist literatures offered incompatible and potentially inaccurate images of engineering, and the suspicion that engineering's status varied from culture to culture, the three arranged to study engineering practice in different countries. Zussman (1985) studied American engineers, Whalley (1984, 1986a, b, 1991) studied British engineers, and Crawford (1989, 1996) studied French engineers. Each conducted multi-method fieldwork using the same basic research design: a comparison of engineers working in a traditional manufacturing firm dominated by production with engineers working in a high-technology firm where research and development played a larger role. Each was also careful to distinguish between different types of engineering in the firms they studied.

Although the details of their ethnographies are far too rich to recount here, individually and collectively Crawford (1989), Whalley (1986b), and Zussman (1985) established three important facts about engineering that subsequent students of technical work ignore only at their peril. First, they made clear that engineering's status is inextricably tied to variations in national and historical contexts. Whalley showed, for example, that British engineering remains more tightly tied to shop-floor traditions and places less emphasis on credentials than engineering in the United States or France. In contrast, French engineers are highly stratified by educational background. Those at the pinnacle, the *ingeniéurs diplomés* who have long been groomed in the *grandes écoles* to lead industry and government, have a more elite status than either American or British engineers (Crawford 1989). American engineering lies somewhere between the British and the French models, but differs significantly from both in that engineering in the United States has long been a path for upward mobility among bright lower class youth.

Second, the Columbia studies demonstrated that the social organization of engineering, the roles that engineers play, the work they do, and how they experience their work vary considerably across industries, and that these variations are tied to differences in product markets, labor markets, technologies, and the pace of technological change. In general, regardless of country, the Columbia researchers found that the organization of engineering in more traditional markets was more bureaucratic: the division of engineering labor was more 'segmented', and engineers were more apt to pursue careers through hierarchical internal labor markets (Crawford 1989: 85; Zussman 1985: 87) and to view management as a career goal (Whalley 1986b). Conversely, in high-technology firms, where technologies were more complex and where the state of the art changed more quickly, the division of labor was project oriented and more tightly interdependent. Engineers in high-tech firms typically pursued careers by changing employers, were more cosmopolitan (Whalley 1986b: 121), more involved in technical problem solving, less involved in supervision (Crawford 1989: 87), and less likely to have a sense of ownership over the products of their work (Zussman 1985: 91–3).

Finally, the Columbia studies pointed to significant differences in the nature of engineering by occupation and function. Unlike earlier researchers, Crawford, Whalley, and Zussman carefully distinguished between the work of production engineers, product engineers, process engineers, designers, service engineers, and R&D engineers. The resulting contrasts led Zussman (1985: 46) to write, 'A comparison of machine design at the two companies suggests that similarities between functions and across industries may well be stronger than those within a single industry and across functions.' Similarly, Whalley (1986b) found that while engineers in his high-tech firm felt more involved and less constrained than engineers in his traditional metalworking firm, there was considerable heterogeneity within each firm by engineering function (occupation).

The message of the Columbia studies for sociologists of work was clear. Neither Weberian nor Marxist theories of technical work adequately capture the status, complexity, or diversity of engineering. Accordingly, theories of technical work need to be built from the ground up, preferably using comparative research designs. Grappling with the role of engineers and other technical workers in contemporary society will, therefore, require sociologists of work to examine what technical workers actually do *in situ*. It will also demand that sociologists remain alert to how organizational, economic, and cultural dynamics shape engineering practice. Finally, the studies underscored that 'engineering' and, by extension, 'technical work', are best treated as cover terms for a set of occupations whose practices and social organization are likely to differ in important ways.

Since the Columbia studies, research on technical work has taken a much-needed ethnographic turn. Although studies of technical work still remain scarce, sociologists have finally begun to lay the foundations for a more empirically accurate understanding of the technical workforce, and several promising lines of scholarship have been developed.

16.4.2 Work Practices

To the degree that sociologists prior to the 1990s concerned themselves with what engineers and other technical workers actually do, their gaze largely stopped at the social: with whom engineers interacted, for what purposes, in what contexts, and how engineers interpreted those interactions and relationships. As a result, sociological images of engineering practice have omitted much of what makes technical work 'technical'.

Beginning in the 1990s sociologists and anthropologists influenced by ethnomethodological studies of scientific laboratories (Amann and Knorr-Cetina 1989; Jordon and Lynch 1992); (Latour and Woolgar 1979; Lynch 1985; Lynch and Edgerton 1988); and by theories of situated practice (Lave 1988; Lave and Wenger 1990; Suchman 1987) began to examine the substantive as well as the social aspects of technical work. To date, the majority of practice-oriented studies have focused on single occupations, most commonly engineering design (Bucciarelli 1988*a*, *b*, 1994; Hargadon and Sutton 1997; Henderson 1991, 1998, 1999; Vincenti 1990), although studies have also examined the work of various technicians' occupations (forthcoming; Barley 1996*b*; Barley and Bechky 1994; Bechky 2003, Nelsen 1997*b*; Nelsen and Barley 1997; Orr 1997; Pentland 1992; Scarselletta 1997; Zabusky 1997; Zabusky and Barley 1996). The most common themes of practice-oriented research are that technical work entails a complex mix of formal, contextual, social, tacit, and explicit knowledge and that technical knowledge is unevenly distributed among practitioners and often travels by word of mouth.

Studies of technical practice pose a significant hurdle that sociologists of work do not face when studying manual and clerical work: to conduct fieldwork on technical practices requires researchers to have at least rudimentary knowledge of the scientific and technical disciplines in which the practice is rooted. It is for this reason that many of those who have studied technical practice have either been trained as engineers and technicians or have worked in technical firms or engineering schools.

Despite this hurdle, studies of technical practice are valuable to sociologists because they provide the details necessary for conceptualizing what technical work involves. This, in turn, provides the basis for developing more finely differentiated distinctions between types of technical work and the roles that technical workers play in different organizations and divisions of labor. As such, studies of practice assemble the type of data necessary for developing new occupational taxonomies and ideal types, more accurate images of how technical work is organized and insights into technical cultures.

16.5 OCCUPATIONAL TAXONOMIES AND IDEAL TYPICAL OCCUPATIONS

Occupational sociologists generally agree that the occupational categories by which the federal government classifies jobs are outdated (Attewell 1990; Miller *et al.* 1980; Spenner 1983, 1995; Steinberg 1990). The US Bureau of the Census initially designed the core of its occupational classification system specifically to chart the rise of industrialism and what were perceived as its associated social problems (Conk 1978). In line with this, Cain and Treiman (1981) reported nearly twenty years ago that 76 percent of the listings in the *DOT* covered blue-collar jobs. Although the *DOT* has subsequently undergone substantial modification, we can still make much finer distinctions among blue-collar work than among managerial, clerical, service, sales, professional, and technical work. Yet, only 24 percent of all employed Americans are blue-collar workers, a decline of 16 percent since 1940 (see Barley 1996*a*; Silvestri 1997). Although the Department of Labor is exploring approaches to occupational classification that should more accurately reflect the division of labor in society and be more sensitive to changes in the nature of work, a new system has yet to be fully authorized or funded (National Research Council 1999). Consequently, we continue to chart trends in the nature of work with occupational categories and systems of analysis developed for an economy that existed somewhere between a quarter and a half a century ago.

The ramifications of outdated and inadequately differentiated occupational categories are considerable. Empirical research is ultimately predicated on the ability to sort phenomena by attributes and to assign appropriate labels or names. Without such conditions, comparisons are impossible. Sociologists have had difficulty coming to terms with engineering's heterogeneity, in part, because they have not been knowledgeable enough to make sufficiently fine distinctions between types of engineers and types of engineering. The problem of taxonomy is more acute for those who wish to study technical occupations about which even less is known.

In some cases, using the techniques of linguistic anthropology (Spradley 1979), researchers can acquire useful taxonomies by learning how insiders map their social worlds (Kling and Gerson 1978; Strauss 1978, 1984). But in some technical worlds, especially those in which technologies are unstable, lines of work may have no name. For instance, in software development, insiders speak of 'skill sets' rather than specialties. 'Skill sets' refer to expertise in specific combinations of technologies, operating systems, languages, and areas of application. Different skills sets often define distinct but overlapping occupational communities.

In short, before sociologists can truly come to terms with the social organization of technical work, they will have to identify, name, and ultimately compare different types of technical work. Research on taxonomies of technical occupations is just beginning to emerge. For example, to study the careers of multimedia developers working in New York City's Silicon Alley, Amanda Damarin (2003) had to first learn how insiders sorted multimedia jobs. An entirely different approach, potentially applicable to software development, would be to develop etic taxonomies by clustering terms for skills mentioned in job announcements.

Closely related to occupational taxonomies is the notion of an ideal typical occupation. Just as one can speak of ideal types that inform our thinking about organizations (Weber 1968/1922), so one can speak of ideal types of work. An ideal typical occupation is an abstraction that captures key attributes of a family of occupations. As Weber noted, ideal types are useful not because they are descriptively accurate but because they serve as models that assist us in thinking about social phenomena. The 'worker-on-the-assembly-line' is one such ideal type. It evokes images of an individual, often in an automobile factory, standing beside a swiftly moving conveyor, repeatedly performing the same operation on each assembly that flows by. Boredom, fatigue, routine, lack of autonomy, and little need for education or thought are the hallmarks of such work. Although factory jobs have always been more varied than this, the ideal type nevertheless evokes a constellation of attributes that capture the family resemblance among many factory jobs.

To date, there have been few attempts to identify ideal types of technical work. The potential of such research, however, was demonstrated by a series of studies of technicians done in the early 1990s at Cornell University with funding from the National Center for the Education of the Workforce. The Cornell researchers conducted ethnographies of medical technicians (Scarselletta 1997), automobile technicians (Nelsen 1997a), science technician (Barley and Bechky 1994), computer technicians (Zabusky 1997: Zabusky and Barley 1996), emergency medical technicians (Nelsen and Barley 1997), library technicians, and engineering technicians (Darr 2000; Darr and Scarselletta 2002). The researchers then did a comparative analysis of the ethnographic data to propose two types of technicians: 'buffers' and 'brokers' (Barley 1996b). Although all technicians' work appeared to have a common 'epistemic core' (taking care of physical systems and inscribing attributes of those systems into symbolic representations), buffers and brokers differ by the nature of their position in occupational divisions of labor. Buffers stand between professionals, such as scientists or engineers, and the physical systems about which the professionals have theoretical knowledge. Brokers, on the other hand, mediate between communities that produce technologies and communities of users who have little or no technical knowledge.

16.6 SOCIAL ORGANIZATION OF TECHNICAL WORK

Understanding technical work also requires research that links activities, tasks, roles, and identities to social organization. We know that different lines of technical work are organized differently. For example, Whalley (1986b) and Zussman (1985) report that production engineering is less likely to be done by teams than is development work. Bailey (Bailey and Gainsburg 2003; Bailey, Gainsburg, and Sept 2003) has shown that structural engineering is more solitary than chip design, and that the distinction is related to differences in the complexity of the technology, the pace of technological change, and the specialization of knowledge around disciplines and subsystems. Although Ritti (1971) wrote about how specialization and complex systems design influenced the experience, perceptions, and attitudes of engineers over thirty years ago, subsequent researchers have largely allowed his insights to lie fallow.

Research on the social organization of project teams has fared better, in large measure because the coordination of collaborative work is a crucial topic in the literature on the management of R&D.[5] Most of the literature on project management is normative and focuses on tools for scheduling, allocating, and organizing work processes. Nevertheless, scattered throughout the literature are hints of social factors and relations that could provide sociologists with important clues about the organization of technical projects, including temporal rhythms, team composition, relations between specialties and functions, and the nature of conflict between managers and technical workers. Especially informative are Kidder's (1981) and Perlow's (1997) ethnographies of development teams in high-tech firms, which document the pressures engineers face, the strategies that managers use to control engineers, and the politics of technical work. Dougherty (1992) and Thomas (1994) have written about the competition and conflict among manufacturing engineers, designers, and other occupational groups that inhabit firms. The social organization of project work is an especially fruitful arena, ripe for exploration by sociologists of work.

The social organization of technical communities also begs for investigation. Sociologists of science have written extensively about the structure of scientific communities (e.g. Burt 1978; Crane 1972; Hagstrom 1965; Hargens 2000; Lievrouw et al. 1987; Mullins 1972, 1973). Although there has been little work on the structure of engineering and other technical communities, the research that has been done suggests that the social organization of engineering differs significantly from that of science. A classic series of studies of R&D labs by Allen and his collaborators (Allen 1977; Allen and Cohen 1969; Katz 1981; Katz and Tushman 1979; Tushman and Katz 1980) showed that communication networks among engineers were less likely to span organizational boundaries than were networks among basic researchers. In development labs, boundary spanning was typically done by a handful of individuals known as 'gatekeepers', who served as bridges to the larger technical community.

Different patterns are suggested by studies of other technical groups. Orr (1997) demonstrated that copier repair technicians participate in and rely on members of regional communities of practice to solve ongoing technical problems. Barley and Kunda's (2004) study of technical contractors suggests that colored graph analysis would show that contractors have ego networks marked by structural holes (Burt 1992), but their networks often contain a 'referral clique' that constitutes a completely connected subgraph at the network's core. Although researchers have suggested that communities of practice (Brown and Duguid 2001; Wenger 1998)

---

[5] The literature on project management is far too large to review. For examples that focus on social dynamics, see Allen (1977); Ancona and Caldwell (1992); Bergen (1986); Katz (1982); and Katz and Allen (1985).

are critical to the flow of knowledge in technical work, scholars have yet to document the structure and composition of such communities.

16.7 Organizational Cultures and Market Influences

Scattered throughout the literature on engineering work are hints that engineering practice is strongly shaped by organizational cultures and by differences in the product and labor markets in which technical workers participate. Ritti (1971) observed that aerospace engineers located in labs further removed from corporate headquarters were less disgruntled, thought they had more influence, and were less underutilized. Importantly, however, Ritti did not argue that engineers would be happier and more productive in the absence of control. Rather, his argument was that engineers were better utilized when they were not subject to the commands of managers who did not understand the nature of technical work but who nevertheless exercised their right to dictate technical direction.

Diane Vaughan's (1996) detailed analysis of the chain of decisions that led up to the destruction of the space shuttle, Challenger, also points to how work and organizational cultures shape engineers' practices, power, and roles. NASA's highly structured and combative bureaucratic review process (designed to uncover unacceptable risks) together with a work culture based on an experiential approach to anomalies and the normalization of deviance fostered a sequence of events stretching over several years that led to the fateful decision to launch Challenger despite evidence that, in retrospect, should have led managers to scrub the launch. NASA's culture contrasts sharply with the cultures of Digital Equipment Company (DEC) (Kunda 1992) and Data General (Kidder 1981), which relied more on normative than bureaucratic control.

The differences in engineering cultures documented by these studies partially reflect different missions and 'markets'. NASA's technology is not only more complex than a minicomputer or microcomputer, but NASA must also contend with national and international political agendas. The market for space flight also entails more costly risks, including the loss of life. Accordingly, one can argue that DEC and Data General's consumer-oriented market allowed for more decentralized control. This conclusion is amplified in studies that examine how product markets shape the contours of technical practice (Darr 2000, 2002, 2003; Darr and Talmud 2003).

Differences in labor markets also affect technical practice. Whalley (1986*b*) and Zussman (1985) argued that to understand engineers one has to understand how their careers unfold. Both argue that the social organization of engineering in traditional metalworking firms differs from the social organization of engineering in high-tech firms because in the former engineers play out their careers within internal labor markets, but not in the latter. Barley and Kunda (2004) explore the experience of technical workers who have chosen to work as contractors. The careers of contractors have an even higher velocity than those of engineers who are permanent employees of high-tech firms. Barley and Kunda argue that the experience of moving from project to project creates a unique orientation to professional practice, which they label itinerant professionalism. The social dynamics of itinerant professionalism differ significantly the dynamics of free and corporate professionalism.

In sum, sociologists of work still have much to learn about the social organization of technical work, and the most productive path to this knowledge will involve comparative fieldwork. The payoff of such research for the discipline is especially high. Armstrong (1984), Barley and Kunda (2001), and others have suggested that as contemporary organizations become less bureaucratically organized and work becomes less manual, organizations appear more like collections of collaborating and competing occupational specialties. If such scholars are correct about what we might call the 'occupationalization' of organizations, understanding the role of technical experts in organizations will be key to developing a theory of organizational life that takes the concept of occupation more seriously. In short, the mandate for studying technical work is nothing less than a reintegration of the study of work, occupations, and organizations.

REFERENCES

ABBOTT, A. (1988). *The System of Professions: An Essay on the Division of Expert Labor.* Chicago: University of Chicago Press.

——(1991). 'The Future of Professions: Occupation and Expertise in the Age of Organization', in P. S. Tolbert and S. R. Barley (eds.), *Research in the Sociology of Organizations,* 8. Greenwich, Conn.: JAI Press.

ABRAHAMSON, M. (1964). 'The Integration of Industrial Scientists'. *Administrative Science Quarterly,* 9: 208–18.

ADLER, P. S. (1992). *Technology and the Future of Work.* New York: Oxford University Press.

ALLEN, T. J. (1977). *Managing the Flow of Innovation.* Cambridge, Mass.: MIT Press.

——and COHEN, S. I. (1969). 'Information Flow in Research and Development Laboratories'. *Administrative Science Quarterly,* 14: 12–19.

——and KATZ, R. (1986). 'The Dual Ladder: Motivational Solution or Managerial Delusion'. *R&D Management,* 16: 185–97.

AMANN, K., and KNORR-CETINA, K. (1989). 'Thinking through Talk: An Ethnographic Study of a Molecular Biology Laboratory'. *Knowledge and Society: Studies in the Sociology of Past and Present*, 8: 3–26.

ANCONA, D. G., and CALDWELL, D. F. (1992). 'Demography and Design: Predictors of New Product Team Performance'. *Organization Science*, 3: 321–41.

ANTLEY, R. M., and ANTLEY, M. A. (1973). 'Automation: Its Impact on the Delivery of Health Care'. *Computers and Automation*, April: 11–14.

ARMSTRONG, P. (1984). 'Competition between the Organizational Professions and the Evolution of Management Control Strategies', in K. Thompson (ed.), *Work, Employment, and Unemployment: Perspectives of Work and Society*. Philadelphia: Open University Press.

ATTEWELL, P. (1987). 'The De-Skilling Controversy'. *Work and Occupations*, 14: 323–46.

—— (1990). 'What Is Skill?' *Work and Occupations*, 17: 422–48.

—— (1992). 'Skill and Occupational Changes in U.S. Manufacturing', in P. S. Adler (ed.), *Technology and the Future of Work*. New York: Oxford University Press.

BAILEY, D., and GAINSBURG, J. (2003). 'Knowledge at Work'. Working Paper, Center for Work, Technology and Organization, School of Engineering, Stanford University.

—— —— and SEPT, L. (2003). 'Apprentices and Gurus: Two Models of Modern Workplace Learning'. Working Paper, Center for Work, Technology and Organization, School of Engineering, Stanford University.

BAILYN, L. (1980). *Living with Technology: Issues at Mid-Career*. Cambridge, Mass.: MIT Press.

—— and LYNCH, J. T. (1983). 'Engineering as a Life-Long Career: Its Meaning, Its Satisfactions, Its Difficulties'. *Journal of Occupational Behavior*, 4: 263–83.

BARLEY, S. R. (1996a). *The New World of Work*. London: British North-American Research Committee.

—— (1996b). 'Technicians in the Workplace: Ethnographic Evidence for Bringing Work into Organization Studies'. *Administrative Science Quarterly*, 41: 404–41.

—— and BECHKY, B. A. (1994). 'In the Backrooms of Science: The Work of Technicians in Science Labs'. *Work and Occupations*, 21: 85–126.

—— and KUNDA, G. (2001). 'Bringing Work Back In'. *Organization Science*, 12: 75–94.

—— —— (2004). *Gurus, Hired Guns and Warm Bodies: Itinerant Experts in a Knowledge Economy*. Princeton, NJ: Princeton University Press.

BECHKY, B. A. (2003). 'Sharing Meaning across Occupational Communities'. *Organization Science*, 14: 312–30.

—— (forthcoming). 'Object Lessons: Workplace Artifacts and Occupational Jurisdiction'. *American Journal of Sociology*.

BELL, D. (1973). *The Coming of Post-Industrial Society: A Venture in Social Forecasting*. New York: Basic.

BERGEN, S. A. (1986). *Project Management: An Introduction to Issues in Industrial Research and Development*. New York: Basil Blackwell.

BIDDLE, J., and ROBERTS, K. (1994). 'Private Sector Scientists and Engineers and the Transition to Management'. *Journal of Human Resources*, 29/1: 92–107.

BLAU, P. M., and SCOTT, W. R. (1962). *Formal Organizations: A Comparative Approach*. San Francisco: Chandler Publishing Company.

BRAVERMAN, H. (1973). *Labor and Monopoly Capital*. New York: Monthly Labor Review Press.

BROWN, J. S., and DUGUID, P. (2001). 'Knowledge and Organization: A Social-Practice Perspective'. *Organization Science*, 12/2: 198–213.

BUCCIARELLI, L. L. (1988a). 'Engineering Design Process', in F. A. Dubinskas (ed.), *Making Time: Ethnographies of High Technology Organizations*. Philadelphia: Temple University Press.

——(1988b). 'An Ethnographic Perspective on Engineering Design'. *Design Studies*, 9: 159–68.

——(1994). *Designing Engineers*. Cambridge, Mass.: MIT Press.

BUCHER, R., and STRAUSS, A. L. (1961). 'Professions in Process'. *American Journal of Sociology*, 66: 325–34.

BURT, R. S. (1978). 'Stratification and Prestige among Elite Experts in Methodological and Mathematical Sociology circa 1975'. *Social Networks*, 1: 105–58.

——(1992). *Structural Holes*. Cambridge, Mass.: Harvard University Press.

CAIN, P. S., and TREIMAN, D. J. (1981). 'The Dictionary of Occupational Titles as a Source of Occupational Data'. *American Sociological Review*, 46: 253–78.

CALHOUN, D. (1960). *The American Civil Engineer: Origins and Conflicts*. Cambridge, Mass.: MIT Press.

CARCHEDI, G. (1977). *On the Economic Identification of Social Classes*. London: Routledge & Kegan Paul.

CARR-SANDERS, A. M., and WILSON, P. A. (1933). *The Professions*. Oxford: Clarendon.

CONK, M. A. (1978). *The United States Census and Labor Force Change: A History of Occupational Statistics, 1870–1940*. Ann Arbor, Mich.: UMI Research Press.

COOLEY, M. (1980). *Architect or Bee: The Human/Technology Relationship*. Boston: South End Press.

CRANE, D. (1972). *Invisible Colleges: Diffusion of Knowledge in Scientific Communities*. Chicago: University of Chicago Press.

CRAWFORD, S. (1989). *Technical Workers in an Advanced Society: The Work, Careers and Politics of French Engineers*. Cambridge: Cambridge University Press.

——(1996). 'The Making of the French Engineer', in P. F. Meiksins and C. Smith (eds.), *Engineering Labour: Technical Workers in Comparative Perspective*. London: Verso.

CROMPTON, R., and REID, S. (1982). 'The Deskilling of Clerical Work', in S. J. Wood (ed.), *The Degradation of Work: Skill, Deskilling and the Labour Process*. London: Hutchinson.

DAMARIN, A. (2003). 'Robust and Modular Occupations: A Labor Flow Analysis of Emerging New Media Work Types'. Paper delivered at the American Sociological Association Annual Meetings, Atlanta, Ga.

DARR, A. (2000). 'Technical Labour in an Engineering Boutique: Interpretive Frameworks of Sales and R&D Engineers'. *Work, Employment and Society*, 14: 205–22.

——(2002). 'The Technicization of Sales Work: An Ethnographic Study in the U.S. Electronics Industry'. *Work, Employment and Society*, 16: 47–67.

——(2003). 'Control and Autonomy among Knowledge Workers in Sales: An Employee Perspective'. *Employee Relations*, 25: 31–41.

——and SCARSELLETTA, M. (2002). 'Technicians, Clients and Professional Authority: Structured Interactions and Identity Formation in Technical Work'. *New Technology, Work and Employment*, 17: 60–72.

——and TALMUD, I. (2003). 'The Structure of Knowledge and Seller–Buyer Networks in Markets for Emerging Technologies'. *Organization Studies*, 24: 435–53.

DERBER, C. (1982a). 'Professionals as New Workers', in C. Derber (ed.), *Professionals as Workers: Mental Labor in Advanced Capitalism*. Boston: G. K. Hall and Co.

——(1982b). 'The Proletarianization of the Professional: A Review Essay', in C. Derber (ed.), *Professionals as Workers: Mental Labor in Advanced Capitalism*. Boston: G. K. Hall and Co.

DOUGHERTY, D. (1992). 'Interpretive Barriers to Successful Product Innovation in Large Firms'. *Organization Science*, 3: 179–202.

DOWNEY, G. L., and LUCENA, J. C. (1995). 'Engineering Studies', in S. Jasanoff, G. Markle, J. Petersen, and T. Pinch (eds.), *Handbook of Science and Technology Studies*. Thousand Oaks, Calif.: Sage.

——DONOVAN, A., and ELLIOTT, T. J. (1989). 'The Invisible Engineer: How Engineering Ceased to Be a Problem in Science and Technology Studies', in L. L. Hargens, R. A. Jones, and A. Pickering (eds.), *Knowledge and Society: Studies in the Sociology of Science Past and Present*, 8. Greenwich, Conn.: JAI.

ENSMENGER, N. (2001). 'The Mongolian Horde versus the Superprogrammer'. Unpublished paper, University of Pennsylvania.

——(2002). 'Letting the "Computer Boys" Take Over: Technology and the Politics of Organizational Transformation'. Unpublished paper, University of Pennsylvania.

——and ASPRAY, W. (2001). 'Software as Labor Process'. Unpublished paper, University of Pennsylvania.

EPSTEIN, K. A. (1986). 'The Dual Ladder: An Attempt at Matching Individual and Organizational Career Needs'. Doctoral Dissertation. Sloan School of Management, Massachusetts Institute of Technology.

FLEISCHER, M., and LIKER, J. K. (1992). 'The Hidden Professionals: Product Designers and Their Impact on Design Quality'. *IEEE Transactions on Engineering Management*, 39: 254–64.

FREIDSON, E. (1970). *Professional Dominance: The Social Structure of Medical Care*. New York: Atherton Press.

——(1973). 'Professionalization and the Organization of Middle Class Labour in Post-industrial Society'. *Sociological Review Monograph*, 20: 47–59.

FRENCH, E. B. (1967). 'The Organization Scientist: Myth or Reality'. *Academy of Management Journal*, 10: 269–73.

GALLIE, D. (1994). 'Patterns of Skill Change: Upskilling, Deskilling or Polarization?' in R. Penn, M. Rose, and J. Rubery (eds.), *Skill and Occupational Change*. London: Oxford University Press.

GLASER, B. G. (1963). 'The Local-Cosmopolitan Scientist'. *American Journal of Sociology*, 69: 249–59.

——(1964). *Organizational Scientists: Their Professional Careers*. Indianapolis: Bobbs-Merrill.

GOLDNER, F. H., and RITTI, R. R. (1967). 'Professionalization as Career Immobility'. *American Journal of Sociology*, 72: 489–501.

GOODE, W. J. (1957). 'Community within a Community: The Professions'. *American Sociological Review*, 22: 195–200.

GORZ, A. (1967). *Strategy for Labor*. Boston: Beacon Press.

——(1976). 'Technology, Technicians, and Class Struggle', in A. Gorz (ed.), *The Division of Labour*. Hassocks: Harvester.

GREENBAUM, J. (1979). *In the Name of Efficiency*. Philadelphia: Temple University Press.

GREENWOOD, E. (1957). 'Attributes of a Profession'. *Social Work*, 2: 45–55.

HAGSTROM, W. O. (1965). *The Scientific Community*. Carbondale: Southern Illinois University Press.

HALL, R. H. (1968). 'Professionalization and Bureaucratization'. *American Sociological Review*, 33: 92–104.

HARGADON, A., and SUTTON, R. I. (1997). 'Technology Brokering and Innovation in a Product Development Firm'. *Administrative Science Quarterly*, 42: 716–49.

HARGENS, L. L. (2000). 'Using the Literature: Reference Networks, Reference Contexts, and the Social Structure of Scholarship'. *American Sociological Review*, 65: 846–65.

HAUG, M. R. (1975). 'The Deprofessionalization of Everyone'. *Sociological Focus*, 8: 197–213.

——(1977). 'Computer Technology and the Obsolescence of the Concept of Profession', in M. R. Haug and J. Dofney (eds.), *Work and Technology*. Beverly Hills, Calif.: Sage.

HENDERSON, K. (1991). 'Flexible Sketches and Inflexible Data Bases: Visual Communication, Conscription Devices and Boundary Objects in Design Engineering'. *Science, Technology and Human Values*, 16/4: 448–73.

——(1998). 'The Role of Material Objects in the Design Process: A Comparison of Two Design Cultures and How They Contend with Automation'. *Science, Technology and Human Values*, 23: 139–74.

——(1999). *On Line and on Paper*. Cambridge, Mass.: MIT Press.

HINRICHS, J. K. (1964). 'The Attitudes of Research Chemists'. *Journal of Applied Psychology*, 48: 287–93.

HUGHES, E. C. (1958). *Men and Their Work*. Glencoe, Ill.: Free Press.

JORDON, K., and LYNCH, M. E. (1992). 'The Sociology of a Genetic Engineering Technique: Ritual and Rationality in the Performance of the "Plasmid Prep"', in A. E. Clarke and J. H. Fujimura (eds.), *The Right Tools for the Job: At Work in Twentieth-Century Life Sciences*. Princeton, NJ: Princeton University Press.

KATZ, R. (1981). 'An Investigation into the Managerial Roles and Career Paths of Gatekeepers and Project Supervisors in a Major R&D Facility'. *R&D Management*, 11: 103–10.

——(1982). 'The Effects of Group Longevity on Project Communication and Performance'. *Administrative Science Quarterly*, 27: 81–104.

——and ALLEN, T. J. (1985). 'Project Performance and the Locus of Influence in the R&D Matrix'. *Academy of Management Journal*, 1: 67–87.

——and TUSHMAN, M. L. (1979). 'Communication Patterns, Project Performance, and Task Characteristics: An Empirical Evaluation and Integration in an R&D Setting'. *Organizational Behavior and Human Performance*, 23: 139–62.

KELLEY, M. R. (1986). 'Programmable Automation and the Skill Question: A Reinterpretation of the Cross-National Evidence'. *Human Systems Management*, 6: 223–41.

——(1989). 'Alternative Forms of Work Organization under Programmable Automation', in S. J. Wood (ed.), *The Transformation of Work?: Skill, Flexibility and the Labour Process*. London: Unwin Hyman.

KIDDER, T. (1981). *Soul of a New Machine*. Boston: Little Brown and Company.

KLING, R., and GERSON, E. M. (1978). 'Patterns of Segmentation and Intersection in the Computing World'. *Symbolic Interaction*, 1: 24–43.

KNORR-CETINA, K., and MULKAY, M. E. (1983). *Science Observed: Perspectives on the Social Study of Science*. Beverly Hills, Calif.: Sage.

KORNHAUSER, W. (1962). *Scientists in Industry: Conflict and Accommodation.* Berkeley: University of California.

KRAFT, P. (1979*a*). 'The Industrialization of Computer Programming: From Programming to Software Production', in A. Zimbalist (ed.), *Case Studies in the Labor Process.* New York: Monthly Review Press.

—— (1979*b*). 'The Routinizing of Computer Programming'. *Sociology of Work and Occupations*, 6: 139–55.

KUHN, S. (1989). 'The Limits to Industrialization: Computer Software Development in a Large Commercial Bank', in S. J. Wood (ed.), *The Transformation of Work?: Skill, Flexibility and the Labour Process.* London: Unwin Hyman.

KUNDA, G. (1992). *Engineering Culture: Control and Commitment in a High Tech Corporation.* Philadelphia: Temple University Press.

LAPORTE, T. R. (1965). 'Conditions of Strain and Accommodation in Industrial Research Organizations'. *Administrative Science Quarterly*, 10: 21–38.

LARSON, M. S. (1977). *The Rise of Professionalism: A Sociological Analysis.* Berkeley: University of California Press.

LATOUR, B., and WOOLGAR, S. (1979). *Laboratory Life: The Construction of Scientific Facts.* Princeton, NJ: Princeton University Press.

LAVE, J. (1988). *Cognition in Practice: Mind, Mathematics, and Culture in Everyday Life.* Cambridge: Cambridge University Press.

—— and WENGER, E. (1990). *Situated Learning: Legitimate Peripheral Participation.* New York: Cambridge University Press.

LAYTON, E. (1971). *The Revolt of the Engineers: Social Responsibility and the American Engineering Profession.* Baltimore: Johns Hopkins Press.

LEE, S. M. (1971). 'An Empirical Analysis of Organizational Identification'. *Academy of Management Journal*, 14: 213–26.

LIEVROUW, L. A., ROGERS, E. M., LOWE, C. U., and NADEL, E. (1987). 'Triangulation as a Research Strategy for Identifying Invisible Colleges among Biomedical Scientists'. *Social Networks*, 9: 217–48.

LYNCH, M. E. (1985). *Art and Artifact in Laboratory Science: A Study of Shop Work and Shop Talk in a Research Laboratory.* London: Routledge.

—— and EDGERTON, S. Y., Jr. (1988). 'Aesthetics and Digital Image Processing: Representational Craft in Contemporary Astronomy', in G. Fyfe and J. Law (eds.), *Picturing Power: Visual Depiction and Social Relations.* London: Routledge.

MCKELVEY, W. W. (1969). 'Expectational Noncomplementarity and Style of Interaction between Professional and Organization'. *Administrative Science Quarterly*, 14: 21–32.

MCKINLAY, J. B. (1982). 'Toward a Proletarianization of Physicians', in C. Derber (ed.), *Professionals as Workers: Mental Labor in Advanced Capitalism.* Boston: G. K. Hall and Co.

MALLET, S. (1975). *The New Working Class.* Nottingham: Spokesman.

MARCSON, S. (1960). *The Scientist in American Industry.* Princeton, NJ: Princeton University, Industrial Relations Section.

MEIKSINS, P. F. (1988). 'The "Revolt of the Engineers" Reconsidered'. *Technology and Culture*, 29: 219–46.

—— and SMITH, C. (1996). 'Introduction: Engineers and Comparative Research', in P. Meiksins and C. Smith (eds.), *Engineering Labour: Technical Workers in Comparative Perspective.* London: Verso.

MERTON, R. K. (1942). 'Science and Technology in a Democratic Order'. *Journal of Legal and Political Sociology*, 1: 115–26.

——(1957). *Social Theory and Social Structure*. New York: Free Press.

MILLER, A., TREIMAN, D. J., CAIN, P. S., and ROOS, P. A. (1980). *Jobs and Occupations: A Critical Review of the Dictionary of Occupational Titles*. Washington, DC: National Academy Press.

MILLER, G. A. (1967). 'Professionals in Bureaucracy: Alienation among Industrial Scientists and Engineers'. *American Sociological Review*, 32: 755–68.

——and WAGER, L. W. (1971). 'Adult Socialization, Organizational Structure, and Role Orientations'. *Administrative Science Quarterly*, 16: 151–63.

MULLINS, N. C. (1972). 'The Development of a Scientific Specialty: The Phage Group and Origins of Molecular Biology'. *Minerva*, 10: 51–82.

——(1973). 'The Development of Specialties in Social Science: The Case of Ethnomethodology'. *Science Studies*, 3: 245–73.

National Research Council (1999). *The Changing Nature of Work: Implications for Occupational Analysis*. Washington, DC: National Academy Press.

NELSEN, B. (1997a). 'Building a Better Worker: An Investigation of the Nature and Implications of Technological Change and the Rise Knowledge Work'. Doctoral Dissertation, Cornell University, Ithaca, NY.

——(1997b). 'Work as a Moral Act: How Emergency Medical Technicians Understand Their Work', in S. R. Barley and J. E. Orr (eds.), *Between Technology and Society: Technical Workers in Modern Settings*. Ithaca, NY: ILR Press.

——and BARLEY, S. R. (1997). 'For Love or Money: Commodification and the Construction of an Occupational Mandate'. *Administrative Science Quarterly*, 42: 619–53.

NELSON, D. (1975). *Origins of the New Factory System in the United States: 1880–1920*. Madison: University of Wisconsin Press.

NOBLE, D. F. (1977). *America by Design: Science, Technology, and the Rise of Corporate Capitalism*. New York: Oxford.

——(1979). 'Social Choice in Machine Design: The Case of Automatically Controlled Machine Tools', in A. Zimbalist (ed.), *Case Studies in the Labor Process*. New York: Monthly Review Press.

——(1984). *Forces of Production: A Social History of Industrial Automation*. New York: Knopf.

ORLIKOWSKI, W. J. (1988). 'The Data Processing Occupation: Professionalization or Proletarianization'. *Research in the Sociology of Work*, 4: 94–124.

ORR, J. E. (1997). *Talking about Machines: An Ethnography of a Modern Job*. Ithaca, NY: ILR Press.

PARSONS, T. (1939). 'The Professions and Social Structure'. *Social Forces*, 17: 457–67.

——(1951). *The Social System*. New York: Free Press.

PELZ, D. C., and ANDREWS, F. M. (1966). *Scientists in Organizations: Productive Climates for Research and Development*. New York: Wiley.

PENTLAND, B. T. (1992). 'Organizing Moves in Software Support Hotlines'. *Administrative Science Quarterly*, 37: 527–48.

PERLOW, L. (1997). *Finding Time*. Ithaca, NY: ILR Press.

PERRUCCI, R. (1971). 'Engineering: Professional Servant of Power'. *American Behavioral Scientist*, 14: 492–505.

——and GERSTL, J. E. (1969). *Profession without Community*. New York: Random House.

POULANTZAS, N. (1978). *Classes in Contemporary Capitalism*. London: Verso.

RITTI, R. R. (1968). 'Work Goals of Scientists and Engineers'. *Industrial Relations*, 7: 118–31.

——(1971). *The Engineer in the Industrial Corporation*. New York: Columbia University Press.

ROBERTS, B. C., LOVERIDGE, R., GENNARD, J., and EASON, J. V. (1972). *Reluctant Militants: A Study of Industrial Technicians*. London: Heinemann Educational Books.

ROBERTS, K., and BIDDLE, J. (1994). 'The Transition into Management by Scientists and Engineers: A Misallocation or Efficient Use of Human Resources.' *Human Resource Management*, 33/4: 561–79.

ROTHSTEIN, W. G. (1969). 'Engineers and the Functionalist Model of Professions', in R. Perrucci and J. E. Gerstl (eds.), *The Engineers and the Social System*. New York: John Wiley and Sons, Inc.

RYNES, S. L., TOLBERT, P. S., and STRAUSSER, P. G. (1988). 'Aspirations to Manage: A Comparison of Engineering Students and Working Engineers'. *Journal of Vocational Behavior*, 32/2: 239–53.

SALZMAN, H. (1989). 'Computer-Aided Design: Limitations in Automating Design and Drafting'. *IEEE Transactions on Engineering Management*, 36: 252–61.

——(1992). 'Skill-Based Design: Productivity, Learning, and Organizational Effectiveness', in P. S. Adler and T. Winograd (eds.), *Usability: Turning Technologies into Tools*. London: Oxford University Press.

SCARSELLETTA, M. (1997). 'The Infamous "Lab Error": Education, Skill and Quality in Medical Technician's Work', in S. R. Barley and J. E. Orr (eds.), *Between Technology and Society: Technical Workers in Modern Settings*. Ithaca, NY: ILR Press.

SHAIKEN, H. (1984). *Work Transformed: Automation and Labor in the Computer Age*. New York: Holt, Rinehart and Winston.

SHAPIN, S. (1989). 'The Invisible Technician'. *American Scientist*, 77: 554–63.

SHELDON, M. E. (1971). 'Investments and Involvements as Mechanisms Producing Commitment to the Organization'. *Administrative Science Quarterly*, 16: 143–50.

SHENHAV, Y. (1999). *Manufacturing Rationality: The Engineering Foundations of the Managerial Revolution*. New York: Oxford.

SHEPARD, H. A. (1958). 'The Dual Hierarchy in Research'. *Research Management*, August: 177–87.

SILVESTRI, G. T. (1997). 'Occupational Employment Projections to 2006'. *Monthly Labor Review*, November: 58–83.

SMITH, C. (1987). *Technical Workers: Class, Labour and Trade Unionism*. London: Macmillan Education Ltd.

SOUDER, W. E. (1974). 'Autonomy, Gratification and R&D Outputs: A Small-Sample Field Study'. *Management Science*, 20: 1147–56.

SPENNER, K. I. (1983). 'Temporal Change in the Skill Level of Work'. *American Sociological Review*, 48: 824–37.

——(1995). 'Technological Change, Skill Requirements, and Education: The Case for Uncertainty', in D. B. Bills (ed.), *The New Modern Times: Factors Reshaping the World of Work*. Albany: SUNY Press.

SPRADLEY, J. P. (1979). *The Ethnographic Interview*. New York: Holt, Rinehardt and Winston.

STEINBERG, R. J. (1990). 'Social Construction of Skill: Gender, Power, and Comparable Worth'. *Work and Occupations*, 17: 449–82.

STRAUSS, A. L. (1978). 'A Social World Perspective'. *Studies in Symbolic Interaction*, 1: 119–28.

—— (1984). 'Social Worlds and Their Segmentation Processes'. *Studies in Symbolic Interaction*, 5: 123–39.

SUCHMAN, L. A. (1987). *Plans and Situated Action: The Problem of Human-Machine Communication*. Cambridge: Cambridge University Press.

THOMAS, R. J. (1994). *What Machines Can't Do: Politics and Technology in the Industrial Enterprise*. Berkeley: University of California Press.

TOREN, N. (1975). 'Deprofessionalization and Its Sources'. *Sociology of Work and Occupations*, 2: 323–36.

TUSHMAN, M. L., and KATZ, R. (1980). 'External Communication and Project Performance: An Investigation into the Role of Gatekeepers'. *Management Science*, 26: 1071–85.

VALLAS, S. P. (1998). 'Manufacturing Knowledge: Technology, Culture and Social Inequality at Work'. *Social Science Computer Review*, 16: 353–69.

—— (2001). 'Symbolic Boundaries and the New Division of Labor: Engineers, Workers and the Restructuring of Factory Life'. *Research in Social Stratification and Mobility*, 18: 3–37.

—— and BECK, J. P. (1996). 'The Transformation of Work Revisited: The Limits of Flexibility in American Manufacturing'. *Social Problems*, 43: 339–61.

VAUGHAN, D. (1996). *The Challenger Launch Decision: Risky Technology, Culture and Deviance at NASA*. Chicago: University of Chicago Press.

VEBLEN, T. (1965/1921). *The Engineers and the Price System*. New York: Viking.

VINCENTI, W. G. (1990). *What Engineers Know and How They Know It*. Baltimore: Johns Hopkins University Press.

WATSON, J. M., and MEIKSINS, P. F. (1991). 'What Do Engineers Want? Work Values, Job Rewards and Job Satisfaction'. *Science, Technology and Human Values*, 16: 140–72.

WEBER, M. (1968/1922). *Economy and Society*. Berkeley: University of California Press.

WENGER, E. (1998). *Communities of Practice: Learning, Meaning and Identity*. Cambridge: Cambridge University Press.

WHALLEY, P. (1984). 'Deskilling Engineers: The Labor Process, Labor Markets, and Labor Segmentation'. *Social Problems*, 32: 117–32.

—— (1986*a*). 'Markets, Managers, and Technical Autonomy'. *Theory and Society*, 15: 223–47.

—— (1986*b*). *The Social Production of Technical Work*. Albany: State University of New York Press.

—— (1991). 'Negotiating the Boundaries of Engineering: Professionals, Managers, and Manual Work', in P. S. Tolbert and S. R. Barley (eds.), *Research in the Sociology of Organizations*, 8. Greenwich, Conn.: JAI Press.

WILENSKY, H. L. (1964). 'The Professionalization of Everyone'. *American Journal of Sociology*, 70: 137–58.

WOOD, S. J. (1982). *The Degradation of Work: Skill, Deskilling and the Labour Process*. London: Hutchinson.

WRIGHT, E. O. (1976). 'Class Boundaries in Advanced Capitalist Societies'. *New Left Review*, July: 3–41.

—— and MARTIN, B. (1987). 'The Transformation of the American Class Structure, 1960–1980'. *American Journal of Sociology*, 93: 1–29.

ZABUSKY, S. E. (1997). 'Computers, Clients, and Expertise: Negotiating Technical Identities in a Non-Technical World', in S. R. Barley and J. E. Orr (eds.), *Between Technology and Society: Technical Workers in Modern Settings*. Ithaca, NY: ILR Press.

——and BARLEY, S. R. (1996). 'Redefining Success: Ethnographic Observations on the Careers of Technicians', in P. Osterman (ed.), *Broken Ladders*. Cambridge: Cambridge University Press.

ZIMBALIST, A. (1979). 'Technology and the Labor Process in the Printing Industry', in A. Zimbalist (ed.), *Case Studies in the Labor Process*. New York: Monthly Review Press.

ZUBOFF, S. (1989). *In the Age of the Smart Machine*. New York: Basic.

ZUSSMAN, R. (1985). *Mechanics of the Middle Class*. Berkeley: University of California.

CHAPTER 17

THE CHANGING NATURE OF PROFESSIONAL ORGANIZATIONS

C. R. HININGS

17.1 INTRODUCTION

AN examination of professional organizations and professionals opens up a very wide range of possibilities, as this has been a central and important topic in the sociology of organizations and occupations for more than four decades. It is not the purpose of this chapter to review the history of developments during that period; that ground has been covered by Abbott (1988), Hall (1968), and Hinings (2001). It has been somewhat less important in organization theory, in spite of Mintzberg's typology (1979). However, there has been something of a change in interest in the past fifteen years, centered on the nature of professional organizations and the ways in which they are changing. It is that burgeoning literature and the questions posed by it that is the focus of this chapter. My aim is to consider changes that are taking place in those professional organizations (and within the relevant occupations) and to examine their impact on management structures and systems. Part of this is also to assess what happens to professionals' power and control of work.

The study of professions in organizations concerns the intersection of two fields that have distinct histories, that is, the study of professions and the study of organizations, but that overlap in the course of those histories. Sometimes they have been strongly related and at other times they have been very separate. The study of professions in organizations has gone through three, overlapping phases since the 1950s. The first phase, from the 1950s and 1960s, critically examined the role of professionals in bureaucratic organizations, seeing the nature of professional and bureaucratic work being in conflict. The second phase, begun in the 1970s and still continuing, criticized the orthodox view of professionals and gave a more power-based, labor market account of their position and how it affected organizational labor markets. The third phase, which originated in the 1960s and 1970s and blossomed in the last fifteen years, emphasizes the dynamic nature of professionals in organizations and acknowledges variety in both organizational locations and professional occupations. It has particularly focused on professional organizations per se rather than professionals in organizations. This chapter is concerned with this third phase, outlining the ways in which professional organizations are managed and how they are subject to change.

17.2 THE MANAGEMENT OF PROFESSIONAL ORGANIZATIONS

In many ways, the origins of the discussion of professional organizations lie in discussions defining characteristics of a profession. The aim was to agree upon a set of structural and value characteristics of a profession (Greenwood 1957). The structural aspects were such things as a full-time occupation, a training and certification system, a professional association, and an ethical code. More important for the study of professional organizations was the extension of Greenwood's notion of a professional culture into a set of values that encompassed peer reference, vocation, public service, self-regulation, and autonomy. While originally, the connection between this work in the sociology of the professions and the sociology of organizations was in terms of the relationship between the values held by professionals and those promulgated by the modern, bureaucratic organization (Hall 1968), it continues to be the basis for conceptualizing how professional organizations are managed. Professionals, this literature has suggested, are socialized into occupations where the key values are autonomy, peer control, and vocation. For example, Hall (1968) operationalized professional values as: the professional organization as a reference; a belief in service to the public; a belief in self-regulation; a sense of calling to the field; and feelings of autonomy. As Powell, Brock, and Hinings (1999: 4) put it, in summarizing this literature, 'The common thread is a set of professional values, beliefs and aspirations woven into the very fabric of professional firms and organizations.'

In his early writing, Scott (1965) distinguished between autonomous and heteronomous professional organizations. (He also dealt with the professional department but this does not concern us here.) In the first type, exemplified by a law firm or a medical clinic, the work of professionals is self rather than externally controlled. It is professionals who design the organization and manage it, since they are the dominant source of authority. Greenwood, Hinings, and Brown (1990) argued that it is the nature of the authority system that is the distinctive mark of a professional organization. Similarly, a number of writers, whose work is based on a wide range of professions, have suggested that it is the emphasis on collegiality, peer evaluation, and autonomy that underpins the distribution of authority in autonomous professional organizations (Blau 1984; Bucher and Stelling 1969; Montagna 1968; Ritzer and Walczak 1988; Smigel 1964).

The heteronomous professional organization is one where professionals provide the core service, as in libraries, hospitals, and universities, but those professional employees are subordinated to an externally derived system. Scott suggests that there is less professional autonomy in these settings. In many ways Scott's heteronomous professional organization is akin to Mintzberg's professional bureaucracy (1979). The key characteristic of this type is that professionals are at the operating core, providing services directly to clients. The control systems are embedded in internalized values and standardization of skills; it is 'clan control' (Ouchi 1980) at work. As Powell, Brock, and Hining (1999) suggest, the professional bureaucracy reflects democratic and collegial values, involving participation and consultation with the professionals seeking collective control over decisions that affect their operational freedom.

In all of this work, the arena of professional work that was largely ignored was that of the professional service firm, per se. This stemmed from the emphasis of research on the professional-bureaucratic relationship, research on professionals working in bureaucratic organizations (i.e. on heteronomous professional organizations or professional bureaucracies). This neglect of professional service firms is particularly striking in light of the fact that the independent professional organizational setting was considered to be very important as the preferred, archetypal work environment for an autonomous professional practitioner. The professional service firm was the ghost at the feast. Interest in the professional service firm was driven out by the concern with the rise of bureaucracy as the dominant organizational form and the response of professionals to it. Thus, the professional service firm was treated as the implicit, professionally hospitable setting that was contrasted with the bureaucratic form. But very little study centered on professionals in professional organizations, although in many cases, this was the main employment context for a given profession. Lawyers, for example, are primarily employed in law firms that are organized as professional partnerships; only a small proportion are employed outside legal practice as corporate counsel or within the public defender justice system. Accountants are split 50/50 between private practice and employment in private and public sector organizations, although almost all accountants are trained in private practice. Similar situations could be outlined for other professions such as architects and consulting engineers.

Work on professional occupations that appeared in the 1970s (and continues today), critically examined the orthodox view of professionals, replacing it with a power-based, labor market analysis. The professional 'project' is to control the conditions of work (the labor process and the labor market) and to increase and maintain status and power (Friedson 1986; Johnson 1972; Larson 1977). Abbott (1988: 15) calls this the 'monopoly school'. It attributes developments in professionalization 'to a desire for dominance or authority'. The basis for this was laid down in critiques of the 'professionals in organizations' approach of the 1960s. Previous research had been firmly anchored in issues of the structure and values of professionalism and paid no attention to power. This approach 'dislocates' the relationship between professionals and organizations, shifting the locus of debate to power and labor markets. The emphasis becomes re-centered on the nature of a profession and the professional project; the claim to professional status is a way to control entry to the occupation and to establish a powerful position in the labor market. Of course, this approach to professional occupations was very much attuned to what was happening generally in the sociology of work and occupations with an emphasis on the labor process (Braverman 1974). The consequence of this 'turn' was a lack of concern with organization.

However, the 1980s and 1990s has seen a rediscovery, reclaiming, and advancement of ideas about professionals in organizations and a particular concern with understanding the nature of the professionally based, private practice organization (Brock, Powell, and Hinings 1999; Nelson 1988). The focus of this work, in its own way, reflects a return to issues of professionalization and bureaucratization. In terms of professionalization, the interest is in professions operating in private practice (the autonomous professional organization) rather than in the professional bureaucracy and it goes beyond law and accounting into management consulting (Abrahamson 1991; Clark and Fincham 2001), engineering consulting (Lowendahl 1997; Malhotra 2003), and architecture (Pinnington and Morris 2002). Bureaucratization has been recast as managerialism and located in the context of knowledge-based organizations and globalization.

As I have suggested, the original lines of research on professionals focused on their situation in bureaucratic organizations with the professional organization taken-for-granted, but not investigated. Greenwood, Hinings, and Brown (1990) suggested that the professional partnership was a form of organization neglected by researchers. Thus, their initial work was concerned with elaborating the distinctive characteristics of the professional service firm, which they labelled the P^2 form. The P is 'squared' because it stands for the two combined elements of professionalism and partnership. The original statement of the P^2 form has been further elaborated in a number of papers (Cooper et al. 1996; Greenwood, Hinings, and Cooper 2004; Greenwood, Suddaby, and Hinings 2002; Hinings, Greenwood, and Cooper 1999). The P^2 is an organization where professionals are both owners and producers. Typically they are from one dominant profession such as accounting, law, architecture, or engineering. The governance system is a partnership where the senior members of the profession jointly and severally take responsibility for the firm.

The idea of the P^2 form derives from the concept of an archetype (Greenwood and Hinings 1993; Hinings and Greenwood 1988). In this context, 'The pattern of an organizational design is a function of an underlying interpretive scheme, or set of beliefs and values, that is embodied in an organization's structures and systems. An archetype is thus a set of structures and systems that consistently embodies a single interpretive scheme' (Greenwood and Hinings 1993: 1055). The interpretive scheme that binds the structures and systems of the P^2 archetype together derives from the special nature of governance and the primary task (Cooper et al. 1996; Greenwood, Hinings, and Brown 1990). In terms of governance, there are strong beliefs in the fusion of ownership and control; some form of representative democracy; a revolving of managerial tasks among the partners; and the immediate locality as the center of commitment. The beliefs around the primary task cover the centrality of professional knowledge; peer control of work; work responsibility as indivisible; widely distributed authority; minimum hierarchy; and strong links with clients.

The organizational consequences of this interpretive scheme are outlined by Greenwood, Hinings, and Brown (1990) in terms of strategic, market-financial, and operational control. Strategic control deals with positioning an organization in the medium and long term, interpreting threats and opportunities, and building capability. Market-financial control involves the clarity of targets and the accountability for those targets, while operating control involves control of major functional areas. They argue that strategic control will be weak in the P^2 archetype. With regard to market-financial control, there will be explicit short-term goals but with very tolerant or loose accountability for achieving those targets. Finally, operating control will be focused on the maintenance of premises, shared overheads, and the selection, training, and promotion of professionals to ensure reliable and appropriate application of professional skills. Cooper et al. (1996) followed this schema but added two structural dimensions to round out the archetype description. They suggested that differentiation would be low and based on personal and professional interests, and that integration would also be low with few policies, rules, and procedures, or specific devices to produce integration. Issues of management and methods of organizing are not issues that are seen as important to discuss in the P² firm. The emphasis is on individual professionals and their ability to do good professional work. Also, following on from Nelson (1988) and Galanter and Palay (1991), Greenwood, Hinings, and Cooper (2004) have suggested that, in human resource terms, the P² form has the 'up or out' system or tournament. Professionals either make it to partner or leave the firm.

There are clearly strong echoes of this organizational form in the discussions that have arisen about the knowledge-based firm with its employment of highly qualified individuals who are applying new, and sometimes esoteric knowledge, and, it is suggested, require freedom and flexibility to achieve results. There is the rise of the 'knowledge-based organization' (Alvesson 1995). The suggestion is that organizations of the new economy are increasingly different from the various kinds of bureaucracy of the old economy. They are more service-based and these services require highly educated employees who, in value terms, are much more like the 'old' professions, being committed to autonomy, vocation, and collegiality. These new organizational forms are seen as much more friendly and hospitable to professionals. Alvesson (1995) and Peters (1992) suggest that the professional service firm is an example of the flexible, knowledge-based organization, that there is a wealth of experience in these organizations from which the newly developing knowledge-based firms can learn.

There is a sense in which the 'evolution' to the elaboration of the P² form shows remarkable continuity over the past forty years. The notion of what values drive professionals and the resultant structures that embody those values has changed little. What has occurred is a more detailed specification of the structures and systems, the organizational form. And it is clear that the P² form thrives in situations where professionals retain high degrees of autonomy in their work because of lack of competition from other professionals and where a particular occupations group is given legitimacy to control specific sets of activities. Also, to ensure a noncompetitive and legitimated work situation, it is necessary that the degree of change is small. Given the collegial nature of this form it is also likely to thrive in smaller rather than larger settings, where partners, in particular, can know each other and interact in authentic ways. These conditions have become increasingly subject to challenge, as a result of which, it has been suggested, many professional organizations are adopting different management structures leading to new organizational forms. It is to that issue of changing management structures to which I now turn.

17.3 Changing Management Structures

Greenwood and Hinings (1996) suggest that professional firms have been changing because of changes in the institutional and market contexts of professional work. There is an increasing emphasis on the dynamic and changing nature of professionals in organizations. At the level of the professional system, Abbott (1988) has pointed out that there are continuous competition and jurisdictional disputes between professional groups over claims to relevant knowledge and expertise. This general issue of interprofessional competition has become sharper with the development of the new economy and the rise of services generally, and business services in particular. The rapid rise in the numbers of management consultants, financial services advisers, software development engineers, information technology consultants, media and marketing occupations, as well as increased demand for accountants, engineers, and lawyers, has changed the dynamics of professional organizations. As a result of these developments, jurisdictional boundaries have blurred and the level of interprofessional competition has increased.

What, then, are the specifics of the pressures for change on professional organizations? There is, of course, an interaction between institutional and market forces, although they are separable analytically. One might argue that it is the changes in market conditions that have a major impact on producing change in institutional contexts. For that reason I will deal with the market context first, then look at the institutional context, after which I will discuss the impact of these changes on organizational forms.

17.3.1 Changing Market Contexts

There have been substantial changes in markets for professional services and, in particular, *growth in the business services market*. This is a mark of a modern economy as a shift takes place from manufacturing to service. Within services generally, the demand for professional business services has increased markedly (Aharoni 1993). It is one of the most rapidly growing sectors in many economies (*The Economist* 1988; *Fortune* 1998). In accounting, for example, mergers and restructuring have produced a decline in audits, but there has been increased business for services such as valuations, insolvency, and consulting, accentuating the shift away from accounting and audit services. While a specific technical expertise is the basis for a legitimate claim to professional status, most professionals have found that their clients have looked for more general business advice (Hinings, Greenwood, and Cooper 1999). The demand for these and other services is from increasingly sophisticated clients. The emphasis of such clients on general business advice has resulted in a rapid growth for management consultancy services and associated work in information technology. Thus, firms such as IBM and Hewlett-Packard have moved increasingly into forms of consulting. Simultaneously, there has been growth in demand for highly specialized services (Lawrence 1993). The success of the corporate law firm is increasingly driven by a demand for advice that goes beyond the details of the law (Gray 1999), setting law firms in an increasingly competitive marketplace. As Flood (1999: 156) puts it, 'Large law firms are intrinsically risk prone enterprises, always in competition with other professional service providers—e.g. accounting firms, investment banks, consultants— for clients, both domestically and internationally.'

Growth in any part of the economy leads to competition as a variety of organizations look to take part in that growth. Powell, Brock, and Hinings (1999) suggest that the markets for all professional services have become more competitive and they cite accounting, law, and health care in particular. Clark and Fincham (2001) have demonstrated the same phenomenon for management consulting. With the development of new business services, there comes the rise of new occupations that claim professional status. In the software development industry there are computer engineers, software engineers, and systems analysts. Financial services have grown rapidly and along with this have come investment analysts, financial planners, mergers and acquisitions specialists whose professional status is unclear, although one sees the same processes as were written about in the 1960s and 1970s, namely those of educational qualifications, professional associations, examinations and designations, and the ideological claim to professional status. These new entrants increase the level of competition for the more established professions.

So, increased competition comes from both new entrants and from a restructuring of existing markets. Part of the market restructuring has been increasingly sophisticated clients dealing with their own pressures to reduce costs. Such clients are now more disposed to switch professional service firms in search of either savings or promised better service (Greenwood *et al.* 1993). Clients are increasingly likely to require professional firms to compete for contracts, give more justification of their fees, or operate within price or cost limits (Powell, Brock, and Hinings 1999).

Interacting with market changes have been *technological developments and changes.* In audit, for example, computer-based audits have reduced both the complexity and labor intensity of the work process and, in doing so, have facilitated the commodification of some services (Brock, Powell, and Hinings 1999; Greenwood *et al.* 1993). Routinization, of course, allows for alternative providers. In law firms, legal documents are now on computer templates. They can be completed by legal assistants. Kondra and Hinings (1998), in dealing with innovation in tightly coupled institutional fields, show how ex-police officers were able to set up specialist practices in competition with lawyers, in part because technology allowed the production of the necessary documentation. Developments in communication produce a freer flow of information for clients, actual and prospective.

A further important aspect of the market context of professional service firms has been the increasing *globalization of services*. As Brock, Powell, and Hinings (1999: 11) put it, 'Multinational companies requiring consistent and uniform services around the globe have spurred the global provision of business services. In addition, professional organizations have followed clients into new markets to provide services to new clients.' This globalization in services of the 1980s and 1990s has been well documented by Aharoni (1993). As the largest clients have moved from being multinationals to being truly international (Bartlett and Ghoshal 1989), they have begun to demand a wide range of services deliverable in consistent form anywhere in the world. Accordingly, the largest professional service firms have stressed the need for tighter coupling of national firms to meet changing client expectations. As the globalization of business corporations has proceeded apace (Appadurai 1996; Latouche 1996), so professional service firms have been impacted.

Apart from the specifics of change in the market context that have been outlined, there are two general features of these changes that are particularly important. First, they have been extremely rapid in ways that were beyond the prior experience of professional firms. Markets have been radically restructured in a decade and changes in demand for various services continue apace. A second important feature is that with these kinds of changes profitability became problematic in some services, a phenomenon that was almost unknown to many professional service firms. Established firms in accounting, law, and management consulting, in particular, faced a very different context by the mid-1990s from the one they had become used to over the preceding twenty years or more.

17.3.2 Changing Institutional Contexts

Traditionally, professional services have been organized within institutionalized and regulated fields (Abbott 1988; DiMaggio 1991; DiMaggio and Powell 1983). One of the elements of a high degree of institutionalization is the existence of a template of organizing, or an archetype around which organizations within the field converge. Strong reciprocal exchanges develop between organizations within the institutional field with strong mimetic, normative, and coercive processes at work (Greenwood and Hinings 1996; Tolbert and Zucker 1983). Two important factors affecting institutional fields are the *extent of tight coupling* and the *extent of sectoral permeability*. In practice there can be variation across sectors in terms of tight coupling (D'Aunno, Sutton, and Price 1991; Fligstein 1990; Oliver 1991). Also, some sectors are more exposed to ideas from other arenas, i.e. they are permeable (Child and Smith 1987). In professional services, institutional boundaries between professions have weakened over the past twenty years as governments have deregulated professional services. There are market forces at work in this, as we have already pointed out, with firms moving to take advantage of new business opportunities (Brock, Powell, and Hinings 1999). For some time now, Western economies have been in a period of deregulation with the ideology of the market being dominant.

At the same time, with the explosion of knowledge-based services and, in particular, the tremendous expansion of business services in OECD economies, there is much more competition over professional jurisdictions. If one takes the example of the 'Big 4' accounting firms (formerly the Big 8 and the Big 10), there has been a continuous expansion of services within these firms and more and more integration across services and across nations (Cooper *et al.* 1998). These processes are at work within a wide range of professional jurisdictions and professional service firms. In law there are strong internationalization pressures. Also, there is considerable discussion over multidisciplinary practice and over allowing nonlawyers to have a controlling interest in law firms. In 2000, the Law Society of New South Wales (calling itself 'the most progressive legal jurisdiction in the world') voted to allow multidisciplinary practices in law firms and also to allow them to incorporate. A further step that has been taken is to take away the requirement for lawyers in that Australian state to be members of their law society. They still have to be issued with a certificate of practice, but do not need to 'buy' all the other services that come with membership, something that alters the role of the professional body substantially.

According to institutional theory, changes in the institutional context (and the market context) should lead to the emergence of alternative archetypes or templates of organizing (DiMaggio and Powell 1991; Greenwood and Hinings 1996; Oliver 1992). Of course, this is unlikely to be an instantaneous process. However, there has been more work suggesting how this might happen. Greenwood, Suddaby, and Hinings (2002) have demonstrated how, over a period of fifteen years, the chartered accountants' professional association in Canada gradually allowed the introduction of the multidisciplinary practice and made it a legitimate way of practicing and organizing. It is here that we see institutional entrepreneurs at work, introducing new ideas (DiMaggio 1988). Since DiMaggio's initial formulation there have been other attempts to illustrate and clarify the concept (Dorado 1999; Garud, Jain, and Kumaraswamy 2002; Lawrence 1999, Suddaby 2001).

For a new archetype to be developed in a field, *theorization, legitimation,* and *dissemination* have to occur (Greenwood, Suddaby, and Hinings 2002; Hinings *et al.* 2003). *Theorization* is the development and specification of a model of new practices and organizational forms, providing a justification for them in the current and future contexts (Strang and Meyer 1993). *Legitimation* then links these new ideas, forms, and practices to sets of values and logics that are held in esteem by field actors. New organizational forms only reach 'taken-for-granted' archetypal status through a process of legitimation. *Dissemination* spreads the new archetype throughout the field, through coercive, normative, and mimetic isomorphism.

17.3.3 Emerging Management Structures

The interactive changes in market and institutional contexts mean that the organizational fields within which professional service firms operate have undergone substantial change. In responding to those changes, professional organizations have changed through internal restructuring, merger, the development of new services, shedding less economically viable divisions, and internationalization (Greenwood and Lachman 1996). Examining all of these changes in structures and systems holistically suggests the emergence of a new professional archetype. In particular the argument is that increasingly competitive markets and professional deregulation have produced more corporate and managerial modes of operation in search of increased efficiency (Brock, Powell, and Hinings 1999; Cooper et al. 1996; Gray 1999; Greenwood, Suddaby, and Hinings 2002; Hinings, Greenwood, and Cooper 1999; Morris and Pinnington 1999).

Cooper et al. (1996) named this new organizational form in professional firms the managed professional business (MPB). Competition leads to a greater focus on business development and the marketing of professional services. Professionalism is centered on business development, hierarchies develop, strategic planning is important, targets become more binding and decision making rests in the hands of management teams rather than the partnership at large. It would seem that work in the MPB becomes somewhat more like that of the professional bureaucracy (Mintzberg 1979) or the heteronomous professional organization (Scott 1965).

The interpretive scheme that binds the structures and systems of the MPB centers on 'effectiveness' and 'efficiency'. There are beliefs in management as a separate skill, in developing organizational strategies, especially in service development and marketing, in rationalizing professional activities and increasing productivity, and in strong, organized client service. Cooper et al. (1996) see the importation of the language and style of the business corporation. Titles shift from Managing Partner to Chief Executive and Practice Leaders to Practice Directors.

The organizational consequence for strategic control in the MPB is increasing analytical rationality and more directive decision making. Strategic control becomes much more important. For market-financial control, targets become more precise both financially and for market penetration. And, in line with the increasing strategic emphasis, long-term timescales are developed, as well as short term. There is less tolerance for missing targets, something that applies to partners as well as more junior staff. With regard to operating control, there is more central involvement and a wider range of behaviors and outcomes are monitored than in the P^2 archetype, including professional standards, quality of service, planning, marketing, and compensation. All of this goes along with increased centralization of decision making. Structurally, specialization increases in two aspects. On the one hand, there is an increase in professional specialization, with professional work being organized into clearly delineated areas. On the other hand, functional professionals are introduced to deal with human resources, marketing, information technology, and finance. There is often a Chief Operating/Administrative Officer who may have partner status without being a core professional. There is an increased use of integrative mechanisms such as cross-functional teams as well as a more clearly delineated hierarchy. More policies, rules, and procedures are introduced to ensure integration and uniformity.

While the MPB has been seen as the dominant archetype by most researchers, Brock, Powell, and Hinings (1999), Gray (1999), Greenwood *et al.* (1998), and Rose and Hinings (1999) have all suggested forms that go beyond the P^2 and MPB. These additions and extensions have essentially focused more closely on changes in scale, governance, strategy, and globalization. Brock, Powell, and Hinings (1999), for example, suggest one addition and one extension. The addition is referred to as the 'Star' form. They characterize it as 'a medium-sized, highly specialized professional firm that persists in that form (i.e. resists merger or significant growth) by a fixation on the highest professional quality standards and a commitment to individual excellence' (Brock, Powell, and Hinings 1999: 227). It is a form that leans toward the P^2, in terms of the lack of management systems and structures, but does emphasize performance-related remuneration and business development. In law, Gray (1999) and Starbuck (1992, 1993) have identified this form, characterized by a specialist strategy and restricted size.

Drawing on the work of Greenwood *et al.* (1998) and Rose and Hinings (1999) on the largest accounting firms (what Rose and Hinings call Global Business Advisory Firms), Brock, Powell, and Hinings (1999) also suggest an extension, an archetype they refer to as the 'Global Professional Network' or GNP. Their characterization of the global professional network also draws on work in international management, particularly that of Bartlett and Ghoshal (1989) and Nohria and Ghoshal (1997). In explaining how multinational corporations operate effectively across borders, particularly when such operations involve knowledge transfer, Nohria and Ghoshal (1997) point to the emergence of an organization that they call the 'differentiated network'. Such an organization is made up of diverse subunits that have their own internal structures and different relationships with headquarters and other affiliates. They share information and resources where appropriate but retain quite distinctive local organizational structures. These organizations very much reflect the sense of 'think global, act local'. Rose and Hinings (1999) saw similar arrangements in their observations of multinational accounting firms. Greenwood *et al.* (1998), while seeing many similarities, suggest that global professional firms can be either confederal (as in the global professional network) or unitary in their organizational forms.

There are two points to be made about these additions. One is that it is probably too early in our research on professional organizations to concentrate on only the P^2 or MPB as the archetypes. Empirically there has, perhaps, been an overconcentration on very large professional service firms and also something of a limitation as to the professional sectors studied. The other point, that has already become a subject of debate, is that of whether there are hybrids and, indeed, whether the P² and MPB are as distinct as some scholars have suggested. It is this second point that I will take up next.

The theory of archetype change emphasizes radical organizational change as the dominant mode of change. While Greenwood and Hinings (1988), Hinings and Greenwood (1988), Greenwood and Hinings (1996), and Kikulis, Slack, and Hinings (1995) have suggested that, at the level of the individual organization, change is not always completed in a radical, transformational fashion, the underlying argument is that over time, within the particular institutional field, radical transformation takes place. Any 'hybrid' or 'schizoid' form is unstable and unsustainable. So, the old design is totally replaced by the new one, even though there are issues of the pace, sequence, and linearity of such a process of radical change (Amis, Slack, and Hinings 2004).

However, there is an alternative view of change processes resting on the notion of *sedimentation*, a process that takes place as new interpretive schemes and their respective structures and systems are layered on preexisting archetypes. This outcome has been suggested by Cooper *et al.* (1996), Kitchener (1999), and Morris and Pinnington (1999). They suggest a more complex process that can contain commitments to two alternative archetypes, resulting in 'sedimented' structures, a layering of one archetype on another. The outcome of change is not radical, in the sense of total replacement. They put forward a strong possibility that change is made up of both radical and incremental elements in line with the work of Brown and Eisenhardt (1997) and Eisenhardt and Tabizi (1995). It also raises the possibility that this is not just a comment on the pace, sequence, and linearity of change, but that the P² and MPB are not as divergent as has been suggested and that a combination of them can be a new and stable organizational form for professionals.

Indeed, Morris and Pinnington (1999: 213) deal directly with continuity and change. They suggest that 'our findings are broadly supportive of the notion of change in professional firms being a partial and recursive process rather than a transformational one'. In particular, the new controls are primarily aimed below the level of partner, and partners continue to espouse values of consultation and a consensus approach to decision making. Kitchener (1999: 197) also reports 'the uneven and inconsistent adoption of change in professional organizations'. This is in line with Oliver's (1991) discussion of buffering tactics, actions that disguise nonconformity with institutional pressures. In a somewhat different context, Ferlie *et al.* (1996) suggest that the introduction of the 'new public management' in the United Kingdom has resulted in hybrid organizational structures and interpretive schemes. At the root of all these reports is the notion that there are changes in the structures and systems of professional organizations, but that professional interpretive schemes are more robust and resilient.

The concept of sedimentation raises two issues that have been the source of discussion. One has to do with processes of change; the other is concerned with the emerging professional organizational form. With regard to change, the argument is about whether change is truly transformational, as suggested by Greenwood and Hinings (1993) and Romanelli and Tushman (1994), or slower and more layered. Cooper *et al.* (1996) say that organizations are actually structures in process and because of this the language of sedimentation is preferable to that of transformation. Kitchener (1999: 198) writes that 'the responses of professional organizations to discontinuous change often accommodate existing together with new forms of organizing'. These kinds of change issues have been taken up by Brown and Eisenhardt (1997), Fox-Wolfgram, Boal, and Hunt (1998), Gersick (1991), and Pettigrew, Woodman, and Cameron (2001) and it is not my concern to pursue them here. Rather, it is the issue of the emerging form of professional firms that is important.

Schwarz and Brock (1998) suggest that hybrid structures are common. They label one form the *coexistent organization*. This organization is characterized by the simultaneous operation of traditional, hierarchical organizational and contemporary network structures. We would thus expect emerging professional service firm archetypes to reflect similar hybrid structures—displaying aspects of both change and continuity. The likelihood is that there are more stable forms than the P^2 and the MPB. Thus, there are new syntheses of interpretive schemes, structures, and systems as professionals find ways of maintaining notions of professionalism with corporate-generated ideas of efficiency. Greenwood, Suddaby, and Hinings (2002) suggest that the notion of 'professionalism' gets reworked in the process of legitimizing the multidisciplinary practice. Abbott (1988) sees the issue of interprofessional competition and jurisdictional disputes as central to the analysis of professionals. Such competition and disputes should have an effect on the types of organizations that emerge in and between professional fields and that to go beyond requires a determination of the extent to which new archetypes have emerged, synthesizing old professional and new business values and beliefs.

17.4 CONCLUSION

So what can we conclude about the state of our current understanding? A continuing important theme is that of the potential conflict between professionalism and bureaucratization. However, the bureaucratization of the 1950s and 1960s has become the managerialism of the 1990s, and the problem has been recast as a conflict between professional values and the forms and cultures of hierarchically organized, profit-driven corporations. The interest in professional service firms and organizations that has developed over the past two decades has begun to deal with the variety of organizational settings that professionals work in and their changing nature. The death of bureaucracy is much overstated, but new organizational forms are emerging that emphasize knowledge acquisition, use, and dissemination, together with flexibility and autonomy in organizational working.

More research needs to be done on the way professional fields are being restructured, the emergence of new occupational groupings, the development of new organizational forms, and changes in organizational–professional relationships. In this chapter, and in most of the new work on professional organizations, there has been a lack of attention to differences between professionals in terms of the organizational settings in which they are located. Hastings and Hinings (1970) showed that accountants seemed to be quite comfortable working in bureaucratic settings, and they explained this in terms of the nature of the work that accountants do, which is to bureaucratize others. Some time ago Stern and Barley (1996) appealed to students of organizations to give greater attention to the work that is actually done in those organizations. So far it has been possible to assume that 'a professional is a professional', but it is now time to examine the validity of this statement. Lawyers, accountants, architects, and engineers share similarities but also exhibit differences. For example, Malhotra (1999), in examining modes of entry into foreign markets, showed that the project-based nature of engineering consulting turned typical notions of entry on their head. Not all professional work is project-based, but much is, and we need to pursue the meaning of this for interpretive schemes and organizational forms.

It is possible to take this argument a stage further. Even within a given form of professional organization, e.g. the P^2 or MPB, there are differences among professionals in the nature of their work and their relationship to the organization. These differences derive from the two basic dimensions of organizational differentiation, vertical and horizontal. Vertically, even though professional organizations have fewer levels than many other organizations, there are at least three levels, of student, associate, and partner (the names may vary). Smigel (1964) showed that associates' work was much more controlled than that of partners. Roslender (1992) emphasizes the technical and social division of labor within accountancy from a labor process perspective. Certainly a key debate in the literature on professional service firms has been around the concept of leverage, the ratio of partners to nonpartners, where value is extracted from associates, students, and accounting technicians to provide earnings for partners (Galanter and Palay 1991; Greenwood and Empson 2003; Maister 1993). Nelson (1988) has a similar account of vertical differences in work. Essentially the work of students and nonpartners is the most controlled, formalized, and subject to rule systems; that of partners is more client-oriented, with a strong relational and business development aspect to it. And the movement toward an MPB organizational form emphasizes hierarchy much more strongly and introduces managerial roles.

Much of the literature on professional service firms treats particular professions as unitary, yet there are strong horizontal work distinctions both professionally and managerially within given organizational forms. Even within the collegially oriented P^2 organization there are horizontal divisions based on different activities and these are much more structured in the MPB. Within law firms, a key distinction is between litigators and corporate/commercial lawyers (Flood 1999; Nelson 1988). The former work in courtroom settings, the latter behind the scenes. In accountancy, strong differences in work and orientation are often perceived between audit practitioners and those involved in business advisory services, with the former being more formalized and structured in their approach to their tasks, and the latter requiring more entrepreneurially oriented approaches (Greenwood, Hinings, and Cooper 2004). And a further element in this mix is that with growth in size, almost all professional firms have added management functions such as accounting/administration, marketing, information technology, and human resource management. Thus, members of other professions join the organization, usually doing work that is more structured in its application.

A further, intriguing topic is the possible convergence of professionals in organizations and organizations of professionals. On the one hand, many 'nonprofessional' organizations are increasingly knowledge-based and it has been proposed that they work through more flexible and autonomy-based organizational forms (Alvesson 1995; Nohria and Ghoshal 1997). As has been argued here, as professional organizations move into new, competitive, markets, they grow in size and change their knowledge base. A response to this development is to become more managed, more strategic, with a decrease in some aspects of autonomy and flexibility (the MPB). Thus, there is a new kind of convergence, combining professionalism and managerialism. And this derives from the increasing role of knowledge in 'post-industrial', service-based economies. We may well be in a period of change in which the professional firm is becoming less distinctive from for-profit business corporations. This is especially true of the larger PSFs, but, with institutional effects, even smaller professional partnerships are increasingly characterized by managerialist tendencies (Greenwood, Hinings, and Brown 1990).

Current research and the debate over 'pure' archetypes, sedimentation, or new archetypes means that research on professional organizations needs to actively look beyond the P^2 or MPB archetypes. This is related to an overconcentration on very large professional service firms, in particular, an issue that tends to be true for organization studies in general. As Brock, Powell, and Hinings (1999) put it, 'The research question is whether the old and the new values, beliefs and structures coexist independently within professional organisations or whether they have merged to form a new reality or a new web of meaning.' The research of Kitchener

(1999) and Morris and Pinnington (1999) proposes a recursive and reflexive situation with old and new values, structures and systems interacting and reinterpreting each other.

REFERENCES

ABBOTT, A. (1988). *The System of Professions*. Chicago: University of Chicago Press.

ABRAHAMSON, E. (1991). 'Managerial Fads and Fashions: The Diffusion and Rejection of Innovations'. *Academy of Management Review*, 16: 586–612.

AHARONI, Y. (1993). 'Globalization of Professional Business Services', in Y. Aharoni (ed.), *Coalitions and Competition: The Globalization of Professional Business Services*. London: Routledge.

ALVESSON, M. (1995). *Management of Knowledge-Intensive Companies*. New York: De Gruyter.

AMIS, J., SLACK, T., and HININGS, C. R. (2004). 'The Pace, Sequence and Linearity of Radical Change'. *Academy of Management Journal* (forthcoming).

APPADURAI, A. (1996). *Modernity at Large: Cultural Dimensions of Globalization*. Minneapolis: University of Minnesota Press.

BARTLETT, C., and GHOSHAL, S. (1989). *Managing across Borders: The Transnational Solution*. Boston: Harvard Business School.

BLAU, J. (1984). *Architects and Firms*. Cambridge, Mass.: MIT Press.

BRAVERMAN, H. (1974). *Labor and Monopoly Capital*. New York: Monthly Review Press.

BROCK, D., POWELL, M., and HININGS, C. R. (eds.) (1999). *Restructuring the Professional Organization: Accounting, Healthcare and Law*. London: Routledge.

BROWN, S., and EISENHARDT, K. (1997). 'The Art of Continuous Change: Linking Complexity Theory and Time-Paced Evolution in Relentlessly Shifting Organizations'. *Administrative Science Quarterly*, 42: 1–34.

BUCHER, R., and STELLING, J. (1969). 'Characteristics of Professional Organizations.' *Journal of Health and Sociological Behavior*, 10: 3–15.

CHILD, J., and SMITH, C. (1987). 'The Context and Process of Organizational Transformation'. *Journal of Management Studies*, 24: 565–93.

CLARK, T., and FINCHAM, R. (eds.) (2001). *Critical Consulting: Perspectives on the Management Advice Industry*. Oxford: Basil Blackwell.

COOPER, D. J., GREENWOOD, R., HININGS, B. and BROWN, S. L. (1998). 'Globalization and nationalism in a multinational accounting form: The case of opening new markets in eastern Europe.' *Accounting Organizations and Society*, 23: 531–48.

——HININGS, C. R., GREENWOOD, R., and BROWN, J. L. (1996). 'Sedimentation and Transformation in Organizational Change: The Case of Canadian Law Firms'. *Organization Studies*, 17: 623–47.

D'AUNNO, T., SUTTON, R., and PRICE, R. (1991). 'Isomorphism and External Support in Conflicting Institutional Environments: A Study of Drug Abuse Treatment Units'. *Academy of Management Journal*, 34: 636–61.

DIMAGGIO, P. J. (1988). 'Interest and Agency in Institutional Theory', in L. Zucker (ed.), *Institutional Patterns and Organizations: Culture and Environment*. Cambridge, Mass.: Ballinger.

—— (1991). 'Constructing an Organizational Field as a Professional Project: U.S. Art Museums, 1920–1940', in W. W. Powell and P. J. DiMaggio (eds.), *The New Institutionalism in Organizational Analysis*. Chicago: University of Chicago Press.

—— and POWELL, W. W. (1983). 'The Iron Cage Revisited: Institutional Isomorphism and Collective Rationality in Organizational Fields'. *American Sociological Review*, 48: 147–60.

—— —— (1991). 'Introduction', in W. W. Powell and P. J. DiMaggio (eds.), *The New Institutionalism in Organizational Analysis*. Chicago: University of Chicago Press.

DORADO, S. (1999). 'Institutional Entrepreneurs: Engineers, Catalysts, and Innovators', presented at the Academy of Management Conference, Chicago.

Economist, The (1988). 'Accountant, Consult Theyself', 10 September: 89–90.

EISENHARDT, K., and TABIZI, B. (1995). 'Accelerating Adaptive Processes: Product Innovation in the Global Computer Industry'. *Administrative Science Quarterly*, 40: 84–110.

FERLIE, E., ASHBURNER, L., FITZGERALD, L., and PETTIGREW, A. (1996). *The New Public Management in Action*. Oxford: Oxford University Press.

FLIGSTEIN, N. (1990). *The Transformation of Corporate Control*. Cambridge, Mass.: Harvard University Press.

FLOOD, J. (1999). 'Professionals Organizing Professionals: Comparing the Logic of United States and United Kingdom Law Practice', in D. Brock, M. Powell, and C. R. Hinings (eds.), *Restructuring the Professional Organization: Accounting, Healthcare and Law*. London: Routledge.

Fortune (1998). 'Consultants Have a Big People Problem'. 13 April: 163–6.

FOX-WOLFGRAM, S. J., BOAL, K. B., and HUNT, J. G. (1998). 'Organizational Adaptation to Institutional Change: A Comparative Study of First-Order Change in Prospective and Defender Banks'. *Administrative Science Quarterly*, 43: 87–126.

FRIEDSON, E. (1986). *Professional Powers*. Chicago: University of Chicago Press.

GALANTER, M., and PALAY, T. (1991). *Tournament of Lawyers: The Transformation of the Big Law Firm*. Chicago: University of Chicago Press.

GARUD, R., JAIN, S., and KUMARASWAMY, A. (2002). 'Institutional Entrepreneurship in the Sponsorship of Common Technological Standards: The Case of Sun Microsystems and Java'. *Academy of Management Journal*, 45: 196–214.

GERSICK, C. (1991). 'Revolutionary Change Theories: A Multilevel Exploration of the Punctuated Equilibrium Paradigm'. *Academy of Management Review*, 16: 10–36.

GRAY, J. (1999). 'Restructuring Law Firms: Reflexivity and Emerging Forms', in D. Brock, M. Powell, and C. R. Hinings (eds.), *Restructuring the Professional Organization: Accounting, Healthcare and Law*. London: Routledge.

GREENWOOD, E. (1957). 'Attributes of a Profession'. *Social Work*, 2: 44–55.

GREENWOOD, R., and EMPSON, L. (2003). 'The Professional Partnership: Relic or Exemplary Form of Governance?' *Organization Studies*, 24: 909–34.

—— and HININGS, C. R. (1988). 'Design Types, Tracks and the Dynamics of Strategic Change'. *Organization Studies*, 9: 293–316.

—— —— (1993). 'Understanding Strategic Change: The Contribution of Archetypes'. *Academy of Management Journal*, 36: 1052–81.

—— —— (1996). 'Understanding Radical Organizational Change: Bringing Together the Old and the New Institutionalism'. *Academy of Management Journal*, 21: 1022–54.

—— and LACHMAN, R. (1996). 'Change as an Underlying Theme in Professional Service Organizations: An Introduction'. *Organization Studies*, 17: 563–72.

——HININGS, C. R., and BROWN, J. L. (1990). 'The P2-Form of Strategic Management: Corporate Practices in the Professional Partnership'. *Academy of Management Journal*, 33: 725–55.

——————and COOPER, D. J. (2004). 'An Institutional Theory of Change: Contextual and Interpretive Dynamics in the Accounting Industry', in W. W. Powell and D. Jones (eds.), *Bending the Bars of the Iron Cage: Institutional Dynamics and Processes*. Chicago: University of Chicago Press.

——SUDDABY, R., and HININGS, C. R. (2002). 'Theorizing Change: The Role of Professional Associations in the Transformation of Institutionalized Fields'. *Academy of Management Journal*, 45: 58–80.

——COOPER, D., HININGS, C. R., and BROWN, J.L. (1993). 'Biggest is Best? Strategic Assumptions and Actions in the Canadian Audit Industry'. *Canadian Journal of Administrative Sciences*, 10: 308–21.

——ROSE, T., COOPER, D. J., HININGS, C. R., and BROWN, J. L. (1998). 'The Global Management of Professional Services: The Example of Accounting', in S. Clegg, E. Ibarra, and L. Bueno (eds.), *Theories of Management Process: Making Sense through Difference*. Thousand Oaks, Calif.: Sage.

HALL, R. H. (1968). 'Professionalization and Bureaucratization'. *American Sociological Review*, 33: 92–104.

HASTINGS, A., and HININGS, C. R. (1970). 'Role Relations and Value Adaptation: A Study of the Professional Accountant in Industry'. *Sociology*, 4: 353–66.

HININGS, C. R. (2001). 'Professions in Organizations', in N. J. Smelser and P. B. Baltes (eds.), *International Encyclopedia of the Social & Behavioral Sciences*. Oxford: Pergamon.

——and GREENWOOD, R. (1988). *The Dynamics of Strategic Change*. London: Blackwell.

——————and COOPER, D. J. (1999). 'The Dynamics of Change in Large Accounting Firms', in D. Brock, M. Powell, and C. R. Hinings (eds.), *Restructuring the Professional Organization*. London: Routledge.

——————REAY, T., and SUDDABY, R. (2003). 'The Dynamics of Change in Organizational Fields', in M. S. Poole and A. Van de Ven (eds.), *Handbook of Organizational Change and Innovation*. New York: Oxford University Press.

JOHNSON, T. (1972). *Professions and Power*. London: Macmillan.

KIKULIS, L., SLACK, T., and HININGS, C. R. (1995). 'Sector-Specific Patterns of Organizational Design Change'. *Journal of Management Studies*, 32: 67–100.

KITCHENER, M. (1999). '"All Fur Coat and No Knickers": Contemporary Organizational Change in United Kingdom Hospitals', in D. Brock, M. Powell, and C. R. Hinings (eds.), *Restructuring the Professional Organization: Accounting, Healthcare and Law*. London: Routledge.

KONDRA, A., and HININGS, C. R. (1998). 'Organizational Diversity and Change in Institutional Theory'. *Organization Studies*, 19: 743–67.

LARSON, M. S. (1977). *The Rise of Professionalism*. Berkeley: University of California Press.

LATOUCHE, S. (1996). *The Westernization of the World: The Significance, Scope and Limits of the Drive towards Global Uniformity*. Cambridge: Polity Press.

LAWRENCE, T. B. (1993). 'Institutional Entrepreneurs in Emerging Industries'. Ph.D. Thesis, University of Alberta.

——(1999). 'Institutional Strategy'. *Journal of Management*, 25: 161–87.

LOWENDAHL, B. (1997). *Strategic Management of Professional Service Firms*. Denmark: Handelshojskolens Forlag.

MAISTER, D. (1993). *Managing the Professional Service Firm.* Boston: Harvard Business School Press.

MALHOTRA, N. (1999). 'International Entry Mode Decisions of Professional Service Firms: The Case of Engineering Consulting'. Ph.D. Thesis, University of Alberta.

—— (2003). 'The Nature of Knowledge and the Entry Mode Decision'. *Organization Studies,* 24: 935–60.

MINTZBERG, H. (1979). *The Structuring of Organizations.* Englewood Cliffs, NJ: Prentice Hall.

MONTAGNA, P. (1968). 'Professionalization and Bureaucratization in Large Professional Organizations'. *American Journal of Sociology,* 74: 138–45.

MORRIS, T., and PINNINGTON, A. (1999). 'Continuity and Change in Professional Organizations: Evidence from British Law Firms', in D. Brock, M. Powell, and C. R. Hinings (eds.), *Restructuring the Professional Organization.* London: Routledge.

NELSON, R. (1988). *Partners with Power: The Social Transformation of the Large Law Firm.* Berkeley: University of California Press.

NOHRIA, N., and GHOSHAL, S. (1997). *The Differentiated Network: Organizing Multinational Corporations for Value Creation.* San Francisco: Jossey-Bass.

OLIVER, C. (1991). 'Strategic Responses to Institutional Processes'. *Academy of Management Review,* 16: 145–79.

—— (1992). 'The Antecedents of Deinstitutionalization'. *Organization Studies,* 13: 563–88.

OUCHI, W. (1980). 'Markets, Bureaucracies and Clans'. *Administrative Science Quarterly,* 25: 129–41.

PETERS, T. (1992). *Liberation Management.* London: Macmillan.

PETTIGREW, A., WOODMAN, R., and CAMERON, K. (2001). 'Studying Organizational Change and Development: Challenges for Future Research'. *Academy of Management Journal,* 44: 697–713.

PINNINGTON, A., AND MORRIS, T. (2002). 'Transforming the Architect: Ownership Form and Archetype Change'. *Organization Studies,* 23: 189–211.

POWELL, M., BROCK, D., and HININGS, C. R. (1999). 'The Changing Professional Organization', in D. Brock, M. Powell, and C. R. Hinings (eds.), *Restructuring the Professional Organization: Accounting, Healthcare and Law.* London: Routledge.

RITZER, G., and WALCZAK, D. (1988). 'Rationalization and the Deprofessionalization of Physicians'. *Social Forces,* 67: 1–22.

ROMANELLI, E., and TUSHMAN, M. (1994). 'Organizational Transformation as Punctuated Equilibrium: An Empirical Test'. *Academy of Management Journal,* 36: 1141–56.

ROSE, T., and HININGS, C. R. (1999). 'Global Clients' Demands Driving Change in Global Business Advisory Firms', in D. Brock, M. Powell, and C. R. Hinings (eds.), *Restructuring the Professional Organization: Accounting, Healthcare and Law.* London: Routledge.

ROSLENDER, R. (1992). *Sociological Perspectives on Modern Accountancy.* London: Routledge.

SCHWARZ, G. M., and BROCK, D. (1998). 'Waving Hello or Waving Good-bye? Organizational Change in the Information Age'. *International Journal of Organization Analysis,* 6: 65–90.

SCOTT, W. R. (1965). 'Reactions to Supervision in a Heteronomous Professional Organization'. *Administrative Science Quarterly,* 10: 65–81.

SMIGEL, E. O. (1964). *The Wall Street Lawyer.* New York: Free Press.

STARBUCK, W. (1992). 'Learning by Knowledge-Intensive Firms'. *Journal of Management Studies,* 29: 713–40.

—— (1993). 'Keeping a Butterfly and an Elephant in a House of Cards: The Elements of Exceptional Success'. *Journal of Management Studies*, 30: 885–921.

STERN, R., and BARLEY, S. (1996). 'Organizations and Social Systems: Organization Theory's Neglected Mandate'. *Administrative Science Quarterly*, 41: 146–62.

STRANG, D., and MEYER, J. (1993). 'Institutional Conditions for Diffusion'. *Theory and Society*, 22: 487–511.

SUDDABY, R. (2001). 'Field Level Governance and the Emergence of New Organizational Forms: The Case of Multidisciplinary Practices in Law'. Ph.D. Thesis, University of Alberta.

TOLBERT, P. S., and ZUCKER, L. G. (1983). 'Institutional Sources of Change in the Formal Structure of Organizations: Diffusion of Civil Service Reform, 1880–1935'. *Administrative Science Quarterly*, 28: 22–39.

CHAPTER 18

PORTS AND LADDERS

THE NATURE AND RELEVANCE OF INTERNAL LABOR MARKETS IN A CHANGING WORLD

PAUL OSTERMAN

M. DIANE BURTON

MANY believe that the nature of careers has changed dramatically in the past twenty years. One scholar writes that internal labor markets have been 'demolished', while a human resources manager at Intel comments that, in contrast to the past, today, 'You own your own employability. You are responsible' (Knoke 2001: 31). The idea of the 'boundaryless career' seems increasingly popular (Arthur and Rousseau 1996).

If it is in fact true that the old rules for organizing work have disappeared, this would represent a fundamental change for employees. It would also have major implications for how scholars think about the labor market. Not surprisingly, the reality is more complicated, with evidence of both change and stability in the nature of the employment relationship. In this chapter we discuss the nature of these developments and their implications for the internal labor market literature.

18.1 WHAT ARE INTERNAL LABOR MARKETS AND WHY ARE THEY IMPORTANT?

In their classic book, *Internal Labor Markets and Manpower Analysis*, Peter Doeringer and Michael Piore (1971) define an internal labor market (ILM) as 'an administrative unit, such as a manufacturing plant, within which the pricing and allocation of labor is governed by a set of administrative rules or procedures' (Doeringer and Piore 1971: 2). Doeringer and Piore described a world in which people were hired at the bottom of a job ladder, in so-called 'ports of entry', and then moved up that ladder over their careers. Wages were open to market forces at these entry points but in setting compensation the firm placed considerable emphasis upon internal equity and customary differentials. Pay determination involved careful analysis of relative wages internally and more casual attention to the external market. Rules regarding work allocation and duty distribution were similarly influenced by tradition. Skills were firm-specific and informal training played an important role in firm operations.

The key insight in the ILM perspective is that organizations are the locus of employment outcomes. The most important decisions regarding wages and employment are made by organizations. While at one level obvious, this perspective contrasted sharply with standard economic theory, which gave almost exclusive attention to the external market. The ILM lens shifted attention to the behavior of organizations and in doing so, alerted scholars from a variety of academic disciplines to the phenomena of careers within organizations.

The recognition that economic outcomes are determined by a complicated mixture of social, political, and economic factors returns to a point made nearly fifty years ago by Alvin Gouldner (1954) in his famous study of how work rules emerge in industrial settings. Gouldner showed in great detail how management and employees interacted in setting the rules that governed the workplace and how the actual system was a political bargain that reflected social as well as economic considerations.

In contrast to the standard economic view, which interprets work rules as the result of optimizing behavior, and in contrast to the Weberian view of bureaucracy, which also emphasizes efficiency and rationality, the ILM perspective forces attention to custom, power, and norms. The intellectual roots of the ILM tradition come from the industrial relations academics—a group of policy-oriented pragmatists who moved easily between academia and practice—who were active during the Depression, World War II, and the postwar period.[1] The ILM perspective, as an interdisciplinary synthesis informed by deep knowledge of work and organizations,

---

[1] These include for example, John Dunlop, Clark Kerr, Charles Meyers, and George Schultz.

offered a realistic view of organizational life and labor market outcomes in a world where most people spent their careers within large bureaucracies.

A key question is whether the insights of the ILM perspective have the same relevance in a world where long-term employment in bureaucratic organizations is less common, academic disciplinary boundaries have become more rigid, and the subjects of scholarly inquiry are increasingly distant from the world of practice. We address this question by explicating what we believe to be the core ideas and values associated with the ILM perspective, assessing the empirical and theoretical progress to date, and proposing a future research agenda.

18.2 CORE IDEAS AND VALUES ASSOCIATED WITH THE ILM PERSPECTIVE

The original Doeringer and Piore analysis asserts the importance of both market and nonmarket forces in shaping ILMs. There is no single clear statement of what these nonmarket forces are, but a reading of the literature suggests that custom, norms, and power are the main considerations (Jacoby 1985). Customs arise because ILMs create stable work groups (or stable work groups create ILMs) and, as a considerable literature documents, this leads to expectations regarding work effort, pay, and the like. There is a long-standing literature on these themes (Crozier 1964; Gouldner 1954; Roy 1952). These expectations can be enforced, even in nonunion settings, by withholding of effort. As a result, firms frequently pay more attention to custom (e.g. in setting wages) than they do to supply and demand in the market.

Norms operate like customs but refer more to the attitudes of management. Throughout most of the postwar period the norms of managers were grounded in the academic literature termed the Human Relations School.[2] As Mauro Guillen points out, the central idea in this line of thought, beginning with Elton Mayo and elaborated by numerous management theorists, was that 'neglecting the morale, sentiments, and emotions of both the worker and manager would set limits to the firm's productivity and profitability' (Guillen 1994: 58).[3] In contrast to the earlier

---

[2] For a summary of the Human Relations School, see Scott (1992: 57–61) Barley and Kunda (1992), and Bendix (1956).

[3] See and Mayo (1945) Roethlisberger and Dickson (1939) for descriptions of the original research that formed the foundation of the Human Relations School. See McGregor (1960), for the most well-known summary of the underlying principles and philosophy of the Human Relations School.

engineering-oriented scientific management approach to boosting performance (Scott 1992: 34–5), the human relations perspective led to the diffusion of human resource practices such as morale surveys and employee suggestion systems. More to the point, it reinforced the norm that the firm should (ideally) make a long-term commitment to its labor force.

Direct exercise of union power and government intervention also shaped ILMs. One of the major goals of unions was to establish predictable rules and procedures that eliminated the arbitrary behavior of foremen under the 'drive system', which typified employment relationships during the first third of the twentieth century. As they gained strength, unions bargained for seniority rights and for job demarcations, which in turn led to job ladders. Sometimes nonunion firms imitated union practice to avoid unionization. In other instances nonunion companies, such as Eastman Kodak, developed their own form of 'welfare capitalism', mixing bureaucratic practices with attention to human relations (Jacoby 1997). The government shaped ILMs by setting rules regarding pay and benefits and by legitimizing union practices such as seniority. A particularly important period was during World War II when the War Labor Board essentially dictated employment practices to firms and to unions.

Economic considerations were also important. For example, Doeringer and Piore gave considerable weight to the role of ILMs in creating a system for efficiently training workers and retaining them. Job ladders accomplish both tasks. Workers higher in the ladder are protected from competition from those below and hence will be willing to provide training. By the same token, the gains to be had from seniority reduce the incentive of trained employees to leave, since they would have to start at the bottom in their next firm.

At the end of the day, the ILM idea is about how social, political, and economic forces act together to determine what happens to people at work. It is this mixture that gives the idea so much interest and power.

18.3 Literature Review and Outstanding Questions

The original Doeringer–Piore formulation focused on blue-collar work in large and medium-sized firms. How well these ideas generalized to the rest of the labor market was unclear. To some extent, Doeringer and Piore generalized via their construct of the secondary labor market to the sector of the economy with no job ladders or other incentives for long-term attachment. However, this idea was mainly aimed at understanding low-wage labor markets and the problem of poverty. What about the rest of the economy, both the white-collar world and also the many nonindustrial firms outside of the poverty job market?

At a theoretical level, scholars have suggested that ILMs referred not to specific practices (e.g. rigid ports of entry), but to the idea that the rules governing work are set administratively and are determined by a range of considerations, economic and noneconomic. Hence, it is not problematic that occupational clusters operate under different ILM rules and constitute different ILM subsystems (Osterman 1987).

Empirical investigations of ILMs in non-blue-collar settings have been relatively rare; however, there are a few notable studies. Rosabeth Moss Kanter's (1977) description of Indsco in *Men and Women of the Corporation* portrays a world of hierarchies and ladders in which upward mobility is the *sine qua non* of success. A seminal study of the California Civil Service (Baron and Bielby 1986) yielded three key insights: first, there are important differences in employment arrangements among firms within an industry or sector; second, the gender composition of jobs influences both the quality and the extent to which they are connected to job ladders that provide upward mobility; and third, job titles—positions on the ladder—and their associated rewards are subject to social and political forces. Other notable studies of managerial careers are those of DiPrete (1989), Jackall (1988), and Rosenbaum (1984). Although they do not all use the ILM vocabulary, their findings are broadly consistent with the ILM perspective.

In the economics literature, Baker, Gibbs, and Holmstrom (1994*a, b*) analyzed career patterns and wages in a bank, using longitudinal personnel data from the 1980s. They found that some of the Doeringer–Piore formulation did not apply in this setting (for example, there were not well defined ports of entry). However, they identified clear job ladders and found wages sheltered from the external market.[4]

All of these studies are rich, detailed examinations of organizational settings over time and are attentive to the social and economic aspects of career dynamics. While the research on ILMs may be overbalanced towards blue-collar work, the existing studies verify that the concept is appropriate for white-collar work.

However, the literature has a bias towards large firms and is virtually silent about how work is organized in smaller firms. This is an important issue, given that most employers in America are small, with under 100 employees, and these firms account of over half of all employment.[5] It is troublesome today because, as we discuss below, many new ideas in employment are emanating from entrepreneurial small firms.

---

[4] They found that there were substantial cohort effects in wage setting, which implies that market considerations were attenuated.

[5] In 1997, 97.6 percent of establishments were under 100 employees and these accounted for 54.6 percent of all jobs (Knoke 2001: 84).

Recent research has elaborated some themes from the original ILM literature. The role of power in shaping work organization is a key element of the ILM perspective and recent work emphasizes alternative conceptions of power. For example, there is evidence that whether or not jobs are part of longer ladders and how work is compensated is influenced by the gender composition of the labor supply (Baron and Newman 1990). Thus, gender considerations affect work organization as opposed to work organization and pay determining who applies for jobs. Similarly, Abbott's work on the dynamics of competition among professions illustrates how professional groups deploy their power within organizations and the licensing power of the state to shape job duties and career paths (Abbott 1988). Additionally, a recent spate of regulations regarding equal employment opportunity has had a substantial impact on how employment is organized within firms. A final social consideration in the construction of ILMs is the power of imitation, or what sociologists refer to as isomorphism (DiMaggio and Powell 1983; Meyer and Rowan 1977). The central idea is that organizations achieve legitimacy by copying the practices of prominent others. While the initial adopters may have had sound reasons for implementing practices, later adopters may be imitating pioneers in order to maintain appearances (Tolbert and Zucker 1983).

These examples illustrate one of the potential extensions of the ILM perspective: considering forms of collective power outside of organizations, including specific work and occupational groups and unions. These forces reassert the importance of the social and the political in the labor market.

The emergence of agency theory and organizational economics has led economic theorists to explanations of ILMs focused on efficiency considerations. In this context, long-term employment relationships are seen as solving incentive and ownership problems. They are interpreted as mechanisms for inducing workers to undertake actions in line with the desires of management, as well as a useful device for solving the challenges of monitoring and enforcement (Gibbons and Waldman 2000). While the economic explanations of ILM practices are useful and important, they treat the organization as simply the transmission belt for a set of considerations that are removed from the dynamics of social and political life. In our view, what gives the ILM idea power, and the reason that it is important, lies precisely in these social and political factors. Social and political factors also introduce inertia and explain why organizations do not immediately adapt when economic incentives change. Therefore, the determination and distribution of economic outcomes, wages, and careers must be understood from a broader perspective.

18.4 The Changing Rules
of Employment

A central challenge confronting the ILM literature is understanding the implications of two decades of organizational restructuring. Thus far, the literature has
been unsuccessful in explaining how ILM structures evolve over time. This was
unproblematic in the context of the long postwar expansion where the basic
structure of the American economy seemed stable. However, beginning in the
mid-1980s, stability was called into question, and firms started to rewrite the
rules of employment. After nearly two decades of turmoil, it is reasonable to ask
whether the ILM idea is still useful, either as a description of reality or as a
theoretical way of understanding the employment relationship.

The earlier discussion points to three questions that go to the heart of whether the
ILM idea still makes sense. First and most basically, do people still have stable careers
within organizations? Second, how have the rules governing employment changed?
Finally, do social forces—customs, norms, power, and imitation—still play any role
in a world in which market forces seem increasingly dominant? As we will see, the
empirical evidence is unclear about the answers to these questions. The next section
reviews what we know about how the rules of employment have changed.

18.4.1 Employment Stability

ILMs cannot exist without employment stability; thus the natural first question is
what has become of job security. There is reason to believe job security has been
undermined for most employees. A much larger fraction of layoffs are now
permanent instead of temporary, and firms are more willing to layoff employees
for reasons other than declining sales. Osterman, using announced layoffs in the
Wall Street Journal, classified the reasons for layoffs in 1974 and 1994 by whether
they were due to poor sales or to restructuring. The fraction due to restructuring
rose to 50 percent from 30 percent (Osterman 1999: 39). In a similar exercise, Farber
and Hallock studied changes in the stock market reaction to layoffs over time and
found that layoffs in the 1990s were seen in a positive light whereas stock prices
previously had been punished (Farber and Hallock 1999).

There are other indications that job security has weakened. Farber (2001)
analyzed biannual data on employee dislocation (permanent layoffs due to

business decisions of firms) and found that while there is a strong cyclical component to dislocation, during the mid-1990s there was more dislocation than would be expected given the tight labor market of that period.

Given these findings one would expect that summary data on job security would show a sharp decline. But this is where the picture gets murky. The best available data are the job tenure information collected every two years in a supplement to the Current Population Survey about the number of years the respondent has worked for the same employer. Table 18.1 provides these data for the entire labor force and for men and women, both with and without age distinctions. The basic story is clear. There is a downward trend in the proportion of men holding long-tenure jobs. The trend is especially pronounced for middle-age men, whom one would expect to be well ensconced in their organizations. However, the trend is quite different for women who, by contrast, have experienced a long-term increase in the fraction holding high tenure jobs. The net effect is a mild decline (but a decline nonetheless) for the labor force as a whole in long-tenure employment.

It is easy to see, from looking at the data for men, why observers may feel that ILMs are crumbling. Although even in 2000 over half of men age 50–54 held long-tenure jobs, the decline has been sharp. Furthermore, the trend, if extrapolated forward, is not promising. However, the longer job tenure of women offsets much of what has happened to men. There is clearly a story to be told about why the fortunes of men and women diverge. But for the purposes of understanding employment systems, the first approximation is that ILMs seem to be in

Table 18.1 Percent of employees with ten or more years of tenure with current employer

	1983	1991	1996	2000
Both sexes 25 and up	31.9	32.2	30.5	31.7
Both sexes age 40–44	38.1	39.3	36.1	35.9
Both sexes age 50–54	53.5	51.4	50.4	48.6
Men 25 and up	37.7	35.9	33.1	33.6
Men age 40–44	51.1	46.3	41.7	40.4
Men age 50–54	62.3	58.5	54.9	51.6
Women 25 and up	24.9	28.2	27.6	29.5
Women age 40–44	23.4	32.0	30.4	31.4
Women age 50–54	42.5	43.4	45.8	45.6

Source: Bureau of Labor Statistics, current population survey.

mild retreat, but nothing as dramatic as the earlier expressions of alarm would suggest.

Additional evidence in the direction of moderation is found in the Bureau of Labor Statistic's survey of contingent work. As part of yet another supplement to the Current Population Survey, respondents are asked every two years about whether they hold contingent jobs. There are three alternative definitions of what is meant by contingent work. The most expansive includes employees who do not expect their jobs to last indefinitely (for reasons other than personal). Among people between the ages of 25 and 64 in the survey of February 2001, 3.2 percent reported that they held contingent jobs. This compares with 3.9 percent in 1995, 3.5 percent in 1997, and 3.3 percent in 1999. There is thus no upward trend in the fraction of the workforce holding precarious jobs.

The mixed story told by these data on tenure and contingent work explains why there is a debate about what is happening to career jobs. A recent exchange between Peter Cappelli (1999) and Sanford Jacoby (1999a, b) does an excellent job of clarifying the disagreement. Cappelli argues that career jobs have been destroyed. He focuses mainly on managers (who are most likely to be men). He discredits the tenure data by pointing out that they reflect quits as well as layoffs—two forces that move in opposite directions and would in aggregate reveal more stability than exists in reality. Finally, he argues that if we focus only on large employers, who are the real drivers of the economy, we would also see much more insecurity than is reflected in the aggregate data. In reply, Jacoby argues that male managers in large firms represent only a small fraction of the economy and that changes elsewhere have been far less dramatic. According to Jacoby, firms have shifted some employment risk to employees; however, this has by no means changed the fundamental character of the employment relationship.

What, then, can we conclude from this conflicting evidence? On their face, the data suggest that ILMs have declined, but that for most people the circumstances of their working life have not changed. We think that this is a fair conclusion, but it overlooks how the changes might affect the attitudes and expectations of employees. A brief parable illustrates this point. Imagine that one hundred people worked together steadily for a number of years with no untoward events. One day someone walks in and summarily fires one person and then walks out. It is true, as the statistician would argue, that only 1 percent of the group has lost their job. However, the world has been turned upside down for everyone. The remaining ninety-nine employees will come to work everyday wondering when their turn will come. This worry will inevitably alter a wide range of behaviors. The actual changes described in this chapter are more extensive than one in one hundred and it is reasonable to believe that their consequences have reverberated broadly.

18.4.2 Temporary and Contract Work

A core characteristic of ILMs is that people who work for the organization are part of the administrative unit that sets employment conditions. Employees are members of the firm. This assumption seemingly has been undermined by the rapid emergence of new ways of organizing work and, in particular, by the growing use of staffing firms and outsourcing contracts. Staffing firms (aka temporary help agencies) supply employees who work on-site in a client firm, whereas outsourcing firms take over activities that were previously done in-house. Both appear to threaten the integrity of ILMs.

According to David Autor (2001), between 1979 and 1995 the temporary help supply industry in the United States increased its daily head count from 435,000 to 2.4 million workers.[6] Although, as Susan Houseman has shown (Houseman 2001), many firms still use temporary help agencies in their old-fashioned role of meeting peak loads and filling temporary vacancies, what is striking about these firms is the new roles they are playing. They have penetrated into a wide range of occupations, and they play an important role in many firms' recruiting and training strategies.

In a similar vein, firms are increasingly contracting out services. This happens at the low end of the labor market where, for example, nearly all building service workers in large buildings now work for contracting firms rather than building owners. However, this also is happening at the high end, as the growth of computer outsourcing by firms such as EDS and IBM testifies.

The most striking pattern in the use of temporary workers is their role in relieving firms of the implicit constraints imposed by ILMs. For example, case studies by Houseman, Kalleberg, and Erickcek (forthcoming) illustrate a widely commented upon pattern: the use of staffing agencies as forms of probationary employment, thereby releasing firms from the constraints of formal probationary periods. Employers use temporary help firms as a recruiting device (as a labor market intermediary) and the movement from 'temp to perm' is not uncommon.[7] In a similar vein, Autor (2001) shows that in those states in which legislation restricted employment-at-will practices temporary help firms grew at a faster pace than average.

The use of staffing firms to loosen the constraints of ILMs goes beyond these examples. Based on their survey of establishments, Abraham and Taylor (1996) concluded that one motivation of contracting out was to induce greater flexibility in the wage structure. Although this is often taken to mean paying lower wages (and avoiding benefits), the use of staffing firms can also sometimes enable

---

[6] According to Autor, '[T]he Temporary Help Supply (THS) industry in the U.S. grew at eleven percent annually—over five times more rapidly than U.S. non-farm employment' (see Autor 2001: 1).

[7] In Osterman's National Survey of Establishments 24 percent of temporaries were eventually hired by firm to which they were assigned. Census data reports that 57 percent of workers in a temporary job were in a permanent job the next year (Cappelli 1999: 142).

Table 18.2 Alternative employment over time (% of labor force)

	1995	1997	1999	2001
Independent contractor or freelance	6.7	6.7	6.3	6.4
On call	1.7	1.6	1.5	1.6
Agency temporaries	1.0	1.0	0.9	0.9
Contract workers	0.5	0.6	0.6	0.5

Source: Bureau of Labor Statistics, current population survey.

firms to pay certain categories of workers higher wages without being forced by the wage structure of the ILM to increase the compensation of all employees. Abraham and Taylor find evidence of this high-wage pattern in their data on contracting out, and Houseman, Kalleberg, and Erickcek (forthcoming) also found examples of exactly this usage in their case studies of temporary workers in health care.

Beyond these specific motivations, the message implicit in the growing use of temporary and contract workers is that the firm no longer considers workers to be part of the organization. Clearly this message is very subversive of ILMs. Table 18.2 shows the fraction of the labor force employed in staffing firms and contracting firms. It turns out that, although the growth rates are quite high when the baseline is the 1970s or early 1980s, the actual numbers are modest and there was relatively little growth in the 1990s. The largest group of employees are independent contractors, but this group differs markedly from the others as evidenced by the fact that the majority of them prefer their employment situation to traditional employment, whereas the majority of temporary and on-call workers would rather have standard jobs (Golden and Appelbaum 1992).

These low numbers are a bit misleading because the high turnover of temporary workers implies that more people flow through these jobs in a given year than appear in them at any point in time. Autor (2001) estimates, for example, that between seven and eight times as many people hold temporary jobs over the course of a year than at any point in time. Nonetheless, from the ILM perspective, these workers do not account for very much of employment.

18.4.3 Wage Setting

Wage setting is obviously a core aspect of the employment relationship[8]. The traditional ILM story was that firms paid more attention to establishing a stable and fair internal wage structure than to rewarding either individual performance or

---

[8] Ruthanne Huising did most of the research underlying this section.

responding to market forces. They did so because customary wage differentials were believed to be essential to the continued social functioning of the firm. The mechanics of wage setting involved extensive attention to internal pay setting (frequently via techniques such as Hay points) and little attention to salary surveys and other market wage data. It is also worth noting that Hay points are allocated to roles rather than individuals and thus give no credit to individual performance.

Increasing wage inequality in the past twenty-five years suggests a potential ILM breakdown. It does not prove the point since inequality could increase via differential growth rates of firms and occupations even in the face of stable internal wage structures. However, growing wage differentials, combined with new managerial rhetoric about pay for performance, implies that something about the wage-setting process has changed.

There are two senses in which ILMs might break down: firms might pay more attention to market wages with ILMs no longer mitigating market forces, or rewards for individual performance might increase and the social strictures on wage differences erode. Either would imply that ILMs have attenuated with respect to pay. However, the evidence suggests the trends are in favor of the former—a breakdown of ILM shelters against market wages.

Observations of wage setting suggest that firms are making increased use of pay surveys[9] and this trend is augmented by the wide availability of salary data via web sites such as salary.com and salaryexpert.com. Furthermore, Levine et al. (2002) show that traditional pay differentials between large and small firms are eroding. They conclude that this cannot be entirely explained by changes in workforce characteristics and that the convergence shows a 'decline in the institutionalist pressures that formerly led to a size-wage effect' (Levine et al. 2002: 73).

The evidence, it should be noted, is not uniformly in the same direction. Levine et al. also find no increase in the sensitivity of employers' wage levels to local labor market conditions. However, other shifts in firms' wage-setting practices add support for the idea that wages are less insulated than in the past. For example, there is growing use of 'broadbanding'—a reduction in the number of pay grades—which enables firms to link individuals' pay more closely both to their performance and to the market wage that they might get (Berger and Berger 2000). Front-line managers who set pay for specific jobs are able to utilize market pay data. Levine et al. (2002: 52) conclude that 'broadbanding results in pay to individuals that is more representative of external market wages for that individual'.

Furthermore, pay-for-performance schemes have been widely adopted both across firms and across categories of employees, and these schemes tend to undermine traditional pay structures. According to one survey, 27.1 percent of nonexempt employees received some of their pay via bonus or incentive plans in 1994

---

[9] Large companies obtain, on average, eleven surveys per year (see Sibson 1990).

and the fraction had increased to 44.8 percent by 1998 (HR Focus July 2000).[10] A survey by the Federal Reserve Bank found that in 1998, 69 percent of lower level employees (i.e. not managers or professionals) received at least one form of variable pay (Lebow *et al.* 1999). Finally, an analysis of Hay data in 1986 and 1992 found that the percentage of employees who received bonuses increased from 19.6 percent to 32 percent (O'Shaughnessy, Levine, and Cappelli 2000).

Taken as a whole, it seems that wage setting is more open to market forces than in the past and that the importance of traditional internal structures has diminished as pay targeted to individuals has increased. This is not to say, however, that pay is now set simply via supply and demand or by individual performance. There is still evidence that internal structures remain important. For example, in their analysis of pay in a large bank in the late 1980s, Baker, Gibbs, and Holmstrom (1994*b*) found clear evidence that the pay level of hiring cohorts relative to each other remained stable over time, a finding that implies that the internal structure shelters pay from the market. Similarly, Levine *et al.* (2002) utilize a community salary survey conducted by the Federal Reserve Bank between 1956 and 1996 in Cleveland to analyze the persistence of internal structure differentials and find them to be relatively constant across the 1980s and 1990s, indicating no increased sensitivity of employer pay practices to market pressures.

The best conclusion, then, is that the role of ILMs in pay setting is weaker than in the past but that they remain an important part of pay determination.

18.4.4 Changing Work Rules

A central element of ILMs, at least in blue-collar settings, was rigid job descriptions. This was particularly true in the union sector but extended into nonunion firms as well. Because firms could lay people off without constraint, unions sought well-defined jobs as a form of protection from employers who would combine assignments in order to increase layoffs. In addition, when promotions and salary increases came from climbing a job ladder, the 'rungs' needed to be well defined.

The system of seniority and tightly defined jobs was rational and effective as long as firms' environment was stable. However, as the product market forced firms to innovate rapidly and focus on quality, the rigidities inherent in the old ILM system became a liability. This became painfully evident as competitors, notably the Japanese, gained better productivity and higher quality from more flexible production methods. The response in the United States was high-performance work systems.

---

[10] This is based on a survey of Fortune 1000 firms by Buck Consulting.

In the past decade and a half many firms, in both manufacturing and services, implemented team-based production, quality programs, job rotation, and other practices that are grouped under the heading of high-commitment or high-performance work systems. Surveys of employers show that these practices have diffused rapidly (Osterman 2000). These work systems require higher levels of skill and ask that employees make a greater commitment to the enterprise by offering ideas and paying more attention to quality. There is compelling evidence that high-performance systems yield enhanced productivity and quality (Ichiowski *et al.* 1996). Although part of the gains are due to intensified effort and peer pressure, employee surveys show that workers prefer these new systems to the alternative (Freeman and Rogers 1999).

The spread and success of high-performance systems appear inconsistent with other developments, notably the rise of insecurity and use of contingent employment. High-performance work systems require a degree of employee commitment, which seemingly is undermined by the other trends. Traditional industrial relations scholars would predict that firms could not successfully obtain the cooperation of their labor force without providing security in return. This, however, seems not to be true. One possibility is that employees sufficiently like the new systems that they are willing to cooperate without a quid pro quo. There is some evidence for this, but the more likely explanation is that the level of employment insecurity is sufficiently high that firms can call the shots without having to offer much in return.

18.4.5 Increased Diversity of Employment Systems

We noted earlier that a nagging question about the accuracy of the original ILM research was how widely it applied to different occupations and types of organizations. Whatever the answer was some twenty years ago, in the past two decades it appears that the amount of diversity in employment models has increased. Prior to the era of restructuring, there were pressures towards uniformity or stability among what were seen as leading firms. In the past two decades much more diversity has emerged even within the core.

Within traditional sectors, new firms have challenged older ways of doing business.[11] For example, automobiles used to be characterized by tight pattern bargaining, in which agreement in one of the Big Three firms was matched in the others. Today the Big Three vary significantly in their agreements. More important, a key nonunion segment—led by Japanese transplants—has emerged whose

---

[11] An excellent study that documents the trends described in this paragraph and makes the point about growing diversity is Katz and Darbishire (2000).

employment practices differ dramatically from the standard model. Likewise, in the large auto parts industry, the spread of an increasingly important nonunion sector has also added to the variation in employment patterns.

Much the same can be said of other industries. In telecommunications, Japanese transplants have not played an important role but the industry has moved a long way from the old world in which AT&T set the dominant pattern for work organization in both local and long-distance service. The breakup of the old AT&T system and the rise of nonunion carriers such as Sprint and MCI have also increased the variation in employment patterns.

One might argue that these examples illustrate growing variety in ILM rules but not a fundamental shift in the ILM idea. However, a more serious challenge to the notion of ILMs has emerged in the Silicon Valley. Many observers believe that how the Valley organizes employment represents a new pattern. The standard perception is that turnover in the Valley is very high and that high-skill employees are motivated by attachment to profession and learning opportunities, not by attachment to firm. Companies that are entirely nonunion work hard to create university-like employment settings (Rogers and Larson 1984). The tenuousness of attachments to firms is emphasized by the fact that the use of temporary help and contract labor is much higher in the Valley than elsewhere in America (Baru 2001).

More detailed research in the Silicon Valley suggests that there is important variation in employment strategies among 'standard' Valley firms. Based on systematic interviews with founders of new Silicon Valley companies, Baron, Hannan, and Burton (2001) identify five distinctive approaches to organizing work and motivating employees. Which strategy is selected has consequences for important outcomes, ranging from the time it takes to launch an Initial Public Offering (IPO) to the bureaucratic structure of the firm and the gender composition of the firm's employees.[12] Whereas the early ILM literature distinguished two types of employment relationships, 'good' and 'bad' (aka core and periphery; primary and secondary; traditional and transformed, etc.), and proposed that ILMs existed in the 'good', there is growing evidence that there are more than two types of employment relationships.

---

[12] These five strategies are termed 'star', 'engineering', 'commitment', 'bureaucracy', and 'autocracy'. They vary according to what kinds of incentives are used to maintain attachment to the firm (e.g. a community of peers, a familial feeling, money), and what kinds of control and career systems are utilized.

18.5 THE RESEARCH AGENDA

It is apparent that there have been substantial changes in how work is organized. There is a great deal of research to be done in understanding what has happened and the implications. In this final section, we describe what we see as an emerging research agenda.

We still lack a good understanding of what is driving many of these labor market developments. The standard list of suspects emphasizes factors that increase the pressure on firms to maximize profits and to reduce the possibilities of slack or rent sharing. These pressures include heightened product market competition, changes in corporate governance, and the role of the stock market. We agree that these are important, but we also believe that some deeper underlying constraints may have changed. For example, there is some evidence—both in the research literature and in policy discussions—that the spread of new technologies has made skills more general (Gould 2002). If this is true, then the gains to be had from ILMs are reduced. Similarly, the spread of information technology has opened the possibilities of new organizational designs (such as increased ability to outsource), which in turn have implications for the structuring of careers. Finally, changes in the broad political environment may have eased constraints managers feel as they consider how to approach their workforce. Understanding the role of these factors is partly the province of the kind of careful historical investigation that characterized the earlier rounds of research on ILMs. It may also be furthered by particular research strategies, such as taking advantage of geographical variation in the constraints facing employers.

A second set of research questions centers on developing a deeper understanding of how the institution of ILMs is evolving. At one level this involves asking about how firms are changing their strategies for organizing work. For example, researchers have noted an increased willingness of companies with long-standing ILMs to open up previously closed job ladders and hire from the outside. How widespread is this and what are the implications? More generally, what do careers now look like within organizations that have flattened their hierarchies and have established partnerships with other firms involving a substantial interpenetration of activities across traditional boundaries? Other researchers have emphasized how the ILMs of newer firms (such as those in the Silicon Valley) differ from older models. Just what these career systems look like and what is the significance of their departures from the standard model seem to us to be important questions. There is also the question noted earlier: how can firms reconcile the implementation of high-performance work systems with continued employment insecurity?

A third set of questions about what is happening emerges from the spread of structured careers outside of traditional firms. Traditionally, careers of this sort have been predominately in either construction craft jobs, certain professions, or in the bad jobs of the secondary labor market. However, the increased importance of contingent employment and independent contractors, combined with the role played by staffing firms in the labor market as well as the spread of peer groups that provide training and job search support (e.g. the International Webmasters Association or the New York New Media Association), suggests that these non-conventional career patterns may be taking on greater importance. Researchers are beginning to investigate these patterns more deeply, and this appears to us to be a fruitful area (Fernandez-Mateo 2002; Kunda, Barley, and Evans 2002).

One implication of the foregoing discussion is that the loosening of ties between employee and firm means that work may increasingly be organized around occupations rather than firms. These 'occupational labor markets' over time may come to replace some of the functions played by firm-based ILMs (Tolbert 1996). Put differently (and using the vocabulary of unions), more work may be organized along craft, as opposed to industrial, lines.

The deepest question, however, is whether the idea of ILMs is still relevant. Recall that in our view the key idea driving the ILM literature is that social forces—customs, norms, power—shape employment relationships. Yet many observers believe that in recent years the market has pushed these considerations aside and that the changes we observe reflect the triumph of market forces. Of course, work is still largely organized within firms and in this, almost tautological sense, ILMs are of continued relevance. But if organizations are merely the transmission belt of the market, then the core idea has lost power.

There is, it seems to us, no doubt that market forces have successfully pushed against the older organizational forms and transformed them (though not as extensively as the more heated popular discussion suggests). The question, however, is whether over time social factors will reassert their importance in determining employment configurations. We suspect that the answer is yes, that what we are witnessing is one stage in a cycle in which market and society push against each other. We think that norms, customs, and power will continue to play important roles even in the kind of new employment arrangements in which people construct careers across boundaries. We certainly believe that this is true within more conventionally defined firms. Over time new customs and norms will arise; these will not simply be reflections of market considerations, and they will take on a power (and inertia) of their own. An important, and open, question is whether the basis of these social pressures will continue to be firms or, rather, whether new configurations will arise around occupations. A substantial shift from the firm to another form of organization would be a substantial change and there are certainly signs (as we have seen) that such a shift is possible. Our best guess is that firms will continue to be the dominant organizing device in the labor market but that occupations will emerge as more important than in the past. We also think that employees will find new ways to deploy power to protect their interests. Mapping and understanding just how all of this plays out will certainly be one of the most important, and interesting, research endeavors in this field.

However, our view that social factors will continue to be important in the labor market should be taken as a hypothesis, one that would constitute a core element in what we see as the emerging research agenda that can only be effectively pursued in a grounded and interdisciplinary fashion.

References

Abbott, A. (1988). *The System of Professions: An Essay on the Division of Expert Labor*. Chicago: University of Chicago Press.

Abraham, K., and Taylor, S. (1996). 'Firms' Use of Outside Contractors: Theory and Evidence'. *Journal of Labor Economics*, 14/3: 394–424.

Arthur, M., and Rousseau, D. (eds.) (1996). *The Boundaryless Career*. New York: Oxford University Press.

Autor, D. H. (2001). 'Outsourcing at Will: The Contribution of Unjust Dismissal Doctrine to the Growth of Employment Outsourcing'. NBER Working Paper No. 7557.

Baker, G., Gibbs, M., and Holmstrom, B. (1994a). 'The Internal Economics of the Firm: Evidence from Personnel Data'. *Quarterly Journal of Economics*, 109: 881–919.

———————— (1994b). 'The Wage Policy of a Firm'. *Quarterly Journal of Economics*, 109: 921–55.

Barley, S., and Kunda, G. (1992). 'Design and Devotion: Surges of Rational and Normative Ideologies of Control in Management Discourse'. *Administrative Science Quarterly*, 37/3: 363–99.

Baron, J. N., and Bielby, W. T. (1986). 'The Proliferation of Job Titles in Organizations'. *Administrative Science Quarterly*, 31: 561–86.

—— and Newman, A. E. (1990). 'For What It's Worth: Organizational and Occupational Factors Affecting the Value of Work Done by Women and Non-Whites'. *American Sociological Review*, 55/2: 155–75.

—— Hannan, M., and Burton, M. D. (2001). 'Labor Pains: Change in the Organizational Models and Employee Turnover in Young High-Tech Firms'. *American Journal of Sociology*, 106/4: 960–1012.

Baru, S. (2001). *Working on the Margins: California's Growing Temporary Workforce*. San Diego: Center on Policy Initiatives.

Bendix, R. (1956). *Work and Authority in Industry: Ideologies of Management in the Course of Industrialization*. Berkeley: University of California Press.

Berger, L. A., and Berger, D. R. (eds.) (2000). *The Compensation Handbook*. New York: McGraw-Hill.

CAPPELLI, P. (1999). 'Career Jobs Are Dead'. *California Management Review*, 42: 146–67.

CROZIER, M. (1964). *The Bureaucratic Phenomenon*. Chicago: University of Chicago Press.

DIMAGGIO, P. J., and POWELL, W. W. (1983). 'The Iron Cage Revisited: Institutional Isomorphism and Collective Rationality in Organizational Fields'. *American Sociological Review*, 48: 147–60.

DIPRETE, T. (1989). *The Bureaucratic Labor Market: The Case of the Federal Civil Service*. New York: Plenum Press.

DOERINGER, P. B., and PIORE, M. J. (1971). *Internal Labor Markets and Manpower Analysis*. Lexington, Mass.: Heath.

FARBER, H. (2001). 'Job Loss in the United States, 1981–1999'. Working Paper No. 453, Industrial Relations Section, Princeton University.

—— and HALLOCK, K. F. (1999). 'Changing Stock Market Response to Announcements of Job Loss: Evidence from 1970–97'. IRRA 51st Annual Paper and Proceedings, 26–34.

FERNANDEZ-MATEO, I. (2002). 'Careers in Boundary Labor Markets: An Empirical Analysis of Creative IT Contractors' Job Histories'. Dissertation proposal, MIT Sloan School.

FREEMAN, R., and ROGERS, J. (1999). *What Workers Want*. Ithaca, NY: Cornell University Press.

GIBBONS, R., and WALDMAN, M. (2000). 'Careers in Organizations: Theory and Evidence', in O. Ashenfelter and D. Card (eds.), *Handbook of Labor Economics*. New York: Elsevier, 3: 2373–437.

GOLDEN, L., and APPELBAUM, E. (1992). 'What Was Driving the 1982–1988 Boom in Temporary Employment?: Preference of Workers or Decisions and Power of Employers'. *American Journal of Economics and Sociology*, 51/4: 473–93.

GOULD, E. (2002). 'Rising Wage Inequality, Comparative Advantage, and the Growing Importance of General Skills in the United States'. *Journal of Labor Economics*, 20/1: 105–47.

GOULDNER, A. W. (1954). *Pattern of Industrial Bureaucracy*. Glencoe, Ill.: Free Press.

GUILLEN, M. (1994). *Models of Management*. Chicago: University of Chicago Press.

HOUSEMAN, S. (2001). 'Why Employers Use Flexible Staffing Arrangements: Evidence from an Establishment Survey'. *Industrial and Labor Relations Review*, 55/1: 149–70.

—— KALLEBERG, A. L., and ERICKCEK, G. (forthcoming). 'Why Employers Use Temporary Help Employment in Tight Labor Markets: Evidence from Case Studies of Hospitals and Auto Suppliers'. *Industrial and Labor Relations Review*.

ICHNIOWSKI, C., KOCHAN, T., LEVINE, D., OLSON, C., and STRAUSS, G. (1996). 'What Works at Work'. *Industrial Relations*, 35/3: 299–333.

JACKALL, R. (1988). *Moral Mazes*. New York: Oxford University Press.

JACOBY, S. (1985). *Employing Bureaucracy: Managers, Unions, and the Transformation of Work in American Industry, 1900–1945*. New York: Columbia University Press.

—— (1997). *Modern Manors: Welfare Capitalism since the New Deal*. Princeton, NJ: Princeton University Press.

—— (1999a). 'Are Career Jobs Headed for Extinction?' *California Management Review*, 42: 123–45.

—— (1999b). 'Reply: Premature Reports of Demise'. *California Management Review*, 42: 168–79.

KANTER, R. M. (1977). *Men and Women of the Corporation*. New York: Basic Books.

KATZ, H., and DARBISHIRE, O. (2000). *Converging Divergences*. Ithaca, NY: Cornell University Press.

KNOKE, D. (2001). *Changing Organization: Business Networks in the New Political Economy*. Boulder, Colo.: Westview Press.

KUNDA, G., BARLEY, S. R., and EVANS, J. (2002). 'Why Do Contractors Contract? The Experience of Highly Skilled Technical Professionals in a Contingent Labor Market'. *Industrial and Labor Relations Review*, 55: 234–61.

LEBOW, D., SHEINER, L., SLIFMAN, L., and STARR-MCCLUER, M. (1999). 'Recent Trends in Compensation Practices'. Working paper, Federal Reserve.

LEVINE, D. I., BELMAN, D., CHARNESS, G., GROSHEN, E. L., and O'SHAUGHNESSY, K. C. (2002). *How New is the 'New Employment Contract'?* Kalamazoo, Mich.: Upjohn Institute for Employment Research.

MCGREGOR, D. (1960). *The Human Side of Enterprise*. New York: McGraw-Hill.

MAYO, E. (1945). *The Social Problems of an Industrial Civilization*. Boston: Harvard University.

MEYER, J. W., and ROWAN, B. (1977). 'Institutionalized Organizations: Formal Structure as Myth and Ceremony'. *American Journal of Sociology*, 83: 340–63.

O'SHAUGHNESSY, K. C., LEVINE, D. I., and CAPPELLI, P. (2000). 'Changes in Managerial Pay Structures, 1986–1992 and Rising Returns to Skill'. *National Bureau of Economic Research*. Working Paper No. 7730, Cambridge, Mass.

OSTERMAN, P. (1987). 'Choice of Employment Systems in Internal Labor Markets'. *Industrial Relations*, 26: 46–67.

—— (1999). *Securing Prosperity: The American Labor Market: How It Has Changed and What to Do about It*. Princeton, NJ: Princeton University Press.

—— (2000). 'Work Reorganization in an Era of Restructuring'. *Industrial and Labor Relations Review*, 53/2: 176–96.

ROETHLISBERGER, F. J., and DICKSON, W. J. (1939). *Management and the Worker*. Cambridge, Mass.: Harvard University Press.

ROGERS, E. M., and LARSON, J. K. (1984). *Silicon Valley Fever: Growth of High-Technology Culture*. New York: Basic Books.

ROSENBAUM, J. (1984). *Career Mobility in a Corporate Hierarchy*. Orlando, Fla.: Academic Press.

ROY, D. (1952). 'Quota Restrictions and Goldbricking in a Machine Shop'. *American Journal of Sociology*, 57: 427–42.

SAXENIAN, A. (1994). *Regional Advantage*. Cambridge, Mass.: Harvard University Press.

SCOTT, W. R. (1992). *Organizations: Rational, Natural, and Open Systems*. Englewood Cliffs, NJ: Prentice Hall.

SIBSON, R. E. (1990). *Compensation*. New York: American Management Association.

TOLBERT, P. S. (1986). 'Organizations and Inequality: Sources of Earnings Differences between Male and Female Faculty'. *Sociology of Education*, 59: 227–36.

—— (1996). 'Occupations, Organizations, and Boundaryless Careers', in M. Arthur and D. Rousseau (eds.), *The Boundaryless Career*. New York: Oxford University Press, 331–49.

—— and ZUCKER, L. G. (1983). 'Institutional Sources of Change in the Formal Structure of Organizations: The Diffusion of Civil Service Reform, 1880–1935'. *Administrative Science Quarterly*, 28: 22–39.

ORGANIZING AND ORGANIZATIONS

INTRODUCTION

STEPHEN ACKROYD

THE question of the organizational composition of the economy is the central concern of the chapters in Part IV. The chapters offer a number of perspectives on the organizational basis of the national and international economy: they consider the way the economy of the advanced regions and their interrelations are now organizationally constituted and the implications this has for contemporary work.

Much has changed in the organization of the economy in the last quarter of a century. There is now greater specialization of activities by organizations, combined with greater interdependence among them. The average size of organizations has decreased. Care must be taken, however, in understanding the nature of these changes. There has not been the creation of an entrepreneurial economy driven by the activities of independent or highly innovative small firms. Rather, there has been the specialization of the activities undertaken by business units and increasing cooperation between them. Large organizations remain important, but they are increasingly made up of interdependent small units, in which self-conscious co-ordination between constituent units is prominent. Large organizations have become deconstructed into constellations of small business units, but they often continue to play a dominant role in economic exchanges. Similar patterns are widespread outside the corporate sector. Through such things as subsidiarization, spin-offs, franchising, and formal alliances as well as varied affiliation arrangements, new patterns of interrelatedness are now ubiquitous. Consequently, considering organizations in isolation from each other as the objects of attention will not yield an understanding of the developments and changes occurring in the corporate economy.

This is in sharp contrast to most organizational research conducted up to and including the 1970s, which was based on the assumption that organizations could be understood and analyzed as independent actors. From the first few decades following World War II to the 1970s, the dominant understanding of organizations was colored by the assumptions and outlook of neoclassical economics, in which individual firms were seen as rational actors and business executives were cast as independent entrepreneurs taking the risks associated with independent operation in the market. Similarly, in organizational analysis, the dominant approach was to the organization, which was seen as the main object of attention (Donaldson 1985; Mintzberg 1983; Pugh and Hickson 1976; Pugh and Hinings 1976). Despite the continued advocacy of contingency theory, and ideas derived from it by a residue of supporters (Donaldson 2002; Mintzberg 1993), this approach has been largely discarded.

There is now more awareness of the increase in interorganizational dependency. Since the beginning of the 1980s, there have been attempts to produce new accounts of the economy that make organizational interdependence central. Arrangements variously defined as interorganizational cooperation (Alexander 1994), network forms of organization (Thompson 2003a; Thompson et al. 1991), organizational networks (Castells 1996), and alliance capitalism (Dunning 1997) have moved center stage. An extreme example of the trend of events is the emergence of widespread franchising. Franchising involves the licensed use of business recipes and is thus a considerable departure from the entrepreneurial idea of business as it has been traditionally conceived (Felstead 1993). Despite the undoubted importance of franchises, due to the conspicuous example of the MacDonald's chain (Ritzer 1993; Smart 1999) and the domination of particular industries by franchising (Schlosser 2002), franchising is just one example of a host of changes involving increased organizational interdependency. More important than franchising, though much less obvious to the casual observer, is the large corporation that is now organized as numerous disaggregated and quasi-independent cost centers, affiliated businesses, and cooperative alliances. More general, but no less significant, are whole industries organized as supply chains, some of which spread across the world.

The Importance of Interorganizational Relations

While the chapters in Part IV and elsewhere in the book consider particular new forms of organizations, they differ from the older tradition of organizational studies in that they offer a new understanding of the social and organizational context that has given rise to such forms. In traditional organizational analysis, of course, a concern for the environment of organizations has been present; but the view has been that the organization was shaped by its context considered as a generalized environment. These days, such views have been largely discarded, in favor of understanding the relationship between organizations as variable, often being both reciprocal and dynamic. Large organizations have probably always affected externalities much more than they were affected by them. Today, for powerful organizations, interorganizational operations are an effective means of environmental management.

Since the first intellectually significant efforts at understanding the importance of intraorganizational connections (Piore and Sabel 1984), it has become clear that such relationships are of increasing importance (see Sayer and Walker 1992 for a review). The proliferation of supply chains, which, as has been noted, for some industries extend across continents linking developed and underdeveloped regions, is a compelling instance of a new type of interorganizational connectedness and dependency. New forms of flexible economic organization themselves achieve a new level of adaptiveness, allowing changes in both the kinds of products and services and their volume to be produced by a firm (or business unit of a larger entity), but these are not nearly so important as the flexibility allowed by new relationships *between* organizations and business units. In the first chapter in this Part, Stephen Procter has a good deal to say about the types of small firms and business units that now make up the economy. He rightly contrasts development in the last few decades as being decisively different from what came before. Hitherto, under the system of mass production often identified as Fordism, productivity had been achieved in large plants, usually at the expense of the quality and variety of output. The organizational basis of this was the highly bureaucratized organization having an extended and elaborate division of labor. By contrast, Procter argues that today we see high productivity being combined with variety of output. This is achieved by: the redesign of jobs involving employees moving between tasks (flexible working); organizations adapting their structures to undertake different activities (flexible organizations); and the development of flexible interorganizational systems. Procter argues that interorganizational arrangements are more contributory to success than intraorganizational efficiency.

Alternative Approaches to Organizational Transformation: Neo-Bureaucracy vs. Networks

How to describe and account for the new modes of articulation between business units is a matter of considerable debate. Hence, there follow two chapters that further explore the question of the structural transformation of the economy from opposite directions. First, there is a chapter by Mats Alvesson and Paul Thompson that looks at the extent to which the bureaucracy, the large-scale and highly structured organization that dominated the economic landscape in developed regions for much of the last century, has been disassembled and replaced with something different. It is, of course, widely argued that organizations have been fundamentally changed in this respect. Allegedly, the bureaucracy has been replaced by post-bureaucratic structures (Heckscher and Donnellon 1994). According to some, the post-bureaucracy is simply an inversion of the bureaucratic form. Where the bureaucracy involved many levels of hierarchy, the post-bureaucracy has few; crucially, where the bureaucracy relied on authority to coordinate activities, allegedly, the post-bureaucracy relies on spontaneous cooperation, and so on (see Ackroyd 2002: 170; Thompson and McHugh 2002: 155).

Through a close analysis of the research record in which corporations have been studied, Alvesson and Thompson show that the simplistic picture drawn by the supporters of post-bureaucratic models is inaccurate. There is not so much the relinquishment of bureaucratic modes of organizational articulation as their augmentation by other modes of control. By such changes, it is possible to understand how it is that major corporations are larger than ever, especially in terms of the assets and resources they have at their command, while seeming to operate on a human scale and to offer unprecedented degrees of autonomy in work performance to employees. Alvesson and Thompson concentrate on considering how corporations exert power within the organizational boundary. But if what has been argued so far is true, that the relationships between organizations are now much more important than they were in the past, then attention needs to be paid equally to the way corporations direct and control the activities of affiliates and partners. Alvesson and Thompson contribute to such analysis. They argue, among other things, that corporations exert control through the use of MIS. Clearly, it does not much matter whether the organizations undertaking joint activities are the business units actually belonging to a large corporation, or are apparently independent entities from a legal point of view. The new modes of control that augment bureaucratic hierarchy can be brought to bear just as effectively on businesses that are merely affiliates or subcontractors. Hence, appropriately considered, the analysis of Alvesson and Thompson does have significance for interorganizational relationships.

By way of contrast to the arguments of Mats Alvesson and Paul Thompson, Grahame Thompson takes a different tack. Thompson suggests that the extent of change in the relationships between firms in the economy has become so extensive that the corporate economy has been fundamentally transformed. He argues that in the past it was realistic to analyze the economy dualistically in terms of, on the one hand, hierarchies (i.e. organizations and institutions of which the most developed form was the bureaucracy), and, on the other hand, markets of various kinds (institutions coordinated by the price mechanism). His analysis proceeds by comparing and contrasting patterns of relationships in organizations and in market contexts and by trying to explain the logic of these alternative modes of allocation. Thompson argues that focusing directly on understanding the pattern of interorganizational relations as a network is also a fruitful way to analyze interorganizational relationships as well as looking at them in terms of hierarchy and market. However, he concedes that any existing network will contain elements of hierarchy and market and only approximate to an idealized form of network.

Considered like this, there is no necessary incompatibility between the positions of Mats Alvesson and Paul Thompson and that of Grahame Thompson. The former are arguing for the recognition of changed patterns of organizational relationships within large firms. They argue that relationships between the constituent parts of such firms have changed from their traditional forms and are now, through modes of augmentation, greatly extended in their reach and effectiveness. Grahame Thompson argues that such is the extent of these and other changes that it is necessary to change the traditional analysis of interorganizational relationships. Insistence on the contrast between hierarchy and market certainly isolates the organization, seeing it as a distinctive kind of structure in the sea of the market. This tends to focus attention on the organization and renders the connections between organizations invisible to the scrutiny of traditional organizational analysis, and, presumably, they can be assumed to be unproblematic. Thus far the argument of Grahame Thompson is logical and defensible and hence highly persuasive in these ways.

However, in common with many theorists of networks, Grahame Thompson, also defines the relations of networks in terms that are fundamentally different from either hierarchy or market. The basis of hierarchy is authority, while that of market is the coincidence of wants mediated by price and backed by contract. Networks, by contrast, are allegedly based on trust. It is implied, moreover, that the discovery of this new (and, by implication, superior) organizational principle accounts for much of the organizational change currently to be observed. Here the approach of Grahame Thompson and that of Mats Alvesson and Paul Thompson, not to mention several other chapters in Part IV, are substantively at odds. It is questionable whether there are any actual examples of interorganizational relationships based purely, or even mainly, on trust. Most also seem to involve authority and other forms of coercion. The chapter of Mats Alvesson and Paul Thompson, indeed, suggests that networks constituted by the extended organization, including those coordinated by large firms, are far from being unlike traditional bureaucratic modes of coordination, i.e. based on the concentration of power and the exercise of authority. Almost any significant example of constellations of firms working together—with the possible exception of the regional industrial cluster—has fairly obvious coercive aspects. This is true, for example, of the arrangements found within many business groups, as well as franchises and other types of business alliances, which are often highly one-sided.

Change in the State Sector and the Multinationals

In the next two chapters, attention is turned to the consideration of two types of formerly large-scale, hierarchically integrated institutions: state organizations and multinationals, both traditionally sites of considerable bureaucracy. The fourth chapter of Part IV, by Robert Hebdon and Ian Kirkpatrick, deals with change in the state sector, while that following it, by Glenn Morgan, examines what is known of change among the multinationals. Both of these also emphasize the increased importance of interorganizational relationships. Although they are clearly changing for different reasons, change in public sector institutions seems to be as widespread as it is in the private sector. In the state institutions, political imperatives are operative as much (if not more) than economic ones. Governments are driving processes of reform. As Hebdon and Kirkpatrick show, change has been continuous in the state sector in all developed economies for some time. The consequence of this has been, in many cases, the adoption of similar organizational forms to those found in the private sector. There is clearly a degree of mimesis underlying this, in that public sector managers, lacking legitimacy, achieve it to some extent by adopting what are taken to be the best practices from the private sector. However, the primary cause of public sector change has been the politically inspired drive to curtail expenditure on public services.

The policy objective of reducing the significance of the public sector has been given point by the development of what is called new public management (NPM). NPM has appeal to right-leaning governments, and the policies indicated by these doctrines have been widely adopted as a means to reducing costs. As Hebdon and Kirkpatrick show, however, the public sector has been an area in which there has been considerable industrial unrest, as NPM led to the adoption of policies contradicting the traditional practices of public sector professionals. Part of the impetus for both the policy of cutting support for the public sector and NPM has been the decline in tax revenues, a trend that can be traced, at least in part, to the activities and policies of the largest companies. Here is yet another piece of evidence that it is not small firms that have been the source of change in recent decades, but the very largest ones. Major companies, especially the largest multinational corporations (MNCs), which contribute disproportionately to both the extent of employment and output, have been adopting policies of internationalization that, among other things, have allowed them to evade taxation and to test the ability of governments to meet the costs of an increasingly expensive repertoire of public sector services. It is thus highly appropriate that changes in public sector organizations are considered alongside changes in multinational corporations.

It should be emphasized that pressures for restructuring, from outside the state itself, do not have uniform effects because of choices made by governments about how to respond. Similarly, reform is mediated by national institutions and the nature and outcome of reform efforts are different in different countries. Hence, in the public domain, it is as difficult to talk in terms of a convergence of organizational models as it is among the largest companies. As Glenn Morgan shows in his contribution to this section, MNCs are an increasingly important feature of the economic landscape, in terms of the proportion of output and employment they account for in all economies in which they operate. Although MNCs originated in traditional areas of manufacture and raw material extraction and processing (and are still strongly concentrated in these economic sectors), they increasingly operate in all areas: in commerce and services and tertiary areas of the economy more generally. Not surprisingly, given their size and importance, an emerging area of debate concerns how the tensions between states and MNCs are resolved. Given that the latter are formidable assemblages of economic assets and other resources, bigger than many of the most populous countries (Anderson and Cavanagh 2000; De Grauwe and Camerman 2002; Sklair 2001, 2002), it is hardly surprising that they should be politically effective and able to evade state policies designed to control them. There is of course considerable controversy about the validity of the comparisons made between corporations and countries. In his work on globalization, Grahame Thompson has introduced an important note of realism into the discussion of the economic resources and the power disposed by major companies and suggested that some of the comparisons between countries and companies are grossly misleading (Thompson 2003b).

Nevertheless, MNCs by any standard are impressive assemblages of capital and have seldom been seen simply as economic agents. The perspective of neoclassical economics has contributed little to accounting for them and their activities. MNCs have demonstrated their importance to national governments in a number of ways. Not only are domestic economies vulnerable to the FDI decisions made by multinationals based in a particular country, but, to make up the shortfall in employment, governments are highly dependent on the incoming FDI of foreign companies. The internationalization activities of the largest companies are seen to be the source of change and to have stimulated the development of small companies, especially business services companies, to support them. Given this, it is understandable that the strategies of the MNCs have become the subject of intense interest and sustained public scrutiny. In his chapter, Glenn Morgan shows that the authoritative accounts of the activities of the MNCs have involved recognition of their political features. He shows that even primarily economic analyses of the activities of MNCs, such as that developed by Dunning (1997), have suggested political motives. Morgan shows just how active the MNCs have been in reorganizing themselves to seek and to operate profitably within new areas of the globe, and what political compromises they have to make to accommodate local conditions. Effective control of such large and complex structures is not straightforward and the emergence of political processes, which affect their internal organization, is not unexpected. Such a conclusion points to the relevance of understanding more fully the governance of major companies.

Restructuring the Economy

It is true that the relationships between organizations of different types have been extensively considered, as when the relationships between organizations and the state were looked at by Hebdon and Kirkpatrick or Morgan. However, none of the contributions considered so far has given attention to changes that are systemic and affect economies considered as wholes. Complex though change at this level is, it has to be considered, for there is no doubt that we are living through a period of systemic change in the organization of the advanced economies, and the US economy has perhaps proceeded further and faster with such change than any other. The task of analyzing economic restructuring is undertaken by William Lazonick, who focuses—primarily but not exclusively—on the restructuring of the US economy in recent decades.

Responding to events in the 1930s, Joseph Schumpeter recognized that capitalism is subject to periodic upheavals during which there is transformation of the organizational infrastructure that he labelled periods of creative destruction. Relating creative destruction specifically to organizational change, Schumpeter (1943: 83) writes that such periods are 'not ... incessant: they occur in discrete rushes, separated from each other by periods of relative quiet'. Lazonick's chapter includes an extended analysis of the destruction and reformation that has been taking place in the largest corporations of the American economy in recent times. What is insightful in this is the way Lazonick brings into the light the mechanisms by which corporations have been transformed. Lazonick argues that this particular sequence of change has been made possible because of financial innovations and ideological changes which, together, have allowed more freedom of action to corporate executives.

Drawing on his earlier work with O'Sullivan (Lazonick and O'Sullivan 2000), Lazonick identifies a change in the character of corporate policy in that what he calls their allocative regime has changed. From being primarily concerned to retain profits and reinvest them in tried and tested technology while simply developing the associated management structures (what he calls the retain and reinvest allocative regime), corporate executives have shifted to a strategy of downsizing their organizations and distributing the realized value (what he calls the downsize and distribute allocative regime). In the jargon of the time, 'leaner and fitter', smaller corporations were created, which nonetheless have superior profitability while continuing to have extraordinary influence in virtue of their pivotal importance in production processes and their control of affiliated companies. Lazonick specifically identifies corporate executives as the prime movers in these changes: using the ideology of shareholder value as the legitimation of their activities, they have reduced and reorganized corporate assets, leaving corporations that are more profitable. In the process, corporate elites have also greatly enriched themselves.

In the course of his discussion, Lazonick is careful to draw the distinction between changes occurring in traditional industries from the new economy, suggesting that it is in the former that the downsize and redistribute allocative regime has been extensively adopted. By contrast, in organizations of the new economy, which have, in a very short time, come to rival the older corporations in size, a variant of the retain and reinvest allocative regime has been adopted. By implication therefore, as the size of the new economy has advanced, some of the more distasteful and socially divisive aspects of the recent period of organizational change have also receded in importance. However, top executives in the new economy too are substantially remunerated through stock options, and, to this extent, some substantial redistributive elements of the new allocation regime are also present in the organizations of the new economy. This suggests that the enrichment of the corporate elite is a permanent change, and one of considerable social as well as economic importance. Not for the first time in this volume, the substantial shift in the proportion of the benefits from major corporations going to different sections of the population have been remarked. Lazonick shows that, in the last two or three decades, the balance of power has swung decisively in favor of capital in corporate America. His findings in this respect echo the conclusion of Kunda and Ailon-Souday in Part II that 'the new corporate division is between top executives and everyone else'.

Lazonick's consideration of the benchmark case of the economy of the United States has relatively little to say about the question of how it compares with other regions of the world. The United States is the world's largest economy, but it is by no means typical. Not only is it very large, but it is also one in which government expenditure on social projects is limited. State expenditure indirectly supports particular sections of the corporate economy, often referred to as the military–industrial complex. It is also an economy in which economic activity is relatively unrestricted; in short, in which the philosophy and practice of laissez-faire is endemic (Hutton 2002). It is therefore an economy in which we might see relatively swift movements between recession and recovery. For these reasons alone, the extent to which the US economy can be regarded as an exemplar, and what the United States does today, sooner or later, other developed regions are bound to follow, is a moot point. For some theorists, the institutional dissimilarities between societies are a significant feature of them (Lane 1995; Whitley 1999). That these differences continue to exist suggests they are self-perpetuating, tending to lock organizational forms and practices into particular and highly distinctive patterns. It is clear, then, that the question of the extent to which the US political economy is an exemplary pattern raises theoretical questions.

In his chapter, which is the seventh and last of Part IV, Chris Smith puts forward a general analytical framework, the SSD model, with which to consider the processes at work in organizational change. Dissatisfied with the approach of institutional writers whose work emphasizes continuity over change (Lane 1995;

Whitley 1999), Smith argues that it is necessary to envisage other processes than those which produce organizational isomorphism, and which tend to shape the institutions of particular societies to adopt readily identifiable recurrent patterns. Smith argues that these researchers have identified important formative processes that do shape organizational practices and structures and he calls them societal effects. Significantly, however, institutional writings that identify societal effects have difficulty accounting for other recurrent features of contemporary capitalism that lead to discontinuity. A key example here might be the kind of epochal change that has occurred in recent years and that was examined in the United States by Lazonick. It seems clear that these stem from general features of capitalism, rather than the arrangements developed in particular societies. However, they are also formative of organizational practices and forms of organization. Smith labels these system effects. In addition to societal effects and system effects, Smith suggests that there are pressures towards emulation which induce firms to adopt ways of organizing that are not part of any indigenous societal pattern, nor do they follow from systemic features of capitalism. Here Smith is primarily concerned with accounting for the tendency for organizations to put in place policies and organizational arrangements copied from what are taken to be the most successful corporations at any given time. These Smith identifies as dominance effects because they are features of the economic organization of the dominant economic power. It is no accident that Taylorism is succeeded by Fordism and Fordism by Toyotaism, as authoritative models for economic organization.

Smith's argument is that there will be various external pressures on the corporation, stemming from societal, system, or dominance effects and these may push firms in different directions and have contradictory implications. Because of this, there is in fact no substitute for the empirical examination of industrial practices and for the researcher to unravel the complex motivations and sources of ideas that are animating managers at any given time and place. It does seem true that although British manufacturing companies were persuaded about the effectiveness and value of Japanese techniques (a dominance effect), they would also be very unlikely to adopt them in their entirety, given the costs involved and the reluctance of British banks to provide long-term low-interest loans (a societal effect). Yet they still had to find a profitable mode of organizing manufacture (the system effect). In sum, Smith's SSD model is a helpful tool for understanding the differences of policy and organization of different economies at different times.

Conclusion: A Global Skepticism?

This discussion of our knowledge of organizing and organized systems began with the recognition that we now inhabit a world in which organizations are pivotal institutions and interorganizational arrangements are increasingly important. At the end of this review, what conclusions can be drawn about the consequences of the organizational changes? Two observations will be made and briefly considered. Both concern the wider implications of the trends that have been analyzed in Part IV and elsewhere in this book, and follow from the recognition that change is being driven by the activities of very large firms. First, there are concerns about the social and economic effects of organizational restructuring within the developed regions. Second, there are concerns regarding the effects of the same trends outside the developed regions in the world at large.

It is undoubtedly true that corporate change has made a contribution to the prosperity of the advanced regions of the world; however, the chief beneficiaries of these changes have been particular groups within a reformulated capitalism. The changes in question have of course proceeded at different rates in different places. However, in Britain and the United States, these changes have initiated profound social reorganization as well as economic developments. We should note the emergence of a transnational capitalist class (Sklair 2001, 2002) and its associated ideologies of managerialism and consumerism. Arguably the effects of these changes are presently mostly hidden from view. In some ways more significant perhaps, the development of footloose corporations owing less and less allegiance to particular nation states has challenged the authority of the state and its ability to raise taxation (Ackroyd 2002; Starbuck 2004). These changes have in some countries undermined and, effectively, cast aside the national settlement between capital and labor, which in earlier decades stabilized economy and society, suggesting that future social stability depends on a high level of prosperity and reasonably full employment, which neither private capital nor nations can any longer guarantee (Hertz 2001).

If change would nonetheless lead to the redistribution of wealth in the world, while risking considerable instability in the developed regions, there might be something to be said for it. However, there is much reason to think that what is happening in economic development is potentially even more challenging when considered in a broader context. The reason for this is that the developments considered here are not to be understood as initiating an inclusive process of economic development having beneficial effects in the whole world. What we are witnessing is not so much economic globalization, as the development of corporations able to compete with large corporations from any part of the world and able to contest with them the yield from the most lucrative of the world's markets. Certainly, large organizations based in the developed world are moving capital (employment and productive capacity) abroad in large amounts, but in doing so they show a marked preference for movement to (a) adjacent economies to the one in which they originated and (b) for making investments in the developed world much more extensively than in the underdeveloped parts of it (Hirst and Thompson 1999).

What we see, then, is a pattern of development that is far from being applicable to the whole world, unless we mean by globalization the emergence in the whole world of a propensity to consume the products of the developed parts of it.

References

ACKROYD, S. (2002). *The Organisation of Business: Applying Organisational Theory to Contemporary Change*. Oxford: Oxford University Press.

ALEXANDER, E. R. (1994). *How Organizations Act Together: Interorganizational Coordination in Theory and Practice*. Luxembourg: Gordon and Breach.

ANDERSON, S., and CAVANAGH, J. (2000). *Field Guide to the Global Economy*. New York: New Press.

CASTELLS, M. (1996). *The Information Age: Economy, Society and Culture*. Vol. 1. *The Rise of the Network Society*. Oxford: Blackwell.

DE GRAUWE, P., and CAMERMAN, F. (2002). *How Big Are the Big Multinational Companies?* Available from: http://www.econ.kuleuven.ac.be/ew/academic/intecon/DeGrauwe.

DONALDSON, L. (1985). *In Defence of Organization Theory*. Cambridge: Cambridge University Press.

——(2002). *The Contingency Theory of Organisation*. London: Sage.

DUNNING, J. H. (1997). *Alliance Capitalism and Global Business*. London: Routledge.

FELSTEAD, A. (1993). *The Corporate Paradox: Power and Control in the Business Franchise*. London: Routledge.

HECKSCHER, C., and DONNELLON, A. (eds.) (1994). *The Post-Bureaucratic Organisation: New Perspectives on Organisational Change*. London: Sage.

HERTZ, N. (2001). *The Silent Takeover: Global Capitalism and the Death of Democracy*. London: Heinemann.

HIRST, P., and THOMPSON, G. (1999). *Globalization in Question*. Cambridge: Polity Press.

HUTTON, W. (2002). *The World We Are In*. London: Little Brown.

LANE, C. (1995). *Industry and Society in Europe: Stability and Change in Britain, Germany and France*. Aldershot: Edward Elgar.

LAZONICK, W., and O'SULLIVAN, M. (2000). 'Maximizing Shareholder Value: A New Ideology for Corporate Governance'. *Economy and Society*, 29: 13–35.

MINTZBERG, H. (1983). *The Structuring of Organizations: A Synthesis of Research*. London: Prentice Hall International.

——(1993). *Structure in Fives: Designing Effective Organizations*. London: Prentice Hall.

PIORE, M., and SABEL, C. (1984). *The Second Industrial Divide: Possibilities for Prosperity*. New York: Basic Books.

PUGH, D., and HICKSON, D. (1976). *Organisational Structure in its Context: The Aston Programme I*. Farnborough: Saxon House.

——and HININGS, C. R. (1976). *Organisational Structure: The Aston Programme II*. Farnborough: Saxon House.

RITZER, G. (1993). *The McDonaldisation of Society*. Newbury Park, Calif.: Pine Forge Press.

SAYER, A., and WALKER, R. (1992). *The New Social Economy: Reworking the Division of Labour*. Oxford: Basil Blackwell.

SCHLOSSER, E. (2002). *Fast Food Nation.* Harmondsworth: Penguin.

SCHUMPETER, J. A. (1943). *Capitalism, Socialism and Democracy.* London: Unwin University Books.

SKLAIR, L. (2001). *The Transnational Capitalist Class.* Oxford: Blackwell.

—— (2002). *Globalization: Capitalism and its Alternatives.* Oxford: Oxford University Press.

SMART, B. (1999). *Resisting McDonaldisation.* London: Sage.

STARBUCK, W. (2004). 'Four Great Conflicts of the Twenty-First Century', in C. L. Cooper (ed.), *The Twenty-First Century Manager.* Oxford: Oxford University Press.

THOMPSON, G. F. (2003*a*). 'Globalisation as the Total Commercialisation of Politics?' *New Political Economy*, 8: 401–8.

—— (2003*b*). *Between Hierarchies and Markets: The Logic and Limitations of Network Forms of Organisation.* Oxford: Oxford University Press.

—— FRANCES, J., LEVACIC, R., and MITCHELL, J. (eds.) (1991). *Markets, Hierarchies and Networks.* London: Sage.

THOMPSON, P., and McHUGH, D. (2002). *Work Organisations* (3rd edn). Basingstoke: Palgrave.

WHITLEY, R. (1999). *Divergent Capitalisms: The Social Structuring and Change of Business Systems.* Oxford: Oxford University Press.

CHAPTER 19

....

ORGANIZATIONS AND ORGANIZED SYSTEMS

FROM DIRECT CONTROL TO FLEXIBILITY

....

STEPHEN PROCTER

19.1 INTRODUCTION: ORGANIZING, ORGANIZATIONS, AND ORGANIZED SYSTEMS

....

THE benefits of organization come from different levels of organized activities, each with distinctive emergent properties. Three levels of organized phenomena are identified: work groups, organizations, and organized systems. It is important how activities are configured at each level and how the different levels of organization are connected and articulated. However, it is an indication of how far modernity has homogenized institutions across the developed world, that it now seems natural not to see these three levels as alternatives to each other. There is not much belief that there is a 'natural economy' of groups and communities that can exist alongside the formal economy or that this is potentially alternative to the organizational economy. Today almost everyone assumes that organizing in groups occurs within organizations (the intraorganizational level), that there is then the organization itself (the organizational level), and that finally there are connections and relations between organizations (the interorganizational or organized system level). This is the age of the organization: it is the pivotal structure of modern times. What we have today is not only an organized world (in that organizations are the central institutions), but an organizational world (in that systems made up of interorganizational connections are becoming increasingly important).

Given the importance of the formal organization in the economy and social affairs, it is surprising how recently any knowledge about it has developed. Clearly there were pioneers in the study of organizing and organization, especially among economists, and although the insights they generated can be seen to be remarkably prescient, it is difficult to regard them as constituting systematic knowledge. Systematic study of this field does not have much history. In fact, a serious concern for organization began with the lowest level distinguished here, intraorganizational relations; and then was concerned almost exclusively with working out why organizations were so effective in production by comparison with traditional arrangements. As it developed, knowledge reflected the interests of those developing or controlling formal organizations. Understanding the properties of organized activities within organizations was sought with the purpose of getting more output from the work groups and the assets belonging to organizations. These are the concerns that connect the earliest writing about organizations, from Smith through Taylor and Ford to the organizational consultants and organizational development specialists of the present day.

By comparison it is surprising how long it took to develop a systematic concern about the organizational level, to gain knowledge of the organization and the role of management in relation to the organization as such. It is difficult to date the serious study of organizations per se much before 1930. Stranger still, interest in the highest level of organization—interorganizational relationships and structures—took longest of all to move to the center stage. Again, there were many people who had insights into this level. Economists, Alfred Marshall (1919) for example, were clearly aware of the importance of interorganizational relationships, but it was not until very recently that this level of organization studies has become the object of sustained attention by scholars. Nevertheless, we have to note that there has been historically a significant broadening of the frame of reference for organization studies, from an almost exclusive concern with intraorganizational relations in the nineteenth and early twentieth centuries, through the study of the organization in the twentieth century, and finally to concern with interorganizational relations. The interorganizational level is perhaps the main concern of organizational analysts today.

These days, the main interest in organizations has shifted in substance and focus. Rather than being overwhelmingly concerned with control of employees and other assets, the benefits of organization are habitually discussed in terms of flexibility

(Carlsson 1989; Sayer and Walker 1992; Volberda 1998). The lack of flexibility in production (the inability to produce goods and services in variety as well as abundance) has been seen as a key limitation of organizing and organizations. The maturation and oversupply of markets in the developed world has much to do with this, and the priority in organizations has dramatically changed direction as a result. The unprecedented abundance in the goods and services now available, and the resulting increase in the discrimination of consumers, has ensured that the variety and quality of what is available is now preeminently important.

Firms always could provide quality goods in almost any form, of course; but only at a price. In recent decades, there was a search for the means to produce quality with variety more cheaply. Flexibility in the design of jobs and organizations has increasingly been seen as the key to solving this problem. In flexibility, it is widely believed, lies the solution to the problem of how to achieve variety at affordable prices. Because of this, the emphasis in organization studies is now on how to develop organizational practices, forms, and systems characterized by greater flexibility.

In this chapter, the argument is that the development of formal knowledge of organization can be understood as a double movement (see Table 19.1): from a narrow focus on work (position 1) to a broad concern with productive systems and, at the same time, from concern about control to concern about flexibility and adaptivity, which may come from less direct control (position 6). Concern in organizational studies has shifted from a desire to understand organization as such (and interest in organizational theory) to recognition of the importance of organized systems. We have moved from thinking that organizations are effective because of their intrinsic properties to thinking that they are effective to the extent that they take their place in particular organized systems. Today, concern of analysts is with:

- *flexible organizations*: including the flexibility of both labor and technology, and the general adaptability of organizational structures (position 4);
- *flexible industrial and economic systems*: the systems within which organizations operate. Such a supra-organizational system might be a large firm or business group, an industry, a region, a national economy, or even the world economy (position 6).

Although it is usual to assume that the modes of organizing below organized systems are effective because of their intrinsic merits, so that there have been sustained attempts to establish the features of organizational flexibility crucial to the effectiveness of the flexible firm, it is unlikely that such organizational features are of crucial importance. In this chapter attention will be paid to the connections between models of flexible firms and the contexts within which firms operate. It is argued that the models are not of universal application and that the patterns of flexibility we observe are a reflection of particular institutional conditions. Consideration of the context is important in trying to answer such questions as why particular forms of organization work effectively. They work because they occupy a

Table 19.1 A typology of organized phenomena

Organizational flexibility	Flexible working (2)	Flexible firms (4)	Flexible economic systems (networks) across industries, regions, and nations (6)
Organizational control	Work design Taylorism (1)	Organizational Fordism (3)	Societal Fordism, bureaucratic society (5)
	Intrafirm organizing (organization behavior)	Constitution of organization (organization theory)	Interorganizational systems

place in a system of production constituted by the interaction of large numbers of organizations.

19.2 ORGANIZING IN HISTORICAL CONTEXT

Until relatively recently, the aim of organizational knowledge was, through the routinization and control of work, to maximize the production of standardized products and services. It was the antithesis of flexibility, seeking to secure regulation and control to ensure conformity of people to processes of production and uniformity in products.

Adam Smith, in *The Wealth of Nations* (1776), illustrates the power of the division of manual labor, but also marvels at the benefits of effective organization. Describing how the manufacture of pins could be broken into eighteen different tasks, Smith argued that a person working alone might not even make a single pin in a day. Ten people, however, by specializing in certain tasks, 'could, when they exerted themselves, make among them about twelve pounds of pins in a day'. This equated to around 48,000 pins, or 4,800 per person.

Towards the end of the nineteenth century the principles on which work should be organized and controlled became a direct concern for those involved in the management of organizations. Prominent here were the ideas of Frederick Taylor (see Taylor 1911), whose main concern was to eliminate what he saw as systematic inefficiencies in the traditional ways work was organized and managed. Under

Taylor's scientific management, work was to be fragmented into its basic components, each to be undertaken in a manner deemed to be the most efficient. There was, in short, a one best way of organizing work (see Kanigel 1997) and achieving this, it was argued, would benefit both workers and employers. Just as important was how this position was to be reached: under scientific management the organization of work was to be the exclusive responsibility of managers. There was thus a separation between those who did the work and those who designed it.

The extent to which these and similar ideas were used, and the nature of their impact on people's work and lives, has generated a great deal of research and discussion. In the 1970s it was widely believed in Britain and America that Taylor's ideas were the dominant force in the organization and control of work from the beginning of the twentieth century. The fragmentation of work and the removal of worker responsibility for its own organization had thus led to industrial work being progressively de-skilled or degraded (Braverman 1974; Thompson 1984). It soon became clear that the extent to which Taylor's and similar ideas were adopted and used varied a good deal. Subsequent research sought to modify Braverman's basic thesis as it applied in different contexts (Friedman 1977; Gospel 1992; Littler 1982; McIvor 2001; Whitston 1996).

De-skilling and the substitution of technology for labor vary systematically between societies and industries. In the United States, de-skilling and technological substitution is deeply embedded and recurrent. David Noble (1977) illustrates this in his account of the development of numerically controlled (NC) machine tools in the United States in the 1940s and 1950s. A key problem lay in how to make a tape-recording of the movements the machine tools would need to follow to give shape to a piece of metal. Although the tape could be made by recording the movements of a skilled machinist, employers were concerned that this would give employees too important a role. The NC system adopted, therefore, was one in which the desired movement of the tool was based on a mathematical translation of an engineering blueprint. More generally, the extensive development of the mass production systems first utilized in the production of motor vehicles by Ford, has subsequently been replicated in many other industries, most recently in the production and distribution of mass produced food (Schlosser 2001).

The adverse effects of a highly developed division of labor were only slowly identified. Problems associated with the simplified and repetitive nature of work under scientific management led to the recommendation of such measures as job rotation and job enlargement (Parker and Wall 1998). From the 1950s onwards more fundamental concerns began to be addressed, as the design of jobs began more systematically to take into account the motivation and satisfaction of employees. Thus, Herzberg's (1966) two-factor theory of worker motivation led to the idea that jobs should be not merely rotated or enlarged but enriched; while Hackman and Oldham's (1976) job characteristics model provided for the design of jobs on the basis of such principles as skill variety, task identity, and task significance.

What is impressive is how slowly such findings were amassed and how they did not lead to much reform. For example, one of the most intellectually impressive practical approaches to organizing was developed by the London-based Tavistock Institute, with their sociotechnical systems approach to workplace organization. The most celebrated use of this approach in the United Kingdom was by the then National Coal Board (Trist and Bamforth 1951; Trist *et al.* 1963). But despite clear promise, proposals using sociotechnical systems were actually little used. Sociotechnical ideas were applied in several other countries, most notably in Scandinavia (Benders and Van Hootegem 1999, 2000). Here we find the most celebrated example of the use of autonomous work groups: in the Kalmar and Uddevalla plants of Volvo (Berggren 1993). But even here the ideas were not without detractors.

By the 1970s, when the work of the sociotechnical systems analysts was finding applications in Scandinavia, knowledge of the organization (as distinct from ideas about the organization of work) remained comparatively underdeveloped. Given the importance of organizations to advanced economies, the knowledge that had been amassed about them and how they work was not impressive. The assumption of the contingency approach to organizations, which was then dominant, was that organizational structures were functional in specific environments. According to this view, there was a need only to identify a small number of distinctive organizational types, each adapted to a distinctive set of environmental circumstances or contingencies. A large and stable market for standardized products would support a large unitary organization (a bureaucracy) while more dynamic conditions required something less mechanical and more organic and adaptable (Burns and Stalker 1966).

It would be only a slight exaggeration to say that organization theory was preoccupied with bureaucracy, and mainly concerned with identifying the circumstances in which bureaucratic designs were not fully applicable. Organizational analysts from the Columbia School (Merton 1949) onwards recognized both the tendency of large organizations to become bureaucratic and some of the drawbacks of this organizational form. However, several decades later, in the work of contingency researchers such as the Aston group (Pugh and Hickson 1976; Pugh and Hinings 1976), whose research was thought to be state of the art in the 1960s and early 1970s, the bureaucracy had been rehabilitated as one of a small number of functional organizational forms. This view was widespread: North American analysts such as Mintzberg (1979) also produced typologies comprising a small number of distinct organizational forms. For these researchers, in the right conditions organizations may be both bureaucratic and efficient. Other structures, such as the multidivisional (or M) form, and the large professional organization (the professional bureaucracy) are also functional in particular contexts.

Although there was recognition of some other possibilities for organizational structures than bureaucracies or variations on them, such as the matrix structure or

Mintzberg's idea of the adhocracy (1979), there was clearly little recognition of any need to fundamentally recast knowledge of organizations or to put effort into understanding interorganizational connections.

19.3 A CHANGE OF DIRECTION: IN SEARCH OF FLEXIBILITY

In the 1980s, and outside the fora within which organizational theory was habitually debated, a new type of writing about organizations emerged rapidly and against expectation. So far as orthodox organizational theorists were concerned, this development was unexpected and unnecessary, provoking heart-searching and pointed defense of orthodoxy (Donaldson 1985). Although highly divergent in philosophy, theoretical assumptions, and attitude towards empirical evidence (Burrell and Morgan 1979), this writing strongly emphasized ways of looking at organizations and organized phenomena distinct from contingency theory. What united writers of otherwise diverse opinions was the need for recognizing new forms of organization which were, in many ways, allegedly, the antithesis of the orderly structures of earlier decades.

There was an explosion of writing about flexibility and flexible forms of organization from a practical as well as a theoretical point of view. In retrospect it is possible to connect this writing with the sustained critique of the consequences of Taylorist and Fordist modes of organizing work alluded to above, on which contingency writing by and large did not draw. Some of this writing concerned specific proposals for a new form of organization called the flexible firm. This proposal is interesting because of its invention outside the framework of orthodox scholarship on organizational structure and because of the controversy that it provoked. It ignored traditional ideas about organization theory and what was known of the history of industrial relations.

After two decades of controversy, the conclusion to be drawn is that there are many forms of new organization. They may be seen as new combinations of labor, technology and management that are adopted mainly because of their location in particular institutional contexts. In the debate, not only have some highly distinctive patterns of organizations been identified, but also different reasons for their variation than those proposed by contingency theory have been clarified. This work brings into relevance the impact of organizational systems as the context shaping particular patterns of organizational design.

19.4 TOWARDS A CONCEPTUALIZATION OF THE FLEXIBLE FIRM

19.4.1 Initial Ideas about the Flexible Firm

Put forward by Atkinson and others (Atkinson 1984; NEDO 1986) in the United Kingdom, the influential early model of the flexible firm claimed that firms were increasingly seeking and achieving flexibility from their workforce in two ways:

- *functional*: 'a firm's ability to adjust and deploy the skills of its employees to match the tasks required by its changing workload, production methods and/or technology' (NEDO 1986: 4).
- *numerical*: 'a firm's ability to adjust the level of labour inputs to meet fluctuations in output' (NEDO 1986: 3–4).

But the flexible firm was just as much a model of work organization (intraorganizational relations) as a model of organizational form. Each of the two main forms of flexibility applied to one of the two groups into which, it was argued, the organization's workforce was divided:

- *core workers*: expected to display functional flexibility in return for security of employment;
- *peripheral workers*: expected to provide the firm with numerical flexibility. This group would be made up of a number of subgroups—part-time workers, contract workers, and so on—each of which would exhibit a particular type of numerical flexibility.

Ideas similar to Atkinson's became widespread. Brewster, Hegewisch, and Mayne's (1994: 189) conclusion from the Europe-wide Cranfield Survey was that 'despite the different legal, cultural and labour traditions around Europe there is a clear general trend amongst employers across the different sectors towards increasing their use of flexibility'. In the United Kingdom, Atkinson's work became the center of an extensive and heated debate. Critics took issue with it theoretically, factually, and ideologically (Pollert 1988, 1991). Its empirical accuracy was one of the most extensively researched aspects.

For numerical flexibility, at least, the work of Casey (1991), Hakim (1990), Marginson (1991), and Penn (1992) provided some support. In addition, data concerning long-term labor market trends showed part-timers accounted for around 25 percent of all UK employment in 1998 (Cully *et al.* 1999: 32). The recent growth rate in such employment, however, has been nothing like that recorded in the 1960s and 1970s, and the growth can in any case be accounted for by changes in the sectoral composition of the economy (Emmott and Hutchinson 1998: 232–3). As critics asserted, to the extent that it existed, numerical flexibility was not new.

This is simply the willingness of employers to lay off workers when they need to, which they do extensively in recessions. This has been traditional practice in both Britain and the United States. Thus, the Atkinson approach to numerical flexibility can be seen as an invitation for employers to continue treating labor as dispensable.

Functional flexibility, on the other hand, is clearly much more important. If it develops, it suggests the emergence of a new and highly skilled and adaptive elite of workers with protected positions in the core of companies. Evidence for functional flexibility was, however, much less easy to identify. According to some commentators, it was on the increase (Cross 1988; Daniel 1987; Elger 1991). However, such direct evidence as there is may be summed up as indicating that such flexibility in the United Kingdom is:

- *negative in nature*: involving the breaking down of lines of demarcation rather than the more positive development of multi-skilled workers;
- *limited in degree*: the most important thing from the employer's point of view is not that individual workers are fully flexible but that the workforce taken as a whole is flexible enough.

In pointing to an emerging group of highly skilled workers, proposals like the Atkinson model were thus inaccurate in key respects. Far from new forms of work organization building and protecting a multi-skilled core of workers, the opposite is true (Hunter *et al.* 1993; Pollert 1988). Again, this is paralleled by research in other countries. Cappelli's (1995: 591) review shows there is little sign of a core–periphery strategy being adopted in the United States: 'There is no evidence that the current changes in the employment relationship in the USA are driven by an interest in buffering core employees.' It seems that the boundaries between core and peripheral workers, insofar as they ever existed, are being broken down, and all workers are being subjected to greater degrees of insecurity. Although the flexible firm model has the merit of combining the two forms of flexibility, Kalleberg (2001) concurs with this view that there is not the evidence to support it in significant aspects.

19.4.2 Reconceptualizing the Problem

In retrospect it became clear that a decisive limitation of the early ideas about the flexible firm was the concentration on labor and the assumption that obtaining flexibility would come from changing its use. In its exclusive focus on manpower, Atkinson implies that the problems of firms are mainly due to their failure to deploy people appropriately. However, this is not to consider the possible contribution of technology to flexible production, and the possibility that lack of investment is potentially as important as the use of labor. We should in fact consider the question of each of the possible sources of flexible output—labor, technology, management, organization and ask why certain recipes for flexibility become widely canvassed and others do not. The point is to explain why flexibility is typically argued for as necessarily taking a particular form (Procter and Ackroyd 2000).

To the finding that British firms have tended to rely on numerical flexibility of labor, we can add that they have not pursued a strategy of technological development either. Much of the early work on advanced manufacturing technology (AMT) concentrated on the diffusion of technologies such as flexible manufacturing systems (FMS) (Rush and Bessant 1992) and computer-integrated manufacturing (CIM) (Edquist and Jacobsson 1988). The conclusion was that take-up was low in the United Kingdom (Tidd 1991). More recent work has looked at how well the individual technologies have been integrated. Waterson *et al.*'s (1997) survey of manufacturing practice found that only just over one in three UK companies reported substantial use of integrated computer-based technology. Accordingly, attention shifted to the question of what differentiates the high-level users from the low-level users (see Jonsson 2000 for Sweden, and Burcher, Lee, and Sohal 1999, for an Australia–UK–Canada comparison). Jaikumar (1986) argues that FMS in the United States are used to intensify mass production rather than introduce flexible production. Similarly, for the United Kingdom, Jones (1989: 116) points to interest in low costs per unit of production, and this is supported by the Waterson *et al.* (1997) survey.

In the United Kingdom, the lack of technological solutions to the problem of flexibility (and the consequent interest in getting labor to close any productivity gap) are plausibly explained by problems in access to finance. Hutton (1995) places emphasis on the financial system's need for liquidity and how this is reflected in its lack of commitment to industry. He sets out how the operation of the banking system leaves industry dependent on expensive short-term funding; while reliance on the stock market forces it into the actions necessary to satisfy shareholders and fend off takeover. This relationship with finance impacts on investment in flexible production technologies in a number of ways. At a general level, Burcher and Lee (1997) demonstrate the pervasive influence of accounting and finance in the consideration, implementation, and operation of AMT. In Hutton's account, the terms on which finance is offered have direct implications for the way labor is managed. This has induced what has been called labor-centered flexibility, which has been increasingly used as short-term pressures on firms have increased over the last twenty or so years.

19.4.3 The Actual Organization of Flexible Production

Looking at how flexible production is organized in the United Kingdom as an example, it is clear this often takes the form of indirect control based on the allocation of costs. What has emerged in manufacturing industry is cell-based production (Ingersoll Engineers 1994), which combines related equipment with the small teams of workers who operate it, into production cells. Cells produce a specific component or family of related products, or undertake a distinct range of activities. The 1998 WERS found as many as 65 percent of all workplaces reporting that most employees worked in formally designated teams (Cully *et al.* 1999: 38), as is required by cellular production. For each product-focused cell, costs and benefits are closely monitored; this allows firms to make decisions about discrete areas of activity based on their costs and to choose whether to subcontract, outsource, or discontinue. In line with more intensive financial pressures and more explicit product strategies, the key organizational differentiation is between products and their related customers. Here, numerical flexibility is achieved by taking on (or dispensing with) not sections of a peripheral workforce but whole sections of the workforce. Using Atkinson's categories, the core has disappeared.

This model, which has been called the New Flexible Firm (Ackroyd 2002; Ackroyd and Procter 1998), has some distinctive implications for labor. It implies a highly limited degree of functional flexibility, in which adaptability is solely as a member of a product-focused work team. The range of tasks to be undertaken and the amount of skill required is therefore severely circumscribed. In this arrangement then, flexible production does not require highly skilled workers: indeed, the new flexible firm model shows that the functional and numerical aspects of flexibility can be substitutes for each other. At the same time, control is effected not by close supervision but through the indirect allocation of costs and the threat of redundancy if productivity is low, while the whole unit is managed indirectly through the readjustments of product portfolios and calculation of costs. From the second Company-Level Industrial Relations Survey (CLIRS), we get some idea of how large British firms use a range of budgetary controls in the relationship between the corporate center and the operating units (Armstrong *et al.* 1996). The most important is the relationship Armstrong *et al.* establish between the use of budgetary controls based on labor cost and labor flexibility. 'The implication,' they argue, 'is that these labour cost ratios are used to impose numerical and/or temporal flexibility on the workforces of large UK companies' (Armstrong *et al.* 1996: 19).

19.4.4 The High-Surveillance Firm

As the implications of the Atkinson model were being tested, other researchers had been examining different patterns of organization. Empirically grounded studies from several parts of the developed world found patterns of internal organization different from those described in the new flexible firm. In these there was often extensive use of new managerial techniques and patterns of work organization, rather than the refurbishment of the old. In the interpretation of these findings, emphasis was placed on the contribution of specific managerial procedures and techniques to secure increased quality and variety of production (Conti and Warner 1993; Delbridge, Turnbull, and Wilkinson 1992; Sewell and Wilkinson 1992). Under these managerial regimes, quite high levels of investment in technology are also essential. However, exclusive or complete reliance on technology is eschewed, and important contributions are sought from workers. In organizations of this type, control is exerted by managers and supervisors monitoring, measuring, and reporting on worker performance. This is achieved in part through discipline imposed by such techniques as just-in-time production (JIT) and total quality management (TQM), but supplementing these are developments making use of the ability of IT-based systems to record and provide information on work performance.

At the extreme, such systems are thought to exercise an absolute control over employees, allegedly providing the modern-day equivalent of the panoptican through which control was achieved in nineteenth-century prisons (Sewell and Wilkinson 1992). These ideas are powerful ones and have exerted considerable influence on debates surrounding work and technology. They have been developed most recently in attempts to analyze the operation of telephone call centers. These have been portrayed as the apotheosis of panoptical control, the success of which is achieved ultimately by its internalization by workers as a result of its ubiquitous nature (Fernie and Metcalf 1997). There are, however, a number of reasons to cast doubt on such conclusions. Perhaps most importantly, the idea of absolute control assumes away the notion of worker resistance, the different forms such resistance can take, and the effects it can have (Taylor and Bain 1999; Thompson and Ackroyd 1995).

In the United States, it has been argued persuasively that a version of this regime, called the high-performance workplace (HPW), has come into existence (Appelbaum *et al.* 2000; Murray *et al.* 2002). In this version, research suggests that high levels of participation are sought and elicited from employees as part of a package of measures to induce high levels of working effort. There is no reason to deny the coherence of models that involve high levels of surveillance and participation. A version that has been identified in the United Kingdom has been labeled the high-surveillance firm (HSF) (Ackroyd 2002; Procter and Ackroyd 2000), and there are clearly many firms operating with this kind of managerial regime.

However, there is controversy concerning just how widespread firms operating these methods are. It is certainly possible that there has been significant copying of these practices in British firms, but the extent to which firms have adopted Japanese methods or simply made expedient and partial use of them is not clear (Ackroyd *et al.* 1989; Oliver and Wilkinson 1992; Procter and Ackroyd 1998).

19.4.5 Other Types of Flexible Organization

The organizational structures considered so far obviously do not identify the complete range of new types of organizations. The conclusion is that although the achievement of flexibility is widely taken to be the goal of contemporary organizational innovation, there is scope for widespread variation in its form. It seems likely that existing research has done little but begin to explore and modify some of the more optimistic ideas about what is happening and how flexibility is realized. Flexible forms of organization, such as the new flexible firm and the high-surveillance firm, are restricted to particular enclaves in particular economies (O'Reilly 1992).

Alvesson and Thompson (in this volume) sound an appropriate note of caution concerning the extent to which traditional bureaucratic organizational forms have been disassembled. It is unlikely that the new flexible firm is a viable model outside the United Kingdom. On the other hand, the high-surveillance firm is likely to be fairly standard in Japanese and other South-East Asian manufacturing, wherever it is located. However, despite the hype, Asian penetration of advanced economies is still small (Procter and Ackroyd 1998). The point is that, apart from developments like the high-surveillance firm, we may expect a good deal of local variation.

Many of the ideas about new forms of organization are of limited application in the industrial sector. The new flexible firm and the high-surveillance firm are most applicable in manufacturing and the commercial sectors of the economy. But these are areas of relative stagnation in the advanced economies. In Britain, the evidence is that only the services sector (and, within this, mainly business services) has shown dynamic growth in the number of firms and the scale of employment in recent decades (Ackroyd 2002). Mainly this is because large firms have reconstructed themselves to outsource many of their activities including business services. For business services companies, there has been less active discussion of specific new organizational forms. The knowledge-intensive firm (or KIF) is perhaps the most widely known (Alvesson 1995; Starbuck 1993). None of the above discussion is to deny that there is a wide variety of organizational structures/forms (many new, quite small, and highly dynamic) emerging in advanced economies. The extent of actual innovation and variation in organizational forms, not to mention the reasons for it, is under researched.

19.5 IDEAS ABOUT FLEXIBLE SYSTEMS

While there has been some headway in research into new types of flexible organization, there has been increasing realization that effectiveness is not attributable solely to the organization as such. Also important is the way organizations are articulated with other organizations: what we have called here the level of organized systems (see postion 6 in Table 19.1). To search for the answer to industrial efficiency (or the lack of it) exclusively at the organizational level is therefore a substantial mistake. This has been easy to overlook, as the key features of organized systems have been changing. Large firms have been reconstituting themselves as constellations of small constituent organizations, but large firms remain, as their overall size indicates, very important in the way that they shape overall levels and directions of industrial activity. Even though organizations seem to be uniformly small, economies are not being changed by innovation from the development of new forms of enterprise, from the bottom up. Thus, research should be on the form of organizations and directed towards understanding interorganizational relationships.

It is a clear implication of the above analysis that the organizational forms now being innovated and diffused are not simply (as contingency theorists proposed) adapted to their market context or environments—understood as an array of abstract contingencies. On the contrary, firms and organizations are adapted to their institutional contexts, and in particular, if the case of the new flexible firm is a reliable guide, to the circumstances of their ownership and the conditions under which they can acquire capital and gain access to key markets. Such considerations bring into focus the importance of how other institutions mediate the environment of firms. The production of goods and services these days is a result of interorganizational relations. The supply chains for components in major industries stretch across the globe and connect advanced economies and less developed parts of the world. The achievement of flexibility is as much an attribute of interorganizational arrangements as it is of the flexible organization of firms themselves.

It is now widely realized how important it is to understand the relationship of organizations to what is outside them. This is understood in terms of interorganizational relations and systems. This topic is large and is also considered in a number of chapters that follow (see chapters by G. Thompson, Hebdon and Kirkpatrick, and Morgan). However, there are general theses about the forms of interorganizational relationships and their causes that merit some consideration here.

19.5.1 Flexible Specialization

The most influential attempt to conceptualize and explain the restructuring of the institutions of the economy in recent decades was Piore and Sabel's flexible specialization thesis. In *The Second Industrial Divide* (1984) they argue that the capitalist world faced a fundamental choice between persisting with an economy based on mass production and fundamentally reorganizing it. In this account, the system of mass production, which had established itself as dominant by the early part of the twentieth century, had been, from the end of the 1960s, under threat. This was partly due to transient crises such as oil price shocks and the effects of political upheavals, but also to the saturation of markets for consumer goods in the developed world. According to these authors, in some enclaves in advanced economies a new pattern of activities developed, which featured a rediscovery of the features of craft production in small firms. This new pattern of production Piore and Sabel identified as flexible specialization.

Under flexible specialization, production is based on flexible networks of small but technologically sophisticated firms employing highly skilled people. The networks are situated in a few regions of developed economies where there had been the spontaneous emergence of dense concentrations of small firms in the same industry. The joint output from such regions would be substantial. In this way, such regions would produce in the kind of volumes required by large consumer markets, yet, at the same time, produce in high quality and great variety. Thus, flexible specialization based on small firms might credibly offer a challenge to the dominance of mass production. The three most prominent and fully considered by these authors were the so-called Third Italy, the area around the city of Salzburg, and the Baden-Württemberg region of Germany. Here pools of expertise, including skilled labor, and suppliers of capitals goods developed, and supporting institutions, such as specialist banks and institutions of local industry, have emerged. Piore and Sabel's argument also implies that local initiatives could be consolidated and developed by regional government, which might, for example, foster appropriate educational provision or ensure appropriate transport and communications.

There are some points of contact with ideas concerning the flexible firm in Piore and Sabel's thesis about flexible specialization. While they do not go into detail about the organization of work in flexibly specialized firms, they argue that the use of flexible capital equipment would be associated with the development of a highly flexible, multi-skilled workforce. As Piore and Sabel express it in their description of the restructuring of the steel and chemicals industries, 'the use of flexible equipment grows out of and requires more flexible use of labor' (1984: 212). Partly as a result of its appeal from a policy point of view, the argument attracted attempts to apply it to the United Kingdom (Hirst and Zeitlin 1989). Phillimore (1990) argued that the features of flexible specialization could be used as a template with which to assess change in the organization of industry, and found evidence of movement towards flexible specialization in several industries. On the other hand, Rowley (1994, 1996) in an extended examination of the ceramics industry, where the conditions for such a restructuring were arguably particularly conducive, found little evidence that the industry was being restructured along the lines of flexible specialization.

A substantial part of the reaction to the idea of flexible specialization was either skeptical or hostile (Amin 1994; Tomaney 1994; Williams *et al.* 1987). That flexible specialization was open to a number of different interpretations clearly was a factor in the influence it enjoyed. Nevertheless, Piore and Sabel take seriously the properties of emergent forms of collective organization in deciding the pattern of activities at firm level.

19.5.2 Lean Production and Global Japanization

An alternative to the thesis of flexible specialization is the thesis of global Japanization (Smith and Elger 1994). In a simple form, this suggests that Japanese production methods are being adopted in all countries because they are inherently superior (for evidence to the contrary, see Munday and Peel 1998). Japanization may occur by Japanese production plants being set up in many countries, or because domestic firms will have to adopt more efficient Japanese methods. The term 'lean production', which supposedly characterizes the system of production originated by the Japanese, was first used by the team reporting on the International Motor Vehicle Program, a fourteen-country research project that resulted in the publication of *The Machine that Changed the World* (Womack, Jones, and Roos 1990). Lean production, it was claimed, 'combines the advantages of craft and mass production, while avoiding the high cost of the former and the rigidity of the latter' (1990: 13), or, more bluntly, it 'uses less of everything compared with mass production' (1990: 13).

The prototype for lean production was a system developed in Toyota in the 1950s. Although mass production was at its zenith at this time, Toyota management, sensibly, did not consider it suitable for the conditions then prevailing in Japan. In particular, production volumes were not considered large enough to justify the use of dedicated machine tools. Instead, emphasis was placed on simplifying tool changes, with responsibility given to production workers. Similarly, rather than have production consolidated in one place, as in the Fordist approach to production, subcontractors could be induced to hold buffer stocks and deliver required components to production lines just in time. This in turn reduced stocks and forced attention on improving product quality. Arguably the original pattern of production was highly adapted to (and therefore not readily transferable from) its context in Japan.

Despite their argument that it emerged in response to the conditions faced by the Japanese economy in the aftermath of World War II, Womack, Jones, and Roos (1990: 88) maintain that 'lean production can be introduced anywhere in the world'. The thesis has been challenged on a number of grounds (Oliver, Delbridge, and Lowe 1996; Turnbull 1988; Williams *et al.* 1992). The view that lean production requires half the human effort is based, argue Williams *et al.* (1992), on focusing on parts of the manufacturing process that together account for less than 15 percent of the total value in production. In defense of these ideas, the Japanese themselves do seem to have been able to make approximations to this pattern of production in various parts of the world, and indeed moving production around, a system called agile production, does seem to be a source of cost reduction. Widespread use has been made of some of the techniques that feature in lean production, so that it is possible to envisage processes of relocation and emulation around the world that we may call global Japanization (Smith and Elger 1994).

Although the argument of global Japanization is theoretically less sophisticated than that of Piore and Sabel's, it does point to important features either not considered or underestimated in that account. It does recognize that large-scale production by major corporations remains very important in shaping properties of organized systems, for example. At the same time there are distinct limits to the extent that Japanese methods can be adopted, and the extent to which production methods will shape productive systems.

19.5.3 Regulation Theory and Post-Fordism

A final account of the importance of organized systems is regulation theory. Originally developed by European Marxist researchers, and retaining characteristics of Marxist thinking, this approach has broad scope. It takes its name from the idea that capitalism is an inherently unstable socioeconomic system and tends to be regulated. Even then, capitalism will have a tendency to crises only resolved by periodic reorganizations. The founders, Aglietta (1979) and Palloix (1976), take the development of capitalism in America as a basic reference point and have popularized the term 'Fordism', which describes not merely the organization of production, but the social system in which it is embedded. There are now many writers regarded as being regulationist in outlook, including Boyer (1988), Jessop (1994), Leborgne and Lipietz (1992), Lipietz (1987), and Peck and Tickell (1994).

These writers postulate that the productive economy develops on its own path and that this drives wider patterns of institutional change. In the normal course of events, as the capitalist economy develops, there is a buildup of tensions between the economy and the rest of the social formation. In the original formulation by Marx, such tensions lead to fundamental transformation of society through revolution. The alternative now proposed suggests that capitalism is more resilient. In particular, corporations and managements are more adaptive and capable of absorbing conflict than was thought possible. Moreover the institutions surrounding the economy also tend to support and regulate the overall system. Nonetheless, capitalism periodically reorganizes itself and in the process breaks out of its regulatory shell, at which point the institutions of society are regrouped around the new relationships.

This is probably the most systematic and far-reaching attempt to clarify the nature of contemporary economic and social change. There are three things worth emphasizing about the regulationist approach. It places in the foreground of analysis the capitalist economy and proposes that change in this initiates other changes. The second point of value lies in the suggestion that changes in other institutions are systematically related to change in underlying economic movements. The breakup of traditional systems of labor recruitment and training, or changes in the provision of welfare services, are not random events, but parts of wider processes of change initiated from within the capitalist economy, and their eventual pattern will be related to this (see also Hebdon and Kirkpatrick, in this volume). On this view, it is not mysterious why the industrial relations system was rapidly disassembled, despite the supposed pressures for continuity which feature so strongly in institutional accounts of change. Third, in the present stage of capitalism, much of contemporary change is caused by the activities of large firms in pursuit of global markets.

19.6 CONCLUSIONS

In conclusion, in looking at the connections between the models of flexible organizations and the ideas about the contexts within which these models might operate, it has been argued that there is little to support the idea that the models of flexibility are of universal application. Considering the extent of the adoption of the new flexible firm, the high-surveillance firm, and lean production shows that none appears to have established itself much beyond the settings in which it was originally established. To gain a fuller understanding of patterns of flexibility we need to look elsewhere, to wider patterns of interorganizational relationships.

The discussion in this chapter suggests that two things are needed. The first is a better understanding of how the intraorganizational, the organizational, and the interorganizational levels of analysis relate to each other. There are some highly suggestive ideas around, as we have seen in Section 19.5 of this chapter, but the extent to which they can be taken as reliable is highly debatable. Most research shows that patterns of flexibility are best understood in the context of the institutional relationships in which organizations make strategic decisions. Second, and finally, therefore, although it is now known that the level of organized phenomena (which have been called organized systems in this chapter) is important in discovering the nature of economic outcomes, there is clearly a need for a great deal more research in this area.

REFERENCES

ACKROYD, S. (2002). *The Organization of Business*. Oxford: Oxford University Press.

——and PROCTER, S. (1998). 'British Manufacturing Organization and Workplace Industrial Relations: Some Attributes of the New Flexible Firm'. *British Journal of Industrial Relations*, 36/2: 163–83.

——BURRELL, G., HUGHES, M., and WHITAKER, A. (1989). 'The Japanization of British Industry?' *Industrial Relations Journal*, 19/1: 11–23.

AGLIETTA, M. (1979). *A Theory of Capitalist Regulation*. London: New Left Books.

ALVESSON, M. (1995). *The Management of Knowledge Intensive Companies*. Berlin: Walter de Gruyter.

AMIN, A. (1994). 'Post-Fordism: Models, Factories and Phantoms of Transition', in A. Amin (ed.), *Post-Fordism: A Reader*. Oxford: Blackwell.

APPELBAUM, E., BAILEY, T., BERG, P., and KALLEBERG, A. (2000). *Manufacturing Advantage: Why High Performance Work Systems Pay Off*. Ithaca, NY: Cornell University Press.

ARMSTRONG, P., MARGINSON, P., EDWARDS, P., and PURCELL, J. (1996). 'Budgetary Control and the Labour Force: Findings from a Survey of Large British Companies'. *Management Accounting Research*, 7/1: 1–23.

ATKINSON, J. (1984). 'Manpower Strategies for Flexible Organizations'. *Personnel Management*, 8: 28–31.

BENDERS, J., and VAN HOOTEGEM, G. (1999). 'Teams and Their Context: Moving the Team Discussion beyond Dichotomies'. *Journal of Management Studies*, 36/5: 609–28.

——(2000). 'How the Japanese Got Teams', in S. Procter and F. Mueller (eds.), *Teamworking*. London: Macmillan.

BERGGREN, C. (1993). *The Volvo Experience: Alternatives to Lean Production in the Swedish Auto Industry*. London: Macmillan.

BOYER, R. (1988). *The Search for Labour Market Flexibility*. Oxford: Clarendon Press.

BRAVERMAN, H. (1974). *Labor and Monopoly Capital: The Degradation of Work in the Twentieth Century*. New York: Monthly Review Press.

BREWSTER, C., HEGEWISCH, A., and MAYNE, L. (1994). 'Flexible Working Practices: The Controversy and the Evidence', in C. Brewster and A. Hegewisch (eds.), *Policy and Practice in European Human Resource Management*. London: Routledge.

BURCHER, P., and LEE, G. (1997). *The Challenge of Investing in Advanced Manufacturing Technologies: A Study of British Manufacturers*. Birmingham: Aston Business School.

———— and SOHAL, A. (1999). 'Lessons for Implementing AMT: Some Case Experiences with CNC in Australia, Britain and Canada'. *International Journal of Operations and Production Management*, 19/5–6: 515–26.

BURNS, T., and STALKER, G. (1966). *The Management of Innovation*. London: Tavistock.

BURRELL, G., and MORGAN, G. (1979). *Sociological Paradigms and Organizational Analysis*. London: Heinemann.

CAPPELLI, P. (1995). 'Rethinking Employment'. *British Journal of Industrial Relations*, 33/4: 563–602.

CARLSSON, B. (1989). 'Flexibility and the Theory of the Firm'. *International Journal of Industrial Organization*, 7: 179–203.

CASEY, B. (1991). 'Survey Evidence on Trends in "Non-Standard" Employment', in A. Pollert (ed.), *Farewell to Flexibility?* Oxford: Blackwell.

CONTI, R., and WARNER, M. (1993). 'Taylorism, Teams and Technology in "Re-Engineering" Work-Organization'. *New Technology, Work and Employment*, 8/1: 31–46.

CROSS, M. (1988). 'Changes in Working Practices in UK Manufacturing 1981–88'. *Industrial Relations Review and Report*, 415: 2–10.

CULLY, M., WOODLAND, S., O'REILLY, A., and DIX, G. (1999). *Britain at Work: As Depicted by the 1998 Workplace Employee Relations Survey*. London: Routledge.

DANIEL, W. (1987). *Workplace Industrial Relations and Technical Change*. London: Pinter.

DELBRIDGE, R., TURNBULL, P., and WILKINSON, B. (1992). 'Pushing Back the Frontiers: Management Control and Work Intensification under JIT/TQM Factory Regimes'. *New Technology, Work and Employment*, 7/2: 97–106.

DONALDSON, L. (1985). *In Defence of Organization Theory*. London: Sage.

EDQUIST, C., and JACOBSSON, S. (1988). *Flexible Automation: The Global Diffusion of New Technology in the Engineering Industry*. Oxford: Blackwell.

ELGER, T. (1991). 'Task Flexibility and the Intensification of Labour in UK Manufacturing in the 1980s', in A. Pollert (ed.), *Farewell to Flexibility?* Oxford: Blackwell.

EMMOTT, M., and HUTCHINSON, S. (1998). 'Employment Flexibility: Threat or Promise?' in P. Sparrow and M. Marchington (eds.), *Human Resource Management: The New Agenda*. London: Financial Times Pitman.

FERNIE, S., and METCALF, D. (1997). '(Not) Hanging on the Telephone: Payment Systems in the New Sweatshops'. Centre for Economic Performance, London School of Economics.

FRIEDMAN, A. (1977). *Industry and Labour*. London: Macmillan.

GOSPEL, H. (1992). *Markets, Firms and the Management of Labour in Modern Britain*. Cambridge: Cambridge University Press.

HACKMAN, J., and OLDHAM, G. (1976). 'Motivation through the Design of Work: Test of a Theory'. *Organizational Behaviour and Performance*, 16: 250–79.

HAKIM, C. (1990). 'Core and Periphery in Employers' Workplace Strategies: Evidence from the 1987 ELUS Survey'. *Work, Employment and Society*, 4/2: 157–88.

HERZBERG, F. (1966). *Work and the Nature of Man*. Cleveland: World.

HIRST, P., and ZEITLIN, J. (1989). 'Flexible Specialisation and the Competitive Failure of UK Manufacturing'. *Political Quarterly*, 60/2: 164–78.

HUNTER, L., McGREGOR, A., MACINNES, J., and SPROULL, A. (1993). 'The "Flexible Firm": Strategy and Segmentation'. *British Journal of Industrial Relations*, 31/3: 383–407.

HUTTON, W. (1995). *The State We're In*. London: Jonathan Cape.

Ingersoll Engineers (1994). *The Quiet Revolution Continues*. Rugby: Ingersoll Engineers.

JAIKUMAR, R. (1986). 'Postindustrial Manufacturing'. *Harvard Business Review*, 64/6: 69–76.

JESSOP, R. (1994). 'Post-Fordism and the State', in A. Amin (ed.), *Post Fordism: A Reader*. Oxford: Blackwell.

JONES, B. (1989). 'Flexible Automation and Factory Politics: The United Kingdom in Current Perspective', in P. Hirst and J. Zeitlin (eds.), *Reversing Industrial Decline?* Oxford: Berg.

JONSSON, P. (2000). 'An Empirical Taxonomy of Advanced Manufacturing Technology'. *International Journal of Operations and Production Management*, 20/12: 1446–74.

KALLEBERG, A. (2001). 'Organizing Flexibility: The Flexible Firm in the New Century'. *British Journal of Industrial Relations*, 39/4: 479–504.

KANIGEL, R. (1997). *The One Best Way: Frederick Winslow Taylor and the Enigma of Efficiency*. London: Little, Brown.

LEBORGNE, D. A., and LIPIETZ, A. (1992). 'Conceptual Fallacies and Open Questions on Post Fordism', in M. Storper and A. J. Scott (eds.), *Pathways to Industrialisation*. London: Routledge.

LIPIETZ, A. (1987). *Mirages and Miracles: The Crises of Global Fordism*. London: Verso.

LITTLER, C. (1982). *The Development of the Labour Process in Capitalist Societies*. London: Heinemann.

McIVOR, A. (2001). *A History of Work in Britain, 1880–1950*. London: Palgrave.

MARGINSON, P. (1991). 'Change and Continuity in the Employment Structure of Large Companies', in A. Pollert (ed.), *Farewell to Flexibility?* Oxford: Blackwell.

MARSHALL, A. (1919). *Industry and Trade*. London: Macmillan.

MERTON, R. (1949). *Social Theory and Social Structure*. Glencoe, Ill.: Free Press.

MINTZBERG, H. (1979). *The Structuring of Organizations: A Synthesis of Research*. London: Prentice Hall International.

MUNDAY, M., and PEEL, M. (1998). 'An Analysis of the Performance of Japanese, US and Domestic Manufacturing Firms in the UK Electronics/Electrical Sector', in R. Delbridge and J. Lowe (eds.), *Manufacturing in Transition*. London: Routledge.

MURRAY, G., BELANGER, J., GILES, A., and LAPOINTE, P. A. (eds.) (2002). *Work and Employment Relations in the High-Performance Workplace*. New York: Continuum.

NEDO (National Economic Development Office) (1986). *Changing Working Patterns: How Companies Achieve Flexibility to Meet New Needs*. London: NEDO.

NOBLE, D. (1977). 'Social Choice and Machine Design: The Case of Automatically Controlled Machine Tools', in A. Zimbalist (ed.), *Case Studies in the Labour Process*. London: Monthly Review Press.

OLIVER, N., and WILKINSON, B. (1992). *The Japanization of British Industry* (2nd edn). Oxford: Blackwell.

——DELBRIDGE, R., and LOWE, J. (1996). 'Lean Production Practices: International Comparisons in the Auto Components Industry'. *British Journal of Management*, 7/special issue: 29–44.

O'REILLY, J. (1992). 'Where Do You Draw the Line? Functional Flexibility, Training and Skill in Britain and France'. *Work, Employment and Society*, 6/3: 369–96.

PALLOIX, C. (1976). 'The Labour Process from Fordism to Neo-Fordism', in C. Palloix (ed.), *The Labour Process and Class Struggle*. London: Lawrence and Wishart.

PARKER, S., and WALL, T. (1998). *Job and Work Design: Organizing Work to Promote Well-Being and Effectiveness*. London: Sage.

PECK, J., and TICKELL, A. (1994). 'Searching for a New Institutional Fix: The After Fordist Crisis', in A. Amin (ed.), *Post-Fordism: A Reader*. Oxford: Blackwell.

PENN, R. (1992). 'Flexibility in Britain during the 1980s: Recent Empirical Evidence', in N. Gilbert, R. Burrows, and A. Pollert (eds.), *Fordism and Flexibility: Divisions and Change*. London: Macmillan.

PHILLIMORE, A. J. (1990). 'Flexible Specialisation, Work Organisation and Skills: Approaching the "Second Industrial Divide"'. *New Technology, Work and Employment*, 4/2: 79–91.

PIORE, M., and SABEL, C. (1984). *The Second Industrial Divide: Possibilities for Prosperity*. New York: Basic Books.

POLLERT, A. (1988). 'The Flexible Firm: Fixation or Fact?' *Work, Employment and Society*, 2: 281–316.

—— (ed.) (1991). *Farewell to Flexibility?* Oxford: Basil Blackwell.

PROCTER, S., and ACKROYD, S. (1998). 'Against Japanization: Understanding the Re-Organization of British Manufacturing'. *Employee Relations*, 20/3: 237–47.

—— —— (2000). 'Strategies for Flexibility: Technology-Centred and Labour-Centred Flexibility in UK Manufacturing'. *International Journal of Manufacturing Technology and Management*, 1/4–5: 366–80.

PUGH, D., and HICKSON, D. (1976). *Organizational Structure in Its Context: The Aston Programme I*. Farnborough: Saxon House.

—— and HININGS, C. (1976). *Organizational Structure: The Aston Programme II*. Farnborough: Saxon House.

ROWLEY, C. (1994). 'The Illusion of Flexible Specialisation: The Case of the Domesticware Sector of the British Ceramics Industry'. *New Technology, Work and Employment*, 9/2: 127–39.

—— (1996). 'Flexible Specialisation: Some Comparative Dimensions and Evidence from the Ceramic Tile Industry'. *New Technology, Work and Employment*, 11/2: 125–36.

RUSH, H., and BESSANT, J. (1992). 'Revolution in Three-Quarter Time: Lessons from the Diffusion of Advanced Manufacturing Technologies'. *Technology Analysis and Strategic Management*, 4/1: 3–19.

SAYER, A., and WALKER, R. (1992). *The New Social Economy: Reworking the Division of Labour*. Oxford: Blackwell.

SCHLOSSER, E. (2001). *Fast Food Nation*. New York: Houghton Mifflin.

SEWELL, G., and WILKINSON, B. (1992). '"Someone to Watch Over Me": Surveillance, Discipline and the Just-in-Time Labour Process'. *Sociology*, 26/2: 271–89.

SMITH, A. (1776). *The Wealth of Nations*.

SMITH, C., and ELGER, T. (1994). *Global Japanisation: The International Transformation of the Labour Process*. London: Routledge.

STARBUCK, W. (1993). 'Learning by Knowledge Intensive Firms'. *Journal of Management Studies*, 29/6: 713–40.

TAYLOR, F. W. (1911). *The Principles of Scientific Management*. New York: Harper and Row.

TAYLOR, P., and BAIN, P. (1999). '"An Assembly Line in the Head": Work and Employee Relations in the Call Centre'. *Industrial Relations Journal*, 30/2: 101–17.

THOMPSON, P. (1984). *The Nature of Work*. London: Macmillan.

——and ACKROYD, S. (1995). 'All Quiet on the Workplace Front? A Critique of Recent Trends in British Industrial Sociology'. *Sociology*, 29/4: 615–33.

TIDD, J. (1991). *Flexible Manufacturing Technologies and International Competitiveness*. London: Pinter.

TOMANEY, J. (1994). 'A New Paradigm of Work Organisation and Technology?' in A. Amin (ed.), *Post-Fordism: A Reader*. Oxford: Blackwell.

TRIST, E., and BAMFORTH, K. (1951). 'Some Social and Psychological Consequences of the Longwall Method of Coal-getting'. *Human Relations*, 4/1: 3–38.

——HIGGIN, G., MURRAY, H., and POLLOCK, A. (1963). *Organizational Choice: Capabilities of Groups at the Coal Face under Changing Technologies: The Loss, Rediscovery and Transformation of a Work Tradition*. London: Tavistock.

TURNBULL, P. (1988). 'The Limits to "Japanization": Just-in-Time, Labour Relations and the UK Automotive Industry'. *Industrial Relations Journal*, 17/3: 193–206.

VOLBERDA, H. (1998). *Building the Flexible Firm: How to Remain Competitive*. Oxford: Oxford University Press.

WATERSON, P., CLEGG, C., BOLDEN, R., PEPPER, K., WARR, P., and WALL, T. (1997). *The Use and Effectiveness of Modern Manufacturing Practices in the United Kingdom*. Sheffield: Institute of Work Psychology.

WHITSTON, K. (1996). 'Scientific Management and Production Management Practice between the Wars'. *Historical Studies in Industrial Relations*, 1: 47–75.

WILLIAMS, K., CUTLER, T., WILLIAMS, J., and HASLAM, C. (1987). 'The End of Mass Production?' *Economy and Society*, 16/3: 405–39.

——HASLAM, C., WILLIAMS, J., and CUTLER, T. (1992). 'Against Lean Production'. *Economy and Society*, 21/3: 321–54.

WOMACK, J. P., JONES, D., and ROOS, D. (1990). *The Machine that Changed the World*. New York: Rawson Associates.

CHAPTER 20

··

POST-BUREAUCRACY?

··

MATS ALVESSON
PAUL THOMPSON

> For 60 years, large companies have been engaged primarily in perfecting
> bureaucracy, but now they are engaged in breaking it.
>
> (Heckscher and Applegate 1994: 1)

20.1 INTRODUCTION

··

IF it is the case that organizations have been perfecting bureaucracy since the 1930s,
it would also be true to say that academics have been engaged in an equally long
battle to demonstrate its imperfections. In this they have had many allies among
intellectuals, politicians, and those in the business world. The traditional commentary and critique of bureaucracy is a well-trodden territory that is unnecessary to
repeat in any detail here. Suffice to say that most academics writing about bureaucracy have operated within either or both of two sets of assumptions. First, that
while bureaucratic rationalization is the dominant organizing logic of modernity
and managerial capitalism, it produces degrees of inefficiency, dehumanization,
and ritualism. Case studies (Blau 1955; Merton 1949) questioned whether the
bureaucratic ideal type was fully rational and efficient, or developed typologies
that emphasized different forms of bureaucracy appropriate to organizational

The authors would like to thank Paul Adler for comments on an earlier draft.

context and type of work. Alongside such neo-Weberian writing was another category of 'structure critics' (including McGregor, Argyris, and Bennis), who emphasized the psychological dysfunctions of bureaucracy and the need for participative work design from a Human Relation's perspective.[1]

Second, that while bureaucracy may be appropriate and indeed functional to particular economic or political environments, it does not 'fit' others, notably where there is a high degree of unpredictability and instability and where innovation and situational adaptability are vital parts of work. This is the foundation of contingency and open systems theory, exemplified in Burns and Stalker's (1961) manufacturing case studies and mechanistic/organic model. Because there is an emphasis on a continuum of models suited to different environments, contingency theory moves away from alternative designs within a purely bureaucratic framework. However, all contingency theorists work within a focus on systems, structure, and strategy, with Mintzberg's (1983) design configuration of adhocracy one of the few to have anticipated future post-bureaucratic models.

Critics of the nature of bureaucracy are still around, their ranks having been swelled by some feminist academics.[2] However, the main development in critique has seen a shift from the limits and dysfunctions of bureaucratic structure and action, to a claim of systemic dysfunctionality—that bureaucracy simply no longer works or is ceasing to be the prime coordination mechanism in a contemporary economy and society. It is now argued that a broad set of powerful economic, social, and technological changes have meant that the days of stable structures and fine-tuning of bureaucratic models are over and those of post-bureaucracies have arrived. As expressed by Child and McGrath (2001: 1136), fixed boundaries and top-down authority 'are maladaptive when massive change, environmental dynamism and considerable uncertainty are the norm'.

In this chapter, we review the nature of these claims and examine the evidence across key territories of change. We accept that bureaucracy is one of a number of competing coordination mechanisms, alongside markets and trust (Adler 2001), and that the balance between such mechanisms changes over time and territory. Nevertheless our review of the evidence far from supports a systemic dysfunctionality argument; it demonstrates that existing and new forms of bureaucratic structure and action remain dominant in most areas, though in more complex hybrids than earlier periods.

---

[1] Among the later critics of the character and costs of bureaucracy were labor process theorists, drawing on Marxism and radical Weberian arguments. Nevertheless, whether historical (Clawson 1980) or contemporary (Edwards 1979), such scholarship saw bureaucratic control as an integral and necessary feature of capitalism, albeit involving arrangements that conferred partial benefits on labor through mutually binding rules and procedures.

[2] See e.g. Bologh (1990) and Ferguson (1984). Their argument focused on the inherent masculinity of bureaucratic rationality, resulting in the marginalization of female interests and ways of organizing based on emotional connection, nurturance, and cooperation.

20.2 POST-BUREAUCRACY AND SHIFTS IN THE GROUNDS OF CRITIQUE

The paradigm of the post-bureaucratic organization (PBO) says that the decentralized, loosely coupled, flexible, nonhierarchical, and fluid organization is or will become dominant. This will operate on the basis of horizontal and vertical networking, and mutual adjustment, and will be guided by visions and shared values rather than command and control. Organizations will be dysfunctional if they do not adapt to the new environment calling for these organizational features. The systemic aspect of that dysfunctionality draws our attention to the inseparability of post-bureaucratic claims from wider conceptions of a paradigm break in socio-economic structure. Every such theory, from post-Fordism through to the knowledge economy, has invoked a break with bureaucracy as cause or consequence of change. In one attempt to explore new organizational forms, Heydebrand (1989: 349) argued that there is an 'intrinsic elective affinity between postindustrialism and postbureaucratic forms'.

Sometimes this is framed in terms of postmodernism. There is a large academic literature on postmodernism and organizations, all focusing on debureaucratization as a means of sustaining a wider vision of paradigm change (Crook, Paluski, and Waters 1992; Palmer and Hardy 2000). The theory and practice of bureaucracy is firmly placed in the past. Clegg argues that 'postmodernism points to a more organic, less differentiated enclave of organisation than those dominated by the bureaucratic designs of modernity' (1990: 181). He draws on the concept of de-differentiation, gives it a different meaning from its usual erosion of boundaries between various branches of the arts, and instead refers to an all-purpose reversal of the division of labor.

Whether postindustrial or postmodern, the organizational dimensions of rival ideal types are held in common. Clegg's list is typical: specialization vs. diffusion, bureaucracy vs. democracy, hierarchy vs. market, disempowerment vs. empowerment, inflexible vs. flexible, individualized vs. collectivized, and mistrust vs. trust (1990: 203). As has been noted elsewhere (Thompson 1993), the lists and typologies bear a remarkable resemblance to those regularly produced in the popular business and management literature. Despite the generalized claims and wide-ranging issues, the more circumspect commentators admit that any changes are at best uneven and in Heckscher and Applegate's words, 'few have moved more than a step or two from traditional structures' and 'we can find no developed exemplars of it' (1994: 2–3). Yet these authors are able to justify their stance on the basis of a compelling need for radical transformation based on new environmental 'logics'. Here again, paradigm break theorists and business writers tend to share identifications of the drivers of change.

All the usual suspects are rounded up: intensification of competition, deregulation, globalization of production, rising rates of product innovation, new forms and increased significance of knowledge and information technology, differentiated and rapidly changing customer preferences, the dominance of intangible services, coping with and encouraging workforce diversity. Above all bureaucracy is held to be unable to cope with the sheer pace of change, thus generalizing observations about turbulent market environments made in earlier decades to the whole economy. Of these factors, probably the most recurrent theme is the determinant role of new forms of information technology. It is seen as embodying a 'techno-logic' that compels democratization of decision making (W. Taylor 1994), or a technocratic rationality based on preprogrammed and internalized formal rules, procedures, and external controls, thus allowing informal relationships, general rules, and a minimal division of labor (Heydebrand 1989: 341).

The currently most favored factor either causing or requiring the break of bureaucracy is the emergence of knowledge as a key dimension in management and organization (Adler 2001; Davenport and Prusak 1998; Spender 1996). There is in fact a double emphasis: on innovation-driven industries, such as computer software and pharmaceutical companies seen as increasingly central in the economy, and on the inherent qualities of knowledge—viewed as increasingly vital across sectors—that require it to be managed through collaborative teams and networks rather than command, control, and rules methods (Hamel and Prahalad 1996). A view of the company as a 'knowledge system' is linked to wider conceptions of learning organizations and 'communities of practice' (Wenger and Snyder 2000). As with knowledge work, the vocabulary in use—community, networks, nurturing social relations—breaks radically with conventional ideas of bureaucracy.

Government and the public sector too have faced pressures to dispense with structured hierarchies, to be driven by missions rather than rules, and to meet the needs of the customer not bureaucracy. While the sector is less subject to market influences, pressure may arise from the need to be seen to be responsive to 'customers' and to adapt to a more entrepreneurial culture. New forms of organization may therefore be seen as institutional isomorphism, as public sector managers seek to gain legitimacy from funders and power holders by implementing private sector ideas and practices. The need to adopt the same post-bureaucratic agenda as private corporations is the line taken by the most influential architects of change (Osborne and Plastrik 1997). However, as their self-confessed influences are management consultants and futurologists such as Peters, Drucker, and Toffler, it is possible that the isomorphism is ideological rather than practical, more salient on the level of talk than materially anchored social practice.

20.3 THE TERRITORIES OF CHANGE

Although post-bureaucratic claims encompass virtually every change undertaken by organizations in the past two decades, in general terms we can state that reversing centralization, a fixed hierarchy, formal rationality, a strong reliance on formal rules and standards, and the division of labor is associated with interrelated internal and external changes. This section outlines those projected changes in a little more detail and discusses what they imply for processes and mechanisms of coordination.

At the heart of projected internal change is functional decentralization of managerial structures. There are a variety of associated forms. For example, Heydebrand (1989: 330–1) argues that profit centers overcome the market–hierarchy dichotomy, reduce the need for CEO control, while encouraging direct negotiation among subunits. An emphasis on horizontal coordination is also applied to the increased use of project and other types of self-governance. Miles *et al.* (1997) argue that more organizational members are expected to develop the ability to self-organize around operational, market, and partnering tasks. This 'cellular' organization allows employees to be more entrepreneurial and to identify customer needs, as well as experience psychological ownership of particular clients, products, and services. While shop-floor work teams are clearly not an alternative means of managerial coordination, they are seen as a central feature of decentralized decision making and delayered structures.

A number of the most fashionable contemporary change programs have been presented by business writers as an integral part of the anti-bureaucratic agenda. Both Total Quality Management (TQM) and Business Process Reengineering (BPR) have been seen as ways of introducing flatter structures and reduced hierarchy. As employees take increased responsibility, conception and execution are reintegrated and more complex jobs are created. Hierarchy is also reduced by a network of interdependencies arising from the necessity for employees to treat each other as internal 'customers'.

While reference to boundaryless organizations is typical business hype, a case can be made for their external relations being increasingly shifting and permeable. Post-bureaucratic claims on this terrain are summarized in the following quote: 'If the old model of organisation was the large hierarchical firm, the model of organisation that is considered characteristic of the New Competition is a network, of lateral and horizontal interlinkages within and among firms' (Nohria 1992: 2).

Restructuring is associated with the process of disaggregation that transforms loose coupling into decoupling. This may take the form of dispersal of business functions to small firms or outsourcing to specialist units and franchises (Perrow

1992). At its most extreme, this may result in the growth of virtual forms of organization (Jackson 1999). The other primary manifestation of external restructuring is the growth of interorganizational networks, whose fluidity and flexibility makes them suited to rapid change.

It is recognized that some of these internal and external changes may lead to problems, particularly on the human resource front. If hierarchies are reduced or eliminated, boundaries become more permeable and roles more flexible, it is difficult for firms to offer career paths and rewards for loyalty and conformity to standardized organizational obligations (Heckscher and Applegate 1994: 7). For some managerial writers, this circle is squared through concepts such as the portfolio worker who, mobile and reliant on his/her own human capital and knowledge, exists largely outside corporate hierarchies, working either simultaneously or sequentially for a number of employers (Handy 1995).

Whether a substantial group of employees exist outside such hierarchies is open to question, but it is clear that in the absence of conventional hierarchies, post-bureaucratic theorists have to conceptualize alternative means of holding organizations together. Once again we can see a convergence between postmodern social theorists and popular business writing (Peters 1989). Parker summarizes the former view: 'The structures that we have been used to since the industrial revolution are fragmenting into diverse networks held together with information technology and underpinned by a "postmodern ... sensibility"' (1992: 9). While we have already commented on the pervasive role allocated to information technology, the 'postmodern sensibility' refers to the role of culture as the means of indirect and internalized control, though some postmodernists do recognize tensions between multiple cultures, and philosophically informed postmodernists would reject a functionalist view of culture as a control system.

The argument set out above is based on the substitution of cultural and other forms of indirect coordination based on trust relations to replace the bureaucratic roles formerly carried out by a rapidly disappearing middle management (Heydebrand 1989: 347; Scarbrough and Burrell 1996). Such delayering is also facilitated by new, horizontal communication channels and devolution of responsibility to self-managing and project teams, reducing division of labor. Nevertheless, there is a further argument used about substitutes for bureaucratic coordination. Direct regulation is also being replaced by the simulation of market disciplines, units are compelled by new ownership and accounting mechanisms to be independent and treat each other as customers (Clegg 1990: 180).

20.4 EVALUATING CLAIMS AND EMPIRICAL WORK

The scope of claims made about post-bureaucracy is, unfortunately, not matched by a similar depth or scope of empirical support. It is one thing to indicate that most organizations have undergone change programs or processes or that there has been a general increase in the pace of change, quite another to demonstrate necessary or specific outcomes. Too often it is simply assumed that by definition bureaucracy cannot adapt or evolve. Far too much of the discussion is speculative and insufficiently specified. For example, Heckscher and Applegate say that, 'Our starting point is not a theoretical concept but a "bin" of empirical developments that tend in one way or another to undermine the pillars of bureaucracy' (1994: 2). Pretty much everything is thrown into that 'bin' from problem-solving task groups to OD initiatives and partnerships. Reliance on new organizational forms and inverted ideal types leads to a failure to be clear enough about the content of bureaucracy and therefore what post-bureaucracy should be evaluated against. In this section we operate within a framework that the central feature of bureaucracy at work is hierarchical authority, underpinned by rationalization and manifested primarily as rule-governed behavior. To explore the nature and extent of change, we examine three areas—work, employment, and decision practices—as well as developments in knowledge-intensive firms as the sector most likely to be moving in a post-bureaucratic direction.

20.4.1 Work Practices

Work practices here refer to the aspects of work organization that are designed to control work behavior, i.e. how specific jobs are being structured and steered. Important changes have taken place since the 1980s. Under the practical and theoretical impact of Japanese competition, employers began to move decisively against key aspects of traditional work rules. Benefits previously accruing to management under systems of bureaucratic control, such as capacity to specify job assignments and motivate workers through job ladders were outweighed by the associated rigidities in organization and performance. Changes made in the name of flexibility were directed largely at practices such as task demarcation and seniority rules governing job protection. Looking back on these changes a reasonable degree of consensus can be found about content and impact. Research into routine manufacturing work under conditions of lean production shows a consistent picture of functional flexibility, teamworking as the organizational form most appropriate to multitasking in the new technical division of labor, and task-centered participation in quality and continuous improvement.

However, increased flexibility does not necessarily mean either the elimination of Taylorism or less rules across the board. While demarcation rules have undoubtedly declined, most other work rules remain intact or have intensified. Extensive formal procedures have been shown to govern most US establishments (Marsden, Cook, and Knoke 1996). While teams undoubtedly provide a framework for functional flexibility and utilization of employee expertise, most remain based on fragmented and highly specified tasks (Findlay *et al.* 2000). Tasks themselves are still subject to high degrees of standardization, testament largely to the continuing use of Taylorist techniques for measuring, timing, and evaluating work (Slaughter 1987; Williams *et al.* 1992). Moreover, the benchmarking systems used to redesign work and drive continuous improvement, such as TQM and BPR, require a concern for standardized procedures and uniform, dependable practices (Wilkinson and Willmott 1994). New computer-based systems are also used to aid task specification and engineered work standards in areas such as warehousing (Wright and Lund 1998). With these processes in mind, Adler's (1993) notion of 'learning bureaucracies' seems to be the most appropriate term for work arrangements in advanced manufacturing.

The shift towards a service economy has long been associated with a postindustrial society, yet a powerful body of evidence has accumulated about the 'industrialization' of services. Evidence about the bureaucratization of service tasks is associated primarily with Ritzer's (1993) McDonaldization of society thesis. He and other writers have convincingly demonstrated that fast food and other retail, leisure, and media operations incorporate classic Weberian processes of calculability, predictability, and quantification. Ritzer pushes the fast-food exemplar beyond the boundaries of useful explanation and in-depth evidence. Other writers see the competitive requirement to meet more sophisticated customer needs as driving standards of service and work requirements upwards, at least in some sectors (Frenkel *et al.* 1999; Korczynski 2002). Yet even they use the term 'customer-oriented bureaucracy' to describe the most common forms of interactive service work, such as those in the fast-growing number of call centers.

Work rules in call centers and settings such as hotel chains focus on the standardization of the service encounter. 'Quality' provision and consistency of product is maintained through mechanisms such as the scripting of language and behavior. When reinforced by high-surveillance technology and procedurally-based software, work tasks are routinized and service operatives experience 'an assembly line in the head' (Taylor and Bain 1998). There has also been a growth of output controls through nontechnological monitoring based on 'control by customers', though there is an element of bureaucratization via report cards and surveys (Fuller and Smith 1991).

A further and well-documented facet of scripting focuses on feelings as well as behavior. Originally identified through Hochschild's (1983) work on flight attendants and other employees involved in emotional labor, what might be described as 'feeling rules' have now been the subject of research in a variety of service settings from insurance, supermarkets, leisure parks, and again call centers (for a review, see Bolton 2004). Scripted and standardized displays of feelings are achieved through 'smile factories', forced niceness, and other forms of verbal interplay and body posture (Van Maanen 1991). The literature on this theme is frequently ambiguous about whether it is the actual feelings or merely the compliant behavior of employees that is being observed. However, irrespective of the exact outcome, the extension of work rules into previously 'private' domains is a significant one. In most cases emotionality is targeted by both bureaucratic rules and 'post-bureaucratic' cultural means such as slogans, rites, selective recruitment, and leadership style. The latter facilitates more flexible 'positive' orientations and more complex interactions rules (Alvesson 1995; Van Maanen and Kunda 1989).

Finally, there are the trends in the sphere of 'knowledge' and knowledge management. The current focus on the importance of knowledge assets reinforces the long understood point that high levels of autonomy are effective preconditions for creative outcomes. Multifunctional project teams, like their equivalents lower down the organizational hierarchy, help to break down bureaucratic hierarchies. Many advocates of knowledge management emphasize networks and the building of knowledge-sharing communities (Swan et al. 1999). Yet the language of much knowledge management—codification, storing, and distribution—also remind us that this frequently takes the form of standardized, highly structured systems in areas such as software design or surveying as well as rules for the use of databases in order to recycle knowledge. Many initiatives involve efforts to develop measures to systematically codify knowledge and then let people follow particular procedures and work according to the associated templates and project metrics (Hansen, Norhia, and Tierney 1999), though the extent to which such measures are used to guide rather than constrain through rules will vary according to context (Alvesson and Kärreman 2001).

As we have already noted, recent public service reform has often been legitimized through attacks on bureaucracy. Yet the focus of reform has tended to be policies to break down producer control and make professionals more accountable to management, the state, funding bodies, or clients. The price of a shift towards professional and performance management, plus enhanced output controls has been a significant growth of centralized audit and monitoring, with a consequent decline in trust and collegiality. While such measures have by no means eliminated professional autonomy and power, they do constitute 'new layers of bureaucracy' (Hoggett, quoted in Clarke and Newman 1997: 158). Among groups such as welfare and social workers, managerial specification of work rules also reflects the need to conform to increased legislation and to avoid costly litigation.

20.4.2 Employment Practices

Employment practices refer to issues such as the recruitment, reward, and representation of labor. There is consensus that considerable changes have taken place compared to postwar industrial relations, which at least in large manufacturing firms, were based on 'inflexible company policy, detailed contract language, legalistic procedures for dispute resolution, and bureaucratic union and management structures' (Fairris 1991: 133). To a large degree work rules generated employment rules, embedded in internal labor markets. Removing the former could, therefore, dispense with some of the need for the latter.

As the chapters elsewhere by Osterman and Burton, Rubery, and Procter make clear, there is little doubt that a variety of measures have been directed towards increasing managerial flexibility in the employment sphere. These include: the use of contingent workers, outsourcing, and temporary contracts that allow firms to escape the obligations imposed by conventional employment rules; some shift away from career hierarchies towards personal 'employability';[3] and decentralized, market-driven, or individualized reward systems. Whereas these chapters outline the extent of and constraints to changes in internal labor markets, what is less obvious is the existence of powerful countervailing tendencies that reimpose other types of employment rules.

First, even with a reduction in the complexity or standardization of pay scales, contemporary performance management systems are grounded in highly bureaucratized metrics and measurement. Second, employment rules are increasingly set through international 'best practice' and thus a process of institutional isomorphism. For example, Ferner (2000) reports, based on case studies, that MNCs move toward more internationally homogeneous, integrated, and centralized approaches to a range of issues in production, marketing, and HRM. This resulted in a pervasive bureaucratization of control, for example, through standardized systems for appraising and rewarding senior managers and for identifying those of 'high potential'.

Third, employment rules and their expression in contracts have moved away from enforcing task to wider forms of behavior. For example, a combination of legislation, perceived best practice, and fear of litigation have led to a significant growth of codes of conduct to deal with a variety of 'inappropriate' behaviors (Ackroyd and Thompson 1999). Equal opportunity policies are probably the most well-known, but many large firms have extended these into wide-ranging harassment codes, or others dealing with issues of health or even romantic liaisons. While, unsurprisingly much of this growth is in the litigation-conscious United States, the

---

[3] Although recruitment is heavily formalized, employability increasingly depends on what Brown and Hesketh (2004) call non-bureaucratic soft currencies such as interpersonal skills, charisma, appearance, and accent.

British Institute for Personnel and Development advises organizations to spell out inappropriate behavior, ideally through or accompanying a contract of employment. Senior National Health Service managers now face dismissal if they fail to comply with a new code of conduct included in their contracts. The public sector is frequently at the forefront of trends towards increased enforcement of wider behavioral norms or codes of conduct, given the prominence of human resource professionals and the concern for standardized and equitable employment criteria.

20.4.3 Decision and Coordination Practices

As we saw earlier, post-bureaucratic arguments rely heavily on notions of decentralization and networks as means of breaking with hierarchical authority. New arrangements are sometimes described as 'heterarchies' that rely instead on collaboration and cooperation (Solvell and Zandar 1995). There are different elements here: the relationship between headquarters and other units, the distribution of decision rules within the operative unit, and the existence of alternative means of cultural or market rather than hierarchical coordination.

With respect to interorganizational relations, neither surveys nor case studies give any significant support to the idea that 'pyramidal hierarchies are replaced by looser networks' (Sennett 1998: 85). In wide-ranging studies, Hill, Martin, and Harris (2000) and Ruigrok et al. (1999) found some structural indicators of PBO, such as business units as profit centers, flattened hierarchies, a reliance on task forces and teams rather than rigid compartmentalization, and extensive use of IT and communication networks. But these results do not support what Ruigrok described as 'far-fetched claims' on the rise of the new organization. Hill, Martin, and Harris reported that decentralization is regulated and restricted by central control of the resource allocation process and target setting; a finding supported by a survey of the largest companies operating in the United Kingdom, 'headquarters exerts tight controls over business unit operations and profitability targets are not devolved' (Armstrong et al. 1998: 13). Interestingly, in Hill, Martin, and Harris's (2000) study, three—out of a sample of ten companies—that were traditionally decentralized were becoming more and not less centralized. Ruigrok et al. (1999: 59–60) provide what seems to be a fair summary of medium-term trends:

Thus, hierarchies still matter (if companies grow, they tend to add layers; there has not been much decentralization of strategic decision making; and companies report a higher increase of vertical than horizontal networking), but they are changing at the same time (there has been a certain degree of delayering; companies do report decentralization of operational decision making; and companies report increasing internal networking).

More sophisticated IT systems facilitate rather than remove managerial power. This may once again be in the form of output controls rather than central direction, but increased capacity to financially monitor, control, and predict performance still constitutes hierarchical authority, even though it deviates from traditional forms of bureaucracy. Integrated computer-based models can be used to predict yield and return, and standardized central planning systems remain a core feature of business practice, retaining hierarchy, though degrees of autonomy may vary across functions (McKinlay 1999).

The most persuasive conceptualization of these developments is provided by Harrison's term 'concentration without centralisation'. The very fact of spatial and functional diversity in networked large organizations or supply chains has led to concentrated economic power changing shape: 'production may be decentralised, while power, finance, distribution, and control remain concentrated among the big firms' (1994: 20). Another way of describing companies such as Benetton, with its tightly integrated and specified outsourced production and franchised distribution, is extended hierarchy (Thompson 1993). In other words, hierarchical relations extend and change their form as organizational boundaries become more permeable. A good example is provided in Pulignano's (2002) account of modular production systems at Fiat, Renault, and Volkswagen. Many service and production units have been outsourced, but operate under the same roof and are regulated both through internal markets and highly specified formal rules for coordinating inter-unit transactions. In his extensive review of the evidence on network forms, Ackroyd (2002: 187) argues that 'the decentred firm is a special kind of network in which significant power is retained by the hub'. Such forms allow corporations to maintain or extend their spheres of interest and control while allowing for greater flexibility and disallowing full costs of ownership. In this sense, networks combine elements of hierarchy and market rather than constituting a separate means of coordination.

What about decision processes and hierarchies within units? Hard evidence for the removal of middle layers and devolution of authority is scarce in case studies and occupational statistics are difficult to interpret given the constant process of renaming and shuffling of managerial jobs. Nevertheless, as we have already noted, there appears to be little doubt that large organizations have become increasingly reliant on cross-functional project teams for coordination and innovation. As with interorganizational relations, the mistake made in some accounts of change is the notion that horizontal forms of coordination replace bureaucratic hierarchy. Intraorganizational developments, however, manifest not an extended but a parallel hierarchy. Horizontal forms of coordination are a kind of 'shadow division of labour', added to and existing alongside conventional hierarchies in order to perform different activities (Warhurst and Thompson 1998: 19). One of the few studies to explicitly examine the 'internal network' argument strongly downplays the extent of change. Using cases from a variety of national and sectoral contexts,

Hales argues that while there was a shift away from managers being held responsible for operational conformance to unit performance, such units 'remained firmly within a system of hierarchical control. Responsibility for unit performance continued to be vested in individual managers who were accountable vertically to identifiable "bosses" and who were judged on the basis of conformance with centrally-imposed rules about appropriate levels of performance' (2002: 61).

Finally, we need to assess parallel changes in the public sector. Despite the introduction of competition and quasi-markets, plus devolved managerial authority, the management of public services remains to a large extent dependent on external political authority and legitimacy. As one British NHS manager observed in Schofield's study, 'There is a bureaucracy, all these hoops you have to jump through. ... They set the rules, we have to meet them' (2001: 86). Put another way, there are inherent constraints to the reconfiguration of decision and coordination rules—public and private organizations remain different in goals and operation, even in the United States (Scott and Falcone 1998). It is hardly surprising, therefore, that empirical studies show limited movement in the direction of post-bureaucracy. For example, studies of public sector change in Australia (Considine 1996; Parker and Bradley 2000) confirm Schofield's (2001) account of the United Kingdom: employees and managers report the continued saliency of central regulation, hierarchical authority, conformity to rules, and bureaucratic values.

20.4.4 Knowledge-Intensive Firms

The increased significance of knowledge and the growth of information-intensive business are often presented as central features in the emergence of post-bureaucratic forms of coordination. The extent of knowledge work, even in knowledge-intensive firms (KIFs), is frequently exaggerated (Thompson, Warhurst, and Callaghan 2001). Nor does knowledge-intensive necessarily imply post-bureaucratic. To use Mintzberg's categories, professional bureaucracies are characterized by highly educated labor using their expertise, while machine bureaucracies call for knowledge-intensive work in the strategic apex and technostructure, but the bulk of the work done is not knowledge-intensive.

Nevertheless, it is reasonable to assume that under knowledge-intensive conditions, such as in science-based organizations or consultancies and other professional service firms, hierarchies, standards, rules, and regulations may diminish in importance and usefulness, as complex issues call for flexibility, autonomy, and exercise of judgment. Case-study evidence indicates considerable diversity in terms of the presence and dominance of bureaucracy in KIFs. Varying modes of control are used ranging from hierarchical and bureaucratic modes, such as monitoring of behavior, rewards such as pay and promotion, to nonpecuniary rewards such as confirmation and status. Most organizations use the entire spectrum, but in very different ways. Some KIFs have relatively strong hierarchical and bureaucratic features (Akehurst 1994; Covaleski *et al.* 1998), others—and probably the most—exhibit the opposite qualities (Alvesson 1995; Morris and Empson 1998; Starbuck 1992). The former tendency is partly related to size, although there are also large firms with a fairly low level of bureaucracy (Kunda 1992). Also organizations working to reuse and implement known solutions can sometimes deviate quite considerably from the organic or adhocratic organizational form. A partnership system—while emphasizing collegiality among senior people—also seems to fuel hierarchy through making the steps between partners and others significant (Maister 1993). In some service companies, transparent charges are a significant measure (Covaleski *et al.* 1998). Here quantifiable performance measures are central and backed up with extensive rewards, as well as status pressures when failing to reach stated objectives. As with some of our previous examples, though there is a focus on output controls rather than direct regulation of behavior, there are typically a wealth of systems, structures, and procedures that support the enhanced efforts to measure outputs.

Despite the variation, control targeted at the values, ideas, beliefs, emotions, and identifications of expert labor, characterize much management in knowledge-intensive companies. This goes beyond what bureaucracy and simple output control can accomplish. Even in those companies trying to standardize their products, 'client involvement adds to task uncertainty, requiring professionals to create their roles to some extent in the course of a client assignment' (Morris and Empson 1998: 619). If bureaucracy is present, it tends to be 'softer' in impact, as employees must adapt to situational circumstances and feel confident to break or bend rules when deemed appropriate.

In a study of a major American high-technology company, Van Maanen and Kunda argue that in circumstances where the formal organization is less important, '"culture" replaces "structure" as an organizing principle and is used both to explain and guide action' (1989: 72). Elsewhere, however, Kunda (1992) maintains that certain elements of bureaucratic control remain in place, even when normative control is predominant. Desirable behavior is, however, achieved as a result of regulations and rules that focus on the individual's experiences and ideas rather than on a direct focus on control of behavior.

To further explore the ambiguities and nuances often buried under the use of one-dimensional labels associated with bureaucratization, we will look more closely at two cases of typical knowledge-intensive firms—a management consultancy firm and a pharmaceutical company (Kärreman, Sveningsson, and Alvesson 2002). In the first, a very large management consultancy firm, called 'Big', power and authority are distributed through hierarchy; work methodologies are standardized; work procedures are fine-tuned toward predictability of outputs, and organizational members are viewed and treated as interchangeable parts. There is also an extensive apparatus with rules, procedures, and checklists for HRM issues such as assessment, feedback, and promotion. It follows that loyalty, so important for knowledge-intensive firms, is secured mainly from an instrumental and calculative point of view, and that social relations and community feelings are not well developed. Impersonal orientations dominate. All this fits comfortably into a traditional concept of bureaucracy.

However, organizational practices at Big also deviate from bureaucratic principles in some instances. The most notable deviation is the way organizational members interact in teams. Here, work is organized in a largely organic and adhocratic way. Members are expected to improvise and contribute regardless of hierarchical standing. Social relations in the team are typically intimate and intense. The bureaucratic modes of operation at Big are, of course, making their presence felt, even in team interaction, but more as a supporting than a regulating structure. It operates more like a vehicle of shared understanding than a protocol for prescribed behavior. In this sense bureaucracy at Big is also a cultural phenomenon: an expression of a particular collective mindset and frame of reference (Kärreman and Alvesson, forthcoming).

As in the case of Big, the pharmaceutical company, called 'Pharma', has clearly established bureaucratic features. More significantly, in key areas such as research and development, it is moving further in a bureaucratic direction, associated with efforts to rationalize and speed up processes. Much managerial talk is clearly based on the assumption that it is possible to formalize and subsequently more consciously manage the project-based research, hence the objective to create a standard model supposedly implemented by managers in all research sites throughout the corporation. R&D is now explicitly described as a 'management process' and the various research sites are commonly referred to as 'industry hotels', signaling a machinelike delivery status.

The belief in technology and the ability to speed up the search for new radical breakthroughs are connected to production-line ideas of mechanization and specialization. The new operative model with its standardized organizing principles and procedures for work processes and responsibility, organizational structure (job design and reporting relationships), and other tasks is a significant industrialization of the former rather organizationally diverse and disparate 'university institution', leading some people to think of the new organization in terms of machine bureaucracy.

In both cases, we can observe systematic examples of *selective bureaucratization*. While the presence of bureaucratic forms of control are significant, they have limited impact on the core work of key categories of consultants and scientists. These findings correspond with those of McKinlay on knowledge management in pharmaceuticals elsewhere in this volume. Summing up this section, we can say that many companies in the KIF sector show characteristics of the PBO prototype. Many KIFs do, however, also include strong bureaucratic features and there are some signs on the strengthening of these. As the two case studies show, it may be misleading to explore bureaucracy only in structural terms. Despite the presence of systems, procedures, and rules, cultural orientations may make these more flexibly used and less constraining, thus in a sense partly transcending bureaucracy.

20.5 CONCLUSIONS AND DISCUSSION: THE DIFFICULTIES OF EXPLORING BUREAUCRACY

As we have seen, many people seem to view the widespread existence and rapid expansion of PBO as a self-evident fact. But it is easy to identify a wealth of powerful counter trends. To sum up, empirical studies of changes reveal relatively modest changes in structural terms; and where change has taken place in some spheres, it is in the direction of more rules, hierarchy, and centralization (Hill, Martin, and Harris 2000; Warhurst and Thompson 1998). Most firms regard hierarchy and formalized procedures as essential tools for assuring efficiency, conformance, quality, and timeliness (Adler 1999: 37). Nor, contrary to some arguments (Heydebrand 1989: 324), are bureaucratic forms confined to a few residual institutional niches such as the public sector. Falls in the size of individual units and decentering of organizations may change the form of bureaucracy, but they do not necessarily diminish its impact. As Hales (2002) observes, 'bureaucracy-lite', with its reduced levels of hierarchy and shift to control over outcomes, may be more consistent with the impersonal, means-end calculations of bureaucratic rationalization.

Examples of PBO are understandably more common in knowledge-intensive firms than in manufacturing and mass service. However, even here bureaucracy remains a vital part of organizational life. Indeed, formerly adhocratic arrangements may move towards more bureaucratic forms of governance over a period of time as such firms look for more effective ways of managing a stable expert workforce (Robertson and Swan 2004).

This is not to deny that important changes (e.g. in the areas of decentralization and disaggregation) are taking place, but they are not producing a fully-fledged post-bureaucratic alternative. Internal forms of horizontal organization and external network-type relations can and do coexist with vertical hierarchies. Most organizations draw upon a spectrum of control forms: from output, bureaucratic, professional/occupational, and customer control to charismatic and authoritative leaders to corporate cultures and emotional control. To some extent this has always been true. But as environments and organizational structures become more complex, a diversification of types of controls and coordination ensues. A good modern example of this is Considine's (1996) account of how a new organizational form, market bureaucracy, has developed in the public sector to deal with changing conditions of risk and taste. Yet it still coexists and competes with other administrative regimes such as procedural, corporate, and network bureaucracies.

In general terms, we can identify a common search across manufacturing, private, and public services for more flexible, responsive ways of organizing, while maintaining a capacity for formalization and central control. Rather than the classic contingency argument of a fit between an organizational structure and its environment, it is better to see contemporary organizational forms as a series of hybrids, within which bureaucratic mechanisms normally remain dominant. This is captured in the emergent vocabularies of contemporary research such as customer-oriented bureaucracies in the service sector (Bourgeois 2001; Frenkel *et al.* 1999) or soft bureaucracy in which decentralized responsibilities are combined with centralized decision making (Courpasson 2000). A degree of employee auton-omy may lead team members to produce and enforce 'quasi-bureaucratic' rules by and on themselves (Barker 1993). Although we are skeptical about Adler's (2001) view that trust is becoming generally more prominent in the mix, he is surely right to identify the task of research as examining how various coordination mechanisms combine in different and more complex settings (see also Kärreman and Alvesson, forthcoming).

To really understand the presence and significance of bureaucracy requires in-depth exploration of organizational practices in different sectors and sections of organization, thus escaping traditional analytical dichotomies such as mechanistic–organic and centralization–decentralization. Forms of control and coordination do not only interact, overlap with, or weaken one another; managers may comply with, reinforce, or circumscribe bureaucracy. For example, organiza-tions may have extensive rules and procedures for HRM issues such as recruitment, compensation, training, development, and promotion, but studies are more skep-tical about the extent to which managers follow them in practice (Jackall 1988). Caution is therefore required before ticking off bureaucratic or post-bureaucratic control forms without checking their meaning and impact carefully and in practice. Superficial studies are likely to register primarily formal arrangements and claims by fashion-conscious corporate actors eager to emphasize progressiveness and to comply with institutional norms (Meyer and Rowan 1977).

Too many contributors to the debate have taken bureaucracy to be a static ideal type, instead of a living, changing, and diverse set of practices. This is often as true of defenders of the abstract and unchanging benefits of hierarchy such as Elliot Jacques (1990), as well as of the paradigm breakers and pop-management authors.

We need to restore some of the features of past debates, where researchers identified variations in bureaucratic form and content, as organizations engaged with new environments and influences. Adler and Borys (1996) remind us of the virtues of Gouldner's work in this respect and develop a new typology based in two generic types of formalization—coercive and enabling bureaucracy. Their purpose is not just to restore diversity and recognize hybridity, but to argue that in contemporary manufacturing environments, some firms (often Japanese transplants) are capable of using participative and collaborative bureaucratic processes to drive learning and innovation.

This is one of a small number of studies going against the grain by stressing potentially positive features of bureaucracy. Such arguments are more often associated, as we saw earlier, with benefits of a distinctive bureaucratic ethos in the public sector. The continued existence of bureaucratic forms and values is used persuasively by du Gay (2000) to support and reinvigorate Weber's arguments concerning the distinctive ethos and 'regime values' of bureaucratic public administration. A 'good bureaucrat' remains someone who adheres to particular standards of procedure, expertise, impersonality, and hierarchy. This, in turn, constitutes 'a positive moral and ethical achievement in its own right' (2000: 7) with respect to the public governance requirements to equitably treat citizens and employees. However, across all sectors bureaucracy can act as a counterweight to arbitrariness and managerial power. While some feminists regard bureaucracy as a form of male rationality, others judge formal equal opportunity policies as an advance on the informal culture and rules of the game within which male power has traditionally operated (Simpson 1997). In her response to Ferguson's critique of bureaucracy, Due Billing makes the wider point that 'rules could also be viewed as an asset for the people working in the organisation' (1994: 183). Even in small feminist organizations, elements of bureaucracy are difficult to avoid (Ashcroft 2001).

Of course, we should not exaggerate the benefits of bureaucracy to either efficiency or mutual gains among organizational participants. Arguments 'bending the stick back' against wholly negative views, should rather be seen as complementary to purely empirical questioning of undifferentiated and one-dimensional analyses of bureaucracy. Post-bureaucracy, for the moment, operates more as a means of legitimating change and marketing new ideas than as a solid empirical indicator of changing forms of work organization. It reflects the strong institutional premium on investigating and labeling what is perceived to be novel. All this is not necessarily bad: it may trigger new ideas and there are reasons to pay extra attention to novel phenomena—even if they are not widely spread. But social scientists need to hold the line against claims, whether from popular business writings or high theory, that are taken as truths irrespective of the evidence.

REFERENCES

ACKROYD, S. (2002). *The Organization of Business*. Oxford: Oxford University Press.

—— and THOMPSON, P. (1999). *Organizational Misbehaviour*. London: Sage.

ADLER, P. S. (1993). 'Time-and-Motion Regained'. *Harvard Business Review*, January–February: 97–107.

—— (1999). 'Building Better Bureaucracies'. *Academy of Management Executive*, 13/4: 36–47.

—— (2001). 'Market, Hierarchy, and Trust: The Knowledge Economy and the Future of Capitalism'. *Organization Science*, 12/2: 215–34.

—— and BORYS, B. (1996). 'Two Types of Bureaucracy: Enabling and Coercive'. *Administrative Science Quarterly*, 41: 61–89.

AKEHURST, G. (1994). 'Brownloaf-MacTaggart—Control and Power in a Management Consultancy', in D. Adam-Smith and A. Peacock (eds.), *Cases in Organisational Behaviour*. London: Pitman.

ALVESSON, M. (1995). *Management of Knowledge-Intensive Companies*. Berlin: de Gruyter.

—— and KÄRREMAN, D. (2001). 'Odd Couple: Making Sense of the Curious Concept of Knowledge Management'. *Journal of Management Studies*, 38/7: 995–1018.

ARMSTRONG, P., MARGINSON, P., EDWARDS, P., and PURCELL, J. (1998). 'Divisionalization in the UK: Diversity, Size and the Devolution of Bargaining'. *Organization Studies*, 19: 1–22.

ASHCROFT, K. L. (2001). 'Organized Dissonance: Feminist Bureaucracy as Hybrid Form'. *Academy of Management Journal*, 44/6: 1301–22.

BARKER, J. R. (1993). 'Tightening the Iron Cage: Concertive Control in Self-Managing Teams'. *Administrative Science Quarterly*, 38: 408–37.

BLAU, P. M. (1955). *The Dynamics of Bureaucracy*. Chicago: University of Chicago Press.

BOLOGH, R. (1990). *Love or Greatness: Max Weber and Masculine Thinking—A Feminist Inquiry*. London: Unwin Hyman.

BOLTON, S. (2004). *Mixed Feelings: Emotion Management in the Workplace*. London: Palgrave.

BOURGEOIS, D. (2001). 'Towards Customer-Oriented Neo-Bureaucracies'. Paper to EGOS Conference, Lyon.

BROWN, P., and HESKETH, A. (2004). *The Mismanagement of Talent: Employability and Jobs in the Knowledge Economy*. Oxford: Oxford University Press.

BURNS, T., and STALKER, G. M. (1961). *The Management of Innovation*. London: Tavistock.

CHILD, J., and McGRATH, R. (2001). 'Organizations Unfettered: Organizational Form in an Information-Intensive Economy'. *Academy of Management Journal*, 44/6: 1135–48.

CLARKE, J., and NEWMAN, J. (1997). *Managerial State: Power, Politics and Ideology in the Remaking of Social Welfare*. London: Sage.

CLAWSON, D. (1980). *Bureaucracy and the Labour Process: The Transformation of US Industry, 1860–1920*. New York: Monthly Review Press.

CLEGG, S. (1990). *Modern Organizations: Organization Studies in the Post-Modern World*. London: Sage.

CONSIDINE, M. (1996). 'Market Bureaucracy? Exploring the Contending Rationalities of Contemporary Administrative Regimes'. *Labour and Industry*, 7/1: 1–28.

COURPASSON, D. (2000). 'Managerial Strategies of Domination: Power in Soft Bureaucracies'. *Organization Studies*, 21/1: 141–61.

COVALESKI, M., DIRSMITH, M. W., HEIAN, J. B., and SAMUEL, D. (1998). 'The Calculated and the Avowed: Techniques of Discipline and Struggles over Identity in Big Six Public Accounting Firms'. *Administrative Science Quarterly*, 43: 293–327.

CROOK, S., PALUSKI, J., and WATERS, M. (1992). *Postmodernization: Change in Advanced Society*. London: Sage.

DAVENPORT, T., and PRUSAK, L. (1998). *Working Knowledge*. Cambridge, Mass.: Harvard Business School Press.

DUE BILLING, Y. (1994). 'Gender and Bureaucracies—A Critique of Ferguson's "The Feminist Case against Bureaucracy"'. *Gender, Work and Organization*, 1/4: 173–93.

DU GAY, P. (2000). *In Praise of Bureaucracy*. London: Sage.

EDWARDS, R. (1979). *Contested Terrain: The Transformation of the Workplace in the Twentieth Century*. London: Heinemann.

FAIRRIS, D. (1991). 'The Crisis in US Shopfloor Relations'. *International Contributions to Labour Studies*, 1: 133–56.

FERGUSON, K. (1984). *The Feminist Case against Bureaucracy*. Philadelphia: Temple University Press.

FERNER, A. (2000). 'The Underpinnings of "Bureaucratic Control" Systems: HRM in European Multinationals'. *Journal of Management Studies*, 37/4: 521–40.

FINDLAY, P., MARKS, A., McKINLAY, A., and THOMPSON, P. (2000). 'Flexible If It Suits Them: The Use and Abuse of Teamwork Skills', in F. Mueller and S. Proctor (eds.), *Teamworking*. London: Palgrave.

FRENKEL, S., KORCZYNSKI, M., SHIRE, K., and TAM, M. (1999). *On the Front Line: Pattern of Work Organisation in Three Advanced Societies*. Ithaca, NY: Cornell University Press.

FULLER, L., and SMITH, V. (1991). 'Consumers' Reports: Management by Customers in a Changing Economy'. *Work, Employment and Society*, 5/1: 1–16.

HALES, C. (2002). '"Bureaucracy-lite" and Continuities in Managerial Work'. *British Journal of Management*, 13: 51–66.

HAMEL, G., and PRAHALAD, C. K. (1996). *Competing for the Future*. Boston: Harvard Business School Press.

HANDY, C. (1995). *The Future of Work*. London: WH Smith Contemporary Papers 8.

HANSEN, M. T., NORHIA, N., and TIERNEY, T. (1999). 'What's Your Strategy for Managing Knowledge?' *Harvard Business Review*, March–April: 106–16.

HARRISON, B. (1994). *Lean and Mean: The Changing Landscape of Corporate Power in the Age of Flexibility*. New York: Basic Books.

HECKSCHER, C., and APPLEGATE, L. (1994). 'Introduction', in C. Heckscher and A. Donnellon (eds.), *The Post-Bureaucratic Organization: New Perspectives on Organizational Change*. London: Sage.

HEYDEBRAND, W. (1989). 'New Organisational Forms'. *Work and Occupations*, 16/3: 323–57.

HILL, S., MARTIN, R., and HARRIS, M. (2000). 'Decentralization, Integration and the Post-Bureaucratic Organization: The Case of R & D'. *Journal of Management Studies*, 37/4: 563–85.

HOCHSCHILD, A. R. (1983). *The Managed Heart: Commercialisation of Human Feeling*. Berkeley: University of California Press.

JACKALL, R. (1988). *Moral Mazes*. New York: Oxford University Press.

JACKSON, P. (ed.) (1999). *Virtual Working: Social and Organisational Dynamics*. London: Routledge.

JACQUES, E. (1990). 'In Praise of Hierarchy'. *Harvard Business Review*, January–February.

KÄRREMAN, D., and ALVESSON, M. (forthcoming). 'Cages in Tandem: Management Control, Social Identity, and Identification in a Knowledge-Intensive Firm'. *Organization*.

——SVENINGSSON, S., and ALVESSON, M. (2002). 'The Return of the Machine Bureaucracy?—Management Control and Knowledge Work'. *International Studies of Management and Organizations*, 32/2: 70–92.

KORCZYNSKI, M. (2002). *Human Resource Management and Service Work: The Fragile Social Order*. London: Palgrave.

KUNDA, G. (1992). *Engineering Culture: Control and Commitment in a High Tech Corporation*. Philadelphia: Temple University Press.

MCKINLAY, A. (1999). 'Recasting the Visible Hand? Strategy, Structure and Process in UK Manufacturing 1970–97'. *Contemporary British History*, 13/3: 148–63.

MAISTER, D. (1993). *Managing the Professional Service Firm*. New York: Free Press.

MARSDEN, P. V., COOK, C. R., and KNOKE, D. (1996). 'American Organizations in Their Environments: A Descriptive Overview', in A. L. Kalleberg, D. Knoke, P. V. Marsden, and J. L. Spaeth (eds.), *Organizations in America: Analyzing Their Structures and Human Resource Practices*. Thousand Oaks, Calif.: Sage.

MERTON, R. K. (1949). *Social Theory and Social Structure*. Glencoe, Ill.: Free Press.

MEYER, J. W., and ROWAN, B. (1977). 'Institutionalized Organizations: Formal Structure as Myth and Ceremony'. *American Journal of Sociology*, 83: 340–63.

MILES, R. E., SNOW, C. C., MATHEWS, J. A., and MILES, G. (1997). 'Organizing in the Knowledge Age: Anticipating the Cellular Form'. *Academy of Management Executive*, 11/4: 7–19.

MINTZBERG, H. (1983). *Structure in Fives: Designing Effective Organizations*. Englewood Cliffs, NJ: Prentice Hall.

MORRIS, T., and EMPSON, L. (1998). 'Organisation and Expertise: An Exploration of Knowledge Bases and the Management of Accounting and Consulting Firms'. *Accounting, Organizations and Society*, 23/5–6: 609–24.

NOHRIA, N. (1992). 'Is a Network Perspective a Useful Way of Studying Organizations?' in N. Nohria and R. G. Eccles (eds.), *Networks and Organizations*. Boston: Harvard Business School Press.

OSBORNE, D., and PLASTRIK, P. (1997). *Banishing Bureaucracy: The Five Strategies for Reinventing Government*. Reading, Mass.: Addison-Wesley.

PALMER, I., and HARDY, C. (2000). *Thinking about Management*. London: Sage.

PARKER, M. (1992). 'Post-modern Organizations or Postmodern Organization Theory?' *Organization Studies*, 13: 1–17.

PARKER, R., and BRADLEY, L. (2000). 'Organisational Culture in the Public Sector: Evidence from Six Organisations'. *International Journal of Public Sector Management*, 3/2: 124–41.

PERROW, C. (1992). 'Small Firm Networks', in N. Nohria and R. G. Eccles (eds.), *Networks and Organizations*. Boston: Harvard Business School Press.

PETERS, T. (1989). *Thriving on Chaos*. London: Pan Books.

PULIGNANO, V. (2002). 'Bureaucracy Insights in Multi-Enterprise Settings: Evidence from the International Motor Manufacturing Industry'. Paper to International Labour Process Conference, University of Strathclyde, April.

RITZER, G. (1993). *The MacDonaldization of Society*. London: Pine Forge Press.

ROBERTSON, M., and SWAN, J. (2004). 'Going Public: The Emergence and Effects of Soft Bureaucracy in a Knowledge Intensive Firm'. *Organization*, 11/1: 123–48.

RUIGROK, W., PETTIGREW, A., PECK, S. and WHITTINGTON, R. (1999). 'Corporate Restructuring and New Forms of Organizing: Evidence from Europe'. *Management International Review*, 39/2: 41–64.

SCARBROUGH, H., and BURRELL, G. (1996). 'The Axeman Cometh: The Changing Roles and Knowledges of Middle Managers', in S. Clegg and G. Palmer (eds.), *The Politics of Management Knowledge*. London: Sage.

SCHOFIELD, J. (2001). 'The Old Ways Are the Best? The Durability and Usefulness of Bureaucracy in Public Sector Management'. *Organization*, 8/1: 77–96.

SCOTT, P., and FALCONE, S. (1998). 'Comparing Public and Private Organizations: An Exploratory Analysis of Three Frameworks'. *American Review of Public Administration*, 28/2: 126–45.

SENNETT, R. (1998). *The Corrosion of Character: The Personal Consequences of Work in the New Capitalism*. New York: Norton.

SIMPSON, R. (1997). 'Have Times Changed? Career Barriers and the Token Women Manager'. *British Journal of Management*, 8/Special Issue (June): S121–S130.

SLAUGHTER, J. (1987). 'The Team Concept in the US Auto Industry: Implications for Unions'. Paper presented at Conference on Japanisation, UWIST.

SOLVELL, O., and ZANDER, I. (1995). 'Organization of the Dynamic Multinational Enterprise: The Home-Based and the Heterarchical MNE'. *International Studies of Management and Organization*, 25/1–2: 17–38.

SPENDER, J. C. (1996). 'Workplace Knowledge as a Competitive Target', in A. Malm (ed.), *Does Management Matter?* Lund: Lund University Press.

STARBUCK, W. (1992). 'Learning by Knowledge-Intensive Firms'. *Journal of Management Studies*, 29/6: 713–40.

SWAN, J., NEWELL, S., SCARBROUGH, H., and HISLOP, D. (1999). 'Knowledge Management and Innovation: Networks and Networking'. *Journal of Knowledge Management*, 3/4: 262–75.

TAYLOR, P., and BAIN, P. (1998). 'An Assembly Line in the Head: The Call Centre Labour Process'. *Industrial Relations Journal*, 30/2: 101–17.

TAYLOR, W. (1994). 'Control in an Age of Chaos'. *Harvard Business Review*, November–December: 64–76.

THOMPSON, P. (1993). 'Fatal Distraction: Postmodernism and Organisation Theory', in J. Hassard and M. Parker, *Postmodernism and Organisations*. London: Sage.

——WARHURST, C., and CALLAGHAN, G. (2001). 'Ignorant Theory and Knowledgeable Workers: Interrogating the Connections between Knowledge, Skills and Services'. *Journal of Management Studies*, 38/7: 923–42.

VAN MAANEN, J. (1991). 'The Smile Factory: Work at Disneyland', in P. Frost, L. F. Moore, M. R. Louis, C. C. Lundberg, and J. Martin (eds.), *Reframing Organizational Culture*. Newbury Park, Calif.: Sage.

——and KUNDA, G. (1989). 'Real Feelings: Emotional Expression and Organizational Culture', in B. M. Staw and L. L. Cummings (eds.), *Research in Organizational Behaviour*, Volume 11. Greenwich, Conn.: JAI Press.

WARHURST, C., and THOMPSON, P. (1998). 'Hands, Hearts and Minds: Changing Work and Workers at the End of the Century', in P. Thompson and C. Warhurst (eds.), *Workplaces of the Future*. London: Macmillan.

WENGER, E., and SNYDER, W. (2000). 'Communities of Practice: The Organizational Frontier'. *Harvard Business Review*, January–February: 139–45.

WILKINSON, A., and WILLMOTT, H. (1994). 'Introduction', in A. Wilkinson and H. Willmott (eds.), *Making Quality Critical*. London: Routledge.

WILLIAMS, K., HASLAM, C., WILLIAMS, J., CUTLER, T., with ADCROFT, A., and JUHAL, S. (1992). 'Against Lean Production'. *Economy and Society*, 21/3: 321–54.

WRIGHT, C., and LUND, J. (1998). ' "Under the Clock": Trade Union Responses to Computerised Control in US and Australian Grocery Warehousing'. *New Technology, Work and Employment*, 13/1: 3–15.

CHAPTER 21

INTERFIRM RELATIONS AS NETWORKS

GRAHAME THOMPSON

21.1 INTRODUCTION

THERE are a number of ways that interfirm relationships can be conceived and organized. The classic dichotomy is between a market form of organization and a hierarchical form. In the first case, interfirm relations take an arm's length, decentralized form where formal contracts between parties, competition between them, and the price mechanism articulate the connections between different firms in a supply chain, value-adding chain, or technological partnership. Alternatively, these relationships are conceived and organized administratively via such bureaucratic means as rules, norms, regulations, and guidelines. These can also take an arm's length form but involve a hierarchical arrangement of superordination and subordination between firms.

These twin traditional approaches constitute different general means of coordination between agents, but both anticipate an ordered relationship emerging between them. Coordination means that the elements in the system are brought into alignment; they act together. Usually these two are run together and to some extent they are on a continuum. At one end we have simple coordination, in which there are processes that just bring together elements into an ordered pattern; that is, not necessarily by intent or design. Here we have non-purposeful outcomes. By contrast, at the other end, administrative coordination is more of a governance relationship in that it implies the management or other regulation of elements. At the governance end, we have mechanisms that order by direction and design; that is, we have purposeful outcomes.

Considered in terms of this continuum, the market appears towards the coordination end while hierarchy appears towards the governance end. Market relationships provide a spontaneous response to the coordination problem, avoiding issues of designed regulation or governance, so markets claim only to coordinate but not to govern. On the other hand, hierarchy claims both to coordinate and to govern. If nothing else, then, this distinction establishes modes of interfirm relations, each claiming a different form of organizational effectiveness, but each located on a continuum from coordination as the bringing together to governance as a securing or regulation of that coordination.

In addition to these traditional approaches towards interfirm connections, there is another claim on how these operate, provided by the network form of organizational relationships. This form also claims a coordination and governance role. In fact, there are two slightly different aspects to network coordination and governance; organized networking activity between firms and self-organizing network activity between them. This is the site of some uncertainty about what is actually involved in the network form of interfirm relationships. In this chapter, the empirical dimensions of interfirm relations and network operations are discussed. These include aspects of interfirm networks such as technological partnerships, knowledge economies, firm clusters, industrial districts, the consequences of introducing ICTs into interfirm relationships, globalization, and internationalization of interfirm networks. While there are a number of theoretical claims to say how networks are most appropriately conceived, the exposition here concentrates on practical issues and concrete organizational forms of interfirm relationships involving networks (see Thompson 2003 for a discussion of these theoretical claims). To the extent that theoretical ideas are considered, they are largely confined to the end of the substantive discussion in this chapter (see below, Section 21.6).

This chapter concentrates on how cooperation and governance are organized in interfirm networks and what networks offer that is different from either strictly market or hierarchical relations between firms. Thus, networks are not seen as simple hybrid organizational forms—occupying a space between markets and hierarchies and involving aspects of them both—but as distinctive, new organizational forms in their own right. They have their own unique characteristics and logic of operation (Grandori and Soda 1995). After setting out an argument to this effect, the discussion critically interrogates evolutionary and biological approaches to understanding networks.

21.2 THE NEW NETWORK INDUSTRIAL SYSTEM

This section examines the long-term relationships between firms and their subcontractors and suppliers, which are often characterized in network terms. Relationships here tend to be informal and cooperative in nature, in large part relying on trust between a main firm and its suppliers. One important stimulus for change comes from technological developments and the need to increase flexibility between a main firm and client firms. Such developments, it is often suggested, lead to the disintegration of the vertically hierarchical character of firms, as more of the production of manufactured parts needed for in-house assembly is outsourced to subcontracting firms.

Under these circumstances, to overcome the possibility of opportunism, trust between companies is needed. To create this trust at least in part, both the subcontracting and the client firms seek to diversify their client base in order to reduce the risk of dependency on any single main firm. All manner of mechanisms operate to secure the idea of a partnership between the firms; mutual dependency and adaptation, discussion and negotiation, honesty, long-term commitments, quality control, benchmarking, and common knowledge shared between them. Two very important aspects of this are the flows of knowledge or information that the network encourages (and not just an exchange of information about prices), and the flows of personnel between the client and subcontracting firms, involving the mutual training in the production practices of each of the firms. Cooperative networks between firms thrive on communication and information flows between their members.

According to the Anglo-American pioneers of this analysis, such as Hirst, Piore, Sabel, and Zeitlin, these examples are not unique (Hirst and Zeitlin 1989, 1991; Piore and Sabel 1984). These authors suggest that the changes just outlined are the tip of a major transformation in the organization of production that promises to engulf much of the advanced industrial economies. This involves a systemic transformation in the way industrial production is being organized. Much of mass production process technology has given way to a flexibly specialized process technology and business strategy. The most appropriate mechanism linking the kinds of firms involved in this production environment can best be described as the network type structure. Often this type of production takes place in highly integrated 'industrial districts' that in some cases eventually expanded to become new regional economies. While this model was argued to be well-established in areas like Emilia-Romagna in Italy, southern Germany, parts of Denmark and France, and in the United States in California and Massachusetts, it was thought to be notable by its absence in others, particularly the United Kingdom (Crouch and Farrell 2001).

Johnston and Lawrence (1988) describe these developments as the generation of value-adding partnerships, a network of interdependent and mutually supportive elements neither formally hierarchically organized nor simply articulated by price relationships. The need for greater flexibility is recognized as central to the reasons for the development of the extended partnership idea. New flexible technologies are an important adjunct to, but not the sole reason for, the changes in the production processes just discussed. One additional point to note from these examples is the way market-type relationships, although not formally the object of the analyses, remain partly present within the explanations of how these instances of networks operate. Thus, we are dealing with an overlapping area when looking at these economic activities. Network and market relationships coexist (along with hierarchical ones), though networking relationships are highlighted as the most important and the ones that impart the other coexisting relationships with their particular specificity.

The above analysis concentrated on the nature of the relationships between firms in the newly evolving production environment. But it is increasingly having implications for how the firm itself might be viewed. The case of vertical (dis)integration has been mentioned in the above discussion. According to Williamson (1975, 1994) vertical integration developed in a period of mass production to reap the scale economies to be had as transactions costs were eliminated with the successive integration of more and more production activity within the (expanding) boundaries of the master firm. The external costs of market transactions were thereby eliminated as these were internalized under an increasingly hierarchical and bureaucratic coordinating mechanism. With the breakup of mass production, however, this process could be in reverse. But will it result in an increasing resort to purely market transactions?

Those committed to the idea of a new era of network firms argue against this. For instance, Sabel (1989) and Sabel, Herrigel, and Kern (1990) have suggested that one of the new organizational forms developing in the wake of the true mass production firm could be termed a quasi-disintegrated firm. This acts as an organizational integrator and specialization coordinator within a collaborative manufacturing environment involving systems of firms. A quasi-vertically disintegrated firm is one where an increasing range of part product processes are externalized from the main firm and located either in their own affiliated organizations or within separated supplier firms. The main firm may keep some of the overall design and R&D functions, but even these are increasingly being located in those organizational units with responsibility for the production of their own discrete part of the overall manufacture. In this way the functions of conception and execution are being re-merged in the variable (sub)units. These subunits are also taking on more of the production process, with their own flexible process technologies. The main firm is thus able to hedge its technological bets under this arrangement for fear of getting burdened with a technology that quickly becomes outdated or redundant.

Under this arrangement the main firm begins to appear as little more than an organizational, and possibly financial, center for the extended network of suppliers and subcontractors. It becomes the systems integrator, organizing the specialist consortia of subunits over which it has no direct control. But the manufacturing system becomes collaborative under these conditions. None of its elements can afford to completely go their own way, yet nor do they want to become totally dependent upon one single dominant firm. As a result of this process Sabel suggests it becomes difficult to specify a clear dividing line between where one firm ends and another one begins. There is no clear boundary around the firm, no internal intrafirm network to pitch against an external interfirm one. This has been designated the Möbius-strip company, with no clear demarcation between its inside and its outside (Sabel 1991).

Many of the attributes of networks thrive in this environment. The relationships between the subunits are too delicate to leave completely to market-type arrangements, with their constant search for new, cheaper suppliers or the ruthless attempt to reduce existing supplier output costs. A long-term collaborative relationship needs to be forged, in which there is a constant exchange of ideas and personnel, requiring trust and loyalty as well as competition. The constant search for better process and product technologies forges a new common interest, one shared by all the members of consortia. But it does not mean that a healthy rivalry between them is absent. It just means that competition is redefined—it is not necessarily strict market competition. Indeed this approach implicates a necessary balance between competition and cooperation for industrial success.

21.3 THE ARGUMENT: TECHNOLOGY, INSTITUTIONS, AND FORMS OF KNOWLEDGE

It is common to view networks in the context of either the analysis of the implications of technology or of the character of emergent institutions. In the first, networks are usually considered in terms of broad technological systems. These are traditionally viewed as functioning in a national context, but which are increasingly being reconsidered in an international environment (Leoncini and Montresor 2000). In the second, networks are viewed in the context of the role of institutions—conceived as configurative arrangements of norms, routines, and habits that impart certain types of behavioral capacities to the agents involved in, or making up, these networked institutional spaces. These two emphases will be considered in the two following central sections of this chapter.

However, it will also be suggested that there are themes that unite these areas of interest. The most obvious common ground here is knowledge. Thus, the argument is that interfirm networks pre-eminently involve the creation and circulation of knowledge. Some have argued that this is the main rationale of these networks so that, for instance, the industrial districts of loosely integrative firms are knowledge economies (Castells 1996) or can be characterized as intelligent regions (Cooke and Morgan 1999). In particular the knowledge accompanying networks enhances the innovative capacity of the systems they engender; they encourage technological advance in a way that neither hierarchical nor strictly market arrangements typically achieve.

21.4 Networks and Technology

21.4.1 Interorganizational Technological Networks and Partnerships

Because of the influence of new technology and the effects of technical innovation, the network form of interfirm relationships has developed strongly. The numbers of collaborative interorganizational networks (sometimes termed strategic alliances) has steadily grown since the 1980s. However, it should not be overlooked that one of the features of these networks is that they are often significantly inter-institutional in nature, since they often involve more than just firms. Public research institutes, government departments, academic institutions, and individual researchers all participate with firms in these situations. Their main objective is to create and further innovation.

The network form of organization lends itself to continuous interaction more comfortably than either market or hierarchical relationships. In advanced knowledge-based technological sectors such as molecular biotechnology, software production, and specialist ICT provision, small dedicated firms, linked into vertical and horizontal collaborative network chains and clusters, are best placed to capitalize on basic research and new scientific developments, and are best at translating these into industrial sectors. The traditional diversified firms, on the one hand, linked into well-established production areas are not adept enough to pick up and run with the rapidly evolving trends in new knowledge-based fields. Thus, the combination of alliances and technology in common has obvious implications for information and knowledge. In particular, a knowledge network is one where the conception, creation, and utilization of knowledge are in continuous interaction, rather than these stages being conceived as separate chronologically and institutionally.

Technological and other partnerships can be of various kinds (Hagedoorn 1990; Hagedoorn and Schakenraad 1990) that can be arranged along the dimension of more to less organizational independence (loose to tight governance):

- *Joint ventures* and specially set up research consortia that share R&D expenditures, usually for specific objectives allowing a high degree of organizational independence.
- *Specific research pacts* covering technological sharing and product development costs. These imply a stronger commitment of companies and higher organizational interdependence.
- *Direct investments*, usually taking the form of equity stakes in other companies. A minority holding in small high-tech companies allows some direct managerial involvement in partner companies. These organizational structures involve more direct forms of governance.
- *Cross-licensing and mutual second sourcing*. Here organizational independence is less and governance stronger. These agreements involve swapping technological information and transferring product technologies, the licensing of patented information/technology, and the transfer of technical specifications. They are highly restrictive in terms of the technology involved but grant wider ranging opportunities for partners to exploit that technology as suits their purpose.
- *Customer–supplier relations*. Here interfirm cooperation takes the form of the lead firm organizing the component supply and assembly production by secondary firms, the outsourcing of some component design and production tasks under lead-firm direction, and the establishment of co-marketing arrangements. Given the lead-firm/supplier/assembly-firm relationships, the level of organizational interdependence is small, governance being organized with a greater degree of centralization.
- *Research contracts* providing a form of R&D cooperation, where the lead firm contracts another party to perform a particular and discrete research task on its behalf. This is a case of little organizational independence in the interfirm cooperation with almost complete closed governance.

21.4.2 Information and Communications Technologies and Networks

The development of information and communication technologies (ICTs) is often thought to radically alter the production environment in which interfirm networks

operate, fostering new ways of organizing supply chains and technological partnerships. This is sometimes placed in the context of an epochal change in the way
economies are organized, namely the transformation to a new economy based
upon ICTs.

Do we have a new ICT-driven economy? (Baily and Lawrence 2001). Very
few analyses have unequivocally supported the idea of a radical new economy, 'e'
or otherwise (see Thompson 2003: ch. 7). At the global level, interfirm B2B revenues
comprise 85 percent of total e-business revenues. Thus, what is going on in
this sector is key to the economic effects of the Internet. But if we examine the
business strategies that it engenders these mainly involve reaping cost efficiencies
from the automation of transactions between businesses (Lucking-Reiley and
Spulber 2001; Wise and Morrison 2000). So these moves look suspiciously like
another step in the relentless downward pressure put on supplier cost margins in an
attempt to take out yet more fat from the supply chain. There is little that looks
radically new here.

It is difficult to know what the long-term implication of e-business will be
for networks. Leamer and Storper (2001) argue that there is a difference between
businesses that require a handshake for the conduct of their activities and
those that merely require a conversation, which can be conducted with the aid of
ICTs at a distance. If, however, new activities increase the complexity of design
and production this might increase the need for face-to-face contact. In
addition the inevitable incompleteness of contracts will always imply the necessity
for handshake transactions and regular face-to-face contact to iron out difficulties.
ICTs complement this; they do not displace it. Information for detailed
product specifications, the organization of production schedules, and the monitoring of quality standards require the continuation of proximity, the clustering
of activities where they can be controlled and monitored through handshake
transactions. There is a limit to the diversification and dispersion of production.
Just-in-time production process technologies (which make full use of ICTs)
concentrate supplier plants around assembly plants, and centralization has grown
here (Klier 1999). And there are just as many good reasons to think that existing
manufacturer supply relations will be strengthened by the advent of ICT rather
than be loosened by it. This is because the efficiency of designing customized
parts is significantly enhanced if suppliers undertake a substantial level of IT
investments, such as the introduction of 3D CAD systems, and the customized
nature of such investments could reduce the number of potential suppliers not
increase them as main manufacturers search brokering sites for standardized
components (Morita and Nakahara 2002). Furthermore, ICT-dependent financial
service industries remain tethered to a few huge cities as agglomeration economies
continue to focus activities around existing centers (Venables 2001).

21.4.3 Commodity or Value-Chains as Networks

A slightly different perspective on the imagery of interfirm relationships is provided by the notion of value-chains or commodity-chains, many of which operate internationally. While value-chains and commodity-chains are somewhat different conceptions, they are often run together (IDS 2001; Johnston and Lawrence 1988). Porter's value-chain (or value-adding) framework concentrates upon the role of the complete firm in the chain of firms that produce goods and services (Porter 1985, 1990). Formally, it stresses the key value-added element in any chain of international production. On the other hand, commodity-chains, while not neglecting the value-added component, tend to stress the various functional activities as discrete stages in the chain and how they are coordinated or governed. Thus, we can think of a move along an agricultural chain, say from farmer, to broker, to basic food processor, to package goods producer, to wholesale distributor, to retailer, and then, finally, to consumer, where the key aspect is the control and coordination of these activities. But the commodity-chain approach can also deal with incomplete firms, so that parts of the chain may fall across firms or several parts fall within a single firm.

The key point about this conception is that the value/commodity-chain is seen as a whole rather than as an aggregation of its individual parts. If each player has a stake in the other's success, the entire value-chain is the competitive unit. But this poses a problem of securing the cooperation between players; hence the emphasis on coordination and governance. Who organizes the chain? Two traditional responses have been forthcoming (Gereffi and Korzeniewicz 1994), producer-driven chains, where the key lead agent is situated at the production end of the chain (say, a manufacturer), and buyer-driven chains, where the lead agent is nearer the consumption end (a retailer, say). For each of these chains, particular agents are seen as taking the responsibility of organizing the governance of the chain, sometimes cooperatively, sometimes through more coercive means. And here is a site of much controversy: (a) can these distinctions between producer-driven and buyer-driven chains be maintained? (b) what is the precise role of power and authority within the chain, and how does it operate? (c) who, as a consequence, appropriates the value-added rents or surpluses and where are these located? (Kaplinski and Morris 2001).

Recently, these two forms of commodity-chain have been supplemented by another emergent form, what Gereffi terms internet-oriented chains (Gereffi 2001a, b) and there have been systematic attempts to empirically verify the approach. There still remain relatively few case studies (Henderson et al. 2002; IDS 2001; Kaplinski and Morris 2001; Raikes, Friis Jensen, and Ponte 2000). The classic global commodity chain (GCC) is to be found in the agricultural, clothing, or footwear sectors (Gereffi 1999). Attempts to extend the GCC approach to more complex manufacturing processes, and into the service sector more generally, have been far less successful (Gereffi 2001*b*). Viewed from the point of view of technology, the question of whether the network type of operation will be any more than an intermediate and temporary form of organization arises. As the dedicated small firms continue their collaboration with the large diversified firm (LDF), after a period of rapid innovation, such a firm could construct a knowledge-based and absorbative capacity of its own, aided by public research institutions. The small dedicated firms, originally emerging to bridge the institutional gap between the LDF and the public research institution, would thus be squeezed, perhaps disappear, and industrial organization would return to the basic dichotomy between market and hierarchy. This is a long-term hypothesis, and one probably too early to pronounce upon. But there seems no clear evidence that such a counter-trend is underway.

21.5 Networks and Institutions

21.5.1 Networks of Interdependent Firms as Institutions

Institutions are sets of rules and constraints that shape human action through inducing patterns of human behavior. Such constraints take the form of formal written rules and codes of conduct that may be transformed by negotiation or political action and represent a framework within which human interaction takes place. The role of institutions is to reduce uncertainty by establishing a stable structure of human interaction through limiting the menus of action given to agents. They stabilize the environment for action, shaping the interactions in networks and the behavioral patterns of the agents involved. Thus, institutionalism denotes a process of attaining a patterned social order by deliberate coordinated action and governance. Networks and network relationships may be considered as emergent institutions.

Clearly there are many types of knowledge that can be identified as important in this institutional context. These are usually divided into two broad categories of codified and tacit knowledge. Codified knowledge bundles up somewhat different phenomena: (a) scientific knowledge or theoretically grounded and publicly reproducible knowledge used to transform material and social processes; (b) knowledge defined as intellectual property such as patents, copyrights, trademarks, licenses, scores, and scripts; and (c) routinized knowledge, sometimes designated as information or data that can be gathered, aggregated, marketed, and disseminated by various means and through various institutional routes. Tacit knowledge is that which cannot be explicitly codified but which rests in implicit personal or institutional practices often associated with craft-like skills, awareness of reputations, and hands on techniques (Ancori, Bureth, and Cohendet 2000; Cowan, David, and Foray 2000). Tacit knowledge cannot be written down or copied. So a further difference between these is that the first type is easily transmissible to others while the second is not.

The point to make is that networks as institutions do not feature one type of knowledge uniquely, but combine them. They are thus unlike traditional communities in which relations are overwhelmingly tacit, but do have this as an essential ingredient. Actually both types of knowledge are necessary for networking-type operations, particularly tacit knowledge. Although some of the results of knowledge production can be readily marketed, the market mechanism is ill-suited to maximize productive outputs because of the public good nature of knowledge (to maximize the production and use of knowledge requires non-excludability, non-rivalry, and transparency, features the market is not always best at providing). Hierarchy is thought to be too inflexible to readily adapt and accommodate to the fast pace of technical advance that characterizes knowledge-based industries.

These issues are particularly acute when it comes to nontransmissible tacit knowledge, since this is by its nature less amenable to effective coordination and governance. Indeed, if these types of knowledge are genuinely uncodifiable and nontransmissible, it is difficult to see how any form of effective coordination or governance could emerge. If such knowledge is so tacit that it is uncommunicable, then it is completely private and secret. Of course, at one level all knowledge is tacit in that it requires at least some hands-on experience to operationalize it.

As a response to this conundrum we need to introduce some conception of the way agents can communicate even if in the first instance they cannot (or do not wish to) completely understand one another. Sabel (2001) has termed such a pragmatic solution pidgin conversations. This is a half language, a colloquial dialogue within and across groups with proximate knowledge that makes intelligible differences between them even as they do not speak exactly the same language. Such pidgin conversations encourage deliberative self-reflection, reinterpretation, and a re-examination of accepted ideas, so that new knowledge can emerge even within fields where deep tacit practices prevail.

This way of thinking about knowledge, and particularly tacit knowledge, parts company with a tradition of thinking about these matters under the heading of the economics of knowledge. In the economic approach to knowledge, knowledge is treated as a form of information. Indeed, a clear distinction is not drawn between these two categories. So what is the difference between them?

Information is passive, static, and discrete. It is something that already exists to be accessed and marshaled for a purpose. Knowledge, on the other hand, requires the application of cognitive capacity: it demands interpretation, understanding, and deployment or use. It is an active category. As information is a presence, knowledge is a process. Knowledge increases understandings and meanings. It implies a labor of conceptualization and a theorization to generate it. Thus, while information is captured, knowledge is produced. In addition, knowledge is not discrete like information. It demands connectivity so that it appears in the form of loosely patterned structures. It is with respect to this conception of genuine knowledge production that interfirm networks are involved, not just with the circulation of existing information.

21.5.2 Are Knowledge Networks Effective as Institutions?

Key features of networks considered as institutions featuring special kinds of knowledge are the habits, routines, conventions, and norms that underwrite the actions of the parties to the network (Lazaric 2000). The question raised by this list is that it tends to emphasize the known over the unknown, about how things are done now rather than how they might be done differently in the future. Thus, there is the danger of building organizational inertia into such a system. Existing practices become institutionalized in the negative sense of that term. In addition, this discussion raises issues about path dependency—the way present configurations of activity have been locked into an institutionalized pattern inherited from the past. Once a pathway is established, for instance, it becomes difficult to escape its limiting and routinized possibilities, which inhibit further adaptation and innovation. A process of cognitive and organizational self-entrapment ensues. Both concerns mean that institutionalized patterns of behavior organized around codes, routines, norms, habits, rules, and custom create severe problems of adaptation to changing circumstances. They could almost guarantee organizational failure rather than success.

The way to get round this problem is to allow history to erupt, to break through the confines of a strictly narrow institutionalist view of knowledge production (or more accurately, its potential nonproduction). This means that, at best, the domain of institutions needs to be expanded to allow for this dynamic to partly undermine its effects while at the same time preserving the benefits of characterizing knowledge in institutional terms. As we shall see, however, quite how, and to what extent, the ordering effects of the institutional complex can be cast aside in a rush to allow the free flow of experimental openness is a difficult issue to deal with.

Finally, not all networks dealing with knowledge are actually involved with the production of new knowledge and innovatory activity. Indeed, even those networks that are discussed explicitly in the context of innovation and new knowledge may also be doing something else. These networks also divide (Riles 2001). They divide both spatially and legally; spatially in the sense that some of those in the network will have full access to the knowledge so produced, and some will not, depending where they are in the network; and legally in the sense of questions of ownership (patents, licenses, copyrights) over outputs and products. The study of how actual networks operate indicates that these inequalities in networks are inevitable. Variations in the pattern of technological specialization and learning of firms in the network depend upon their different positions within it (Shachar and Zuscovitch 1990). Whatever arrangements there are to cooperate and collectively share outputs, it is impossible for some not to be advantaged, or to take better advantage, than others.

21.5.3 Embeddedness and Weak and Strong Ties

A key term deployed in the analysis of interfirm networks is embeddedness. This has its contemporary origins in the work of Granovetter (Granovetter 1973, 1985). Embeddedness refers to how socioeconomic actions and outcomes are affected by dyadic relations, and how actors are placed in the overall network structure. This approach emphasizes the ongoing process of construction and reconstruction of interactions in a network context, linking embeddedness to a continuous process of evolutionary change and complexity.

Embeddedness is closely associated with another concept introduced by Granovetter, that of weak ties. Networks benefit from weak or loose ties in a number of ways. They prevent locking-in of close and strong organizational couplings. These can inhibit interactive learning and innovation as actors are given the opportunity to search for other linkages in the network if they are not committed strongly to any single set of relationships. In addition, weak ties help against the establishment of exclusive networks of closely knit insiders who look with suspicion on outsiders and thereby jealously guard their own privileged access to the network resources at all costs. In order to thrive, networks need to share those resources beyond an immediate circle of favored partners. Weaker ties to distant actors prevent an untimely closure of the network. And finally, this allows for some redundancy or slack, so that ineffective ties and relationships can be terminated, and new ones kindled if things do go wrong.

Granovetter emphasizes that size of the network matters only when it adds to the diversity of the connections. More ties by themselves are not useful. It is only if increasing size adds to diversity that it is positively viewed. This is what Burt has phrased the effectiveness of structural holes in networks (Burt 1992). Structural holes refer to the idea that there should not be too much overlap between network participants and clusters that simply duplicate connections to resources. Some redundancy in a network is useful for lubricating the wheels of change. This is particularly so when it involves key links in the structure, the absence of which could otherwise lead to a rapid undermining of the network. Efficiency, by increasing dependency, also increases vulnerability, and can thus contribute to, rather than decrease, the liabilities associated with newness (Steier and Greenwood 2000).

Finally, embeddedness may have a dual specificity in multidimensional networks. In an attempt to empirically establish the nature of the connections between manufacturing and financial firms, for instance, Uzzi has emphasized the benefits of network complementarity in synthesizing the ties between different organizational entities (Uzzi 1997, 1999). Network complementarity relates to an integrated mix of embedded ties and arm's length market ties. The most robust networks, and those that promoted coordinated adaptation, were those combining a judicious mix of the two; a hybrid of networks and markets. Arm's length ties enabled manufacturing firms to reap the benefits of scanning the market for best deals and broker information among banks, and thus avoid the overattentiveness to local resources and inherited conventions. On the other hand, embedded ties offered all the advantages of collaborative knowledge and the longer-term facilities of partnering. Combining these two maximized the range of available action.

21.6 EVOLUTION, BIOLOGY, COMPLEXITY, AND THE SELF-ORGANIZATION OF NETWORKS

Discussion of the way knowledge is generated in interfirm networks does give rise to the consideration of some key theoretical issues. One of the most interesting of these is the extent to which networks may be considered in terms of evolutionary or biological theories of organization. There are two conceptions of this evolutionary economy, both pose the question of how far this process is self-organizing as opposed to consciously organized. In the above discussion networks were characterized in both these terms. In fact they sit rather uneasily between the two. The reason for this has in large part to do with the level of abstraction at which the discussion is pitched and part to do with exactly which analogy of the system is adopted. Two main analogies are discussed: the Darwinian self-selection biological analogy and the evolutionary population ecology analogy (Foster 1997, 2000). Both claim to say something about how self-organization works, which is the focus here.

The Darwinian self-selection analogy is the more conventional of the two. It is biological in origin, concerned with how competition between atomistic units produces evolutionary adaptation and change. This neatly fits with the homo economicus of traditional economic theory. Fitness (profit) is maximized while adverse mutations (inefficiencies) are minimized as competitive selection processes steer the system towards a potential, if only temporary, equilibrium with optimal properties. This process of competition can limit variety as the weak are eliminated and the strong and more efficient rewarded. As a result, homogeneity emerges and economic evolution would, at least temporarily, cease.

Against this can be pitched a version of evolutionary population ecology. This stresses the notion of mutualism (cooperative trade and contracting) over competition as the dynamic of the system. This does not rely on well-developed markets, but on a continual, spontaneous generation of novelty—the work of homo creativus, capturing the creative and adaptive aspects of human behavior and thereby cutting any necessary biological link between selection and variety. Novelty and variety generation become decisive, with competitive selection becoming dependent upon this primary aspect not its progenitor. It is not the market system that generates variety—that is secured by the creativity, innovation, and entrepreneurialism shown by adaptive agents. Rather, the market system presents opportunities to test out variety and novelty. Selective competition follows varietization, not the other way around. There is no equilibrium or disequilibrium operating here, only nonequilibrium involving complex feedback loops that encourage the internalization of selection and adaptation.

Variety is endogenously created, not the result of an encounter with an external environment as in the biological case. Indeed, this endogeneity is one of the defining features of self-organization. There is no arranged external stimulus. Order happens not because of selection but despite it, a function instead of the spontaneous propagation that is self-organization. The learning that is involved in these systems is not, then, equivalent to the classic systems-environment model, where the adaptation of the system to its environment is controlled externally and occurs in the course of a learning process. Rather this is replaced by a systemic closure. This closure is operational in so far as the effects produced by the system are the reasons for the maintenance of systemic organization. Where there is sufficient complexity, the system performs internal self-organization and exerts self-control. The information the system provides thereby on its environment is a system-internal construct. Any reference to outside is merely a special case of self-reference (Krohn, Küppers, and Nowotny 1990: 7).

To establish order, there must be neither too many connections nor too few. Too few, and the network energy is too low, so collapse threatens. But at the limit of full connectivity with every element connected to every other the system becomes hopelessly unstable (Simon 1996). What is needed is a system of loosely coupled connections (a decompositional hierarchy) so that most components receive inputs from only a few of the system's/network's other components enabling change to be isolated into local neighborhoods. This controls the rate of change and establishes order in the network/system.

Clearly, stable states are delicately balanced. The more connections there are and the greater the potential network energy, the more likely the internal system will be thrown into turmoil. And there is a tendency for the system to gravitate towards maximum connectivity or edge of chaos, since this gives it the advantage of maximum energy. But if there are too many of these connections, when the system is perturbed, elements/agents will fly off from one attractor to another. This accounts, then, for both the idea of change in these kinds of networks—they evolve as the system moves from one attractor to another creating new connections—and why the question of stability and order are the flip side of this evolution. The system is always delicately poised between stability and disorder. It can also theoretically account for Granovetter's strength of loose ties idea (Granovetter 1973, 1985). Looser and less dense connections are strengths, necessary for stability and network robustness.

Hence, if networks were genuinely self-organizing, there would be no reason for managerial intervention. The fact that it becomes a reasonable requirement to prevent the descent into chaos raises a genuine issue as to networks' true self-organizing status. Admittedly, if left entirely to themselves these systems would eventually return from chaos, but at what cost and under what circumstances? The temptation to managerially intervene, in an attempt to avoid this cost, is clearly present, and indeed is the main way that this complexity/self-organizational discussion has entered the managerial and organizational literature involving inter-firm relationships (Anderson 1999).

Finally, the capacity for self-organization of networks might best be seen not through the traditional lens of specialization and tacitness, but through that of varietization and formalization. Too much specialization of functions by agents in networks reduces their capacity for pragmatic self-reflectiveness, and too great a taciticity increases the possibility of cognitive entrapment. On the other hand, an emphasis on variety and diversity open up opportunities for agents, and formalization of otherwise tacit practices equally enables concurrent learning between parties, encouraging mutual innovation. This has important implications for the types of industrial districts mentioned above. Traditionally the old craft-based industrial districts relied on a specialization of functions for their competitive advantage (hence the emphasis on flexible specialization). But the new districts need to emphasize pragmatic varietization if they are to preserve their self-organizational flavor and retain their competitive advantage against the large oligopolistic and hierarchically organized firm, or if they are not to retreat into market forms of coordination.

21.7 CONCLUSIONS: THE FATE OF INDUSTRIAL DISTRICTS AND OTHER IMPLICATIONS OF INTERNATIONALIZATION

The earlier discussion of global commodity chains as a form of interorganizational network suggests the importance of discussing the relationship between interorganizational networks and internationalization/globalization more generally. The context for the emergence of networks is not merely regional or national but international. For many, the last of these is decisively important.

In this conclusion, discussion will initially focus on two examples. The first concerns the fate of collaborative industrial districts and the innovation systems they support, along with the issue of national systems of various kinds in which they are set (national business systems, national production systems, national innovations systems, national financial systems). The second example concerns the linked issue of transnational corporations (TNCs) and how these might be reacting to ICT developments as globalization pressures reconfigure their organizational forms into network-like operations.

During the 1980s there was a flurry of new analytical work identifying the importance of industrial districts and regional economies as key elements in the competitiveness of national economies. These industrial districts were argued to embody a new local economy that was robustly organized in networked terms, reliant upon flexible-specialization process technologies and lean-production techniques, and dependent upon the innovativeness of small and medium-sized enterprises.

During the 1990s there was a reaction against this model. The argument developed that these local networked economies were almost uniquely vulnerable to the new forces of globalization (Amin and Robins 1990; Amin and Thrift 1992; Harrison 1994). Rather than offering a different trajectory for economic development and remaining robust in the face of oligopolistically organized corporate giants, local industrial districts were likely to be internationally integrated into global networks dominated by TNCs, shaking out small firms dependent upon tasks no longer performed locally. This was part of a general process of the local being overrun by the global, reconfiguring, and downgrading the former as just a pale outline lurking in the shadow of the latter.

More recent evidence has demonstrated that this pessimistic prognosis is far from the actual outcome. Industrial districts remain alive and continue to thrive. They have quite effectively bounced back from the threat of obscurity announced by the strong globalization thesis (Crouch *et al.* 2001; Whitford 2001). Insofar as TNCs have had an effect on local industrial districts, they may have actually reinforced their competitive advantage rather than undermined it (Hirst and

Thompson 1999: ch. 3). Italian industrial districts in particular, which amounted to something of the paradigm case for the original flexible-specialization and networked industrial district thesis, while having to reinvent themselves around diversification rather than specialization, have nevertheless proved robust enough to compete with whatever the forces of globalization might have thrown at them (Burroni and Trigilia 2001; Locke 1995; Whitford 2001). In different ways, this is true for the other areas and countries mentioned above (Crouch *et al.* 2001).

The second issue raised in the context of globalization is the role attributed to the activities of TNCs, since these are the crucial agents in the dissemination of technological advance and reconfiguring dynamic comparative advantage as be-tween different countries. But TNCs are important for another reason. Their operations in the age of globalization are increasingly being rethought through the metaphor of a network—the network enterprise. The technological transfers that they are involved in controlling, and the wider aspects of their business strategies, are being transformed largely because of increased international invest-ment integration. This is itself heavily aided by the advent of new ICTs, like the Internet, the www, and internal intranets. TNCs are able to effectively operate in this newly internationalized environment precisely because of the advent of these and other communication technologies.

First, what does the idea of a network enterprise mean? One of the most forceful exponents of this development is Castells, who links it to the advent of a new network age:

[this is] the organizational form built around business projects resulting from cooperation between different components of different firms, networking among themselves for the duration of a given business project, and reconfiguring their networks for the implementa-tion of each project. The network enterprise evolved from the combination of various networking strategies. First, the internal decentralization of large corporations, which adopted lean, horizontal structures of cooperation and competition, coordinated around strategic goals for the firm as a whole. Secondly, the cooperation between small and medium sized businesses, pulling together the resources to reach critical mass. Thirdly, the linkage between these small and medium business networks, and the diversified components of large corporations. And, finally, the strategic alliances and partnership between large corporations and their ancillary networks. Taken together, these trends transform business management into a variable geometry of cooperation and competition depending upon time, space, process, and product. (Castells 2001: 67)

Grabher (2001) has suggested that the network enterprise has been adopted in respect to a particular business sector—the US and UK advertising industry—which he calls a project model approach. Such a project model involves time-limited collaborative relationships between parties to complete a specific task which then dissolve as new projects demanding new collaborative partners arise. He argues this is emblematic of wider changes in networking structures that could affect all business relationships as a result of the emergence of ICTs. But while it may operate quite well for creative enterprises in the advertising sector, it does not look an attractive or viable option for the production of complex manufacturing goods, for instance, which require the establishment of enduring and long-term relationships. The characteristics of these longer-term relationships were discussed earlier in this chapter.

For Castells, TNCs are subject to these processes just as much as domestic firms. TNCs are now estimated to conduct up to a third of all international trade in the form of intrafirm trade (that is trade within the boundaries of the firm but which stretch across national frontiers). These intrafirm trade networks have been built on the back of the TNCs' prime activity, the within-firm reorganization of international production networks via the deployment of foreign direct investment. In addition to this, TNCs are increasingly responsible for international financial investments of various kinds (such as M&A activity), for internal-to-the-firm but across border labor deployment (a form of international migration), and for various interfirm partnerships and agreements. All of these can be considered in terms of cross-country networks operating within or between TNCs.

As far as the empirical basis for these networks is concerned, data limitations prevent any clear confirmation that there are robust business networks operating in any depth, though there are signs that large TNCs are spreading their affiliation relationships globally so there is some locational diversification. But there seems still to be high single ownership advantages, and diversified organizational advantages are as yet difficult to discern. Overall, however, Ietto-Gillies (2002) sees a process of international fragmentation amidst integration developing in this field, led by TNCs. In these cases it is the role of ICTs that is stressed as a force for transforming the whole nature of TNC operations and leading the new business networks. In addition, as the discussion of ICTs indicated earlier, the introduction of these technologies might not be quite as transformative as is suggested here.

Finally, the connections between interfirm relationships and networks are strong ones both analytically and empirically, but these should not be viewed as exclusive. However, the network imagery has proved a most robust and enduring one for summing up interfirm relationships. It is the network form that gives other coexistent coordination and governance mechanisms their particular specificity in explaining many interfirm connections, reminding us that complex organizational hybrids require careful analytical elaboration to uncover their subtle characteristics and logic. This can only be done once the specific attributes of interfirm networks have been uncovered.

REFERENCES

AMIN, A., and ROBINS, K. (1990). 'The Re-Emergence of Regional Economies: The Mythical Geography of Flexible Accumulation'. *Environmental Planning D: Society and Space*, 8: 7–34.

——and THRIFT, N. (1992). 'Neo-Marshallian Nodes in Global Networks'. *International Journal of Urban and Regional Research*, 16/4: 571–87.

ANCORI, B., BURETH, A., and COHENDET, P. (2000). 'The Economics of Knowledge: The Debate about Codification and Tacit Knowledge'. *Industrial and Corporate Change*, 9/2: 255–87.

ANDERSON, P. (1999). 'Complexity Theory and Organizational Science'. *Organization Science*, 10/3: 216–32.

BAILY, M. N., and LAWRENCE, R. Z. (2001). 'Do We Have a New E-economy?' *American Economic Review Papers and Proceedings*, May: 308–12.

BURRONI, L., and TRIGILIA, C. (2001). 'Italy: Economic Development through Local Economies', in C. Crouch, P. Le galès, C. Trigila and H. Voelzkow (eds.), *Local Production Systems in Europe: Rise or Demise?* Oxford: Oxford University Press.

BURT, R. S. (1992). *Structural Holes: The Social Structure of Competition*. Boston: Harvard University Press.

CASTELLS, M. (1996). *The Rise of the Network Society*. The Information Age: Economy, Society and Culture, Volume 1. Oxford: Blackwell.

——(2001). *The Internet Galaxy*. Oxford: Oxford University Press.

COOKE, P., and MORGAN, K. (1999). *The Associational Economy*. Oxford: Oxford University Press.

COWAN, R., DAVID, P. A., and FORAY, D. (2000). 'The Explicit Economics of Knowledge Codification and Tacitness'. *Industrial and Corporate Change*, 9/2: 211–53.

CROUCH, C., and FARRELL, H. (2001). 'Great Britain: Falling through the Holes in the Network Concept', in C. Crouch, P. Le galès, C. Trigila and H. Voelzkow (eds.), *Local Production Systems in Europe: Rise or Demise?* Oxford: Oxford University Press.

——LE GALÈS, P., TRIGILIA, C., and VOELZKOW, H. (eds.) (2001). *Local Production Systems in Europe: Rise or Demise?* Oxford: Oxford University Press.

FOSTER, J. (1997). 'The Analytical Foundations of Evolutionary Economics: From Biological Analogy to Economic Self-Organization'. *Structural Change and Economic Dynamics*, 8: 427–51.

——(2000). 'Competitive Selection, Self-Organization and Joseph A. Schumpeter'. *Evolutionary Economics*, 7: 311–28.

GEREFFI, G. (1999). 'International Trade and Industrial Upgrading in the Apparel Commodity Chain'. *Journal of International Economics*, 48: 37–70.

——(2001a). 'Beyond the Producer-Driven/Buyer-Driven Dichotomy: The Evolution of Global Value Chains in the Internet Era'. *IDS Bulletin*, 32/3: 30–40.

——(2001b). 'Shifting Governance in Global Commodity Chains with Special Reference to the Internet'. *American Behavioral Scientist*, 44/10: 1616–37.

——and KORZENIEWICZ, M. (eds.) (1994). *Commodity Chains and Global Capitalism*. Westport, Conn.: Praeger Publishers.

GRABHER, G. (2001). 'Ecologies of Creativity: The Village, the Group, and the Hierarchic Organization of the British Advertising Industry'. *Environment and Planning A*, 33: 351–74.

GRANDORI, A., and SODA, G. (1995). 'Inter-Firm Networks: Antecedents, Mechanisms and Forms'. *Organization Studies*, 16/2: 183–214.

GRANOVETTER, M. (1973). 'The Strength of Weak Ties'. *American Journal of Sociology*, 78: 1360–80.

——(1985). 'Economic Action and Social Structure: The Problem of Embeddedness'. *American Journal of Sociology*, 91: 481–510.

HAGEDOORN, J. (1990). 'Organizational Modes in Inter-Firm Cooperation and Technological Transfer'. *Technovation*, 10/1: 17–30.

—— and SCHAKENRAAD, J. (1990). 'Strategic Partnering and Technological Cooperation', in B. Dankbaar, J. Groenewegen, and H. Schnek (eds.), *Perspectives in Industrial Economics*. Dordrecht: Kluwer.

HARRISON, B. (1994). *Lean and Mean*. New York: Basic Books.

HENDERSON, J., DICKEN, P., HESS, M., COE, N., and WAI-CHUNG YEUNG, H. (2002). 'Global Production Networks and the Analysis of Economic Development'. University of Manchester: Mimeographed.

HIRST, P. Q., and THOMPSON, G. F. (1999). *Globalization in Question* (2nd edn). Cambridge: Polity Press.

—— and ZEITLIN, J. (eds.) (1989). *Reversing Industrial Decline?* Oxford: Berg.

————(1991). 'Flexible Specialization versus Post-Fordism: Theory, Evidence and Policy'. *Economy and Society*, 20/1: 1–56.

IDS (Institute for Development Studies) (2001). 'The Value of Value Chains: Spreading the Gains from Globalization'. *IDS Bulletin Special Issue*, 32/3: July.

IETTO-GILLIES, G. (2002). *Transnational Corporations: Fragmentation amidst Integration*. London: Routledge.

JOHNSTON, R., and LAWRENCE, P. R. (1988). 'Beyond Vertical Integration—The Rise of the Value-Adding Partnership'. *Harvard Business Review*, July–August: 94–101.

KAPLINSKI, R., and MORRIS, M. (2001). *A Handbook for Value Chain Analysis*. Brighton: Institute of Development Studies.

KLIER, T. H. (1999). 'Agglomeration in the US Auto Supply Industry'. *Economic Perspectives*. Chicago: Federal Reserve Bank of Chicago.

KROHN, W., KÜPPERS, G., and NOWOTNY, H. (eds.) (1990). *Self-Organization: Portrait of a Scientific Revolution*. Dordrecht: Kluwer Academic Publishers.

LAZARIC, N. (2000). 'The Role of Routines, Rules and Habits in Collective Learning: Some Epistemological and Ontological Considerations'. *European Journal of Economic and Social Systems*, 14/2: 157–71.

LEAMER, E., and STORPER, M. (2001). 'The Economic Geography of the Internet Age'. *Journal of International Business*, 32/4: 641–65.

LEONCINI, R., and MONTRESOR, S. (2000). 'Network Analysis of Eight Technological Systems'. *International Review of Applied Economics*, 14/2: 315–34.

LOCKE, R. M. (1995). *Remaking the Italian Economy*. Ithaca, NY: Cornell University Press.

LUCKING-REILEY, D., and SPULBER, D. F. (2001). 'Business-to-Business Electronic Commerce'. *Journal of Economic Perspectives*, 15/1: 55–68.

MORITA, H., and NAKAHARA, H. (2002). 'Impacts of the Information-Technology Revolution on Japanese Manufacture–Supplier Relationships'. Mimeographed.

PIORE, M., and SABEL, C. (1984). *The Second Industrial Divide*. New York: Basic Books.

PORTER, M. (1985). *Competitive Advantage: Creating and Sustaining Superior Advantage*. Basingstoke: Macmillan.

—— (1990). *The Competitive Advantage of Nations*. Basingstoke: Macmillan.

RAIKES, P., FRIIS JENSEN, M., and PONTE, S. (2000). 'Global Commodity Chain Analysis and the French Filiere Approach: Comparison and Critique'. *Economy and Society*, 29/3: 390–417.

RILES, A. (2001). *The Network Inside Out*. Ann Arbor: University of Michigan Press.

SABEL, C. (1989). 'Flexible Specialization and the Re-Emergence of Industrial Districts', in P. Q. Hirst and J. Zeitlin (eds.), *Reversing Industrial Decline? Industrial Structure and Policy in Britain and Her Competitors*. Oxford: Berg.

—— (1991). 'Moebius Strip Organizations and Open Labour Markets', in P. Bourdieu and J. S. Coleman (eds.), *Social Theory for a Changing Society*. Boulder, Colo.: Westview Press.

—— (2001). 'Diversity, Not Specialization: The Ties That Bind the (New) Industrial Districts'. Conference paper, Complexity and Industrial Clusters: Dynamics and Models in Theory and Practice. Milan, June 19–20.

—— HERRIGEL, G., and KERN, H. (1990). 'Collaborative Manufacturing', in H. G. Mendius and U. Wendeling-Schröder (eds.), *Zulieferer im Netz-Zwischen Abhängigkeit und Pärlnerschaft*. Köln: Bund Verlag.

SHACHAR, J., and ZUSCOVITCH, E. (1990). 'Learning Patterns within a Technological Network: The Case of the European Space Program', in B. Dankbaar, J. Groenewegen, and H. Schenk (eds.), *Perspectives in Industrial Organization*. Dordrecht: Kluwer Academic Publishers.

SIMON, H. A. (1996). *The Sciences of the Artificial* (3rd edn). Cambridge, Mass.: MIT Press.

STEIER, L., and GREENWOOD, R. (2000). 'Entrepreneurship and the Evolution of Angel Financial Networks'. *Organization Studies*, 21/10: 163–92.

THOMPSON, G. F. (2003). *Between Hierarchies and Markets: The Logic and Limits of Network Forms of Organization*. Oxford: Oxford University Press.

UZZI, B. (1997). 'Social Structure and Competition in Interfirm Networks: The Paradox of Embeddedness'. *Administrative Sciences Quarterly*, 42: 35–57.

—— (1999). 'Embeddedness in the Making of Financial Capital: How Social Relations and Networks Benefit Firms Seeking Financing'. *American Journal of Sociology*, 64/4: 481–505.

VENABLES, A. J. (2001). 'Geography and International Inequalities: The Impact of New Technologies'. Background paper for Globalization, Growth and Poverty. World Bank, Washington, 2002.

WHITFORD, J. (2001). 'The Decline of a Model? Challenge and Response in Italian Industrial Districts'. *Economy and Society*, 30/1: 38–65.

WILLIAMSON, O. E. (1975). *Markets and Hierarchies: Analysis and Antitrust Implications*. New York: Free Press.

—— (1994). 'Transaction Cost Economics and Organization Theory', in N. J. Smelser and R. Swedberg (eds.), *The Handbook of Economic Sociology*. Princeton: Princeton University Press.

WISE, R., and MORRISON, D. (2000). 'Beyond the Exchange: The Future of B2B'. *Harvard Business Review*, November–December: 88–96.

CHAPTER 22

....

CHANGES IN THE ORGANIZATION OF PUBLIC SERVICES AND THEIR EFFECTS ON EMPLOYMENT RELATIONS

....

ROBERT HEBDON

IAN KIRKPATRICK

22.1 INTRODUCTION

....

FEW observers would dispute the fact that radical changes have been attempted in the funding and organization of public services in most developed countries. Some argue that established modes of public administration are being superseded by a new global paradigm of public management (OECD 1995; Osborne and Gaebler 1992). Increasingly the trend is said to be away from 'outmoded traditional ways of organizing and conducting public business towards up-to-date, state-of-the-art methods and styles' (Hood 1998: 196). Such change is thought to have had implications for employment relations. According to Farnham and Horton (1996: 331) traditions of paternalism, emphasizing fairness and employee welfare, have given way to a harder more rationalist style of management. The primary goal of the state as employer is now one of achieving effective job performance, high quality of output, service to customers, and value for money.

However, questions remain as to how far these moves to restructure or modernize public services have been translated into practice (Lynn 1998). A growing body of research points to the resilience of older forms of public administration and underlying values. There are also numerous studies that question the idea of convergence between national systems (Bach 1999; Flynn and Strehl 1996; Hood 1995; Kickert 1997; Pollitt and Boukaert 2000). These emphasize the way national institutions and political dynamics are likely to shape the timing, pace, and content of restructuring. In this light talk about 'a public services version of the "End of History"' seems at best premature and ill-founded (Bach and Della Rocca 2000: 95).

In this chapter our aim is to present a critical overview of recent debates about the nature and consequences of public sector restructuring. To do so we first describe some of the main characteristics of public service organizations and how these have been largely embedded in national-level institutions and policy traditions. Following this, the chapter analyses the forces that have driven restructuring and looks at how, in most developed countries, change has been associated with attempts to reshape public services through privatization and management reform. Finally we turn to the question of the consequences of this process for employment relations and joint regulation in public services.

22.2 THE NATURE AND SCOPE OF PUBLIC SECTOR SERVICES

22.2.1 The Organization of Public Services

There is considerable variety in the way public services are organized. Across OECD countries there are obvious differences in the structure of each nation's public sector. In federal states (Germany, Australia, and the United States) regional and local administrations take responsibility for the bulk of services. In centralized unitary states (France, the United Kingdom) the tendency is for control to be concentrated at high levels (OECD 1997b). National systems also vary in the extent to which public services are administered through a hierarchy (at central or local levels) or though quasi-contractual relationships. In some countries (such as France and, until the early 1990s, the United Kingdom) decision making was traditionally centralized with a high degree of vertical integration between policy-making, planning, and service provision. Elsewhere public services have been more fragmented in overall structure. In The Netherlands many services (including health, social security, education, and justice) are provided by nonprofit, para-governmental agencies with semi-independent legal status (Flynn and Strehl 1996: 87–8). In the United States, federal government also failed to develop a unified structure with core functions dispersed between cabinet departments, independent executive agencies, independent regulatory commissions, and public corporations (Peters 1995).

For many, public sector organization is typically an approximation to Weber's (1947) ideal type of bureaucracy (Schofield 2001). Civil service administrations have tended to be hierarchical, with specialization, formalization, rigid career structures based on merit and seniority and a focus on standard rules and procedures. Linked to this has been the dominance of a set of administrative values or doctrines that reinforce and justify bureaucratic behavior. Hood and Jackson (1991) refer to theta-type administrative values stressing the importance of fairness, honesty, integrity, transparency, and democratic accountability. From this perspective bureaucracy is judged to be a most appropriate mode of organizing not only to coordinate services but also to combat favoritism, corruption, and political interference in the work of officials (Du Gay 2000).

Some public organizations have tended to be less bureaucratic than others (Hoggett 1994). This is true of labor-intensive services such as health, education, and social care. These services, employing large numbers of qualified professionals, are different from pure bureaucracies. They involve what Clarke and Newman (1997) describe as a bureau-professional mode of organizing. A key feature of this arrangement is that, within broad legal and financial constraints, producer groups are able to exercise degrees of autonomy over the means and (sometimes) ends of service delivery. Such autonomy results from the complex and inherently discretionary nature of the tasks being performed. But also important is the success many professions have had in negotiating and defending special privileges. Crucial to this is a powerful service ethic or ideology emphasizing the trustworthiness of the professions and both the necessity and desirability of a form of control based on self-regulation and limited managerial interference (Friedson 1994; Wilding 1982).

Distinctive variations in bureaucracy can also be linked to national institutions and state traditions. An important distinction is often made between administrative systems influenced by notions of Rechtstaat (prevalent in central Europe and Germany) and those common in the Anglo-Saxon world shaped by values of public interest (Pollitt and Boukaert 2000: 52–4; Ridley 1996). In the former the state is regarded as a central integrating force within society (a kind of transcendent entity) focused on the development and perpetuation of laws (R. Rhodes 2000: 70). Within this tradition civil servants are not merely public employees but legitimate representatives of state authority (subject to statute and administrative law). Also implied is a form of legalistic bureaucracy far closer to the Weberian ideal that might be found in the United States or the United Kingdom. Much greater emphasis is placed on ensuring conformity with rules and norms and pursuing change only if it is first sanctioned through wider changes in the overarching legal framework (Flynn and Strehl 1996: 12).

22.2.2 Types of Welfare Regimes

These differences in public services can be explained by the institutional characteristics of each country and the nature of welfare regimes (Zeltin 2003). Esping-Anderson (1990) argues that it is possible to generalize about a small number of welfare state forms, each characterized by different sociopolitical origins and degrees of decommodification (the extent to which social rights are detached from market forces). Focusing on the experience of Sweden, Germany, and the United States, he identifies three dominant regimes of welfare capitalism—social democratic, conservative, and liberal. These, he argues, have important consequences for the nature and extent of public service provision (with social democratic and conservative regimes, on the whole, being far more generous than liberal) and for levels of state employment. Important for the latter is not only the size of public spending but also the orientation of a regime, or the extent to which welfare is provided through direct wage employment or some other means (Rubery and Grimshaw 2003: 92).

From this perspective the social democratic or Nordic states have been prone to develop a large public sector workforce. Here 'the provision of benefits and services (including a vast range of health and social services) is under the direct responsibility of (central and local) public authorities' (Ferrara 1998: 83). In conservative regimes high levels of public expenditure (close to around 50 percent of GDP in France, Germany, and The Netherlands) do not always translate into direct employment. In this context more emphasis is placed on achieving welfare goals through transfer payments to families than direct provision funded out of taxation. There is also a greater role played by social partners and nonprofit organizations in the management and delivery of public services (Ferrara 1998: 86). Finally, in liberal regimes (the United States and Australia) the tendency has been to rely on a residual welfare state with minimal investment in direct provision through wage employment and a greater reliance on the private sector. The only exception to this has been the United Kingdom, which developed a welfare model based on universal citizen entitlements funded from direct taxation and with the central and local state acting as a near monopoly provider (Harris and McDonald 2000; Wincott 2001).

Regime characteristics therefore account for many differences in the level of public sector organization and employment. But added to this must be some recognition of the role of contingent political factors. In some southern European countries, the state has historically acted as an employer of last resort, public sector expansion being used explicitly to mop up unemployment and maintain macroeconomic stability (Bach 1999). Political dynamics have also been important in determining levels of public ownership of utilities or commercial enterprises (Lane 1997). In France waves of political enthusiasm for direct state intervention in economic planning (the most recent being in 1982) led to a marked expansion of the public enterprise sector. Even in the late 1990s this sector remained important, with approximately 1.5 million employees (Mosse and Tchobanian 1999).

22.3 RESTRUCTURING PUBLIC SERVICES

Despite these differences in the organization of the state sector, there have been sustained efforts in developed countries to restructure public services, to control expenditure, and, through measures such as privatization, to reduce the size and scope of the state sector. Related to this have been attempts to implement new forms of management and organization within public services. These developments have had important consequences for the nature of employment relations. But prior to considering these, it is necessary to outline the forces driving change.

22.3.1 General Pressures for Change

In recent literature on state restructuring, emphasis is placed on broad macroeconomic pressures as key drivers of change. This kind of explanation begins with the notion of a state fiscal crisis (Foster and Plowden 1996; O'Connor 1973). Fiscal crisis, it is argued, intensified from the mid-1970s as levels of public expenditure in developed countries grew at a rate that outstripped revenues from taxation. In the United Kingdom between 1965 and 1975, social expenditure grew at 5.9 percent per annum (deflated), while the growth rate of GDP was only 2.6 percent (Pollitt 1993: 29). This process coincided with a period of rising inflation, unemployment, and sluggish economic growth in a context of worldwide recession. Added to this were increasingly unfavorable demographic trends (population aging) and growing citizen demands for improvements in the quality of public services (Clarke and Newman 1997). These developments are said to have placed all nation-states under pressure to control public expenditure, or at least be seen to be doing so, for purposes of legitimation (Flynn 2000).

Related to the above are demands for change arising from wider shifts in the global economy. It is argued that the globalization of capital markets and the expansion of international trade reduced the room for maneuver of nation-states. Increasingly governments had less freedom to pursue demand-led macro-economic policies, especially if these involved raising public expenditure through taxation (OECD 1997b). For many, such change implies nothing less than a radical shift in the role of the nation-state (Burnham 1999; Palan and Abbott 1996; Whitfield 2001). Jessop (1994: 263), for example, talks about the emergence of a hollowed-out neo-Schumpeterian workfare state in which the focus is on a 'productivist reordering of social policy'. In such a state, government interest shifts decisively towards supply-side policies aimed at promoting national competitiveness. The emphasis is on seeking to reduce the burden of welfare expenditure and improving efficiency.

These pressures have made some kind of restructuring of welfare regimes unavoidable. However, as Hood (1995: 103–4) reminds us, there is no straight correlation between the macroeconomic performance of nation-states and the likelihood of restructuring. Countries with relatively healthy economies, such as Sweden and Switzerland, were just as willing to change as those with rising levels of national debt and unemployment. It is also notable that it is in the United States, with a minimal welfare state (public expenditure never exceeding 33 percent of GDP through most of the 1980s and 1990s), where demands to reform government have been most vocal (Flynn 2000).

These observations have led to calls for a nuanced and less deterministic account of state restructuring. Central to this is an understanding of how broad macroeconomic demands have been mediated through national state institutions and how change is likely to be path dependent. Linked to this is a need to acknowledge the role of political dynamics in driving (or hindering) change. As Pollitt and Boukaert (2000) suggest, the timing, pace, and content of restructuring in each country has been determined in large part by the willingness of political elites to act.

22.4 THE EXTENT AND NATURE OF PUBLIC SECTOR RESTRUCTURING

From the mid-1980s many states sought ways of reducing (or minimizing) the overall cost of services (Whitfield 2001). This was pursued by strengthening the hand of central finance ministries to impose cash limits on spending (Pollitt and Boukaert 2000), targeting services and benefits (through means testing) or cutting services and transferring responsibility to individuals and families (Ferrarra 1998; Ferrara and Hemerijck 2003). These policies were adopted in most OECD countries, but taken furthest in liberal regimes such as the United States, New Zealand, and the United Kingdom. In the United Kingdom there has been a steady downsizing in the level of entitlements to benefits and services (especially for health, social care, and housing) since the mid-1980s, a trend not significantly reversed under the current Labour government (M. Rhodes 2000).

Associated with this process of cost minimization were attempts to reshape the management and organization of public services. One aspect of this was a movement across developed countries to privatize public services. Also important were attempts to adopt managed forms of service delivery and the practice of reorganization. In what follows each of these changes is described in more detail.

22.4.1 Privatization

The most extreme way sought to reshape the public sector is through privatization (Pitelis and Clarke 1993), the transfer of ownership to the private sector through the sale of stock. This has been undertaken extensively when state-owned public utilities (public utilities and transport, telecommunications, financial services) have been transferred to private ownership; The impact has been considerable: over the past twenty years the size of the public enterprise sector fell by approximately 50 percent in developed industrial nations (OECD 2000a: 154). However, it is important to note variations between countries in the pace of change. During the 1990s the highest rates of privatization were in the United Kingdom, Australia, France, Germany, Italy, Japan, and Spain. In the United States there has been less activity, probably because there was less nationalized industry in the first place. Nevertheless the backwardness of the United States in this respect may soon change with the start of ambitious plans announced in November 2002 to privatize as many as 850 federal government jobs. Under the initiative, private contractors will be able to compete with current government non-management employees.

Given that public provision of services is the dominant form of service delivery in the United States and private provision (in theory) appears to be more cost-efficient, researchers have tried to answer the question of why more services have not been privatized (Lopez-de-Silanes and Vishny 1997). As a restructuring form, privatization has undoubtedly commanded interest, due to the specification of the restructuring decision as a dichotomy between keeping services public and shifting them to the private sector. Focusing on the case of New York State, Warner and Hebdon (2001) discovered that the decision by local government to change the form of service delivery is more complex than a choice between public and private provision. Despite the avowed political commitment to privatization (Lauder 1992) only 17 out of 133 counties and townships surveyed had introduced such change by 1996. Many respondents indicated their governments had pursued other strategies short of privatization to achieve similar goals. Warner and Hebdon (2001) distinguish four: intermunicipal cooperation (mutual aid, joint production, creation of a special district, or contracting with another governmental unit); reverse privatization (contracting back in); governmental entrepreneurship (government contracts its services to private or nonprofit sector clients); and cessation of services.

22.4.2 Management Reform

There have also been moves to shift from traditional public service administration to managed provision. This strategy originated in the United States and United Kingdom but later spread more widely, including to countries with strong trad-itions of state administration such as Sweden and Denmark (Flynn and Strehl 1996; Hood 1995). By the mid-1990s ideas about management reform had become mainstream, articulated and widely disseminated by consultants, academics, think tanks, and a range of international agencies, including the IMF, the World Bank, and the OECD. A key feature of change has been to persuade public organizations to adopt similar practices to those of private firms, to develop strong executive management roles, creating more visible, active, and individualistic forms of leadership (Ferlie *et al.* 1996). Managers, it is argued, must be given discretionary powers to challenge the power of professionals and unions and if necessary alter work organization. Also implied is the adoption of techniques and practices from the corporate sector, such as financial control and accounting systems.

Interest in management reform was fuelled by a critique of existing modes of public administration (Aucoin 1990). Public choice theorists argued that public organizations were captured by self-interested, budget maximizing producer groups (such as officials, professionals, and trade unions) and were therefore inefficient. Others focused on more general failings of bureaucracy as a mode of coordination that was incapable of change. Osborne and Gaebler (1992: 11) suggest that 'centralised bureaucracies ... no longer work very well' and have become 'bloated, wasteful, ineffective'. Almost everywhere attention is focused on the so-called weaknesses of the public service employment model. This was seen to be inflexible and hierarchical, producing a workforce that is over protected, incompetent, and poorly motivated (OECD 1995).

Emerging from this critique came numerous proposals for the reform of public organizations collectively known as New Public Management (NPM) (Hood 1991; Metcalf and Richards 1990; McLaughlin, Osborne, and Ferlie 2002; Pollitt 1993). The literature disagrees over what NPM stands for, although most tend to refer to the classic formulation of it first proposed by Hood (1991). According to Hood (1991) NPM is rooted in sigma-type values emphasizing the need to match resources to tasks, focusing on avoiding waste, and increasing efficiency. More specifically the NPM implies a departure from two core principles of older administration. First is the idea that the public sector should converge with and seek to emulate the structures and management practices found in corporate firms. Second is the assumption that public services will operate more effectively if managers are empowered and not fenced in by explicit standards and rules (Hood 1995: 95).

Recently doubts have been expressed about the extent to which NPM represents a coherent program of reform (Lynn 1998). One problem concerns the appropriateness of exporting private sector management values and practices into the public domain (Stewart and Walsh 1992). Following Allison (1979) many argue that public and private sectors are alike in all unimportant aspects and that attempts to transfer practice will be difficult and costly. Beyond this are questions about the internal consistency of the NPM package itself (McLaughlin, Osborne, and Ferlie 2002; Newman 2000). Finally, despite its claim to have universal appeal, it is argued that NPM ideas are deeply rooted in the North American culture of business management (Kickert 1997: 38). This may limit their relevance in the European context.

These criticisms are important in debunking the myth that NPM represents a coherent global paradigm for reform. However, looking across the OECD, it is possible to identify common themes that have informed processes of management restructuring.

22.4.3 Organizational Restructuring

Accompanying the development of NPM has been the reorganization of public sector services. Across developed countries (OECD 1995) there have been moves to break up monolithic and centralized public service organizations into smaller, specialized quasi-autonomous agencies or business units. This led to the decentralization of various management and budgetary responsibilities to lower level organizations or (in many continental European states) tiers of government. Also implied is a shift in the mode of control, from a system based on hierarchy to one rooted in quasi-contractual relationships between central government and semi-autonomous agencies (Hoggett 1994). As one might expect, the extent of reorganization varied between states, being most profound in the United Kingdom and New Zealand. It should also be noted that not all countries began to change from the same starting point. In the United States, as noted earlier, management and political responsibility for many public services have traditionally been devolved and fragmented (Peters 1995).

A further aspect of reorganization was the attempt to extend market disciplines into the public domain. In Europe and North America it has been widely assumed that de facto, contract-based competitive provision should be substituted for bureaucracy wherever possible (Hood 1995: 96). In France, Germany, and Spain this led to piecemeal moves to contract out services such as hospital catering, garbage collection, and highway maintenance (Bach and Della Rocca 2000: 90–1). By contrast, in the United Kingdom outsourcing was extended to professional services (Colling 2000) and, most recently, under the private finance initative, to the running of entire schools or departments within hospitals (Grimshaw, Vincent, and Willmott 2002). Even in those services not subject to privatization, there have been growing pressures to become more competitive (Hoggett 1994). One aspect of this is policies, such as those adopted in health care services in the United Kingdom and Denmark, leading to the construction of internal markets and formalized purchaser and provider roles within public organizations (Le Grand and Bartlett 1993).

Despite political enthusiasm for markets in public services, evidence that such change produces cost savings or improved quality remains thin. In the United States, studies show some subcontracting cost savings, others indicate cost increases after subcontracting (i.e. municipal services could be provided cheaper by public employees), but most show no significant differences between the costs of private, contracted-out services and those provided by municipal employees (Hebdon 1995). Research conducted in the United Kingdom also casts doubt on the idea that outsourcing has universally delivered cost savings and improvements in services. Boyne (1998) notes rising transaction costs associated with contracting for street cleaning and refuse collection in local government that largely cancel out short-term efficiency gains.

22.5 CONSEQUENCES OF RESTRUCTURING

Given moves to downsize public services, it might be expected that levels of public service employment would decrease. Indeed, if one focuses on aggregate statistics compiled by the OECD, this does appear to be the case (OECD 2001). In many countries, including those with a strong commitment to public services (Germany and Sweden), public service employment as a proportion of the total did fall during the 1990s. This was also the case in the United Kingdom, where the proportion declined from 19.5 percent in 1990 to 12.6 percent in 1999. To avoid layoffs, many governments offered hiring freezes, early retirements, transfers, and other voluntary departure incentives.

However this downward trend should not be exaggerated. With the exception of the United Kingdom and New Zealand, the fall in public services employment has not been dramatic. Even in the United States, a country where political elites expressed anxiety over public spending, employment levels in the late 1990s remained roughly the same as in 1985 (around 15 percent) (ibid.). One should also note that in some countries—Spain, France, and Finland—the size of the workforce grew during the 1990s. Finally it is also possible that official statistics exaggerate the nature of decline, especially when they fail to account for transfers of public service workers to newly established agencies or public enterprises (OECD 1997a).

In terms of overall employment, therefore, the impact of public service restructuring has not been that dramatic. However a key question is whether or not this also applies to the way in which employment relations are managed? In what remains of this section, our aim is to address this matter. To do so the following are considered: the nature of personnel policy and practice, joint regulation, and the impact of outsourcing.

22.5.1 The State as Employer: Changes in Personnel Policy and Practice

In many countries the trend was for employment relations in the public sector to be distinct from those of private firms (Farnham and Horton 1996; Sparrow and Hiltrop 1994). This was reflected most obviously in high levels of job security and employment protection enjoyed by public service employees. In some countries (France, Germany, and Spain) civil servants were (and remain) tenured, subject to separate statute and administrative rather than private employment law. Closely related to this is an emphasis on strong internal labor markets in public services (Bach and Della Rocca 2000: 83; Wise 1996). In many countries a majority of senior posts in public administration continue to be reserved exclusively for those who have risen up a civil service hierarchy. Finally one finds in many countries a style and ethos of personnel management in the public sector (Bach 1999). In the United Kingdom this took the form of a paternalistic approach towards staff and an explicit emphasis on the state acting as a progressive or model employer (Fredman and Morris 1989). Implied were policies aimed at ensuring continuity of employment, procedural fairness in collective bargaining, investment in training and development, and equal opportunities (Colling 2001: 601).

To be sure, in most developed countries this model of personnel practice did not apply universally. In Europe traditionally there has been a high degree of segmentation within the public service workforce with clearly defined core and periphery groups. In Germany, for example, only a fraction of the total workforce (32 percent) enjoys the full legal status (and protection) of core civil servants (Beamte) (Rober 1996: 171–2). In many countries significant numbers of public service employees (mainly women) are employed on nonstandard (part-time/temporary) terms and conditions. These facts remind us that while public services employment was (and in many respects, still is) distinct, some of the benefits that flow from it have been unequally distributed.

It is now widely believed that many aspects of traditional people management in public services have been eroded. One aspect of this has been to reduce employment protection and tenure of career civil servants and weaken internal labor markets through more open recruitment at senior levels (Bach 1999). This change was marked in New Zealand and, to a lesser extent, the United Kingdom. In New Zealand, the 1988 State Services Act abolished the notion of a unified civil service transferring responsibility for the determination of employment conditions to the chief executive of each department (Boston, Pallot, and Walsh 1996). In continental Europe there have also been moves in this direction. In Italy a far-reaching reform was introduced in 1993 privatizing the employment relationship, placing civil servants on the same employment contracts as their counterparts in the private sector (Bordogna, Dell'Arigna, and Della Rocca 1999).

Running parallel have been downward pressures in many countries on the level of compensation of public sector employees. In Canada a primary focus of restructuring was on controlling labor costs, as these ranged from 65 to 85 percent of total costs (Rose 1995). In the 1990s three models of wage restraint emerged: legislated controls (e.g. federal, New Brunswick, Newfoundland, and Manitoba); hard bargaining (e.g. Saskatchewan and the local level in most provinces); and a third alternative, the Ontario New Democratic Party government's social contract (Swimmer and Thompson 1995). In the United Kingdom, central governments also sought to hold down public sector pay through tight cash limits and annual targets for efficiency gains in national agreements (Colling 2001; White 1999). One consequence has been to significantly restrict the growth of pay in public services relative to the private sector (Elliott and Duffus 1996).

Related have been attempts to introduce human resource management techniques into the public sector. In the United Kingdom, for instance, there has been interest in techniques such as team working, total quality management, and business process reengineering—although the extent to which these have altered practice is questionable (Cully *et al.* 1999; Foster and Hoggett 1999). More generally, across developed countries, there has been experimentation with systems of variable or performance-related pay in public services (Hood 1995: 98; OECD 2000*b*). One can therefore find evidence of restructuring leading to changes in personnel policy, gradually eroding the distinction between employment relations in the public and private sectors. However it is important to recognize that these tendencies are not universal. In many countries, including Germany and France, civil service reforms have been piecemeal and strongly resisted. Even in the United States, despite the rhetoric of modernizing government, little progress has been made in practice.

22.5.2 Joint Regulation

When focusing on joint regulation in public services a starting point is to understand how national systems continue to be shaped by state policies and wider institutions of collective bargaining and codetermination (Ferner and Hyman 1998). In countries like France and Spain, union density has historically been low (approximately 10 percent of civil servants in France), while in the United Kingdom one finds high levels of unionization (61 percent in 1997). Even in the United States where, in recent years, unions have been placed under pressure (Appelbaum and Batt 1994), density levels remain high in comparison to the private sector.

This picture of divergence also applies to the arena of collective bargaining and pay determination (Olsen 1996). According to Traxler, Blaschke, and Kittel (2001), it is possible to identify three patterns of joint regulation in public services. First are those countries where collective bargaining is the sole or primary method of determining pay and employment terms and conditions (as in Denmark, Italy, and Sweden). A second approach includes states such as Spain, Austria, and The Netherlands where, until recently, government has tended to determine employment conditions unilaterally. Here unions might organize but are permitted only consultative rights. Finally, it is possible to identify a mixed pattern of regulation consisting of both collective bargaining and unilateral regulation. This latter model applies to Germany where two distinct subsystems exist, one for core civil servants (subject to administrative law) and another for public employees, based on joint regulation (Keller 1999). The United Kingdom also combines long-standing institutions for peak-level collective bargaining (the Whitley council system) with a variety of national pay review bodies (for groups such as police doctors and teachers) (Bach and Winchester 2003).

Where collective bargaining institutions exist one finds variation in their level and scope. With regard to level the trend in many countries has been for bargaining to be highly centralized, conducted at national levels (ILO 1997). This is true even of the United Kingdom, despite the fact that in the private sector the trend has been towards decentralized, enterprise-level bargaining (Winchester and Bach 1999). However, not all national systems are equally centralized. In the United States, while the terms and conditions of some groups of federal employees are centrally negotiated, this does not apply to the public sector as a whole (Katz and Kochan 1992). Here there is greater emphasis on collective bargaining and pay determination at state, county, or city level. In twenty-four states there are comprehensive laws that impose a duty to bargain on public employers for all public employees—state, teacher, police, fire, and other municipal employees.

We should note differences in the scope or coverage of collective bargaining. Given the points already made, it is not surprising that in some countries (such as Sweden or Italy) there is wide, almost universal coverage. Elsewhere collective bargaining is restructured to selective groups and issues. In the United States, there are numerous public sector labor laws that limit the scope of bargaining for public employees under archaic notions of sovereignty (Hebdon 1994). Unlike private sector collective bargaining, most public employee unions do not have a legal right to strike. As a matter of policy, the services provided are viewed as too essential to permit disruptions. Strikes may threaten health and safety. Even in states where public sector strikes are legal, strikes may be stopped by injunction if thought to pose a threat to public security and welfare. In the United States, bargaining is also noteworthy for its restricted scope. By 1977, 28 states had management rights clauses enshrined in law (Hebdon 1994). At the federal level Title VII of the Civil Service Reform Act effectively bans wages and benefits from the bargaining table.

Turning to the impact of restructuring a complex picture emerges of change and continuity. In many countries the model of centralized collective bargaining was strongly criticized in the 1990s and became a focus of reform (Corby and White 1999: 18). One aspect of this was an attempt to decentralize pay determination to regional or organizational levels. In the United Kingdom, limited regional pay bargaining in the 1980s gave way to more radical policies aimed at devolving bargaining for employment conditions and some aspects of pay to local authorities, executive agencies, and NHS trusts in the 1990s (White 1999). In some continental European states—such as Denmark—one can note similar, albeit less radical, moves to weaken the regulatory impact of national agreements (Bach and Della Rocca 2000).

A further change worth noting is with regard to procedures for conflict resolution in public services (Hebdon 1996). In some states public sector bargaining is regulated by detailed legal arrangements that aim to minimize the risk of strike action. In the United States, there has been considerable experimentation in this area over the past twenty years (McKersie 1988). Procedures such as interest-based bargaining abound at federal, state, and local levels of government covering a wide range of occupations from blue-collar municipal employees in Wisconsin to clerical and administrative employees in the Federal Department of Labor. In Wisconsin, the Wisconsin Employment Relations Commission (WERC 1992) offers training in consensus bargaining, a problem-solving approach to negoti- ations and dispute resolution. However, in recent years, public sector strikes declined and new issues of concern emerged, associated with wage freezes, layoffs, restructuring, contingent workers, privatization, and employee benefits. In this environment policymakers have reassessed the necessity of procedures that focus on avoiding strike outcomes, and not the process for dealing with change and adjustment. There have also been secular declines in strike frequency and the number of workers involved in many countries. What appeared a few years ago as acceptable dispute resolution methods are increasingly under assault from taxpayers, employers, and politicians.

There are therefore important indications of change in the nature of joint regulation in public services. But it would be a mistake to exaggerate this trend. In some countries, notably in France and Germany, there have been no significant moves to decentralize collective bargaining for core public services staff. Even in the United Kingdom, national frameworks for pay determination and tight fiscal controls remain important (Colling 2001). This has led many to refer to 'the apparent paradox of increased central control set against the Conservative govern- ment's rhetorical support for management devolution' (Bach and Winchester 2003: 289). Finally, in most countries levels of unionization in public services have not fallen nor has there been significant decline in the coverage of collective bargaining.

With regard to unionization, in some states, public sector restructuring was aimed at weakening collective organization and bargaining rights (Colling 2000). This was especially true of the United Kingdom, where density levels fell during the 1980s, as did union membership—by approximately 2 percent in 1979 and 1996 (Corby and White 1999). But this trend is not apparent elsewhere. In most continental European states, union membership either remained stable or, in the case of Spain, rose over the past two decades (Jodar, Jordana, and Alos 1999). A similar story can be told in relation to developments in North America. In Canada union density remained high (at about 70 percent) despite frequent legislative restrictions into collective bargaining and the rights of unions. Over the 1991–1999 period union density declined slightly for the federal, local, and education sectors, but it stayed the same in the provincial sector and increased in the health and social sector. In the United States, union density also remained stable from 1978 to 1999. Here too public employees were under attack on the related fronts of job security and compensation through privatization and challenges to collective bargaining rights. But while this has led to decline in selected occupations (such as sanitation workers) these losses were offset by organizing gains for electrical and gas workers, safety workers (fire and police), and education personnel over the same period (BLS 2000).

A further sign of continuity is that, in most states, there has been no marked decline in the coverage of collective bargaining in public services. While there have been piecemeal attempts by governments to de-recognize unions and establish unilateral pay determination this has not resulted in fundamental change. In continental Europe the general trend has been towards the recognition of collective bargaining rights for larger groups of public employees (Bach 1999: 12). In the United States, despite the challenges of public sector collective bargaining over the last four decades, it remains a popular mechanism for providing employees a voice in the workplace. After the growth period in the 1960s, close to 40 percent of public service employees at the local, state, and federal levels of government are covered by collective bargaining. Even in the United Kingdom, where there have been moves to de-recognize unions and establish unilateral pay determination (for some professional groups), public sector workforces remain predominantly collectivized (Cully et al. 1999: 92).

22.5.3 Outsourcing and the Creation of a Two-Tier Workforce

Finally, we turn to the question of the impact of outsourcing activity on public sector employment relations. A key finding from the US research is that privatization has had negative consequences for employees and levels of unionization. According to Chandler (1994), the threat of privatization in collective bargaining had a negative effect on the wages of unionized sanitation workers. Similarly, Thompson (1995) found that privatization and contracting out may result in the loss of union members and may reduce levels of employment and wages. Such findings are supported in a recent study by Hebdon and Stern (2003), focusing on seventy-one cases of restructuring in towns and counties in upstate New York. Respondents were asked questions about the fate of affected workers and conditions of employment in the privatized firm. The survey showed that a broad range of services was affected (payroll, school bus drivers, solid waste, snow plowing, ambulance, airport management, and human services). The results suggest that private contractors were more likely to pay lower wages compared to the local government wages. The worker characteristics of those employees affected by privatization were compared with New York county averages using New York 1990 census of government data. The results show that women and visible minorities were more likely to be adversely impacted by privatization and contracted out workers were significantly less likely to be unionized. Out of 134 unionized employees before contracting out, 99 lost union membership and only 1 gained membership when transferred to a private employer. This means that 73 percent of all unionized jobs in the survey lost their union status after contracting out.

UK-based research has also tended to point to negative consequences of privatization. Marsh (1991) suggested the main impact of the UK experience with privatization on employees was deterioration in pay and conditions and loss of jobs. Later studies of compulsory competitive tendering in local government also identify costs for the workforce. There is evidence that during the 1990s outsourcing was associated with cuts in employment, declining wages, work intensification, and a deterioration in benefits—especially for a majority of women on part-time contracts (Colling 1999; Elliott and Duffus 1996).

These findings suggest that in the United Kingdom, as in the United States, privatization may be producing a two-tier workforce (Bach 2002: 329). However in the United Kingdom the impact of restructuring is slightly more complex as there has been a less marked decline in union membership or bargaining rights (Colling 1999, 2000). While collective bargaining became more fragmented and narrower in content, outsourcing did not lead to a retreat from it in principle (Bach and Winchester 2003). The process of tendering is also subject to European Union laws governing the transfer of undertakings (Rubery *et al.* 2002). While the effectiveness of this regulation is widely questioned, it does appear to have slowed down slightly the process of change in employment conditions following privatization.

22.6 CONCLUSIONS

This chapter provides an account of change in public service employment relations in developed countries. It has been argued that a series of macro-pressures led to attempts to restructure public services in broadly similar ways. Across developed countries the focus has been on fiscal control, privatization, and management reform. Linked to this have been moves to reduce the size of the public sector workforce and introduce a variety of changes in the nature of employment regulation.

A major consequence of these changes is that in most countries the once sharp distinction between employment relations in public and private sectors has been eroded (Bach 1999: 10). However also notable is the robust and resilient nature of public sector employment institutions. Even in the United Kingdom, central governments were unable to convert their enthusiasm for change into a coherent and effective program of reform. Beyond this one should note the uneven pattern of change across developed countries. As Hood (1995: 99) suggests, there would appear to be a wide gap separating a high NPM group of countries (including New Zealand, Australia, and the United Kingdom) and a low NPM group consisting of Germany and Japan. Full convergence between national systems of public administration has yet to occur and there is little sign that it will do so in the near future.

When seeking to understand this uneven and incomplete pattern of change in public services a number of points can be made. First, there are the different goals that have informed the process of reform in developed countries (Flynn 2000; Kickert 1997). According to Pollitt and Boukaert (2000: 93–4), it is possible to identify contrasting visions of desired future arrangements that were expected to follow from management restructuring. In some countries, such as the United Kingdom, the emphasis was on revolutionary change, dismantling existing structures, and moving towards a minimalist or night watchman state. In mainland Europe and Canada political elites had far less radical objectives in mind. Here the focus has been on either modernizing public services or, as was the case in Germany, seeking only to maintain the status quo while making it work better (ibid.). These different visions were also important in shaping the way change was implemented. In the United Kingdom, restructuring was largely imposed by central government with only minimal consultation. Unions and professions, in this context, were viewed as part of the problem rather than the solution (Colling 2001). Elsewhere the process of change was more consultative. For example, in Italy unions participated in and largely accepted wide-ranging changes in the contractual status of public officials (Bordogna, Dell'Arigna, and Della Rocca 1999).

A second explanation is the variable strength of resistance to change. In all countries there has been opposition to restructuring, not least from unions and entrenched groups of professionals (Clarke and Newman 1997). But this opposition has clearly been more effective in some contexts than in others. In the United Kingdom and New Zealand, central governments were able to drive through changes in organization and personnel policy with relative ease (Boston, Pallot, and Walsh 1996; Colling 2001). By contrast, in France, attempts to modernize public services and alter the contractual status of civil servants, have met with powerful and sustained opposition from administrative elites, unions, and politicians (Clark 1998).

Finally, uneven development can be attributed to the differential capabilities of different political regimes to implement change (Hood 1995). In Germany the logic of the federal system ensures that 'public sector reform activities are bound to proceed in a disjointed and incrementalist rather than a comprehensive and wholesale manner' (Schroter and Wollmann 1997: 188: quoted in Pollitt and Boukaert 2000: 49). The German constitution also affords civil servants a degree of legal immunity from interference by politicians making it hard, if not impossible, for government to unilaterally impose change (Rober 1996). By contrast, in more centralized unitary states (such as the United Kingdom and New Zealand) fewer constitutional constraints exist. In these contexts there is less extensive legal regulation of employment in public services. National governments, especially those enjoying a parliamentary majority, have been able to either legislate or simply impose restructuring (using crown prerogative and other executive powers) (Bach and Winchester 2003). Hence, one might understand variations in the pattern of change not only in terms of differing goals but also in terms of the capability of national governments to implement reform.

References

ALLISON, G. (1979). 'Public and Private Management: Are They Fundamentally Alike in All Unimportant Aspects?' Reprinted in J. Shafritz and A. Hyde (eds.), *Classics in Public Administration*. Belmont: Wadsworth.

APPELBAUM, E., and BATT, R. (1994). *The New American Workplace*. Ithaca, NY: ILR Press.

AUCOIN, P. (1990). 'Administrative Reform in Public Management: Paradigm, Principles, Paradoxes and Pendulums'. *Governance*, 3: 115–57.

BACH, S. (1999). 'Europe: Changing Public Service Employment Relations', in S. L. Bach, G. Bordogna, G. Della Rocca, and D. Winchester (eds.), *Public Service Employment Relations in Europe: Transformation, Modernisation or Inertia?* London: Routledge.

——(2002). 'Public-Sector Employment Relations Reform under Labour: Muddling Through or Modernisation?' *British Journal of Industrial Relations*, 40/2: 319–39.

——and DELLA ROCCA, G. (2000). 'The Management Strategies of Public Sector Employers in Europe'. *Industrial Relations Journal*, 31: 82–96.

——and WINCHESTER, D. (2003). 'Industrial Relations in the Public Sector', in P. Edwards (ed.), *Industrial Relations* (2nd edn). Oxford: Blackwell.

BLS (US Department of Labor, Bureau of Labor Statistics) (2000). *Union Densities in 1999*.

BORDOGNA, L., DELL'ARIGNA, C., and DELLA ROCCA, G. (1999). 'Italy: A Case of Co-ordinated Decentralisation', in S. Bach, L. Bordogna, G. Della Rocca, and D. Winchester (eds.), *Public Service Employment Relations in Europe: Transformation, Modernisation or Inertia?* London: Routledge.

BOSTON, M. J., PALLOT, J., and WALSH, P. (1996). *Public Management: The New Zealand Model*. Auckland: Oxford University Press.

BOYNE, G. A. (1998). 'Competitive Tendering in Local Government: A Review of Theory and Evidence'. *Public Administration*, 76/Winter: 695–712.

BURNHAM, P. (1999). 'The Politics of Economic Management in the 1990s'. *New Political Economy*, 4/1: 37–54.

CHANDLER, T. (1994). 'Sanitization, Privatization and Sanitation Employees' Wages'. *Journal of Labor Research*, 15/2: 137–53.

CLARK, D. (1998). 'The Modernisation of the French Civil Service: Crisis, Change and Continuity'. *Public Administration*, 76/1: 97–115.

CLARKE, J., and NEWMAN, J. (1997). *The Managerial State*. London: Sage.

——(1999). 'Tendering and Outsourcing: Working in the Contract State?' in S. Corby and G. White (eds.), *The Public Services: Themes and Issues.* London: Routledge.

——(2000). 'Personnel Management in the Extended Organisation', in S. Bach and K. Sisson (eds.), *Personnel Management.* London: Blackwell.

——(2001). 'Human Resources in the Public Sector', in I. Beardwell and L. Holden (eds.), *Human Resource Management: A Contemporary Perspective* (3rd edn). London: Pitman.

CORBY, S., and WHITE, G. (1999). 'From the New Right to New Labour', in S. Corby and G. White (eds.), *The Public Services: Themes and Issues.* London: Routledge.

CULLY, M., WOODLAND, S., O'REILLY, A., and DIX, G. (1999). *Britain at Work: As Depicted by the 1998 Workplace Employee Relations Survey.* London: Routledge.

DU GAY, P. (2000). *In Praise of Bureaucracy.* London: Sage.

ELLIOTT, R., and DUFFUS, K. (1996). 'What Has Been Happening to Pay in the Public Service Sector of the British Economy? Developments over the Period 1970–92'. *British Journal of Industrial Relations*, 34/1: 51–85.

ESPING-ANDERSON, G. (1990). *The Three Worlds of Welfare Capitalism.* Cambridge: Polity Press.

FARNHAM, D., and HORTON, S. (eds.) (1996). *Managing People in the Public Services.* London: Macmillan.

FERLIE, E., ASHBURNER, L., FITZGERALD, L., and PETTIGREW, A. (1996). *The New Public Management in Action.* Oxford: Macmillan.

FERNER, A., and HYMAN, R. (eds.) (1998) *Changing Industrial Relations in Europe* (2nd edn). Oxford: Blackwell.

FERRERA, M. (1998). 'The Four "Social Europes": Between Universalism and Selectivity', in M. Rhodes and Y. Meny (eds.), *The Future of European Welfare: A New Social Contract?* Baisingstoke: Macmillan.

——and HEMERIJCK, A. (2003). 'Recalibrating Europe's Welfare Regimes', in J. Zeltin and D. M. Trubek (eds.), *Governing Work and Welfare in a New Economy.* Oxford: Oxford University Press.

FLYNN, N. (2000). 'Managerialism in the Public Services: Some International Trends', in J. Clarke, S. Gerwitz, and E. McLaughlin (eds.), *New Managerialism New Welfare?* London: Sage.

——and STREHL, F. (eds.) (1996). *Public Sector Management in Europe.* London: Prentice Hall, Harvester Wheatsheaf.

FOSTER, C., and PLOWDEN, F. (1996). *The State under Stress.* Buckingham: Open University Press.

FOSTER, D., and HOGGETT, P. (1999). 'Changes in the Benefits Agency: Empowering the Exhausted Worker?' *Work, Employment and Society*, 13/1: 19–39.

FREDMAN, S., and MORRIS, G. (1989). *The State as Employer.* London: Mansell.

FRIEDSON, E. (1994). *Professionalism Re-born: Theory, Prophesy and Policy.* Cambridge: Polity Press.

GRIMSHAW, D., VINCENT, S., and WILLMOTT, H. (2002). 'Going Privately: Partnership and Outsourcing in UK Public Services'. *Public Administration*, 80/3: 475–502.

HARRIS, J., and McDONALD, C. (2000). 'Post-Fordism, the Welfare State and the Personal Social Services: A Comparison of Australia and Britain'. *British Journal of Social Work*, 30: 51–70.

HEBDON, R. (1994). 'The Perils of Privatization: Lessons for New York State'. Mimeograph, Cornell University.

—— (1995). 'Contracting Out in New York State: The Story the Lauder Report Chose Not to Tell'. *Labor Studies Journal*, 20/1: 3–29.

—— (1996). 'Public Sector Dispute Resolution in Transition', in D. Belman, M. Gunderson, and D. Hyatt (eds.), *Public Sector Employment in a Time of Transition*, Annual Research Volume, Industrial Relations Research Association.

—— and STERN, R. (2003). 'Do Public Sector Strike Bans Really Prevent Conflict?' *Industrial Relations*, July: 493–512.

HOGGETT, P. (1994). 'The Politics of the Modernisation of the UK Welfare State', in R. Burrows and B. Loader (eds.), *Towards a Post Fordist Welfare State*. London: Routledge.

HOOD, C. (1991). 'A Public Management for All Seasons'. *Public Administration*, 69/1: 3–19.

—— (1995). 'The "New Public Management" in the 1980s: Variations on a Theme'. *Accounting Organisation and Society*, 20/2–3: 93–109.

—— (1998). *The Art of the State: Culture, Rhetoric and Public Management*. Oxford: Clarendon Press.

—— and JACKSON, M. (1991). *Administrative Argument*. Aldershot: Dartmouth.

ILO (1997). *World Labour Report 1988–1998: Industrial Relations, Democracy and Social Stability*. Geneva: ILO.

JESSOP, B. (1994). 'Post-Fordism and the State', in A. Amin, *Post Fordism: A Reader*. Oxford: Blackwell.

JODAR, P., JORDANA, J., and ALOS, R. (1999). 'Spain: Public Service Employment Relations since the Transition to Democracy', in S. Bach, L. Bordogna, G. Della Rocca, and D. Winchester (eds.), *Public Service Employment Relations in Europe: Transformation, Modernisation or Inertia?* London: Routledge.

KATZ, H. C., and KOCHAN, T. (1992). *An Introduction to Collective Bargaining and Industrial Relations*. New York: McGraw-Hill.

KELLER, B. K. (1999). 'Germany: Negotiated Change, Modernisation and the Challenge of Unification', in S. L. Bach, G. Bordogna, G. Della Rocca, and D. Winchester (eds.), *Public Service Employment Relations in Europe: Transformation, Modernisation or Inertia?* London: Routledge.

KICKERT, W. (ed.) (1997). *Public Management and Administrative Reform in Western Europe*. Cheltenham: Edward Elger.

LANE, J. E. (ed.) (1997). *Public Sector Reform: Rationale, Trends and Problems*. London: Sage.

LAUDER, R. S. (1992). *Privatization for New York: Competing for a Better Future. Report of the New York State Advisory Commission on Privatization*. Edited by E. S. Savas. Albany, NY.

LE GRAND, J., and BARTLETT, W. (1993). *Quasi Markets and Social Policy*. Basingstoke: Macmillan.

LOPEZ-DE-SILANES, A., and VISHNY, R. (1997). 'Privatization in the United States'. *Rand Journal of Economics*, 28/3: 447–71.

LYNN, L. (1998). 'The New Public Management as an International Phenomenon: A Sceptical Viewpoint', in L. Jonesa and K. Schedler (eds.), *International Perspectives on the New Public Management*. Greenwich, Conn.: JAI Press.

McKERSIE, R. B. (1988). 'Productivity Bargaining in New York: What Went Wrong?' An Afterword, in D. Lewin, P. Feuille, T. A. Kochan, and J. Delaney (eds.), *Public Sector Labor Relations: Analysis and Readings*. Lexington, Mass.: Lexington Books.

McLaughlin, K., Osborne, S. P., and Ferlie, E. (eds.) (2002). *New Public Management: Current Trends and Future Prospects*. London: Routledge.

Marsh, D. (1991). 'Privatization under Mrs. Thatcher: A Review of the Literature'. *Journal of Public Administration*, 69/Winter: 459–80.

Metcalf, L., and Richards, S. (1990). *Improving Public Service Management*. London: Sage.

Mosse, P., and Tchobanian, R. (1999). 'France: The Restructuring of Employment Relations in the Public Services', in S. Bach, L. Bordogna, G. Della Rocca, and D. Winchester (eds.), *Public Sector Employment Relations in Europe: Transformation, Modernisation or Inertia?* London: Routledge.

Newman, J. (2000). 'Beyond the New Public Management? Modernizing Public Services', in J. Clarke, S. Gerwitz, and E. McLaughlin (eds.), *New Managerialism New Welfare?* London: Sage.

O'Connor, J. (1973). *The Fiscal Crisis of the State*. New York: St. Martin's Press.

OECD (1995). *Governance in Transition: Public Management Reforms in OECD Countries*. Paris: OECD.

—— (1997a). *Family, Market and Community: Equity and Efficiency in Social Policy*, Social Policy Studies, No. 21. Paris: OECD.

—— (1997b). *Measuring Public Employment in OECD Countries: Sources, Methods and Results*. Paris: OECD.

—— (2000a). *OECD Economic Outlook 2000*. Paris: OECD.

—— (2000b). *Recent Developments and Future Challenges in Human Resource Management in Member Countries*. Paris: PUMA/OECD.

—— (2001). *Highlights of Public Sector Pay and Employment Trends*. Paris: PUMA/OECD.

Olsen, T. (1996). *Industrial Relations Systems in the Public Sector in Europe*. Fredrich Ebert Foundation. Oslo, Norway: EPSC.

Osborne, D., and Gaebler, T. (1992). *Reinventing Government: How the Entrepreneurial Spirit is Transforming the Public Sector*. Reading, Mass.: Addison Wesley.

Palan, R., and Abbott, J. (1996). *State Strategies in the Global Political Economy*. London: Pinter Press.

Peters, G. (1995). 'Bureaucracy in a Divided Regime: The United States', in J. Pierre (ed.), *Bureaucracy in the Modern State: An Introduction to Comparative Public Administration*. Aldershot: Edwin Elger.

Pitelis, C., and Clarke, T. (eds.) (1993). *The Political Economy of Privatisation*. London: Routledge.

Pollitt, C. (1993). *Managerialism and the Public Services: The Anglo American Experience* (2nd edn). London: Macmillan.

—— and Boukaert, G. (2000). *Public Management Reform: A Comparative Analysis*. Oxford: Oxford University Press.

Rhodes, M. (2000). 'Desperately Seeking a Solution: Social Democracy, Thatcherism and the "Third Way" in British Welfare', in M. Ferrera and M. Rhodes (eds.), *Recasting European Welfare States*. London: Frank Cass.

Rhodes, R. A. W. (2000). 'Governance and Public Administration', in Jon Pierre (ed.), *Debating Governance: Authority, Steering and Democracy*. Oxford: Oxford University Press.

Ridley, F. (1996). 'The New Public Management in Europe: Comparative Perspectives'. *Public Policy and Administration*, 11/1: 16–29.

Rober, M. (1996). 'Germany', in D. Farnham, S. Horton, J. Barlow, and A. Hondeghem (eds.), *New Public Managers in Europe: Public Services in Transition*. London: Macmillan.

Rose, J. (1995). 'The Evolution of Public Sector Unionism', in G. Swimmer and M. Thompson (eds.), *Public Sector Collective Bargaining in Canada*. Kingston, Ont.: IRC Press.

Rubery, J., and Grimshaw, D. (2003). *The Organisation of Employment: An International Perspective*. London: Palgrave Macmillan.

——Earnshaw, J., Marchington, M., Cooke, F. L., and Vincent, S. (2002). 'Changing Organisational Forms and the Employment Relationship'. *Journal of Management Studies*, 39/5: 645–72.

Schofield, J. (2001). 'The Old Ways are Best? The Durability and Usefulness of Bureaucracy in Public Sector Management'. *Organization*, 8/1: 77–96.

Schroter, E., and Wollmann, H. (1997). 'Public Sector Reforms in Germany: Whence and Where? A Case of Ambivalence'. *Administrative Studies / Hallinnon Tutkimus*, 3: 184–200.

Sparrow, P., and Hiltrop, J. M. (1994). *European Human Resource Management in Transition*. New York: Prentice Hall.

Stewart, J., and Walsh, K. (1992). 'Change in the Management of Public Services'. *Public Administration*, 70: 499–518.

Swimmer, G., and Thompson, M. (1995). 'Collective Bargaining in the Public Sector: An Introduction', in G. Swimmer and M. Thompson (eds.), *Public Sector Collective Bargaining in Canada*. Kingston, Ont.: IRC Press.

Thompson, M. (1995). 'The Industrial Relations Effects of Privatization: Evidence from Canada', in G. Swimmer and M. Thompson (eds.), *Public Sector Collective Bargaining in Canada*. Kingston, Ont.: IRC Press.

Traxler, F., Blaschke, S., and Kittel, B. (2001). *National Labour Relations in Internationalised Markets: A Comparative Study of Institutions, Change and Performance*. Oxford: Oxford University Press.

Warner, M., and Hebdon, R. (2001). 'Local Government Restructuring: Privatization and Its Alternatives'. *Journal of Policy Analysis and Management*, 20/2 (Spring): 315–36.

Weber, M. (1947). *The Theory of Social and Economic Organization*. Translated by T. Parsons. New York: Free Press.

WERC (Wisconsin Employment Relations Commission) (1992). *Biennial Reports, State of Wisconsin*.

White, G. (1999). 'The Remuneration of Public Servants: Fair Pay or New Pay?' in S. Corby and G. White (eds.), *The Public Services: Themes and Issues*. London: Routledge.

Whitfield, D. (2001). *Public Services or Corporate Welfare? Rethinking the Nation State in the Global Economy*. Sterling, Va.: Pluto Press.

Wilding, P. (1982). *Professional Power and Social Welfare*. London, Boston: Routledge and Kegan Paul.

Winchester, D., and Bach, S. (1999). 'Britain: The Transformation of Public Service Employment Relations', in S. Bach, L. Bordogna, G. Della Rocca, and D. Winchester (eds.), *Public Service Employment Relations in Europe: Transformation, Modernisation or Inertia?* London: Routledge.

Wincott, D. (2001). 'Reassessing the Social Foundations of Welfare (State) Regimes'. *New Political Economy*, 6/3: 409–24.

Wise, L. (1996). 'Internal Labour Markets', in H. Bekke, J. Perry, and T. Toonen, *Civil Service Systems in Comparative Perspective*. Bloomington: Indiana University Press.

ZELTIN, J. (2003). 'Introduction: Governing Work and Welfare in a New Economy: European and American Experiments', in J. Zeltin and D. M. Trubek (eds.), *Governing Work and Welfare in a New Economy*. Oxford: Oxford University Press.

UNDERSTANDING MULTINATIONAL CORPORATIONS

GLENN MORGAN

23.1 INTRODUCTION

IN 1993 Ghoshal and Westney stated that 'organization theory and the study of the MNC have not had a particularly close relationship. Organization theorists have rarely taken the MNC as an arena for study' (Ghoshal and Westney 1993: 1). In the ten years since then, however, academics and researchers have taken a lot more interest. The result has been a confluence of interests across international business and organization studies around the internal structure of the multinational, and we have witnessed the emergence of a new era in which the internal dynamics of these organizations is of greater interest and is being actively studied.

In this chapter, issues that have captured the attention of researchers are discussed and the emerging research agenda is laid out. The first part focuses on understanding the history, and contemporary scale and significance of multinationals as economic actors. The second part considers influential theoretical approaches to the MNC offering different accounts of why they exist. Two opposing perspectives are distinguished, the economic and the political. In the past, there was a rigid divide between these but, increasingly, researchers are using elements of both perspectives to understand the dynamics of multinationals. The crucial additional feature here is the importation of insights from institutionalist literature on the relationship between firms and national contexts. The third part of the chapter therefore reviews how research deriving from an institutionalist perspective complements existing approaches by directing attention to the social embeddedness of multinationals and their subsidiaries.

A minimal definition of the multinational is any company that has an organizational presence in two or more national jurisdictions. However, even quite small companies have international affiliations and alliances these days (Buckley and Ghauri 2000). Conventionally, the study of the MNC is confined to the consideration of the largest companies of the developed world. However, as will be suggested, these are better understood as MNCs as opposed to global corporations (Doremus *et al.* 1998; Morgan 2001c).

23.2 THE HISTORY AND CONTEMPORARY IMPORTANCE OF THE MNC

23.2.1 Origins and History

Historically the multinational organizational form begins in the late seventeenth and early eighteenth centuries with the establishment of corporate bodies such as the East India Trading Company in Britain. Trading companies were more concerned with buying and selling products than the production of goods and services outside the home economy. The key point in the emergence of multinationals was when firms began to invest abroad and manage those investments through organizational forms such as subsidiaries and affiliates (Teichova, Levy-Leboyer, and Nussbaum 1986; Wilkins 2001).

This process began in the nineteenth century as part of more general internationalization of economies. The dominant form of foreign investment at this time was portfolio investment: it occurred through the intermediaries of the financial system (particularly the City of London) and involved individual investment in the shares or bonds launched by overseas-based companies such as in railway companies. These stock issues were sponsored by merchant banks (mainly in Britain and France); in return for the sponsoring (which guaranteed the willingness of European investors to buy the stocks), banks took a commission.

Alongside this there was the development of foreign direct investment where firms established activities across national boundaries. The dominant form of this investment in the late nineteenth and early twentieth centuries was based on raw material extraction as European and US companies sought to secure access to resources such as rubber, oil, coffee, iron ore, gold, diamonds, tobacco, and sugar in an era of imperial competition. It was in this era that multinationals such as Royal Dutch Shell, British Petroleum, Standard Oil and its successors, British American Tobacco, Rio Tinto, Dunlop, Lever Bros., and Tate and Lyle emerged. Such firms were highly interdependent with the formal and informal imperial relationships of their home societies.

Imperial power opened up regions for economic exploitation managed by the emerging multinationals (Cain and Hopkins 1993). Also, in the late nineteenth and early twentieth century, the struggle for power in Europe was given impetus by the drive for colonies where the necessary raw materials for economic and military expansion were assumed to be located. Banking institutions also began to internationalize in this period, setting up branch offices and subsidiaries in countries where they were investing or organizing the provision of capital. At the same time, there was a small-scale creeping internationalization of manufacturing production. The Scottish thread manufacturer, J. P. Coats, had global manufacturing operations before World War I as did UK companies such as Courtaulds, Nobel, Vickers, and Pilkingtons (Wilson 1995: 111). Some US and German companies also began to set up production facilities in other countries.

In the interwar years, the unstable political and economic situation militated against a smooth continuation of this trend. There were some examples of internationalization across national borders (such as the arrival of Ford and General Motors in the United Kingdom), but these were limited. After the Wall Street Crash of 1929, US overseas investment ceased for a time. On the other hand, protectionism and the imperial preference movements in the 1930s served to tighten some of the economic linkages between metropolitan territories and their formal and informal colonies, thus solidifying the imperial nature of companies like Imperial Tobacco and Imperial Chemical Industries in the United Kingdom (Cain and Hopkins 1993). In Europe, protectionism helped large firms establish near monopoly positions within home markets. This became the basis of international cartels in certain technology and knowledge-intensive sectors (such as electricity generation) where multinational firms that were monopolists in their own home states divided the other markets of the world between themselves (mostly on the basis of already existing informal and formal imperial relationships) (Glimstedt 2001).

Although World War II shook the foundations of these firms, many (from both sides) survived the war. For US companies in particular, during the immediate postwar period, the switch back to peacetime production was supported by the opportunities available in Europe where devastation of the industrial base had been huge. The Marshall plan and the role played by organizations such as the Ford Foundation, paved the way for a gradual expansion of US FDI and US multinationals into the United Kingdom and Europe (Djelic 1999; Zeitlin and Herrigel 2000).

While the oil and other raw material multinationals of the United Kingdom and The Netherlands rapidly recovered their position, European manufacturing and financial multinationals were slower to re-emerge.

By contrast with British and Dutch, the expansion of Japanese, German, and French FDI, for example, only really began in the late 1980s. In 1980, the outward FDI stocks of Germany were around 20 percent of those of the United States; by 2001, they were 37 percent. Similar figures for Japan are 9 percent in 1980 and 21 percent in 2001 and for the United Kingdom, 37 percent in 1980, growing to 68 percent in 2001. In the late 1990s the United Kingdom's outward flow of funds surpassed that of the United States. In 2000, UK outward FDI flows were around $254 billion, while those of the United States were $164 billion. From the early 1980s, FDI flows became increasingly large, reaching an average annual growth rate of 40.1 percent in the period 1996–2000. In this process, the predominant form of investment was either between developed countries or between developed countries and a small number of developing ones, particularly in East Asia (Hong Kong, Singapore, Korea, Taiwan, and lately China) and Latin America (especially Mexico and Brazil). In 2001, 68.4 percent of FDI flows were between developed countries; 13.9 percent were into Asia and the Pacific, and 11.9 percent into Latin America and the Caribbean. These flows were primarily into the manufacturing and service sectors of these societies compared to the flows of the pre-World War I period where investment was directed mainly at the raw material and extractive industries.

23.2.2 The Rise of Multinational Services

Despite the growing importance of the service sector to most developed economies, multinationals remain predominantly based in manufacturing or raw material extraction. While financial institutions (such as banks and insurance companies) are deliberately excluded from the UNCTAD data due to the difficulties of acquiring comparable data, the number of nonfinancial firms in the UNCTAD top 100 list that are not in either the manufacturing or the service sector is eighteen overall.

Nevertheless, the last two decades have seen major developments in the internationalization of services in the tertiary sector and the degree to which service firms can become multinational has been widely debated. In 2001, 25 of the 113 cross-border merger and acquisitions deals in that year worth $1 billion or more, involved services companies in telecoms, management consultancy, and information retrieval (figures calculated from UNCTAD 2002). Miozzo and Soete state that 'such mergers have enabled increasingly international service conglomerates of a hybrid nature ... to acquire the capacity to penetrate foreign markets with a diversified, albeit integrated, range of services or goods. The transnationalization process is more advanced in advertising, accounting, tourism, banking, insurance

and wholesale. ... The most rapid recent internationalization is in the management and computer-based service firms' (Miozzo and Soete 2001: 177).

Unlike the manufacturing and extractive sectors, service companies do not invest
in large fixed assets and their pattern of internationalization is subject to strong
cyclical effects dependent on economic conditions. This also means that their
actual importance is often underestimated by data based on the consideration of
assets. Indeed, the internationalization of enterprises of this type will influence
practices within host societies profoundly, for example, the influence of management consultancies and accounting companies in transferring particular business
practices or the influence of investment banks in enforcing conformity to certain
international or US-based standards of reporting and transparency.

23.2.3 The Contemporary Importance of the MNC

The 2002 World Investment report lists the world's 100 largest nonfinancial transnational corporations (UNCTAD 2002). This report ranks firms by foreign assets
(in 1999) and also provides a transnationality index (based on the average score of
proportion of assets/sales/employment outside the home base). The top ten companies by foreign assets are still dominated by the raw material producers in the
shape of oil companies (Exxon Mobil is 2nd, Royal Dutch Shell 3rd, Totalfina 8th,
and BP 10th). Car companies (Ford at 5th, General Motors at 4th, DaimlerChrysler
at 7th, and Toyota at 6th) are the second most important group. The final two in the
top ten are General Electric (at no. 1) and IBM (9th). These are not, however, the
most transnational companies in the sense of having the widest overseas spread not
just of assets but also sales and employment.

Multinationals have certainly become of increasing economic significance to
developed countries as a source of inward investment as can be seen from Table
23.1 detailing the impact of manufacturing FDI. In recent years this trend has been
driven by acquisition and merger rather than investing in new capacity. Thus, FDI
has increasingly become a way of restructuring the ownership of existing capacity.
This in turn reflects the importance for multinationals of their relationships with
capital markets. To access capital for such activities, multinationals have to become
increasingly financially internationalized. They cannot generate sufficient funds
internally for the large merger and acquisition deals that became common in the
late 1990s, nor can such funds be generated from their home capital markets, for
reasons of size and broader regulatory issues. For example, to make an acquisition
in the United States via a share-swop deal, a firm must be able to offer investors
shares quoted on US stock markets. This requirement has been one of the pressures

Table 23.1 Importance of MNCs to national economies

	Employees of foreign affiliates in manufacturing (thousands of employees)	As % of total employment in manufacturing	No. of parent company MNCs in country	Foreign affiliates located in country	FDI inward stock as % of GDP 2000
UK	745.8	18%	3,208	8,609	30.5%
US	2,274.8	11%	3,263	15,699	12.4%
France	807	21%	1,922	9,473	19.9%
Germany	N/A	N/A	8,522	13,267	24.1%
Japan	177.5	1.4%	3,786	3,359	1.1%

Source: Adapted from UNCTAD (2002): data based on latest year available.

forcing particularly German firms to seek US listings. Such listings bring with them a number of formal and informal requirements: for complying with accounting standards, for transparency, for reporting mechanisms and for investor relations that may substantially differ from those in the home base.

The growth of FDI and the emergence of huge multinational corporations led to debates about the political significance of such phenomena. For example, Anderson and Cavanagh claim that of the 100 biggest economies in the world, 51 are multinational corporations and only 49 of them countries (Anderson and Cavanagh 2000). This is part of a critique of the power of multinationals going back to the 1950s and 1960s and continuing into the current era of antiglobalization movements. In this critique, multinationals are so big and powerful that they can override democratic governments. Others have been skeptical about such size comparisons suggesting that on a like-for-like basis (comparing company value-added to national GDP in a year), 'of the 100 largest economies, 63 are countries and 37 are corporations ... among the top 50 economies only 2 are corporations ... the large countries in the world are much larger than the largest corporations' (De Grauwe and Camerman 2002: 4). In De Grauwe and Camerman's methodology, the largest corporation is Wal-Mart (at 44 in the top 100 economies), just below Chile and just above Pakistan, Peru, and Algeria. Size, of course, is not the only determinant of influence and power as De Grauwe and Camerman assume.

23.3 THEORIES OF THE MNC

Theoretical views of the MNCs are divided into two camps: those who seek to explain their existence by applying an economic logic to firm development and foreign direct investment and those who apply instead a political/power logic to the internationalization process.

23.3.1 Economic Logic

It is interesting to note that the dominant theoretical approach to the MNC has not been neoclassical economics. Gilpin, for example, states that 'despite the importance of multinational corporations in the functioning of the international economy neoclassical economists have remarkably little to say about them' (Gilpin 2001: 279). In fact the economic perspective on multinationals has been dominated by the self-proclaimed eclectic approach, developed by Dunning (Dunning 1998, 2001). Dunning's argument is that it is possible to understand processes of FDI and firm internationalization by reference to three sets of assets: ownership, location, and internalization assets.

The concept of ownership assets refers to the firm having developed in its home country certain specific assets; these may be production techniques, management techniques, particular products, or brand identities that can be used in other countries. Thus, the initial investment can be paid back more effectively as a result of utilizing it in new markets. This does not explain why the firm does not simply franchise or contract out its expertise rather than go to all the trouble of setting up operations in another country. The second element of the eclectic model then comes into play. This develops from the transaction cost approach and considers the circumstances under which firms internalize transactions (organize them as part of their internal hierarchy of command) or externalize (buy on the marketplace). Thus, the firm that wishes to engage in international operations faces the choice of externalizing, entering into a relationship with a company in the targeted country for that company to produce the product, or setting up its own facility in the country. The latter is clearly more expensive and requires more investment than the former, so why do firms bother to do it?

For the economists, the answer must be that the costs of maintaining a relationship with another firm (and all that this implies in terms of transferring some of its key ownership assets to an outsider, monitoring the costs of potential opportunism on the part of the other company, and insuring against the risks of losing control of key elements of knowledge or reputation) must ultimately be higher than the costs of setting up the subsidiary. The firm therefore internalizes the operation and sets up a subsidiary. The third element of the model is the locational advantage of the new site. In this discussion, there is a broad distinction between asset exploiting reasons for location, for example, access to markets (by getting behind potential tariff barriers), and asset acquiring reasons for location, for example, accessing new knowledge assets by locating in areas with specialist firms. Dunning's model is based primarily on economic efficiency considerations as interpreted by senior managers in the MNC's headquarters. Firms pursue internationalizing processes in an eclectic way to grow and expand (Dunning 1998, 2001).

23.3.2 Political Power Perspectives

The economic approach has always coexisted with more political interpretations of why multinationals exist. For Hymer (1968), the need for overseas expansion derived essentially from the limits of the home market. Using Marxian theory, Hymer (1968, 1972) argues that this expansionist tendency derives from the falling rate of profit in the metropolitan countries. Continued growth required the opening up of new markets and new sources of cheap labor and raw material by multinationals without restriction from foreign governments. Hymer's work therefore surfaced a number of themes that became increasingly predominant in the critical, political perspective on multinationals. His focus on the importance to the MNC of finding new sites of cheap labor (to undercut trade union power in Western social democracies), on the exploitation of the resources of the developing countries (by driving down the prices of raw materials and neglecting the broader environmental consequences for such societies), on the collusion of the home country state in this process (and the weakness of peripheral host states in opposing the process), on the consequent control over and homogenization of tastes and consumption around the world as MNCs grew to dominate national markets, became themes in the radical critique of multinationals as it later developed. Essential to these themes was the issue of power, a term missing in Dunning, as in most economic analyses. In the radical approach, multinationals were involved in two power struggles—with labor and with governments.

MNCs and Labor

The basic issue with labor was how conditions of work were affected by the existence of the multinational. In 1980 Frobel argued that there is a new international division of labor that emphasized the relative ease with which firms could relocate assembly line production to areas of cheap labor. This became a threat hanging over trade unions in the developed world. The result was the use of coercive comparisons in which managers of multinationals used the threat of relocation to restructure labor practices in the metropolitan area (reducing wages and conditions). In some industries, this was a meaningful threat.

Where production systems were relatively standardized and Taylorized, managers only needed to find a semi-skilled workforce with the rudiments of industrial discipline in a political system that was stable and welcoming of foreign capital to be able to carry out the threat. Although attempts were made to forge cross-national alliances of trade unionists within multinationals, the difficulties of developing coordinated action across national sites with different institutional contexts, meant that most of these came to nothing, although more recent efforts to establish an institutional framework for this (in the EU directive on European Works Councils), might suggest a revival of these activities (Marginson 2000; Whittall 2000). Similarly, attempts to raise standards in developing countries up to somewhere near the level of the industrialized world (through ILO action) and thereby undermine the possibility for coercive comparisons have generally been unsuccessful.

However, it gradually became obvious that not all production systems (or services) could be easily relocated. As analysts became more interested in post-Fordist systems, based on smaller product runs, higher inputs of technology and expertise, continuous innovation and quality improvement, the importance of a skilled and knowledgeable workforce came to the fore. This was reflected in statistics showing that, in terms of total FDI, the bulk is not going to low-wage developing countries but to other industrialized countries. In 2000, 82 percent of inward flows of FDI went to the developed countries (UNCTAD 2002).

Service sector multinationals in banking and finance, consultancy, and business services were even more likely to concentrate their investments in areas of developed concentrations of expertise and demand (Miozzo and Soete 2001). These two tendencies—of removing standardized tasks to low-wage areas but shifting more complex processes to industrial districts and clusters where expertise and knowledge is more readily available—indicate the role of multinationals in a growing disaggregation of the value chain (see Dicken 1998; also Gereffi 1995; Gereffi and Tam 1999). This creates complex coordination problems for the managers of the MNCs, as it means a dispersal of tasks across many different institutional settings.

MNCs and Governments

The second element of the radical critique also emphasizes the arbitraging capacity of the multinational vis-à-vis governments. In this argument, governments are increasingly weak in relations to MNCs, and particularly in respect to their capacity to induce large business to sustain domestic employment and to pay corporation tax in the home economy. In this view, governments are desperate to encourage inward FDI for its potential spillover effects, in boosting the local economy (through providing more jobs either directly or indirectly), in creating new skills among the workforce and among suppliers, and in encouraging other firms to invest (see Gereffi's discussion of local upgrading through participation in global commodity chains; Gereffi 1995; Gereffi and Tam 1999).

Such enthusiasm may be so great as to encourage governments to offer among other things subsidies of various kinds, reduced taxes, and softer regimes of labor and environmental regulation. Many MNCs supply their subsidiaries internally or from already established contractors. Therefore the impact on the economy through boosting local suppliers may be low. Internal pricing regimes also make it relatively difficult for outsiders to scrutinize the profitability of local plants either for taxation purposes or in the event of threats of closure and demands for extended government support or cheaper labor. Finally, MNC subsidiaries may lobby, overtly or covertly, against tightened government regulation of the environment or employment conditions. However, localities, particularly those in developed nations, often have particular combinations of skills and capabilities that cannot be accessed elsewhere and governments are not therefore in such a weak position as is often implied (Hirst and Thompson 1999). Another important factor is the degree of sunk costs that manufacturing MNCs have committed to a certain locality and which cannot simply be abandoned once they have been made.

23.3.3 More Recent Developments in Theory

In the 1980s, the study of multinationals was dominated by theorizing linked to the kind of eclectic model proposed by Dunning (1998). The most common approach tended to be based on contingency logic. The structure of the MNC flowed from strategy that in turn related to the markets in which it was located (Bartlett and Ghoshal 1989). Thus, firms in highly standardized markets, where brand identity and economies of scale were major factors, would be likely to replicate the organizational forms and practices of the home economy. On the other hand, firms in markets where local responsiveness was required, different models would be adopted. Thus, these writers presented the MNC as a rational economic actor following the dictates of the market. Management would translate those dictates into appropriate organizational structures. They displayed little interest in the internal or external politics of the MNC or in the idea that there might be different interests with different objectives inside the firm. This was paradoxical, since their major interest was in the increasing importance of the footloose truly transnational firm (see also the further development of this model in Nohria and Ghoshal 1997) where power was increasingly dispersed. Some attempts have been made within this tradition to take seriously the diversity of external and internal environments in the MNC. The two most significant are the neocontingency approach to MNC structure and the more politically aware approach, which involves paying attention to managing internal tensions.

Neocontingency Writing

The integration-responsiveness model put forward by Prahalad and Doz (1987) suggested that there was a tension between the MNC being responsive to local markets, on the one hand, and, on the other hand, the firm-maximizing economies of scale by standardizing and integrating products and processes across its various divisions and subsidiaries. In organizational terms, this was strongly related to how subsidiaries were managed and controlled. In Prahalad and Doz's model, where subsidiaries were producing distinctive products for local markets, there was likely to be a high level of autonomy for the local management. Where subsidiaries were reproducing standardized products based on a predetermined model, then they would be tightly controlled and constrained by head office.

In 1989 Bartlett and Ghoshal developed this further by identifying four main types of organizational structure in internationalizing firms, which they labelled as multinational, international, global, and transnational (Bartlett and Ghoshal 1989). Multinational firms were those in which responsiveness to the local market was paramount. Therefore the MNC was run almost as a set of independent national companies. International firms contained subsidiaries that were locally oriented but key aspects of the home-based assets of the firm (such as technology or management systems) were transferred from the center. Global firms were based on economies of scale with key decisions taken centrally about how to develop products and processes. Standardized products were produced for the global market and the task of the local subsidiary was to fit into that model rather than focus on supply of the local market. Transnational firms were identified in terms of an integrated network of interdependent subsidiaries. Rather than information simply flowing backwards and forwards between headquarters and subsidiaries, people, information, and ideas flow in multiple directions.

Thus, according to Bartlett and Ghoshal, firms in highly standardized markets where brand identity and economies of scale were major factors would be likely to adopt the global model. Firms in markets where local responsiveness was significant but where ownership advantages were high (due, for example, to the development of particular types of production processes) would tend to adopt the international model. The multinational model reflected a portfolio approach to firm growth where the headquarters was mainly concerned to identify profitable opportunities wherever they might appear. The transnational firm was likely to exist in markets requiring a mix of local responsiveness and economies of scale and where innovation requirements were high.

Managing Internal Tensions

An earlier theorist who had speculated along similar lines but had produced a more radical view of the impact of this change in the nature of the MNC was the Swedish scholar, Gunnar Hedlund. Hedlund had identified a tendency towards heterarchy in multinationals (Hedlund 1986, 1993). By this he aimed to emphasize the contrast between firms in which the headquarters took a dominant and controlling interest in the actions of subsidiaries and those firms where there was recognition that subsidiaries had their own set of capabilities and competences (whatever might have been transferred from headquarters). In the latter cases, multinationals could either ignore those locally based capabilities and try to impose a standard format or they could seek to take advantage of diversity and difference in the organization by giving the subsidiaries a more open role in the firm. This would require a loosening of central control, a reduction of the power differential between the headquarters and the subsidiary, and an opening up of the organization to multiple flows of information and personnel across various directions. Thus, from having one central site of power and control, the firm would have multiple focal points, networked together in a nonhierarchical, heter-archical way.

Hedlund thought that the resulting tensions could be managed through the creation of a strong corporate culture that permeated all the different parts of the organization. While this was clearly naive and under-theorized, his idea that the MNC faced much more complex coordination problems than the economic rationalists supposed was correct. Hedlund raised the possibility that this rosy picture might be organizationally unattainable. Responding to Hedlund's challenge researchers began to look at the relationship between headquarters and subsidiaries in more detail (Birkinshaw 1997, 2000, 2001; Birkinshaw and Hood 1998; Bresmen, Birkinshaw, and Nobel 1999; Taggart 1998). Birkinshaw, in particular, has contributed to the debate by arguing that subsidiaries can take initiatives to extend their charters and the range of activities that they undertake. In part, this is based on the opportunities that arise as the headquarters evolves new plans and seeks ways of implementing them (e.g. to invest heavily in a new process). Subsidiaries may then become involved in a process of bidding and negotiation to show that such investments should come their way. At one level, Birkinshaw implicitly leads back to the idea that the MNC is a political system in which there are different groups competing for power and using the resources that they control in order to exert power over others (see also Westney and Zaheer 2001); at another level, however, he retains an apolitical approach, assuming that this market competition is essentially explicable in terms of the market efficiency effects of subsidiary strategies.

23.4 INSTITUTIONS AND MULTINATIONALS

Interest in bargaining and competition within multinationals is now widespread. However, this has yet to be translated into a systematic framework that incorporates the political aspects of multinationals as well as the economic aspects. In the rest of this chapter the argument is made that, by combining the existing focus on head office–subsidiary relations in MNCs with a more political and social conception of the firm (as currently being developed in institutionalist accounts of economic processes), it is possible to construct a research agenda that will match the complexity of multinational organizations with a corresponding degree of analytical sophistication.

23.4.1 Recent Institutional Accounts

The objective of a number of recent institutionalist accounts has been to understand economies in terms of the preservation of national systems of institutions (Dore, Lazonick, and O'Sullivan 1999; Hall and Soskice 2001; Hollingsworth 1997; Quack, Morgan, and Whitley 2000; Soskice 1999; Whitley 1999). The approach has been to understand the historical construction of capacities and capabilities in firms and their implications for strategy, structure, and operation. In these approaches, actors and the national business systems they produce (at the inter- and intraorganizational levels) derive from a path-dependent process of institution building. Actors use the resources (financial, legal and regulatory, cultural and skill/knowledge-based) that are available to them in order to build organizational systems. These resources have generally coevolved in a way that creates institutional complementarities between them. They take a particular shape in national systems due to the distinctive historical pathways of institutional development that have occurred. Firms are therefore seen as representative of distinctive and even divergent national economic systems (Whitley 1999).

The application of this approach to the study of multinationals can broadly be argued to have proceeded through three main phases, the hegemonic, the hybridization, and the transnationalism approach.

The first approach can be summarized in the words of an influential article entitled 'Global Firms Are National Firms with International Operations' (Hu 1992). Hu's argument was that multinational firms reproduced their home-based practices in their international operations. He gave little attention to how internationalizing the firm might impact on these home-based practices. It was sufficient to understand the institutional context of the multinational's home base in order to understand how it would control and coordinate its subsidiaries. The headquarters was hegemonic in the sense that it sets all the key parameters for subsidiaries. Hirst and Thompson (1999) reinforced this by arguing that the degree of transnationality in many multinationals was much lower than seemed assumed in many discussions of globalization. Thus they showed that the asset base of most large MNCs was still predominantly in their home country as was the bulk of employment, R&D, and ownership of company shares.

23.4.2 Patterns of Hybridization

More recent empirical research at the organizational level has suggested that this underestimates the degree to which the MNC has to adapt its practices to the different host environments. This has given rise to the second approach of hybridization. In this approach, while head office and home patterns are still dominant, the argument is made that they have to be negotiated when they are implemented in specific contexts. Out of this process of negotiation emerges a hybrid model in the host context. Whereas the hegemonic approach focuses entirely on the head office, the hybridization model examines primarily the dyadic relationships between particular subsidiaries and the headquarters where actors within the subsidiary have power to resist the impositions of the head office. This causes some variability in the ways in which head office practices are implemented in subsidiaries. The institutionalist approach to hybridization goes beyond the integration-responsiveness model described earlier as it emphasizes particularly the power relations and conflicts between local employees and trade unions and the headquarters, with a particular emphasis on this conflict being structured by the specific institutionalist context of different forms of capitalism.

The hybridization perspective was particularly stimulated by the expansion of Japanese firms in the 1980s and 1990s into the United Kingdom and the United States. A series of studies in the late 1980s and 1990s sought to understand how the Japanese multinational adapted to operating in a completely different institutional environment (Elger and Smith 1994). In the United States and the United Kingdom, studies such as Abo (1994) and Liker, Fruin, and Adler (1999) argued that there was a process of hybridization, particularly in terms of certain aspects of the human resource system and the supply management system. In human resources, Japanese firms did seek to provide long-term employment but their commitment (while greater than comparable US and UK firms) was not as great as it was to their Japanese employees. Similarly, the wage system tended not to incorporate key elements of the system in Japan such as seniority-based rewards (Ishida 1986). The company union system that characterized Japan was unworkable in these settings and meant that Japanese MNCs were faced with the choice of becoming nonunion or negotiating single union deals. Similarly, the Japanese MNC did seek to build close relationships with suppliers but they tended to favor suppliers from Japan and were more wary about the level of information exchange and participation in joint projects than they would be in Japan (Morgan *et al.* 2002).

These findings were backed up with a range of qualitative case studies of various degrees of depth, which also emphasized that the Japanese made adjustments to their practice in recognition of the distinctive institutional environment in which they were located (Beechler and Bird 1999; Campbell and Burton 1994; Delbridge 1998; Elger and Smith 1998; Graham 1995).

By the late 1990s, more interest was being paid to German MNCs. By this time, German MNCs were becoming major investors in the United Kingdom and the United States, often through acquisition. As with the Japanese, the clash between a liberal market institutional setting and a coordinated capitalism system was seen as the key issue. How would German MNCs adapt to this process? In the event, however, the findings of the research revealed a much more complex picture than in the Japanese case and in doing so contributed to the rise of the third approach of transnationalism. The reason for this was that one of the key findings in studies of German firms was that any particular act of internationalization was part of a broader strategy of change for the MNC. International operations were often part of a circumspect strategy to find new ways of doing things that could be transferred back to Germany or to other parts of the MNC (Child, Faulkner, and Pitkethley 2000, 2001).

German managers typically did not impose German ways, preferring instead to introduce some new (often relatively loose) financial and operational reporting measures, while gradually getting to know the strengths and weaknesses of the foreign operation. Over a period of time, technical and financial support might be made available for changes in the acquired subsidiary, but more important was the effort to learn from the subsidiary, about labor practices in a liberal market economy, about management skills in such a setting, and about corporate finance and access to capital markets outside Germany (Bluhm 2001; Ferner and Quintanilla 1998; Ferner and Varul 2000; Lane 1998, 2001). This learning would gradually be made available more broadly in the organization as other subsidiaries were established.

The German example therefore revealed that hybridization as conceived in the Japanese case, that is, a process of headquarters–subsidiary processes of accommodation was not a very useful concept for German MNCs. Indeed, it was more likely that the Japanese MNCs were the exception rather than the rule because power has remained very centralized in Japanese MNCs and the headquarters tends to insulate itself from either dependency on particular subsidiaries or learning from subsidiaries.

23.4.3 Transnationalization: Understanding Contemporary Practice

This leads into the third approach deriving from the institutionalist perspective, which has been labelled here transnationalism. In this approach, the MNC is seen as a bounded social space encompassing distinctive institutional settings and social actors. Arguably, this approach began to emerge as industrial relations experts examined more closely the dynamics of power within the multinational insofar as it affected the ways in which different groups of workers could make their interest felt (Edwards *et al.* 1996; Ferner 1997; Ferner and Edwards 1995). More recently, however, it has been developed in a series of studies deliberately seeking to understand how firms from different national institutional contexts international-ize and with what effect (Kristensen and Zeitlin 2001; Morgan 2001*a, b, c*; Whitley 2001). In these discussions, the national institutional setting constitutes the social context of routines, practices, skills, and careers. The distinctiveness of the multi-national is that it creates a common social space in which different institutional settings are encapsulated.

In this perspective, we can therefore distinguish two distinct and cross-cutting forces inside the multinational. The first is the social embeddedness of the subsid-iary in the local institutional context. This depends on a variety of factors such as the nature of the activity (the degree of integration of the task into a broader global value chain), the degree of investment and assets that have been sunk into the local context, the composition of the workforce (the size and significance of expatriates and more generally the degree of social cohesion between different levels of the workforce within the workplace) and the linkages into the broader social context (reliance on local suppliers and customers, participation in local training and skill institutions). As Solvell and Zander (1998) have pointed out, there is a tendency in some manufacturing cases for the degree of local embeddedness of the subsidiary to increase as contacts with the local context are increased and deepened. This sets up a centripetal logic in the manufacturing MNC.

The second process is one of standardization and increasing control from the headquarters as management tries to tie the various institutionally distinct settings together. A preliminary list of such mechanisms, drawing on the traditional preoccupations of organization theory, would include the following:

- *Organization structure*: how individuals, plants, and offices are brought together within and across national boundaries to constitute subsegments of the organiza-tion that can be monitored and controlled
- *Performance measures*: what performance measures are to be monitored over what period in the organizational subunits and with what consequences? Obvious differences exist between the use of tight financial controls backed by

strong intervention when targets are not met versus performance measures based primarily on other criteria such as market share, productivity, headcount

- *Standardization of procedures*: human resource procedures (recruitment, appraisal and reward systems, management development programs, attitudes towards trade unions) or in terms of standard operating procedures for technology or other aspects of the organization process, or relations with suppliers
- *Best practices benchmarking and transfer*: this also relates to measurement but in a more proactive way so that high-performing sites become exemplars for others and find there are attempts to abstract practices from local settings and transfer them to other sites. Such processes can be formalized into a knowledge management database for the organization
- *Creation of standardized management careers*: allowing transfer across national boundaries as a means of both imposing standardization and also picking up new learning experiences.

As Birkinshaw suggested, a crucial additional feature consists of the headquarters' ability to act as a bank that distributes rewards to high-performing subsidiaries in the form of capital for investment. It is the headquarters that links in with capital markets and ultimately takes decisions on how internally generated funds will be used and how and when to raise additional funds on these markets. In effect, the headquarters operates a carrot and stick approach to controlling the subsidiaries. However, even this has its limits as subsidiaries may envisage a future outside their current organization if the particular carrot and stick is not deemed suitable. In other words, subsidiaries may seek to put themselves into play on the market for corporate control if relations with headquarters begin to seriously fail. This obviously assumes that there is a viable business at the subsidiary level, something that may be hard to establish in financial terms (due to the complexities of internal pricing regimes in MNCs) and in reputational terms. This also depends on factors such as how tightly integrated the production process and the organization structure of the local site is with the global value chain and structure of the MNC, how cohesive the local managers and workforce are (in terms of cooperating for survival and growth), what support can be obtained from the local community, and whether there are either potential buyers or financial institutions that may fund a management buyout.

Some of these features are, of course, strongly related to the local institutional context while others relate to how the headquarters has integrated the various parts of the firm and tied them together in ways that make unbundling difficult. On the other hand, the headquarters itself will often require the flexibility for unbundling in order to respond to requirements for restructuring that may arise from stock market pressures. Thus, the MNC itself will often be involved in disposing of subsidiaries as it rationalizes and refocuses its activities. Therefore the headquarters is trapped in an inescapable dilemma; it wants to maximize the dependency of the subsidiary on the center to reduce the centripetal tendencies referred to earlier, yet it wants to maintain sufficient flexibility to be able to dispose of subsidiaries should circumstances so require it. The result is that the subsidiary is bound to live in a state of permanent insecurity where the search for (or at least consideration of) alternative futures is likely. This in turn relates to the fundamental instability of the multinational form itself. Whereas economic rationalists have tended to see this as a non-problem, organizational research is increasingly showing up the precariousness of multinational firms and attempts to create cross-national teams, cross-national knowledge-sharing, and cross-national management career structures.

In distinction to the other institutionalist approaches, therefore, the transnational approach attempts to encompass the totality of the social space of the multinational in which there are multiple flows of people, information, procedures, and practices occurring all the time. These flows interact with the socially embedded nature of actors and subsidiaries to create the context in which the battle for survival, both at the level of subsidiaries and sites and at the level of the MNC itself, must be understood. This suggests that, in methodological terms, the study of the MNC has to match the complexity of the firm itself. The task facing those wishing to pursue the transnationalism research agenda is therefore large. For obvious financial and logistical reasons, few studies have come close to this. However, there is Belanger et al.'s study of ABB (1999), which has the considerable virtue of bringing together a series of country-level studies that reveal the variable levels of embeddedness of the firm's subsidiaries. There is also the work of Kristensen and Zeitlin (2001), who have examined the development of a UK-headquartered MNC and considered the bargaining that has gone on between subsidiaries located in the United States, Germany, Denmark, and the United Kingdom. These two studies are noteworthy for their intrinsic interest and because they are so rare. Such studies bring together ideas from institutionalism with those that have developed in the international business literature concerning subsidiary autonomy and development.

23.5 CONCLUSIONS

This chapter has sought to achieve three objectives. The first has been to provide a historical account of the multinational and its current development. The largest MNC in the current period (measured by assets) are based in manufacturing and extractive industries and their headquarters are located in the major economies. The second objective has been to critically examine the literature accounting for the existence of multinationals and their activities. Here, the economic approach (in particular, Dunning's eclectic theory) was contrasted with approaches emphasizing issues of power and control. More recent research, however, has begun to unify these two approaches by looking at subsidiary–headquarters relations. In these recent perspectives, a combination of political and economic factors is seen to determine the overall structure and strategy of the firm. The third objective was to signal the current stage of knowledge and to argue that further progress in understanding these internal markets requires the incorporation of insights from institutional theory.

Three approaches were distinguished under this broad heading. However, it was argued that only the third approach deals sufficiently with the distinctive nature of multinationals, that is, the diffuse and complex flows of labor, capital, technology, and knowledge across multiple national boundaries. This creates a transnational social space defined by two cross-cutting features. On the one hand, each set of actors is embedded in their distinctive local institutional context; from this context, actors develop distinctive powers and capabilities. In general, there is a tendency to deepen this local embeddedness as time goes on and local networks become stronger. On the other hand, the headquarters of the MNC implements systems of control and management that aim at various levels of standardization across the organization (in terms of organization structure, financial or other reporting, procedures, management careers).

This tension is further overlaid by the control the headquarters has over access to capital, though this is accompanied by the direct pressure that the headquarters feels from capital markets for performance. The headquarters therefore controls the purse strings for the subsidiaries, but this can have a negative effect for the overall cohesion of the MNC because the insecurity felt by the subsidiary in terms of its continued development within the MNC can push it further down the line of increasing its local embeddedness and loosening its dependence on the MNC headquarters. Conceptualizing these processes in terms of transnational social spaces opens up the possibility of a much deeper understanding of the dynamics of MNCs than either the subsidiary strategy/internal markets point of view that has developed in the international business literature or the limited considerations of certain institutionalist approaches. It also provides the opportunity of integrating the study of MNCs with traditional preoccupations of organizational and industrial studies. Given the current size and importance of multinationals, that can surely only be a good thing.

References

Abo, T. (1994). *Hybrid Factory: The Japanese Production System in the United States.* Oxford: Oxford University Press.

ANDERSON, S., and CAVANAGH, J. (2000). *Top 200: The Rise of Corporate Global Power.* Washington, DC: Institute for Policy Studies.

BARTLETT, C. A., and GHOSHAL, S. (1989). *Managing across Borders: The Transnational Solution.* London: Century Business.

BEECHLER, S. L., and BIRD, A. (1999). *Japanese Multinationals Abroad: Individual and Organizational Learning.* New York: Oxford University Press.

BELANGER, J., BERGGREN, C., BJORKMAN, T., and KOHLER, C. (1999). *Being Local and Worldwide: ABB and the Challenge of Global Management.* Ithaca, NY: ILR imprint, Cornell University Press.

BIRKINSHAW, J. (1997). 'Entrepreneurship in Multinational Corporations: The Characteristics of Subsidiary Initiatives'. *Strategic Management Journal,* 18: 207–29.

—— (2000). *Entrepreneurship in the Global Firm.* London: Sage.

—— (2001). 'Strategy and Management in MNE Subsidiaries', in A. Rugman and T. L. Brewer (eds.), *The Oxford Handbook of International Business.* Oxford: Oxford University Press.

—— and HOOD, N. (1998). *Multinational Corporate Evolution and Subsidiary Development.* London: Macmillan.

BLUHM, K. (2001). 'Exporting or Abandoning the "German Model"?: Labour Policies of German Manufacturing Firms in Central Europe'. *European Journal of Industrial Relations,* 7: 153–73.

BRESMAN, H., BIRKINSHAW, J., and NOBEL, R. (1999). 'Knowledge Transfer in International Acquisitions'. *Journal of International Business Studies,* 30/3: 439–62.

BUCKLEY, P. J., and GHAURI, P. (eds.) (2000). *Internationalization of the Firm.* London: Thompson.

CAIN, P. J., and HOPKINS, A. G. (1993). *British Imperialism: Innovation and Expansion 1688–1914.* London: Longman.

CAMPBELL, N., and BURTON, F. (1994). *Japanese Multinationals.* London: Routledge.

CHILD, J., FAULKNER, D., and PITKETHLEY, R. (2000). 'Foreign Direct Investment in the UK 1985–1994: The Impact on Domestic Management Practice'. *Journal of Management Studies,* 37: 141–66.

———— (2001). *The Management of International Acquisitions.* Oxford: Oxford University Press.

DE GRAUWE, P., and CAMERMAN, F. (2002). 'How Big Are the Big Multinational Companies?' Available from http://www.econ.kuleuven.ac.be/ew/academic/intecon/DeGrauwe/PaulDeGrauwe.htm

DELBRIDGE, R. (1998). *Life on the Line in Contemporary Manufacturing.* Oxford: Oxford University Press.

DICKEN, P. (1998). *Global Shift* (3rd edn). London: Paul Chapman Publishing.

DJELIC, M.-L. (1999). *Exporting the American Model: The Post-War Transformation of European Business.* Oxford: Oxford University Press.

DORE, R., LAZONICK, W., and O'SULLIVAN, M. (1999). 'Varieties of Capitalism in the Twentieth Century'. *Oxford Review of Economic Policy,* 15: 102–20.

DOREMUS, P. N., KELLER, W., PAULEY, L., and REICH, S. (1998). *The Myth of the Global Corporation.* Princeton, NJ: Princeton University Press.

DUNNING, J. (1998). 'Reappraising the Eclectic Paradigm in an Age of Alliance Capitalism', in M. Colombo (ed.), *The Changing Boundaries of the Firm.* London: Routledge.

—— (2001). 'The Key Literature on IB Activities: 1960–2000', in A. Rugman and T. L. Brewer (eds.), *The Oxford Handbook of International Business*. Oxford: Oxford University Press.

EDWARDS, P., ARMSTRONG, P., MARGINSON, P., and PURCELL, J. (1996). 'Towards the Transnational Company? The Global Structure and Organisation of Multinational Firms', in R. Crompton, D. Gallie, and K. Purcell (eds.), *Changing Forms of Employment: Organisations, Skills and Gender*. London: Routledge.

ELGER, T., and SMITH, C. (1994). *Global Japanization?* London: Routledge.

—— —— (1998). 'New Town, New Capital, New Workplace? The Employment Relations of Japanese Inward Investors in a West Midlands Industrial Town'. *Economy and Society*, 22: 523–53.

FERNER, A. (1997). 'Country of Origin Effects and HRM in Multinational Companies'. *Human Resource Management Journal*, 7: 19–37.

—— and EDWARDS, P. (1995). 'Power and the Diffusion of Organizational Change within Multinational Enterprises'. *European Journal of Industrial Relations*, 1: 229–57.

—— and QUINTANILLA, J. (1998). 'Multinationals, National Business Systems and HRM: The Enduring Influence of National Identity or a Process of "Anglo-Saxonization"'. *International Journal of Human Resource Management*, 9: 710–31.

—— and VARUL, M. (2000). '"Vanguard" Subsidiaries and the Diffusion of New Practices: A Case Study of German Multinationals'. *British Journal of Industrial Relations*, 38: 115–40.

FROBEL, F. (1980). *The New International Division of Labour*. Cambridge: Cambridge University Press.

GEREFFI, G. (1995). 'Global Production Systems and Third World Development', in B. Stallings (ed.), *Global Change, Regional Response*. Cambridge: Cambridge University Press.

—— and TAM, T. (1999). 'Industrial Upgrading and Organizational Chains', in Chieh-hsuan Chen (ed.), *Business Transformation and Social Change*. Taipei: Linking Publishing.

GHOSHAL, S., and WESTNEY, D. E. (1993). *Organization Theory and the Multinational*. London: Macmillan.

GILPIN, R. (2001). *Global Political Economy*. Princeton, NJ: Princeton University Press.

GLIMSTEDT, H. (2001). 'Between National and International Governance: Geopolitics, Strategizing Actors and Sector Coordination in Electrical Engineering in the Interwar Era', in G. Morgan, R. Whitley, and P. H. Kristensen (eds.), *The Multinational Firm*. Oxford: Oxford University Press.

GRAHAM, L. (1995). *On the Line at Subaru-Izusu*. Ithaca, NY: ILR imprint, Cornell University Press.

HALL, P. A., and SOSKICE, D. (2001). *Varieties of Capitalism*. Oxford: Oxford University Press.

HEDLUND, G. (1986). 'The Hypermodern MNC—A Heterarchy?' *Human Resource Management*, 25: 9–35.

—— (1993). 'Assumptions of Hierarchy and Heterarchy: An Application to the Multinational Corporation', in S. Ghoshal and D. E. Westney (eds.), *Organization Theory and the Multinational Corporation*. London: Macmillan.

HIRST, P., and THOMPSON, G. (1999). *Globalization in Question* (2nd edn). Oxford: Polity Press.

HOLLINGSWORTH, J. R. (1997). 'Continuities and Changes in Social Systems of Production: The Cases of Japan, Germany and the United States', in J. R. Hollingsworth and R. Boyer (eds.), *Contemporary Capitalism: The Embeddedness of Institutions*. Cambridge: Cambridge University Press.

HU, Y. S. (1992). 'Global or Stateless Firms are National Corporations with International Operations'. *California Management Review*, 34: 107–26.

HYMER, S. H. (1968). 'The Large Multi-National "Corporation"', in M. Casson (ed.), *Multinational Corporations*. Aldershot: Edward Elgar.

—— (1972). 'The Multinational Corporation and the Law of Uneven Development', in J. N. Bagwati (ed.), *Economics and World Order*. London: Macmillan.

ISHIDA, H. (1986). 'Transferability of Japanese Human Resource Management Abroad'. *Human Resource Management*, 25: 103–20.

KRISTENSEN, P. H., and ZEITLIN, J. (2001). 'The Making of a Global Firm', in G. Morgan, R. Whitley, and P. H. Kristensen (eds.), *The Multinational Firm: Organizing across Institutional and National Divides*. Oxford: Oxford University Press.

LANE, C. (1998). 'European Companies between Globalization and Localization: A Comparison of the Internationalization Strategies of British and German MNCs'. *Economy and Society*, 27: 462–85.

—— (2001). 'The Emergence of German Transnational Companies and Their Impact on the Domestic Business System', in G. Morgan, R. Whitley, and P. H. Kristensen (eds.), *The Multinational Firm: Organizing across Institutional and National Divides*. Oxford: Oxford University Press.

LIKER, J., FRUIN, W. M., and ADLER, P. (1999). *Remade in America: Transplanting and Transforming Japanese Management Systems*. New York: Oxford University Press.

MARGINSON, P. (2000). 'The Eurocompany and Euro Industrial Relations'. *European Journal of Industrial Relations*, 6: 9–34.

MIOZZO, M., and SOETE, L. (2001). 'Internationalization of Services: A Technological Perspective'. *Technological Forecasting and Social Change*, 67: 159–85.

MORGAN, G. (2001a). 'The Development of Transnational Standards and Regulations and Their Impacts on Firms', in G. Morgan, R. Whitley, and P. H. Kristensen (eds.), *The Multinational Firm: Organizing across Institutional and National Divides*. Oxford: Oxford University Press.

—— (2001b). 'The Multinational Firm', in G. Morgan, R. Whitley, and P. H. Kristensen (eds.), *The Multinational Firm: Organizing across Institutional and National Divides*. Oxford: Oxford University Press.

—— (2001c). 'Transnational Communities and Business Systems'. *Global Networks*, 1: 113–30.

—— WHITLEY, R., SHARPE, D., and KELLY, W. (2002). 'The Future of Japanese Manufacturing in the UK'. *Journal of Management Studies*, 3: 1023–44.

NOHRIA, N., and GHOSHAL, N. (1997). *The Differentiated Network: Organizing Multinational Corporations for Value Creation*. New York: Jossey-Bass.

PRAHALAD, C. K., and DOZ, Y. (1987). *The Multinational Mission: Balancing Local Demands and Global Vision*. New York: Free Press.

QUACK, S., MORGAN, G., and WHITLEY, R. (2000). *National Capitalisms, Global Competition and Economic Performance*. Amsterdam: John Benjamins Publishing.

SOLVELL, O., and ZANDER, I. (1998). 'International Diffusion of Knowledge: Isolating Mechanisms and the Role of the MNE', in A. D. Chandler, O. Solvell, and P. Hagstrom (eds.), *The Dynamic Firm: The Role of Technology, Strategy, Organization and Regions*. Oxford: Oxford University Press.

SOSKICE, D. (1999). 'Divergent Production Regimes: Coordinated and Uncoordinated Market Economies in the 1980s and 1990s', in H. Kitschelt, P. Lange, G. Marks, and J. D. Stephens, (eds.), *Continuity and Change in Contemporary Capitalism*. Cambridge: Cambridge University Press.

TAGGART, J. H. (1998). 'Strategy Shifts in MNC Subsidiaries'. *Strategic Management Journal*, 19: 663–81.

TEICHOVA, A., LEVY-LEBOYER, M., and NUSSBAUM, H. (1986). *Multinational Enterprise in Historical Perspective*. Cambridge: Cambridge University Press.

UNCTAD (2002). *World Investment Report 2002*. Geneva: UNCTAD.

WESTNEY, E., and ZAHEER, S. (2001). 'The Multinational Enterprise as an Organization', in A. Rugman and T. L. Brewer (eds.), *The Oxford Handbook of International Business*. Oxford: Oxford University Press.

WHITLEY, R. (1999). *Divergent Capitalisms*. Oxford: Oxford University Press.

—— (2001). 'How and Why Are International Firms Different?' in G. Morgan, R. Whitley, and P. H. Kristensen (eds.), *The Multinational Firm: Organizing across Institutional and National Divides*. Oxford: Oxford University Press.

WHITTALL, M. (2000). 'The BMW European Works Council: A Cause for European Industrial Relations Optimism?' *European Journal of Industrial Relations*, 6: 61–83.

WILKINS, M. (2001). 'The History of Multinational Enterprise', in A. Rugman and T. L. Brewer (eds.), *The Oxford Handbook of International Business*. Oxford: Oxford University Press.

WILSON, J. F. (1995). *British Business History 1720–1994*. Manchester: Manchester University Press.

ZEITLIN, J., and HERRIGEL, G. (2000). *Americanization and Its Limits: Reworking US Technology and Management in Post-war Europe and Japan*. Oxford: Oxford University Press.

CHAPTER 24

CORPORATE RESTRUCTURING

WILLIAM LAZONICK

24.1 INTRODUCTION: THE BUSINESS CORPORATION AND RESTRUCTURING

BUSINESS corporations are central to economic activity nationally and globally. In 2002 there were thirteen corporations in the world with revenues in excess of $100 billion, six of them American, three Japanese, two German, one British, and one British-Dutch. Of the world's fifty biggest employers—ranging from Wal-Mart, with 1,300,000 employees to Peugeot with 198,600 employees—eighteen were American, nine French, seven German, six Chinese, four Japanese, two British, and one each Dutch, British-Dutch, Russian, and Swiss. In 2002 the 500 largest corporations by revenues employed an average of 92,985 people each (Fortune 2003).

At some point in history—although in many cases that history goes back more than a hundred years—even the largest of these business corporations did not exist. They grew large over time by developing the productive capabilities of their investments in physical and human capital and then realizing returns on these investments through the sale of goods and services. As they captured a larger extent of the market, they benefited from economies of scale and scope. In retrospect, that

Some of the research underlying this chapter was supported by the Russell Sage Foundation.

growth was not inevitable (even if, with careful research, it may be explicable), and one cannot assume that any particular corporation will be able to sustain its current levels of revenue and employment in the future. Industrial corporations that have grown large often undergo major restructuring.

At any point in time, the structure of the corporation is the result of an evolutionary process that reflects strategic investment decisions to serve particular markets, engage in particular activities, and produce in particular locations. Restructuring occurs when the corporation is not willing or able to utilize the capabilities and assets that are the legacy of past decisions. Within any company, the incomes, employment opportunities, and career paths of large numbers of people may be affected. Long-term employees may find that the corporation no longer requires their services. Whether and how they secure new employment will depend on labor market conditions and their own marketability. Other employees may find themselves compelled to work for different companies and/or in different locations. In most cases of restructuring, these changes in work will be beyond the control of most employees. The main exception is a management buyout where divisional managers, motivated by the possibility of exercising more control over the conditions of and returns from their employment, take the initiative in removing a division from the existing corporation.

Under adverse economic conditions that cut across industrial sectors or firms within a sector, large numbers of companies in the same nation or region may engage in restructuring at the same time. Such restructuring can have a negative impact on national or regional employment, especially when restructuring involves large-scale downsizing or the closing or locational shift of a labor-intensive facility. Thus, restructuring can have profound impacts on the quality and quantity of jobs available in the economy. It may render uncertain the livelihoods of large numbers of people within a region or nation for whom the industrial corporation provided stable employment. At the same time, however, corporate restructuring may be a necessary response to changing technological, market, and economic conditions if the firms that provide employment are to remain competitive. Through an analysis of corporate restructuring, we can gain insights into the larger questions of who gains and who loses in a rapidly changing global economy and how the regulation and governance of the corporation can promote stable and equitable economic growth.

24.1.1 Analyzing Corporate Restructuring

Corporate restructuring entails a significant reduction in the resources that a corporation allocates to product markets or process activities or geographical locations in which it had previously been engaged. Such a reduction may be part of a process of reallocating corporate resources to new growth areas, but corporate restructuring always entails a retrenchment of resource commitments to one or more specific markets, activities, or locations. For any corporation the starting point for restructuring is an existing organizational structure that employs a certain number of people in particular locations to serve markets by engaging in particular activities.

Restructuring can take six forms: buyout, divestiture, outsourcing, relocation, downsizing, and bankruptcy. A buyout occurs when managers within a particular unit in the corporation secure the financing required to turn the unit into a separate company. A divestiture occurs when the corporation sells a particular business unit to outsiders, in some cases by spinning off the unit and listing it on a stock exchange. An outsourcing occurs when the corporation enters into a supply or distribution relation with another company to engage in activities that the corporation previously performed. A relocation occurs when the corporation shifts an activity from one place to another with a substantial change in whom it employs. A downsizing occurs when the corporation permanently reduces its employment level without necessarily abandoning a product market, process activity, or geographic location. A bankruptcy occurs when a firm fails to meet or renegotiate its obligations to its creditors and may be preceded by any or all of the other forms of restructuring.

Corporate executives generally argue that the purpose of corporate restructuring is renovation, not redistribution. In downsizing they might argue that, notwithstanding its redistributive impact, the termination of the employment of some people is an essential prelude to rightsizing the company so that it can invest in innovations that will make the remaining labor force more competitive. However, decision-making power is unequally distributed among participants in the corporation. Even when renovation is a goal, those who have more power may use the process to improve or maintain their own welfare while foisting the costs of restructuring on others. An analysis of corporate restructuring should ask by whom and for whom the corporation is run, and how renovative outcomes might be achieved while mitigating the losses of those who are not given the opportunity of sharing in the gains of renovation.

The main focus of this chapter is corporate restructuring as it has occurred in the United States over the past two decades. The United States is not only the world's largest economy but also the one in which managerial prerogative in restructuring the industrial corporation has been least constrained, especially in terms of laying off existing employees and creating new firms. Nevertheless, in the post-World War II decades, up to the 1970s, most established US industrial corporations—ones that we would now label old economy—pursued investment strategies that have been called elsewhere retain and reinvest (Lazonick and O'Sullivan 2000a); they retained corporate revenues and reinvested in the growth of the corporation. During the 1980s and 1990s, however, many of these established corporations engaged in investment strategies that we have called downsize and distribute; they have downsized corporate labor forces and distributed corporate revenues. During the same decades, however, a new breed of corporation drove the growth of the US economy, based on a new retain and reinvest regime—to the point where by the late 1990s they formed the foundation of a new economy. As a prelude to discussions of the restructuring of the old economy corporation and the rise of the new economy corporation in the 1980s and 1990s, the following section summarizes the key features of the historical evolution of the US industrial corporation to the 1970s.

24.2 THE EVOLUTION OF THE US CORPORATION: HISTORICAL BACKGROUND

In the 1950s the United States dominated the world economy. Its level of per capita income was well ahead of fast-growing nations such as Germany and Japan (Maddison 1994: 22). The industrial corporation was central to US economic power, and within the United States a small number of corporations had attained immense control over the allocation of the economy's resources. In 1959 forty-four of the world's fifty largest corporations in terms of revenues were US-based, with the remaining six headquartered in Europe. Corporations represented 9.6 percent of US business enterprises, but 79.3 percent of business revenues. US corporations with assets of $100 million or more accounted for one-tenth of 1 percent of corporations, but 55.4 percent of corporate assets, 54.5 percent of before tax corporate profits, and 67.9 percent of corporate dividends (Kaysen 1996: 25; US Bureau of the Census 1976: Series V, 182–96).

24.2.1 Managerial Revolution

The central characteristic of the US corporation in the post-World War II decades was managerial organization. The corporations that dominated the US economy into the 1970s grew large by investing in the organizational capabilities of professional, technical, and administrative personnel, resulting in what Chandler (1977) called 'the managerial revolution in American business'. By the 1920s, when major US industrial corporations consolidated their positions across a range of research-intensive and capital-intensive industries, the managerial revolution was complete

(Chandler 1962, 1977; Lazonick 1986; Noble 1977). In 'The Rise of Administrative Overhead in the Manufacturing Industries of the United States, 1899–1947', Melman (1951) showed that the number of salaried employees in US manufacturing rose from 0.35 million in 1899 to 1.50 million in 1929 and then to 2.58 million in 1947, with the ratio of salaried employees to 100 wage earners rising from 7.7 in 1899 to 17.9 in 1929 and to 21.6 in 1947 (Melman 1951: 66). In 1929 industries with the highest ratios of salaried employees to wage earners included drugs and medicines (61.5), soap (42.3), flour (39.4), business machines (36.9), photoengraving (35.1), printing and publishing (33.4), structural steel (25.4), lithographing (24.7), and electrical machinery (24.6).

24.2.2 Transforming Technologies, Supervising Workers, Accessing Markets

What did all these salaried managers do? One critical role of the managerial organization was to transform technologies. During the first decades of the twentieth century, many high-technology companies such as General Electric, Eastman Kodak, AT&T, and Du Pont created in-house R&D labs. Between 1899 and 1946 US manufacturing companies put in place almost 2,200 laboratories for industrial research, of which 26 percent were in chemicals and 20 percent in machinery. These research labs employed 2,775 scientists and engineers in 1921, 6,320 in 1927, 10,927 in 1933, and 27,777 in 1940, so that even the Great Depression did not curb corporate investments for transforming technologies. Government funding of corporate R&D during World War II helped increase the number employed scientists and engineers to 45,941 by 1946, representing 0.40 research personnel for every 100 wage earners in that year (Mowery and Rosenberg 1989: 62–71).

A second critical role of managerial organization was to supervise the work of wage earners. In transforming technologies, a central focus of the US managerial corporation was to take skills off the shop floor by embedding craft capabilities in machine processes. These changes eliminated the craft-worker, but replaced him with the semi-skilled operative whose job it was to perform routine manual tasks on a repetitive basis as a complement to the high-speed capabilities of mass-production machines. Managers supervised these mass-production operatives to ensure that they maintained the pace of work. The ratio of supervisory personnel to production workers in US manufacturing increased by 15 percent between 1900 and 1910, and by another 35 percent in the following decade, after which this ratio stabilized (Lazonick 1990: ch. 7).

A third critical role of the managerial organization was to access product markets. Without access to markets to sell corporate products, the high fixed costs of developing technology and investing in production facilities would have resulted in high losses. In making investments in production capabilities, therefore, industrial corporations also had to make investments in distribution capabilities, including sales, offices, advertising, and even customized transportation facilities to ensure that they would be able to sell the goods they produced. As Chandler (1990) has shown, from the late nineteenth century, a three-pronged investment in production, distribution, and management was a necessary condition for the growth of the industrial enterprise.

In the first stage of growth, the industrial enterprise sought to build distribution capabilities for national markets, an effort facilitated in the last decades of the nineteenth century by the construction of transcontinental railroads and a national telecommunications system. From the 1920s this infrastructure was augmented by the development of the world's leading air transportation system, whose growth was closely linked to the rise of a national and international airmail service (Heppenheimer 1995). The organizational capabilities developed within the leading industrial corporations that enabled them to dominate national markets subsequently laid the foundations for multinational expansion.

24.2.3 The Trajectory of Development

There was a general slowdown in multinational expansion between the world wars, but, according to Jones (2002: 4607), '[b]etween 1945 and the mid-1960s the USA may have accounted for 85 percent of all new flows of [foreign] direct investment'. This global expansion was mainly in manufacturing facilities in other advanced economies that gave the multinational companies better access to foreign markets. By 1980, Britain, which served as a production location for goods sold throughout Western Europe, was the recipient of more foreign direct investment than all of Africa and Asia combined (Dunning 1993: 20; Jones 2002: 4607). In the 1980s and 1990s there was a tendency for multinational corporations to locate activities such as R&D and marketing in different parts of the world, so that intrafirm trade became a significant share of world trade. In 1989, for example, cross-border transactions in goods and services between US-based firms and their foreign affiliates or parent companies accounted for about 42 percent of US exports and 49 percent of imports (Dunning 1993: 386–7).

As they expanded, US industrial corporations diversified into new lines of business. Capabilities developed for one product market could be used as a basis for gaining entry to new product markets. Moreover, as companies were successful, they could use internally generated revenues to finance new investments, including R&D. Federal government and business spending on R&D doubled in real terms between 1953 and 1959, and doubled again between 1959 and 1982. R&D as a proportion of GNP increased from 1.40 percent in 1953 to 2.53 percent in 1959 to 2.61 percent in 1982, with a peak of 2.96 percent in 1964. In that year, the proportion of R&D spending from the federal government also peaked at 66.5 percent, gradually declining to 46.1 percent in 1982 (Mowery and Rosenberg 1989: 126–7).

During the postwar decades, therefore, US industrial corporations had access to unprecedented amounts of new technology that they could exploit commercially. For transforming knowledge into revenue-generating products, they had access to an unparalleled communications infrastructure and had, over the previous decades, built up formidable organizational capabilities. The golden age of the 1950s and 1960s, moreover, provided industrial corporations with favorable demand conditions on both home and foreign markets (Marglin and Schor 1990).

24.2.4 The Rise of the Multidivisional Enterprise

In the early decades of the twentieth century, industrial corporations had discovered that success in one product market could provide them with privileged access to technological, organizational, and financial resources that could be used for entry into new product markets. By the 1920s a small number of leading industrial corporations had begun to cope with the problem of how to organize different business units within one coherent corporate organization. The result in the ensuing decades was the transition from a functional to a multidivisional organization of the enterprise (Chandler 1962).

The multidivisional structure vested control over the integration of specialized functions such as purchasing, production, and sales within divisions that operated as profit centers, with their focus on developing products for sale in particular markets or geographical areas. Besides controlling staff functions (legal, accounting, finance, human resource, industrial relations, research) at the corporate level, corporate headquarters maintained strategic control over major decisions for expansion in or withdrawal from lines of business and geographic locations. Chandler (1962: 11) depicted corporate headquarters as making entrepreneurial decisions and the divisions as making operational decisions, where 'entrepreneurial decisions and actions refer to those which affect that allocation or reallocation of resources for the enterprise as a whole, and operating decisions and actions ... refer to those which are carried out by using the resources already allocated'.

In his seminal book, *Strategy and Structure*, Chandler (1962: 369) held up General Electric (GE) as a model of 'future trends in the organization of the most technologically advanced type of American industrial enterprise'. He noted how in the 1950s the company implemented the multidivisional structure by breaking down its organization into twenty operating divisions that administered the work of functional departments, whose total numbers grew from 70 in 1950 to 105 in 1960

(Chandler 1962: 368). While Chandler (1962: 369) expressed concern that GE had perhaps created too many operating units to be administered effectively, he argued that the organizational changes in the company in the 1950s had 'undoubtedly facilitated General Electric's recent diversification into nuclear power, jets, computers, industrial automation systems and other new fields as well as the expansion of the company's resources abroad'.

Based on the multidivisional structure, however, over the next two decades GE became an unwieldy conglomerate that failed to transform its considerable capabilities in electronics into competitive advantage in semiconductors, computers, and factory automation. Moreover in the 1950s it was GE that was foremost among US companies in creating the ideology that by learning general principles of how to manage the work of others (laid out in the company's five-volume manual, 'Professional Management in General Electric') a well-trained manager could manage any type of business (O'Sullivan 2000: 118–21). In the 1960s this ideology became standard fare in US graduate business schools. It was used to justify the growth of the US corporation through diversification, often by means of mergers and acquisitions, even if many of the lines of business in these conglomerates had no technological or market relation to one another.

During the 1960s the conglomerate movement significantly reshaped the organization of the US industrial corporation. The mean number of lines of business of the top 200 US manufacturing corporations ranked by sales rose from 4.76 in 1950 to 10.89 in 1975. For the 148 corporations of the 200 largest in 1950 that still existed in 1975 the mean number of lines of business rose from 5.22 to 9.74. In the conglomerate movement of the 1960s, annual average mergers and acquisitions (M&A) announcements increased from 1,951 in 1963–7 to 3,736 in 1968–72, with a peak level of 5,306 in 1969 (Merrill Lynch Advisory Services 1994). Between 1950 and 1978 Beatrice Foods did 290 acquisitions, W. R. Grace 186, IT&T 163, Gulf and Western 155, Textron 115, Litton Industries 99, and LTV 58 (Ravenscraft and Scherer 1987: 30, 32, 38, 39). Scherer and Ross (1990: 157) have shown that, of assets that large manufacturing and mining companies acquired when they bought other companies, 10.1 percent were in the pure conglomerate category in 1948–55, 17.7 percent in 1956–63, 34.8 percent in 1964–71, and 45.5 percent in 1972–9.

This corporate growth from the 1950s to the 1970s was also reflected in average employment of the largest corporations by revenues. The 50 largest US industrial corporations by revenues averaged 87,080 employees in 1957 (the first year for which we have Fortune 500 data), 117,393 in 1967, and 119,093 in 1977. In total, in 1957 these 50 companies employed 4.4 million people (equivalent to 6.4 percent of the US civilian labor force), in 1967 5.9 million (7.5 percent), and in 1977 6.0 million (5.8 percent) (it should be noted that these data refer to worldwide employment by the corporations so that these percentages somewhat overstate their importance to total US employment). Table 24.1 shows the changes in employment over this period for the twenty largest employers in 1957 and in 1977.

Table 24.1 Employment, 1957–1977, of the twenty largest US corporate employers in 1957 and 1977

Company	Rank 1957	1957	1962	1967	1972	1977	Rank 1977
General Motors	1	588,160	604,278	728,198	759,543	797,000	1
General Electric	2	282,029	258,174	375,000	369,000	384,000	3
US Steel	3	271,037	194,044	197,643	176,486	165,845	8
Ford Motor	4	191,759	302,563	394,323	442,607	479,000	2
Bethlehem Steel	5	166,859	122,089	131,000	109,000	94,000	22
Standard Oil (NJ)/Exxon[a]	6	160,000	150,000	150,000	141,000	127,000	14
Western Electric	7	144,055	151,174	169,700	205,665	162,000	9
Chrysler	8	136,187	77,194[b]	215,907	244,844	250,833	6
Westinghouse Electric	9	128,572	109,966	132,049	183,768	141,394	11
ITT	10	128,000	157,000	236,000	428,000	375,000	4
Goodyear Rubber and Tire	11	101,386	95,740	113,207	145,201	159,890	10
Boeing	12	94,998	104,100	142,700	58,600	66,900	42
Sperry Rand	13	93,130	103,545	101,603	85,574	85,684	28
General Dynamics	14	91,700	84,500	103,196	60,900	73,268	36
Du Pont (E.I.) de Nemours	15	90,088	93,159	111,931	111,052	131,317	13
Firestone Tire & Rubber	16	88,323	83,909	95,500	109,000	115,000	18
Douglas/McDonnell Douglas[c]	17	78,400	44,000	140,050	86,713	61,577	47
RCA	18	78,000	87,000	128,000	122,000	111,000	20
Socony Mobil Oil/Mobil Oil/ Mobil[d]	19	77,000	74,900	75,800	75,400	200,700	7
Swift/Esmark[e]	20	71,900	54,200	48,300	33,600	44,700	85
OTHER COMPANIES AMONG TOP 20 EMPLOYERS IN 1977							
IBM	26	60,281	81,493	221,866	262,152	310,155	5
United Aircraft/United Technologies[f]	24	61,688	63,461	78,743	63,849	138,587	12
Eastman Kodak	37	50,300	47,800	105,600	114,800	123,700	15
Gulf & Western Industries[g]	N/A	N/A	N/A	46,000	65,000	116,600	16
North Amer. Aviation/ Rockwell Int'l.[h]	30	54,660	97,728	115,326	80,045	115,162	17
Union Carbide	23	64,247	58,798	99,794	98,114	113,669	19

[a] Standard Oil of New Jersey (Esso) changed its name to Exxon from 1972.
[b] US employment only.
[c] Douglas Aircraft merged with McDonnell Aircraft in 1967 to form McDonnell Douglas.
[d] Socony Mobil Oil changed its name to Mobil Oil in 1966, and then to Mobil in 1976.
[e] Swift became the core company of Esmark in 1977.
[f] United Aircraft changed its name to United Technologies in 1975.
[g] Founded in 1956, Gulf & Western Industries had its origins as a Michigan autoparts distributor that in 1966 acquired Paramount Pictures and became a major conglomerate.
[h] North American Aviation merged with Rockwell-Standard in 1967 to create North American Rockwell, and then changed its name to Rockwell International in 1973.

Sources: Fortune 500 lists, *Fortune*, June 1958, July 1963, June 15, 1968, May 1973, May 8, 1978.

The sectors with the largest employers included automobiles, tires, steel, electrical machinery, electronics, aerospace, oil refining, and chemicals. Over this period, IBM increased its employment fivefold, rising from the 24th largest employer in 1957 to the 5th largest in 1977 as it transformed itself from a business machine company to the world's dominant computer company. On the list as well are two major conglomerates, ITT and Gulf & Western, companies that grew very large during the conglomerate movement of the 1960s.

24.3 THE RESTRUCTURING OF THE US CORPORATION SINCE THE 1970S

24.3.1 A Change of Allocation Regime

Into the 1970s corporate managers had been engaged in a retain-and-reinvest allocation regime: they retained substantial corporate revenues and reinvested in growth. From the early twentieth century, the retain-and-reinvest regime resulted in innovation that generated gains for shareholders, employees, suppliers, consumers, communities, and governments (Lazonick 1990, 1992; O'Sullivan 2000). Yet by the 1960s and 1970s the strategy of retain-and-reinvest was failing to generate innovation. In many companies it resulted in an overextension and overcentralization of the corporation that made it financially vulnerable, especially in an economic downturn.

The rise of innovative foreign competitors exacerbated this vulnerability, and typically forced some type of restructuring, particularly downsizing, on the part of US corporations that lost market share. The most formidable foreign challenge came from Japan. Building on the development of innovative capabilities in their home markets during the 1950s and 1960s, Japanese companies gained competitive advantage in the US markets for steel, memory chips, machine tools, electrical machinery, consumer electronics, and automobiles in the 1980s and 1990s. These were industries in which US companies entered the 1970s as world leaders. Initially, as Japanese exports to the United States increased in the last half of the 1970s, observers attributed the success of the Japanese to their lower wages and longer working hours. By the early 1980s, however, with real wages in Japan continuing to rise, it became clear that Japanese advantage was based on organizational learning that resulted from a more thoroughgoing organizational integration of participants in an enterprise's functional and hierarchical divisions of labor (Lazonick 1998). Indeed, during the 1980s, Japan exported management practice as well as material goods to other advanced economies, and from the second half of the 1980s, with the yen strengthening and Japan's trade surpluses generating political backlash, Japanese companies made a transition to direct foreign investment.

24.3.2 The Role of Finance in Restructuring

With the downturn in the US economy in the early 1970s, it became apparent that resource allocation in US corporations had become overcentralized. The problem was not size per se but rather that strategic decision makers, isolated at the top, had lost touch with the types of resource allocation required for innovative enterprise. In addition, by the end of the 1960s, the growth of conglomerates through M&A had been debt-financed. Quite apart from the negative effect of conglomeration on the innovative capabilities of the companies concerned, there was financial pressure on the corporations to shed some of the businesses they had taken on. The conglomerate movement of the 1960s turned into the deconglomeration movement of the 1970s (Merrill Lynch Advisory Services 2002).

By the mid-1980s many divestitures occurred in the aftermath of hostile takeovers. Corporate raiders looked for companies undervalued relative to the breakup value of their various divisions, used debt-finance to acquire the companies, and then sold divisions to pay the debt (Long and Ravenscraft 1993). The junk bond was widely favored as a debt instrument in hostile takeovers (Taggart 1988). Initially, junk bonds were previously issued investment-grade corporate securities, the ratings of which had been lowered. Since these bonds could be bought at a deep discount, they offered a high, if risky, yield. In the first half of the 1970s Michael Milken of the Wall Street firm, Drexel Burnham Lambert, made a market in junk bonds by convincing institutional investors to include these securities in their portfolios (Bruck 1989). Liquidity was thus bestowed on the junk-bond market, while, in a period in which escalating inflation was eroding real interest rates, institutional investors welcomed the higher risk-adjusted returns that these securities offered.

By the late 1970s it became possible to issue new junk bonds to finance leveraged buyouts (LBOs). Most of these were divisional buyouts in which the top managers of a division sought to recapture strategic control over resource allocation. Specialized Wall Street LBO firms, of which KKR was the most prominent, would finance the LBO to reap returns when the newly formed private firms could do an initial public offering (IPO) (Gaughan 1996: 293; Jensen 1989: 65).

The ideology that rationalized the hostile takeover movement was that the corporation should be run to maximize shareholder value (Lazonick 1992; Lazonick and O'Sullivan 2000a, b; O'Sullivan 2000). The main charge of the proponents of shareholder value was that many corporate managers were making poor allocative decisions. By exercising their influence through the market for corporate control, so the argument went, shareholders could alter the allocative decisions of managers, change the managers themselves, or disgorge the free cash flow of the corporation to shareholders so that they themselves could reallocate the economy's resources to their best alternative uses. In fact, it was top corporate managers who in the 1980s embraced shareholder value ideology because their own personal rewards were increasingly based on boosting their corporations' stock prices and because it provided legitimacy to their restructuring activities.

24.3.3 Higher Financial Yields

For the most part, the hostile takeover movement of the 1980s affected corporations in stable-tech sectors of the economy (Hall 1994). These were sectors in which enterprise capital-intensity was high enough to create formidable barriers to new entrants, but where companies could generate substantial revenues without engaging in continuous innovation. Stable-tech industries included those that required large investments in advertising and distribution to attain and maintain brand-name recognition (for example, processed foods), in exploration and conservation to replenish the sources of raw materials (oil refining and timber products), or expensive purchased equipment (airlines) (Lazonick 1992: 470).

In such industries, established companies could reduce reinvestment over the medium term and still sell their products at competitive prices. In low-tech sectors, firms did not have such accumulated assets, whereas in high-tech sectors there was an imperative to replace old capabilities with new capabilities on a continuing basis. Moreover, given that the most critical assets in high-tech tend to be embodied in human beings, a financially driven hostile takeover would likely result in the firm's most valuable assets walking out the door.

In stable-tech industries, low share prices and large cash balances invited hostile takeovers. Managers in these industries took steps to lift their share prices by increasing the level of dividend payouts and engaging in large-scale stock repurchases. Stock options, which had since the 1950s become an important form of executive compensation, gave top managers of the major corporations a powerful personal stake in modes of resource allocation that boosted stock price (Hall and Leibman 1998; Lewellen 1968).

As Table 24.2 shows, the returns to corporate securities increased substantially in the 1980s and 1990s, mainly because of increases in the price yields of stocks. To what extent were these higher yields the result of redistributive or renovative restructuring, or alternatively the growth of new innovative firms? Given the competitive challenges that US industry faced in the 1970s and 1980s, the augmented dividend yields in both the 1970s and 1980s suggest a redistributive effect,

Table 24.2 US corporate stock and bond yields, 1960–2002 (average annual % change)

	1960–9	1970–9	1980–9	1990–9	2000–2
Real stock yield[a]	6.63	−1.66	11.67	15.01	−9.76
Price yield	5.80	1.35	12.91	15.54	−8.52
Dividend yield	3.19	4.08	4.32	2.47	1.89
Change in CPI[b]	2.36	7.09	5.55	3.01	2.60
Real bond yield[c]	2.65	1.14	5.79	4.72	4.47

[a] Stock yields are for Standard and Poor's composite index of 500 US corporate stocks.
[b] Consumer Price Index.
[c] Bond yields are for Moody's Aaa-rated US corporate bonds.

Source: Updated from Lazonick and O'Sullivan (2000a), using US Congress (2003: tables B62, B73, B953).

especially when it is recognized that it has been the practice of new economy companies such as Intel, Microsoft, and Cisco not to pay dividends. At the same time, companies such as these that grew from new ventures to going concerns over these decades were having a renovative impact on the economy as a whole; their stock prices rose as they expanded employment and paid their employees more while supplying customers with higher quality products at lower prices. Such renovative impacts helped increase the aggregate price yields, notwithstanding overspeculation at certain times in the stocks of the companies concerned.

24.3.4 Increasing Income Inequality

The extent of corporate downsizing and worsening of the household distribution of income that occurred in the 1980s and the 1990s suggests that a significant portion of the increase in real stock yields represented redistribution from labor to capital. The era of corporate downsizing took hold in the recession of 1980–2 when hundreds of thousands of stable, well-paid blue-collar jobs were lost and never subsequently restored. The number of people employed in the US economy as a whole increased between 1979 and 1983 by 0.4 percent. But over the same period employment in mass-consumption durable-goods manufacturing, which supplied most of the economy's stable, well-paid blue-collar jobs, declined by 15.9 percent (US Congress 1992: 344). In 1978 union membership in the United States had reached a peak of 23.6 percent of the nonagricultural labor force, but, as a result of the downsizing of the early 1980s, had fallen by 1983 to 20.1 percent.

The subsequent boom years of the mid-1980s witnessed hundreds of plant closures. Between 1983 and 1987, 4.6 million workers lost their jobs, of which 40 percent had been employed in manufacturing. During the deal decade of the 1980s, job security decreased markedly for salaried managers and production workers. In the white-collar recession of the early 1990s tens of thousands of professional, administrative, and technical employees found their jobs had been eliminated, although blue-collar workers bore the brunt of the downturn.

In 1980 manufacturing employment was 22 percent of the labor force; by 1990 it had fallen to 17 percent and by 2001 to 14 percent. The rate of job loss was about 10 percent in the 1980s and 14 percent in the first half of the 1990s. Those with less education experienced a higher rate of loss, and the wages of displaced workers when re-employed were about 13 percent lower than in their previous jobs (Farber 1997; Schultze 1999). While the employment picture improved during the new economy boom of the late 1990s, job cutting remained a way of life for major US corporations. According to data on layoff announcements by companies in the United States collected by the recruitment firm, Challenger, Gray, and Christmas, announced job cuts averaged just under 550,000 per year for the period 1991–4, 450,000 per year in 1995–7, and 656,000 per year during the boom years 1998–2000. These figures were, however, far surpassed in the recent economic decline, with 1.96 million layoff announcements in 2001 and 1.47 million in 2002 (Challenger Employment Report, cited in news articles).

24.3.5 Restructuring the Old Economy Corporation

At the center of the restructuring that occurred in the 1980s and 1990s were the old economy corporations that over the previous decades had grown to be enormously large. Table 24.3, which picks up in 1977 where Table 24.1 left off, shows the trend toward reduced levels of employment, as well as the disappearance of companies as legal entities among US corporations that were the largest employers in 1977. In that year these twenty companies employed 4.5 million people, in 2002 only 1.9 million. The following paragraphs summarize how the restructuring of these twenty companies occurred over this quarter century, and the implications for their changed levels of employment.

In steel the trend toward reduced employment began in the 1970s and continued on a major scale in the 1980s and 1990s. US Steel remained a large corporation by transforming itself into an oil-refining company, and changing its name to USX, although recently it has restructured itself by spinning off its steel business under its original name; the company that was US Steel is now Marathon Oil, while the present-day US Steel is a new company. In the oil industry itself there was consolidation with the largest employer in 1977, Mobil, being absorbed by Exxon in 1999.

Table 24.3 Employment, 1977–2002, of the twenty largest US corporate employers in 1977

Company	Rank 1977	1977	1982	1987	1992	1997	2001	2002
General Motors	1	797,000	657,000	813,400	750,000	608,000	365,000	350,000
Ford Motor	2	479,000	379,229	350,320	325,333	363,892	352,748	350,321
General Electric	3	384,000	367,000	302,000	268,000	276,000	310,000	315,000
ITT	4	375,000	283,000	120,000	[a]			
IBM	5	310,155	364,796	389,348	308,010	269,465	319,876	315,889
Chrysler	6	250,833	73,714	122,745	128,000	121,000	[b]	
Mobil	7	200,700	188,000	120,600	63,700	42,700	[c]	
US Steel/USX/Marathon[d]	8	165,845	119,987	53,522	45,582	40,894	30,671[e]	28,166[e]
Western Electric/Lucent[f]	9	162,000	153,000	[g]	[g]	134,000	77,000	47,000
Goodyear Rubber and Tire	10	159,890	131,096	114,658	95,712	95302	96,430	92,000
Westinghouse/CBS[h]	11	141,394	145,251	112,478	109,050	51,444	[i]	
United Technologies	12	138,587	184,000	190,000	178,000	180,100	152,000	155,000
Du Pont (E.I.) de Nemours	13	131,317	165,013	140,145	125,000	98,396	79,084	79,000
Exxon/Exxon Mobil	14	127,000	173,000	100,000	95,000	80,000	97,900	92,500
Eastman Kodak	15	123,700	136,500	124,400	132,600	97,500	75,100	70,000
Gulf & Western Industries	16	116,600	107,900	[j]				
Rockwell Int'l/ Automation[k]	17	115,162	100,271	116,148	78,895	45,000	23,100	22,000
Firestone Tire & Rubber	18	115,000	53,500	53,500	[l]			
Union Carbide	19	113,669	103,229	43,119	15,075	11,813	[m]	
RCA	20	111,000	[n]					

[a] As a result of divestitures, ITT Corp. ceased to be on the Fortune 500 list. ITT last reported sales in 1996 and was acquired by Starwood Hotel & Resorts in 1998.

[b] Acquired by Daimler-Benz in 1998.

[c] Acquired by Exxon in 1999, to become Exxon Mobil.

[d] After having acquired Marathon Oil in 1982 and Texas Oil & Gas in 1986, US Steel changed its name to USX. On December 31, 2001, USX spun off its steel business at United States Steel and renamed itself Marathon Oil.

[e] The employment figures are for Marathon Oil only. The newly spun-off United States Steel first appeared on the 2002 Fortune 500 list with 36,251 employees.

[f] In 1985 Western Electric became a division of AT&T (AT&T Technologies), which in 1996 was spun off, along with AT&T's Bell Labs to become Lucent Technologies.

[g] A division of AT&T.

[h] Westinghouse bought CBS in 1995, divested all of its non-entertainment divisions in 1996, and changed its name to CBS Corp. in 1997.

[i] Time Warner acquired CBS in 2000.

[j] Subsequent to the death of Gulf & Western founder, Charles Bluhdorn in 1983, the new CEO, Martin Davis, sold off many of the conglomerate's businesses. In 1989 Gulf & Western was renamed Paramount Communications, and in 1994 Paramount Communications was acquired by Viacom.

[k] Having spun off its avionics and communications unit as Rockwell Collins, Rockwell International changed its name to Rockwell Automation to reflect its new focus. Rockwell Collins had 17,500 employees in 2001 and 14,500 in 2002.

[l] The Japanese tire company, Bridgestone, acquired Firestone in 1988.

[m] Dow Chemical acquired Union Carbide in 2001.

[n] GE acquired RCA in 1986 and dissolved the company into its consumer electronics business, retaining only the RCA brand. In 1988 GE sold its consumer electronics business, along with the RCA brand to the French company, Thomson.

Sources: Fortune 500 lists, *Fortune*, May 2, 1983; April 25, 1988; April 19, 1993; April 27, 1998; April 15, 2002; April 14, 2003.

But the 2002 employment of Exxon Mobil was just 28 percent of the combined employment of Mobil and Exxon in 1977.

Automobile companies are still among the largest corporate employers but they are smaller than in the late 1970s. In 1998 Chrysler, the smallest of the big three automobile companies, was acquired by Daimler-Benz of Germany and ceased to be an American company. In other industries, Eastman Kodak (photography), Goodyear (tires), and Rockwell International (electronic equipment) cut back employment in the face of loss of market share, especially to Japanese competition. In consumer electronics, RCA succumbed to Japanese competition as its attempts at innovation in the late 1970s and early 1980s failed (Graham 1986), while a Japanese tire company, Bridgestone, gobbled up Firestone. Union Carbide was acquired by Dow Chemical in 2001, its financial condition having been overly weakened by litigation stemming from the 1984 Bhopal disaster in India when poisonous gas leaked from its pesticide plant and its role in supplying cancerous silicone to producers of breast implants.

ITT and Gulf & Western, the two largest companies to emerge from the conglomerate movement of the 1960s, shed assets and by the 1990s had been absorbed into other companies. Westinghouse, the electrical power company that like its counterpart GE, had become an unwieldy conglomerate by the late 1970s, also rid itself of assorted assets but unlike GE met its demise. Before the legal entity that had been Westinghouse vanished in 2000 (acquired by Time Warner), it had been run since 1997 under the name of a television company, CBS. In contrast, General Electric, which was dramatically restructured in the 1980s and 1990s under the rule of Neutron Jack Welch, became a successful financial services company supported by its traditional strengths in aircraft engines, medical equipment, and electric power. Through divestiture, outsourcing, and downsizing, and notwithstanding numerous acquisitions, GE cut its employment into the mid-1990s—its lowest level was 221,000 at the end of 1994—but by 2002 employed more people than it did fifteen years earlier.

With its domination of the mainframe computer industry combined with its expansion in the 1980s into personal computers (for which it set the standard), IBM increased its employment by 26 percent from 1977 to 1987. It cut back employment, however, when its mainframe computers failed to remain competitive with microcomputers. Through subsequent restructuring that has focused on software rather than hardware, IBM has regenerated its ability to grow (Gerstner 2002).

United Technologies, a diversified corporation in aerospace products and building systems, that bought and sold businesses throughout the 1980s and 1990s, employed more than 150,000 people in 2002 despite job cuts at the end of the period. Du Pont expanded employment in the early 1980s, especially when it acquired the oil company Conoco in 1981, but in the 1990s contracted employment as it sought to focus on its core chemical operations, including the spinoff of Conoco in 1998. Du Pont, too, has cut back employment in the recent recession.

In 1985 Western Electric, which had been a wholly owned subsidiary of AT&T, became AT&T Technologies, an internal division of AT&T. In 1996 AT&T spun off AT&T Technologies into the independent company, Lucent Technologies, which incorporated within it Bell Labs. During the following years, Lucent sought to make the transition from the old to the new economy by acquiring data communications companies, many of which were revenue-less start-ups, and by extending stock options to high-tech personnel. From 1996 through 1999 Lucent's stock price skyrocketed, but then in 2000–2002 plummeted further. In the downturn, the company found itself on the brink of bankruptcy—a fate avoided by slashing its workforce from 126,000 at the end of 2000 to 47,000 just two years later (Carpenter, Lazonick, and O'Sullivan 2003). As part of its restructuring process in 2001 and 2002, Lucent began rationalizing its operations through outsourcing to contract manufacturers. This restructuring boded ill for unions. In 1996, 36.3 percent of Lucent's worldwide employees and 46.0 percent of its domestic employees were union members; in 2002 these numbers were 14.5 percent and 21.3 percent, respectively. In September 1999 Lucent employed 46,818 union employees, an increase of over 1,700 from three years earlier. In September 2002 Lucent only employed 6,800 union members, representing a loss of over 40,000 union jobs in three years.

24.4 CORPORATE RESTRUCTURING IN THE NEW ECONOMY

During the winter of 1996, corporate restructuring was a major theme in the US news media. In late December 1995, AT&T had announced that as part of the process of breaking itself up into three separate companies (one of which was Lucent) it would be cutting 40,000 jobs. AT&T was a company that could trace its origins to the 1870s. It had created the world's most advanced telephone system, was the home of the famous Bell Labs, and employed 300,000 people. Now AT&T became emblematic of the failure of US old economy corporations to continue to provide employment opportunities. In the 1996 presidential election, Patrick Buchanan, a right-wing politician, caught the attention of the media by denouncing the highly paid executives of AT&T and other downsizing corporations as corporate hit men (Pearlstein 1996). Fuel was added to the fire by the revelation that, in the name of creating shareholder value, 'Chainsaw' Al Dunlap had in 20 months as CEO of Scott Paper, devastated the 115-year-old company to his immense personal gain. Brought in as CEO of Scott Paper in April 1994, within a couple of months Dunlap had terminated 11,000 people, representing 35 percent of the labor force including 71 percent of the staff at corporate headquarters, 50 percent of managers, and 20 percent of production workers. He moved the headquarters of the company from Philadelphia to Boca Raton, Florida, and, by the time that he had sold Scott Paper to its long-time rival, Kimberley Clark, Dunlap had reaped $100 million for himself. Pictured on the cover of *Business Week* as 'The Shredder' on January 15, 1996 (Byrne and Weber 1996), Dunlap was a dramatic example of downsize-and-distribute under the guise of creating shareholder value (Byrne 2002).

In March 1996 the *New York Times* ran a seven-part news series called, 'The Downsizing of America', subsequently released as a paperback. By the spring of 1996, however, the furor over corporate downsizing had disappeared as Americans discovered the new economy. The roots of the new economy lay in the post-World War II boom when the US government and the research laboratories of old economy companies had combined to develop ICT technologies. The development of computer chips from the late 1950s provided the technological foundation for the microcomputer revolution from the late 1970s, which in turn provided the technological infrastructure for the Internet boom of the 1990s. Each wave of technological innovation created opportunities for the emergence of start-up companies central to the commercialization of the new technologies.

The new economy corporation differed from its predecessor in significant ways, some of which reflected the youth of these companies and others the result of strategic choices related to the employment of labor and the mobilization of finance. Being young, new economy companies sought to grow by developing capabilities for a particular product market. These companies were the antithesis of multidivisional structures and conglomerates spawned in the old economy, notwithstanding the fact that the personnel of the new economy firms had often acquired their knowledge in the old economy corporations.

In Silicon Valley many high-tech start-ups were backed by venture capitalists who insisted on highly focused business strategies and recruited experienced managers to ensure this focus. These young companies tended to employ a high proportion of university-educated personnel, and it became the norm to use stock options as a compensation tool to attract and retain them (Lazonick 2003). At the same time, these companies shunned investments in factories that employed blue-collar workers, preferring to outsource the manufacture of components and sub-assemblies to specialized contractors. As a result the new economy companies tended to be union-free (Sturgeon 2002).

New economy companies tended to do an initial public offering (IPO) more quickly after being founded than had been the case for old economy companies (Hobijn and Jovanovic 2000), in part to raise cash but also to give liquidity to the stock that their employees received when they exercised their stock options. They relied on internally generated revenues to fund their growth and tended to pay no dividends. With the markets for their products booming in the 1980s and 1990s, some of these companies grew rapidly as can be seen in Table 24.4. While these companies do not dominate the US economy, they have been central to a critical high growth sector. During the last two decades of the twentieth century, these companies manifested a new retain-and-reinvest regime that to some extent offset the tendency of old economy companies to downsize and distribute.

For a high-tech company the new economy model meant a focus on employing highly educated and skilled people in high value-added activities such as R&D, new product development, and marketing. Contract manufacturers such as Solectron, Celestica, Sanmina-SCI, Jabil Circuit, and Flextronics, to whom lower value-added activities were outsourced, were nonunion and adept at moving production from high-wage to low-wage areas of the world. In the past such relocations had been constrained in the case of high-end work by the need to be close to the customers' home bases (typically in high-wage regions) and by the lack of skills in low-wage regions. In recent years developments in communications technology have overcome the need for the geographic proximity of users and producers while in the low-wage regions such as Southeast Asia and Eastern Europe, where contract manufacturers increasingly operate, there has been substantial augmentation of the skills and experience of local labor forces.

Ironically, during the new economy boom there was an accelerated flow of highly educated human capital from the low-wage regions to high-wage regions, with hundreds of thousands of foreign-born scientists and engineers entering the United States to work at high-tech firms on temporary (H-1B) visas. This influx of personnel was in addition to those scientists and engineers who worked in the United States as permanent residents, naturalized citizens, or exchange visitors. Many of these people had entered the United States through enrolment in graduate schools, where in many programs they constituted the majority of students (Johnson, Rapoport, and Regets 2000).

The globalization of labor markets was made possible by investments in skill formation in developing countries, with India and China being important examples (Guo 2000; Wad 2000). Over the past three decades there has been an increasing trend to globalization of R&D by major industrial corporations in the advanced economies (Archibugi and Michie 1995; Cantwell 1997; Michie, Oughton, and Pianta 2002), with a heavy emphasis on locating in other advanced economies. Often the choice of global location has depended on the specific advantages developed in industrial districts. During the 1990s, moreover, it became possible to locate certain R&D functions, particularly those related to software engineering in new product development, in developing nations (Best 2001; Mytelka 1999), with India emerging as a prime location over the past few years (Kripalani, Engardio, and Hamm 2003). In effect, industrial corporations now make use of, and contribute to, national skill-formation systems around the world by employing foreign labor that migrates to the home bases of these corporations and by foreign

Table 24.4 Employment, 1993–2002, new economy ICT companies with the largest revenues in 2002 (number of employees, except sales in $ billions)

Company (date of founding and 2002 Fortune ranking in parentheses)	2002 sales $b	1993	1996	1999	2000	2001	2002
Dell Computer (1984; 34)	35.4	5,950	10,350	36,500	40,000	34,600	39,100
Microsoft (1975; 47)	28.4	14,430	20,561	31,396	39,100	47,600	50,500
Intel (1968; 58)	26.8	29,500	48,500	70,200	86,100	83,400	78,700
Cisco Systems (1984; 95)	18.9	1,451	8,782	21,000	34,000	38,000	36,000
Sun Microsystems (1982; 155)	12.5	13,323	17,400	29,000	38,900	43,700	39,400
Solectron (1977; 158)	12.3	4,545	10,781	37,396	65,273	60,000	73,000
Oracle (1977; 190)	9.7	9,247	23,111	43,800	41,320	42,297	42,006
Sanmina-SCI (1980; 214)[a]	8.7	703	1,726	7,220	24,000	48,774	46,030
Nextel (1987; 216)	8.7	773	3,600	15,000	19,500	17,000	14,900
Scientific Applications Int'l (1969; 288)	6.1	14,872	22,600	39,078	41,500	40,400	38,700
Apple Computer (1976; 300)	5.7	14,938	10,896	9,736	8,568	9,603	10,211
EMC (1979; 308)	5.4	2,452	4,800	17,700	24,100	20,100	17,400
Applied Materials (1967; 327)	5.1	4,739	11,403	12,755	19,220	17,365	16,077
EchoStar Communications (1980; 341)	4.8	500	1,200	6,048	11,000	11,000	15,000
Charter Communications (1992; 362)	4.5	N/A	2,000	11,909	13,505	17,900	18,600
Gateway (1985; 387)	4.2	2,832	9,700	21,000	24,600	14,000	11,400
Maxtor (1982; 421)	3.8	8,900	8,940	5,133	8,551	9,811	12,449
Jabil Circuit (1966; 441)	3.5	997	2,649	6,554	19,115	17,097	20,000
Affiliated Computer Services (1988; 488)	3.1	2,200	5,850	15,700	18,500	21,000	36,200
Qualcomm (1985; 489)	3.0	1,262	6,000	9,700	6,300	6,500	8,100
Average number of employees[b]		6,731	11,542	22,341	29,158	30,007	31,189

Note: For inclusion on this list, a company had (a) to be an ICT company (as indicated below), (b) to be founded 1965 or later, (c) to not have been established by spin-off from an Old Economy company, and (d) to not have grown through acquisition of, or merger with, an Old Economy company. As categorized in the 2002 Fortune 500 list, the ICT industries include computer and data services (Affiliated Computer Services, Scientific Applications International), computer peripherals (EMC, Maxtor), computer software (Microsoft, Oracle), computers, office equipment (Dell Computer, Sun Microsystems, Apple Computer, Gateway), network and other communications equipment (Cisco Systems, Qualcomm), semiconductors and other electronic components (Intel, Solectron, Sanmina-SCI, Applied Materials, Jabil Circuit), and telecommunications (Nextel Communications, EchoStar Communications, Charter Communications). In 2001, Compaq Computer, with $33.6 billion in revenues and 70,950 employees, was high up on this list, but in 2002 was acquired by Hewlett-Packard.
N/A: data not available.

[a] Sanmina until 2001, when it merged with another contract manufacturer, SCI.

[b] In doing the calculation for 1993, it was assumed that Charter Communications had 1,000 employees in that year.

Sources: Fortune 500 list, *Fortune*, April 14, 2003; www.hoovers.com.

direct investment that creates employment opportunities for educated labor in the host countries.

24.5 TOWARD A COMPARATIVE PERSPECTIVE ON CORPORATE RESTRUCTURING

This chapter has provided an overview of the evolution of corporate restructuring in the United States. The starting point was the growth of the managerial corporation, a phenomenon that occurred in a number of major economies during the first half of the twentieth century (Chandler, Amatori, and Hikinol 1997) but in which the United States particularly stood out. Initially the growth of the corporation came from its ability to innovate and to generate higher quality, lower cost products without lowering the wages of employees. By the second half of the twentieth century, however, many of the largest US industrial corporations had grown too big to remain innovative in their main markets. The overgrowth of the US industrial corporation, as manifested in the conglomerate movement of the 1960s, created a need to reintegrate strategic decision making with the organizational structures required to implement corporate strategy, a process that was partially achieved through divestitures and leveraged buyouts in the 1970s and 1980s. In addition, the Japanese challenge to US industry in these decades also placed pressure on US industrial corporations to relocate, downsize, and outsource. Much of this restructuring activity was necessary for US industrial corporations to put in place the types of organizations that could respond to the new realities of international competition. The prevalence of restructuring activity, combined with financial deregulation also created an opportunity for financial interests to take over corporations and then break them up for their own financial gain.

This financial engineering, with its emphasis on downsize and distribute, found justification in the ideology of maximizing shareholder value, and in fact resulted in much higher returns on corporate securities in the 1980s and 1990s than in the previous two decades. However, a new retain-and-reinvest regime was developing in the ICT sectors of the economy. The 1980s and 1990s saw the growth of high-tech ventures that outsourced routine manufacturing processes and employed a skill base of highly educated and highly mobile personnel. These new high-tech companies challenged traditional corporations, and in the new economy boom of the late 1990s old economy companies sought to restructure themselves on the new economy model.

In Western Europe and Japan, corporate growth and restructuring occurred in different ways, shaped by different political constellations of managerial, labor, and financial interests and, different systems of corporate governance (Dore *et al.* 1999; Lazonick and O'Sullivan 2002). In Germany codetermination at the level of the enterprise governs restructuring (O'Sullivan 2000), whereas in France the state has played the dominant role. In France, for example, a combination of the Mitterand program of nationalizations in 1982–83 and subsequent privatizations from 1986 secured the dominant positions of a number of capital-intensive, high-technology companies, including Compagnie Générale d'Electricité (CGE) in electrical equipment, Rhône-Poulenc in chemicals, Saint-Gobain-Pont à Mousson in glass, paper, and metals, and the combination of Sacilor and Usinor in steel (Schmidt 1996: 116). As nationalized enterprises the state exercised strategic control and provided financial commitment to restructure to compete globally. As privatized enterprises were protected from external interference by a French cross-shareholding arrangement known as *noyau dur*, these restructured companies were able to grow through mergers and acquisitions. The French state was also often directly involved in downsizing these companies by using tax revenues to fund early retirement programs. French companies also restructured to focus their competitive capabilities on particular industrial sectors, as in the case of Alcatel which, evolving out of the CGE conglomerate, shed a number of businesses to focus on the telecommunications industry.

In Japan corporate enterprises evolved within industrial groups, with the result that individual enterprises did not grow as large or diversified as their US counterparts, even when they became major competitors in their particular markets. These corporations maintained a commitment to lifetime employment for their male production workers and managerial personnel. At the same time, they limited the size of the permanent, directly employed labor force by outsourcing components to tiers of suppliers. When a company ran into financial difficulty, firms involved in its network of business relations became involved in its restructuring, with emphasis being placed on maintaining the commitment to lifetime employment or reallocating displaced workers to new jobs.

With the collapse of the Japanese stock and land markets at the beginning of the 1990s, many Western observers thought that Japanese corporations would embark on a downsize-and-distribute regime to restore profitability, with lifetime employment disappearing in the process. Despite the pressures of the prolonged recession of the Japanese economy in the 1990s and into the 2000s, this type of restructuring of Japanese companies has not taken place. The major industrial corporations (as distinct from banks) entered the 1990s in solid financial condition, and most have remained highly competitive. There has been, moreover, considerable flexibility within the system of lifetime employment to adjust the size and cost of permanent labor to cope with the depressed economic environment (Lazonick 1999).

While distinctive national differences remain, there are powerful pressures on companies to adopt a global model of corporate organization. In the first decade of the twenty-first century, the US new economy model remains the one with the most influence on a global scale. It is one, however, that has been central to an economy fraught with instability and inequality. In-depth comparative research is needed to determine whether other models of corporate restructuring can deliver more stable and equitable economic growth.

REFERENCES

ARCHIBUGI, D., and MICHIE, J. (1995). 'The Globalisation of Technology: A New Taxonomy'. *Cambridge Journal of Economics*, 19/1: 121–40.

BEST, M. (2001). *The New Competitive Advantage: The Renewal of American Industry*. Oxford: Oxford University Press.

BRUCK, C. (1989). *The Predators' Ball*. Harmondsworth: Penguin.

BYRNE, J. (2002). 'Chainsaw Al Dunlap Cuts His Last Deal'. *Business Week Online*, September 6.

—— and WEBER, J. (1996). 'The Shredder'. *Business Week*, January 15.

CANTWELL, J. (1997). 'The Globalisation of Technology: What Remains of the Product Cycle Model?' in D. Archibugi and J. Michie (eds.), *Technology, Globalisation and Economic Performance*. Cambridge: Cambridge University Press.

CARPENTER, M., LAZONICK, W., and O'SULLIVAN, M. (2003). 'The Stock Market and Innovative Capability in the New Economy: The Optical Networking Industry'. *Industrial and Corporate Change*, 12/3: 963–1034.

CHANDLER, A. (1962). *Strategy and Structure: Chapters in the History of the American Industrial Enterprise*. Cambridge, Mass.: MIT Press.

—— (1977). *The Visible Hand: The Managerial Revolution in American Business*. Cambridge, Mass.: Harvard University Press.

—— (1990). *Scale and Scope: The Dynamics of Industrial Capitalism*. Cambridge, Mass.: Harvard University Press.

—— AMATORI, F., and HIKINO, T. (eds.) (1997). *Big Business and the Wealth of Nations*. Cambridge: Cambridge University Press.

DORE, R., LAZONICK, W., and O'SULLIVAN, M. (1999). 'Varieties of Capitalism in the Twentieth Century'. *Oxford Review of Economic Policy*, 15/4: 102–20.

DUNNING, J. (1993). *Multinational Enterprises and the Global Economy*. Addison-Wesley.

FARBER, H. (1997). 'The Changing Face of Job Loss in the United States'. Washington, DC: Brookings Papers in Microeconomics.

Fortune (2003). 'Global 500: The World's Largest Corporations'. *Fortune*, July 21: F1–F43.

GAUGHAN, P. (1996). *Mergers, Acquisitions, and Corporate Restructurings* (2nd edn). New York: John Wiley and Sons.

GERSTNER, L. (2002). *Who Says Elephants Can't Dance? Inside IBM's Historic Turnaround*. New York: Harper Collins Business.

GRAHAM, M. (1986). *RCA and the Videodisk: The Business of Research*. Cambridge: Cambridge University Press.

GUO, Y. (2000). 'Graduate Education Reforms and International Mobility of Scientists and Engineers in China', in *National Science Foundation, Graduate Education Reform in Europe, Asia and the Americas*, Proceedings of National Science Foundations Workshop on the International Mobility of Scientists and Engineers NSF, April.

HALL, B. (1994). 'Corporate Restructuring and Investment Horizons in the United States, 1976–1987'. *Business History Review*, 68/1: 110–43.

—— and LEIBMAN, J. (1998). 'Are CEOs Really Paid Like Bureaucrats?' *Quarterly Journal of Economics*, 113/3: 653–91.

HEPPENHEIMER, T. (1995). *Turbulent Skies: The History of Commercial Aviation*. New York: John Wiley.

HOBIJN, B., and JOVANOVIC, B. (2000). 'The Information Technology Revolution and the Stock Market: Evidence'. *NBER Working Papers*, No. 7684.

JENSEN, M. (1989). 'Eclipse of the Public Corporation'. *Harvard Business Review*, 67/5: 61–74.

JOHNSON, J., RAPOPORT, A., and REGETS, M. (2000). 'US Graduate Education', in *National Science Foundation, Graduate Education Reform in Europe, Asia and the Americas*, Proceedings of National Science Foundations Workshop on the International Mobility of Scientists and Engineers NSF, April.

JONES, G. (2002). 'Multinationals', in M. Warner (ed.), *International Encyclopedia of Business and Management* (2nd edn). Thomson Learning.

KAYSEN, C. (1996). *The American Corporation Today*. New York: Oxford University Press.

KRIPALANI, M., ENGARDIO, P., and HAMM, S. (2003). 'The Rise of India'. *Business Week*, December 8, 2003: 66–74.

LAZONICK, W. (1986). 'Strategy, Structure, and Management Development in the United States and Britain', in K. Kobayashi and H. Morikawa (eds.), *Development of Managerial Enterprise*. Tokyo: University of Tokyo Press.

—— (1990). *Competitive Advantage on the Shop Floor*. Cambridge, Mass.: Harvard University Press.

—— (1992). 'Controlling the Market for Corporate Control'. *Industrial and Corporate Change*, 1/3: 445–88.

—— (1998). 'Organizational Learning and International Competition', in J. Michie and J. G. Smith (eds.), *Globalization, Growth and Governance*. Oxford: Oxford University Press.

—— (1999). 'The Japanese Economy and Corporate Reform: What Path to Sustainable Prosperity?' *Industrial and Corporate Change*, 8/4: 607–33.

—— (2003). 'The Evolution of Stock Options as a Mode of High-Tech Compensation'. Working paper.

—— and O'SULLIVAN, M. (2000a). 'Maximizing Shareholder Value: A New Ideology for Corporate Governance'. *Economy and Society*, 29/1: 13–35.

—— —— (2000b). 'Perspectives on Corporate Governance, Innovation, and Economic Performance'. Report prepared for the project on *Corporate Governance, Innovation, and Economic Performance* under the Targeted Socio-Economic Research Programme of the European Commission, June (www.insead.edu/cgep).

—— —— (eds.) (2002). *Corporate Governance and Sustainable Prosperity*. London: Palgrave.

LEWELLEN, W. (1968). *Executive Compensation in Large Industrial Corporations*. New York: Columbia University Press.

LONG, W., and RAVENSCRAFT, D. (1993). 'Decade of Debt: Lessons from LBOs in the 1980s', in M. Blair (ed.), *The Deal Decade*. Washington, DC: Brookings Institution.

MADDISON, A. (1994). 'Explaining the Economic Performance of Nations, 1820–1989', in W. Baumol, R. Nelson, and E. Wolff (eds.), *Convergence of Productivity: Cross-National Studies and Historical Evidence*. Oxford: Oxford University Press.

MARGLIN, S., and SCHOR, J. (eds.) (1990). *The Golden Age of Capitalism: Reinterpreting the Postwar Experience*. Oxford: Oxford University Press.

MELMAN, S. (1951). 'The Rise of Administrative Overhead in the Manufacturing Industries of the United States, 1899–1947'. *Oxford Economic Papers*, 3/2: 62–112.

Merrill Lynch Advisory Services (1994). *Mergerstat Review*. W. T. Grimm.

—— (2002). *Mergerstat Review*. W. T. Grimm.

MICHIE, J., OUGHTON, C., and PIANTA, M. (2002). 'Innovation and the Economy'. *International Review of Applied Economics*, 16/3: 253–64.

MOWERY, D., and ROSENBERG, N. (1989). *Technology and the Pursuit of Economic Growth*. Cambridge: Cambridge University Press.

MYTELKA, L. (1999). *Competition, Innovation and Competitiveness in Developing Countries*. Paris: OECD Development Centre.

New York Times (1996). *The Downsizing of America*. New York: Times Books.

NOBLE, D. (1977). *America by Design: Science, Technology, and the Rise of Corporate Capitalism*. New York: Oxford University Press.

O'SULLIVAN, M. (2000). *Contests for Corporate Control: Corporate Governance and Economic Performance in the United States and Germany*. Oxford: Oxford University Press.

PEARLSTEIN, S. (1996). 'AT&T's '95 Pay Package for Chief: $16 million; Firm Defends Chairman as Criticism Mounts'. *Washington Post*, February 28: C1.

RAVENSCRAFT, D., and SCHERER, F. (1987). *Mergers, Sell-Offs and Economic Efficiency*. Washington, DC: Brookings Institution.

SCHERER, F., and ROSS, D. (1990). *Industrial Market Structure and Economic Performance* (3rd edn). Boston: Houghton Mifflin.

SCHMIDT, V. (1996). *From State to Market?: The Transformation of French Business and Government*. Cambridge: Cambridge University Press.

SCHULTZE, C. (1999). 'Downsized & Out: Job Security and American Workers'. *Brookings Review*, 17/4: 9–17.

STURGEON, T. (2002). 'Modular Production Networks: A New American Model of Industrial Organization'. *Industrial and Corporate Change*, 11: 451–96.

TAGGART, R. (1988). 'The Growth of the "Junk" Bond Market and Its Role in Financing Takeovers', in A. Auerbach (ed.), *Mergers and Acquisitions*. Chicago: University of Chicago Press.

US Bureau of the Census (1976). *Historical Statistics of the United States from the Colonial Times to the Present*. Washington, DC: US Government Printing Office.

US Congress (1992). *Economic Report of the President*. Washington, DC: US Government Printing Office.

—— (2003). *Economic Report of the President, 2003*. Washington, DC: US Government Printing Office.

WAD, A. (2000). 'Issues in Human Resources in Science and Engineering: India', in *National Science Foundation, Graduate Education Reform in Europe, Asia and the Americas*, Proceedings of National Science Foundations Workshop on the International Mobility of Scientists and Engineers NSF, April.

....

BEYOND CONVERGENCE AND DIVERGENCE

EXPLAINING VARIATIONS IN ORGANIZATIONAL PRACTICES AND FORMS

....

CHRIS SMITH

25.1 INTRODUCTION

....

THE collapse of Eastern European state socialism and marketization within China suggest that capitalism has triumphed in the world. But significant puzzles remain about the nature of capitalism: is it a single world political and economic system or is it, rather, only a quasi-homogeneous system that appears as a set of rival models

Acknowledgements to Tony Elger, who provided very detailed comments on this chapter and with whom many of the ideas presented have been tested and refined; to Stephen Ackroyd for his very thorough revision of the paper; to Peter Meiksins, who was my co-writer on the earlier paper from which this chapter has been developed; and finally to Paul Thompson for getting me to write this chapter and debating the ideas.

derived from the differential role of the state, market, capital, and labor within a series of fragmented, historically divergent, national economies? In short, is there or is there not a coherent, singular political economy called capitalism, and how does this bear on the question of the forms being adopted by firms and their subsidiaries?

This chapter outlines different approaches to the analysis of contemporary capitalism and considers what role they allocate to the business organization. Three distinct positions are distinguished. First, there are those who cling to the idea of distinctive national business systems and retain a belief in the organization of work, management, and employment relations characterized by a national system of institutions. Such writers argue for the persistence of national differences and the continuation of diversity. Second, there are those who argue for the importance of globalizing trends and the convergence between organizational forms and policies and, by extension, more general features of economic organization. Such arguments are far removed from the naive convergence arguments of earlier generations. Today it is argued that convergence forces are carried forward by worldwide agencies, in particular, transnational corporations (TNCs) and their global institutional supporters, such as the World Trade Organisation (WTO). This is an argument that suggests the gradual removal of diversity and increased homogenization. Third, between the extremes, there are arguments that suggest a small number of patterns, of distinctive varieties of capitalism, can be distinguished.

It is proposed that there is merit in all these positions, but none recognizes the complexity of real economies and none are able to explain the extent of change and continuity actually existing. The patterns of work and organization in the contemporary international organization are more complex than local/global, national/universal, and divergence/convergence dichotomies suggest. As an alternative, an argument is developed in favor of the system, society, and dominance (SSD) model (Smith and Meiksins 1995). In the central sections of the chapter, then, it is argued that capitalism, as a political economy (based on distinctive property rights, accumulation through competition, and incessant innovation of the means and forces of production) possesses a generic form, but one which reveals distinctive characteristics according to the organization of institutional actors, especially firms, labor, and the state (Elger and Edwards 1999).

However these forms are not fixed, as there are globalizing forces tending to produce convergence operating on all businesses, but particularly those exposed to internationalizing markets (Traxler, Blaschke, and Kittel 2001). Moreover such forces are filtered through nationally distinctive institutional settlements, which have societal effects (Maurice, Sellier, and Silvestre 1986) on the way work is organized, authority constructed, and patterns of industrial relations enacted. Within the international firm, we therefore have permanent, three-way tensions between (a) generic features of capitalism and (b) particular forms of management and labor derived from the nationally embedded contexts (where the firm originated and the subsidiaries are currently located) and (c) standardizing forces derived from dominant or global actors as they represent best practices to the firm. There is a context of complexity. The chapter will advance a model of cross-national organizational analysis that will provide understanding of this growing complexity.

25.2 ALTERNATIVE ACCOUNTS OF CONTINUITY AND CHANGE

25.2.1 National Business Systems

An approach to understanding the organization of economic relations that emphasizes national patterns emerged within organizational sociology in the 1970s and produced ideas spreading across industrial sociology, industrial relations, and labor process analysis.

Arguments of this kind make conditional or context-dependent statements about the world and work organizations. The approach emphasizes the persistence of the variations within capitalism carried by cultural or ideational uniqueness located in national and subnational institutions. These can be national innovation systems (Nelson 1993); business systems (Whitley 1992a, b; Whitley and Kristensen 1997); training systems (Crouch, Finegold, and Sako 1999); education systems (Dosi and Kogut 1993; Lorenz 2000); trade unions (Ferner and Hyman 1992; Hyman 2001; Katz and Darbishire 2000; Streeck 1992; Traxler, Blaschke, and Kittel 2001); or management styles and philosophy (Redding 1990). Against generalizations about globalization, convergence, or the dominance of neoliberal practices (such as shareholder value, open capital markets, and flexible labor markets), such writers insist on the power of the past to continue to deliver significant, nontrivial national differences within capitalist societies. They continue to invest value in path dependencies to reproduce national specificities (Sorge 1991).

The condensation of business systems—distinctive ways of doing things—within particular territories is observable across time and these do exhibit some path-dependent features. In Britain, for example, the technical education of workers is of a lower magnitude compared to Germany or Japan. In addition the hierarchical ordering of management specialisms is also different and persistently so, with accounting and finance in a dominant position in the United Kingdom, relative to the power of engineers. In Germany and Japan, the relationships are reversed (Meiksins and Smith 1996). Raising capital has also been consistently different, with greater reliance on stock markets, and less on industrial banks (which do not really exist in Britain), rather than interfirm investments and investment through retained profits, which are more common in Japan and Germany (Lane 1997). We can continue to elaborate the facts of comparative difference, but they only speak to one constituent of practices within firms, namely that which is given by a particular national set of institutional arrangements.

In practice the systemic features of capitalist development are not simply expressed in a uniform fashion across the global economy. Capitalist institutions crystallized in a distinctive fashion within specific nation-states, and national characteristics continue to shape relationships. Furthermore, national institutional patterns are not confined to the environments of corporate enterprises, but penetrate powerfully into their internal operations. It is such features that have been highlighted, but, in turn, overstated, by the contemporary family of theories of societal effects, institutional settlements, and national business systems. These approaches tend to reify societal influences as a configuration of self-contained determinants of organizational arrangements within the ambit of each specific nation-state (Hollingsworth, Schmitter, and Streeck 1994; Lane 1995; Maurice and Sorge 2000b; Sorge 1991; Whitley 1992a, b).

Typically these approaches argue that the national ownership of firms matters, because the firm absorbs the practices, ideas, and culture from institutions within the state or national level (education, training, employers' associations, organization of capital supply, interfirm relations, and worker–manager relations). In other words, firms are embedded and marked by their national origins in profound and lasting ways. However, firms, especially large ones, are also key actors in shaping their environments, because they have desirable or scarce products, locational choice, or power, they can regime shop or use their bargaining power to create conditions within states that favor their interests. Firms exist more within the terrain of competing practices, with senior management cadres drawn from different business systems, different sectors, different national educational backgrounds and training, which means that the firm is far less likely to be nationally homogenous. In other words, firms and states are in a contradictory not corresponding relationship.

This approach also ignores firms that borrow and adopt practices, say by employing managers from firms from other territories, or by learning through partnerships or transplant operations. Moreover, societal effects theory operates with an oversocialized view of action: action is determined by inputs or the supply side with different ingredients producing different national cakes. This ignores cross-national learning through the transnational firm; and internal variation within states based on region, ethnicity, and the embeddedness of particular industrial complexes and sectors (Smith and Elger 2000). In other words composite, large-scale societies contain variety, not uniform societal effects, and sectors are diverse within national territories, responding to global or international pressures in different ways, depending upon their exposure to world markets, global competition, and international technological forces (Hollingsworth, Schmitter, and Streeck 1994).

A key problem for such arguments is the difficulty of explaining not the persistence of local practices but those that seem to be global in their diffusion and that should not exist if the nation is the boundary of economic activity.

25.2.2 Convergence through Globalization

Today it is evident that there are convergence forces that are carried by worldwide agencies. In particular there is the transnational corporation, the policies of which are producing an emergent process of globalization. As Sklair (2001: 48) has noted: 'globalizing corporations are those consciously denationalizing from their domestic origins in the course of developing genuinely global strategies of operation'. Here globalizing is a verb, a process and practice, rather than something that already exists. Thus 'transnational corporations are said to be globalizing, not global, [they can be so] to the extent that they operate in a world made up of nation states, though not necessarily dominated by them economically, politically or in terms of culture-ideology' (ibid.). Because this is an argument for a long-term tendency, it is not similar to the technological determinism of Kerr *et al.* (1960) or production determinism suggested by Braverman (1974) or the naive views of 'one best way' principles of business organization of Taylor, Mayo, and Fayol.

Alongside these wide policy and structural convergence forces, we also have within the firm management being subject to globalizing management concepts as fashions, practices, and professional projects of competing management cadres. For example in the 1980s and 1990s, it was lean production and associated Japanization that spread through the business schools and into practicing management. Later it was business process reengineering, which emerged as an American reaction to non-American rationalization recipes. But such recipes are carried within TNCs, and the strategies they are pursuing on a global basis. Further, the internationalization of consumer markets means that global brands and TNCs are challenging local producers with bigger marketing budgets and more purchasing power. TNCs are forcing globalizing of brands and internationalizing of production. They create pressures on price, which reinforce cost reduction through an international division of labor (Frobel, Heinrichs, and Kreye 1980), forcing manufacturers to flee from embedded, high-cost institutional environments to source parts and assembly processing in low-cost areas, such as China and ASEAN countries, Mexico and South America, or Central and Eastern Europe. Exporting assembly jobs creates longer production chains, integrates new states into the global market, and undermines national institutional settlements, which are predicated on national manufacturing and corporate bargaining.

It is important not to exaggerate or misunderstand what is being claimed here. In its most effective form this is largely a structural argument. It is to be distinguished from arguments for globalization based on the diffusion of consumption patterns. The McDonaldization thesis of Ritzer (1993), for example, suggests that national boundaries are being dissolved. But talk of global consumption standards, of world factories, and shared management education through such programs as the MBA is as sterile and unbalanced as the national partisanship of the business systems approach. Clearly, there is also a need to avoid polarized general theory—convergence or divergence, national versus global, particular societies versus international practices. Rather we should seek to capture the contradictions between the different structures and actors (states, markets, regional blocs, globalizing firms, employers' and workers' organizations) at the same time as being careful with both level and unit of analysis and being clear what it is we are trying to demonstrate—difference or similarity.

25.2.3 Varieties of Capitalism

The divergence and convergence arguments considered so far might be resolved by the varieties of capitalism approach to comparative analysis (Albert 1993; Boyer *et al.* 1998*a*; Coates 2000; Crouch and Streeck 1997; Esping-Anderson 1990; Hall and Soskice 2001) or rival capitalist business models (Chandler 1990; Lazonick 1991). Such approaches argue that there are distinctive patterns of institutions that allow societies displaying similar institutional configurations to be identified. Such arguments typically focus on the role of state policy and practice, welfare or societal institutions—such as industrial relations or the organization of business and management—in furnishing distinctiveness and diversity. These approaches mainly offer an assessment of national political economies as both self-contained and stable spaces for the reproduction of difference. However, the constancy of state-welfare and differing institutional practices has been called into question by the challenges to the nation-state posed by internationalizing product and service markets, globalizing or transnational companies, and the general increased mobility and de-territorialization of capital (Sklair 2001, 2002).

The stability of the nation-state during the postwar boom was supported by welfarism, Keynesianism, financial or exchange controls on the movement of capital, and nationally centered pacts between states, employers' and workers' organizations. The resurgence of the market, international capital, and the greater mobility of financial and physical capital through the transnational corporation (TNC) challenged these policies and institutional arrangements from the late 1970s. Therefore the competing capitalism's perspective has been threatened by resurgence of neoliberalism and international market forces (Traxler, Blaschke, and Kittel 2001).

States, rather than reinforcing national institutional settlements and differences on the basis of competition with other states, begin to come under pressure from internationalizing firms to deregulate (or homogenize) their national territories, open up state activities to market forces, and transform the state practices into a common agenda of a competition state (Cerny 1990). Such states have standard policy incentives to pull in foreign direct investment (FDI), increase flexibility of the workforce, deregulate labor markets, and weaken trade unions and local institutional actors. Beginning in more marketized economies—Australia, the United States, and United Kingdom—this liberal market philosophy has been spreading to corporatist, regulated, and more embedded institutionalized states, such as Germany (Jurgens, Naumann, and Rupp 2000) and Japan (Dore 2002; Morgan and Takahashi 2002).

25.2.4 States, Firms, and Change

It is sensible to concede that national, state, and institutional arrangements within countries create practices that are relatively stable. States (and the social institutions within them) do not encounter profound ownership change in the same way as private firms, but they do make structural adjustments, such as the shift from Keynesianism to neoliberalism since the late 1970s. However, international competitiveness between states is unlike that between firms because states do not go bankrupt or get taken over, and therefore behave differently from firms (Krugman 1994). We therefore need to separate states and firms in comparative analysis and to note the patterns of interaction between them.

Firms do carry the traits of national environments. Furthermore, although both states and firms change, states do so more slowly than firms, so they can be seen plausibly as the context within which firms operate. However they are not constrained by these, as capital is mobile, labor is mobile through and between the firm, and increasingly state policy is transferred through what Sklair (2001) calls transnational practices and institutions, such as the European Union. But states and national institutions change more slowly because they are not as subject to the rationalizing forces of international markets, competition, and technological forces of capitalism. Firms are more dynamic—changing ownership, and integrating activities cross-nationally, operating with a global reach that few states (or national institutions) can possess as they are tied to territory in a way that capital, and to a lesser extent labor, are not.

Firms are more receptive to change than states. Moreover, production systems may be more heterogeneous, combining elements of old (Fordist) and new (innovative or experimental) practices. Further, firms unlike states can experiment within national systems, and across national territories, because capital, unlike national institutions, is mobile (and increasingly so under neoliberal economic management practices). The recent Japanese transplant debate (Abo 1994; Ackroyd et al. 1988; Elger and Smith 1994; Kenney and Florida 1993; Liker, Fruin, and Adler 1999; Milkman 1991; Oliver and Wilkinson 1992; Womack, Jones, and Roos 1990), discussion on the diffusion of management ideas (Kogut 1993), the role of international business consultants (Kipping and Engwall 2002) and of international firms in diffusing transnational or world best practice (Morgan, Kristensen, and Whitley 2001; Sklair 2001) make firms less, not more likely to exhibit tensions within their practices, rather than homogeneous national traits implied by societal effects theory (Maurice and Sorge 2000a; see also Morgan, in this volume).

Capital takes many forms, some with more mobility than others. But because of system effects it cannot take any form. Firms and sectors, while representing more or less continuous institutional practice, are not necessarily spatially bounded to national localities. Technologies—hardware, information, and knowledge—are more mobile and are dissolving these spatial distances and challenging the need to have production and services in physical proximity. Production of mass consumer commodities is increasingly spatially disaggregated through long subcontracting chains with enormous geographical spread according to the logic of accumulation. Consumer services (finance, banking, insurance, travel, and telecommunications) are similarly increasingly breaking free from local high streets into regional and national concentrations. One interesting indication of this is call centers, geographically dispersed from clients, but linked through product standardization and common technology. In general, we need to characterize labor processes and business organizations more generally as sitting within competing and emergent globalizing and localizing pressures, rather than as having become universal or remained separate and unique.

25.3 An Alternative Framework: Distinguishing System, Societal, and Dominance Effects

By way of critique of the arguments outlined above within comparative organizational analysis, it can be shown that the international firm will be a site for the social interaction of distinct forces, and not simply a universal set of economically efficient organizational practices versus a local set of institutional rules, customs, laws, and relations. This model of system, society, and dominance effects grew out of comparative research on the engineering profession (Smith 1990; Smith and Meiksins 1995) and was extended through research on Japanese transplants in Britain (Smith and Elger 1997, 2000). The model is an attempt to create a dynamic, synthetic, and integrated approach to cross-national organization analysis and was built upon and reacted to the work of Child (1981) and Lane (1989).

The usefulness of the analysis is demonstrated by the fact that international organizations reflect a three-way interaction of contextual and interest group effects from different structural sources. This triple determination may be stated as follows: first, there is political economy or mode of production (system effects); second, there is the effect of unique national institutions, cultures, and histories (societal effects); and, third, there is the diffusion of best practices or modernization strategies by the society-in-dominance at any particular period of global competition (dominance effects). In recent decades it has been the United States or Japan that has exercised these dominance effects.

The value of the approach has been highlighted in a number of ways. It has been considered in reviews of British economic sociology (e.g. Dodd 2000), applied in understanding international human resource management (Edwards 2004), and diffused through influential critical British organization studies textbooks, especially Thompson and McHugh (2002). The latter elaborated the model by Smith and Meiksins with political economy (system effects), national institutions (societal effects), and global forces (dominance effects) mutually interacting together and upon work organization (2002: 82–3). More recently, Rubery and Grimshaw (2003: 47) have built a model of the international pressures on societal employment systems that 'has close parallels to that proposed in the various writing of Elger, Meiksins and Smith'. In particular they accept the idea of dominance and see it as being an advance on the ideas of the institutionalist writers who emphasize societal effects. They use the SSD model to identify the competing pressures of divergence and convergence within the firm as introduced by different forces.

Other writers have used the model to critique cultural and institutional approaches and stress the importance of system features of generic conflict in employment relations in the globalization of the service sector (Sturdy 2001); or in debate on new production concepts diffused by Japanese firms (Delbridge 1998; Sharpe 2001). Those closer to the societal effects model have tried to test and weigh the relative importance of societal effects against dominant country effects, and they have concluded that societal institutions carry more effect on, in this case, supply relations, than current global best practice, such as vogue solutions from Japan (Lane 1997). But, as Sharpe (2001: 198) notes, 'Smith argues that companies selectively transfer value and operational capacities to fit local labour markets and product markets, hence reinforcing existing patterns of diversity rather than leading to a homogenization effect' (Smith 1996: 3). Hence, it is not the aim of the SSD model to elevate one effect above another, but rather to analytically locate the sources of pressures to change and/or continuity within the international firm.

Thus, there is not necessarily any disgreement with the conclusions of some critics. For example, Maurice and Sorge (2000b: 391–2), defending the societal effects approach against criticism from the SSD model, argue that societal effects may be amplified by globalization forces, reinforcing existing structures, rather than changing them. This may indeed occur. On the other hand, the opposite may be true. Work on Japanese transplants in Britain highlights the subnational variations in practice applied by TNCs, and the innovative practices developed by dominant players within particular societal conditions, rather than simply the further reproduction of the same institutional practices and effects (see also Morgan, in this volume). One of the locational preferences for international firms, especially mass manufacturing companies, appears to be for clustered concentrations in special zones, new towns, or growth regions, which frequently lie outside national rules of the game or permit experimentation within national rules, often influenced by alliances between local states and international capital. In these contexts general societal values and rules may not apply in the same way to international firms (Smith and Elger 2000).

The SSD model is not unidirectional and overly structural in emphasis. It allows that the firm does select policies and options and often does shape its environment. Research in Japanese TNCs in the United Kingdom based on the SSD model highlights the agency of the firm in managing its environment (Elger and Smith 1998; Smith and Elger 1998). This research is supported by the work of others (Clark and Mueller 1996), who have tried to interrogate the action of the large firm within the context of societal constraints, developing what Mayer and Whittington (1999: 936) call a reflexive recombination of local and international practices. Therefore, this work on Japanese transplants has supported the agency of the firm in shaping and not simply carrying its context.

It is an inappropriate use of the model to rank the relative importance of different effects as is attempted by Lane (1997). The assumption is that system, society, and dominance effects may all be present and may work in inconsistent or consistent directions. Discussion of the intervention of a dominant player with global work organization practices in the United Kingdom in the form of Japanese TNCs highlights their selective application of their own business systems, selective disregard of national practices and innovation, and varying degrees of resistance from employees. Rather less than complete subordination of British workers (e.g. employment relations and work organization practices) to Japanization was found (Elger and Smith 1998; Smith and Elger 1998). Lane's case study in a sector not exposed to international competition might explain why she found societal arrangements intact rather than complicated by dominance effects.

25.3.1 System Effects: Universalism

To begin to explore the three effects in more detail, system is understood in a broad sense. System is political economy, which produces common interests and similar problems, regardless of the country context within which, say, capitalist social relations are located. Under consideration here are effects that come through common social relations or purposes—for example, the desire to work for private gain, rather than enhanced community status or common bonds of group or collective interest. System means fundamentally shared factors, however specifically they may have been introduced or arrived at. State Socialism had generic features, typically an accentuated role for the state in economic affairs, the planning and management of the firm, control of labor allocation, and constraints on managers' freedom to hire and fire workers. System is therefore political and economic. In addition, system can refer to global technology or techniques and ways of working that are diffused as common standards through such channels as management textbooks. Capitalist competition, technological dynamism, and capital–labor conflict underpin and exert common pressures on all specific manifestations of capitalist social relations, within enterprises, sectors, or national economies. It is these underlying dynamics, with their associated conflicts and uncertainties that go under the heading of system imperatives.

Systemic features of capitalism begin with property rights, owners and non-owners and the capitalist employment relationship. Paid work in a capitalist society requires waged labor dependent on employers for work and is structured by the drive for capital accumulation and profitable production. This motivates firms, which are activated by managers and workers drawn into definite social relations for this purpose. Workers are motivated (compelled and facilitated) to sell their labor power to survive. Managers have to take this human raw material and combine it with social forces of production (tools, equipment and technology, and material objects for work) and a purpose, profitable production, which animate the rules of capitalist economic action. Within relations between waged workers and employers (or their representatives), there is an exchange, an employment relationship in which wages are exchanged for labor services. However, the precise amount of work or labor effort to be expended for economic return is left open-ended, as is the precise nature of the tasks to be performed, their sequencing, the particular standard of work, the performance criteria, the quality of the authority, and human relations between those who employ and those who are employed.

Universal or systemic theorizing assumes a standardized or standardizing workplace in which technology, science, and managerial discourse aims at creating common methodologies regardless of the sector or country in which the firm is operating. System thinking is common to all deductive reasoning, which builds on abstract concepts, in which context-dependent rationality is suspended for the purposes of building ideal or pure typologies. Following a realist method, system represents an underlying dynamic, which nevertheless appears in varied manifestations.

25.3.2 Societal Effects: National Divergence

While there clearly are societal, industry, and even specific community effects on the organization of businesses, a key theoretical question concerns how formative they may be. In what circumstances can they be overridden or bypassed? The societal effects school frequently suggests an irreducible diversity to work organization, regardless of common factor inputs or modes of systemic rationalizing (Maurice and Sorge 2000b). This is because the rules of the game under which managers and workers interact are formed by nationally specific cultural and institutional codes. As these codes or rules emerge through the historical process within each country, they are unique. Any systemic thinking on work organization, according to this logic, will be filtered through distinctive, inimitable agencies, and therefore be set to perpetually reproduce diversity. A country's history cannot be wiped clean, or only in exceptional circumstances of wars or colonization, and even then cultural differences persist at subnational levels:

By means of cross-national comparisons of organizational units which were fairly identical with regard to acknowledged contingencies, this Group has identified quite a large cross-national variety of organizational forms and practices which though unrelated to task context or performance difference, is very closely bound to institutionalized human resources (education, training, work careers), social stratification and industrial relations. (Sorge 1991: 162)

In extreme form, this school does not merely discount the idea of the capitalist labor process, but denies it; all that exists are national variants of ways of working, a menu of social relations prepared by national histories and not economic or functional structures of a supranational capitalist system. British writers using this approach (Lane 1989) have critiqued the universalism of Braverman's de-skilling thesis, for example, by bringing into focus different patterns of training and skill formation between capitalist societies, suggesting that social institutions mold capitalist social relations in distinctly national ways, so that there is no generalized tendency for capitalism to de-skill or for the labor process to express the same antagonistic relationships between labor and capital as seen in the United Kingdom or United States. Workers' and managers' expectations of and perceptions of each other are partially cultural; i.e. they are informed by historical experience and are partially the products of institutional genesis.

According to this view, more generally:

National-sectoral regimes of economic governance *evolve over time* and constitute *historically grown social facts* for each generation of traders. At any given point, economic actors are confronted with a legacy of local social institutions that are not of their making; not subject to their choosing; not in principle amenable to contractual reordering; and whose functional and evolutionary logic is different from that of a market or a formal-organisational hierarchy. At the centre of this logic is the ability of governance regimes to impose *socially constructed collective obligations* on individuals, if necessary against their resistance. ... In the real world, the 'givenness' of an industrial order is visible in its ability to *socialize* its subjects into distinctive identities. While individuals 'belonging to' a particular order may undertake to remake it—for example, in line with the perceived imperatives of efficiency and 'economizing'—in doing so they are forced to observe its present modus operandi and the constraints it imposes upon them (in other words, to accept its 'path dependency'). (Hollingsworth, Schmitter, and Streeck 1994: 278–9) (emphasis in the original)

Country boundaries around work (through social institutions, laws, values, and attitudes) remain one of the key features by which organizations are distinguished in this model. Supranational forces—technology, science, management best practices, international firms—operate to make a nation's economic base diverse and are not simply reflective of internal national institutional rules of the game. On the other hand, it is clear that many organizations move between societies and are not nationally bounded, but draw from an internationally diverse range of practices (see Morgan, in this volume). It becomes an open research question whether host or home practices, or a hybrid or combination of the two, shape work organization and employment relations in these firms. The range of practices brought into action means the transnational firm is able to draw upon divergent policies, practices, and individuals with differing orientations to work than those simply present within the host society. This diversity produces varied organization learning and the leverage of coercive comparison.

25.3.3 Dominance Effects

The third element in the argument concerns the uneven nature of economic power, and the tendency for one society to take the lead in evolving work organization or business practices considered more efficient than those operating within other countries. These lead societies create dominance effects, which circulate as best practices or global standards that are emulated by other societies (see also Strang and Kim, in this volume). In this way, societies do not face each other as equals, but with uneven capabilities, which encourages the process of learning and borrowing or diffusion and dominance. Added to which, the globalization of capital means international companies operate in several regions and societies, and home practices might only be retained if they are judged to yield competitive advantage to the firm.

Within the contemporary debate, there are those who emphasize a plurality of equally effective national solutions to common economic problems, and those who search for a best solution, and hence an arrangement of social institutions that delivers superior economic performance. But as Crouch (2001: 132) has noted, the search for the best model—Sweden, Germany, or Japan in recent years—has short-term currency, as the economies of these countries begin to underperform, as did the American and other companies taken as representative of excellence by Peters and Waterman (1982). What Crouch does not explain is why the search for excellence or the best model of capitalism continues. This is because of both systemic competition between states and capital, and the idea of unevenness between societies and dominance.

Within the debate on the Japanese model, we have seen a clear relationship between the economic success of Japan, and the intense interest by firms and governments in wishing to learn from and borrow Japanese ideas. But in order to make these more acceptable or to neutralize their societal origins, systemic and nonsocietal technical terms are invented, such as lean production or TQM or continuous improvement. While originating in Japan, circulation creates a different discourse, and association with the Japanese context may be broken—this was especially important as the dominance of the Japanese economy faded in the 1990s. Dominance effects signal the idea that one society originates ideas, and may seek to diffuse these, as new standards, but through the process of diffusion, there occurs a distillation of the ideas into societal and systemic elements. This is clear in the Japan debate and was also evident in earlier debates on Taylorism:

Taylorism ... was initially bounded by the constraints of American capitalism; but its diffusion transformed it into a 'best practice' which was seen as a system requirement in some economies. ... The identification of Taylorism with American economic success made it difficult to resist. Disentangling the three influences of society, system and dominance has always been part of the critique of Taylorism as it became a dominant ideology and began to diffuse to Europe and Japan; but we could say that it was only with the emergence of other dominant capitalist states, in Europe and Japan, that such a critique has been able to separate these levels, and identify what in Taylorism is specific to America, what is part of capitalism, and what held sway only through American economic hegemony and not intrinsic qualities of Taylorism itself. (Smith and Meiksins 1995: 263–4)

Dominance may also be symbolic, tied to cyclical patterns of economic success of one nation or region. Because efficiency is institutionalized in the form of a strong society or country case, rather than simply abstracted concepts of growth, output, and productivity, it is inevitable that comparative modeling and diffusion has a cognitive and symbolic dimension. Following institutional theory, one would expect that the urge to emulate these perceived (and real) dominant economies is stimulated as much by conformity, fashion, and the need to overcome the uncertainties of capitalist competition (DiMaggio and Powell 1983). For example, Japan and the so-called Asian Tiger economies, founded as they were on export processing and not import substitution strategies, were successful, dominant, and therefore worthy of both emulation, promoted through management and firms, and coercive isomorphism fostered through state direction. But when the cycle moves, stars of yesterday become dogs of today, and learning from literatures moves on to new talents. In this way, dominance rotates and has a cognitive or perceived/symbolic element, as well as representing real efficiency differences between societies.

25.4 APPLYING THE SSD MODEL

While there are undoubtedly some important societal effects, the most significant problem for this approach is in explaining theoretically why there are continued convergence pressures within supposedly nationally bounded economies? The imperative of efficiency (i.e. abstract economic or market principles) applies to all capitalist societies as system imperatives. However, establishing the efficiency even of non-complex and bounded systems is notoriously difficult. On the other hand, it is clear that dominant countries provide models of best practice that involve the packaging of national operations into apparently neutral requirements, which actually involve the selective borrowing of best practices from national agendas. This is because of the economic inequality between societies and the nature of capitalist competition.

Thus, while the theorists of societal effects have begun to develop valuable accounts of the sources of diversity in national trajectories of capitalist development and class relations, these accounts have concentrated upon the internal logics of institutional development that are held to explain persistent distinctiveness, while giving little attention to the ways in which evolving relations among states alter the terrain upon which national systems operate.

25.4.1 Dominance and Diffusion

The SSD model suggests that capitalist production rationalization has national traits, such as the link between Taylor, Taylorism, and the United States; or Ford, Fordism, and the United States. But also that diffusion of new production and employment ideas through international firms, consultancy channels, academic discourse, and universal management educational processes (such as the global commodity of an MBA), aims to delink the sources of ideas (Taylorism and Fordism in the United States, Toyotaism in Japan) from national contexts through the process of diffusion (Kogut and Parkinson 1993; Smith and Meiksins 1995; Wood 1991). Delinking stresses the universal efficiency gains that all organizations will receive from the adoption of new best practices. Nevertheless, application and adaptation of novel practices within the workplace, especially the TNC subsidiary, will raise themes of ownership, until techniques become global best practices (Sklair 2001, 2002), denationalized, and diluted or altered through the diffusion process.

The system, society, and dominance model aims to capture the complexity of transfer within the modern, internationalized workplace. It locates the sources of difference that come into the firm through home or local practices (societal contexts), standard or system forces, given by definite relations of production of a particular political economy and the importance of a society-in-dominance or standard setter for modern employment and work relations, which continually fuels competition between companies and nations by holding up the latest business, production, or employment practice originated in an apparently more efficient/dominant society or company within a market, sector, or region, and diffused through various agencies that gain from packaging and trading best practice knowledge and information.

25.4.2 An Appropriate Consideration of Complexity

As research into the activities of Japanese transplants reveals, while there is not a simple diffusion of something called the Japanese model or a generic process of Japanization, there are certainly real traces of borrowing, learning, transfer, and transformation through the interaction of internationally dominant TNCs in national economies (Smith and Elger 2000). Throughout the 1980s and 1990s there was an active debate on the transfer of Japanese management techniques from Japan into the West through the agency of the Japanese transnational company. At different moments and in different societal contexts, applying Japanese practices to new locations was considered straightforward, due to their inherent and irresistible efficiency superiority, thus normatively essential for the competitive survival of the Western firm (Florida and Kenney 1991; Womack, Jones, and Roos 1990). At other times it was regarded as a more interactive and problematical process of application and adaptation, involving considerable compromise for the Japanese firm (Abo 1994; 1998; Itagaki 1997) or as very creative and dynamic, where relocation produced new work forms, different from both those in Japan and within the host society, and therefore unanticipated and unimagined prior to the process of Japanese subsidiary formation (Boyer *et al.* 1998*a*; Freyssenet *et al.* 1999; Jurgens, Malsch, and Dohse 1993; Kenney and Florida 1993; Liker, Fruin, and Adler 1999; Smith 1996).

However, TNCs affect global, regional, and trans-state forms of interdependence and integration, often based on cost-driven and market-driven business strategies or the construction of different global commodity chains (Gereffi and Korzeniewicz 1994). These, while not suppressing institutional and value differences between societies, tend to create common policy response/instruments within states desperate to attract FDI—such as low/no tax incentives, special labor codes, as found in new towns, and special development regions and zones (Dicken 1998; Sklair 2002). The competition state (Cerny 1990; Elger and Burnham 2001) and globalization reinforce each other, and the national is not a source of simple diversity, but convergence to standards that fit the process of the internationalization of capital. It is the adoption of these common policy instruments designed to pull investment, and the consequent clustering of manufacturing capital, that create distinctive management and labor responses—especially high turnover and management retention/adaptation strategies such as process de-skilling, interfirm collusion, contract segmentation, neopaternalism, and worker substitution (Smith and Elger 2002).

Capitalist firms in different societies are not all equivalent in terms of efficiencies and productivity, and where economic goods are tradable through TNCs, such differences inform location choices, but also national policymakers, who place comparative economic advantage on the agenda, and press towards the adoption of modern technologies, techniques, and practices to compete with the best. Such emulation—again present in the Japanization debate—creates homogenization or globalization pressures, which tend to test and erode local or national institutional rules and practices. The comparative evaluation of the economic performance between countries raises borrowing as a possibility, even though in practical terms, taking practices and policies from one country and transferring them to another is far from straightforward—as discussed above. Nevertheless the fact that the idea of transfer occurs repeatedly needs explaining and is not self-evident from a pure societal effects perspective in which countries compete with each other through divergent, but functionally equivalent organizational means and methods. This leads to a discussion of differences between societies, and the dominance effects these create through the competitive pressure of the global marketplace.

Despite evident system properties, every consideration of the social relations in organizational change must take into account actor consciousness, the actions and reaction of groups of actors. This was either not considered by societal effect theorists, or if it was, it was treated as marginal to the theme of transfer and transplantation, which was a largely mechanical or technical process, and not one mediated through human agency and so did not require interpretation. Modern management practices and production systems were judged like bits of technology and thought capable of isolation and transfer (Ferner 1997). However, ethnographic accounts of workers' life on the line in Japanese subsidiaries or emulator plants highlighted a much more mundane, routine, and pressured picture of work and authority relations (Delbridge 1998; Graham 1995; Palmer 1996; Sharpe 1997, 1998). But this research also highlighted movable and immovable practices. Delbridge (1998: 203–4), for example, noted that certain technical aspects of the Japanese production system were present in his two case companies—quality regime, inventory control, and grouping of activities. But none of the social side of the Japanese model was present—security of employment, teamworking, and seniority pay— echoing earlier work by Milkman (1991) in the United States and Dedoussis (1995) in Australia.

25.4.3 Transnational Firms and SSD Model

Transnational companies are globalizing, not globalized, as Sklair suggests, and therefore their organizations will be marked by both their origins and the strength of the local practices embedded within any particular subsidiary, as well as the prevailing forces within the world market and production system. States or national business systems are always penetrated by the international division of labor, the world market, and competition between rival capitalist societies and are never islands of self-sustaining diversity. However, the idea that globalization, best practices, or the latest 'one best way' modernization recipe will sweep away diversity is misleading. What flows from the arguments within this chapter is that the interplay of different processes, often pulling in contradictory directions, is a more feasible scenario. As such, the new international division of labor within global capitalism may confirm some countries within already dependent, peripheral, or subordinate positions within the order of global capitalism. But new entrants may also create different ways of organizing the firm, employment relations, work organization, and supplier relations and redefine themselves and influence others in the system. Japan played this role in the 1980s with a profound influence on work organization outside of Japan. Finally, whatever value there is in particularizing the nature of organization, work, and employment relations by reference to country or production metaphor (e.g. Fordism or Toyotaism), the universal or systemic social relations given by political economy will always be present within all these diverse representations or appearances. In other words, capital–labor contestation is structurally endemic to capitalism, but is expressed in manifold ways and mediated through a great variety of institutional forms.

The transferred or internationalized workplace condenses the effects of globalizing capitalist forces, national institutional rules, and world best practice work and employment standards within local and unique work situations. But it is only through social interaction that groups and individuals negotiate which of these different (and perhaps competing) ways of working, standards of quality, authority relations, and methods of employment will actually shape particular work situations. It is therefore important to retain a research focus on the workplace, as it is here that the working out of workplace rules and practices emerges. The unpredictability of workplace relations comes from the system effects within employment relations but also the impossibility of knowing, from the outside, how the contingent combinations of particular workers and managers, in particular locations, sectors, and contexts, will actually interact to produce definite work and employment relations. It is both the systemic and contingent contradictions that necessitate empirical enquiry, as social agents are reflexive and have choices over how they interact within the constraints of their situation.

REFERENCES

ABO, T. (ed.) (1994). *Hybrid Factory: The Japanese Production System in the United States.* Oxford: Oxford University Press.

—— (1998). 'Hybridization of the Japanese Production System in North America, Newly Industrializing Economies, South-East Asia and Europe: Contrasting Configurations', in R. Boyer, E. Charron, U. Jürgens, and S. Tolliday (eds.), *Between Imitation and Innovation: The Transfer and Hybridization of Production Models in the International Automobile Industry.* Oxford: Oxford University Press.

ACKROYD, S., BURRELL, G., HUGHES, M., and WHITAKER, A. (1988). 'The Japanization of British Industry?' *Industrial Relations Journal,* 19/1: 11–23.

ALBERT, M. (1993). *Capitalism against Capitalism.* London: Whurr.

—— CHARRON, E., JURGENS, U., and TOLLIDAY, S. (eds.) (1998a). *Between Imitation and Innovation: The Transfer and Hybridization of Productive Models in the International Automobile Industry.* Oxford: Oxford University Press.

BRAVERMAN, H. (1974). *Labor and Monopoly Capital.* New York: Monthly Review Press.

CERNY, P. G. (1990). *The Changing Architecture of Politics: Structure, Agency and the Future of the State*. London: Sage.

CHANDLER, Jr., A. D. (1990). *Scale and Scope: The Dynamics of Industrial Capitalism*. Cambridge, Mass.: Harvard University Press.

CHILD, J. (1981). 'Culture, Contingency and Capitalism in the Cross-National Study of Organisations', in B. Staw and L. L. Cummings (eds.), *Research in Organizational Behaviour*, Volume 3. Greenwich, Conn.: JAI Press.

CLARK, P., and MUELLER, F. (1996). 'Organisations and Nations: From Universalism to Institutionalism'. *British Journal of Management*, 7: 125–40.

COATES, D. (2000). *Models of Capitalism: Growth and Stagnation in the Modern Era*. Cambridge: Polity Press.

CROUCH, C. (2001). 'Heterogeneities of Practice and Interest'. *New Political Economy*, 6: 131–5.

—— and STREECK, W. (eds.) (1997). *Political Economy of Modern Capitalism: Mapping Convergence and Diversity*. London: Sage.

—— FINEGOLD, D., and SAKO, M. (1999). *Are Skills the Answer? The Political Economy of Skill Creation in Advanced Industrial Societies*. Oxford: Oxford University Press.

DEDOUSSIS, V. (1995). 'Simply a Question of Cultural Barriers? The Search for New Perspectives in the Transfer of Japanese Management Practices'. *Journal of Management Studies*, 32: 731–46.

DELBRIDGE, R. (1998). *Life on the Line in Contemporary Manufacturing: The Workplace Experience of Lean Production and the 'Japanese' Model*. Oxford: Oxford University Press.

DICKEN, P. (1998). *Global Shift: Transforming the World Economy* (3rd edn). London: Paul Chapman.

DiMAGGIO, P., and POWELL, W. (1983). 'The Iron Cage Revisited: Institutional Isomorphism and Collective Rationality in Organizational Fields'. *American Sociological Review*, 48: 147–60.

DODD, N. (2000). 'Economic Sociology in Britain'. *Economic Sociology European Electronic Newsletter*, 2/1: 3–12.

DORE, R. (2002). 'Stock Market Capitalism and Its Diffusion'. *New Political Economy*, 7: 115–21.

DOSI, G., and KOGUT, B. (1993). 'National Specificities and the Context of Change: The Co-evolution of Organization and Technology', in B. Kogut (ed.), *Country Competitiveness: Technology and the Organizing of Work*. Oxford: Oxford University Press.

EDWARDS, T. (2004). 'The Transfer of Employment Practices across Borders in Multinational Companies', in A. W. Harzing and J. V. Ruysseveldt (eds.), *International Human Resource Management* (2nd edn). London: Sage.

ELGER, T., and BURNHAM, P. (2001). 'Labour, Globalization and the "Competition State"'. *Competition and Change*, 5: 245–68.

—— and EDWARDS, P. (1999). 'An Introduction', in P. Edwards and T. Elger (eds.), *National States and the Regulation of Labour in the Global Economy*. London: Mansell.

—— and SMITH, C. (1994). 'Introduction' and 'Global Japanization? Convergence and Competition in the Organization of the Labour Process', in T. Elger and C. Smith (eds.), *Global Japanization? The Transnational Transformation of the Labour Process*. London: Routledge.

——— (1998). 'New Town, New Capital, New Workplace? The Employment Relations of Japanese Inward Investors in a West Midlands New Town'. *Economy and Society*, 27: 578–608.

ESPING-ANDERSON, G. (1990). *Three Worlds of Welfare Capitalism*. Princeton, NJ: Princeton University Press.

FERNER, A. (1997). 'Country of Origin Effects and HRM in Multinational Companies'. *Human Resource Management Journal*, 7: 19–37.

—— and HYMAN, R. (eds.) (1992). *Industrial Relations in the New Europe*. Oxford: Blackwell.

FLORIDA, R., and KENNEY, M. (1991). 'Organisation versus Culture: Japanese Automotive Transplants in the United States'. *Industrial Relations Journal*, 22: 181–96.

FREYSSENET, M., MAIR, A., SHIMIZU, K., and VOLPATO, G. (eds.) (1999). *One Best Way? Trajectories and Industrial Models of the World's Automobile Producers*. Oxford: Oxford University Press.

FROBEL, F., HEINRICHS, J., and KREYE, O. (1980). *The New International Division of Labour: Structural Unemployment in Industrialized Countries and Industrialization in Developing Countries*. Cambridge: Cambridge University Press.

GEREFFI, G., and KORZENIEWICZ, M. (eds.) (1994). *Commodity Chains and Global Capitalism*. Westport, Conn.: Praeger.

GRAHAM, L. (1995). *On the Line at Subaru-Isuzu: The Japanese Model and the American Worker*. New York: ILR/Cornell University Press.

HALL, P. A., and SOSKICE, D. (2001). 'An Introduction to Varieties of Capitalism', in P. A. Hall and D. Soskice (eds.), *Varieties of Capitalism: The Institutional Foundations of Comparative Advantage*. Oxford: Oxford University Press.

HOLLINGSWORTH, J. R., SCHMITTER, P. C., and STREECK, W. (eds.) (1994). *Governing Capitalist Economies: Performance & Control of Economic Sectors*. Oxford: Oxford University Press.

HYMAN, R. (2001). *Understanding European Industrial Relations: Between Market, Class and Society*. London: Sage.

ITAGAKI, H. (ed.) (1997). *The Japanese Production System: Hybrid Factories in East Asia*. London: Macmillan.

JURGENS, U., MALSCH, T., and DOHSE, K. (1993). *Breaking from Taylorism: Changing Forms of Work in the Automobile Industry*. Cambridge: Cambridge University Press.

—— NAUMANN, K., and RUPP, J. (2000). 'Shareholder in an Adverse Environment: The German Case'. *Economy and Society*, 29: 54–79.

KATZ, H. C., and DARBISHIRE, O. (2000). *Converging Divergences: Worldwide Changes in Employment Systems*. Ithaca, NY: ILR Press.

KENNEY, M., and FLORIDA, R. (1993). *Beyond Mass Production: The Japanese System and Its Transfer to the US*. Oxford: Oxford University Press.

KERR, C., DUNLOP, J. T., ARBISON, F., and MYERS, C. A. (1960). *Industrialism and Industrial Man*. Cambridge, Mass.: Harvard University Press.

KIPPING, M., and ENGWALL, L. (eds.) (2002). *Management Consulting: Emergence and Dynamism of a Knowledge Industry*. Oxford: Oxford University Press.

KOGUT, B. (ed.) (1993). *Country Competitiveness: Technology and the Organizing of Work*. Oxford: Oxford University Press.

—— and PARKINSON, D. (1993). 'The Diffusion of American Organising Principles to Europe', in B. Kogut (ed.), *Country Competitiveness: Technology and the Organizing of Work*. Oxford: Oxford University Press.

KRUGMAN, P. (1994). 'Competitiveness: A Dangerous Obsession'. *Foreign Affairs*, March/ April: 28–44.

LANE, C. (1989). *Management and Labour in Europe*. Aldershot: Edward Elgar.

—— (1995). *Industry and Society in Europe: Stability and Change in Britain, Germany and France*. Aldershot: Edward Elgar.

—— (1997). 'The Governance of Inter-Firm Relations in Britain and Germany: Societal or Dominance Effects?' in R. Whitley and P. K. Kristensen (eds.), *Governance at Work: The Social Regulation of Economic Relations*. Oxford: Oxford University Press.

LAZONICK, W. (1991). *Business Organisation and the Myth of the Market Economy*. Cambridge: Cambridge University Press.

LIKER, J. K., FRUIN, W. M., and ADLER, P. S. (1999). 'Bringing Japanese Management to the United States: Transplantation or Transformation?' in J. K. Liker, W. M. Fruin, and P. S. Adler (eds.), *Remade in America: Transplanting and Transforming Japanese Management Systems*. Oxford: Oxford University Press.

LORENZ, E. (2000). 'The Transfer of Business Practices to Britain and France', in M. Maurice and A. Sorge (eds.), *Embedding Organizations*. Amsterdam/Philadelphia: John Benjamin.

MAURICE, M., and SORGE, A. (2000a). 'Conclusions', in M. Maurice and A. Sorge (eds.), *Embedding Organizations: Societal Analysis of Actors, Organisations and Socio-Economic Context*. Amsterdam: John Benjamin.

—— —— (eds.) (2000b). *Embedding Organizations: Societal Analysis of Actors, Organisations and Socio-Economic Context*. Amsterdam: John Benjamin.

—— SELLIER, F., and SILVESTRE, J. J. (1986). *The Social Foundations of Industrial Power: A Comparison of France and Germany*. Cambridge, Mass.: MIT Press.

MAYER, M. C. J., and WHITTINGTON, R. (1999). 'Strategy, Structure and "Systemness": National Institutions and Corporate Change in France, Germany and the UK, 1950–1993'. *Organization Studies*, 20: 933–59.

MEIKSINS, P., and SMITH, C. (1996). *Engineering Labour: Technical Workers in Comparative Perspective*. London: Verso.

MILKMAN, R. (1991). *Japan's California Factories: Labor Relations and Economic Globalisation*. Los Angeles: IIR, University of California.

MORGAN, G., and TAKAHASHI, Y. (2002). 'Shareholder Value in the Japanese Context'. *Competition and Change*, 6: 169–91.

—— KRISTENSEN, P. H., and WHITLEY, R. (eds.) (2001). *The Multinational Firm: Organizing across Institutional and National Divides*. Oxford: Oxford University Press.

NELSON, RICHARD R. (ed.) (1993). *National Innovation Systems: A Comparative Analysis*. Oxford: Oxford University Press.

OLIVER, N., and WILKINSON, B. (1992). *The Japanisation of British Industry: New Developments in the 1990s* (2nd edn). Oxford: Blackwell.

PALMER, G. (1996). 'Reviving Resistance: The Japanese Factory Floor in Britain'. *Industrial Relations Journal*, 27: 129–43.

PETERS, T. J., and WATERMAN, R. H. (1982). *In Search of Excellence*. New York: Random House.

REDDING, S. G. (1990). *The Spirit of Chinese Capitalism*. Berlin: De Gruyter.

RITZER, G. (1993). *The McDonaldization of Society*. London: Sage.

RUBERY, J., and GRIMSHAW, D. (2003). *The Organization of Employment: An International Perspective.* Basingstoke: Palgrave.

SHARPE, D. (1997). 'Managerial Control Strategies and Sub-cultural Processes: On the Shop-Floor in a Japanese Manufacturing Organisation in the UK', in A. Sackmann (ed.), *Cultural Complexity in Organisations: Inherent Contrasts and Contradictions.* London: Sage.

——(1998). 'Shop Floor Practices under Changing Forms of Management Control: A Comparative Ethnographic Study'. Ph.D. thesis, University of Manchester.

——(2001). 'Globalization and Change: Organizational Continuity and Change within a Japanese Multinational in the UK', in G. Morgan, R. Whitley, and P. H. Kristensen (eds.), *The Multinational Firm: Organizing across Institutional and National Divides.* Oxford: Oxford University Press.

SKLAIR, L. (2001). *The Transnational Capitalist Class.* Oxford: Blackwell.

——(2002). *Globalization: Capitalism and Its Alternatives.* Oxford: Oxford University Press.

SMITH, C. (1990). 'How Are Engineers Formed? Professionals, Nation and Class Politics'. *Work, Employment and Society*, 3/4: 451–67.

——(1996). 'Japan, the Hybrid Factory and Cross-National Organisational Theory'. Special Issue, 'Vernetzung und Vereinnahmung-Arbeit zwischen Internationlisierung und neuen Manaegmentkonzepten'. *Osterreichische Zeitschrift fur Soziologie*, 3: 105–30.

—— and ELGER, T. (1997). 'International Competition: Inward Investment and the Restructuring of European Work and Industrial Relations'. *European Journal of Industrial Relations*, 3: 279–304.

—— ——(1998). 'Greenfields and "Wildebeestes": Management Strategies and Labour Turnover in Japanese Firms in Telford'. *Employee Relations*, 20/3: 271–84.

—— ——(2000). 'The Societal Effects School and Transnational Transfer: The Case of Japanese Investment in Britain', in M. Maurice and A. Sorge (eds.), *Embedding Organizations: Societal Analysis of Actors, Organisations and Socio-Economic Context.* Amsterdam: John Benjamin.

—— ——(2002). 'The Transferred Workplace—Towards a Theory of Work in the Transnational Firm'. *EGOS Colloquium*, Barcelona, July.

—— and MEIKSINS, P. (1995). 'System, Society and Dominance Effects in Cross-National Organisational Analysis'. *Work, Employment and Society*, 9: 241–68.

SORGE, A. (1991). 'Strategic Fit and the Societal Effect: Interpreting Cross-National Comparisons of Technology, Organisation and Human Resources'. *Organisation Studies*, 12: 161–90.

STREECK, W. (1992). 'National Diversity, Regime Competition and Institutional Deadlock: Problems in Forming a European Industrial Relations System'. *Journal of Public Policy*, 12: 301–30.

STURDY, A. J. (2001). 'The Global Diffusion of Customer Service—A Critique of Cultural and Institutional Perspectives'. *Asia Pacific Business Review*, 7: 73–87.

THOMPSON, P., and MCHUGH, D. (2002). *Work Organisations* (3rd edn). Basingstoke: Palgrave.

TRAXLER, F., BLASCHKE, S., and KITTEL, B. (2001). *National Labour Relations in Internationalized Markets.* Oxford: Oxford University Press.

WHITLEY, R. (1992a). *Business Systems in East Asia.* London: Sage.

—— (ed.) (1992*b*). *European Business Systems: Firms and Markets in Their National Contexts*. London: Sage.

—— and KRISTENSEN, P. K. (eds.) (1997). *Governance at Work: The Social Regulation of Economic Relations*. Oxford: Oxford University Press.

WOMACK, J. P., JONES, P. T., and ROOS, D. (1990). *The Machine That Changed the World: The Triumph of Lean Production*. New York: Rawson Associates.

WOOD, S. (1991). 'Japanization and/or Toyotaism?' *Work, Employment and Society*, 5: 567–600.

FOR REFERENCE
Do Not Take From This Room